THE RENAISSANCE IN SCOTLAND

BRILL'S STUDIES IN INTELLECTUAL HISTORY

VOLUME 54

THE RENAISSANCE IN SCOTLAND

Studies in Literature, Religion, History and Culture Offered to John Durkan

EDITED BY

A. A. MacDONALD, MICHAEL LYNCH

AND

IAN B. COWAN

E.J. BRILL
LEIDEN · NEW YORK · KÖLN
1994

The paper in this book meets the guidelines for permanence and durability of the Committee on Production Guidelines for Book Longevity of the Council on Library Resources.

Library of Congress Cataloging-in-Publication Data

The Renaissance in Scotland : studies in literature, religion, history, and culture offered to John Durkan / edited by A. A. MacDonald, Michael Lynch, and Ian B. Cowan.
p. cm. — (Brill's studies in intellectual history, ISSN 0920-8607 ; v. 54)
Includes bibliographical references.
ISBN 9004100970 (cloth)
1. Scotland—History—16th century. 2. Scotland—History—15th century. 3. Renaissance—Scotland. I. MacDonald, A. A. (Alasdair A.) II. Lynch, Michael, 1946– . III. Cowan, Ian Borthwick. IV. Series.
DA784.R47 1994
941.104—dc20 94-26032
CIP

Die Deutsche Bibliothek - CIP-Einheitsaufnahme

The Renaissance in Scotland : studies in literature, religion, history and culture offered to John Durkan / ed. by A. A. MacDonald ... - Leiden ; New York ; Köln : Brill, 1994
(Brill's studies in intellectual history ; Vol. 54)
ISBN 90-04-10097-0
NE: MacDonald, Alasdair A. [Hrsg.]; Durkan, John: Festschrift; GT

ISSN 0920-8607
ISBN 90 04 10097 0

PRINTED IN THE NETHERLANDS

CONTENTS

ACKNOWLEDGEMENTS

The editors wish to record their gratitude to their fellow contributors and to thank Mrs Anna Cowan and Mr J.J. Robertson, literary executor of the late Professor Ian B. Cowan, for permission to include his essay in the volume. We are indebted to the Columba Trust for a generous subsidy to aid costs of publication. We wish to acknowledge the assistance of the National Library of Scotland and Glasgow University Library in granting permission to reproduce the illustrations, drawn from their respective collections. We also acknowledge the permission given by Oxford University Press to reproduce the text of a poem from *The Poems of Robert Henryson*, edited by Denton Fox (Oxford, 1981).

A.A.M.
M.L.

CONTRIBUTORS

Peter Asplin is Senior Assistant Librarian, Special Collections, Glasgow University Library

Priscilla Bawcutt is a Teaching Fellow in the Department of English, University of Liverpool

Tom Birrell is Emeritus Professor of English Literature, University of Nijmegen

Alexander Broadie is Professor of Philosophy, University of Glasgow

Ian Cowan (*d.* 1990) was Professor in Scottish History, University of Glasgow

Ian Cunningham is Keeper of Manuscripts, Maps and Music, National Library of Scotland, Edinburgh

Mark Dilworth is Abbot of Fort Augustus Abbey, Invernessshire

Robert Donaldson was formerly Keeper in the Department of Printed Books, National Library of Scotland, Edinburgh

Kenneth Elliott is Senior Lecturer in Music, University of Glasgow

William Gillies is Professor of Celtic, University of Edinburgh

Theo van Heijnsbergen is Lecturer in the English Department, University of Groningen

Brian Hillyard is Assistant Keeper in the Department of Printed Books, National Library of Scotland, Edinburgh

James Kirk is Reader in Scottish History, University of Glasgow

Mark Louglin is Head of the History Department at Charterhouse

Michael Lynch is Professor of Scottish History, University of Edinburgh

Alasdair MacDonald is Professor of Mediaeval English Language and Literature, University of Groningen

Leslie Macfarlane is Honorary Reader in History, University of Aberdeen

Hector MacQueen is Senior Lecturer in Scots Law, University of Edinburgh

Sally Mapstone is a Fellow of St Hilda's College and University Lecturer in Medieval English, University of Oxford

Stephen Rawles is Principal Assistant Librarian, Arts & Humanities, Glasgow University Library

Allan White is Catholic Chaplain at the University of Cambridge and Lecturer in Church History at Blackfriars, Oxford

Michael Yellowlees completed his doctoral thesis in the Scottish History Department, University of Edinburgh

ABBREVIATIONS AND CONVENTIONS

The following is a list of abbreviations of libraries and depositories and of abbreviated titles of works commonly referred to in the text. The latter generally follows the styles recommended in 'List of abbreviated titles of the printed sources of Scottish history to 1560', *SHR*, xlii (1963). Place of publication is given, here and in the notes to chapters, unless it was London.

Aberdeen Council Register	*Extracts from the Council Register of the Burgh of Aberdeen*, 2 vols. (Spalding Club, 1844-8).
Aberdeen Ecc. Recs.	*Selections from the Records of the Kirk Session, Presbytery and Synod of Aberdeen* (Spalding Club, 1846).
Aberdeen Fasti	*Fasti Aberdonenses*, ed. C. Innes (Spalding Club, 1854).
Aberdeen St Nicholas Cartularium	*Cartularium Ecclesiae Sancti Nicholai Aberdonensis*, 2 vols. (New Spalding Club, 1888-92).
ADCP	*Acts of the Lords of Council in Public Affairs, 1501-1554: Selections from Acta Dominorum Concilii*, ed. R.K. Hannay (Edinburgh, 1932).
Aldis	H. G. Aldis, *A List of Books printed in Scotland before 1700* (2nd edn., Edinburgh, 1970).
Amours	*Scottish Alliterative Poems*, ed. F.J. Amours, 2 vols. (STS, 1892-7).
Anderson, *Early Sources*	*Early Sources of Scottish History, 500 to 1286*, ed. A.O. Anderson (Edinburgh, 1922).
APS	*The Acts of the Parliament of Scotland*, ed. T. Thomson and C. Innes, 12 vols. (Edinburgh, 1814-75).
ARCR	*Contemporary Printed Literature of the Counter-Reformation, 1558-1640*, eds. A.F.

	Allison and D.M. Rogers (Aldershot, 1989).
Asloan MS	The Asloan Manuscript (NLS, MS 16500).
Asloan MS.	*The Asloan Manuscript,* ed. W.A. Craigie, 2 vols. (STS, 1923-5).
AUL	Aberdeen University Library.
AUR	*Aberdeen University Review,* Aberdeen.
Balfour, *Works*	*The Historical Works of Sir James Balfour,* 4 vols. (Edinburgh, 1824-5).
Bamff Chrs	*Bamff Charters, 1232-1703,* ed. J.H. Ramsay (Oxford, 1915).
Bann. Club	Bannatyne Club, Edinburgh.
Bann. Misc.	*The Bannatyne Miscellany,* 3 vols. (Bannatyne Club, 1827-55).
Bann. MS	Bannatyne Manuscript (NLS, Adv. MS.1.1.6).
Bann. MS.	*The Bannatyne Manuscript,* ed. W. Tod Ritchie, 4 vols. (STS, 1928-34).
Bann. MS. (fac)	*The Bannatyne Manuscript,* facsimile edn. W. Ringler and D. Fox, (London, 1980).
Bannatyne, *Memorials*	Richard Bannatyne, *Memorials of Transactions in Scotland, 1569-1573,* ed. R. Pitcairn (Bann. Club, 1836).
Binns Papers	*The Binns Papers, 1320-1864,* ed. J. Dalyell of Binns and J. Beveridge (SRS, 1938).
BL	British Library, London.
Black, *Surnames*	G.F. Black, *The Surnames of Scotland: their Origin, Meaning and History* (New York, 1946).
BN	Bibliothèque Nationale, Paris.
BOEC	*Book of the Old Edinburgh Club,* Edinburgh.
Buchanan, *Vernacular Writings*	*Vernacular Writings of George Buchanan,* ed. P.H. Brown (STS, 1892).
BUK	*Acts and Proceedings of the General Assembly of the Kirk of Scotland,* ed. T. Thomson, 3 vols. (Bann. Club, 1839-45).

C&M	Walter Chepman and Androw Myllar, various prints, 1508, reprinted in *Pieces from the Makculloch and the Gray MSS.*, ed. G. Stevenson (STS, 1918).
Calderwood, *History*	*History of the Church of Scotland by Mr David Calderwood,* 8 vols. (Wodrow Soc., 1842-9).
Camb. Reg.	*Registrum Monasterii S. Marie de Cambuskenneth* (Grampian Club, 1872).
Catholic Narratives	W. Forbes Leith, *Narratives of Scottish Catholics under Mary Stuart and James VI* (Edinburgh, 1885).
Chron. Picts-Scots	*Chronicles of the Picts: Chronicles of the Scots,* ed. W.F. Skene (Edinburgh, 1867).
Complaynt of Scotland	*The Complaynt of Scotland,* ed. A.M. Stewart (STS, 1979).
Cowan & Easson, *Religious Houses*	*Medieval Religious Houses: Scotland,* ed. I.B. Cowan and D.E. Easson (2nd edn., 1976).
CPL	*Calendar of Entries in the Papal Registers relating to Great Britain and Ireland: Papal Letters,* eds. W.H. Bliss *et al.* (1896-).
CSP Scot.	*Calendar of State Papers relating to Scotland and Mary, Queen of Scots, 1547-1603,* eds. J. Bain *et al.*, 13 vols. (1898-1969).
CSP Spain	*Calendar of State Papers, Spanish,* eds. G. Bergenroth *et al.*, 13 vols. (1862-1954).
CUL	Cambridge University Library.
Dempster, *Historia*	T. Dempster, *Historia ecclesiastica gentis Scotorum,* ed. D. Irving, 2 vols. (Edinburgh, 1829).
Diurnal	*A Diurnal of Remarkable Occurents ... since the Death of King James the Fourth till the year 1575* (Bann. Club, 1833).
DNB	*Dictionary of National Biography* (1885-).
DOST	*Dictionary of the Older Scottish Tongue,* Chicago and Aberdeen.

Dowden, *Bishops*	J. Dowden, *The Bishops of Scotland* (Glasgow, 1912).
Dryburgh Liber	*Liber S. Marie de Dryburgh* (Bann. Club, 1847).
DSCHT	*Dictionary of Scottish Church History & Theology*, eds. N.M. de S. Cameron, D.F. Wright, D.C. Lachman and D.E. Meek (Edinburgh, 1993).
Dunbar, ed. D. Laing	*The Poems of William Dunbar*, ed. D. Laing (1834).
Dunkeld Rentale	*Rentale Dunkeldense*, ed. R.K. Hannay (SHS, 1915).
Durkan & Ross, *Libraries*	J. Durkan and A. Ross, *Early Scottish Libraries* (Glasgow, 1961).
DVS	Sir John Skene, *De Verborum Significatione* (Edinburgh, 1597).
Edin. Recs.	*Extracts from the Records of the Burgh of Edinburgh*, 5 vols. (Scottish Burgh Records Soc., 1869-92).
Edinburgh Burgesses	*Roll of Edinburgh Burgesses and Guild-Brethern, 1406-1700*, ed. C.B.B. Watson (SRS, 1929).
EETS	Early English Text Society, London.
EHR	*English Historical Review*, London.
ER	*The Exchequer Rolls of Scotland*, eds. J. Stuart *et al.* (Edinburgh, 1878-1908)
EUJ	*Edinburgh University Journal*, Edinburgh.
EUL	Edinburgh University Library.
Ep. Regum Scotorum	*Epistolae Jacobi Quarti, Jacobi Quinti et Mariae Regum Scotorum*, ed. T. Ruddiman (Edinburgh, 1722-4).
FBD	*The First Book of Discipline*, ed. J. K. Cameron (Edinburgh, 1972).
Fowler, *Works*	*The Works of William Fowler*, ed. H.W. Meikle, 3 vols. (STS, 1914-40).
Fox	*The Poems of Robert Henryson*, ed. D. Fox (Oxford 1981).
Fraser, *Haddington*	W. Fraser, *Memorials of the Earls of Haddington*, 2 vols. (Edinburgh, 1889).
Fraser, *Menteith*	W. Fraser, *The Red Book of Menteith*

	(Edinburgh, 1880).
Fraser Papers	*Papers from the Collection of Sir William Fraser* (SHS, 1924).
Frasers of Philorth	*The Frasers of Philorth*, ed. A. Fraser, 3 vols. (Edinburgh, 1879).
GKW	*Gesamtkatalog der Wiegendrucke* (Leipzig etc., 1925-).
Glasgow Univ. Munimenta	*Munimenta Alme Universitatis Glasguensis*, ed. C. Innes, 4 vols. (Maitland Club, 1854).
Grampian Club	Grampian Club, London.
GUL	Glasgow University Library.
Hailes, *Annals*	Sir David Dalrymple, Lord Hailes, *Annals of Scotland from the Accession of Malcolm III to the Accession of the House of Stewart*, 3rd edn. (Edinburgh, 1819).
Hain	L. Hain, *Repertorium Bibliographicum* (Stuttgart, 1826-38).
Haws, *Parish Clergy*	*Scottish Parish Clergy at the Reformation, 1540-1574*, ed. C.H. Haws (SRS, 1972).
Highland Papers	*Highland Papers*, ed. J.R.N. Macphail, 4 vols. (SHS, 1914-34).
HKJVI	*The Historie and Life of King James the Sext*, ed. T. Thomson (Bann. Club, 1825).
Holyrood Liber	*Liber Cartarum Sancte Crucis* (Bann. Club, 1840).
IHS	*Irish Historical Studies*, Dublin.
Inchaffray Chrs	*Charters, Bulls and other Documents relating to the Abbey of Inchaffray* (SHS, 1908).
Inchaffray Liber	*Liber Insule Missarum* (Bann. Club, 1847).
Inchcolm Chrs	*Charters of the Abbey of Inchcolm*, eds. D.E. Easson and A. Macdonald (SHS, 1938).
Index	*Index of Middle English Verse*, ed. C. Brown and R. H. Robbins (New York, 1943); *Supplement*, ed. R. H. Robbins and L. Cutler (Lexington, 1965).
IR	*The Innes Review*, Glasgow.

J. Ecc. Hist.	*Journal of Ecclesiastical History*, Cambridge.
Jacobean Union	*The Jacobean Union*, eds. B.R. Galloway and B.P. Levack (SHS, 1985).
James IV Letters	*The Letters of James the Fourth, 1505-13*, eds. R.K. Hannay and R.I. Mackie (SHS, 1953).
James V Letters	*The Letters of James V*, eds. R.K. Hannay and D. Hay (Edinburgh, 1954).
Keith, *History*	Robert Keith, *History of the Affairs of Church and State in Scotland, from the Beginning of the Reformation to the Year 1568*, 3 vols. (Spottiswoode Soc., 1844-50).
Kinsley	*The Poems of William Dunbar*, ed. J. Kinsley (Oxford, 1979).
Knox, *History*	*John Knox's History of the Reformation in Scotland*, ed. W.C. Dickinson, 2 vols. (Edinburgh, 1949).
Knox, *Works*	*The Works of John Knox*, ed. D. Laing, 6 vols. (Wodrow Soc., 1846-64).
L&P Henry VIII	*Letters and Papers, Foreign and Domestic., of the Reign of King Henry VII*, eds. J. Brewer and J. Gairdner, 21 vols. (1862-1910).
Laing Chrs	*Calendar of the Laing Charters, 854-1837*, ed. J. Anderson (Edinburgh, 1899).
Life of Blair	*The Life of Mr Robert Blair* (Wodrow Soc., 1848).
Lindsay, *Works*	*The Works of Sir David Lindsay of the Mount, 1490-1555*, ed. D. Hamer, 4 vols. (STS, 1930-36).
Mackenzie	*The Poems of William Dunbar*, ed. W.M. Mackenzie (1932).
McRoberts, *Essays*	D. McRoberts (ed.), *Essays on the Scottish Reformation, 1513-1625* (Glasgow, 1962).
Maitl. Fol. MS.	Maitland Folio Manuscript (Cambridge, Magdalene College, MS. 2553).

Maitl. Folio MS.	*The Maitland Folio Manuscript*, ed. W. A. Craigie, 2 vols. (STS, 1919-27).
Maitland Misc.	*Miscellany of the Maitland Club*, 4 vols. (Maitland Club, 1833-47).
Manual	*A Manual of Writings in Middle English, 1050-1500*, ed. J. Burke Severs and A. E. Hartung (New Haven, 1967-).
Melville, *Diary*	*The Autobiography and Diary of Mr James Melville*, ed. R. Pitcairn (Wodrow Soc., 1843).
MB XV	*Musica Britannica* (3rd edn., 1975), vol. xv: *Music of Scotland*, ed. K. Elliott and H.M. Shire.
MLN	*Modern Language Notes*, Baltimore.
NLS	National Library of Scotland, Edinburgh.
New Grove	*New Grove Dictionary of Music and Musicians*, ed. S. Sadie (1980).
NRA	National Register of Archives, Edinburgh.
OED	*Oxford English Dictionary* (2nd edn., 1989).
Patrick, *Statutes*	*Statutes of the Scottish Church, 1225-1559*, ed. D. Patrick (SHS, 1907).
PEBS	*Papers of the Edinburgh Bibliographical Society*, Edinburgh.
Pitcairn, *Trials*	*Criminal Trials in Scotland from 1488 to 1624*, ed. R. Pitcairn, 3 vols. (Edinburgh, 1833).
PRO	Public Record Office, London.
Procs. Brit. Acad.	*Proceedings of the British Academy*, London.
PSAS	*Proceedings of the Society of Antiquaries of Scotland*, Edinburgh.
Richardinus, *Commentary*	*Commentary on the Rule of St Augustine by Robertus Richardinus*, ed. G. Coulton (SHS, 1935).
RMS	*Registrum Magni Sigilli Regum Scotorum*, eds. J.M. Thomson *et al.*, 12 vols. (Edinburgh, 1882-1912).
Rollock, *Works*	*Select Works of Robert Rollock*, ed. W.M.

	Gunn, 2 vols. (Wodrow Soc., 1844-9).
Row, *History*	John Row, *History of the Kirk of Scotland from the Year 1558 to August 1637* (Wodrow Soc., 1842).
RPC	*The Register of the Privy Council of Scotland*, eds. J.H. Burton *et al.*, 14 vols. (Edinburgh, 1877-98).
RSCHS	*Records of the Scottish Church History Society*, Edinburgh.
RSS	*Registrum Secreti Sigilli Regum Scotorum*, eds. M. Livingstone *et al.*, 8 vols. (Edinburgh, 1908-).
St A Acta	*Acta Facultatis Artium Universitatis Sanctiandree, 1413-1588*, ed. A. I. Dunlop, 2 vols. (SHS, 1964).
St A Recs.	*Early Records of the University of St Andrews* (SHS, 1926).
Satirical Poems	*Satirical Poems of the Time of the Reformation*, ed. J. Cranstoun, 2 vols. (STS, 1891-3).
Scot. Stud.	*Scottish Studies*, Edinburgh.
Scot, *Apologetical Narration*	William Scot, *An Apologetical Narration of the State and Government of the Kirk of Scotland since the Reformation* (Wodrow Soc., 1846).
Scots Peerage	*The Scots Peerage*, ed. Sir J. Balfour Paul, 9 vols. (Edinburgh, 1904-14).
Scott, *Fasti*	*Fasti Ecclesiae Scoticanae*, ed. H. Scott, 7 vols. (rev. edn., Edinburgh, 1915-).
SGS	*Scottish Gaelic Studies*, Edinburgh.
SHR	*Scottish Historical Review*, Edinburgh and Aberdeen.
SHS	Scottish History Society, Edinburgh.
SLJ	*Scottish Literary Journal*, Aberdeen.
SP	State Papers Collection, Public Record Office, London.
Spalding Club	Spalding Club, Aberdeen.
Spalding Misc.	*Miscellany of the Spalding Club*, 5 vols. (Spalding Club, 1844-52).
Spottiswoode, *History*	*History of the Church of Scotland ... by the Right Rev. John Spottiswoode*, eds. M.

	Russell and M. Napier, 3 vols. (Spottiswoode Soc., 1847-51).
Spottiswoode Misc.	*The Spottiswoode Miscellany*, 2 vols. (Spottiswoode Soc., 1844-5).
Spottiswoode Soc.	Spottiswoode Society, Edinburgh.
SRO	Scottish Record Office, Edinburgh.
SRS	Scottish Record Society, Edinburgh.
SSL	*Studies in Scottish Literature*, Columbia, South Carolina.
Stair Soc.	Stair Society, Edinburgh.
STAKSR	*Register of the Minister, Elders and Deacons of the Christian Congregation of St Andrews, 1559-1600*, ed. D.H. Fleming, 2 vols. (SHS, 1889-1890).
STC	*A Short-Title Catalogue of Books printed in England, Scotland & Ireland 1475-1640*, compiled by A. W. Pollard and C. R. Redgrave; 2nd edn. by W. A. Jackson, F. S. Ferguson and K. F. Pantzer (1976-86).
STS	Scottish Text Society, Edinburgh and London.
TA	*Accounts of the Lord High Treasurer of Scotland*, eds. T. Dickson and Sir J. Balfour Paul (Edinburgh, 1877-1916).
TEBS	*Transactions of the Edinburgh Bibliographical Society*, Edinburgh.
TDGAS	*Transactions of the Dumfriesshire and Galloway Natural History and Antiquarian Society*, Dumfries.
TGSI	*Transactions of the Gaelic Society of Inverness*, Inverness.
Thre Prestis of Peblis	*The Thre Prestis of Peblis*, ed. T.D. Robb (STS, 1920).
Thirds of Benefices	*Accounts of the Collectors of Thirds of Benefices, 1561-1572*, ed. G. Donaldson (SHS, 1949).
TLS	*Times Literary Supplement.*
TRHS	*Transactions of the Royal Historical Society*, London.
TSES	*Transactions of the Scottish Ecclesiological*

	Society, Aberdeen.
Warrender Papers	*The Warrender Papers*, ed. A.I. Cameron, 2 vols. (SHS, 1931-2).
Watt, *Fasti*	*Fasti Ecclesiae Scoticanae Medii Aevi ad Annum 1638*, ed. D.E.R. Watt (SRS, 1969).
Wigt. Chrs	*Wigtownshire Charters*, ed. R.C. Reid (SHS, 1960).
Wodrow, *Biog. Colls.*	*Collections upon the Lives of the Reformers and Most Eminent Ministers of the Church of Scotland*, 2 vols. (Maitland Club, 1834-48).
Wodrow Misc.	*The Miscellany of the Wodrow Society* (Wodrow Soc., 1844).
Wodrow Soc.	Wodrow Society, Edinburgh.

ILLUSTRATIONS

FOREWORD

This volume brings together a group of new essays, all of which bear on the general theme of the Renaissance in Scotland. Various aspects of cultural history are discussed: literature, printed books, manuscripts, libraries, music, universities, philosophy, law, religion and society. It is the hope of the editors that through these detailed studies light will be cast on the general complex of issues conventionally labelled 'the Renaissance'.

There can be no scholar working in this area who has not benefited from the manifold researches and publications of Dr John Durkan, who, through a long career, latterly from a base within the Scottish History Department of the University of Glasgow, has done more than any other to make the field of the Scottish Renaissance his own. At the same time, John Durkan has generously shared the fruits of his erudition with his fellow scholars, both within Scotland and furth of it. He has been a source of particular inspiration and help to successive generations of younger scholars, who are well represented in this collection.

'In any age there is nothing more difficult to pin down than a climate of thought', wrote John Durkan, 'and nothing more necessary to reckon with'. There can be few if any who have contributed more to the understanding of the age of the Scottish Renaissance than the scholar known to many simply and affectionately as the 'master'. It is truly fitting that a list of John Durkan's publications should be included within this volume, since this remarkable corpus in itself provides an excellent map for anyone investigating this area of study. The editors, on behalf of all the contributors to this book, are happy to record here their indebtedness to John Durkan's scholarship: further individual acknowledgements of John's scholarly influence appear in the notes to the various articles. All the contributors wish him many more enjoyable and productive years of research.

The idea of assembling such a collection of essays was first discussed by the editors in 1988. After the tragic death of Ian Cowan, in 1990, Michael Lynch agreed to become the co-editor of the volume. Had he lived, Ian Cowan might well have written on a topic different from the one included in this volume. Sadly, no trace has survived of the contribution on which he was working.

The editors are nonetheless glad to be able to include an essay by Ian Cowan, and they are particularly obliged to Dr Michael Yellowlees for bringing a draft manuscript into a publishable form.

THE SCOTS *BUKE OF PHISNOMY* AND SIR GILBERT HAY

Sally Mapstone

In the century after his death Sir Gilbert Hay's reputation was a high one. He was honourably included by two sixteenth-century poets in their catalogues of Scottish makars. Dunbar commemorated him in *Lament for the Makars*, and Lindsay in *The Testament of the Papyngo* wrote of him as one of those who 'Thocht thay be ded, thar libells bene leuand'.[1] Both Dunbar and Lindsay were probably thinking of Hay primarily as a poet, for their lists celebrate 'makaris' and 'poetis'. In other words, they had more in mind the Hay who wrote an Alexander romance than the Hay who translated the three pieces in the so-called prose MS.

Hay's name has commonly been associated with *The Buik of King Alexander the Conquerour* (hereafter *BKA*), thought by its editor John Cartwright and by *DOST* to have been composed c.1460 for Lord [Thomas] Erskine. That work is extant now in two manuscripts copied c.1530 and c.1580-90 (hereafter collectively MSS *A*). But the lacunous and confusing conclusion to the poem states that it was either copied or revised in 1499 from an earlier version of the work by Gilbert Hay (*BKA*, 19287-19369); the relationship of the *BKA* as it now stands to Hay's original work remains in dispute.[2] The view taken in this essay is that the version

---

[1] Kinsley, 180; Lindsay, *Works*, i, 56. There is another possible contemporary reference to Hay that ought to be better known. The mid fifteenth-century MS of the *Scotichronicon* in Corpus Christi College, Cambridge, contains as a half leaf in its preliminary material (19v) the following: 'I schreu hiȝ hert and al ye harnis in hiȝ heid/y*at* tuk out yis half lef gif it weȝ dun in/my keing q*uod* gilbert ye hayes' (M.R. James, *A Descriptive Catalogue of the Manuscripts in the Library of Corpus Christi College, Cambridge*, (Cambridge, 1912), i, 391). There is obviously no confirmation that this is Hay the poet, but the association of a Gilbert Hay with the 'keping' of a MS is worth comparison with the ascription of part of an MS of legal material, copied c.1455-60, now Edinburgh, NLS, Adv. MS 25.4.14 (1), as 'per manum venerabilis viri G.H.' (f.90v). Other contemporary references to Hay in court records are discussed in Sally Mapstone, 'The Advice to Princes Tradition in Scottish Literature, 1450-1500' (Oxford University D.Phil., 1986), 48-54.

[2] All references to the text are to *The Buik of King Alexander the Conquerour*, ed. J. Cartwright, 2 vols. (STS, 1986-90; a final volume, with commentary, is awaited.) The MSS are BL, Add. MS 40732 and SRO, GD 112/71/9. The attribution of the *BKA* to Hay has been most extensively disputed by M.P. McDiarmid:

of the *BKA* that survives is a revised one, compiled (by an unidentified writer) around 1499, and that it makes substantial use of an earlier poem by Hay, along with other material by him or associated with him.

Both the manuscripts of the *BKA* were owned in the late sixteenth century by Duncan Campbell, 7th laird of Glenorchy, and the later manuscript is apparently a copy made for him from the earlier one.[3] These are late witnesses of the poem, but their references to Hay by name give further testimony to his continuing reputation in the sixteenth century, even while the extent of his own contribution to the work is unresolved. By contrast, the three prose works, *The Buke of the Law of Armys*, *The Buke of the Ordre of Knychthede*, and *The Buke of the Governaunce of Princis*, written around 1456 for William Sinclair, earl of Orkney and Caithness, survive in one copy made in the late 1480s, probably for Sinclair's son Oliver, and there is little evidence that they were well known outside the family.[4]

There is another valuable piece of evidence for Hay's literary status in the early sixteenth century: the inclusion of his name in the contents list of the Asloan MS.[5] It was not very common for writers to be so identified in this table. Only six names are included altogether, the others being Ireland, Henryson, Dunbar and Kennedy, and Chaucer. It is probable that Asloan did not know the names of all the authors whose writings he copied, but the fact that he did know Hay's and listed him in this talented company suggests that Hay's literary reputation was of some weight. Equally interesting is the context in which his name is used. For this curious part of the contents list, detailing a considerable section of the manuscript which is now lost, raises a number of questions about Hay's poetic writing, in particular

---

see e.g. the introduction to *Barbour's Bruce*, eds. M.P. McDiarmid and J.A.C. Stevenson 3 vols. (STS, 1980-85), i, 27-32. A full statement of his views is forthcoming in an issue of *SSL*.

3 *BKA*, ii, pp. vi-xvii.

4 J.H. Stevenson (ed.), *Gilbert of the Haye's Prose Manuscript*, 2 vols. (STS, 1901-14) i, pp. xxviii-xxxiv; R.J. Lyall, 'Vernacular prose before the Reformation' in R.D.S. Jack (ed.), *The History of Scottish Literature*, i (Aberdeen, 1988), 163-82 (167-70). It is possible, however, that the author of *Lancelot of the Laik* knew *The Buke of the Governaunce of Princis*. I discuss this question in a forthcoming study of Scottish advisory literature.

5 *Asloan MS*, i, pp. xiii-xv. For discussion of the contents list see the comments by I.C. Cunningham in the present volume, and Catherine van Buuren (ed.), *The Buke of the Sevyne Sagis* (Leiden, 1982), 414-19. R.J. Lyall's researches on the compilation and make-up of the MS have yet to appear in print.

whether his reputation rested on other works besides his *Alexander* romance, and whether that poem was most widely known in its full version.

Hay's name is mentioned in one of the three items that come in between the mysterious '... of þe angell/Deid/quhyte dragoun Devill wysman blak dragoun ȝoung man and of þe sawlis in hell' and 'Itm a ballat of þe Incarnacioun'. They are:

Itm þe buke of curtasy and nortur'
Itm þe docume*nt* of Sir gilbert hay
Itm þe Regiment of king*is* w*ith* þe buke of phisnomy[6]

The second and third of these items have hitherto been tentatively aligned with some of Hay's prose works.[7] But there are problems with such hypotheses: the titles do not tally, and *The Buke of the Governaunce of Princis,* which might be called a 'Regiment', does not contain a physiognomy section. Moreover, the inclusion of any of Hay's prose pieces at this point in the Asloan MS, besides vastly increasing the bulk of the manuscript, would have been out of keeping with its organisation. In so far as we can reconstruct the contents of the manuscript, they divide (with the interesting exception of *The Buke of the Chess*) into prose up to the *Sex Werkdayis and Agis,* and verse thereafter.[8] The three items here fall into the verse section.

The document of Sir gilbert hay, the one item definitely, if vaguely, assigned to him, is thus more likely to have been in verse than prose. Some sense of what its character was may be gleaned by considering the probable nature of the two items on either side of it. But the cases for associating Hay with these items are of different kinds. In both cases the evidence for his authorship of them is largely circumstantial, but it is far stronger in the case of *The Regiment of kingis with the buke of phisnomy.* It is thus with this text that we shall deal first at length, returning later to the question of *The*

---

[6] *Asloan MS,* i, p. xiv.

[7] R.J. Lyall, 'Politics and poetry in fifteenth and sixteenth century Scotland', *SLJ,* iii (1976), 5-29 (28), and, with a different argument, 'The lost literature of medieval Scotland' in J. D. McClure & M.R.G. Spiller (eds.), *Bryght Lanternis, Essays on the Language and Literature of Medieval Scotland* (Aberdeen, 1989), 33-47 (40-41). Also J. Cartwright, 'Sir Gilbert Hay's *Buik of Alexander the Conquerour,* a Critical Edition of Lines 1-4263' (Toronto University Ph.D., 1964), pp. xvii-xviii.

[8] *The Buke of the Chess* may be placed where it is simply because it came into Asloan's hands at this point, but he may also have felt it to be more fittingly included among the serious moral works which the prose section contains.

buke of curtasy and nortur, and indeed to the nature of the *Document.*

If Hay's *The Buke of the Governaunce of Princis* did not contain a physiognomy, the *BKA* did. The 'phisnomy' section of that massive poem is itself a substantial portion (nearly 350 lines) of the 'Regiment' (the term used by Aristotle at 9356), inserted about half-way through it.[9] The 'Regiment' is loosely based on the pseudo-Aristotelian *Secretum Secretorum.* But whereas it is possible to identify which recension of the *Secretum* Hay was using for his translation of *The Buke of the Governaunce of Princis,* the *BKA* 'Regiment' is treated with such freedom and imagination (particularly in its inset 'inner council' allegory) that the likelihood that that 'Regiment' was a direct translation of a still unidentified recension of the *Secretum* is remote.[10] The presence of such a 'Regiment' in an Alexander romance is itself distinctive. Neither of the *BKA*'s major sources, the Latin *Historia de Preliis* nor the French *Roman d'Alexandre* contained such material; and although it was not entirely unknown for versions of the Alexander story to include tracts of advisory matter, it was hardly a common feature.[11] In the context of this Scottish romance, however, it makes good sense. As John Cartwright has shown, the advice on good government which Aristotle's 'Regiment' offers to Alexander is entirely in keeping with the presentation of Alexander as an exemplary model for Christian knighthood and kingship.[12]

Despite the general thematic accord between the 'Regiment' and the rest of the romance, the 'Regiment', however, retains the

---

[9] The 'Regiment' is at *BKA*, iii, 9464-10555, with the 'phisnomy' beginning at 10108. The 'Regiment' has no separate rubric in the MSS, but they do rubricate 'Off the phisnomye'.

[10] M.A. Manzalaoui (ed.), *Secretum Secretorum, Nine English Versions* (EETS, 1977) [hereafter *9EV*], i, p. xxxvi; Mapstone, 'The Advice to Princes Tradition', 93-142, where the relation of *The Buke of the Governaunce of Princis* to its French source is discussed in detail and the 'inner council' section of the *BKA* analysed. A new edition of Hay's prose MS by Professor Jonathan Glenn will shortly be published by STS.

[11] J. Cartwright, 'Sir Gilbert Hay and the Alexander tradition' in D. Strauss and H.W. Drescher (eds.), *Scottish Language and Literature, Medieval and Renaissance* (Frankfurt, 1986), 229-38. One manuscript of the *Old French Prose Alexander* contains extracts from the *Secretum Secretorum,* but there is nothing to link it with Scotland or Hay: W. Söderhjelm, 'Notice et extraits du MS. fr. 51 de la Bibliothèque Royale de Stockholm', *Mémoires de la Société Néophilologique de Helsingfors,* vi (1917), 305-33. See also George Cary, *The Medieval Alexander,* ed. D.J.A. Ross (Cambridge, 1957), 29-33, 38-58.

[12] 'Hay and the Alexander tradition', passim.

decidedly detachable character of a piece of argument imposed on a narrative sequence that would not be greatly disturbed by its omission. The inclusion of a work entitled *The Regiment of kingis with the buke of phisnomy* in close proximity to the name of Hay in the Asloan list thus prompts speculation whether this item was the *BKA* 'Regiment', either excerpted from the long poem or preserved in the form in which it had been originally composed, possibly by Hay, before being inserted into the romance? The title certainly fits very well with the *BKA* material. As we have seen, the term 'Regiment' is used by Aristotle; 'kingis' (rather than 'princis') are continually referred to in its course; and the phrase 'þe buke of phisnomy' is actually used at the opening of that section (10111). Moreover Asloan's phrase 'with the buke of phisnomy' would make sense in the context of MSS *A*, where that part of the 'Regiment' is separately rubricated. Asloan might well have arrived at his title by looking quickly through his exemplar and spotting the distinguishing rubric.

However, the phrasing 'with þe buke of phisnomy' could also suggest that the *Phisnomy* was perceived as a discrete unit, itself capable of detachment from the *Regiment*;[13] and this indeed is to some extent borne out by analysis of its likely source material. For whereas the majority of the 'Regiment' cannot be traced to any one recension of the *Secretum*, the physiognomy section, as we shall see, does broadly follow the pattern of one tradition. It is thus possible that this *Phisnomy* had a separate textual history before being united to the *Regiment*. Some very interesting information that alters the balance in favour of one set of these speculations has recently come to light.

In 1987 Mrs Joyce Sanderson published an account of 'A recently-discovered poem in Scots vernacular: "Complections of Men in Verse"'.[14] The poem is preserved in two late seventeenth-century manuscripts in the NLS, Adv. MSS 34.3.11 and 34.3.12 (hereafter collectively MSS *B*). They are themselves partial transcriptions of the 'Historical Collections' of Sir Lewis Stewart of Kirkhill (1586-1655), now extant in Adv. MS 22.1.14, in which, regrettably, the folios that might have contained the poem do not

[13] Cartwright ('A Critical Edition', pp. xii-xiii) posited the idea that the item was composed of two works, a 'Regiment' without a physiognomy section, and a separate physiognomy.

[14] *Scottish Studies*, xxviii (1987), 49-68.

survive;[15] it seems, in fact, quite possible that the *B* MSS were made from another complete copy of Stewart's writings which is no longer extant.[16] That the two transcripts from this common source were also made independently of each other is evident from the inclusion in the later manuscript, Adv. MS 34.3.12, of two lines (157, 291) not found in Adv. MS 34.3.11. Moreover, Adv. MS 34.3.12 appears both a more accurate and a more faithful copy of the exemplar. One possible explanation for this is that it was copied by the antiquary Robert Mylne.[17] It was from this

---

[15] ibid., 49-50. A page from Adv. MS 34.3.12 is reproduced on p. 51. Mrs Sanderson notes that Sir Lewis's mother was Katherine Bannatyne, sister of George. More information on Sir Lewis and his family is to be found in J.M. Sanderson, 'Two Stewarts of the sixteenth century: Mr William Stewart, poet and William Stewart, elder, depute clerk of Edinburgh', *The Stewarts*, xvii, no. 1 (1984), 25-46 (38-41).

[16] The following table (for which I am indebted to Ian Cunningham) shows the correspondences in material between the three manuscripts. (Adv. MS 22.1.14 and Adv. MS 34.3.11 are foliated, the latter also having older pagination; Adv. MS 34.3.12 is paginated):

item	22.1.14	34.3.11		34.3.12
	f.	p.	f.	p.
list of relig. inst.	152-6			
		(5 ff. lost)		
Scottish kings (del.)	157v			
concordance of yeiris	158v			
list of events	159r	1	1r	3-4
Scottish kings	159v	3	2r	vi
minute Reg. Melrose	160-1, 5-7	3-4	1-2	
castle wards	162r	10-11	5v-6	
peerages		8	4v	7
charter to T. Adam		8-9	4v-5	8-9
misc. hist. notes		9	5	9
notes re. parl. etc		10	5v	10
colleg. churches		11-12	6	11-13
phisnomy poem		13-16	7-8v	14-17
Douglas forfeitures	162v-170	16-32	8v-16v	18-42

(Following are blank: 22.1.14, ff.156v, 157r, 161v; 34.3.11, pp.2,4 = ff.1v, 2v).

Mrs Sanderson suggested that the poem was included in the five folios missing between ff.156-7 in Adv. MS 22.1.14. But it will be seen that MSS *B* start their copying at the equivalent of f.159r in Adv. MS 22.1.14, that is, after the point at which the poem should have been included. As the order of items in all three manuscripts is different at this point, that argument is not totally conclusive. But it should also be noted that 22.1.14 moves directly on at f.162 from material on castle wards to an item on Douglas forfeitures, whereas 34.3.11 and 34.3.12 have six items including the poem between these two entries. This difference in order suggests that, though there would have been space for the poem and the other missing material in the five absent folios in 22.1.14, the poem might not have been copied into that manuscript in the first place.

[17] Sanderson, 'A recently-discovered poem', 50, 66.

version that Mrs Sanderson printed the poem, and the same manuscript is used as the copy-text for the transcription printed in the Appendix to this essay, with emendation from Adv. MS 34.3.11 where necessary.

Mrs Sanderson's conclusion that the poem 'could have been written in the late fifteenth, or early sixteenth, century' was an accurate one.[18] For 'Complections of Men in Verse' (one of the titles given to it in Mylne's MS[19]) is in fact the physiognomy in the *BKA*, separated from its 'Regiment' and with an introductory section on the four humours, or complexions, which is not found in the surviving MSS of the whole physiognomy poem. This is not, then, quite the same thing as Asloan's *Regiment of kingis with the buke of phisnomy*, but we have already seen that the physiognomy could be perceived as a separable piece.

Comparison of the *A* and *B* texts of the physiognomy shows that the new witnesses have considerable textual value in recovering previously lost lines and some original readings. In order easily to demonstrate this, the *A* text of the physiognomy is also included in the Appendix. *B*'s worth will further be illustrated through an examination of the texts in relation to the source material of the physiognomy, for MSS *B* are again of help in allowing more to be said about the model of the physiognomy, and the imaginative revision of it for which Hay may have been responsible.

The physiognomy that ultimately lies behind this Scottish poetic version is, as Cartwright suggested, that found in the Latin recension of the *Secretum*, probably produced in the first half of the thirteenth century by Philippus Tripolitanus, from which further versions, known generally as the 'Vulgate' tradition, descended.[20] That simple statement made, anything said beyond it—as is so often the case with the *Secretum Secretorum*—must be heavily qualified. That this Scots physiognomy is in this tradition is indubitable. As we shall see, not only does it provide the organisational model, but some of the Scots phrasing can be traced back to the Latin. But the transmission of the physiognomy—as part of the *Secretum* and also separately from it—is of such complexity that it would be a vain hope to identify the specific manuscript

---

18 ibid., 67.

19 The 'Complections' title is in a secondary index; in Mylne's main index it is called 'Vertues and vices of persons showin from the featers of thr bodyes the tones of thr voices etc In a Monastick Ryme' (p. x).

20 'Hay and the Alexander tradition', 235. *9EV*, pp. xiv-xxii.

used for this version, were it indeed to survive. Many manuscripts also remain unpublished.[21] We can, nevertheless, state that the 'phisnomy' abides quite strictly by the pattern established in Philippus, though it does have some sections in a different order and both expands and condenses others.[22] In this respect, the treatment of the physiognomy is in keeping with the employment of sources in the *BKA* as a whole, if not with its 'Regiment'. Cartwright's description of what he sees as Hay's use of the *Roman d'Alexandre* fits equally for the approach to the physiognomy: 'he usually expands what he takes over, adding comment and detail'. And, as he also notes of the *BKA*'s physiognomy itself, this detail has a 'vigorous and colloquial' character 'of a kind not to be found in any other version of the *Physiognomy*'.[23] The additions are humorous and inventive, and they transform the character of the physiognomy from a sober catalogue to a far more evocative, even idiosyncratic, set of observations.

MSS *B* contain 42 lines not preserved in MSS *A*, many of which have a good claim to authenticity.[24] This is especially important in

[21] See F. Wurms, *Studien zu den deutschen und den lateinischen Prosafassungen des pseudo-aristotelischen 'Secretum Secretorum'* (Hamburg, 1970).

[22] The pattern of the 'phisnomy' may be compared with that of the Philippus version (see n.25 below) as follows:

Philippus	*Phisnomy*
hair	hair
eyes	eyes (including brows)
brows	
nose	nose
mouth, face, lips	mouth and lips
and temples	face and temples
	head
ears	ears
voice	voice
neck	
belly, chest, back	chest, back,
and shoulders	and shoulders
arms	arms
hands and fingers	hands and fingers
	belly
	ideal man
legs, feet, and knees	legs
pace	pace
ideal man	ideal man

[23] 'Hay and the Alexander tradition', 233, 235.

[24] *B*, 1-20, 34, 36, 43-4, 49-50, 52, 57, 84-7, 295, 297, 304-05, 318-21, 338-9. I have included here only lines for which there is nothing corresponding in *A*. There are a quantity of instances where equivalent lines in *A* and *B* differ particu-

the case of the opening passage on the complexions (*B*, 1-20) because there is no direct precedent for this in the Philippus physiognomy.[25] What it did have at this point was a passage on the different 'colours' of men, which are indirectly associated with the complexions.[26] But as Mrs Sanderson has pointed out, the translation of the *Secretum* made by the Anglo-Irish writer James Yonge in 1422 has a passage on the complexions which, like *B*'s, specifically names and describes them.[27] Yonge was working from a French revision of the Vulgate made by Jofroi de Waterford and Servais Copale in the late thirteenth century. This version and Yonge's translation contain, unusually, two successive forms of the physiognomy: the first, of psychological and physical characteristics, including the humours, taken over from the Latin physiognomy by Bartholomew of Messina, and the second the more familiar Vulgate version.[28] As Mrs Sanderson noted, the complexions section in *B* has similarities to the opening of the first physiognomy in Yonge, while the rest of *B*'s rendition has correspondence with the second.[29] There is, however, no question of the Scots account being drawn from Yonge's version, and it would be an exaggeration to say that, apart from dealing with the

larly noticeably from each other, e.g.: *A* 41-8, *B* 51-60; *A* 52, *B* 62; *A* 54, *B* 64; *A* 57-8, *B* 67-8; *A* 71-2, *B* 81-2; *A* 200, *B* 211; *A* 286, *B* 299; *A* 302-03, *B* 316-17; *A* 331, *B* 345.

[25] References to the Philippus physiognomy are to the most accessible and cited modern edition, in the recension by Roger Bacon: *Opera hactenus inedita Rogeri Baconi*, ed. R. Steele, fascicule v (Oxford, 1920; hereafter *Bacon*). On the dissemination of the Latin text, pp. vii-lxiii.

[26] *Bacon*, 166-7. This is perhaps best illustrated by reference to the translation in MS Ashmole 396 (see below, n.30), 90-92.

[27] 'A recently-discovered poem', 59-75, with detailed comparisons, which are thus not repeated. Yonge's version is in *Three Prose Versions of the Secreta Secretorum*, ed. R. Steele (EETS, 1898) [hereafter *3PV*]. Reference here is to 219-20.

[28] M.A. Manzalaoui, 'The *Secreta Secretorum* in English Thought and Literature from the Fourteenth to the Sixteenth Century, with a Preliminary Survey of the Origins of the *Secreta*', 2 vols. (Oxford University D.Phil., 1954), i, 366-75; G.L. Hamilton, 'The sources of the *Secret of Secrets* of Jofroi de Waterford', *The Romanic Review*, i (1910), 259-64; J. Monfrin, 'La place du *Secret des Secrets* dans la littérature française mediévale' in W.F. Ryan and C.B. Schmitt (eds.), *Pseudo-Aristotle: 'The Secret of Secrets', Sources and Influences*, Warburg Institute Surveys, ix (1982), 73-113. I have been able to consult only one MS of Waterford/Copale: BL, Royal MS 20 B v, an abbreviated version, in which a truncated form of the physiognomy appears as an item separated from the rest of the work on f.156. Comparison showed the closeness of Yonge's translation, and gave no reason to associate the 'phisnomy' more definitely with this recension. In the textual discussion below, reference is made to Yonge as the most accessible edition.

[29] 'A recently-discovered poem', 60.

humours, Yonge's resembles it more strongly than do the relevant parts of the several English fifteenth-century translations of the *Secretum* in the Vulgate tradition, three of which will be used in the comparisons that follow here.[30]

Nevertheless, the conjunction of a passage on the humours with a physiognomy could suggest that the author of the 'phisnomy' was working with a French MS in the Waterford/Copale recension. But set against this must be the fact that, as we shall see, there is a closeness between some of the Scots phrasing and the Latin Vulgate's that suggests no French intermediary. Moreover, striking as the overlap of material between the 'phisnomy' and Yonge/Waterford/Copale is, the verbal correspondences are not strong enough to give conclusive proof of a textual relationship, not least because the subject-matter was commonplace. If discussion of the humours was not a dominant part of the physiognomy tradition,[31] it was a staple part of the *Secretum* and related literature. We have already seen that the 'colours' section in the *Secretum* physiognomy was related to the theory of the four humours. The chapters on diet and the seasons in the *Secretum* made much explicit reference to them, and Hay himself had described the need for 'equaliteis of complexiouns' in his translation of *The Buke of the Governaunce of Princis*.[32] Further, from the thirteenth century the dissemination into popular literature of theory on the humours through short groups of mnemonic verses, first in Latin then in the vernaculars, through treatises such as the *Regimen Salernitatum*, had become widespread.[33] Mrs Sanderson noted the links between these sorts of verses and the phrasing in *B*.[34] The continuing appeal of this type of literature

---

[30] Those consulted are MS Lambeth 501, from French, early fifteenth century (*3PV*); MS Sloane 213, from Latin, in which a translation of the Vulgate physiognomy is accompanied only by the onomantic art of the *Secretum*, early fifteenth century (*9EV*); and MS Ashmole 396, from Latin, which has an extended, combined physiognomy, in a revised version of the Vulgate type, mid-fifteenth century (*9EV*, see p. xviii).

[31] In addition to Bartholomew of Messina; R. Förster (ed.), *Scriptores physiognomonici graeci et latini*, 2 vols. (Leipzig, 1893), contains one Latin version, the Pseudopolemonis, which includes a section thereon, ii, 150-60 (158-9).

[32] *Prose MS*, ii, 114.

[33] R. Klibansky, E.Panofsky, & F. Saxl, *Saturn and Melancholy* (1964), 112-23.

[34] With particular reference to John Russell's *Boke of Nurture*, but the material was widely current ('A recently-discovered poem', 60-61).

for Scottish readers is illustrated by the verses on 'complexiounis' copied into Patric Scot's medical book in the early seventeenth century.[35] A considerable amount of the material in this compilation may itself be traceable back to the *Secretum*. It is thus possible that the author of the 'phisnomy' himself drew the connection between the humours and the rest of the physiognomy, but it is more probable that it had already been made in his source physiognomy, through the sort of resources described above.

The textual relationship of MSS *A* and *B* is a far from direct one. The 42 lines present in *B* but not the earlier *A* make it clear that *B* descends from a different group of exemplars. But if *B* has lines not in *A*, *A* contains 29 not found in *B*.[36] The most textually interesting passages are at the beginning and end of the physiognomy, where the major divergences between the two sets of manuscripts occur. In a substantial number of other cases the two groups of witnesses contain lines which differ markedly from each other in phrasing, though they come at the same place and are making broadly the same point.[37] In some instances the looseness of expression is such that it would be difficult to ascribe a 'better' reading.[38] It is here that cross-referencing with the Latin text can be extremely useful. But MSS *A* do remain manifestly the more reliable witnesses: they have fewer garbled lines and more narrative coherence.[39] Even so, the very late witnesses *B* retain a considerable textual interest.

The most striking testimony of this is found at the beginning of the physiognomy, where there is excellent reason to believe that MSS *B* contain 20 lines which have dropped out of the *A* text,

---

[35] On the book see H. Hargreaves, 'Patric Scot's medical book' in M. Benskin and M.L. Samuels (eds.), *So Meny People Longages and Tonges* (Edinburgh, 1981), 309-21. The MS is BL, Harley 1734, and the poem is on f.35. There are a number of interesting verbal correspondences with Hay's poem, but this probably points to the commonplace nature of the subject rather than to any borrowing. The sanguine man is described as 'Syngand, hardy ... Luiffand' (cf. *B*, 9-10); the choleric is said to be 'Off wit full large *and* hardy als' (cf. *B* 13-14) and the phlegmatic is 'Intill spitting in habundance' (cf. *B*, 6).

[36] *A*, 1-14, 31-2, 49-50, 77-8, 116, 319-26.

[37] See n.24, above.

[38] Cf. the discussion of a poem with greater looseness of phrasing and late witnesses, Sally Mapstone, '*The Thre Prestis of Peblis* in the sixteenth century' in A. Gardner-Medwin & J.Hadley Williams (eds.), *A Day Estivall* (Aberdeen, 1990), 124-42.

[39] *B*, for example, lacks the second half of a couplet after 127, and has several hopeless efforts, e.g. 211.

possibly through a bad case of eye-skip.[40] This is the section on the four complexions with which the *B* text rather abruptly opens, in contrast to *A*'s more gradual introduction on the choosing of officers in battle. But it is easy to see exactly where in *A B*'s section on the complexions should be inserted, for *A* itself raises the question of 'complexioun' as one of the physiognomical features of which Alexander should take note (ll. 13-14). At this point there should follow *B*'s 20 lines designating the four types. The two texts then come together (*A* 15ff, *B* 21ff) on the necessity to avoid dealings with deformed men. The complexions theme is indeed a recurrent one in the 'Regiment'. In the development of the 'little world of man' idea earlier on, it had stated, 'And, fra oure gud complexioun changit be,/Bot we haue some remed, þan mon we de.' (9811-12). And in MSS *A* the physiognomy section is followed by the exemplum of how Hippocrates resisted the signs of his outward complexion in order to act virtuously. The authenticity of this passage in *B* seems unquestionable on internal grounds. There is, moreover, a relevant piece of external evidence. Mrs Sanderson noted that the prologue to John Rolland's mid-sixteenth-century *Court of Venus* appears to quote from these lines on the complexions.[41] This could be, indirectly, further proof of the dissemination of Hay's writing in the sixteenth century, though we cannot tell whether Rolland knew the physiognomy as part of the *BKA*, or as a poem on its own.

The physiognomy then proceeds through its customary head to foot course. Comparison with Philippus and the translations will often show an indebtedness to the Vulgate tradition, but just as often it reveals a striking originality. A few examples from the early parts of the physiognomy will illustrate this.

The first section, on the hair, displays both the 'phisnomy''s debts to its source and its colourful expansions of it. On plenitude of hair, the various accounts read thus:

Phillipus: Multitudo eciam pilorum in pectore et ventre reperta declarat horribilitatem et singularitatem nature, et diminucionem apprehensionis et amorem injuriarum, et sapiencie innuit paucitatem.

---

[40] *B*'s opening 'The first complextioun ...' (1) should be inserted before the line in *A* that starts 'And oure all thing first counsale I ...' (15). It is possible that a scribe resuming his copying jumped down to the second instance of the use of 'first'.

[41] 'A recently-discovered poem', 62-3.

Lambeth: Many heres in þe brest or in þe wombe bytokyns horibilyte and singularyte of kynde, *and* lessenyng of þe resceyt, and loue of wronges.
Yonge: Plente of her*e* in wombe and in breste, tokenyt oribilite and syngulerte of kynde and smalnys of vndyrstondynge and loue of body.[42]
'Phisnomy': When beard *and* breist *and* brouis all overgroun,
Ry*ch*t vnfrilie w*ith* birnand eyn þat glowis,
And of the laife vngudlie of portiriture,
That is great taikin of mervellous nature,
Of nature horribille *and* vnreasonabill,
And perallus, *and* till all vyces able. (*B*, 53-8)

The 'phisnomy''s text is quoted from *B* (cf. *A*, 42-6) because it preserves a reading, lost in *A*, which catches the meaning of the Latin in a more imaginative manner than any of the translations. The phrase in question is 'horribilitatem et singularitatem nature'. All the translations, from Latin, or through French, render the epithets very literally.[43] It is the *B* MSS, by contrast, that have a more effective rendering of 'singularitatem' in 'mervellous nature' (56) which, despite the repetition of 'nature' in the next line, looks both better and more appropriate than 'taking of grete diuersite' at the equivalent place in *A* (42).[44] We can also see in this passage how far the Scots author will move away from the matter of the Latin text. In his hands *pectore et ventre* (in the translations always 'brest' and 'wombe') become the expanded, alliterative, 'beard *and* breist *and* brouis', picking up an idea from a later section 'de superciliis'.[45] The burning eyes are an added detail in the 'phisnomy'; indeed it has transformed the hirsute man into a more alarming and dangerous proposition altogether.

This discussion of hair is longer and more varied than most of

---

42 *Bacon*, 167; *3PV*, 114, 233. Lambeth has been taken as representative of the English versions, for Sloane and Ashmole are very similar (*9EV*, 11, 93, and n.43 below).

43 ibid., Sloane, 'horribilté and syngulerté of kynde'; Ashmole, 'horribilité and singularité of nature'.

44 Another fifteenth-century poet made a similar translation: 'Merveyllous of complexio*un* and singuleer in nature', R. Steele (ed.), *Lydgate and Burgh's Secrees of Old Philisoffres* (EETS, 1894). There is no other reason to associate this translation with the Scots version.

45 'Supercilium quod habet multos pilos ...', *Bacon*, 168.

those texts, apart from Ashmole, with which we are comparing the Scots physiognomy, and this general principle holds good for many sections that follow. Nowhere is this more so than in the treatment of eyes, where there are elaborate and vivid variations on the arguments set out in the source, and much more besides. Only Ashmole is as varied and longer, but this is a translation, whereas the author of the 'phisnomy' appears to be working from his own invention. His account contains nearly all the details in Philippus, and there are again several close parallels of expression. He blends two sentences from the Latin: 'Qui habet oculos magnos, invidus est et inverecundus, piger inobediens.... Cum vero habet oculos extensos cum extensione vultus talis est maliciosus nequam'[46] to produce:

> And quha hes ene goigland out oure his face,
> Betaiknys ire and pride and wilfulnes,
> Inwye, but schame, swere, inobedient, (*A*, 63-5)

Here we should note *B*'s noun 'inobedience' (75), the last in a series of nouns, though the rhyme with 'entent' in the next line (*A*, 66, *B*, 76) would call it into question as a preferable reading. The idea of bulging eyes is mistranslated by Yonge or his source, and he also lacks a translation for Philippus, 'Cum vero oculi sint mediocres declinantes ad celestem colorem', which Lambeth, Sloane and Ashmole all translate, and the 'phisnomy' renders as, 'the ene of quhilk þe sterne drawis to the blew,/That maist is liknynit to þe hevinlie hew' (*A*, 59-60).[47] Distinctions such as this heighten the case for the Scots version's indebtedness to a Latin text descended from Philippus, rather than a French MS in the Waterford/Copale line.

The textual worth of MSS *B* is evident again in the discussion of red eyes. Here Philippus' 'Si vero oculi fuerint rubei, ille cujus sunt est animosus et fortis et potens'[48] becomes in *A*:

> And quha sa hes rede ene, w*it*houtin dout,
> Thay salbe fund blak, hardy, and stout, (69-70)

but *B*'s version of the trio, 'bald, hardie *and* stout' (80) makes more sense (cf. similar phrasing at *A*, 207, *B*, 218), and 'bald' is an entirely acceptable translation of *animosus*.

This pattern of a skeletal framework of translation, onto which is

---

[46] ibid.
[47] ibid. *3PV*, 233, 115; *9EV*, 11, 95.
[48] *Bacon*, 168.

built a sharp and often humorous set of observations of the Scottish author's own devising is repeated throughout the sequence of bodily features and habits which is then pursued. In the process much is done to transform an essentially denotive system of physiognomical explication into something far more distinctive, as if the poet finds as much pleasure in evolving metaphors and similes as in their quasi-scientific application.

It is this enjoyment of the apt phrase that leads him into such image-making as 'grete lang nos, haukbeik, before dippand/Hie in þe mydd*is*, as griffoun beik rysand' (*A*, 113-14), 'keppand nois, oure-hingand as a barge' (*A*, 146), or 'fatt pudding leggis' (*A*, 271). In passages such as this the emphasis is moving away from the characteristic it explains, and towards the wittiness of the expression that evokes it. Thus 'Et qui habet tempora inflata et venas plenas est valde iracundus'[49] becomes

> Quha has ane vissage fatt, schorte, and suollyn,
> With keppand nois, w*ith* cheikis and tempillis bollyn,
> Wyth litill hew, of culloure vermyllioun,
> Orpy growis in þare arbere all sessoun. (*A*, 169-72)

One striking passage which well reveals the stylish interpretation of the source is that on speech. It is also one in which the concentration of good or better readings in *B* is especially dense. At its opening the 'phisnomy' is following the pronouncements of Philippus with some attention. 'Et qui habet grossam vocem et sonoram est bellicosus et eloquens'[50] expands to:

> And quha-sa has his speiche gros and ground,
> W*ith* wourd*is* clere, vnwe*m*myt, hale and sound,
> He is baith bald and stout, of gude langage,
> Off eloquence, of gud witt and knawledge; (*A*, 205-8)

B's main contribution here is 'round' in the first line (*B*, 216), a better rendering of *sonoram* than the 'ground' of *A* (presumably 'sharpened', but perhaps produced through association with the opening letters of 'gros'). Philippus next deals with the well-modulated voice and the swift speaker, whether of loud or quiet tones. The 'phisnomy' omits the first and second, characterizes the 'pipand voce and small' (*A*, 209) in a manner unrelated to anything in the Latin, and introduces the idea of defects such as stuttering or stammering, but also including rapid speech. Some

---

49 ibid., 169.
50 ibid.

of the epithets may be loosely lifted from the Latin, but the correspondence of characteristics is not one to one.[51] The Scottish poet develops his catalogue to include the man 'Quha quhilum spekis swift, and quhilu*m*is slaw' (*A*, 219), the token of a 'diuers nature' (*A*, 220) and then draws near again to an idea in Philippus: 'Et qui habet dulcem vocem invidus est et suspiciosus. Pulcritudo eciam vocis indicat stolidatem et insipienciam et magnanimitatem'.[52] But for our author this provides the stimulus for a small sequence of semi-proverbial and metaphorical comparisons. In the two following quotations from *A*, possible emendations from *B* are italicized in the margin:

Quha has a voce slekit, baith soft and swete,
And in his mouth melt buttir will no*ch*t lete,
Thay draw oft out of men w*ith* þare langage,
And garris þame wene þai haue a gude marage - *curage* (*B*, 237)
As ane fowllare, quhan he wauld foulis tak, *his pluvars get* (*B*, 238)
With his suete note he drawis þame to the nett. (*A*, 224-8)

There is no precedent for these ideas in the Latin, and none of the vernacular translations has anything similar. The man in whose mouth butter would not melt, and the devious fowler are the Scottish poet's own. *B* has a considerable amount to offer at a point where for several lines the MSS of *A* show signs of an unusual quantity of scribal disturbance and alteration. *B*'s 'curage' (237) makes more sense than *A*'s rather desperate 'marage' (227). Its 'pluvars' (238) is a harder reading than 'foulis' (*A*, 227); and its 'get' (238) is clearly correct over *A*'s 'tak' (227), as the rhyme with 'nett' in the next line proves.

The section on speech in the 'phisnomy' concludes with another pair of distinctions, between the garrulous man and the taciturn man, for which there is again no model in Philippus, which at broadly this point is comparing those who move their hands when speaking with those who do not. The Scottish poet's continuation shows his appealing weakness for proverbial illustration. Once more *B*'s readings are important:

[51] E.g. 'inprobus, stolidus, importunus et mendax .... iracundus et precipitans, male nature' (*Bacon*, 169-70), with 'Invious, sturtand, crabbit, and vnkynde,/Pres[u]mpteous, haisty, and wþeris wald supprise' (*A*, 214-15).

[52] *Bacon*, 170.

Quha spekis oure oft, and ay is traitland new,	
He may never laik of lyere and vntrew:	*he may never fail ȝee of law and vertew* (*B*, 241)
And he þat oure soildin is, and spekis oure still,	*and wha sa seildin speiks and is our still* (*B*, 242)
Traist wele he has ane hede vnwourthy wyll -	
The wattir þat rynnys is clere and kyndly gude,	*the rynand water* (*B*, 244)
Ane standand watt*er* ay stinkis in þe mvde (*A*,229-34)	*and standand water is stinkand of the mude* (*B*, 245)

As it stands, *A* makes little sense. The last couplet suggests a contrast between the good nature of the loquacious speaker and the corruption of the untalkative man. But the opening lines appear to say that the talkative man will never be lacking of the liar. Cartwright's notes show that as originally written line 230 in *A* had the form, 'He may never laik of lere and vertew'.[53] This is much closer to *B*'s 'he may never faiȝee of law and vertew' (*B*, 241), an approving statement which fits far more sensibly into this context. It would seem that *A* has a misplaced correction of a line in its exemplar that in *B* has remained unaltered. Similarly, *B*'s 'and wha sa seildin speiks and is our still' (242) is a much more coherent argument than 231 in *A*, and the parallel phrasing 'rynand ... standand ... stinkand' (244-5) in *B* is more attractive than the contrasting forms in *A*.[54]

There are other instances where emendation from *B* should be seriously considered,[55] but the last major passage of textual difference is in the conclusions to the two versions. Both appear to have lost different parts of the delineation of the ideal man—a two-stage account in the 'phisnomy' which quirkily begins its discussion before the final physical section on the feet.[56] The loss is more severe in *B*, but it yet retains some authentic-looking lines which have dropped out of *A*. Put together, they make an effective finale to the physiognomy.

---

53 *BKA*, iii, 257.

54 Hay could have found the idea in the *Secretum*; cf. *Prose MS*, ii, 138-9.

55 For example *A*, 35, *B* 41, where *B*'s 'clemens' is better sense and a better rhyme than *A*'s 'clenes'. Or *A*, 285, *B*, 298: Cartwright has corrected *A*'s 'of kittill' to 'and kittill'. *B* reads 'of kittill will', which is a better translation of the Latin, 'male voluntatis', *Bacon*, 171.

56 Cf. *A*, 263-70, a very near translation of the description in Philippus, *Bacon*, 171.

The perfect physiognomy is one that conforms to the ideal man, 'In mydlin way of all his governance/In all proportioun als betwene þai tua' (*A*, 312-13). At *A* 302, *B* 313 begins a short divergence in line-order and other textual differences between them. While *B* suspiciously almost repeats a line (318 and 322) here, it also has a couplet on eloquence and prudence (320-1), not present in *A*, which has a plausibly recapitulatory character. When the two versions join together again, *A* has eight lines (319-26) not found in *B*; but *B* in return has a couplet on speech and pace (238-9), which well rounds off the physiognomy, and ends 'sic men as thir sould be about a king', indicating that it should probably be inserted after *A* 326. Moreover, *B*'s 'loff' at 341 has a good claim as a harder reading than *A*'s 'love' (328). And its final line, 'in weir and peace in houshald or battell', neatly finishes off the physiognomy by looking back to the idea of battle expounded in the opening lines of *A*.

At this point *A*, by contrast, is arguing, 'Thare is na reule bot sum tyme it will falȝee' (*A* 332), and it then pursues the theme of conquering an adverse physiognomy through the story of Hippocrates. The customary position of this exemplum was at the start rather than the conclusion of the physiognomy,[57] but the relocation of it in the *BKA* provides its poet with a means of getting out of that section and into the final part of his 'Regiment', in which the king is urged to rule through the exercise of reason, something which may involve the necessary restraining of his bad instincts. As the *BKA* poet, recalling surely the earlier comments on the complexions, puts it:

And tocht þow find be þe complexioun
Thy will inclynit to ill conditioun,
Think wele þan þat þi merite is gretar
Na it in þi awne nature growin war, (10494-7)

But what is of further interest is that the Hippocrates episode is within the *Secretum* a separable sub-section of the physiognomy proper. Thus Manzalaoui assigns it a separate sigil in this categorisation of the *Secretum*'s constituent parts.[58] In other words, the physiognomy could occur without the exemplum. Thus it may be of significance that MSS *A*, which have the physiognomy inserted

---

[57] As, for example, in Philippus, *Bacon*, 165; Lambeth, *3PV*, 113; Sloane, *9EV*, 10-11; Ashmole, *9EV*, 90. It is not in Yonge.

[58] *9EV*, p. xiii.

in a 'Regiment' based on the *Secretum*, include the Hippocrates story in keeping with many recensions of that work. MSS *B*, which have the physiognomy on its own, do not have the anecdote and finish instead where the physiognomy usually ended. One way of interpreting this evidence would be that MSS *B* represent the physiognomy as it was originally written, as a separate poem, which was inserted in two later stages: first into the 'Regiment', at which point the Hippocrates story was added to it, and its erstwhile final couplet altered, and thereafter into the *Alexander*. This would make sense of the title *The Regiment of kingis with the buke of phisnomy* in the Asloan MS which, as we have noted, allows for the possibility that these are two distinct works, yoked together.

The likelihood that the 'Regiment' and its 'phisnomy' existed as a separate entity or entities which later were taken into the *BKA* during the process of its re-composition or revision is heightened by another piece of previously unnoticed evidence. For this huge poem contains other material which can definitely be demonstrated to have been appropriated from another poetic work with independent circulation.

Lines 8477-592 of the 'Voeux du Paon' section of the *BKA*, a part of it already rather loosely based on the equivalent section of the *Roman d'Alexandre*,[59] contain a discussion under the aegis of the 'King of Lufe' of the 'thewis of ane gud women' (8478) which is in large part lifted from the Scots poem on that subject, extant now in two manuscripts: CUL, MS Kk.1.5 (6), written c.1480, and Cambridge, St John's College, MS G. 23, written in 1487. In the first of these the text is headed 'The thewis off gudwomen'.[60] The *BKA* 'thewis' cannot be shown to derive directly from either of these MSS—indeed it shares different readings with both of

[59] Comparison may most easily be made with the text printed in vol. ii of *The Buik of Alexander*, ed. R.L. Graeme Ritchie, 4 vols. (STS, 1921). The statement made by Cartwright, that in the treatment of the *Voeux du Paon* 'Hay [*sic*] tactfully condenses a poem of 8800 lines to 1800, keeping the main line intact and adding some touches of his own' ('Hay and the Alexander tradition', 233) needs qualification. The 'thre questionis' (8007) that Betis, as King of Love, determines to ask of each of the participants in the court of love, and of which the 'thewis of ane gud women' is a part, is a very distinctive addition in this Scots version.

[60] See T.F. Mustanoja (ed.), *The Good Wife Taught Her Daughter* ... (Helsinki, 1948) and R. Girvan (ed.), *Ratis Raving* (STS, 1937). On the relation of the two texts, Mustanoja concludes '... neither of the texts is a faithful copy of the original. Nor can either of them be a copy of the other.' (155)

them—but that this part of the *BKA* is an indirect descendant from the *Thewis* and not an original component of the poem is clear. Mustanoja and Girvan concur in dating the *Thewis* around 1450,[61] which would itself date the work earlier than both dates now ascribed to the *BKA* (1460 and 1499). Moreover the *BKA* contains only a portion of the *Thewis*: Kk.1.5 has 294 lines, the St John's MS 306, the *BKA* version 115. But perhaps the most conclusive piece of evidence is metrical. The two earlier versions are in 'remarkably regular' octosyllabic couplets;[62] in the *BKA* these have been transformed into decasyllabic verses.

That the reviser of the *BKA* should have felt such a freedom to incorporate a portion of the *Thewis* into the romance he was reworking may lie in his perception of it as material amply amenable to this kind of appropriation. The most recent scholar to work on the *Thewis* and its neighbours in Kk.1.5, *Ratis Raving*, *The Foly of Fulys and the Thewis of Wysmen*, and *The Consail and Teiching at the Vys Man Gaif his Sone*, Denton Fox, explains the verbal resemblances and other oddities of style between the poems in the form 'we now have them' as due to the fact that 'people seem to have regarded them as miscellaneous collections of good advice rather than poetic masterpieces, and writers seem to have felt completely free to make additions, deletions and changes as they saw fit'.[63] That the *BKA* reviser viewed these poems in this manner is given further support by the presence in the same part of the poem, at 8573-7, near the end of the *Thewis* borrowing, of five lines which are based on 251-5 of *The Consail and Teiching* ....[64]

But the *BKA* reviser may also have felt the use of the *Thewis* material appropriate for a reason that takes us back to the question of the identity of those two other items that precede the *Regiment* and *phisnomy* in Asloan's contents list. Is it possible that *The buke of curtasy and nortur* is a title for one, or more, of the Kk.1.5 pieces? From the title it must be some form of one of the courtesy books, the manuals of manners and etiquette whose popularity was growing and whose audience was widening throughout the fifteenth century. Indeed, most English versions date from the mid-fifteenth century, and the inclusion of such a piece in Asloan's collection probably reflects a similar broadening

---

61 *The Good Wife*, 155-6; *Ratis Raving*, p. lxxiv.

62 *The Good Wife*, 136.

63 '*DOST* and evidence for authorship: some poems connected with *Ratis Raving*', in C. Macafee & I. Macleod (eds.), *The Nuttis Schell: Essays on the Scots Language* (Aberdeen, 1987), 96-105 (102, 101).

64 I owe this reference to Miss Katherine Stephenson.

of the Scottish audience to whom they appealed, from the aristocracy to merchants and craftsmen.[65]

The pieces in Kk.1.5 are not strictly courtesy books of the ilk of Lydgate's *Stans Puer ad Mensam*,[66] (the most popular English poetic version), but they are the only surviving fifteenth-century Scottish works of this type. It is at least worth considering that Asloan might have copied together a group of works (*Regiment* and *phisnomy*, *Thewis*, and possibly *Consail and Teiching*) which commonly circulated together, and that, before him, the *BKA* reviser might have found them in a similar textual relationship.[67]

We now come to the other item in the contents list, *The document of Sir gilbert hay*. There is one poetic candidate for identification with this item, which has not previously been canvassed, but for the consideration of which there is some good circumstantial evidence. We surmise this item to be a piece of verse; we know it to be instructional, and we find reference to it just before the *Regiment*, a piece dealing with kingship. One work which would fit with all of these features and facts and which is the right sort of date is the poem variously known as *De Regimine Principum* (the title preferred here), the *Harp*, and *Ane Buke of Gud Counsall to the King*.[68] This poem was written in the 1450s and contains governmental advice to the king. It was presumably intended for James II and his advisers, though the king is not named in it. *De Regimine Principum* was a popular poem, being copied as late as c.1570 into the Maitland MS. It was also one of the earliest pieces of Scottish verse to be put into print, among the Chepman and Myllar prints, in 1508. Its apparent absence from the Asloan Folio MS is thus the more noticeable, since there is considerable overlap between Chepman and Myllar and Asloan, and it has been well argued that Asloan probably copied some of his material from 'prints closely related to, but not identical with, the surviving Chepman and Myllar prints'.[69]

This speculation is made the more interesting when allied to the

---

65 J.W. Nicholls, *The Matter of Courtesy, Medieval Courtesy Books and the Gawain-Poet* (1985), 69-73, 145-76.

66 ibid., 193.

67 The *BKA* and the Kk.1.5 poems also have in common the device of a concluding 'epilogue' (found in both the *Thewis*, 295-316, and *Ratis Raving*, 1799-1814) in which the writers speak, as revisers, of their debts to earlier works of a similar nature. Given Asloan's *Document* title, it is worthy of note that the *Thewis* epilogue refers to 'sindry documentis ... of wysmen' (299-301). See also Fox, '*DOST* and evidence for authorship', 101.

68 The most accessible edition of the poem is in *Maitl. Folio MS.*, ii, 74-91.

69 D. Fox, 'Manuscripts and prints of Scots poetry in the sixteenth century',

fact that the *BKA* 'Regiment' has a number of unmistakable verbal and situational similarities to *De Regimine Principum*. One example will suffice as illustration. *De Regimine Principum*'s lines

> It is degradying till a kyngis croun
> To mell hym with smale wrechit besynes ...
> & specialie þe ryale mageste
> Suld neuer be traueld bot in materis hee.[70]

may be compared with 9905-7 of the *BKA* 'Regiment'

> ... Nocht mell him with small wrechit besines -
> His small materis with small men ay repes,
> On he materis ay travell his prudence;

These, however, are not straightforward appropriations into the 'Regiment', as in the case of the *BKA*'s borrowings from the *Thewis*. Rather, they look like the reworking by the same author in one context (the 'Regiment') of material first used in another (*De Regimine Principum*). In other words, it is unlikely that the *BKA* reviser, already probably borrowing the 'Regiment' for his poem, would then go to the trouble of adding into it phrases and ideas from *De Regimine Principum*; it is more likely that these 'borrowings' were already put there to start with by the *Regiment*'s author.

If the Asloan MS *Document of Sir gilbert hay*[71] were indeed to be *De Regimine Principum*, the connections between that poem and the 'Regiment' necessarily suggest—to bring the argument full circle—that the 'Regiment', and its closely associated 'phisnomy', could themselves be works by Hay. Two interpretations of this evidence are possible: either that the 'Regiment' and 'phisnomy' were inserted into the *BKA* by its later reviser as pieces known to him to have been of Hay's composition; or that Hay himself incorporated this material into the poem, having originally composed it separately. Either of these explanations would help to

in A.J. Aitken, M. McDiarmid & D.S. Thomson (eds.), *Bards and Makars* (Glasgow, 1977), 156-71 (158).

[70] *Maitl. Fol. MS.*, ll. 99-105 (correctly, 92-8). Further examples of the relationships between *De Regimine Principum* and the 'Regiment' are discussed in my forthcoming study of Scottish advisory literature and in Mapstone, 'Advice to Princes Tradition', 136-41.

[71] 'Document', in the sense of instruction or piece of teaching, is a word often used by Hay himself in his prose works: Mapstone, 'Advice to Princes Tradition', 62; Lyall, 'Lost literature', 40-41. It is striking that the *BKA* 'Regiment' is introduced by Aristotle: 'Tharefore haue me excusit, I the require,/And tak þir documentis þat I leif þe here' (9461-2).

account for the strong links in subject matter between the strictures in the 'Regiment' on good kingship and the many other passages of this type in the course of the *BKA*; and the second possibility—that this part of the revision was actually Hay's—would also explain the relatively smooth transition effected by the addition of the Hippocrates story to the 'revised' 'Regiment', as the kind of thing the original author might be more likely to produce.

This line of argument cannot quite be used for the *Thewis* material, which fits less obviously into the *BKA* as a whole, and which has been shown to have a different type of textual tradition. If, however, as suggested, the *Thewis* material did circulate in conjunction with a separated 'Regiment' and 'phisnomy', as is possibly indicated under Asloan's *Buke of curtasy and nortur*, its appropriation by the 1499 reviser of the *BKA* makes a certain amount of sense. Whether the *Thewis* and the other works associated with it should actually be more closely linked still with Hay remains unproved. What we can, however, conclude is that there are good arguments for associating Asloan's *Regiment of princis with the buke of phisnomy* with Hay—even if they are not, yet, conclusive ones. The study of both the *BKA* and the Kk.1.5 poems is still in its infancy, but it is to be hoped that further exploration of these complex relationships will clarify more about the processes of their composition.

Let us return finally to the 'phisnomy' poem. For its Scottish author—be it Hay or another—the physiognomy provided an opportunity for poetic invention which he clearly took with pleasure. For Asloan it was a text of a piece with other works of a didactic but less heavy character than those included in his prose section; like *The buke of curtasy and nortur* it offered advice applicable to all socially ambitious men. Robert Mylne's motive in copying the manuscript at the end of the seventeenth century was an antiquarian one. Less apparent, and worthy of further investigation, is why earlier in the century Sir Lewis Stewart should have wanted a copy of the poem.[72] Further study of his Collections, an interesting miscellany of the historical, the legal, and the literary, may reveal

[72] Mrs Sanderson notes that the poem is 'the only non-factual item in the [Stewart] Collections', 'A recently-discovered poem', 49.

it.[73] The textual history of this Scottish 'phisnomy' certainly offers a small but illuminating view of changing cultural tastes from the fifteenth to the seventeenth centuries.[74]

Appendix

The *A* physiognomy is quoted from John Cartwright's STS edition, which takes the earlier of the two *Alexander* manuscripts as its copy-text. I have also used those of Cartwright's textual notes (here numbered 1-15) which refer to his emendations (often also in square brackets) of *A* which can now be either confirmed or qualified by the *B* witnesses as indicated. (Cartwright does not include textual variants from the later manuscript in his apparatus after 5000; thus reference here is only to his copy-text.) I am grateful to Dr Cartwright and to the Scottish Text Society for permission to use this material. To facilitate comparison this section of the *Alexander* has been renumbered 1-332, but the line numbers of the full poem are also given in parenthesis. The *B* physiognomy is transcribed from NLS, Adv. MS 34.3.12, with emendations from Adv. MS 34.3.11 as noted. Punctuation and capitalisation are editorial, following generally the practice in Cartwright's edition. Square brackets are used here for small corrections of spelling, which otherwise remains unaltered. All abbreviations are expanded and italicised as indicated. The scribe of Adv. MS 34.3.12 makes a number of other marks, particularly over *u*, which have no abbreviatory force and are thus not recorded. I am grateful to the trustees of NLS for permission to publish this transcription, and to Mrs Sanderson for very considerable assistance in its making.

---

[73] Compare the comments on the wide cultural value of legal material in J. Durkan, 'The early Scottish notary', in I.B. Cowan & D. Shaw (eds.), *The Renaissance and Reformation in Scotland* (Edinburgh, 1983), 22-40 (40).

[74] I am most grateful to Mrs Sanderson for generously sharing her past and present researches on the poem with me.

Physiognomy A

Off the phis*no*mye

Till all thy batallis ordand gouernouris,
In quham þow may maist traist in þine hono*uris*,
f.142r And cheis þe men w*ith* all gud proporteis,
As in þe buke of phisnomy þow seis,
Baith stark and stoure, of gud proportioun;
And alsua langand þare conditioun,
Quhare þow sall se þare proporteis alhale,
Quhome to refuse, quhome to þi *ser*vice wale,
Baith of þare fassoun and þare phisnomy,
And all þare feris, and giftis of þare body,
Thare hyde, þare hare, þare fassoun, and þare semblance,
Thare speiche, þare luke, þare gang, þare contenance,
Thare voce, þare hew, and þare complexioun,
Be all þe part*is* of þe body, vp and doun.
And oure all thing first counsale I þat þow
Fra man mysmade of nature vmbechew,
[M]ankit,[1] dememberit fra nature of mankynd,
For co*m*monly þa[i][2] haue ane aukwart strynd,
For [quhay-sa] falt has in his natiuitie,
In his conditioun fa[l]tles[3] sal no*ch*t be,
Bot gif þat þai throw vertew þame refrenne,
And throw þare witt þare wikkit will *con*strenȝe.
And first at ma*n*nys hare þow tak knawlege:
Giff þai be ȝoung, bot no*ch*t oure tend*er* of age,
Giff it be dosk, ȝellow, broun, or blak,
Eftir þe land, the hare is no*ch*t to lake;
Giff it be rede, be wer, for few is wise
Quhan hede and berd is hewit on sindry wise -
Thay can of falshede and subteletie,
And to begyle þai ar richt wound*er* sle,
And quhare þe falt of falsett rigna*n*d is,
Thare may na vertew ring þare, as I wis.

---

[1] *MS* Nankit: *B*, 23, mankit.
[2] *MS* þane; *B*, 24, they.
[3] *MS* fatles; *B*, 26, faultles.

Soft ȝellow hare is takin of gude ingine,
And abill baith to craft and clergy syne,
W*ith* mansuetude of swetnes and clenes,
W*ith* habilnes of witt and hie prudence.
Richt reuch of hare betaknys scharpe nature,
And hie of blude, w*ith* gudlie protrature,
W*ith* gude culloure and gude chere of wissage,
And wele favorit of fassoun of corssage;
And, be [thay][4] no*ch*t wele favorit, but vnfre,
f.142v That is takin of grete diuersitie,
Of nature horabill and vnressonabill,
And perrellus and till all vicis habill.
Quhan breist and bak and browis all ouregrow*is*,
Vnfrely made, w*ith* birna*n*d ene þat glowis,
It is no*ch*t spedefull w*ith* þame to haue dail
Na hald þame into cumpaney speciall,
Bot gif þai contrar to þare nature be,
And governe þame be law and veretie.
  Ane large forehede, w*ith* browis semlie sett,
Nocht rouch, hary, w*ith* campis hingand plett,
Bot small and lengȝhe, and of gude compas,
W*ith* vþer properteis endlang þe f[a]ce,[5]
With b[l]ak[6] or broun or gray, fare ene and grete,
Nocht goigland, or fer out na fer in sett -
Thir ar the takny*n*nis of wisdome and iustice,
Off luffe and lawte and to [be] kyndlie wise.
The ene of quhilk þe sterne drawis to þe blew,
That maist is liknynit to þe hevinlie hew,
That is ane takin of pece and equitie,
Off gud witt, lufe, prudence, and cheretie;
And quha hes ene goigland out oure his face,
Betaiknys ire and pride and wilfulnes,
Inwye, but schame, swere, inobedient,
And, be þare wauwill, þe war in þare entent.
Quha sa has ene rynnand co*n*tynuallie,
It is ane full ill takin, traist wele treulie;
And quha sa hes rede ene, w*ith*outin dout,
Thay salbe fund blak, hardy, and stout,

---

[4] *MS* thay *omitted*; *B*, 51, they.
[5] *MS* force; *B*, 63, face.
[6] *MS* brak; *B*, 65, blak.

And, be it woma*n*, scho salbe bald of kynd,
And vnschemfull to wreik quhan scho is leynd.
Bot ene of twyn cullouris all men may rew
Quhan ilkane e is of ane sindry hew:
Bot gif vertew haue dominatioun,
That ressoun may be lord attoure passioun,
Thay ar þe werst þat euer bare creature,
Or euir war made or ordand by nature -
Saiffand þe ene þat ar of alkin hewis,
Quhilk God and nature of all ma*n*kynd rewis:
Quhan alkin hewis ar spruttit in þe ene,
f.143r With spottis of blak and rede and quhyte betwene,
Thare followis oft my[s]fassoun[7] of wissage,
And mekill mare of conscience and corage,
And as-like ene oft schawis litill mude,
And mekill quhite waverand ene war neuer gude,
And sand-blind ene ar schamefull, co*m*mounly,
And feneȝeis oft, becaus þai ar fawte;
And glowrand ene ar corsand in þe sicht,
Ar thrawin, and full of subtell[e][8] and slicht;
And quha sa skellyis, w*it*h ane e lukland by,
Thay ar inclynit to vicis co*m*mounly.
Quha stotand, glourand, w*it*h ane sembland stout,
Thay ar no*ch*t hale in harnis, haue ȝe na dout,
For in þare forehede fallis sum franyssing,
Quhilk bring*is* þame oft tymes in a rauyssing,
That sic ane francyis, and ane fantasye
Makis þame, but raddour, abill to folie.
And quha w*it*h sade chere hes ene dede and still,
Incly*n*nit ar reddie till vncouth ill;
And quha sa lurkand ene has, ay lauchand,
To lichory ar mekill inclynand,
And als to dissaue and sleith þare nature is,
And mak sembland þat þai can do na mys.
Quha wynkis, w*it*h his ene, and nod*is* als,
It cu*m*mys wele of kynd for to be fals;
Quha lukis on side, and haldis þare hede on wrey,

[7] *MS* myfassoun; *B*, 95, misfassioun.
[8] *MS* subtell; *B*, 102, sutteltie.

And fenȝeis to mak small ene dangerusly,
Thay ar dissimiland, fenȝeand, and vntrew
Off luffe, and abill to dissaue ynew.
Quha has ane lenȝhe neis, thyne and wele made,
Ar hichty, brethfull, and full of lichtlyhede;
Bot grete lang nos, haukbeik, before dippand,
Hie in þe myddis, as griffoun beik rysand,
Ar wicht and ma*n*full, as co*m*mounlie is pruvit,
In pece and were richt wourthy to be luvit;
And quha hes neis in mydwart law and schorte,
Keppand before, ȝow may wele knaw þat sort -
Thay ar aukward and illwilly of kynd,
Donsocht, crabbit, angry quhan þai ar teynd,
f.143v To murthur and mysdede reddie ay,
And will nowther kepe kyndnis, lawte, nor fay,
And reddie will mak ane forfattoure,
Bot grace and vertew bridell þare nature.[9]
Giff þai be no*ch*t oure snak, bot mesurabilly,
Vpsett before, sic takynnis ar wourthy;
Weill favorit in þe visage and þe ene,
Off hide and hare and voce and cullo*ure* clene,
Blayith lauchand chere, traist þare cu*m*paney,
And kynd for kyndnes sall do reddely -
Gude fallowschip þai luffe attoure all thing,
Cur[t]es[10] and fre and gentill of þare spending.
Giff þai be nerrow-thirllit, of speiche rous,
Thai ar donsocht, to ansure at rabous;
Quha hes nois bra[i]d,[11] [t]akin at mydwart,
And schorte before, fer keppand vpwart,
Has mony wourd*is* fals, and litill effect,
With vþer faltis followand in þe nek -
Quhen þow þi s*er*uand*is* to þe were wauld wale,
Do thame nane ill, nor haue w*ith* þame na dale.
Ane mydlin nois, þat nowthir oure hie nor law is,
Quhilk in a gudlie phisnomy men knawis,
Attoure þe laif suld maist co*m*mendit be,
With wþer proporteis, as forsaid haue we.
Quha has ane mekill mouthe, wide and large,

[9] *MS* þat þare nature; *B*, 135, þ*er* nature.
[10] *MS* Curles; *B*, 143, Curtise.
[11] *MS* braud; *B*, 146, braid.

W*ith* keppand nois, oure-hingand as a barge,
Thai ar manfull and hardy men of prufe,
Gude of langage, and worthy for to luffe,
Quha hes thik lippis, grete and vngudely,
Ill maid, vnhartfull, all laith and vnlufely,
Ar oft tyme full of foly, and fulich,
Nocht wise, ewill taucht, full of vngudely speiche.
f.144r Quha sissoure-lippit is, scharpe and thyn,
Scharpe of þe nabe, and scharpe als of þe chyn,
Traist wele þai ar bayth nerrow and nedy,
Baith covatus, fast-haldand, and gredy,
And has a toung to sett þare wourd*is* sharply,
To flite and chide, and to speik velany.
Quha hes fatt face, ill favourit and flechly,
Thik and churylly, w*ith* lumpis vnlufely,
Thay seme to be vnhabill be nature,
For God giffis oft wisdome a gud figure.
Quha has ane lenȝe vysage, of gude fassoun,
Weill favorit, betakny*is* gude perfectioun:
Sa hede and hare and hew accorde þaretill,
He sould be ressoun haue ane gudely will,
And habill als to craft and clergy,
And wele i*n*clinit to vertew co*m*monly.
Quha has ane vissage fatt, schorte, and suollyn,
With keppand nois, w*ith* cheikis and tempillis bollyn,
Wyth litill hew, of culloure vermyllioun,
Orpy growis in þare arbere all sessoun.
Quha has ane blosit face, w*ith* hevy cors,
Son of gluttony mon be on force.
Quha has ane vissage schorte attoure mesour*e*,
With nek and body schorte of portratoure,
With nois and lippis listand vp agane,
To fle fra his cu*m*paney mak þe be ane -
Quhare nature falȝeis his proportionis,
Thare followis oft tymes ewill conditionis.
And quha sa visage has oure lang, vnfre,
Giff it ill favorit and ill collorit be,
Traist wele þat persoun is iniurious,
Subtell, invius, and malicius.
f.144v Quha has ane hede excedant grete and fatt,
Nocht till his vþer memberis accordant þat,
It signefeis beistiall conditionis,

Wyth carnelle appetete, and but ressouns.
Quha has ane crag vncumly, lang, and small,
With litill dotill hede, and round w*ith*all,
And oure grete body to avenand,
Thay ar co*m*monly þe maist cu*n*nand.
Quha has schorte nek, w*ith* schulderis hie and stricht,
Suppois þe laif wele fassonit be at richt,
He is subtell, fals, fleischeand till his lorde,
And of few men þe gude he sall recorde.
Quha has þe crag grete, swoun hede and body,
Off kynd he is þe sonn of lichery,
Or of glutony, or baith togidder tua,
And co*m*monlie þare followis faltis ma.
Quha-sa has mekill eris, syde hingand,
It is grete takin he is vncu*n*and;
And quha oure litill eris has to his stature,
It is ane takin of sum falt in nature.
And quha-sa has his speiche gros and ground,
  W*ith* wourd*is* clere, vnwe*m*myt, hale and sound,
He is baith bald and stout, of gude langage,
Off eloquence, of gud witt and knawlege;
And quha-sa has ane pipand voce and small,
And waik and wayndand in þare sprete withall,
That is ane takynning of ane vaik corage,
And baith w*ith* falt of lawte and langage.
  Or quha-sa stutis and mantis, or spekis haistaly,
Ar covatus, fast-haldand, and gredy
W*ith* mony wilis and subtelleis of mynd,
Invious, sturtand, crabbit, and vnkynde,
Pres[u]mpteous,[12] haisty, and wþeris wald supprise,
And laith to do ressoun, mony wayis.
f.145r   Quha quhilum spekis swift, and quhilu*m*is slaw,
Be þat a diuers nature may men knaw,
For hide invy and fellony is no*ch*t schawin
Quhill ma*n* in his conditionis be knawin.
Quha has a voce slekit, baith soft and swete,
And in his mouth melt buttir will no*ch*t lete,
Thay draw oft out of men w*ith* þare langage,

[12] *MS* Pres-ȝ[...]pteous; *B*, 228, Presumteous.

And garris þame wene þai haue a gude marage -
As ane fowllare, quhan he wauld foulis tak,
With his suete note he drawis þame to the nett.
Quha spekis oure oft, and ay is traitland new,
He may never laik of lyere and vntrew;[13]
And he þat oure soildin is, and spekis oure still,
Traist wele he has ane hede vnwourthy will -
The wattir þat rynnys is clere and kyndly gude,
Ane standand watt*er* ay stinkis in þe mvde.
  Quha has ane large breist, w*ith* schulderis brede,
W*ith* memberis mete, and tharefore manly maid,
With lang armys, and hand*is* fare and sture,
With all þe laif of memberis of measure,
That is ane takyn of grete stremyte,
In dede of were or battell for to be.
And quha-sa has ane waldin subtell bak,
Is pridfull, sle, invious, leif to lak;
And quha lute-bakkit is, withouttin were,
Is hudepik, hirtoun, wreth in all maner.
Thyn, nerrow schulduris is hurtland and sogrand—
Thai ar disparit of grete God all-wieldand,
And evir to want gude ar in drede and dout,
And wynnys þis warldit sall falȝie þame all out.
  Lang armes ar takin of larges,
Gentreis, fredome, w*ith* strenth and hardines,
f.145v And schorte armes ar takynnying of discorde
And nerrownes, is evill settand till ane lord.
Lang armes, w*ith* lang fengeris, waldin and fare,
Till all craftis richt wounder habill ar,
Bot schorte hand*is*, w*ith* schorte fingeris and grete,
On subtell craft sall neuer be wele sett.
And quha mekill wame has, wittirly,
It is ane takin of hicht and lichery,
Off gluttony, presumptioun, and arrogance,
And but riches, of sympill governance.
  Thik hanchis brade, w*ith* fillattis stark and stoure,
Grete brawnit, and wele made at all mesure,

---

13 *MS* first has 'He may never laik of lere and vertew'. 'Lere' is then altered to 'lyere', and 'vertew' is cancelled and 'vntrew' written instead. Original readings confirmed by *B*, 241.

W*ith* gudlie fassoun, baith of fute and hand,
And weill breistit, of visage wele farrand,
In mydlin way of compositioun,
Off hare als dosk, or ȝellow, blak, or broun,
W*ith* gudlie chere, wele favorit in visage,
Myngit w*ith* rede, and of gud mesurage,
Broun, blak, or gray þe roundale of his eye,
Clere-vocit and hale—þat is a man for the.
Quha has fatt pudding leggis, vnlufely made,
Lous-fleschit, with mysfassounit fete and brade,
It is to traist þat all þe remona*n*d
Is no*ch*t to prise quhan þat is mysfarand,
For efter þat þare followis co*m*monly
Misgoverance, wanwitt, and grete foly.
And litill feitt is takin of narrones,
And hard of nature, and ful of wrechitnes,
That excedis, be mesure of nature,
Les na it aw to be of portrature.
Quha sa in ganging ha[s][14] stedfast pais,
Thare followis oft proporteis of grace,
And quha sa nym*m*yll gais, and haistalie,
And schapis to do his dedis suddanly,
Sic men ar importune [and][15] kittill,
And habill als ane richteous caus to spill.
  Quha is of feris licht, and cast of hede,
And can no*ch*t stedfastly stand in a stede,
f.146r All men may wele consaue and vnderstand
Lichtnes of witt cu*m*myis efter followand.
Ane man that kekis and copyis vþer men,
And smyrk lauchtand gais but and ben,
In kirk or m*er*cat or in wþer place,
Thow sall knaw be þe compas of his face
That of his ded*is* þare sall litill prow -
Quha luffis his hono*u*re, sic ane suld vmbeschew.
  Bot will þow cheis of man of all bewteis,
Quhat man of gudlie fassoun þat thow seis
Is manly maid in all his portratoure,
And has ane gudlie favore in his figure,

---

[14] *MS* had; B, 292, hes.
[15] *MS* of kittill; *B*, 298, of kittill will. (See n.55, above.)

And hald*is* gude mesure in all his proportioun,
Off hede, of body, of ly*m*mes vp and doun,
Wele collorit and wele fleschit, as efferis,
And in his visage gudlynes apperis,
And is of feris cu*n*and and manlike,
And that na faltis forsaid him intertrik.
Bot haue in mynd þir vþer proporteis,
As in þis buike before wrettin þow seis.
Sett þow no*ch*t by of quhat hare þ*at* he be,
Sa dowbill rede hare haue na dail w*it*h þe;
Off stedfast blyith luke, hale of countenance,
In mydlin way of all his governance,
In all proportioun als betwene þai tua,
Nor hie nor law, nor fatt nor lene alsua,
Nor in his sicht þare be no lake to se,
For mony falt*is* ar knawne be þe eye -
The gudly suete luke co*m*monly is kynd,
And soft-hydit ar gude of witt and mynd,
And gudly face, no*ch*t oure fatt nor o*ure* large,
Off quyk culloure, no*ch*t oure lang at outrage,
No*ch*t ledin-hewit, nor blawin, blak, nor bare -
W[ele]-favorit blake is gudly w*it*h sic hare;
No*ch*t suelland-chekit, no tempillis risand hie,
Bot efter his gudlie mak and quantetie;
No*ch*t oure grete wame, no cleyngit in þe breist
f.146v In mydlin way þe wertew is evir neist.
And gadder in þai mynd þir poyntis hale,
Nocht all to lake, no*ch*t all to love and waile,
Bot haue ay gude consideratioun
Off forme and culloure and conditioun—
It sall the mekill proffeitte and avail3e.
Thare is na reule bot sum tyme it will fal3ee ...

Physiognomy B

p. 14 The first complectioun is called flew*m*[atik],[1]
The tother sangui[n]e, the thrid is colerik,
The feird *and* the last is called melancholly,
Thir four all nature governs all generally.
Flewmen is fatt *and* slaw, sweir *and* sliparie,
Whyt-spittand, ay blunt-wittit and drasie.
Sanguin is fair *and* fat be measur, reid *and* whyt,
Luifand *and* larg, *and* lachand with delyte,
In blythnes ay singand and wys hardy -
It is the best complextioun soveranly.
A crabit complectioun is colerik,
A far mair noble is na flewmatik,
For it is frie, bayt*h* lairg, hardy, *and* stout,
Mair subtill wys *and* mair worthy allout;
Bot small *and* lenyee ar they, broun of face,[2]
Far mair of vndertakin, *and* hering.
The worst co*m*plection is melancholly,
For it is sour, invyous, cald *and* dry,
Gredie, untrue,[3] dreidfull *and* ay drowpan,
And leidin hewit, *and* full seildum lachand.
Alse of a thing I cou*n*sall the that thow
Fra man mismaid in his person vnbe[c]how,
Whilk is mankit fra members of mankynd,
For co*m*monly they haue ane akwart strynd;
For wha falt bearis of his nativitie,
In his co*n*ditioun faultles sall not be,
Bot give þ*at* throw vertew him refrainyee,
And throw his wit his wickit will co*n*strenyee.
And first at mans hair thow take knawledge:
Gife they be young *and* not our te*n*der of age,
Gife it be dosk or yallow, broun or blake,
Efter þe lande, the hair is not to lake;
Gif it be reid be war, for I warn yow,

---

[1] MS flew*meg*; *Adv. 34.3.11* flew*m*ett. The form at l. 13, 'flewmatik', fits the rhyme.

[2] *Adv. 34.3.11* reads 'are þe broun of face', which is also possible.

[3] MS virtew; *Adv. 34.3.11* untrue. This confusion is recurrent See n.31, below, and Physiognomy *A*, n.13.

Whair ane is trew twe*n*tie is not to trow,
Whare head *and* beard is hewit of sindrie wyse
I red thow hald thame not in thy service.
For to begyll they ar ay wonder slee,
And mekill tane of slicht *and* sitteltie.

Bot yallow hair is taken for guid ingyne,
And habill bayth to craft *and* clergy fyne,
W*ith* ma*n*suetude of swetnes *and* clemens,
And governes be wisdome *and* prudence,
That is to say, with vther properties,
As afterwart of þ*am*e declairit beis.
Right roch of hair betaikins stark nature,
And hee of blood, bot langand ther figure;
Have they guid collour, wel-favored in visage,
And als of guide fassioun in þ*er* corsaig,
W*ith* guidly ferys *and* giftis remanend,
Thow may weill hald þ*am*e to thyne avin servand.
And be they ry*ch*t evill-favored *and* vnfrie,
And in þ*er* ferys als vngodly bee,
When beard *and* breist *and* brouis all overgroun,
Ry*ch*t vnfrilie w*ith* birnand eyn þ*at* glowis,
And of the laife vngudlie of portiriture,
That is great taikin of mervellous nature,
Of nature horribille *and* vnreasonabill,
And perallus, *and* till all vyces able.
I reid with sic men þ*at* thow have litill deall,
Na hald not in thy houshald speciall.
A large forehead w*ith* browis semlie set,
Nocht our feir out na mekill hair ourfreit,
W*ith* uþer guid bewties endlang the face,
The corpis inclynit till all guidlines,
W*ith* blak, or gray, or broun eyn *and* gryte,
Not gogland, over fair out na far inset -
Thir ar guid taikins w*ith* the remanend
Of p*ro*perteis q*uhi*lk*is* are after tidand.

The eyn of q*uhi*lke the stern draws to the blew,
Whilk maist is liknit to the heavinlie hew,
That is guid taikin of peace *and* equitie,
Of guid wit, prudence *and* of cheritie;
And wha hes great eyn gogland over þ*er* face,

Betaiknis pryde *and* ire and wilfullnes,
Invy, but shame, sweir inobedience,
And be they wa[*u*]will,[4] the war is þ*er* intent.
Wha hes eyn rinand ay co*n*tinuallie,
It is a full evill taikin, traist trewlie;
Bot swa sa hes reid eyn with[out]in dout,
They shall be fundin bald, hardie *and* stout,
And be it woman, she beis dow[b]ill hardie -
I will not say that is in villany.[5]
Bot eyn of twyn cullors are not guidly,
Bot are inclynit to vyce *and* villany,
Gif þ*er* maister followis ther p*ro*perties,
That are inclynit to all iniquities,
Thay are inclynit meikill baill to brew
When everilk eye is[6] of a sindrie hew,
Bot gif virtew have domina*tio*une,
That prudence m*aister* his co*m*plectioun.

Be war with eyn whilk are of sindrie hews,
Whilks God *and* nature *and* all guid men rewis,
With spots of whyte and reid blew-blak betuein;
When alkin hewis are sprutit in the eyn
Ther followis misfassioun of vissage,
And mekill mair of co*n*science and curage.[7]

p. 15 And aynslyk eyn oft shawis littill mude,
And oure mekill whyte waule[8] ey wes never guid,
And sand-blind eyn ar shamfull, comou*n*lie,
And fenyeis oft, for caus they ar faultie.

And glowrand ene are corssand in þ*e* sycht,
Are thrawin, *and* full of[9] sutteltie and sly*ch*t;
And wha sa skellis with ane eye luikand by,
They are inclynit to vyces co*m*monly.

---

[4] MS wā will; *Adv. 34.3.11* wawill; *A*, 66, wauwill.

[5] *Adv. 34.3.11*'s 'I will not say yt is ane villany' is a viable alternative, but *A* 71-2 is the better couplet altogether.

[6] *MS* eyes; *Adv. 34.3.11* eye is. Cf. *A*, 74.

[7] *MS*, curge; *Adv. 34.3.11* curage.

[8] *MS* waule; omitted *Adv. 34.3.11*. *A* has 'waverand' (86). *B*'s exemplar may have had a form of 'wa[u]will', with which the scribe earlier had trouble (see n. 4, above).

Wha stutand glowres w*ith* a sembland stout,
They are not haill in harnes, haif na dout,
Sa in ther forehead fallis a vanishing,
Whilke brings them often in ramessing,
W*ith* sick a frenseis and a fantasie,
Makis þ*em*, but reddour, abill to foly.
And wha with sad chere[10] hes eyn deid and still,
Are reddely inclynit to vncouth ill.

And wha lurkand eyn hes, ay lachand,
Till licherie are mekill inclynand,
Alse to dissave and fleche þ*er* natur is,
And make sembland that they can do na mis.
Wha winkis w*ith* his eyn and nodis als,
It cumes them weill of kynd for to be fals;
Wha luikis on syde, and haldes his heid awry,
And fenyeis to make small eyn denyouslie,
They are dissembland, coveit *and* vntrew
Of luf, and abill to dissave anew.

Wha hes ane lenyee nois, thin *and* weill made,
Are ly*ch*tlie,[11] breathfull, of lichtlie heid;
Bot great lang nos, hauk-beik, befor dipand,
Hee in the midis, as gryffone beik rysand,
Are wicht *and* manfull, co*m*monlie, *and* proved[12]...

And wha hes nos in midwart law *and* short,
Kepand before, men may weill knaw þ*er* sort -
They are akwart *and* evill willy of kynd,
Donsoth,[13] crabit, and angrie q*uhe*n thai are tein,
To murther *and* to misdeid reddy are,
And nowther will keep kyndes lawtie na fay,[14]
And reddely will make a forfaltour,
Bot grace *and* vertew brydill þ*er* nature.

---

[9] of, supplied from *Adv. 34.3.11.*

[10] *MS* with said other; *Adv. 34.3.11* with sad chere. Cf. *A*, 99.

[11] MS ly*ch*tlie; *Adv. 34.3.11* lightlie. *A* has the harder 'hichty' (112). *B*'s may come from association with 'lichtlie heid' later in the line. Cf. n.29, below.

[12] *MS* proven; *Adv. 34.3.11* proved. Cf. *A*, 115. A line is missing after this one; cf. *A*, 115-16.

[13] *MS* donsthotle; *Adv. 34.3.11* donsoth.

[14] *MS* far; *Adv. 34.3.11* fay. Cf. *A*, 121-2.

Gif they be not our snak, bot messurablie,
Vpset befor, sick taking is worthie;
Weill-favoured in the visage, the eyn,
Of hyd *and* hair, of voce *and* cullour clean,[15]
Blythe, lachand thair,[16] traist þ*er* guid co*m*pany,
And kynd for ki[n]dnes[17] shall be reddely,
And guid fellowship they loue attour all thing,
Curties and kend *and* gentill of þ*er* spending.
Gif they be narrow thirlit with speech rouss,
They are donesoth of anser at rebouss;
Wha hes the nos braid in the midlewart,
And short befor, for keepand wpperwart,
Hes mony fals wordis of littill effect,
With oþ*er* faltis foloand in the net -
When thow servandis to þe wer suld waill,
Do þ*em* na evill, na haif w*ith* þ*em* na daill.

A midlin noss, whilk nother oure hee na law is,
Whilke in a guidlie phisnomy men knawes,
With uther properties, as forsaid haue we,
Before the laif suld maist co*m*me*n*dit be.

Wha hes ane mekill mouthe, *and* wyd *and* large,
With keppand noss, or hingand as ane barge,
They are manfull *and* hardie men of pruife,
And of langage, and wortthie for to loue.

Wha hes gryte lips, thik and vnguidlie,
Ill maide, vnhartfull, laith[18] *and* vnlouelie,
Are oft tyme full of fuly, *and* fulache,
Nather wyse na weill tacht, *and* of vnguidlie speich.

Wha sesour lipit is, and sharpe *and* thin,
Small in the neb, *and* sharp als of the chin,
Trust well they are baith narow *and* nedy,
Baith cuvetous, fast-haldand and gredy,

---

[15] *MS* cleir; *Adv. 34.3.11* clean. Cf. *A*, 127-8.

[16] *MS* thair; *Adv. 34.3.11 þer*. This is possible, but a mistranscription of a form of *A*'s 'chere' (129) may be more likely.

[17] *MS* kindes; *Adv. 34.3.11* kyndnes.

[18] *MS* laiche; *Adv. 34.3.11* laith. Cf. *A*, 150.

And hes a tung to set ther word sharplie,
To flyt *and* chyde and to speik villanie.

Wha hes fatt face, ill-favoured *and* fleshly,
Thik *and* threwyllie,[19] w*ith* lumpis vnlouely,
They seme to be vnhabill by natur,
Ffor God gives of wisdome guid figur.

Wha hes a lang visage, of guid fassoun,
Well-favoured, betaikins guid perfectioun,
Sa hyde *and* hew and hair accord then till,
They suld be reasone haue a guidly will,
And abill als to craft and to clergie,
And well inclynit to vertew com*m*onlie.

Wha hes ane visage short *and* fatt *and* suollen,
And keepand noss, with chekes bolne,
With lytill hew, of cullour wermelin,
Orpie growis in his herbe all sessoun.

Wha hes a blusit face, of hevie corss,
The sone of lichorie he man be of forss.

Wha hes a visage short attour*e* mesour*e*,
Bayth neck *and* bodie short of portrature,
With neis and lipis liftand up agane,
p. 16 To flie fra his cumpany all suld be fane—
Wher nature failyeis his proportiouns,
Ther folies oftymes evill co*n*ditiouns.

And wha visage hes our lang, vnfre,
Gif it evill favoured *and* evill cullorit be,
Traist weill that persone is vniurious,
Sutell, invyous, and eik malicious.

Wha hes ane heid exceiding gryte and fatt,
Noth to his vther me*m*bers accordand that,
It signifies bestiall co*n*ditioun,
Of carnall apetyte and vnreasoun.

[19] *MS* threwyllie; *Adv. 34.3.11* threwlly. Probably a corruption from *A*'s 'churylly' (160).

Wha hes ane craig vncumly lang *and* small,
With lytill dotleheid,[20] and round with all,
And our mekill bodie to the awennand,
They are not co*m*monlie the maist emenand.[21]

Wha hes short neck w*ith* shoulders hie *and* stricht,
Suppose the laue will fassonit be at ry*ch*t,
He is suttell, false fletchand to his lord,
And of few men the gude will he record.

Wha hes gryte heid, craig, and fat body,
Traist well they are inclynit to licherie,
And to glutry, sleathe, *and* vyces ma,
Give they be not, the tyme is passtt of they.[22]

Wha hes mekill earrys, thik *and* syde hingand,
Gryte taikin is that he is uncu*n*and.

Wha earris hes our lytill to his stature,
It is gryte taikin of sume falt of nature.

And wha is of speikin gross and round,
With words cleir, vnwe*m*mit, haill *and* sound,
He is bayt*h* bald and stout, *and* gude langage,
Gude witt, gude eloquens *and* gude knawledge.

And wha sa hes a pypand voyce *and* small,
And waik *and* wandand in þ*er* speich w*ith* all,
That is taikin of waik curage,
And bayt*h* with falt of lawtie and langage.

And wha sa stutes or mantis, or speik[s][23] hastie
Are cuvatus, fast-haldand, and gredie,
With mony wyles *and* suttelteis of mynd,
Invyous, sturtand,[24] crabit and vnkynd,

---

[20] *MS* dottitlheid; *Adv. 34.3.11* dotlehead. Cf. *A*, 191.

[21] *MS* eñand; *Adv. 34.3.11* emenand. This is possible, but a mistranscription of *A*'s cu*n*nand (192) is also likely.

[22] A weak line-filler, though *B*'s 210 is as attractive as *A*'s 199.

[23] *MS* speik; *Adv. 34.3.11* speiks.

[24] *MS* sturt *and*; *Adv. 34.3.11* sturtand.

Presumteous, hastie, *and* reddy to suppryse,
And lay*th* to pairtt with geir in ony wyse.

Wha whylum speiks swyft, and whylum sla,
Be that a divers nature men may knaw,
For hid faultis in mony men ar not shawin,
Whill sick men in co*n*ditiounes be well knawin.

Wha hes ane sleikit voce, *and* swyft *and* sweit,
And in his mouthe melt butter will not lett,
They draw oft out of men w*ith* þ*er* langage,
And garis þ*e*m weyn that they haue a guid curage,
As fouller when he wald his pluvars get,
With his sweit not he draws þ*e*m to the net.

Wha alwyse speikand is, *and* tratland new,
He may never failȝee of law and vertew;
And wha sa seildin speaks *and* is our still,
Traist weill he hes a hyd vnworthie wyll,
The rynand water is cleir and ky*n*dlie guide,
And standand water is stinkand of the mude.

Wha hes a large brest w*ith* shulders braid,
W*ith* members meit, þ*er*fore, *and* manly maid
Wicht lang armes, *and* hands fair *and* sture,
And uþ*er* me*m*bers all of guid measour,
That is a taikin of great stremute,
In deid of wer or battell for to be.

And wha sa hes a waldin suttill bak,
Is prydfull, slee, invyous, leif to lak.

And wha lute bakit is, with[out]in were,
Is hudpyk hurcheon, wrocht in all maner;
Thin narow shalders ay hurkland *and* figand—
Thai ar dispaireit of great God all-wieldand,
And ever to want gude are in dreid *and* dout,
And wenis[25] the wardle will failȝie[26] þa*me* all out.

[25] *MS* weimis; *Adv. 34.3.11* wenis. *A* (248) has 'wynnys'.
[26] *MS* faylyet; *Adv. 34.3.11* failȝie.

Lang armes [ar][27] taikin of largenes,
Gentreis, fredome w*ith* strenthe *and* hardines;
And short armes are taikin of discord
And narow heart, evill sittand to ane lord.

Lang armes with waldyn finger fair,
Till all crafts ry*ch*t wonder abill ar;

Bot short armes with short fingers *and* great,
On suttell craft shall never be seimlie set.

And wha sa great swollin wame hes, vtterly,
It is a taikin of pryde and lichourrie,
Of gluttoun, presumptioun, *and* arrogance,
And bot riches, of simpill governance.

Thik braid hoches, with filletis stark *and* sture,
Great brandis, *and* weill made at measour,
With gudlie fassioun, baythe of fute *and* hand,
And weill breistit, of visage well-farand,
In hair als dosk, yallow, blak, or broun,
In midlin way of co*m*positioun,
W*ith* guidlie cheir, well favored in visage,
Myngit w*ith* reid *and* guid messurage,
p. 17 Broun, blak, or gray the roundall of the ey,
Cleir voceit and haill, þ*at* is a man for the.

Wha hes fatt pudding leges, vnfrielie maid,
Lous flechit, w*ith* misfassionit feit *and* braid,
It is to traist þ*at* all the remanend
Suld not be weill whan þ*at* is misfara[n]d,
For after þ*at* followis com*m*only
Misgovernans, wanwit *and* gryte folie.

And lytill feit is taikin of narrownes,
And hard of nature, full of wretchitnes,
Whilk our skant is of measour be nature,
Les na it aw to be of portratur.

---

[27] ar, both MSS read 'in', probably through anticipation of 'taikin'. Cf. *A*, 249.

Wha sa in ganging hes a steadfast pace,
Ther followis oft prosperitie and grace.

And wha sa nimlie gais *and* spedilie,
Bot gife he have a ry*ch*t great cause *and* why,
And settis to do his deidis all in haist,
They are lyke guidlie purpose for to waist,
For they are inoportwn *and* of kittill will,
And oft þ*er* purpose comes not weill þ*e*m till.[28]

Wha ever be lyght[29] of feris *and* cast of head,
And haldis not purpose steadfast in a steid,
All men may will considder *and* vnderstand,
Lightnes of witt is after followand,
And when the witt is light *and* richt cha*n*geable,
Sic men sall never be to hono*ur* abill.

What man þ*a*t kekland copes vther men,
And smyrkand, lauchand, gois but *and* ben,
In kirk *and* in mercat or in vther place,
Thow knaw be the figur of his face
That of his deidis þ*er*[30] sall cum lytill prove -
Wha luifis hono*ur*, sick men suld umbe[c]how.

What man of guidly fassioun that thow sees,
When thow will cheis a man w*it*h all ve[r]chewis,[31]
Is manly maid of gude portiritur,
Bayt*h* guidlie *and* weill favored of figure,
After the tennor of all proportioun,
As we haif said in our discriptioun,
Weill cullourit *and* weill maid as effeiris,
Weill favourit in his feiris and maners,
Of hyd *and* hair and hew *and* eloquence,
With pleasant presenta*tio*une of prudence,
Weill collourit *and* weill fleshit as effeiris,
And in his visage guidlynes appears,

---

[28] *MS* and oft þ*er* pupose andis not weill þ*e* thamee till; *Adv. 34.3.11* And oft þ*er* purpose comes not weill þem till. But *A*, 285, is very different.

[29] lyght, *MS* is very indistinct, *Adv. 34.3.11* light. Cf. *A*, 288.

[30] *MS* thand; *Adv. 34.3.11* þ*er*. Cf. *A*, 295.

[31] Both MSS read 'vechewis', where *A* (297) has 'bewties'.

And in all thing is cu*n*and and manlyke,
And at na forsaid faultis entertryke.

Bot have in mynd thair vþer properteis,
As in this book befor writtin thow sees,
And set not[32] by of what hair that he be,
So doubill reid hair haue na daill w*ith* the;
Of stadfast blyt*h* luik, haill of countenance,
In midlin way of all his governans,
In all proportioun als betuixt the twa,
Nather hee nor law, nor fatt nor lyn alswa,
Na in his sight þ*er* be na laik to see,
For mony a fault is knawin be the ey -
The guidlie sweit luik co*m*mounlie is kynd,
And soft of hyd is guid of witt *and* mynd;
Of mesoured speeche *and* stadfast in ganging,
Sic men as thir sould be about a king.
And guider in thy mynd thir poy*n*ts haill,
Not all to lake na all to loff and waill,
Bot haue ay guid considderatioun
Of fforme and cullo*ur* *and* co*n*ditioun -
It sall be mekill profeit and availl
In weir and peace, in houshald or battell.

---

[32] *MS* int; *Adv. 34.3.11* not.

THE LATIN ORIGINAL OF ROBERT HENRYSON'S ANNUNCIATION LYRIC.

A.A. MacDonald

The Middle Scots poem, *Forcy as deith is likand lufe*, is a religious lyric on the subject of the Annunciation.[1] In the one manuscript in which it is preserved (NLS Adv. MS 34.7.3, the so-called Gray Manuscript) it is attributed to 'Ro. Henrisoun', and this colophon is by general consent taken to refer to the author of the *Fables*, the *Testament of Cresseid* and the *Orpheus and Eurydice*.[2] More will be said about this lyric below; the main purpose of the present contribution, however, is to call attention to the hitherto unknown fact that the Middle Scots poem is a direct translation from a Latin original.

TEXTS OF THE LATIN POEM

Henryson's model, *Fortis ut mors dilectio*, is at present known from four manuscripts, all of the fifteenth century.[3] On the basis of the names of the towns in which these manuscripts are found—Trier, Utrecht, Cambridge and Edinburgh—the sigla **T**, **U**, **C** and **E** have been awarded respectively.

T. (fifteenth century)

In Max Keuffer's descriptive catalogue of the manuscripts in the Stadtbibliothek in Trier this codex is listed as no. 306, and is said, without further precision, to date from the fifteenth century.[4] The

---

[1] *The Index of Middle English Verse*, ed. C. Brown and R.H. Robbins (New York, 1943), no. 856.

[2] *The Poems of Robert Henryson*, ed. D. Fox (Oxford, 1981), pp. cxv (introduction), 154-6 (text), 426-33 (notes). Fox's text is reproduced below, by permission of Oxford University Press.

[3] *Repertorium Hymnologicum* [etc.], ed. U. Chevalier, 6 vols. (Louvain, 1892-1920), no. 26761, referring to T and U. The poem is not recorded in Walther: *Initia Carminum ac Versuum Medii Aevii Posterioris Latinorum*, ed. H. Walther (Göttingen, 1959); *Ergänzungen und Berichtigungen* (Göttingen, 1969).

[4] *Beschreibendes Verzeichnis der Handschriften der Stadtbibliothek zu Trier*, ed. Max Keuffer, 10 parts (Trier, 1888-1931). The MS (now known as Hs.306/1978 8o) is described in part iii (1894), 'Die Predigt-handschriften', 121-5. I am much

manuscript (282 ff.) was compiled by a Carmelite of Worms, who, however, had originally professed at Trier. A fifteenth-century hand has written on the first folio: 'Detur fratribus Carmelitis treverensibus', and a seventeenth-century addition reports that the possessor of the manuscript, being at Worms, bequeathed the volume to his mother house. It is a typical friar's miscellany, and consists of a collection of religious texts which, one presumes, would come in useful in connection with preaching activity. With the exception of three (not two, as Keuffer declares) poems on Our Lady (ff.174-175), whereof the first is the lyric under discussion here, the contents are in prose, and with the exception of one item (ff.48v-49v), which is in German, all the texts are in Latin. The largest items in the collection consist of a series of sermons (ff.71v-165), and an 'Alphabetum morale' of similitudes (ff.179-257) according to the moral and spiritual senses. In between these works there are sundry short items, including an alphabetical list of heretics (ff.165v-169), a jumbled list of *quaestiones* and propositions (ff.170-174), and the three hymns on Mary (ff.174-175).[5] The manuscript is all in one hand; however, bound in with it at the end, and beginning on f.259, we find a quite different manuscript, written in an early fifteenth-century hand.

The Trier poem has been printed, in the *Analecta Hymnica*, where seven stanzas are reproduced.[6] This contrasts interestingly with **U**, **C** and **E**, and with the Scottish translation, all of which have only six stanzas, and the discrepancy prompts one to suspect the extra lines in **T** (see Textual Notes, below). In this context the following facts may be noted: a) whereas the first six stanzas have 12 short lines each (written out in the manuscript as six long lines), the seventh stanza has 16 short (eight long) lines; b) the rhyme scheme of the first six stanzas (which, *pace* Keuffer, is ababbaabbaab) differs from the (not quite perfect) scheme of the last stanza (abababababababab); c) the first six stanzas are followed by the words 'Aue Maria gratia plena', whereas the seventh is followed merely by 'Amen'. The natural conclusion is that these

obliged to Dr G. Franz, Ltd. Bibliotheksdirektor, Stadtbibliothek Trier, for generously providing a photocopy of the lyric from Hs. 306/1978 8o.

[5] The folio references used here follow the modern, pencil, numbering, which differs slightly from that of Keuffer.

[6] *Analecta Hymnica Medii Aevi*, ed. Cl. Blume and G.M. Dreves, 55 vols. (Leipzig, 1886-1922; reprint New York, 1961), xlvi, 123-4 (no. 76).

final lines are not part of the original poem, but that Keuffer in his inventory of the contents of the manuscript has erroneously conjoined two separate items. The mistake may be attributable to the presence of seven prominent red lombards, each at the beginning of its respective group of lines; another possible consideration is the fact that the 'seventh' stanza continues the theme of Marian devotion of the preceding stanzas. In any event, Blume and Dreves were suspicious of this poem: 'Str. 7 scheint—Inhalt und Form legen dies gleichmäßig nahe—kaum zu vorstehendem Liede zu gehören.'

U. (1477)

Unlike all the other witnesses, this manuscript (207 ff.), which is preserved in the University Library, Utrecht, is dated: 1477 (f.206). It comes originally from the Carthusian monastery Nieuwlicht (Novae Lucis), founded by Zweder van Gaasbeek in May 1392 at Bloemendaal, close to Utrecht. The charterhouse was a victim of Reformation vandalism, and, beginning in 1579, the buildings were demolished. Before then, however, the monks had departed into the nearby city, taking their books with them, so that many works from this important library have survived.[7] In the catalogue of the manuscripts in the University Library at Utrecht this item is listed as No.369.[8] The manuscript was written by Nicolaus Tsgravenzande, a Carthusian of Nieuwlicht, said to have died c.1499.[9] The contents of the manuscript consist entirely of devotional material. *Fortis ut mors dilectio* appears on ff.87v-88, and was printed from this manuscript by Blume and Dreves.[10]

An intriguing feature of this text of the Latin poem is that it is incorporated into a long work (ff.34v-146v), called in the colophon 'orationes rigmatice gloriose virginis Marie frequentande'. This is a series of prayers designed to be used for meditations throughout the whole year. These verse prayers, seldom shorter

---

[7] K.O. Meinsma, *Middeleeuwsche Bibliotheken* (Amsterdam, 1902), 154-60; J.P. Gumbert, *Die Utrechter Kartäuser und ihre Bücher im frühen fünfzehnten Jahrhundert* (Leiden, 1974), 23-41.

[8] *Catalogus Codicum Manu Scriptorum Bibliothecae Universitatis Rheno-Traiectinae*, ed. P.A. Tiele and A. Hulshof, 2 vols. (Utrecht and The Hague, 1887-1909), i, 122; ii, 55-6.

[9] *Manuscrits datés conservés dans les Pays-Bas*, ed. G.I. Lieftinck and J.P. Gumbert, 2 vols. (Amsterdam and Leiden, 1964-88), ii, 204-05 (here listed as no. 696).

[10] *Analecta Hymnica*, xxxi, 134-5 (no. 134).

than 20 or longer than 120 lines, are arranged in groups of seven, with one for each day of the week, from Sunday to Saturday. They comprise a protracted laudatory address to Mary, and, as the rubrics to weeks 1-6, 28-9, 31-3, 35-7, 49 and 50 declare, the main subject is the Angelic Salutation. In this manuscript, uniquely, *Fortis ut mors dilectio* is preceded by six lines (see Textual Notes, below) rhyming aabbcc (ff.87-87v). There is no reason, however, to consider these six lines, which do not fit in with the rhyme scheme of the remainder, as an integral part of the poem. Beginning with the poems of the thirteenth week, one observes in the opening words within each group a pattern which most often displays the sequence: Ave, Salve, Gaude, Vale, Salve, Gaude, Vale. Other orders are possible, and, in particular, the words 'Salve' and 'Gaude' may be exchanged, but there is manifest regularity in the use of 'Ave' for each Sunday, and of 'Vale' for both Wednesday and Saturday. *Fortis ut mors dilectio* is the Saturday poem for week 25, and thus, in order to fit the pattern, has to begin with a 'Vale'. This is doubtless the explanation for the appearance of the supernumerary lines at the head of our poem, in contradistinction to the other witnesses. At the beginning of the meditation of each week the reader greets Mary through the words of the poem, and he takes his leave again at the end of the week; we may also note here that, rounding off the entire series of prayers, there are two concluding poems, beginning respectively with 'Ave' and 'Vale'.

The other works in the manuscript are in prose. The first item (ff.1v-5) is the *Soliloquium Jesu* of Eckbert of Schönau (d.1184), also attributed to St Anselm (1033-1109).[11] There follows (ff.5-12) *Centum Meditationes sive Articuli passionis Jesu Christi*, a work which is customarily associated with the *Horologium aeternae Sapientiae* of Henry Suso (1300-63).[12] Next comes a series of *Orationes de vita Iesu Christi*, in two sections which embrace the verse prayers (ff.12v-34, 146v-175v). The final work is the *Septem horulae operum*

[11] *Soliloquium seu Meditationes,* in *Patrologia Latina,* 195, 105-14; *PL,* 158, 773-9.

[12] *Heinrich Seuses 'Horologium Sapientiae',* ed. P. Künzle, OP (Freiburg-Schweiz, 1977). A convenient English translation is: H. Suso, *Little Book of Eternal Wisdom* and *Little Book of Truth,* trans. and ed. J.M. Clark (1953), 159-66. See also J. Deschamps, 'De Middelnederlandse Vertalingen en Bewerkingen van de *Hundert Betrachtungen und Begehrungen* van Henricus Suso', *Ons Geestelijk Erf,* lxiii (1989), 309-69.

divinorum (ff.176-206). With the exception of the *Soliloquium Jesu*, all these various prose works have been harnessed by the compiler into a series of meditations for the whole year: the *Centum Meditationes* provides the material for week 1, the *Orationes* that for weeks 2-17 and 18-43, and the *Septem horulae* that for weeks 44-52. The manuscript thus provides a double series of meditations; this is announced already on the title page, wherein the reader is exhorted to perform the exercise of repeating the prose and verse devotions, on Jesus and Mary respectively, at the proper times of each day.[13] The manuscript thus gives an insight into the devotional practices of the Carthusians of the time, and is a most interesting compilation.

C. (late fifteenth century)

This text (Emmanuel College Cambridge MS 84; 45 ff.) is described by Montague Rhodes James as: 'cent. xv late, written in France for Scotch use'.[14] It contains the following items: a kalendar (ff.1-6v); a prose salutation to Our Lady, beginning 'Missus est Gabriel' (ff.7-10v); a collection of *memoriae sanctorum* (ff.11-42v); three poems (written out as prose) to Mary (ff.43-45v). *Fortis ut mors dilectio* is the last item in the manuscript (ff.44v-45v).[15]

James's opinion as to the French origin of the manuscript seems to have been based partly upon the script and partly on the kalendar: certain saints who find a place therein—Hugh the archbishop (9 April), Eutropius (30 April), Fiacre (30 August) and Remigius (1 October)—have strong French connections. That the manuscript was intended for use by a Scot, or for use in Scotland, was inferred by James from the inclusion in the kalendar of St Ninian (16 September (in gold); his translation is noted for 31

---

[13] 'Item nota. Hic incipit devocionale novum sive exercitium devote frequentandum Videlicet singulis diebus atque singularibus oracionibus infrasignatis Unde qui vult gaudere consolatione protectione gratia atque devocione dicat primum oracionem de ihesu ante prandium Item post prandium oracionem de domina Item post vesperas martirologium in oratorium vel post missas in ecclesia qui non habet librum Et tunc oracionem domini post prandium Item post vesperas oracionem de domina quod nota.'

[14] *The Western Manuscripts in the Library of Emmanuel College: A Descriptive Catalogue*, ed. M.R. James (Cambridge, 1904), 75-6. The MS is no. 54a in *Catalogue of Scottish Medieval Liturgical Books and Fragments*, ed. D. McRoberts (Glasgow, 1953), 10. I am much obliged to Mrs Priscilla Bawcutt for drawing this text to my attention, and also to Dr F.H. Stubbings, Honorary Keeper of Rare Books at Emmanuel College, for facilitating the inspection of the MS.

[15] James, *Descriptive Catalogue*, gives the *incipit* as: *(M)ortis ut mors dilectio.*

August), and from the appearance, among the suffrages, of SS Kentigern, Columba, Duthac and Ninian.

In certain respects, however, James's discussion requires qualification. Most importantly, it should be noted that the manuscript is a composite. James himself suspected that the second item (the prose salutation) was written in a different, and possibly English, hand, and his theory is confirmed by a rubric (possibly overlooked by him) within this devotional exercise: 'say x. tymes' (f.8). Moreover, the rough quality of the parchment in this second section of the manuscript sets this portion off against the others, which are all written on smooth, thin vellum. Whether the hand of the first item is the same as that of item three is not (*pace* James) altogether clear; but in any case the hand of item four is somewhat different yet again. Item four begins acephalously, and there is no saying how many folios have been lost before the present f.43. There is no trace in item four of the early foliation found in item three. The only illumination in the manuscript is found on the outer margins of the pages of the kalendar (which is now incomplete, lacking the months January-March, May, November-December); here we find highly competent floral decorations, albeit that these have been damaged by the excision of rectangular pieces of vellum, which may have contained pictorial illustrations. In the light of the foregoing, it may be concluded (a) that the assertion of a French origin for this manuscript is only justified in relation to the first item contained within it, and (b) that the various items now found in the manuscript need not be closely contemporaneous with each other. Moreover, it is entirely possible that the association of items two, three and four with the kalendar only took place within Scotland itself.

Nor does this exhaust the interest of the manuscript. If the appearance of St Ninian may be said to give the kalendar a Scottish caste, what then of the inclusion of such English saints as Edward, King and Martyr (translation, 21 June), Thomas à Becket (translation, 7 July), Swithin (15 July), Oswald (5 August) and Cuthbert (translation, 4 September)? The last two of these, of course, also enjoyed a considerable cult in Scotland. A further interesting feature is the inclusion of the Holy Helpers among the *memoriae* (they are listed among the martyrs, after the apostles, and before the confessors and virgins). While the present manuscript mentions 15 Helpers, the regular number of the auxiliary saints was one less, and the extra name is that of St Magnus.

The cult of the Holy Helpers in the fifteenth century was characteristic of Germany, and it would seem to have been especially prevalent in the Rhineland, Franconia and Bavaria. In the diocese of Augsburg (as also, occasionally, elsewhere) it was customary to add to the group of saints a fifteenth: in this case St Magnus (of Füssen).[16] The appearance of the name 'Magnus' in the list of auxiliary saints cannot, therefore, be held to corroborate the Scottish aspect of the manuscript.[17] The third item in **C** may, therefore, be freed from the imputation of a French background, and may, rather, be thought of as sharing the German and/or Low Countries background of two of the other manuscripts discussed here. Whether this has implications for the fourth item within the manuscript is not clear, but there is, at least, no need to locate this final item within a French context.[18]

E. (c.1498)

The Scottish connections of the fourth text (NLS MS 10270; 153 ff.) are much more secure; they have been studied in detail by David McRoberts, who has also given a full description of the manuscript.[19] The owner of the manuscript was James Brown, born c.1456 (perhaps in Angus), student at St Andrews in the 1470s, and dean of Aberdeen from 1484 until his death in 1505. Brown was probably a relation of George Brown, who was chancellor of Aberdeen until 1483 before being appointed bishop of Dunblane (d.1515).[20] There are several references in the manuscript to one Elizabeth Lauder, daughter of Sir Robert Lauder of the Bass (1450-95).[21] This lady, it is mentioned, died in June 1494 and was buried in the choir of the Dominican church in

---

[16] See *The New Catholic Encyclopedia*, 'Holy Helpers'.

[17] This would seem, nonetheless, to have been the view of the compilers of the catalogue, *French Connections: Scotland and the Arts of France* (Edinburgh, 1985), 143; they also point to SS Eustace, Giles and Margaret in this context. Since the cult of the latter saints (three more of the Holy Helpers) was so widespread, however, these names suggest little as to the origin of the MS.

[18] It remains the case that the script used in items one, three and four of the MS is of a generally French type (as opposed to German); this fact, however, need be indicative of no more than the place of training of the scribe or scribes. Moreover, this type of hand, it seems, was also common in the Burgundian Netherlands.

[19] D. McRoberts, 'Dean Brown's Book of Hours', *IR*, xix (1968), 144-67; no. 75 in McRoberts, *Scottish Medieval Liturgical Books and Fragments*, 13.

[20] Watt, *Fasti.*

[21] On her family see: J. Young, *Notes on Historical References to the Scottish Family of Lauder* (Glasgow, 1884; reissued Paisley, 1886); J. Stewart Smith, *The Grange of St*

Edinburgh; on ff.152v-153 there are some Latin verses on her death, written from the standpoint of a person evidently close to her. A later hand has added the information that she was the mother of William and Janet Brown, and this has led McRoberts (p.164) to conclude that 'the relations between James Brown and Elizabeth Lauder were not strictly in accord with Canon Law'.

The manuscript was written and illuminated in Flanders, in Bruges or Ghent, and probably during the months (May to October, 1498) that James Brown spent there, in between his coming back from Rome (where he had lobbied successfully for the appointment of James IV's brother, the Duke of Ross (d.1504), to the archbishopric of St Andrews) and his return to Scotland. Brown's stay in the Low Countries is recorded in the accounts of Andrew Halyburton, Conservator of the Privileges of the Scottish Nation in the Netherlands; Halyburton's wife, it may be noted, was a member of the celebrated Bening family of Bruges miniaturists.[22]

The manuscript has some preliminary matter (*rotae* for the Golden Number, Indiction and Dominical Letter, together with a kalendar) then four further sections, each of which is preceded by a full-page miniature. The kalendar (ff.4-15v), as McRoberts points out, is appropriate to the cathedral of Aberdeen; moreover, it is distinguished by the inclusion of saints from all over Scotland, as is the case with the list which bishop William Elphinstone was to insert into the printed Aberdeen Breviary of 1510.[23] The death of Elizabeth Lauder on 11 June 1494 is recorded, next to the name of St Barnabas the Apostle. The first main section (ff.17v-50) contains the text of 11 psalms; the second (ff.50v-90) contains various *memoriae*, together with short prayers (the Latin poem appears here, on ff.61-62); the third (ff.90v-111) contains the Penitential Psalms and the Litany of the Saints; and the fourth (ff.111v-153v) contains the Vespers, Matins and Lauds of the Dead, with, at the end, a list of the books of the Old Testament and the verses on Elizabeth Lauder already mentioned. In

---

Giles, the Bass, and the other Baronial Homes of the Dick-Lauder Family (Edinburgh, 1898), 168-88; C.A.B. Lawder, *The Lawders of the Bass and their Descendants* (Belfast, 1914).

[22] *Ledger of Andrew Halyburton, 1492-1503*, ed. C. Innes (Edinburgh, 1867), 205-17. See also: D. McRoberts, 'Material destruction caused by the Scottish Reformation', in McRoberts, *Essays*, 415-62 (457).

[23] L.J. Macfarlane, *William Elphinstone and the Kingdom of Scotland 1431-1514: The Struggle for Order* (Aberdeen, 1985), 231-46.

view of the many personal touches visible in this manuscript, it seems not unlikely that Dean Brown commissioned it for his own use. It is the prayer book of one individual, and, as the title of McRoberts' article indicates, bears a close resemblance to a Book of Hours.[24]

On the basis of the texts at our disposal no clear stemma can be constructed, which might show the relationships between the four versions of the Latin poem. There are no grounds for thinking that the text of any one of the versions discussed above is derived from any of the others. The omission in **U** of one line, together with the presence of several lines peculiar to this witness, means that **U** cannot have been a source for **T**, **C** or **E**; in view of what is known of the origin, history and date of **E**, this manuscript cannot have been the source of **U** or **T**, and it is perhaps unlikely to have been the source of **C**; since there is no reason to suppose that **T** ever travelled further than from Trier to Worms and back again, it is unlikely that **T** was the source of **U**, **C** or **E**; the date of **C** rules it out as a source of **U**, and there is no particular ground for supposing it to have been a source for either **T** or **E**. It is clear from the textual variants listed below that **T**, **C** and **E** exhibit considerable agreement between themselves as against **U**, which emerges by comparison as a less satisfactory witness. There are a few places where **C** and **E** agree with each other as against **T** and **U**, but there are even more places where **C** and **E** differ from each other. In view of the uncertain transmission of the poem, the choice of **E** as copytext for the present edition has been governed by the following considerations: **E** is the most carefully prepared of the various witnesses and presents perhaps the best text; furthermore, **E** has unambiguous Scottish connections, and was produced close in time to the presumed date of composition of Henryson's poem.

It should perhaps be added that there is no reason to suppose that **E** was ever seen by Henryson, and in any case, though we have no precise date for the poet's death, **E** is probably slightly too late for him.[25] Since so little can be said with certainty concerning the date, history and ownership of **C**, it would be unsafe to assume that this manuscript was the route through which Henryson came

[24] The Hours of the BVM, however, are absent: cf. V. Leroquais, *Les Livres D'Heures Manuscrits de la Bibliothèque Nationale*, 2 vols. (Paris, 1927); R.S. Wieck, *Time Sanctified: the Book of Hours in Medieval Art and Life* (New York, 1988).

[25] Henryson's date of death cannot be precisely determined, but may have occurred in the 1490s. All that safely can be said is that he had died sometime be-

to know the Latin poem (though the possibility, manifestly, cannot be altogether ruled out). It is, however, perhaps significant that at one place where **C** and **E** give divergent readings, the Scottish translation seems somewhat closer to **E**: Henryson's rendering, 'To be moder and madyn meir' (31) brings out the paradox of the **E** reading ('Virgo mater efficitur') rather than the bland statement of **C** ('mira res efficitur'). At the other places where **C** and **E** differ, however, it is not possible to be sure which version Henryson is following.

The existence of four texts of the Latin poem suggests that this lyric enjoyed a certain popularity in the late fifteenth century. It is interesting to observe the differences between the types of manuscripts in which the poem is preserved: a Carmelite friar's collection of memoranda, for use in preaching; a Carthusian's book of devotional exercises, for use in meditation throughout the year; a unknown reader's book of prayers to saints; the prayers and devotions assembled for personal use by a member of the secular clergy. The quality of the manuscripts, moreover, varies with their function: **T** is little more than a convenient notebook, of paper; **U** is an unpretentious but well organised manuscript, mostly of paper but with some leaves of vellum, and has highlighting in red, together with red and blue lombards; apart from its attractive kalendar (with blue, red and gold lettering and floral margins), **C** is a plain and functional collection of devotional texts, on vellum of varying quality; **E** is in every way a fine production on vellum, with some full-page illustrations, much illumination and many gold and coloured capitals. The author of the Latin poem is not known; the provenance of at least two of the manuscripts might perhaps suggest that the poem enjoyed a currency in the Low Countries, but religious lyrics are notorious for being widely copied, and no hasty conclusions as to place of composition should be drawn. It is evident, however, that the lyric had an attraction for readers in Scotland.

---

fore 1505, since he is mentioned in William Dunbar's *Timor mortis conturbat me*, which cannot have been composed before that year. See D. Gray, *Robert Henryson* (Leiden, 1979), 2-3; *Poems of Henryson*, ed. Fox, pp. xiii-xxii.

Fortis ut mors dilectio

Fortis ut mors dilectio,
Qua durum fit suaue;
Ut refert sancta lectio,
Nil est amanti graue.
Amor nos traxit a ue,
Dum de celesti solio
Fit Gabrielis missio
In virginis conclaue.
O felix, inquit, aue,
In te fiet conceptio
Sed non pudoris lesio,
Tu tantum deo faue.

Auditis his subticuit
Puella deo grata,
Et, ut pudicam decuit,
Silebat salutata;
Ne fieret turbata,
Mox angelus retexuit,
Modum partus exposuit,
Quo foret illibata.
Qua serie prolata,
Ara celestis claruit,
Dum virgo verbo paruit
Et mansit impregnata.

Archangelus regreditur,
Qui venit hec narrare,
Et grauida relinquitur
Puella sine pare.
O decus singulare;
Virgo mater efficitur,
Creator est, qui gignitur,
Et dei salutare.
O pectus puellare,
Thesaurus in te tegitur,
Virtute cuius regitur
Celum, tellus et mare.

Forcy as deith is likand lufe

Forcy as deith is likand lufe,
Throuch quhom al bittir suet is;
No thing is hard, as writ can pruf,
Till him in lufe that letis;
Luf ws fra barret betis.
Quhen fra the hevinly sete abufe
In message Gabriell couth muf,
And with myld Mary metis,
And said, 'God wele the gretis;
In the he will tak rest and rufe,
But hurt of syn or ȝit reprufe;
In him sett thi decret is.'

This message mervale gert that myld,
And silence held but soundis,
As weill aferit a maid infild.
The angell it expoundis,
How that hir wame but woundis
Consave it suld, fra syn exild;
And quhen this carpin wes compilit,
Brichtnes fra bufe aboundis.
Than fell that gay to groundis,
Of Goddis grace na thing begild;
Wox in hir chaumer chaist with child,
With Crist our kyng that cround is.

Thir tithingis tauld, the messinger
Till hevin agane he glidis;
That princes pure with-outyn peir
Full plesandly applid is,
And blith with barne abidis.
O worthy wirschip singuler,
To be moder and madyn meir,
As Cristin faith confidis;
That borne was of hir sidis
Our makar, Goddis sone so deir,
Quhilk erd, wattir, and hevinnis cleir
Throw grace and virtu gidis.

Magna sunt hec miracula,
Que manant ex amore;
Amoris ardet facula
Nec uritur ardore.
De Gabrielis ore
Dum virgo sumit verbula,
Frondescit Aaron virgula
Omni carens humore,
Et vellus madet rore,
Nec terram tangit stillula,
Dum virgo sine macula
Meretur mater fore.

The miraclis ar mekle and meit
Fra luffis ryuer rynnis;
The low of luf haldand the hete
Vnbrynt full blithlie brinnis;
Quhen Gabriell beginnis
With mouth that gudely may to gre
The wand of Aaron, dry but wete,
To burioun nocht blynnis;
The flesch all donk within is,
Vpon the erd na drop couth fleit;
Sa was that may maid moder suete
And sakeles of all synnis.

Mira matris integritas
In ventre deum vexit,
Et sola diuinitas
Portantem se protexit;
Pro nobis se despexit
Vera dei sublimitas,
Dum infirmatur sanitas,
Que mori non neglexit.
Sed, quando resurrexit,
Vera patebat deitas,
Et sic probatur caritas,
Qua deus nos dilexit.

Hir mervalus haill madinhede
God in hir bosum bracis,
And hir diuinite fra dreid
Hir kepit in all casis.
The hie God of his gracis
Him self dispisit, ws to speid,
And dowtit nocht to dee on deid;
He panit for our peacis,
And with his blude ws bacis,
Bot quhen he ras vp, as we rede,
The cherite of his Godhede
Was plane in euery placis.

O domina dulcissima,
Vultu nitens decoro,
O mater clementissima,
Virili carens thoro,
Te postulans exoro,
Ut, que feci, nequissima
Pellantur et turpissima,
Ne demon trahat loro.
Condonans quod ignoro,
Ad gaudia clarissima
Nos transfer, beatissima,
Ducensque celi choro. Amen.

O lady lele and lusumest,
Thy face moist fair and schene is;
O blosum blith and bowsumest,
Fra carnale cryme that clene is;
This prayer fra my splene is,
That all my werkis wikkitest
Thow put away and mak me chaist
Fra Termigant that teyn is,
And fra his cluke that kene is,
And syn till hevin my saule thou haist,
Quhair thi makar, of michtis mast,
Is kyng, and thow thair quene is.

Prose translation of the Latin lyric

1. Love is as strong as death, and through it what is hard is made soft; as the holy lesson tells us, nothing is difficult to the lover. Love drew us from despair, when Gabriel was sent on an embassy from the seat of heaven to the room of a virgin. O blessed one, he said, hail; in thee shall a conception be accomplished, but there shall be no injury to thy modesty; only incline thy will to that of God. (12)

2. Having heard these things, the maiden beloved of God spoke not, and, as befitted a modest woman, she who had been greeted remained silent. Lest she should be troubled, the angel straightway revealed and expounded the manner of that birth, how she should be unharmed. When this tale was told, the heavenly altar began to shine brightly, while the virgin was obedient to the word, and remained pregnant thereof. (24)

3. The archangel who came to tell these things departs and the peerless maiden is left heavy with child. O singular honour! A maiden is become a mother, and He who is engendered is the Creator and the divine salvation. O virginal bosom, a treasure is locked away within thee, by the power of which heaven, earth and sea are governed. (36)

4. Great are these miracles which spring from love; the torch of love burns yet it is not consumed by the heat. When the virgin hears the words from the mouth of Gabriel, the rod of Aaron begins to put forth leaves while devoid of all sap. Also, the fleece is soaked with dew, yet no droplet touches the earth, when the virgin immaculate deservedly becomes a mother. (48)

5. The wonderful chastity of the mother bore God within her womb, and only this Godhead protected the one bearing Itself. The true sublimity of God despised Itself for our sake, when, His strength turning to weakness, He did not shrink even from dying. But, when He rose again from the dead, the true divinity was obvious, and thus is demonstrated the love by which God has loved us. (60)

6. O sweetest lady, splendid in the beauty of thy face; O most gentle mother, innocent of union with manly flesh, as a suppliant I entreat thee, that the very wicked and shameful things which I have done be banished, lest the devil should drag me away in his noose. Forgiving what I no longer remember, transport us, most blessed one, to the most radiant joys, and lead us into the company of heaven. Amen. (72)

Punctuation and textual notes

It is clear that the stanzas of the Latin poem fall basically into three units, each of four lines, and this is reflected in the punctuation of the texts of **T** and **U**, as given in the *Analecta Hymnica.* Curiously, however, the scribe of **E** has provided illuminated capitals at the beginning of the first, sixth and tenth lines of each stanza, even though such a pattern does not suit the sense of the poem nearly so well. One can only guess at the reasons for this arrangement: could it, for example, be that the lyric had a musical dimension, now lost, which demanded such a division into units of five, four and three lines? At any rate, the punctuation adopted in the Latin text above is the one which seems best to bring out the sense of the lines as the poet intended them. Capitalisation is editorial, and abbreviations are silently expanded.

In the list which follows only those readings in **U**, **T** and **C** which differ from **E** in choice of wording or in word-order are noted. Note that the texts as given in *Analecta Hymnica* are not altogether accurate in some small details, such as spelling.

1 *Fortis*; in **C** the space left for a large capital letter is not filled in (M.R. James proposed to read *Mortis*; see above). In **U** the text is preceded by the following lines:
Vale, dei genetrix,
Virgo inestimabilis,
Vale, caelestis pietas,
Et pietatis caritas,
Sic serui tui, deprecor,
Immeriti non esto immemor.

3 **U**: *Ut sacra refert lectio*; **T**: *Ut sancta refert lectio.*

4 **U** omits.

5 *traxit*; **U** gives *transfert,* subpuncted, then *traxit. aue*; **U**: *a ve*; **T**: *aue,* with a vertical line separating the first two letters: this was

a common play on words.[26]

7 *Gabrielis*; **E**: *Gabriel. missio*: **U** omits.

8 *In virginis*; **C**: *virginis in.*

12 *tantum*; **E**: *tam* (with nasal mark above *m*; = tamen?); **U**: *tm* (with nasal mark above *m*).

13 *subticuit*; **U**, **T**: *obstupuit.*

19 *partus*; **U**: *prius. exposuit*; **C**: *apposuit.*

20 *foret*; **T**: *floret.*

22 *Ara*; **C**: *aula. Ara celestis*; **U**: *Vexillum crucis.*

23 *virgo verbo*; **C**: *verbo virgo.*

25 *Archangelus*; **C**: *angelus.*

30 *Virgo mater*; **C**: *mira res.*

33 *puellare*; **U**: *singulare.*

34 *Thesaurus in te*; **C**: *in te thesaurus.*

36 *et*: **U** omits.

38 *manant ex*; **C**: *veniunt.*

40 *ardore*; **T**: *amore*, corrected to *ardore.*

42 *sumit*; **C**, **E**: *sumpsit.*

50 *vexit*; **E**: *nexit.*

51 **C** and **E** lack one syllable. **T**: *Ut solis divinitas*; **U**: *Et sobolis divinitas.*

52 *se*; **T**: *te.*

61 **U**: *Virgo mente purissima.*

62 **U**: *Te reus hinc honoro.*

63 **U**: *Dei mater castissima.*

68 *demon*; **U**: *hostis. loro*; **T**: *lora*; **U**: *oro.*

69 *Condonans*; **C**: *condolens.*

72 *Ducensque celi*; **U**: *Iungens celesti. Amen*: **T** omits.
The text in **T** continues with the following lines:
O mater humilitatis,
In qua deus incarnatur,
Pulchra et admirabilis,
Cui nulla comparatur,
Gaude, nam tuis brachiis
Divina virtus portatur
Foveturque obsequiis
Atque mamilla lactatur,
Tuis favet imperiis
Nec non precibus placatur,

[26] For an example in an English text: *The Commonplace Book of Robert Reynes of Acle*, ed. C. Louis (New York and London, 1980), 300 and 489.

Impetra nobis miseris,
Ut mox ad te dirigatur
Spiritus et his gaudiis
In sempiternum fruatur,
Et populus incredulus
Ad Iesum per te convertatur.

Henryson's rendering

Not the least of the interests of the Latin lyric is that it affords a unique glimpse into the Scottish poet's methods of composition; none other of Henryson's works is (as far as is known) a direct translation. As with the Latin original, each of Henryson's stanzas is essentially organised in three groups of four lines, despite the structure suggested by the illuminated capitals in **E** (see above). Nonetheless, the first stanza of the Scottish version does fall more naturally into the 5-4-3 pattern, and this is reflected in the text (reproduced above) as given in the edition of Denton Fox. The third stanza also begins with a syntactic unit of five lines, since Henryson has delayed by one line his rendering of 'O decus singulare'. This element of structural uncertainty in the stanzas, the significance of which ought not, perhaps, to be exaggerated, may result merely from an attempt to cope with the dense brevity of the Latin lines, many of which, as independent phrasal units, lend themselves to being linked in more than one way with those around them.

On occasion Henryson succeeds in achieving almost literal translation, as with the opening lines, where 'Fortis ut mors dilectio,/ Qua durum fit suaue' becomes 'Forcy as deith is likand lufe,/ Throuch quhom al bittir suet is'. Other felicitous examples would be: 'Pro nobis se despexit' / 'Him self dispisit, ws to speid' (53), and 'Vultu nitens decoro' / 'Thy face moist fair and schene is' (62). Sometimes Henryson is able to make small improvements on the original, as when 'Ut refert sancta lectio' becomes the more economical 'as writ can pruf' (3), or when 'Archangelus regreditur/ Qui venit hec narrare' is rendered 'Thir tithingis tauld, the messinger/ Till hevin agane he glidis' (25-6), where the reader is vouchsafed a hint of angelic locomotion. There are almost no absolute losses: one, however, is 'Condonans quod ignoro' (69), and another (8) concerns the Virgin's 'conclaue' (but this will return in 23).

In certain lines Henryson's choice of words alters the sense of the original. The specific reference to conception in line 10 gives way to the more vague 'In the he will tak rest and rufe'. In 27-8 the maiden heavy with child ('grauida...puella') is raised to the status of 'princes pure', before in the final line becoming 'quene'. When 'Mira matris integritas' is given as 'Hir mervalus haill madinhede' (49), Henryson may be said to be highlighting the paradox of conception by a virgin; in changing 'O mater clementissima' into 'O blosum blith and bowsumest' (63) he seems to opt for increased physical awareness. There are also some places where Henryson introduces entirely new ideas: in one such we gain the poetically effective image of the river of love (38), in another an allusion to the topic of the coronation of the Virgin (71-2). A change typical of the vernacular is that of 'demon' (68) to 'Termigant'. The only passage which might be described as free translation is found in lines 23-4, which are rendered thus:

Than fell that gay to groundis,
Of Goddis grace na thing begild;
Wox in hir chaumer chaist with child,
With Crist our Kyng that cround is.

Here Henryson's words evoke the scene of the Annunciation as it is represented in countless pictures and manuscript illustrations; the latter, in turn, are doubtless influenced by works of popular theology and affective expositions of the Bible narrative, such as the *Meditationes Vitae Christi* attributed to St. Bonaventure, translated into English in the early fifteenth century by Nicholas Love, prior of Mount Grace charterhouse.[27]

The Scottish poem is remarkable for the amount of alliteration which it contains. This, as might be expected, has the effect of increasing the incisiveness of the lines; it is a technique which is particularly suited to the articulation of proverbs (of which there are many in Henryson) and frequent alliteration is a characteristic of Henryson's verse. The Latin poem itself contains not a little alliteration, and when this falls on a key word, it is carried over into the Scots translation. One may, for example, compare the following passage:

[27] Nicholas Love's *Mirror of the Blessed Life of Jesus Christ*, ed. M.G. Sargent (New York and London, 1992). At the pages dealing with the Annunciation Sargent notes influences from SS Elizabeth of Hungary and Bernard of Clairvaux: 21-30, 260-62 (on the precise identity of the former, see pp. xvii-xix).

Magna sunt hec miracula,
Que manant ex amore;
Amoris ardet facula
Nec uritur ardore (37-40)

with the translation:

The miraclis ar mekle and meit
Fra luffis ryuer rynnis;
The low of luf haldand the hete
Vnbrynt full blithlie brinnis.

Though the number of syllables remains the same, the number of words, and thus the possibility of alliteration, is considerably increased; this contributes to the lapidary style of the Scottish version. All in all, Henryson's translation may be pronounced a remarkably successful achievement.

Throughout the foregoing discussion it has been taken for granted that the Scottish translator was indeed Robert Henryson, but one must not neglect to note, for the sake of completeness, that some doubts have been raised hereanent. These doubts concern the trustworthiness of the colophon in the Gray MS (which attributes another familiar Middle English poem,[28] in Scottish guise, to one 'Glassinbery', otherwise unknown), and also certain suspicious rhymes. The first of these points is of little relevance to the Annunciation poem, unless one invoke the principle of guilt by association; the second was signalised by G. Gregory Smith (it concerns the rhyming of open and close *e*), who felt almost compelled 'to consider the poem a direct Northern version of a Southern text'.[29] For his part, Denton Fox was less troubled by the linguistic evidence and he accepted the poem into the canon of Henryson's works, albeit with the caveat: 'It should probably be classified among the more doubtful of the attributions'. Fox also observed that 'the poem does not in any way resemble Henryson's other poems', while conceding that it is 'clearly the work of a competent poet'.[30] These linguistic and stylistic considerations do

[28] *Index of Middle English Verse*, no. 3612.

[29] *The Poems of Robert Henryson*, ed. G. Gregory Smith, 3 vols. (STS, 1906-14), i, p. lxxiii. On the same page, however, Gregory Smith also declares: 'Against the ascription to Henryson, given on the authority of a MS. almost contemporary (c.1500), no serious argument can be offered, though the differences of style are striking.'

[30] *Poems of Henryson*, ed. Fox, 428. Nothing daunted, Fox gives this lyric pride of place among Henryson's minor poems.

not seem strong enough to undermine the traditional ascription of this poem (now known to be a translation) to Henryson. Moreover, the fact that the Latin poem has no known connection with England, while it is found in Scotland, the Low Countries and the Rhineland, is something that may provide negative evidence against Gregory Smith's speculation as to a Southern (i.e. English) source.

The poem, *Forcy as deith is likand lufe*, is a religious lyric, and may be viewed in the context of the other Middle Scots specimens of the genre.[31] Though most of these poems are anonymous, nearly every mediaeval Scottish poet composed at least one, while the lyrics of William Dunbar are outstanding, in terms both of number and of poetic quality. Among the other short poems of Henryson one may mention here: 'The Abbey Walk', an injunction to be obedient to God; 'The Bludy Serk', a religious fable on Christ the lover-knight; 'Ane Prayer for the Pest', a collective confession of sin and appeal to God for mercy.[32]

The subject of *Forcy is deith is likand lufe* is the Annunciation, in which the Angelic Salutation inaugurates the latest, and most significant, stage in the history of the redemption of man. As is to be expected, this episode looks forward to the eventual sacrifice of Christ on the Cross, and to his subsequent Resurrection. Throughout the poem the figure of Mary is central, together with the role which she, as virgin and mother, played in the divine scheme. Within the overall theme of the contact between the human and the divine, this paradoxical encounter, leading to the conception of Christ, is the greatest of the miracles of love; and love, as the opening quotation from the *Song of Songs* (8: 6) declares, is as strong as death.

Religious lyrics of this type are designed to be used for personal meditation, leading to the inculcation of devotion.[33] This poem of Henryson's displays some affinity with Dunbar's 'Ane Ballat of Our Lady': *Hale, sterne superne; hale, in eterne.*[34] Both poems are in twelve-line stanzas, with lines of four and three feet (the rhyme schemes are not identical, however, nor are the metrical

[31] A.A. MacDonald, 'The Middle Scots Religious Lyrics' (Edinburgh University Ph.D., 1978), esp. 160-68; idem., 'Religious poetry in Middle Scots', in *The History of Scottish Literature Vol. I*, ed. R.D.S. Jack (Aberdeen, 1988), 91-104.

[32] *Poems of Henryson*, ed. Fox, 156-8, 158-62, 167-9.

[33] R. Woolf, *The English Religious Lyric in the Middle Ages* (Oxford, 1968), 1-15; D. Gray, *Themes and Images in the Mediaeval English Religious Lyric* (London and Boston, 1972), 31-58.

[34] *The Poems of William Dunbar*, ed. J. Kinsley (Oxford, 1979), 4-7.

patterns). Henryson's lyric may lack the flamboyant aureation of Dunbar's poem, but the insistent alliteration suggests an equivalent level of artistic virtuosity. Dunbar's poem is unified through the recurrence of the Latin refrain, 'Ave Maria, gracia plena', which appears as the ninth line of each of the seven stanzas and establishes the lyric as a rhetorical expansion upon the words of the Archangel Gabriel. In this context it is notable that these same Latin words appear between each stanza of the original poem as preserved in **T** (see above). Clearly these two lyrics of Henryson and Dunbar have a common background in Marian devotion.

The Scottish manuscript which contains the largest number of short, anonymous religious lyrics is BL Arundel MS 285 (c.1550).[35] Like Dean Brown's MS, this is a collection of prayers and devotions, in prose and verse, in both Latin and Scots, and there is a certain overlap in the contents of the two manuscripts. Arundel MS 285 resembles a Book of Hours even less, however, and it is rather a collection of popular devotional texts; in such a manuscript Henryson's poem would in no way have been out of place. As it is, the preservation of *Forcy as deith* owes everything to the fact that the poem happened to appeal to the taste of the scribe and notary, James Gray, who jotted it down in his notebook sometime between 1503/4 and 1532.[36] Other scribes likewise inserted poems on available blank pages and fly-leaves, as one finds, for example, in the Makculloch MS;[37] fairly recently two further Marian lyrics have been discovered on a bifolium bound in with a manuscript of the *De Consolatione Philosophiae* of Boethius.[38] During the Reformation no kind of mediaeval Scottish verse was so thoroughly suppressed as were poems expressing Marian devotion;[39] in such a lacuna Henryson's lyric stands out as a fortunate survival, and the awareness of the Latin original helps

[35] *Devotional Pieces in Verse and Prose*, ed. J.A.W. Bennett (STS, 1955). See also J.A.W. Bennett, 'Scottish pre-Reformation devotion: some notes on British Library MS. Arundel 285', in *So meny people longages and tonges*, ed. M. Benskin and M.L. Samuels (Edinburgh, 1981), 299-308.

[36] *Poems of Henryson*, ed. Fox, 426-7.

[37] *Pieces from the Makculloch and the Gray MSS, together with the Chepman and Myllar Prints*, ed. G. Stevenson (STS, 1918), pp. xiv-xv.

[38] I.C. Cunningham, 'Two poems on the Virgin (National Library of Scotland, Adv. MS 18.5.14)', *TEBS*, v (1985-7), 32-40.

[39] A.A. MacDonald, 'Poetry, politics and Reformation censorship in sixteenth-century Scotland', *English Studies*, lxiv (1983), 410-21.

somewhat to illuminate the context of literary composition in Scotland in the late fifteenth century.[40]

[40] Several friends and colleagues have kindly given me the benefit of their time and expertise in connection with this poem; in particular I am indebted to Dr F. Akkerman, Mr I.C. Cunningham, Prof. Dr J.P. Gumbert, Dr Jos M.M. Hermans, and the late Dr E.R. Smits. Any remaining errors are my own responsibility.

WILLIAM ELPHINSTONE'S LIBRARY REVISITED

Leslie J. Macfarlane

Years ago, while searching *seriatim* through the medieval manuscripts and incunables held in the library of King's College, Aberdeen, the present writer brought together and analysed the contents of 28 books which had once belonged to William Elphinstone, bishop of Aberdeen between 1483 and 1514, and founder of its University in 1495.[1] All of them bore his signature of ownership, and, judging from the notes he made in the margins of many of them, it was clear that they had once formed a part of his own working library, which he had either gifted to King's College between 1505 and 1512, or bequeathed in his will to his young University just before his death in 1514. This collection, the first and largest single gift of books to the University in this early phase of its history, became the nucleus of the College library, to which, shortly, were to be added others donated by those regent masters and officials who had been associated with the University project from the beginning. The collection was first housed in the Scorpio Chamber, located at the junction between the Great Hall and the south range of the College buildings, probably in the Round Tower.[2] Sometime between 1532 and 1542, however, it was transferred to the two-storied structure abutting the south side of the Chapel, which Bishop William Stewart had erected especially to accommodate the sacristy below and the College library above. And there, in order to comply with the College's constitution, which required an annual inspection of the library, this early group of manuscripts and incunables was first catalogued, although it is evident that the printed books were from the start given a separate classification and shelved separately from the manuscripts.

A recent search through King's College Library failed to produce any more manuscripts or early printed books which bore

---

[1] L. Macfarlane, 'William Elphinstone's Library', *AUR*, xxxvii (1958), 253-71.

[2] *Fasti Aberdonensis*, ed C. Innes (Spalding Club, 1854), 576; J.R. Pickard, *A History of King's College Library, Aberdeen, until 1860*, i (Aberdeen 1987), 5-6.

Elphinstone's signature of ownership. But it did reveal that in the course of its long history and growth up to 1870, when it was rehoused again, the Library had been recatalogued three or four times. Moreover, a close look at its earliest pre-1560 catalogue numbering of manuscripts showed that with one or two missing numbers, Elphinstone's identifiable manuscript collection had been numbered sequentially. When therefore, on examination, other late medieval manuscripts in the Library were discovered which supplied the actual missing numbers in this sequence of Elphinstone's collection, it was not unreasonable to deduce that, although they lacked his signature of ownership, they had once formed a part of his collection, which he had either given to the College in its early years, or bequeathed it to it in his will in 1514. The following study, then, will argue for their inclusion on the basis of this probability. At the same time, it will provide the opportunity to comment further on the content of his library, and to correct a few errors in the present author's 1958 article.

The earliest University catalogue of this collection of manuscripts begins with the numeration as given in the left hand column of the table on page 68. From this table we note, first, that four manuscripts which bear Archibald Whitelaw's signature of ownership, and one each which had once been in the hands of Andrew and Gavin Leslie, and Hector Boece, are to be found in the heart of the Elphinstone corpus. Now on the face of it, it could be argued that this corpus was no more than a random early grouping of manuscripts on hand when the cataloguer came to catalogue the Library and to which he merely gave this sequence. Closer analysis, however, points towards the conclusion that they were all once in Elphinstone's possession and a part of his collection when donated by him to the University. Before turning to the Whitelaw manuscripts 199^{1-2}, 200, 257 and 214, however, a few words must first be said about this most accomplished humanist scholar.

A graduate of St Andrews and later a teacher at the University of Cologne, Archibald Whitelaw was royal secretary to both James III and James IV between 1462 and 1493.[3] A friend of Elphinstone's, he worked closely with him in the King's Daily Council for twenty years, and accompanied him on several ambassadorial

[3] Watt, *Fasti*, 168, 173, 235, 240, 313, 354; N. Macdougall, *James III: a Political Study* (Edinburgh, 1982), passim; N. Macdougall, *James IV* (Edinburgh, 1989), 51, 73, 105, 284.

Earliest Catalogue Number	Present Catalogue Number	Signature of Ownership	Brief description of manuscript
0.1.1	MS 12	Wm Elphinstone	Nicolaus Tudeschis, *Commentaria in Decretales* I, tit 1-6
0.1.2	MS 15	Wm Elphinstone	ibid., II, tit 24-30
0.1.3	MS 16	Wm Elphinstone	ibid., III, tit 1-50
0.1.4	MS 14	Wm Elphinstone	ibid., II, tit 1-13
0.1.5	MS 13	Wm Elphinstone	ibid., I, tit 29-43
0.1.6	MS 17	Wm Elphinstone	Dominicus de S. Geminiano, *Recollecta super Sexto* III, tit I-V, tit 11
0.1.7	MS 199[1-2]	A Whitelaw	Author unidentified, *Commentaria in Decretales* II, tit 23-30
0.1.8	MS 195	Wm Elphinstone	Henricus Retheri, *Lecturae super Digestis*
0.1.9	MS 196	Wm Elphinstone	Henricus de Piro, Johannes Groesbek, Ricardus de Turnaco, *Lecturae super Codice et Institutionibus*
0.1.10	MS 197	Wm Elphinstone	Johannes Groesbek, Ricardus de Turnaco, Henricus Retheri, *Lecturae super Digestis et Libris Feudorum*
0.1.11	MS 198	Wm Elphinstone	Nicolaus Tudeschis, *Commentaria in Decretales* IV; *Glose Clementinarum* I-V
0.1.12	MS 222	Wm Elphinstone	Laurentius Valla, *Elegantiae Latinae Linguae*
0.1.13*	MS 223	A & G Leslie	Porphyry's *Isagoge super Organon* [*scored through]
0.1.14	MS 200	A Whitelaw	Several authors, *Lectura super Clementinas*
0.1.15	MS 201	Wm Elphinstone	Johannes de Imola, *In Constitutiones Clementinas* I-V
0.1.16	MS 262	Wm Elphinstone	Petrus de Ancarano, *Lectura Repetita Sexti et Clementinarum*
0.1.17	MS 257	A Whitelaw	Author unidentified, *Commentarium in Decretales* III, tit 1-24
0.1.18	MS 264	Hector Boece*	Johannes de Irlandia, *Super Sentenciarum Petri Lombardi* [*Boece's ownership inferred]
0.1.19	MS 214	A Whitelaw	Paulus Orosius, *Historiarum initium ad Aurelium Augustinum*; Lucius Amneius Florus, *Romana historia*

missions. Considering that Whitelaw was one steeped in the liberal arts rather than canon law, it comes as a surprise to find that MSS 199^{1-2}, 200 and 257 are, in fact, fifteenth century commentaries on the *Decretals* of Gregory IX and lectures on the *Constitutions* of Clement V; and moreover, that Whitelaw had worked his way systematically through the texts, as the marginal comments scattered throughout them in his own neat, unmistakably humanist hand makes abundantly clear. From these comments, then, it would appear that he was more familiar with the problems affecting the canonists of his day than may previously have been supposed. But Elphinstone, as one of the most distinguished canonists in late medieval Scotland, was already familiar with these commentaries, and had long since possessed his own copies of them, so clearly he did not need them for himself. What is suggested here, therefore, is that Elphinstone had discussed the founding of his University with Whitelaw around the latter's retirement from office in 1493, when Whitelaw was well over 70 years of age and would have had no more use for these manuscripts; and that as a gesture of his enthusiastic support, Whitelaw had, before his death in 1498, either given or bequeathed them to Elphinstone for the use of the University's young Law Faculty, then certain to be short of useful texts like these. And this, too, might explain why Elphinstone did not put his signature of ownership on them, since he wished them to be remembered as Whitelaw's manuscripts, rather than his own.

This supposition is reinforced when we come to look more closely at the other Whitelaw manuscript 214. Orosius's commentary on St Augustine's *City of God*, his *History against the Pagans*, was widely read throughout the Middle Ages, and became a particular favourite among humanists in the Renaissance period. It is much less surprising, then, to find that Whitelaw not only possessed a copy of this work, but that he had also annotated it throughout in his own hand. Now it so happened that Elphinstone, as a humanist himself, had brought over Hector Boece from Paris in 1497 precisely to introduce humanist studies into the liberal arts syllabus at King's College; and given that Hector Boece's name (though not in his own hand), appears on the first folio of this Whitelaw manuscript, it seems likely that as a keen reader of Roman history himself, Boece would have introduced this text to his first-year Arts students when it became available to him, since it included not only Orosius's work, but Florus's four books on Roman history as well as an exposition on the Trojan war: a probability strengthened by the name (not the attribution of ownership) of Alexander Galloway, an early student of Boece's at King's College, which also appears on the first folio of the manuscript, perhaps as a borrower, like Boece. If between 1493 and 1498, then, Whitelaw did gift these four manuscripts to Elphinstone for his University venture, they would certainly have been put to good use from its earliest years onwards, or as soon as they were placed in the Library.

The argument for the inclusion of the other two manuscripts in the Elphinstone collection, other than on the basis of their catalogue numeration, is much more conjectural but still feasible. MS 223, Porphyry's *Isagoge*, the long-standing introduction to Aristotle's *Categoriae*, was frequently given as a set book in logic for first-year Arts students in the medieval universities. Elphinstone himself had been taken through it by his regent, master Duncan Bunch, when a student at Glasgow, and it was clearly a set book at Aberdeen from its earliest years. Elphinstone's signature of ownership nowhere appears in this manuscript. But on folio 58v, in a different and later hand than that of the scribe, occur the words: 'Liber Andree Leslye Studentis alme universitatis aberdonensis per donum reverendissimi ...', the writing then becoming too faint under violet light to read; and on folio 160v occurs: 'Magister Gawinus Leslye est huius libri possessor manu propria Jesus Maria Amen'. Folio 202v also has 'James ... primus annus sui pontificatus' and 'Gallowaye', in addition to a number of pen trials, some in Scots.

We lack the matriculation rolls of King's College for this period, but the Cathedral register informs us that master Andrew Leslie was admitted as a notary public for the diocese of Aberdeen on 13 April 1540,[4] so he is likely to have been a student of the University in the late 1530s. He tells us that the manuscript had been given to him by a senior ecclesiastic ('reverendissimus'). This could have been Gavin Leslie, an earlier graduate of King's College and almost certainly a relative of Andrew, a chaplain at the altar of the Three Kings in the parish church of St Nicholas, Aberdeen in the 1520s,[5] and shown on f.160v as the possessor of this manuscript. But the inclusion of names on f.202v in hands

[4] *Registrum Episcopatus Aberdonensis*, ed. C. Innes (Spalding and Maitland Clubs, 1845), ii, 323-4.

[5] *Cartularium Ecclesiae Sancti Nicholai Aberdonensis*, ed. J. Cooper (Spalding Club, 1892), ii, 320-21.

contemporaneous or even earlier than Gavin Leslie's suggests that the manuscript was being used or borrowed by others in King's College as early as 1514—at least if the James referred to on that folio was James Ogilvie, nominated in that year, though unsuccessfully, to the bishopric of Aberdeen ('primus annus sui pontificatus'). How the manuscript came into the hands of either Gavin or Andrew Leslie we now have no means of knowing, but it seems that when catalogued, the cataloguer believed it to be a part of Elphinstone's original collection since he gave to it the serial number 0.1.13, and then altered it (presumably mistakenly) to 0.1.12, since 0.1.12 had already been assigned to Elphinstone's Valla manuscript.

The *Sentences* of Peter Lombard had been a set text for all students of theology at the University of Paris long before John Ireland taught in its Faculty from the 1460s onwards, and there can be little doubt that MS 264, Ireland's Commentaries on the 3rd and 4th Books of the *Sentences*, was a copy of a part of his lecture course while there. Now Elphinstone had laid it down in his constitution that the Faculty of Theology at his University should follow that at Paris, so that it is safe to assume that Peter Lombard's *Sentences* would have been a set text at Aberdeen from the time teaching began, even before King's College was built and had begun to function, in 1505. There were, for example, several copies of the *Sentences* available in the Cathedral Library of St Machar when James Ogilvie, James Brown or James Aitkenhead were teaching in their cathedral manses to the first batch of Dominican theology students by 1497. There were also commentaries on the *Sentences* by other theologians available at the Cathedral at this time, though not those of John Ireland.

Elphinstone had been a student and teacher himself at Paris between 1465 and 1470, when John Ireland was teaching there, and, like many of his fellow Scots, would almost certainly have been present at the ceremony when Ireland was elected Rector of the University on 10 October 1469. Elphinstone also met John Ireland when the latter came from France on two diplomatic missions to Scotland in 1479 and 1480. By the 1490s, therefore, Elphinstone would have been very well aware of Ireland's distinguished reputation as a theologian, and would certainly have given his approval for the use of his Commentary on Peter Lombard's *Sentences* in his own Faculty of Theology at Aberdeen. His signature of ownership does not appear on any of the folios of this manuscript. Indeed, f.ii of MS 264 distinctly tells us that it was gifted to the College by Hector Boece, its Principal.

This entry, however, is in a later hand, and not in Boece's own distinctive hand as its owner. It is true that after he was appointed Principal by Elphinstone in 1505, it was incumbent upon Boece to teach the theologians, and he may well have used this copy of Ireland's Commentary within the agreed framework of Elphinstone's syllabus for the Faculty. But Alexander Galloway's name also appears on f.1r at the beginning of the actual text; and since Galloway never read theology at King's, but liberal arts and canon law, it is arguable that like the Orosius MS 214 and indeed the Porphyry MS 223, the John Ireland MS 264 may also have been a part of the original Elphinstone collection which Galloway, as the official of the diocese and executor of the bishop's will, transferred to the College library shortly after Elphinstone's death in 1514. Hector Boece used the Ireland MS when teaching in the Faculty of Theology, just as he would have used the Orosius manuscript when teaching in the Arts Faculty; it is, therefore, also arguable that, being found in his keeping on his death in 1536, MSS 264 and 214 were inscribed, like the rest of Boece's own books, as having been gifted by him to the College before being returned to their original place on the shelf according to their catalogue sequence within the Elphinstone collection.

A description of each of these six additional manuscripts to the Elphinstone Corpus has been given elsewhere, and need not be repeated here.[6] But this revisit to his Library does provide the opportunity to look again at the many comments Elphinstone made in the margins of his manuscripts, first as a student and lecturer in Canon Law at Paris, then as a diocesan official, and later as a bishop; from these comments it is possible to discern some of the most controversial legal, social and ecclesiastical problems of his age, still awaiting resolution. As for the seven books Elphinstone purchased at Paris as a student and lecturer between 1465 and 1470,[7] these covered the commentaries of Nicholas Tudeschis on Books I-IV of the *Decretals* of Gregory IX, the commentary of Dominic of St Geminiano on Books III-V of

---

[6] For MSS 199[1-2], 200, 257 and 264, see N.R. Ker, *Medieval Manuscripts in British Libraries*, (Oxford, 1977), ii, 14-15, 18-19; for MSS 214 and 223, see M.R. James, *A Catalogue of the Medieval Manuscripts in the University Library, Aberdeen* (Cambridge, 1932), 59-60, 66-7.

[7] MSS 12-17, 198.

the *Sext* of Boniface IX, and those of Nicholas and Dominic on the *Constitutions* of Clement V, leaving him without further learned opinion only on Book V of the *Decretals*, Books I-II of the *Sext*, and Books I-V of the *Extravagantes* of John XXII. The last named text had not yet been authoritatively edited for use in the Law Faculty at Paris, while it is possible that Book V of the *Decretals* and Books I-II of the *Sext* may not have been lectured on at the time. From this it is clear that Elphinstone, in his years at Paris, was well briefed on the latest jurisprudential thinking on most of the accepted text of the *Corpus Iuris Canonici*. And while it would be rash to assume that those titles and chapters which he most heavily annotated in these manuscripts were those he actually lectured on himself, it is evident that these were the ones to which he gave his closest attention at this stage in his career.

These marginal notes occur mainly in MSS 14, 15 and 198, and concern those areas which tried to define the limits proper to secular and ecclesiastical jurisdiction, those on the validity of oaths, and those on customary and statutory law. By the mid fifteenth century, none of these problems had gone away. Indeed, the running conflict between popes, emperors and kings over the nomination of bishops and abbots, the taxation of the clergy and the amount of canonical injunctions which secular rulers could accommodate from visits of papal legates, had occupied the minds of civil and canon lawyers ever since Gregory IX's *Decretals* and Gratian's earlier *Decretum* had been lectured upon in the universities of western Europe from the thirteenth century onwards. But by now canonists like Nicholas Tudeschis were having to wrestle with far more sophisticated anti-papal legislation coming from the courts of European monarchs. Moreover, when we read Tudeschis' commentaries on these areas of conflict, we begin to realise how far the Church's position had been challenged by secular rulers as a result of the Schism and the ensuing Conciliar Movement, and how far Tudeschis was aware of this, thus giving us a rare insight into the way he sought to come to terms with these problems and tried to resolve them.

Basically, although a moderate conciliarist himself, Tudeschis stood at the end of a long line of classical canonists who believed in the pre-eminence of the spiritual power, namely, that popes finally had the right to judge kings and emperors. But he qualified this by stating that popes should confine their authority to spiritual matters—to matters affecting the Christian faith or sin, such as heresy, usury, divorce, concubinage, defamation of character, the breaking of contracts and the like; a qualification with which, on the face of it, few secular authorities at the time would have disagreed. Indeed monarchs, if watchful of their rights, had long since recognised the value of spiritual authority as exercised in their ecclesiastical courts. But the real struggle lay elsewhere and was much more threatening to both the spiritual and the temporal powers. Thus in order to satisfy their political ambitions, secular monarchs by now demanded the same kind of dedicated loyalty and service from their bishops and abbots as they required of their lay counsellors and government officials: hence their need to nominate their own candidates to these offices, and to force the papacy to accede to their choice. But how far was this a purely secular matter? Already Tudeschis had watched civil lawyers strengthening their masters' hands, as in France, by claiming that secular rulers were emperors in their own kingdoms, and thus held full authority over those not subject to them even in temporal matters (*Commentaria in Decretales,* Lib II, tit XXVI, c 13: *Ad audientiam*). Hence his argument that this could result in an emasculated episcopacy unable or unwilling to defend even the legitimate rights of the Church.

The nomination of bishops and abbots, therefore, required much more careful procedures (Lib I, tits IV, V and VI), which in years to come, when James IV obtained the archbishopric of St Andrews, first for his brother, and then for his illegitimate son aged eleven, Elphinstone would have had cause vividly to remember. And yet Tudeschis was equally aware that the papacy, by involving itself so heavily in the secular politics of the day, had already lost much of its spiritual credibility. Much better then, he argued, that whenever the papacy intended to pass judgement on kings and emperors in what appeared to be purely temporal matters, it should do so by invoking the process of the *denuntiatio evangelica,* basing its cause *ratione peccati,* on sacred scripture rather than on papal constitutions. This happened, for instance, when rulers committed perjury or serious breaches of the peace by forswearing their solemn oath on a peace treaty (Lib II, tit I, c 13: *Novit ille*)—a vital issue which would come to haunt Elphinstone in 1482 and 1513, when both James III and James IV, each in turn, went back on their solemn oaths to keep the peace with England, hard pressed though they were. But canon lawyers who drafted treaties saw things differently from their royal masters. For them, national honour and political expediency had also to be considered within a framework of moral obligation; a point which comes home to us when we read Elphinstone's marginal notes on Tudeschis's detailed commentary on the taking and validity of oaths in his 36 chapters of Lib II, tit XXIV of the *Decretals*: *De Iureiurando*, in MS 15.

When Elphinstone became Official of Glasgow in 1471, and then of Lothian in 1478, he was plunged into the daily grind of adjudicating *ex officio* and *ad instantium partium* causes until 1488; this explains his gradual accumulation of reference books and further legal commentaries.[8] To judge from his lengthy marginal notes in MSS 15-17, 198 and 202, and INC 40, together with a fragment from one of his Court books, the two most difficult problems he had to deal with throughout these years were those concerning marriages and benefices. As to the former, great care had to be taken by Officials to ensure that when contracted, marriages were free from canonical impediment and had been lawfully witnessed. Those seeking to free themselves from the marriage bond, therefore, had to prove the existence of an initial impediment—like the lack of consent by one or other of the partners, or their being related within the fourth degree, namely, having common great grandparents, which latter required a papal dispensation before marriage. The prevalence of handfasting in Scotland at this time, however, gave Officials cause for even greater concern, the dense coverage of Elphinstone's marginal notes on f.9v of MS 198 dealing precisely with the many complications this custom produced. Here, in the text on betrothals *Veniens* (Lib IV, tit 1 *De Sponsalibus et Matrimoniis*, c XV), Tudeschis argues that if intercourse took place after a promise to marry, this *sponsalia de futuro* constituted a valid marriage, even when unwitnessed, since it affected the possible legitimation of heirs and heiresses; and this was why, in order to minimise causes coming before the courts of Officials, handfasting should be made a public act, before witnesses in a church.

This was a clear opinion which Elphinstone weighed here, as elsewhere in the whole of Tudeschis' Commentary on Book IV of the *Decretals* (whose 21 titles deal with every aspect of matrimonial law), against the text of the *Decretals* themselves and its Gloss; as for example in tit VI, *Qui Clerici vel Voventes Matrimonium Contrahere Possunt*, where Tudeschis and Elphinstone agree 'that clerks in minor orders may lawfully contract marriage, but once they are in

[8] MSS 184, 201, 202, 262, and INC 40, as described in Macfarlane, 'William Elphinstone's library', 260-64.

major orders as subdeacons, deacons and priests, they may not; and if they do, such marriages are null and void'. Elphinstone's *nota bene* against this first chapter of tit VI may have some added weight here, given that he was the son of a cleric in minor orders who went on to become a priest on the promise of a canonry at Glasgow Cathedral and who thus committed his son to the illegitimate state.

Elphinstone's father's early career, in fact, highlights the state of the whole system of benefice holding in the later Middle Ages, which by then had become almost unworkable. The system was already complicated enough, with widespread plural benefice holding and with too many clerics chasing too few vacant benefices, thus causing patrons to compete with each other. But faced with grave financial difficulties of its own, the fourteenth-century papacy had legislated to reserve to itself the right to nominate additional kinds of benefices, and had later widened this right to include expectative graces, namely the right to nominate clerics to benefices before they became vacant. Not unnaturally, all of this was fiercely resisted by both lay and ecclesiastical patrons, causing further endless litigation and frustrating delays in appointing beneficees. This was especially so in Scotland, where most benefice appeals against the claims of the papacy or other rival patrons went straight to the Roman Rota as appeals of the first instance, rather than, as in most other countries, to the ecclesiastical courts of their metropolitans for their first appeal hearing. For this reason Scottish Officials had to be particularly careful of the procedures governing the hearing and settling of benefice disputes, and it is not surprising to find that sometime during his career as the Official of Glasgow, Elphinstone either bought or came into the possession of MS 202, a collection of 451 causes put to the Roman Rota, some of which contain procedural guidance. Bound with this volume, too, is a huge legal dictionary, its largest entry, on Benefices, occupying several pages and covering every conceivable method of benefice holding and the problems likely to occur when disputes arose. What Elphinstone thought of all this is perhaps best seen when we look at his notes in the margins of MSS 16 and 17, where many problems relating to benefices come under the close scrutiny of Nicholas Tudeschis and Dominic of St Geminiano.

Both these canonists had become disturbed over the increase in expectative graces and papal dispensations for incompatible plural benefices, which they saw as violations of earlier papal injunctions and dubious in law. For this reason, Tudeschis examined with some care the proper use of the dispensing power of popes and bishops and the rights of patrons in his Commentary on Book III of the *Decretals*, especially in title V *De Praebendis et Dignitatibus*, title VIII *De Concessione Praebendae*, title XII *Ut Ecclesiastica Beneficia Sine Deminutione Conferantur*, and title XXXVIII *De Iure Patronatus*, on many chapters of which Elphinstone made notes in the margins of MS 16. Similarly, we find him writing additional notes on the same titles of Dominic of St Geminiano's Commentary on the *Sext* in MS 17.

When we look, then, at the many marginal notes that Elphinstone made in his manuscripts and incunables, both as a student and teacher at Paris and as an Official of two busy dioceses, we begin to see how he gradually built up his reputation as an outstanding canonist himself; but more interestingly, we can see the strong, formative influence which acute minded canonists like Tudeschis and his school had on his jurisprudential thinking. This became increasingly critical and reformist the more Elphinstone became involved with the Scottish crown and the papacy and the tensions between them from 1478 onwards, when he became a Lord of Council; and it enables us to understand what he was trying to achieve both as a bishop of a diocese and as a drafter of treaties in public international law for his royal masters.

It explains why he fought both the crown and the papacy on those very principles outlined by Tudeschis, Dominic of St Geminiano and Peter of Ancarano on the nature and function of spiritual and secular authority and their proper spheres of jurisdiction, on oaths and oath taking, on the validity of customary law, and on the need of the papacy to return to the use of the *denuntiatio evangelica*. He deplored, for instance, the crown's abuse of nominating bishops and abbots purely for financial gain, like James IV's nominations of his brother and son to the archbishopric of St Andrews in 1497 and 1504; but equally he fought off both the crown and the papacy over the right to nominate his own diocesan officials, when they wished to fob him off with candidates of their own. But on the whole, in this sphere of papal and royal politics, when both were ranged against him, he could not win. It could well be argued, of course, that such jurisprudential principles failed to take into account the complex problems affecting both the papacy and European monarchs in the late fifteenth and early sixteenth centuries, each party with its own fiscal needs and political rivalries; and that the use of the *denuntiatio evangelica*, with its ultimate threat of excommunication, no longer carried any real weight—although it might be remembered that James IV was deeply troubled over such a threat in 1513. It was, in any case, all too late. Perhaps all that might usefully be said here is that such voices were prophetic, and that such principles needed to be stated clearly if the papacy were ever to regain its spiritual credibility; and that there were still reforming bishops around in Europe at that time who were prepared to stand by such principles as long as they were scripturally based.

Elphinstone did, however, have greater freedom to exercise his reforming instincts in his pastoral duties. We may note, for instance, his purchase as a bishop of INC 34, *Manuale parrochialium sacerdotum*, which was a standard guide on the administration of the seven sacraments, with useful additional notes on feast days and fast days. Another purchase, his INC 190 *Modus Confitendi*, discussed the moral aspects of confessional practice, and both, clearly, were intended to be used as text books in his programme for the training of priests either at the Grammar School in Old Aberdeen, or more likely, after 1505, in the Faculty of Theology at King's College. Both of these books have to be placed within the context of his diocesan Constitutions of 1506, his production of the *Aberdeen Breviary* for the use of the Scottish Church in 1510, and the other reforms he initiated as bishop of Aberdeen between 1488 and 1514.

Reading the marginal notes which Elphinstone set against the texts of many of these legal commentaries, then, may tell us more about the Europe of his age than we may first suppose. On the surface, they show us a professional at work on practical disputes; but further down are the fundamental issues to be wrestled with and resolved. While none of these shrewd comments and observations can bring the man to life, the fortunate survival of three of his books, in themselves, enables us to catch a revealing glimpse of his inner self, his private face.[9] These are chiefly collections of sermons, meditations on the passion of Christ and other devotional reading in which he has underlined favourite passages, repeated memorable phrases in the margins and scattered them with *nota benes*. All of these confirm, with unusual force, Boece's

[9] These are INC 9, 17, 37, 188, 190 and 200, all bound into one volume; INC 45 bought by the bishop in 1505; and INC 148 given to King's College by him in 1510.

own comments (often thought to be absurdly hagiographical) on Elphinstone's personal austerities during Lent, and his frequent reading of the Scriptures in later life: 'He found delight in the frequent commemoration of Christ's saving sufferings, a topic on which he used to discourse with much learning and devoutness. The night before Good Friday he spent in prayer....[10] In the leisure of old age he took great delight in the Scriptures, the memorials of the prophets, the apostles, the interpreters of Holy Writ; sometimes, too, of the philosophers whose works chiefly conduce to a holy life'.[11] An examination of the marginal notes in these three books affords us a fresh and perhaps surprising view of a man known chiefly to most modern scholars as the one-time Chancellor of the Kingdom, Keeper of the Privy Seal, auditor of the Exchequer, and member of the King's Daily Council, hearing causes year in year out which had all but foundered in the lower courts. With all that, it would seem that Elphinstone was the King's servant, but God's first.

A Handlist of William Elphinstone's Library

The following works, which are to be found in King's College Library Aberdeen today, distinguish those known to be his from those possibly gifted to him for his University. The manuscripts are given their present catalogue number, but the incunables follow their more easily identifiable older numeration.

1 Manuscripts and incunables acknowledging Elphinstone's ownership

CANON LAW

MS 12	Nicholas Tudeschis, *Commentaria in Decretales* I, tit 1-6
MS 13	Nicholas Tudeschis, *Commentaria in Decretales* I, tit 29-43
MS 14	Nicholas Tudeschis, *Commentaria in Decretales* II, tit 1-13
MS 15	Nicholas Tudeschis, *Commentaria in Decretales* II, tit 24-30
MS 16	Nicholas Tudeschis, *Commentaria in Decretales* III, tit 1-50
MS 17	Dominicus de S Geminiano, *Recollecta super Sexto* Lib III, tit 1—Lib V, tit 11

[10] *Hectoris Boetii Murthlacensium et Aberdonensium Episcoporum Vitae*, ed. J. Moir (New Spalding Club, 1894), 111.

[11] ibid., 101.

MS 184 Henricus de Bohic, *Commentaria in Decretales* I and IV
MS 198 Nicholas Tudeschis, *Commentaria in Decretales* IV; *Glossa Clementinarum* I-V
MS 201 Johannes de Imola, *Commentaria in Clementinas* I-V
MS 202 *Decisiones Rotae; Lexicon Iuridicum*
MS 262 Petrus de Ancarano, *Lectura Repetita Sexti et Clementinarum*[12]
INC 40 Nicholas Tudeschis, *Commentaria in Decretales* IV and V

CIVIL LAW[13]
MS 195 Henricus Retheri, *Lecturae super Digestis*, XLV, tit 1; XXIV, tit 3; XXV, tit 1; XXVIII, tit 1-3; XXIX, tit 2, XXX unfinished
MS 196 Johannes Groesbek, Henricus de Piro and Ricardus de Turnaco, *Lecturae super Codice et Institutionibus*[14]
MS 197 Johannes Groesbek, Ricardus de Turnaco and Henricus Retheri, *Lecturae super Digestis et Libris Feudorum*[15]

LEGAL DICTION
MS 222 Laurentius Valla, *Elegantiae latinae linguae*

PASTORAL AND SCRIPTURAL
INC 32, *Manuale parrochialium sacerdotum*
INC 193, *Andreas de Escobar, Modus confitendi*
INC 157.1 Nicholas de Lyra, *Glossa Ordinaria in Vetus Testamentum*, vols 2, 3 and 4[16]

---

[12] Line 18 of the poem given in Macfarlane, 'Elphinstone's Library' (1958), 264, should read L semel, *not* IV semel.

[13] MSS 195, 196 and 197 were the lecture notes taken down by William Elphinstone's father and his fellow student Michael Collace when studying Civil Law at the University of Louvain between 1431 and 1433. I am very grateful to both Professor Robert Feenstra and Neil Ker for having corrected my previous attempt to identify their lecturers, and for providing the more accurate information as given in this list. Professor Feenstra is making an exhaustive study of these manuscripts and their unique survival.

[14] MS 196. Professor Feenstra gives the lecturer on Institutes IV, 6 as Henricus de Piro; on Codex I, II, III and VI as Johannes Groesbek, and on Codex VII as probably Ricardus de Turnaco.

[15] MS 197. The lectures on Digest XII and XIII were given by Johannes Groesbek; that on Digest VI by Ricardus de Turnaco; those on the *Libri Feudorum* by Henricus Retheri.

[16] For an interesting commentary on these volumes see G. Patrick Edwards, 'William Elphinstone, his College Chapel and the Second of April', *AUR*, li (1985), 1-17.

DEVOTIONAL AND HOMILECTIC

INC 9	*Sermones Sancti Augustini ad heremitas*
INC 17	Guilermus Textor, *Sermones tres de passione Domini; Dialogus Beati Anselmi; De passione Ihesu Christi et beate Marie virginis; Tractatus Beati Bernardi, De planctu beate Marie virginis*
INC 37	*Dialogus inter clericum et militem; De nativitate et moribus antichristi*
INC 45	*Homeliarius doctorum*
INC 148	*Sermones Quadragesimales de penitencia Roberti de Liteo*
INC 188	*Tractatus Sancti Bonaventure*
INC 190	St Isidore, *Colloquium peccatoris et crucifixi Ihesu Christi*
INC 200	Lucius Annaeus Seneca, *De quattuor virtutibus*

NATURAL PHILOSOPHY

INC 28	Bartholomaeus Anglicus, *De proprietatibus rerum*

2 Manuscripts not acknowledging Elphinstone's ownership, but possibly gifted to him or purchased by him

MS 199$^{1-2}$	*Commentaria in Decretales* II, tit 23-30
MS 200	*Lectura super Clementinas*
MS 214	Paulus Orosius, *Historiarum initium ad Aurelium Augustinum*; Lucius Amneius Florus, *Romana historia*; *Historia de origine Troianorum*; *De Excidio Troie*; *De Bello Troiano*
MS 223	Porphyry, *Isagoge super Organon*
MS 257	*Commentarium in Decretales*
MS 264	Johannes de Irlandia, *Super Sentenciarum Petri Lombardi*

JAMES LIDDELL ON CONCEPTS AND SIGNS

Alexander Broadie

Jacobus Ledelh,[1] hereafter James Liddell, was an Aberdonian who like many other young Scots of the latter part of the fifteenth century attended the University of Paris. His name ('Jacobus Leadell, dyoc. Sancti Andree') appears on a Paris list in 1481, and in 1483 he took his master's degree.[2] In 1484 he began teaching at that university, and in the same year was appointed to the administrative post of procurator. Two years later he was appointed examiner of the Scottish bachelors at Paris. It is not known in what year he ceased to teach at the University, nor when he died. But evidence may be gleaned from the *Duellum Epistolare* (Lyons, 1519) of Symphorien Champier, then physician to the duke of Lorraine. In that work, which also contains a letter by Robert Cockburn, bishop of Ross, 'James Ledelh, a Scot by nationality' is mentioned as a friend of Robert Cockburn.[3] John Durkan, who has studied this document, has argued that the context of the reference suggests that Liddell was still alive when the *Duellum* was published.

NLS has a small book by Liddell, dated 1495. It contains two treatises, one on concepts and signs (*Tractatus conceptuum et signorum*), and the other on obligations exercises (*Ars obligatoria logicalis*), exercises in which a student demonstrates his competence at avoiding falling into contradiction. The book is important historically for, on the basis of the evidence of Champier's *Duellum*, Liddell is the first Scot to have had a book of his printed in his own lifetime. Works by Scots, in particular by Duns Scotus, had of course been printed earlier than 1495 but those works appeared after their author's death.

Liddell's treatise on concepts and signs is the subject of this essay. Though the treatise is important historically, this is not to imply that it does not speak to present-day philosophers about

---

[1] I am grateful to John Durkan, who first drew my attention to the small volume by Jacobus Ledelh in NLS.

[2] For an account of Liddell's career see W. Beattie, 'Two notes on fifteenth century printing: I. Jacobus Ledelh', *TEBS*, iii (1950), 75-7.

[3] For details see J. Durkan, 'Robert Cockburn, bishop of Ross, and French humanism', *IR*, iv (1953), 121-2.

topics currently under investigation, particularly topics in the field of semiotics. Liddell's work in its own day could not have been considered an original contribution to philosophy; and he himself states in his introductory remarks that he is going to expound common positions.[4] It is a particularly clear exposition of a set of doctrines which were in common currency at that time. But since those doctrines would interest present-day philosophers if only they knew them, some of the doctrines at issue will be discussed here.

The treatise has two parts, for there are two basic kinds of sign, natural and conventional. The distinction is easy to grasp, though the full articulation of the distinction involves complex and subtle argumentation. Let us consider an example. Thunder is a sign of rain. Perhaps, then, we should say that the sign-relation is a relation between two terms, a sign and a significate, in this case the thunder and the rain. But a third term is involved, namely a knower, for a sign signifies something to someone. Thunder does not merely signify rain; it signifies rain to someone for whom the thunder has that significance. It would not signify rain in a world in which there was no perceiver who could grasp the relation between thunder and rain. The reason thunder has the significance that it has for us is simply that we are familiar with the relation. In general, thunder is followed by rain, and our awareness of this natural relation between the two is a partial cause of the formation within us of a notion or concept of rain when we hear thunder. We do not by an act of will impose this particular significance on thunder, that is, we do not voluntarily treat it as a sign of rain. This is how we find the world, and this is how, quite naturally, we respond cognitively to it.

The situation is the same in a great variety of cases, some of which were common examples in the medieval logic textbooks. Liddell employs the standard example of groaning, which is a sign of sickness. Others took the examples of a smile as a sign of joy, smoke as a sign of a fire and barking as a sign of a dog. In each of these cases there is a natural relation between sign and significate. One further such case should be described here because of its role in Liddell's treatise. In thinking about an object, a notion or concept of it is formed. This concept, as the representative in the mind of the object in the external world, signifies that of which it

[4] sig. a 1r.

is a concept. That the concept should signify the object is not a matter of choice; Liddell would say that it signifies the object because it is its nature to do so. If it signified something else, it would not be the concept that it is. And in so far as it is natural for the concept to signify what it does signify, there is a natural relation between the concept in the mind and the object outside. Put otherwise, the concept is a sign and the external object is its natural significate.

In contrast to the kinds of sign so far discussed, all of which signify their significates naturally, there are signs which signify by convention. Liddell mentions the frequently cited example of a barrel hoop placed outside a tavern as a conventional sign that wine is available within,[5] and also gives the example of a military standard raised before an army as a sign of battle.[6] But the conventional signs upon which Liddell concentrates are the words and propositions to be found in human language. There is, of course, no natural connection between the word 'house' and houses. That the word signifies what it does is due to our imposing a given significance on the word. The crucial point is that, for us, groaning is a sign of pain not because we have imposed that significance upon groans but because groans are a natural expression of pain. The contrast with the significance of words could not be plainer.

This is not to say that a single utterance or inscription may not at the same time signify both naturally and conventionally, a point Liddell develops. For example, a person's utterance has not only its conventional significance but also a natural significance in so far as it is a sign of his presence. Thus if a caller's opening words on the telephone are 'How are you?', not only will the sense of the words be grasped but the words will also be a sign of who is speaking, in so far as the voice is recognised. Likewise, a handwritten message not only has its conventional significance but also a natural significance in so far as the handwriting is a sign of the writer—in that sense the whole inscription, not just the hand written name at the end of the message, is his signature.

But the fact that one thing, an utterance or inscription, can signify both naturally and conventionally at the same time, does not contradict the thesis that these are two radically different sorts

---

[5] sig. b 2r.
[6] ibid.

of signifying; rather it highlights the thesis. The two parts of Liddell's treatise deal respectively with the two sorts of signifying just discussed, with the first part on natural signifying, and the second on conventional.

Having stated that there are these two sorts of signifying Liddell immediately states the fundamental relation between them. Concepts, as we noted earlier, signify naturally whatever they signify, and words which express those concepts signify conventionally what the concepts signify naturally. Thus, for example, in thinking about Glasgow Cathedral a concept of the cathedral is thereby formed. The utterance 'Glasgow Cathedral' expresses that same concept and signifies the very same thing signified by the concept. What is the relation between concept and utterance? Liddell's answer is that it is one of subordination, with the utterance subordinate to the concept.

The utterance is subordinate in that it depends for its existence upon the concept, and the concept does not depend for its existence upon the utterance. Once a person has a concept he can employ an utterance to enable him to give public expression to his concept. That is, the utterance can be used to represent the concept to others. It is in virtue of this relation between the utterance and the concept that the utterance has its significance. It is a conventional (and therefore a public) sign of that which the concept signifies naturally. Except as expressing a concept, the utterance lacks conventional significance. On the other hand a person can have a concept for which there is no corresponding conventional sign. Of course, a sound can be uttered for which there is no corresponding concept, but in that case the utterance is a nonsense sound (*vox non significativa*), and hence we are not dealing with an utterance which, though not linked to a concept in the way described above, somehow manages to have conventional significance—hence Liddell's insistence that signs which signify conventionally are subordinate to concepts.

According to this doctrine there is a triangle of relations between (1) concept, (2) conventional sign and (3) significate. The concept and the conventional sign each immediately signify the significate. Thus the concept of Glasgow Cathedral and the utterance 'Glasgow Cathedral' each immediately signify the building. But the conventional sign is also in one sense a sign of the concept as well as of the building in so far as the conventional sign signifies the presence of the concept it expresses. It would, however, be a mistake to suppose that whenever a person says something which has conventional significance he must also be having at the same time the corresponding concept. We can, after all, speak without attending to what we are saying, and on such occasions what we say manages to make sense. The reason for this is that once a given significance has been imposed on an utterance of a certain type such an utterance has that significance whatever (if anything at all) is going on in the mind of the speaker. He does not require to have the corresponding concept for the utterance to be significant. But there has to be such a concept for the utterance to acquire its significance by imposition, and for a listener to understand the utterance is for him to form that corresponding concept. Thus we need not after all abandon the earlier thesis concerning the subordination of conventional signs to concepts.

There now follows an examination in greater detail of Liddell's account of the nature of a sign. And since what makes something a sign is what it does, viz. signify, we have to consider a sign in respect of its distinctive act, and examine the act of signifying.

Liddell gives the following definition: 'To signify is to represent something or some things or in some way (or somehow) formally and instrumentally to a cognitive power, vitally changing the power'.[7] A number of these clauses, perhaps all of them, call for clarification, and Liddell, well aware of the difficulties in the definition, proceeds immediately to the task of clarification. He does not, however, deal with the word 'represent', perhaps because he feels he can safely assume the requisite background knowledge, but it would be helpful to begin by making some points about the word.

According to the definition, signifying is a kind of representing. Considerations of the structure of *repraesentare* can usefully be brought to bear here. For X to represent something, as Liddell employs the term, is for X to be a re-presentation of the thing; it is for the thing to be present again in virtue of the presence of X. But the thing which is re-presented is present again not *in propria persona* but in its representative, viz. X. Thus, by convention the utterance 'Glasgow Cathedral' represents the building—it does so in virtue of the convention established by an act of imposition; and by its nature my concept of Glasgow Cathedral represents

[7] sig. a 1r.

that same building. It is the natural representative within the mind of the building without.

Those familiar with the version of the theory of ideas which is associated most especially with Descartes and Locke know that this way of speaking has pitfalls. According to Locke's theory, there are within us concepts, also called 'ideas', which are representatives of things outside our minds, and through which we come to a knowledge of them. Locke, in particular, is commonly credited (or discredited) with the view that the ideas are the immediate objects of knowledge, and the things of which they are ideas are known only mediately via our knowledge of the ideas themselves. This position is open to the criticism that it leads to scepticism about the existence of objects outside the mind. For any claim to knowledge of an external object is in principle uncheckable. It is not just that we cannot check whether external things have the precise properties we think they have; we have no means, even, of checking whether external things exist. Cognitively speaking, we are trapped within our world of ideas.

Liddell's own position is not open to this line of attack. As he uses the term 'concept', it is not to be equated with a Lockean idea, viz. a mental entity through knowledge of which we arrive at a knowledge of the object of which we have the idea. Instead, a concept, as Liddell uses that term, is an act of the cognitive power, it is the very cognizing of the object. Thus to have a perceptual concept of an object is to be perceiving that object; to have a memory concept of it is to be remembering it, and so on. In each case we have to understand talk about having a concept in terms of talk about acts of the cognitive power. Hence in having a perceptual concept of a given external object a person does not first perceive the concept and then know the object of which the concept is a concept. Instead, to have the perceptual concept is to be in immediate perceptual contact with the external object. For this reason Liddell's position does not give rise to scepticism about the external world in the way in which Locke's theory of ideas does.

In clarification of his definition of 'signify', Liddell tells us that he uses the phrase 'cognitive power' [*potentia cognitiva*] advisedly, for to signify is to represent to a cognitive power and not only to the intellect.[8] The intellect is one part of the cognitive power of a

[8] sig. a 1r-v.

human being, and is distinguished from other parts, for example, the sensory part, by its distinctive acts, in particular the acts of conceiving non-sensible things, that is, things which are of such a nature as not to be available for sensory inspection. Of this kind are cognitive acts, and the power of cognition itself. And in so far as we form a concept of God we form a concept of a non-sensible being, and in so doing our intellect is engaged.

A further kind of concept, the 'common' concept, was also thought by some to require the activity of intellect, though there was a good deal of controversy concerning this. Liddell discusses this concept at some length.[9] His discussion centres on the division of concepts into those which are singular and those which are common. This important topic shall now be addressed.

A singular concept, he tells us, is one which represents one thing singularly; a common concept is one which represents many things divisibly, and can stand for them divisibly.[10] Both of these definitions call for explanation. Suppose that there is in fact only one sun in the world and that a concept of a sun is formed. The concept represents that one sun. It must represent some sun or other, since it is a concept of a sun. And it does not represent another sun, for there is no other. Yet Liddell would say that the concept is not singular, for it does not represent that one sun singularly. The reason for this is that the concept is of such a nature as to be able to represent suns other than the one that actually exists in the world. In fact it only represents the one sun, but if there were another sun in the world, the concept could represent that other sun just as well. The crucial point is that there is nothing about the concept that prevents it representing many things.

That concept must therefore be contrasted with a concept which not only represents one thing but is in addition of such a nature that it is not possible for it to represent anything other than the one thing that it does represent, for example a person's concept of his friend X. The concept represents X and cannot represent anyone or anything else. After all, if it represents Y, then the concept is not a concept of X. Routinely in the textbooks by medieval logicians proper names are said to be singular in the way just described, but proper names need careful handling, for

[9] sigs. a 6v-b 1r.
[10] sig. a 6v.

many people can share a proper name, and on that account a proper name might be thought to be common. Nothing is lost, however, by invoking proper names in this context, so long as it is borne in mind that what is truly singular is not the name itself but the concept of the individual bearing that name.

A common concept, in contrast, is one which has such a nature that it can represent many things. Thus, to return to the earlier example, the concept of a sun would be common even if there were only one, for if there were other suns the concept would represent each one of them just as well. The concept of a donkey, not of this donkey but of a donkey, is likewise common. Thus people have a concept of a donkey on the basis of which one can point to any donkey whatsoever and say truly, 'That falls under my concept of a donkey'. If, on the other hand, the concept is of such a nature that there can be only one donkey, say Browney, who falls under the concept, then that concept of a donkey is singular, being a concept not of just any donkey but of that one.

What should be said about the concept of the population of Scotland? Is the concept singular or common? It might be said that it is common, for a population is composed of many persons. But Liddell would not accept this argument. And his rejection follows from his employment of the term 'divisibly' in his definition of 'common'. Though there are indeed many people in a population, not one of them can be brought separately, or as Liddell would say 'divisibly', that is divided from the other members of the group, under the concept of the population of Scotland. Thus X, Y, Z, and so on, are jointly the population of Scotland, but X is not the population of Scotland, neither is Y, and so on. There is no doubt that Liddell would hold that the concept of the population of Scotland is singular and not common, for the concept is of such a nature that one and only one population can be brought under it.

One interesting feature of Liddell's discussion is his introduction of the notion of vagueness. A singular concept, he holds, can be determinate or vague, and vagueness itself admits of degrees. He writes: 'When we think of a singular thing according as it differs from every other thing, that concept is properly called a determinate singular concept'.[11] Thus the thought of a friend X is of a given person as different from every other person. But if Y

---

[11] sig. a 7r.

says that he met a man, the listener thereupon forms a concept of a man, not of just any man, but of that man, viz. the one Y met. The listener does not, however, know whether that man is Tom, Dick or Harry, and in that sense the concept, though singular since it is of that man and of no other, is nevertheless indeterminate or vague. But not very vague, for at least it is known what the species is—for it was a human being who was met.

On the other hand, if Y says that he saw an animal, the listener forms a concept of what it was that Y saw. But this concept, though singular, is vaguer than the concept just spoken of, for this time the listener does not know, for he has not been told, what species of animal it was that Y saw—whether it was a dog or a lion, and so on. But, as Liddell points out, we can form a concept vaguer still, for if Y says that he saw a substance, we form a concept of what Y saw, without knowing whether the substance was animal, vegetable or mineral. But despite the vagueness of our concept it is nevertheless singular, for it is a concept of that substance, viz. the one seen by Y. And as Liddell points out, a singular concept can be vaguer still, for we can form a concept of this entity without the concept being precisely of a substance or of an accident. It is important to note that when Liddell speaks about a vague singular concept, what is vague is the concept and not the singularity. For Liddell, it makes no sense to ascribe vagueness to singularity. In the cases of our concepts of that man, that animal, that substance and that entity, the concepts are all equally, because absolutely, singular.

It is interesting to note that in his discussion of singularity Liddell reveals his debt to Duns Scotus. The debt concerns the relation between accidental and specific difference.[12] Two things of different species are said to be specifically different. Two things of the same species differ not specifically but accidentally, that is, in respect of their accidents. We know that two things of the same species are two, and not one, because differences in their accidents reveal this fact. But, asks Liddell, if we are presented with an egg and then with another egg and they have the same accidents, how do we tell the two eggs apart? Or, to put the question more starkly, if while our gaze is averted from an egg a second egg indistinguishable from the first in respect of its accidents is put in its place, can we, on redirecting our gaze, tell that the replace-

[12] sig. a 7v.

ment has occurred? The answer is that in this life we cannot. But Liddell, in the footsteps of Duns Scotus, invokes the concept of a proper difference, as contrasted with a specific difference. In this life all we have upon which to base our judgment are the accidents, and *ex hypothesi* these are of no help. But there is also the sheer thisness of a thing, that which, other than its accidents, distinguishes the thing from other members of the same species. But the thisness, though detectable, is not detectable by us on our pilgrim-way.

Our singular and common concepts represent things to us, but we should remind ourselves that in his definition of 'signify' Liddell tells us that to signify is to represent some thing or some things or in some way or somehow to a cognitive power. Our discussion of singular and common concepts covers that part of the definition which refers to 'some thing or some things'. I should like now to turn briefly to the next clause, viz. 'in some way (or somehow) [*aliquo modo vel aliqualiter*]'.

These two phrases are being used as synonyms, and for convenience just one of them, 'in some way', will be employed here. Liddell informs us that he employs this phrase 'on account of syncategorematic words [*propter dictiones syncategorematicas*]'.[13] Syncategorematic words are words which do not themselves signify anything but which, in the context of a complex expression, affect the way that we take other terms in the complex expression. Among the words he has in mind are 'every', 'some', 'no', 'only', 'and', 'or' and 'if', and he held that to each of these terms there corresponds a concept.

Consider the proposition: 'Every fish is a swimmer'. 'Fish' signifies anything that can be pointed to while saying truly 'That is a fish'. But 'every' cannot signify anything, for there cannot be anything such that it is possible to point to it and say truly 'That is every'. 'That is every' is not even a grammatically well formed proposition. But that is not to imply that 'every' is not a significant part of the proposition 'Every fish is a swimmer'. 'Every' clearly signifies, even though it does not signify some thing. Instead it was said to signify 'in some way' [*aliquo modo or aliqualiter*]. In what way? The short answer is 'universally'. Thus in thinking about every fish, we form a concept of fish and think about it universally. Likewise, in thinking that no fish has feathers, we are thinking

[13] sig. a 1v.

universally and negatively about fish. And as regards that latter proposition we are also thinking predicatively about feathers, and the predicativeness of our thinking is marked by the term 'is' in the proposition. Likewise 'if' does not signify any thing, but it is none the less significant. Thus suppose we are thinking that if it does not rain we shall go for a walk. The 'if' signifies the way in which we are thinking about going for a walk, for we are thinking about it conditionally, that is we are thinking of our going for a walk as conditional upon its not raining. The notion of a syncategorematic concept is of central importance, for it is precisely such concepts upon which the discipline of logic is focused.

Liddell's definition of 'signify' includes the clause 'formally and instrumentally'. The term 'instrumentally' is included, Liddell tells us,[14] because God represents principally. The implication of this explanation is that 'sign', which is employed by Liddell as a technical term and has to be understood on that basis, refers in Liddell's treatise to something with the status of intermediate cause. An instrument is moved by something and towards some end. But God, as first cause, cannot be an intermediate cause, and therefore cannot be an instrument. Hence he cannot *be* instrumentally, and neither therefore can he represent instrumentally. This does not, of course, prevent our saying that, as first cause, he can represent principally. And indeed we have to say just that, for everything is represented in God. Whatever exists is a sign of God, for everything in the created order owes its existence to God. God however is not a sign of anything.[15]

But why does Liddell say that a sign represents formally [*formaliter*]? The answer is that there is more than one way in which one thing can represent another, and certain of these ways have to be ruled out. We learn from Liddell that it was a custom in the Church for a person to beat his breast when reciting the formula 'I confess to God in heaven [*Confiteor deo caeli*]'.[16] For this reason the formula came by custom [*ex consuetudine*] to represent the beating of the breast. Nevertheless, using 'signify' in its technical sense, we have to say that the formula does not signify the beating of the breast, for to represent merely *ex consuetudine* is not to represent *formaliter*. 'I confess to God in heaven' has a certain

[14] ibid.
[15] Cf. Thomas Aquinas, *Summa Theologiae*, 3,62,5 c.
[16] sig. a 1v.

significance because the individual terms in the phrase have acquired significance by imposition, and the order in which the terms appear in the phrase also makes, by convention, a distinctive contribution to the significance of the phrase as a whole. The phrase represents formally some thing, or in some way, in virtue of its significance as thus acquired, and only what is represented formally is said to be signified.

Finally, note should be taken of Liddell's thesis that to signify involves vitally changing a cognitive power. As with the previous clauses considered, we have to ask what it is that Liddell is thereby excluding. His own highly schematic account of the matter is this: 'even though something changes a cognitive power deprivatively, it is not on that account said to signify'.[17] Many sorts of thing have a deprivative effect on a cognitive power, for example, a sleeping draught or a blow to the head, that is, anything which interferes with the proper activity of a cognitive power, the activity of thinking. But in fact, as is clear from writings of his close contemporaries, especially writings by Scottish philosophers, there is more to the notion of 'vitally changing a cognitive power' than is indicated by Liddell's remarks. For a cognitive power to be changed vitally is for it to be exercising its proper power, and such an exercise consists in the act of thinking. This is not to say that the possession of a concept as such consists in a vital changing in a cognitive power. A distinction must here be made between two sorts of possession of knowledge. Almost all of any person's knowledge is dispositional. Each of us has a vast range of knowledge, though almost all of that knowledge is not the object of present attention. We know all those things in the sense that if asked we can provide from within our own minds the right answers, but years can go by without our attention being focused on that which, all the same, counts as knowledge. Knowledge which is possessed though not exercised is merely dispositional, classified by the late-medieval thinkers as a *habitus*. Such knowledge is to be contrasted with knowledge which is being exercised. For knowledge to be exercised is for there to be a vital change in the cognitive power. When we not only have knowledge but are thinking about that which we know, this act of thinking represents whatever it is that we are thinking about, and represents in such a way that it can be said to signify its object. On the other hand, the

[17] ibid.

knowledge which is merely disposition does not signify anything. All that can be said is that it would signify if the knowledge were being exercised.

With this last point, all the clauses in Liddell's account of the nature of a sign have been dealt with, even if briefly. In fact, this account has considered only a very few of the many points he makes in his brief though dense treatise, but it should be clear that there is much interesting philosophy in that first ever book by a Scottish author to be printed in that author's lifetime. If, as can be argued, Scotland has as great a claim as any country to be regarded as the nation of philosophers,[18] there is a singular propriety in the fact that that first printed book was a treatise on epistemology.

---

[18] See A. Broadie, *The Tradition of Scottish Philosophy* (Edinburgh, 1990), and idem, 'A nation of philosophers', in P.H. Scott (ed.), *Scotland: A Concise Cultural History* (Edinburgh, 1993), 61-76.

NEW LIGHT ON GAVIN DOUGLAS

Priscilla Bawcutt

His Career in the Church

We know much more about Gavin Douglas than about other early Scottish poets.[1] Son of the fifth earl of Angus, provost of St Giles, Edinburgh, and bishop of Dunkeld, Douglas—together with his family, friendships, and career—seems remarkably well documented. Yet there is still much in his life that is obscure, and any supplement to our knowledge is very welcome. The material to be discussed in the following notes derives from the archives of the Vatican Library.[2]

i. The first is an entry in the Register of Supplications for 13 February 1489:

> Gavin Douglas, clerk of St Andrews diocese, of illustrious and comital parentage on both sides and in his 13th year; that even now in his 13th year you would dispense him to hold a canonry and prebend, and two other benefices with cure or otherwise incompatible, etc.[3]

This petition contains the earliest surviving reference to Douglas, ante-dating the St Andrews University record that he matriculated in 1490.[4] It shows how early he was designed for a career in the church, and clearly implies the advantage of having aristocratic

---

[1] For fuller information, see P. Bawcutt, *Gavin Douglas: a Critical Study* (Edinburgh, 1976), esp. 1-46; also the full 'Biographical Introduction', in *The Works of Gavin Douglas*, ed. J. Small, 4 vols. (Edinburgh, 1874), i, pp. ii-cxxvii.

[2] In what follows I am much indebted to John Durkan for drawing to my attention items ii-iv, which have been calendared in recent volumes of *Entries in the Papal Registers relating to Great Britain and Ireland.* I am equally indebted to Dr Alan Macquarrie for drawing to my attention the three unpublished and previously unnoticed references to Douglas (items i, v and vi), in the Register of Supplications and Archive of the Sacred Penitentiary. Microfilm of material in the Vatican archives relating to Scotland is deposited in the Department of Scottish History, University of Glasgow. See I.B. Cowan, 'The Vatican Archives: a report on pre-Reformation Scottish material', *SHR*, xlviii (1969), 227-42.

[3] Register of Supplications, vol. 899, f.102v.

[4] *St Andrews Univ. Recs.*, 187.

parents. It also helps to establish a little more precisely the date of his birth, which had previously been conjecturally estimated as c.1474-5. If, however, one assumes that Douglas was probably thirteen by the end of 1489, his birth-date must have been 1476, slightly later than the usual reckoning. Yet such a date would not be inconsistent with Douglas's own rather vague words to the Lords of Council in July 1515, that he was 'ane man of xl yeris of age or tharby [thereabouts]'.[5] This petition is said to have been conceded, but there is no indication as to whether it was acted upon immediately.

ii. The following dispensation, dated 25 February 1495, is singled out by the editor of *Entries in the Papal Register for Pope Alexander VI* as a letter of outstanding interest:

> To Gavin Dowglas, cleric, d. Glasgow, M A, dispensation—at his supplication—to him, who, as he asserts, is of noble birth by both parents and by one of them of the stock of earls, and is in his twentieth year of age, to receive and retain together for life any three benefices, with cure or otherwise mutually incompatible .... With the proviso that the incompatible benefices in question shall not, on this account, be defrauded of due services and the cure of souls therein (if any) shall not be neglected.[6]

It has been noted that behind every letter in the Papal Registers, such as this one, there lay a petition or a supplication, such as Douglas's of 1489. It was common for quite a long time to elapse between the drafting of a suppliant's petition and the formal dispatch of a 'letter of grace'.[7] Nonetheless in this case the interval of six years seems unusually long, and there are slight discrepancies between this document and the preceding one, both as to Douglas's age (this suggests a birthdate of 1475) and as to diocese (Glasgow here, rather than the more likely St Andrews). It is just possible, therefore, that this dispensation may refer not to the poet but to a less well known Gavin Douglas, son of the laird of Drumlangrig, who matriculated at Glasgow University in 1489, and would therefore have been a close contemporary.[8] Yet the words 'who, as he asserts, is of noble birth by

---

[5] Douglas, *Works*, i, p. lxi.

[6] *CPL*, xvi (Alexander VI Lateran Registers Part One: 1492-1498), ed. A.P. Fuller (Dublin, 1986), no. 391; see also p. xviii.

[7] *CPL*, xv (Innocent VIII Lateran Registers: 1484-1492), ed. M.J. Haren (Dublin, 1978), pp. xv-xxiv: 'The Papal Chancery at the end of the fifteenth century'.

[8] *See Glasgow Univ. Munimenta*, ii, 103.

both parents and by one of them of the stock of earls' seem highly appropriate to the son of the fifth earl of Angus; and on balance it seems likely that this is indeed a reference to the poet.

iii. The chancery registers of Alexander VI—like those of other popes—suffered great losses over the centuries. But there survives an Index to Alexander's registers, produced in the middle of the eighteenth century, that furnishes clues, often in bizarre spelling, to the contents of some of the missing letters. Two of these *rubricellae*, or rubrics, which relate to the fourth year of Alexander's papacy (1495-6), concern Gavin Douglas.[9] One (no. 1298) notes that 'Garivinus de Uglas' sought the archdeaconry of St Andrews. There is no other evidence, however, to confirm that he received—or even sought—this important administrative office. The other entry (no. 1348) implies that 'Gowinus de Wglas' had been granted the *decanatus* of Dunkeld. This is valuable, since it pre-dates the earliest Scottish evidence of Douglas's interest in the deanery of Dunkeld, vacant since the death of Alexander Inglis (25 February 1496). Despite a reference to Douglas as 'Dene of Dunkeldene' (January 1497), this benefice was vigorously contested by George Hepburn, both before the Lords of Council and in Rome; his persistence seems to have been successful, and he was still in possession in 1527.[10]

iv. A letter from the Registers of Julius II (23 July 1508) has particularly interesting implications:

> To the archbishop of St Andrews, the bishop of Lismore and the abbot of the monastery of Kelso, d. St Andrews, mandate as below in favour of Gavin Do'gles, cleric, d. St Andrews. The pope has learned that a canonry of the church of Glasgow and the prebend of Dongles, in the same, formerly held on apostolic dispensation by John, late bishop of Ross, are vacant *certo modo* and have been for so long that by the Lateran statutes their collation has lawfully devolved on the apostolic see although Walter Kenedi, who claims to be a cleric, has detained them without any title or support of law in respect of them but of his own temerity and *de facto* for a certain time, as he still does. He therefore orders the above three, or two or one of them, to summon Walter and others concerned and if they find the said canonry and prebend, of which the annual rent does not exceed 50 pounds sterling, to be vacant ... to collate and assign

[9] See further *CPL*, xvi, pp. xlix-liv.
[10] See Bawcutt, *Gavin Douglas*, 6-7; Watt, *Fasti*, 105.

> them to Gavin, inducting him, etc., having removed Walter and any other unlawful detainer.[11]

I take this Gavin Douglas, 'cleric, d. St Andrews', to be indeed the poet, although it is perhaps a little strange that he is not here entitled provost of St Giles, Edinburgh (an office that he had held since 1503 at the latest). There seems no evidence, however, that Douglas ever wrested possession of these benefices from members of the Kennedy family. It should be noted that the identity of 'Walter Kennedi', in 1508 *de facto* canon of Glasgow and rector of Douglas, is debatable. I think that he is likely to be the poet of that name, son of Gilbert, first Lord Kennedy of Dunure; he was probably closer in age to Dunbar than to Douglas, since he graduated at Glasgow University in 1478.[12] This Walter Kennedy (**I**) is said to have had a son, also called Walter Kennedy (**II**), who in 1517 inherited from his father the lands of Glentig, and presumably also his benefices. It is known that Walter Kennedy **II** was incorporated at Glasgow University in 1511 and elected as rector in 1525; he too was a canon of Glasgow and rector of Douglas, and from 1525-1540 provost of the collegiate church of Maybole.[13]

v. A further document is in the Archive of the Sacred Penitentiary (30 July 1510):

> Gavin Douglas, provost of the collegiate church of St Giles, Edinburgh, St Andrews diocese, shows to the pope that many Scottish families wish to contract marriages between *consanguinei* for making of peace and avoidance of bloodshed, but the distance from Rome makes it inconvenient to obtain a dispensation. He therefore supplicates that the pope would grant him a special faculty for four years from the present date to dispense ten couples to marry within the fourth degrees of consanguinity and affinity.[14]

We have more evidence for Douglas's involvement in secular affairs, when he was provost of St Giles—completing his translation of the *Aeneid*, for instance, and attending meetings of the

---

[11] *CPL*, xviii (Pius III and Julius II Vatican Registers: 1503-1513, Lateran Registers 1503-1508), ed. M.J. Haren (Dublin, 1989), no. 38.

[12] For discussion of Kennedy's life, see J.W. Baxter, *William Dunbar* (Glasgow, 1952), 62-3; also *Glasgow Univ. Munimenta*, ii, 227-8.

[13] See D. Cowan, *Historical Account of the Noble Family of Kennedy* (Edinburgh, 1849), 24-5; also *Glasgow Univ. Munimenta*, ii, 125, 150, 154.

[14] Archive of the Sacred Penitentiary, vol. 55, f.433.

Lords of Council.[15] The chief interest of this document therefore is that it records some of his activities as a churchman.

vi. The final document, also from the Archive of the Sacred Penitentiary (23 May 1517), relates to Douglas's difficulties in obtaining the bishopric of Dunkeld, after the death, in 1515, of Bishop George Brown:

> Gavin Douglas, bishop of Dunkeld, shows to the pope that when the see of Dunkeld was vacant by the death of George, last bishop, and Gavin had papal provision and possession, in fear of death and imprisonment he agreed to pay a pension of 40 marks Scots to Andrew Stewart, bearing himself a canon of Dunkeld, until Andrew should have provision to a benefice or benefices of like value, to be drawn from the fruits of his [Gavin's] mensal churches of Alyth and Cargill, and this was confirmed by apostolic letters dated Rome, 16 November 1516, as is more fully contained therein; since, however, Gavin was induced by force and fear of the nobleman John, duke of Albany, at present Governor of the kingdom of Scotland, he should not be bound by his oath and begs to be absolved therefrom.[16]

Douglas's candidature was indeed opposed by the Duke of Albany; he was charged with breaking the laws concerning the purchase of benefices at Rome, and even imprisoned for a while. In 1516, though officially admitted to the temporalities of Dunkeld, he still had to contend with the claim of Andrew Stewart, brother of the Earl of Atholl, to be the rightful bishop, elected by the chapter of Dunkeld. Alexander Myln gives a graphic account of the armed resistance of Stewart and his supporters, shooting from the steeple of the cathedral and the episcopal palace.[17] As this document shows, Douglas was highly resentful of the pressure put upon him by Albany, but a settlement was eventually reached. Albany recommended Stewart for the see of Caithness, and on 14 December 1517 he was provided to it by the pope, his annual pension from the fruits of the churches of Alyth and Cargill in the diocese of Dunkeld being extinguished.[18]

---

[15] Cf. Bawcutt, *Gavin Douglas*, 8-10.

[16] Archive of the Sacred Penitentiary, vol. 62, ff.955v-956v.

[17] See *Vitae Episcoporum Dunkeldensium*, in *Dunkeld Rentale*, 331-4; also Bawcutt, *Gavin Douglas*, 13-15.

[18] Cf. Dowden, *Bishops*, 248-9.

Conscience

Much of the new material presented above reinforces what is known from other sources concerning Gavin Douglas's ambition to multiply benefices and gain worldly wealth; in a letter to his agent, Adam Williamson (January 1515), he speaks quite openly of Dunkeld as 'an rycht gud Byschopry of rent and the thryd Seyt of the realm'.[19] There may seem a curious irony therefore in the attribution to him of a short moral poem in the Maitland Folio Manuscript, usually known as *Conscience.* Yet I see little reason to reject it from the canon, unlike the longer and better-known poem, also in the Maitland Folio, *King Hart.*[20] Douglas would hardly be unique if he failed in life to act upon principles that he professed in writing; and there is indeed an element of self-reproach in the poem's last line: 'God send defens with conscience in till *ws*'. Douglas makes a similar attack on the greed of churchmen in *Eneados* (Prologue VIII, 105 ff.), and *Conscience* has affinities, in style and diction, with his other poetry. Yet there has been little critical attention paid to this poem, despite its arresting play on words:

> Quhen halie kirk first flurist in ȝouthheid,
> Prelatis wer chosin of all perfectioun;
> Off conscience than the brydill had to leid,
> And conscience maid the hale electioun.
> Syn eftir that come schrewit correctioun,
> And thocht that conscience had our large ane weid,
> And of his habite out cuttit thay ane skreid.
>
> And fra conscience the con thay clip away,
> And maid of conscience science and na mair;
> Bot ȝit the kirk stude weill full mony day,
> For it wes rewlit be mene of wit and layre.
> Syn eftir that sciens began to payr,
> And thocht at sciens was our lang ane iaip.
> The sci away fast can thay rub and scraip.

[19] Douglas, *Works*, i, p. xxxvi; also Bawcutt, *Gavin Douglas*, 13.

[20] See Bawcutt, *Gavin Douglas*, 48, and, more fully, 'Did Gavin Douglas write *King Hart*?', *Medium Aevum*, xxviii (1959), 31-47; also F. Ridley, 'Did Gawin Douglas write *King Hart*?', *Speculum*, xxxiv (1959), 402-12.

And fra sci of science wes adew,
Than left thai nocht bot this sillab ens,
Quhilk in our language singnifies that schrew,
Riches and geir, that gart all grace go hens;
For sciens both and faythfull conscience
So corruptit ar with this warldis gude
That falset ioukis in everie clerkis hude.

O hungrie ens, cursit with caris calde!
All kynd of folk constrenis thow to wirk:
For the that theif Iudas his maister sald,
For the Symon infectit halie kirk.
To poysoun iustis thow dois never irk.
Thow fals ens, go hens, thow monsture peralous!
God send defens with conscience in till ws.[21]

Only one parallel to this has hitherto been noted, an anonymous poem in the Bannatyne Manuscript, which is short enough to quote in full:

Quhen doctouris prechit to win the joy eternall,
Vnto the hevin eftir our lordis assense,
Thay causit iustice but bud or fauour carnall,
Thay causit be pvnist fleschly vyle offense,
Gaif banyfice to clerkis of conscience;
And sa the feind had sic invy thairon,
Gart skraip away of conscience the con
And sa behind wes levit bot science.

Than wer all clerkis for science promovit,
And thay that wald to study maist apply.
Bot ȝit the feind at science wes commovit:
Gart skraip away of science the sci,
And sa levit ens be his fals sle invy,
Quhilk suld be for gold or geir exponit,
Quhairby benifice ar now of dayis disponit,
But science or conscience for to sell and by.

---

[21] For an unpunctuated transcript, see *Maitland Folio MS.*, i, 217. See also *The Shorter Poems of Gavin Douglas*, ed. P. Bawcutt (STS, 1967), 137.

O souerane lord and most excellant king,
Gar put the con and sci again till ens,
And rewll thy realme with iustice in thy ring.
Gife benifice to clerkis of consciens,
Off wisdome and honour, to stand at thy defens.
Se in thy court that conscience ay be clene,
For corruptioun befoir thy deyis hes bene,
Aganis iustice, with vthir grit offens.[22]

The resemblances between these two pieces are obvious. Both are concerned with the spiritual deterioration of the church from its beginnings, or 'ȝouthheid'; both speak of a decay in learning and attack the cupidity of clerks, manifest in the election of prelates and the disposition of benefices. Both do this by means of the same piece of word-play: the reduction, syllable by syllable, of *conscience* to *ens*. Both poets also, while attributing the same meaning to *ens*, feel constrained, somewhat awkwardly, to explain that meaning:

this sillab ens,
Quhilk in our language singnifies that schrew,
Riches and geir ...

And sa levit ens ...
Quhilk suld be for gold or geir exponit.

There is indeed an oddity about their usage. *Ens* was not an everyday word in the Scots vernacular; indeed it receives no entry in *DOST*.[23] *Ens* was employed chiefly by scholars and philosophers. It was one of those highly abstract words, like *objectum* and *subjectum*, which, in Douglas's own words:

... ar als ryfe amangis clerkis in scuyll
As evir fowlis plungit in laik or puyll.
(I Prol, 375-6)[24]

Ens, 'being', was often used synonymously with *esse*; a back-formation from words like *potens*, it was employed by Boethius to translate Greek *on*, and thenceforward figured repeatedly in the subtle metaphysical distinctions drawn by medieval philosophers between existence and essence, and substance and accidents.[25]

[22] See *Bann. MS.*, ii, 234-5.

[23] It does not figure in *The Middle English Dictionary* either; *OED*'s first entry (from Sir Philip Sidney) is dated 1581.

[24] *Virgil's 'Aeneid' Translated into Scottish Verse*, ed. D.F.C. Coldwell, 4 vols. (STS, 1957-64), ii, 14.

The only other early Scots vernacular use known to me is of this scholastic nature: John Ireland, expounding 'Qui es in celis', a phrase from the Paternoster, writes:

> God alanerly is the thing that is, for thar is na thing eternall, na propirly ens bot he that is durabile without begynnyng ore ending.[26]

I am not aware of evidence for the sense-development of *ens* to 'riches and geir', i.e. material wealth, in Scots or in other languages, and it appears strange, though not totally inexplicable. The two poets, in their effort to make a striking moral point, seem to be straining normal linguistic usage. There is possibly a late and distant echo of this word-play in the saying recorded by James Carmichaell: 'Con was hanged and left onlie science behind' (cf. the Bannatyne poem, 7-8); but if so, the point about *ens* has been jettisoned as if it were meaningless in the vernacular, or too abstruse.[27]

There exists, however, an earlier and more pointed use of this word-play, which throws some light on how these poems originated. In 1488 the Minister General of the Franciscans, Francis Nanni, or Samson (1414-99), addressed the Chapter General at Cremona, and rebuked the Conventuals for their increasing laxity:

> Hic [generalis] in Capitulo generali Cremone celebrato, attendens qualiter semper in peius fratres Conventuales laxabantur et declinabant, studia quoque Ordinis minuebantur, ingemiscens coram toto Capitulo dicebat notabile verbum: Heu, inquit, patres et fratres! olim in Ordine nostro multis temporibus solebat esse et dominari vera conscientia; tandem intrante et regnante scientia, paulatim dimissa est prima sillaba, videlicet *con*, et solum remansit quod sequitur, videlicet *scientia.* Nunc vero fratrum malicia et negligentia deperit et secunda sillaba, videlicet *sci,* quia scientia et studia deperiunt in Ordine et solum remanet nunc quod sequitur in dicto vocabulo, videlicet *entia,* quia fratres moderni tanquam lapidei,

---

25 See E. Gilson, 'Notes sur le vocabulaire de l'être', *Mediaeval Studies,* viii (1946), 150-58.

26 *The Meroure of Wysdome,* vol. i, ed. C. Macpherson (STS, 1926), 31. The punctuation is slightly modernised. A later, and probably post-Reformation Scots use occurs in 'The Prophecy of Gildas': 'When Idolatrie is in Ens, and Re' (*Ancient Scottish Prophecies in Alliterative Verse* [1603], ed. D. Laing (Bann. Club, 1833), 43). Here *ens* appears to signify 'material objects'.

27 *The James Carmichaell Collection of Proverbs in Scots,* ed. M.L. Anderson (Edinburgh, 1957), no. 426.

> bestiales et mali sine conscientia et sine scientia remanent velut entia bruta. Et iuxta verbum Apostoli facti sunt primum *velut es sonans*, postea velut terra et lapides invicem seipsos collidentes.[28]

A very similar account of this incident is given by the Polish friar, John Komorowski, in his *Memoriale Ordinis Fratrum Minorum*, and is there entitled, 'Declaracio de nomine consciencia'.[29] In this case the rebuke was directed specifically to the Conventual branch of the Franciscans, not—as with the Scottish poets—to `halie kirk' as a whole. What is more, the word-play was in Latin, and addressed to an audience that ought, presumably, to have been familiar with the word *ens* and its plural *entia*, as well as with its employment by great scholastic thinkers in their own order, such as Thomas of York, John Pecham, Roger Bacon and Duns Scotus.[30] The word is here employed in a way consonant with medieval Latin usage; the friars, through their lack of spiritual qualities, are said to be reduced to mere existence, something which they share with animals and even stones.

How did Douglas encounter this word-play? Although such a device might well have been a preaching-aid long used by other friars (and indeed by other clerics), it seems associated particularly with the name of Francis Nanni, and with the time when he was Minister General of the Franciscans. Statute 4 of the Chapter General held at Casale in 1485, dealing with the subject of studies, reads:

> Quod habeatur bona cura de studiis ut, si sine conscientia sumus, cum qua incepit Ordo noster, adminus habeamus scientiam, quia nunc, amisso con. et sci. solum remanserunt nobis entia; quod unusquisque tendit ad avaritiam.[31]

It seems likely that such a sarcastic witticism—a *notabile verbum*—would have been circulated rapidly, by word of mouth as well as in writing, and was probably not long confined to the friars. The Franciscans had many houses in Scotland, and the Observants, or reformed branch of the order, were particularly favoured by

[28] See P. Salvator Tosti, OFM, 'Ordinationes Fr. Min. Conventualium Generales et Provinciales Marchiae Saeculi XV', *Archivum Franciscanum Historicum*, xvi (1923), 370; also J. Moorman, *A History of the Franciscan Order* (Oxford, 1968), 504-05, which briefly summarises this passage.

[29] See *Monumenta Poloniae Historica*, vol. v (Lwow, 1888), 212-13; also Moorman, *Franciscan Order*, 546-7.

[30] Cf. D.E. Sharp, *Franciscan Philosophy at Oxford in the Thirteenth Century* (Oxford, 1930), 87-8, 132, 184, 382-3, and *passim*.

[31] *Archivum Franciscanum Historicum*, xvi (1923), 372.

James IV.[32] But other Scottish churchmen, travelling in Italy, might well have brought the jest back to their own country. The ingenious word-play, however, began to lose some of its point, when transferred from Latin into the vernacular and when the first clerical listeners were replaced by a wider audience unfamiliar with philosophical subtleties about *ens* and *entia*.

So far I have stressed what these two poems have in common, but there are also striking differences between them. Douglas's poem perhaps reveals a slight trace of the Latin original in its employment of the grammatical term *sillab* (16), which does not appear in the Bannatyne poem. It also seems to me by far the neater and more rhetorically polished of the two; the Bannatyne piece has inept repetitions at lines 5 and 20, and 7 and 12, and is metrically clumsy. Douglas is concerned primarily with the choice of prelates, those who ruled the church (11), and who 'the brydill had to leid' (3). His poem indeed interestingly resembles a passage in a late fifteenth-century work, *The Thre Prestis of Peblis*, which also laments the decline of the church from 'auld tymes', and traces the cause to changes in the way bishops were elected and to the prevalence of simony.[33] The Bannatyne poem seems wider in scope, yet more specific in its audience: referring repeatedly to 'justice' (3, 19, 24), it links the corrupt bestowal of benefices directly to the misgovernment of the realm; and whereas Douglas exhorts churchmen in general, including himself, to reform, this poem is explicitly addressed to a 'king'.

That king is most likely to have been James V. Since the Bannatyne Manuscript was completed by 1568, it is improbable that this piece was intended for the infant James VI. What is more, it has a revealing position in the manuscript, forming one of a small cluster of 'Advice to princes' poems. It is immediately followed by Alexander Scott's New Year greeting to Mary Queen of Scots (1562), and surrounded by other admonitory pieces, most of which are definitely addressed to James V. One is written by Alexander Kyd and four by William Stewart—both poets

---

[32] See further, J. Durkan, 'The Observant Franciscan province in Scotland', *IR*, xxxv (1984), 51-6; also W. Moir Bryce, *The Scottish Grey Friars* (Edinburgh and London, 1909).

[33] See *Thre Prestis of Peblis*, 355-430; with *Conscience*, 2-4, cf. 'The second is be way of Electioun, / Ane Persone for to cheis of perfectioun' (389-90). On this poem's popularity, see S. Mapstone, '*The Thre Prestis of Peblis* in the Sixteenth Century', in *A Day Estivall*, ed. A. Gardner-Medwin and J.H. Williams (Aberdeen, 1990), 124-42.

associated with James V's court—and several of the poems contain datable allusions: to the aftermath of Flodden, for instance, or to the problems caused by the king's 'tendir aige', or minority.[34] James V is notorious for his 'disreputable' appointments to bishoprics and abbeys;[35] he used the Church to enrich himself and his illegitimate sons, who were provided, while still infants, to the abbeys of Melrose, Kelso and Holyrood, and to the priories of St Andrews and Coldingham. This anonymous poem is brief and comparatively tactful; a good commentary on it is provided by Lindsay's scathing indictment of James V and the Scottish church in *The Testament of the Papyngo*, 961-1031.

Of these two poems Douglas's is undoubtedly the wittier, and probably served as a model for the later and clumsier piece in the Bannatyne Manuscript. Such re-working of older material was a common practice among poets at this time. It would be ridiculous to claim that either poem has very high literary value; nonetheless they are small illustrations of the liveliness and complexity of sixteenth-century Scottish culture, and its many close ties with the Continent.

---

[34] For these poems, see *Bann. MS.* ii, 221-57.

[35] The epithet is Gordon Donaldson's; see his *Scotland: James V to James VII* (Edinburgh, 1965), 54.

THE ASLOAN MANUSCRIPT

I.C. Cunningham

The Asloan Manuscript (NLS, MS. 16500, previously MS. Acc. 4233) of the early sixteenth century is, even in its present lamentably imperfect condition, one of the most important sources for Scottish prose and verse of the period. Several of the pieces included in it, especially those in prose, are not preserved elsewhere. Some are also found in the approximately contemporary and equally fragmentary prints of Chepman and Myllar; more appear in later manuscripts, such as the Bannatyne and Maitland Folio. In the latter cases Asloan is always an important witness, even if obviously less crucial than in the first. It is also interesting as a manuscript book, whose production and history can be traced in some detail.

The manuscript first came to scholarly attention at the beginning of the nineteenth century. Its then owner, Sir Alexander Boswell, 1st Bart., of Auchinleck, in collaboration with the Deputy Keeper of the Records of Scotland, Thomas Thomson, had several items from it printed at his private press (see below I, no.xii (*bis*), xvi and xviii). Substantial extracts were transcribed by William Gibb for George Chalmers (now EUL, MS. La.III 450), and these were used by David Laing for Bannatyne Club and other publications.[1] About 1890 the manuscript itself was for a short period deposited in the British Museum, but later attempts to ascertain its whereabouts and gain access were fruitless.[2]

In 1917, however, agreement was reached between the owner, Lord Talbot de Malahide, and the Scottish Text Society on the publication of a complete transcript. The editor, W. A. Craigie, worked from a set of photographs (now NLS, MSS. 335-6), and the edition was published in two volumes in 1923-5. Later editions of individual works and spot checks by myself show this to be what was intended, a serviceable and substantially accurate guide to the text (the notes are less full than they might be), but it cannot be of much help in codicological matters.

---

[1] In particular *Select Remains of the Early Popular Poetry of Scotland* (1822), *Holland's Howlat* (1823), and *The Poems of William Dunbar* (1834).

[2] See e.g. correspondence in the *Athenaeum* (1906) i, 422, 482, 516, 671.

Only with the purchase of the manuscript by the National Library in 1966 did it become fully accessible. Since then editors of individual pieces have used it; among these Dr Catherine van Buuren (see below I, no.xxi) calls for special mention. The present paper tries to bring together existing information and add some new facets, to give as complete a description of the manuscript as is at present possible.

I. Contents

The original contents are known from a list on ff.iii-iv compiled by the principal scribe, John Asloan (see below, IV), and headed 'Heir begynis [the contents of the] buke follow[and]'. This comprises 71 numbered items (not strictly 71 separate pieces: i-xii go together, xii (*bis*) has to be added and liiii subtracted). Of these 34 are totally lost, and seven are imperfect. The following tabulation gives Asloan's own numbers and titles as in his list (the numbers on the first page of the list, as far as xxv, are lost; these are supplied from the headings; viii is totally omitted in the list); also, for those which survive, folio numbers and headings and subscriptions; then information about other sources and modern editions and literature (the latter selective). In transcription I generally follow van Buuren rather than Craigie (except for final *ss*).

(i-xii) John Ireland, 'Treatise on the Passion, etc.', c.1490 (no general title in the contents-list or in the text). Unique. *Asloan MS*, i.1. For the author see the edition of his *Meroure of Wisdom* by C. Macpherson, F. Quinn and C. McDonald (STS, 1926, 1965, 1990); and J.H. Burns, 'John Ireland: theology and public affairs in the late fifteenth century', *IR*, xli (1990), 151-81.

i, [ii] In P*ri*mis ane chapit*ur* schawin be master Ihon yrland of þe w*er*tewe of þe glorius passoun of Ihesu nixt efter þat he h... þe causs of this compilacoun Ca*pitulo* primo & s*ec*u*n*do

ff.1, 4v [no headings or subscriptions, but (as also in the following) there are chapter summaries]

iii I*tem* of þe sacrament & w*er*tewe of pen*n*ance in generale

f.5v [no heading or subscription]

iiii I*tem* of confessioun sacramentale w*ith* co*n*dicionis & profettis þ[arof]

f.5v [no heading or subscription]

v Item of confessioun sacramentale with þe secund part of pennance
f.7v [no heading or subscription]
vi Item of satisfactioun sacramentale in generale
f.11v [no heading or subscription]
vii Item of þe deidis of almoss and mercy spirituale and corpo[rale]
f.17 [no heading or subscription]
viii [Item of vertuoss fasting and meritur]
f.19 [no heading or subscription]
ix Item of prayer and vrisoun and wertuiss yarof
f.21 [no heading or subscription]
x Item of þe noble and excellent werteu of cherite
f.25v [no heading or subscription]
xi Item of mercy mast proper to þe hie devyne maieste
f.28 [no heading or subscription]
[xii] Item The table of confessioun efter master Ihon Irland
f.33 [no heading]
f.40v [no subscription]
xii(bis) Item þe buke callit þe chess
f.41 Heir begynnis The buke of þe chess
f.76v heir endis þe buke of þe chess

A unique Scots translation, of unknown authorship and date, of the Latin text of Jacobus de Cessolis, *De ludo scachorum* (first printed at Utrecht, 1475 [GKW 6523]), abridged towards the end. Printed by Sir Alexander Boswell, *The buke of the Chess*, Auchinleck Press, 1818 (*Frondes Caducae*, vol. VII). *Asloan MS*, i.81.

xiii Item ane tractat callit þe cart schortly drawyn
f.77 Heir followis þe diuisioun of all þe world callit þe cart schortly drawyn In yngliss
f.86 Heir endis þe cart of þe warld

Ranulf Higden, *Polychronicon*, bk 1, ch. 5-7, 11, 9, in the translation by John of Trevisa, 1387 (printed by Caxton, 1482 [Hain 8659]; see the edition of Higden by C. Babington, Rolls Ser., 1865-86). Ed. G.G.J. Weijnen (Nijmegen thesis, 1983). *Asloan MS*, i.153.

xiiii Item þe buke of þe Portuuss of nobilness
f.86 Heir followis þe Wertuiss of nobilness and portratouris þarof Callit þe Portuuss and matynnis of þe samyn
f.92v heir endis þe porteouss of nobleness

A fragment (from f.90v) of this *Porteous of Nobleness* also in C&M, no. I, 1508 (Aldis 13, *STC* 20120), where the colophon states that it was translated from French by Androw Cadiou, tentatively identified by Beattie with Dom. Andreas Cadoen of the diocese of Aberdeen, B.A., who was received in the English nation of the University of Paris in 1472 and was later an advocate in Aberdeen. The French original is Alain Chartier, *Le Bréviaire des Nobles* (first printed at Bréhaut-Loudéac, 1485 [GKW 6560]). *Asloan MS*, i.171.

xv I*tem* ane tractat callit þe Scottis originale

f.93 Heir begy*n*nis the Scottis originale

f.98v Heir endis þis small tractat of þe Scottis originale

Another version in a Panmure manuscript of c.1460 printed in *Bann. Misc.* iii, 35-42. *Asloan MS*, i.185.

xvi I*tem* ane tractat of certane kyngis of yngland schawand of þar [evill governance]

f.99 Heir followis ane tractat of a Part of þe yngliss cronikle schawand of þar kingis Part of þar ewill & cursit governance

f.108 blank.

Incomplete; unique. Printed by Sir Alexander Boswell, *Ane Tractat* ..., Auchinleck Press, 1818 (*Frondes Caducae*, vol. VI). *Asloan MS*, i.197.

xvii I*tem* ane tract of þe kingis of scotland begy*n*nand i*n* þe thrid [age of þe warld]

f.124 Heir begy*n*nis ane tractat drawin owt of þe scottis cornikle begynnand in þe thrid age of þe warld

f.136v [no subscription]

Asloan MS, i.245.

xviii I*tem* ane addicioun of scottis corniklis and deidis

f.109 Heir followis ane schort memoriale of þe scottis corniklis for addicoun

f.123v [no subscription]

Unique. Edited by Thomas Thomson, *The Auchinleck Chronicle*, printed c.1810 but not published till 1877, with an introductory note by T. G. Stevenson, when the incorrect date 1819 was added to the title. For the text and a historical discussion, see C. McGladdery, *James II* (Edinburgh, 1990), 160-73 and 116-24. *Asloan MS*, i.215.

xix I*tem* þe buke callit þe spectakle of lufe

f.137 Heir begy*n*nis þe lytill buk entitillit and callit the Spektakle of luf Or delectatioun of luf of wem*en* quhilk Is devydit in viij partis f.150v Explicit þe spectakle of luf

Unique. Translated, 1492, from an unidentified original. Printed in *Bann. Misc.* ii, 121-47. *Asloan MS*, i.271.

xx I*tem* þe figuris of þe ald testament *con*forme till þe newe according to þe vj werk dayis aggreand w*ith* sex agis

f.151 Heir begy*n*nis ane extract of þe bibill of þe sex werkdays according to þe sex agis q*uh*ilkis restit in þe sevynt And figuris of þe ald testament & newe

f.166v Heir endis þe figuris of þe ald testament conforme till þe new testament acording vj werk dayis till þe vj agis and restand in þe vij day & age

Unique. Ed. L.A.J.R. Houwen (Groningen, 1990). *Asloan MS*, i.299.

xxi I*tem* þe buke of þe sevyne sagis

f.167 Heir begy*n*nis þe buke of þe sevyne sagis

f.209v Heir endis þe sevyn sagis

The Seven Sages of Rome. A unique Scots version, c.1470, probably from a Latin *Historia septem sapientium*, ed. C. van Buuren, (Leiden, 1982). *Asloan MS*, ii.1.

xxii I*tem* þe Iustis betuix þe talȝeour & þe sowtar

f.210 The Iustis betuix þe talȝeour & þe sowtar

f.211v *Quod* dunbar

William Dunbar, 'The Tailor and the Soutar'. Also in Bann. MS. f.111 (no. 172) and Maitl. Fol. MS. p.161. In Kinsley given as part B, 'The Turnament', of 'Fasternis Evin in Hell', no. 52, p.154. *Asloan MS*, ii.89. *Index* 2289.8. *Manual* (4) x.79.

xxiii I*tem* a ballat of þe abbot of tungland

f.211v Off þe fenȝeit falss frer of tungland

[after f.212 end lost]

William Dunbar, 'The Abbot of Tongland'. Only ll.1-69. Complete in Bann. MS. f.117 (no. 181). Kinsley no. 54, p.161. *Asloan MS*, ii.92. *Index* 417.5. *Manual* (4) x.59.

xxiiii I*tem* þe testament of Cresseid

Robert Henryson, *The Testament of Cresseid.* Fox, 111. David Laing conjectured that a Chepman and Myllar print has also been lost. The text now depends on later prints.

xxv I*tem* þe disputacioun betuix þe ny*cht*tingale .(.)av.[3] [...] merle

[3] The reading of this word, thanks to staining and tearing in the paper, is very uncertain. The first letter might be 'm' but equally well and perhaps better 'in'. The common reading 'mavis' is unlikely and its removal reduces the chances

William Dunbar, 'The Nightingale and the Merle'. Bann. MS. f.283 (no. 272), Maitl. Fol. MS., 165. Kinsley, no. 16, p.60. *Index* 1503.5. *Manual* (4) x.84.

xxvi [ ] goldin targe

William Dunbar, 'The Golden Targe'. Bann. MS. f.345 (no. 396), Maitl. Fol. MS. p.64, C&M, no. IV, n.d. (Aldis 7, *STC* 7349). Kinsley, no. 10, p.29. *Index* 2820.5. *Manual* (4) x.77.

xxvii I*tem* mast*er* Robert hend*er*so*n*nis Dreme On fut by forth

Robert Henryson, 'On Foot by Forth'. Lost; also mentioned in *The Complaynt of Scotland*, f.50v (p.50 in the edition by A.M. Stewart (STS, 1979)).

xxviii I*tem* [ ] sawis of þe angell Deid quhyte dragoun Devill wysman blak dragoun ȝoung man and of þe sawlis in hell

xxix I*tem* þe buke of curtasy and nortur

Possibly connected with the following, though none of Hay's known works has this as title.

xxx I*tem* þe document of sch*ir* gilbert hay

On Hay and his writings see *Gilbert de la Haye's Prose Manuscript*, ed. J. H. Stevenson (STS, 1901-14), and *The Buik of King Alexander the Conquerour*, ed. J. Cartwright (STS, 1986-). For a tentative identification of this piece see S. Mapstone, 'Sir Gilbert Hay's *Buke of Phisnomy*', in the present volume.

xxxi I*tem* þe Regiment of kingis w*ith* þe buke of phisnomy

Pseudo-Aristotle, *Secreta secretorum* (see Roger Bacon, *Opera hactenus inedita*, ed. R. Steele, fasc. 5, Oxford, 1909). Apparently not Sir Gilbert Hay's version ('The Buke of the Guvernaunce of Princes') as it omits the physiognomy, but possibly from *The Buik of King Alexander* (Mapstone, ibid.).

xxxii I*tem* a ballat of þe Incarnacoun

xxxiii I*tem* a ballat of steidfastness

xxxiiii I*tem* a ballat of recompence

xxxv I*tem* a ballat of o*ur* lady of pete

xxxvi I*tem* a ballat of disputacoun betuix þe body & saull

xxxvii I*tem* a ballat of þe devillis Inquest

xxxviii I*tem* a ballat of our lady

xxxix I*tem* þe buke of colkelby

---

of this being a different poem from Dunbar's. What follows the 'v' is equally uncertain. These are the results of an examination under UV light by Prof. A.A. MacDonald and myself, following a suggestion of Mrs. P. Bawcutt.

Colkelbie Sow. Bann. MS. f.357 (no. 401). G. F. Jones, *Wittenweiler's Ring and Colkelbie Sow* (Chapel Hill, 1956). *Colkelbie Sow and the Talis of the Fyve Bestes*, ed. G. Kratzmann (New York and London, 1983), who thinks this may have been a different version. Mentioned by Gavin Douglas in *The Palace of Honour* (1501), l.1712, and elsewhere.

xl I*tem* þe buke of the otter and þe ele

xli I*tem* þe flyting betuix Ke*n*nyde & dunbar

Flyting between Dunbar and Kennedy. Bann. MS. f.147 (no. 219); Maitl. Fol. MS. p.53; later parts C&M, no. VII, n.d. (Aldis 9, *STC* 7348). Kinsley no. 23, p.76. *Index* 3117.8. *Manual* (4) x.28.

(xlii-xlvii) Robert Henryson, *Fables*. Fables XIII, VIII, VII, III, IV, V in Fox. All in Bann. MS., BL, Harl. MS. 3865, prints by Charteris (1570), Bassandyne (1571), etc.

xlii I*tem* þe fablis of Esope And first of the paddok and þe mouss

xliii I*tem* þe preching of þe swallow

xliiii I*tem* þe lyoun and þe mouss

xlv I*tem* of chanticler and þe fox

xlvi I*tem* of þe tod and þe wolf

xlvii I*tem* þe pa*r*liament of bestis

xlviii I*tem* By a palace as I couth pass

xlix I*tem* a ballat of treuth

l I*tem* þe buke of þe howlat

f.213 Heir begy*n*nis þe buke of þe howlat

f.228v Heir endis þe buke of þe howlat

Richard Holland, *The Howlat*, c.1450. Bann. MS. f.302 (no. 383); C&M, fragment (Aldis 17, *STC* 13594). Ed. D. Laing (Bann. Club, 1823); Amours no. II. *Longer Scottish Poems*, vol. i, 1375-1650, ed. P. Bawcutt and F. Riddy (Edinburgh, 1987), 43-72 (with bibliography). *Asloan MS*, ii.95. *Index* 1554. On the author M. M. Stewart, 'Holland of the *Howlat*', *IR*, xxiii (1972), 3-15.

li I*tem* þe talis of þe fyvc bestis

[before f.229 beginning lost]

f.235v Heir endis The Talis of þe fyve Bestis

Of unknown authorship and date. D. Laing, *Ancient and Popular Poetry of Scotland*, ed. J. Small (1885), 281-93. *Colkelbie Sow and the Talis of the Fyve Bestes*, ed. G. Kratzmann (New York and London, 1983). *Asloan MS*, ii.127.

lii I*tem* þe wyplandis mouss & borowstovnis

f.236 Heir begynnes The tale of þe wplandis mouss and þe borowstoun mouss

f.240 heir endis of þe twa myss

Robert Henryson, *Fables.* Fable II in Fox. Sources as for items xlii-xlvii, above. *Asloan MS,* ii.141.

liii I*tem* þe maner of þe crying of a play

f.240 Heir followis þe maner of þe crying of ane playe

[after f.242 end lost]

'The Crying of a Play'. End lost; 165 ll. Bann. MS. f.118v. (no. 182) (136 ll.). *Asloan MS,* ii.149. Sometimes attributed to Dunbar (STS edn., 314-20; Mackenzie (1932), 170). G.F. Jones, *MLN,* lxix (1954), 479-80, dates to after 1509.

liiii I*tem* ane ballat of luf

ff.243-6. Part of lx. On the transposition of folios see below III (i).

lv I*tem* þe buke of sch*ir* orpheus & erudices

f.247 Heir followis þe tale of orpheus And Erudices his quene

f.256 Explicit þe buke of orpheus

Robert Henryson, *Orpheus and Eurydice.* Bann. MS. f.317 (no. 387) (longer); C&M, no. VIII, n.d. (Aldis 11, *STC* 13166). Fox, 133. *Asloan MS,* ii.155. *Index* 3442. *Manual* (4) x.5.

lvi I*tem* þe talis of þe thre prestis of peblis

f.257 Heir begy*n*nis þe buke of þe thre prestis of peblis how þai tald þar talis

[after f.262 end lost]

Three Priests of Peebles, ll.1-359 only. SRO RH 13/35 (S. Mapstone, '*The Thre Prestis of Peblis* in the sixteenth century', in A. Gardner-Medwin and J.H. Williams (eds.), *A Day Estivall* (Aberdeen, 1990), 124-42). Charteris 1603. T. D. Robb, STS (1920), who dates 1484-8. *Asloan MS,* ii.175. Attributed to Henryson by D. MacDonald, *Neophilologus,* li (1967), 168; rejected by Fox, p.xxviii, n.3.

lvii I*tem* þe buke of þe contemplacoun of sy*n*naris

f.263 Heire ffollowis The comtemplacioun of sy*n*naris appliand for eu*er*ilk day of þe oulk And first for monunday of þe blyndand blunder and viciouss wanyte of þis warld

f.290 Heir endis þe buke of þe contemplacoun of synnaris

William of Tours, *The Contemplation of Sinners.* Also in BL, Arundel MS. 285, Harl. MS. 6919 (J. A. W. Bennett, *Devotional Pieces in Verse and Prose* (STS, 1955)). Wynkyn de Worde, 1499 (anglicised). Ed. D. J. Young (Oxford B.Litt., 1955). *Asloan MS,* ii.187. See A. A. MacDonald, *IR,* xxxv (1984), 58-87.

lviii Item ane ballat of þe passioun
f.290v Heir begynnis þe passioun of Ihesu
f.292 *Quod* dunbar

William Dunbar, 'The Passioun of Crist'. Also in Maitl. Fol. MS. p.203 (+ 6 ll.); BL, Arundel MS. 285, f.170 (16 stanzas) (Bennett, op. cit.). Kinsley no. 3, p.7. *Asloan MS*, ii.242.

lix Item ane ballat of our lady
f.292 heir followis ane ballat of our lady
[after f.292 end lost]

Bodleian Library, MS. Arch. Seld. B 24, f.137v., attributed to Chaucer (denied by W. W. Skeat, *Complete Works* (Oxford, 1894-7), i, 47). *Asloan MS*, ii.245.

lx Item þe maying & disport of chaucer
f.293 Heir begynnis þe mayng and disport of chauceir
f.300v heir endis þe mayng and disport of chaucer

John Lydgate, *Complaynt of the Black Knight*, early 15th cent. (Lydgate, *Minor Poems*, ed. J.N. MacCracken (EETS, 1934), 382). Also attributed to Chaucer in Bodleian Library, MS. Arch. Seld. B 24 (also a Scottish manuscript, late 15th cent.), and C&M, no. VI, 1508 (Aldis 4, *STC* 5099); cf. Skeat, *Complete Works*, vii, pp. xliii, 245. *Asloan MS*, ii.247.

lxi Item ane ballat of our lady
f.300v heir followis diuerss ballatis of our ladye (heading also for lxii and lxiii)
f.301v finis

Also in NLS, Adv. MS. 18.5.14, f.i(v); EUL, Makculloch MS. (La.III 149, f.183). Ed. I. C. Cunningham, *TEBS*, v, part 5 (1988), 32-40. *Asloan MS*, ii.271.

lxii Item ane ballat of our lady
f.301v [no separate heading]
f.303 *Quod* Kennyde

Walter Kennedy, ed. J. Schipper (Vienna, 1901), no.4, p.17 (reprinting Dunbar, ed. D. Laing, vol. ii,93). *Asloan MS*, ii.272.

lxiii Item ane ballat of our lady
f.303 [no separate heading]
f.304v *Quod* dunbar

William Dunbar, 'Ane Ballat of Our Lady'. Unique. Kinsley no. 2, p.4. *Asloan MS*, ii.275.

lxiiii Item þe buke of ralf colȝear

The Taill of Rauf Coilȝear, an alliterative poem preserved in a unique copy of a print by Robert Lepreuik, St Andrews, 1572 (Aldis 113, *STC* 5487; facsimile, ed. W. Beattie, Edinburgh, 1966).

Amours no. III. The tale is mentioned by Gavin Douglas in *The Palace of Honour*, l.1711, and by Dunbar, 'To the King' (Kinsley, no. 42, l.33). Beattie, op. cit., p.v, suggests that it may have been printed by C&M.

lxv The buke of sch*ir* gologruss & schir gawane

Sir Gologrus and Sir Gawain, preserved only in C&M, no. II, 1508 (Aldis 12, *STC* 11984).

lxvi I*tem* þe disputacoun betuix þe merle & þe ny*cht*tingale

'The merle and the nightingale', presumably another copy of xxv.

lxvii I*tem* Dunbarris Derige of Edinburgh & strivling

William Dunbar, 'Lament for Edinburgh and Stirling'. Also in Bann. MS. f.102 (no. 166), Maitl. Fol. MS. p.290. Kinsley no. 22, p.72. *Index* 3870. *Manual* (4) x.51.

lxviii I*tem* ane ballat of all officeris

lxix I*tem* ane ballat of making of

lxx I*tem* ane ballat of pacience

lxxi I*tem* ane ballat of wardlie plesance

II. Present Condition

Before going on to discuss how the manuscript was created, it is necessary to describe its later physical vicissitudes and its present state.

Before the eighteenth century, various transpositions and the losses of gatherings and leaves, which have so reduced its extent, had already occurred. One of the former indeed took place before Asloan compiled his contents-list (see I, item liiii); those in xii (*bis*) and xvii-xviii are later. Some small repairs to the paper had also been made. Only then was the manuscript foliated, apparently by Lord Auchinleck (see VI), for the first and only time.[4]

About 1812 the manuscript was given to the Edinburgh binder Abram Thomson for treatment.[5] Whether the original gatherings

[4] In foliating he repeated the number 140. This was later noticed and partial correction made: the original 140 to 188 were altered to 141 to 189; but the process was taken no further, so that 189 is now repeated.

[5] Van Buuren in her description of the manuscript confuses the binder Abram Thomson with the record scholar Thomas Thomson. The former operated in Edinburgh's Old Fishmarket Close from at least 1807 to 1836; from 1825 he was *praeses* of the Master Bookbinders (I am grateful to my colleague John Morris for this information). Several others of his bindings are known; in particular he treated the Bannatyne manuscript in a very similar way to the Asloan about a dozen years later.

were still wholly or partially intact is not known; if they were Thomson cut them into single leaves. He repaired the leaves and trimmed them (cropping parts of the folio numbers 87, 93 and 214 and various upper-case letters). Each leaf was then inlaid into new paper (with dated watermarks from 1804 to 1812, but mostly 1811)[6] measuring 398 x 300 mm. One transposition was corrected: ff.112-13 were restored to their proper place after f.118. Seven gaps or supposed gaps were marked by the insertion of blank leaves after ff.63, 66, 116, 167, 228, 242 and 246. These sheets, plus endpapers of thick brown paper, were sewn on four double cords and fixed to thick boards. The joints were formed and the boards covered with brown russia leather. The outside of both covers, the outer 25 mm. of each side of the inside covers (to which the pastedowns do not extend), and the spine were decorated with geometrical and botanical designs, tooled in gilt. The edges of the paper were also gilt. Title and date were stamped on the spine: "SCOTTISH / TRACTS / IN / PROSE & VERSE", "MS. TEMP. JAC. V". The binder fixed his label on the front endpaper.

Thomson's work has lasted well for over one and a half centuries, protecting the precious leaves. It is pointless to complain that he did not respect the original format or leave a record of his treatment. Such things were simply unknown in his time.

III. Original Format

As the manuscript stands we can see that the page size (trimmed as already noted) is 230 x 170 mm. The text is written in single columns of from 29 to 34 lines; the written area is from 200 to 215 mm. high, and from 125 to 150 mm. (prose) or 95 to 100 mm. (poetry) wide. There are no bounding or guide lines. To find out more we require (i) to consider the gaps and transpositions indicated by the text and (ii) to examine the watermarks of the paper. From these, taken together, can be deduced (iii) the original division into gatherings. Finally the manuscript can be shown (iv) to have consisted of a series of fascicles.

(i) Sequence of folios

Errors have occurred at various times. One goes back to before the compilation of the contents-list: ff.243-8 appear there as the

[6] Van Buuren is mistaken in stating that some of these are dated 1822.

item liiii, 'ane ballat of luf', but they are in fact part of Lydgate's *Complaynt of the Black Knight* and should follow f.298 (as a nineteenth-century pencil annotator saw). Others had happened by the time of the inlaying. The correct sequence in xii (*bis*) (ff.53, 59-63, 54-8, 64-5, 75, 70, 72, 68, 67, 74, 73, 69, 71, 66, 76) was established by the pencil annotator, certainly on textual grounds. The interchange of xvii and xviii was obvious from the numbers, but the full solution has remained uncertain (see below). (The explanation of these transpositions will be given below (iii).)

Losses have occurred after f.212 (large but incalculable), ff.228 and 242 (1 sheet), f.262 (probably one gathering), ff.278 and 292 (1 sheet), and f.304 (large but incalculable). Except for those at ff.278 and 292 these were noted by the pencil annotator.

In xviii the lacuna between ff.118 and 119 was noted by an eighteenth-century reader; it was filled by the transposition there of ff.112-13 at the time of the inlaying. The other gaps, after ff.111, 120 and 123, were noted by the pencil annotator. The sequence is not quite certain. This 'Addition to the Scottish Chronicle' begins on f.109 and ends on f.123v; f.122 is textually linked to f.123, and f.121 probably is to f.122. Between these fixed points comes a large section, ff.117-20 (with 112-13 after 118), whose leaves are all textually linked, and two smaller sections, ff.110-11 and ff.114-16, likewise linked internally; the relative position of these cannot be textually established with certainty. Nor does chronology provide a guide, because the text does not proceed in linear fashion through the fifteenth century, but goes back from 1446 to 1445 (f.111), from 1452 to 1451 (ff.117-18), from 1454 to 1448 (ff.112-13), and in f.121 is back in 1420. When one takes into account the occurrence of watermarks (below (ii)) on ff.114, 117, 118, 113, 121 and 122, as well as the textual linkings, the only plausible sequence is ff.109-11, 1 leaf lost, ff.114-16, 1 leaf lost, ff.117-20, 1 leaf lost, ff.121-3, 1 leaf (presumably blank) lost.[7]

(ii) Watermarks

No fewer than nine differently watermarked papers are used in the surviving parts of the manuscript. Four of them are seen, if I may anticipate the results of the next section, to be restricted to

[7] Craigie, who had no knowledge of the watermarks, restored two imperfect series, covering the years 1428-60 and 1420-55, by placing ff.114-16 after f.123. This also ignores that f.123v is the end of the text.

one gathering: *c* to iii, *e* to v, *h*, *i* and *j* to xxi. Another three are found in only two gatherings: *a* in i and ii, *d* in iv and vi, *g* in xix and xx. The remaining two are much more frequent: *b* in vii to xii, and *f* in xiii to xviii. They are variously from France and the Netherlands and of the early sixteenth century, more closely the second and third decades.[8]

a A five-spoked wheel, with a central line from the top surmounted by a quatrefoil and the letters I and P to the sides. The total height is 48 mm.; the width is 26 mm. The chain-lines are 26 mm. apart, so that the mark fits exactly between them. Identical to Briquet 13519 (France, 1521-7). (ff.3, 15, 16, 17, 18, 23, 24, 25, 26.)

b A shield containing the letter R with a crown above and a fleur-de-lys at each side of it. The height and width are both 32 mm. The chain-lines are 28 mm. apart; one runs through the centre of the mark. The closest published form is Briquet 8987 (Northern France and the Netherlands, 1493-1523), but the curl at the foot of the R is different and the chain-lines are to the side. (ff.4, 5, 6, 9, 10, 52, 77, 80, 81, 82, 83, 84, 90, 91, 95, 96, 97, 98, 99, 101, 107, 124, 126, 127, 129, 130, 131, 135, 110, 117, 118, 113, 121, 122, 114, 137, 138, 141, 142, 144, 147, 148, 152, 155, 156, 158, 160, 163, 164, 166.)

c A unicorn with stripes across its body. The chain-lines are 22 mm. apart. The mark is placed between them, but at an angle so that the back of the body does not touch the line, while the front legs and part of the head have it through them; the stripes are at an angle to the body and parallel to the chain-lines. None of the examples in Briquet or Piccard x.2213 sqq. have these details. (ff.29, 34, 36, 37, 38, 39.)

d A six-spoked wheel with six spikes, with a central line from the top surmounted by a five-petalled flower and another flower at each side. The total height is 48 mm. The chain-lines are 30 mm. apart; the mark fits between them, with the spikes and side flowers sometimes touching them, sometimes with a gap of 2-4 mm. It is almost identical to Briquet 13370 (France, 1518-25). (ff.42, 47, 48, 49, 50, 68, 67, 69, 71, 66, 76.)

e A Gothic P surmounted by a quatrefoil. The total height is 64 mm. The chain-lines are 27 mm. apart and the mark is placed be-

[8] See C.M. Briquet, *Les Filigranes*, repr. ed. A. Stevenson (Amsterdam, 1968); also *Die Wasserzeichenkartei G. Piccard im Hauptstaatsarchiv Stuttgart* (Stuttgart, 1961–).

tween them, one form centrally, the other touching the left line with its middle and top. The mark itself is identical to Briquet 8702 (Northern France, 1508-14), but the distance between the chain-lines in it is 24 mm. (ff.59, 60, 54, 55, 56.)

f A shield containing three fleur-de-lys, surmounted by a crown and having below the letter t. The total height is 62 mm. The chain-lines are 24 mm. apart; the mark at its greatest is slightly wider so that the lines run through it at each side. The mark is identical to Briquet 1748 (Northern France, 1509-24), but the position of the chain-lines differs, going through the fleur-de-lys. (ff.168, 169, 170, 171, 173, 175, 177, 182, 183, 188, 190, 191, 193, 194, 195, 196, 198, 203, 206, 207, 209, 210, 211, 212, 213, 215, 216, 218, 219, 220, 224, 227, 230, 231, 234, 235, 238, 239, 242, 248, 249, 250, 251, 252, 255, 256, 262.)

g Generally similar to *f*, but with a five-petalled flower above the crown, and a curled tail below. The total height is 72 mm. The chain-lines are 26-28 mm. apart; one runs through the centre of the mark. Briquet 1774 (Northern France, 1519-20) is similar, but the tail is different. (ff.263, 264, 269, 271, 273, 274, 275, 276, 279, 280, 284, 286, 288, 289, 290.)

h A shield containing one fleur-de-lys with two diamonds above, surmounted by a cross with the letters I and C at each side. The total height is 35 mm. The chain-lines are 26-28 mm. apart; one runs through the centre of the mark. Briquet 1613 (Northern France and the Netherlands, 1515-23) is very similar, except that the mark is positioned between the chain-lines, which are 23 mm. apart. (ff.296, 297, 298, 243, 245, 302.)

i and *j* may be the two forms of the same mark. It is a unicorn with a band across the middle; the legs differ slightly, the length and angle of the horn more considerably. Piccard, x.2206 and 2205 respectively are very similar. (ff.303 and 304.)

(iii) Gatherings

The original make-up of the manuscript, destroyed when it was cut into single sheets to be inlaid (if not before), can be recovered with almost total certainty, largely from the sequence of leaves with and without watermarks (each original sheet having the watermark on one half only; which half this is and which way up the watermark is depends on how the sheet was turned and folded when originally used and is immaterial for the present purpose). If there ever were quire-signatures or catchwords (which is far from certain) they have been trimmed off. In the following diagrams the leaves with watermark are starred.

i^{16}

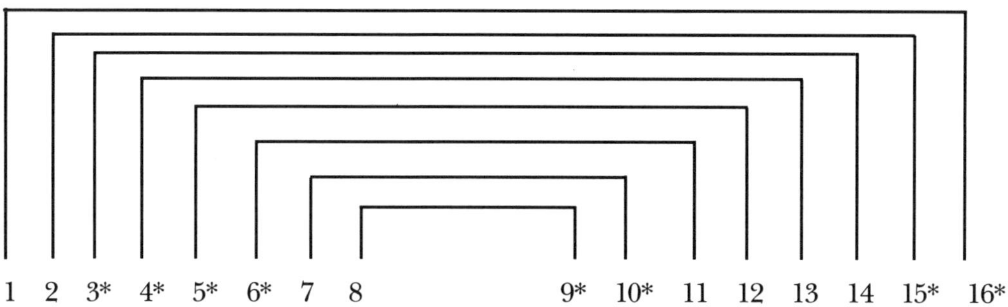

ii^{12}

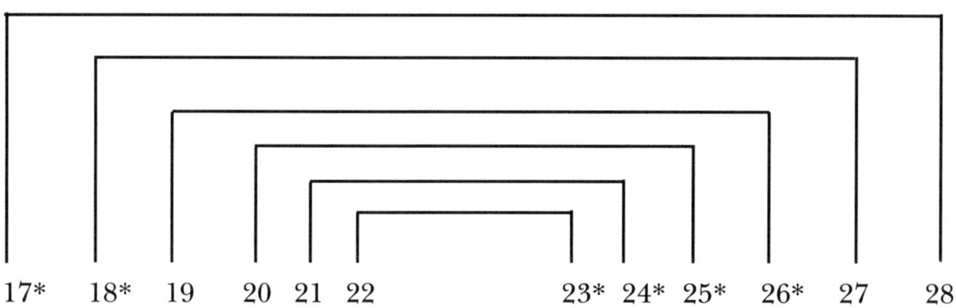

iii^{12}

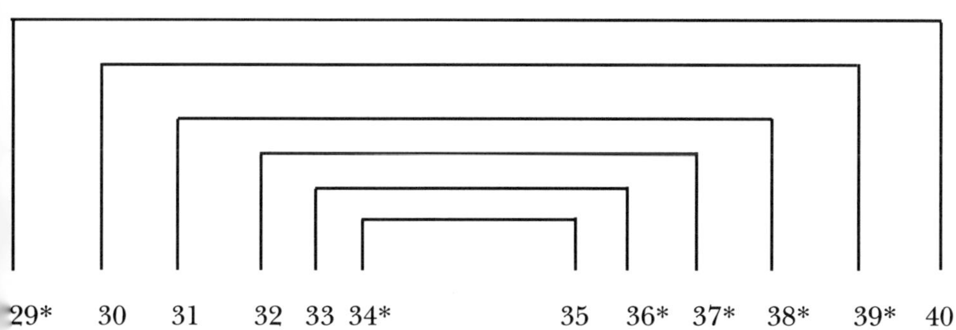

iv^{12}

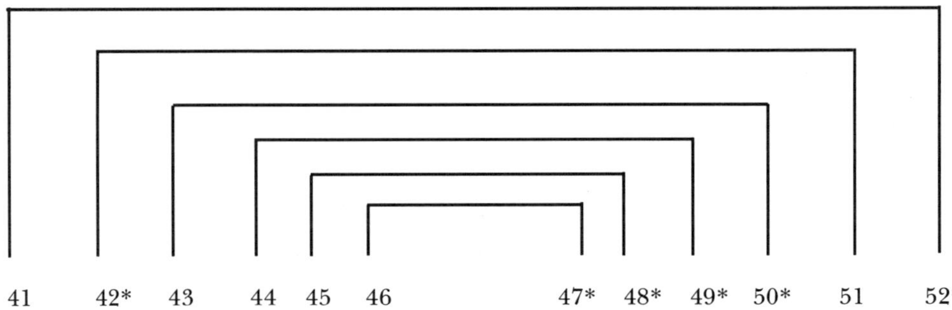

v^{12}

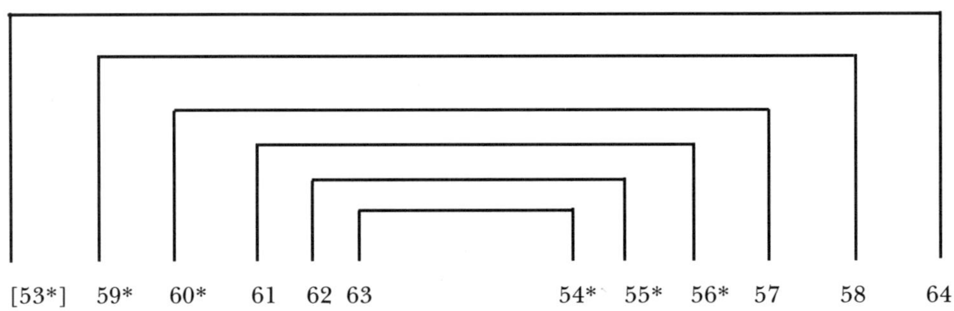

The present f.53 is a later substitute; it is assumed that the original was watermarked, as the conjugate of f.64. After it had been lost the remaining sheets were folded inside out, thus giving the present sequence, and the single f.64 remained at the end.

vi^{12}

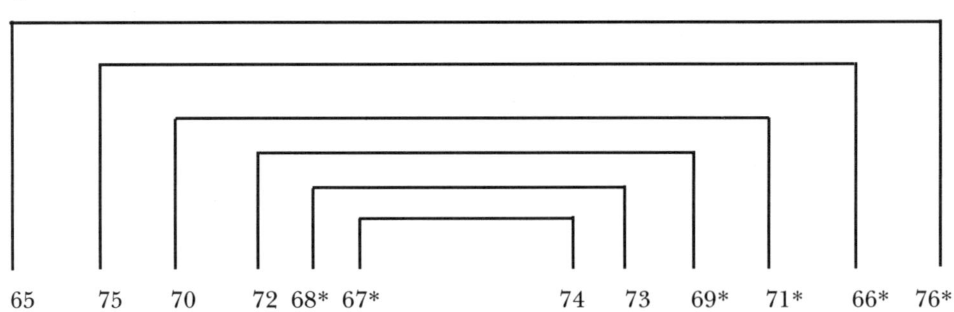

The second and fourth sheets (ff.75/66 and 72/69) were folded the wrong way, and the third to sixth were reversed in order.

vii^{16}

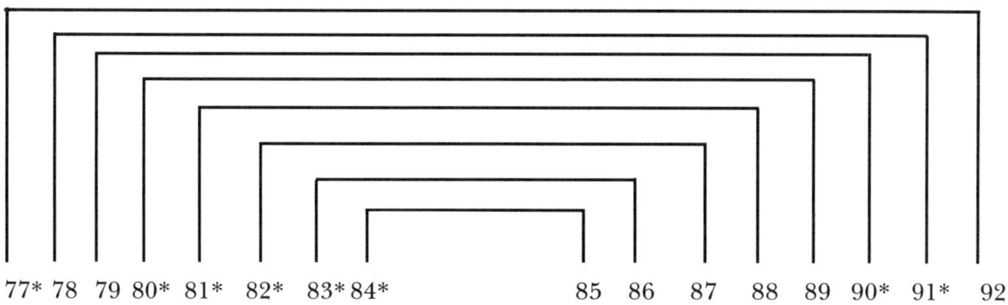

viii^{16} (-16)

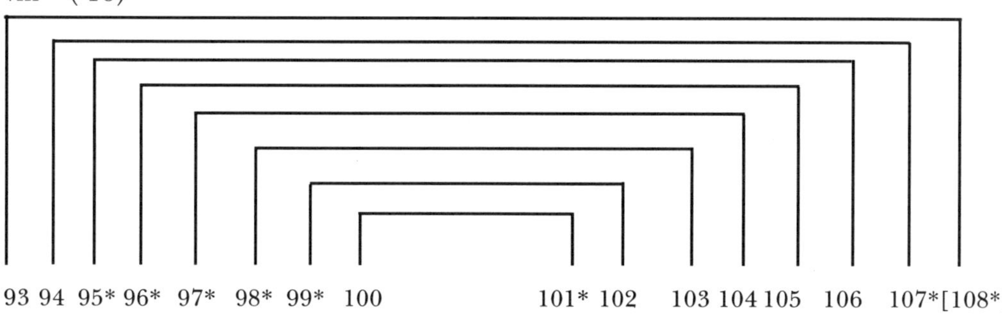

f.108 is a later substitute for a presumably blank and watermarked original.

ix^{16}

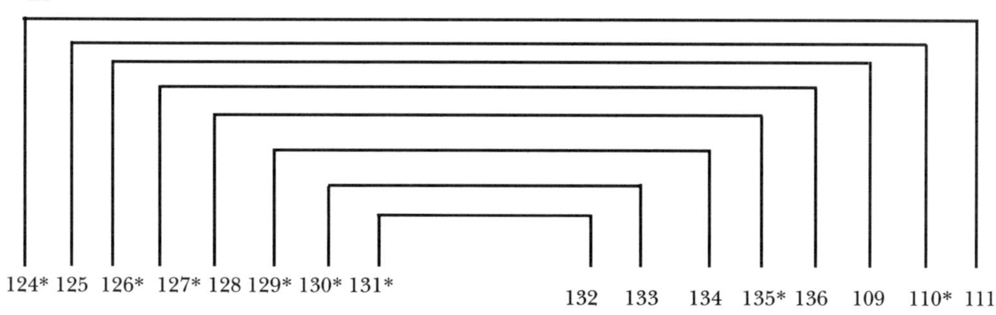

The first three sheets were folded the wrong way and placed separately at the beginning of the gathering; the centre sheet of the following gathering and the rest of that gathering were then placed in the centre of these three sheets.

x^{16} (-1,5,12,16)

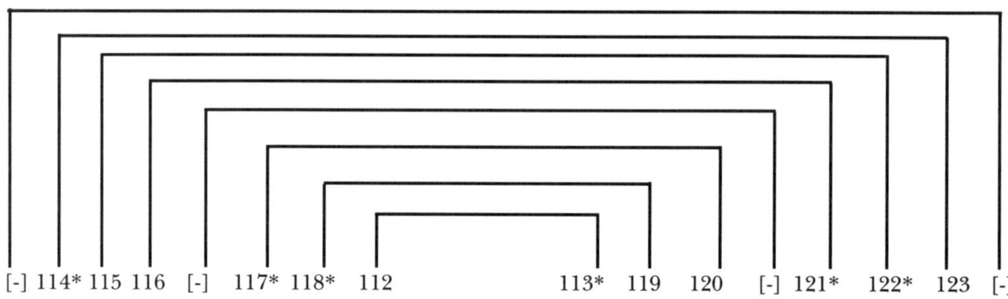

16 was probably blank. For the inferred losses see above (ii).

xi^{14}

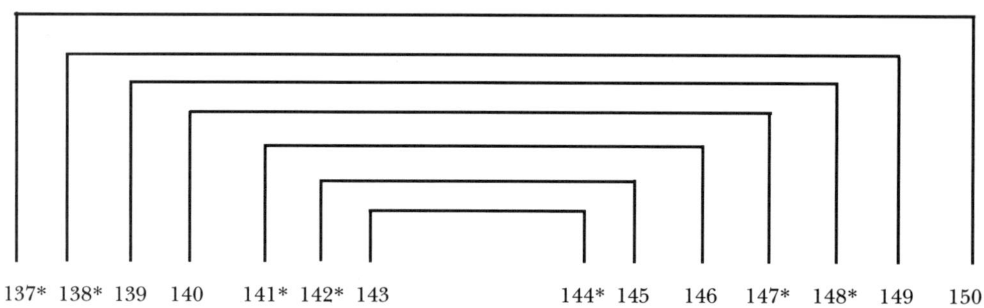

xii^{16}

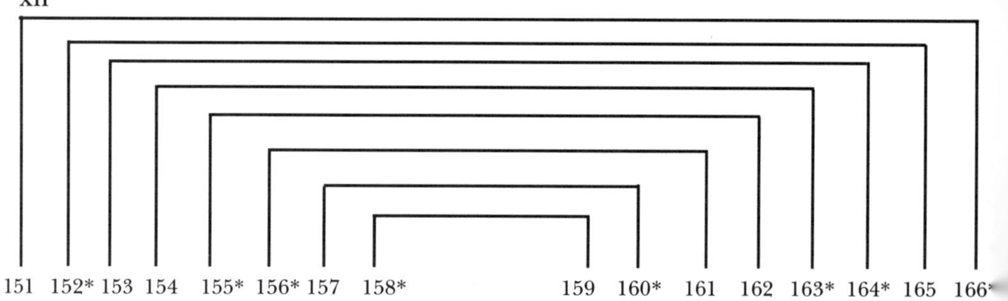

xiii^{16}

Van Buuren's rejection of a lacuna after f.167 is confirmed.

xiv^{16}

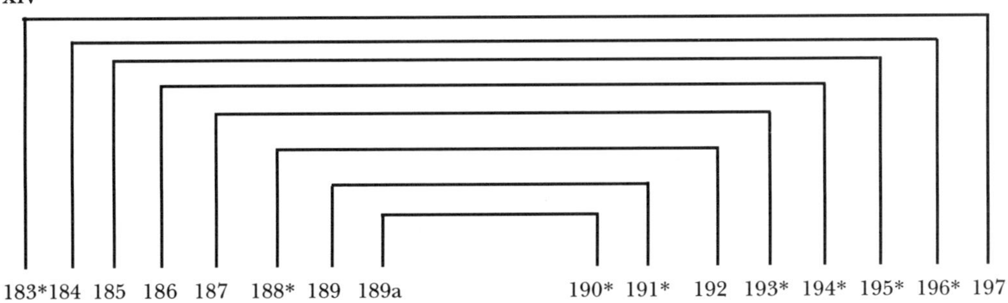

xv^{16} (-16)

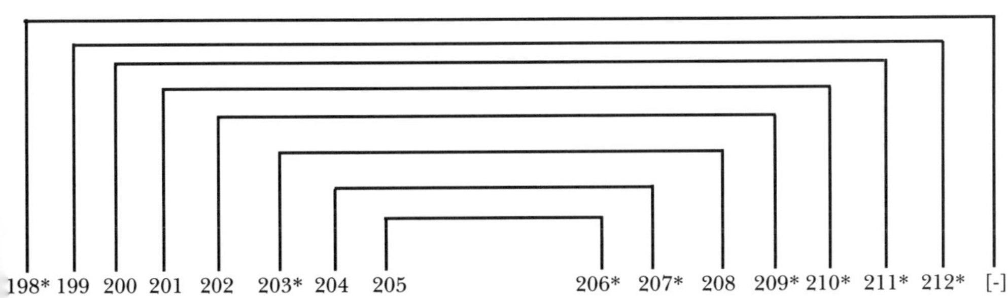

[Gap in MS]

xvi^{16}

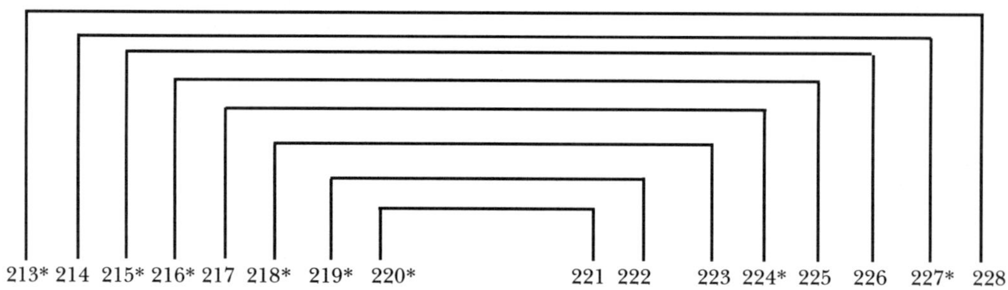

xvii^{16} (-1,16)

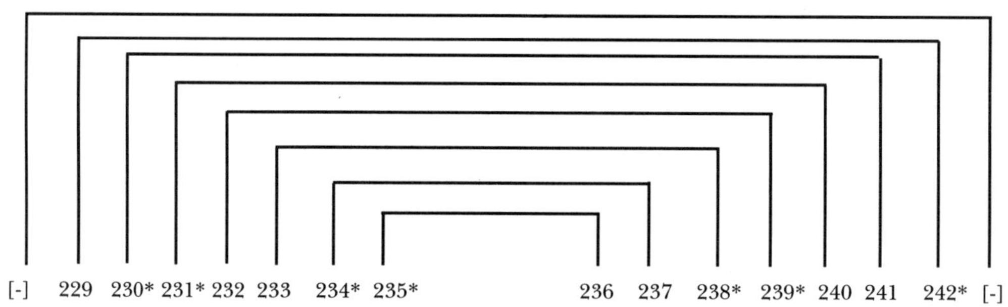

xviii^{16}

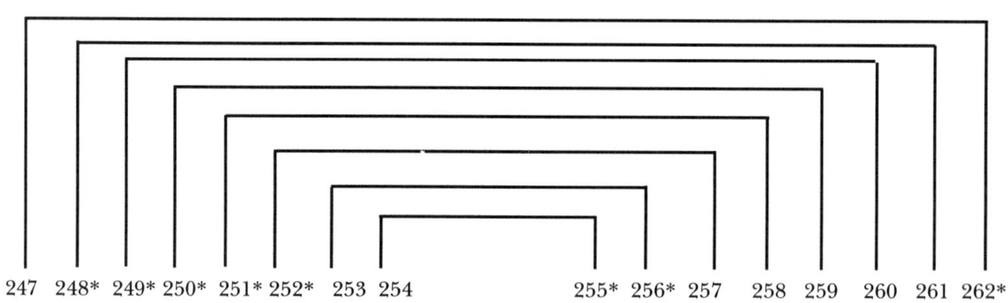

[Gap in MS]

xix^{16}

xx^{16} (-1,16)

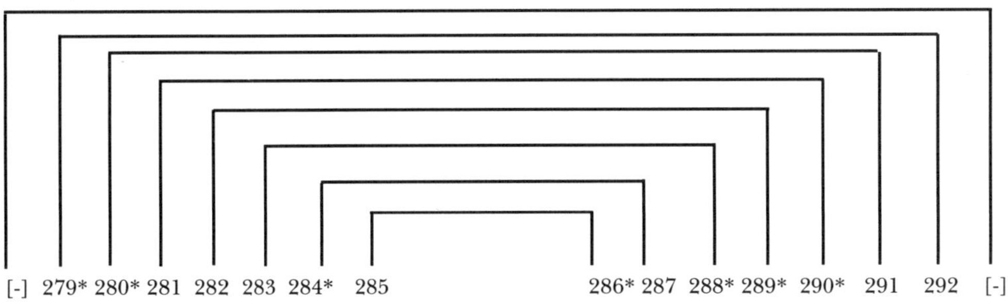

xxi^{16}

The two inside sheets fell out and were replaced between gatherings xvii and xviii.

[Gap in MS]

The great majority of the restored gatherings are of 16 leaves: 13, plus another two probably so (x and xvii). Only 5 are of 12 (ii-vi), and one of 14 (xi). The latter anomaly will be dealt with later (below IV).

(iv) Fascicles

There is a remarkably good correlation between the inferred gatherings (which I should repeat were reconstructed solely from the watermarks and gaps without further consideration of the content) and the items of the manuscript, as the following table shows.

gathering i	= ff.1-16		items i-vi
ii	17-28	}	vii-xii
iii	29-40	}	
iv	41-52	}	
v	53-64	}	xii (*bis*)
vi	65-76	}	
vii	77-92		xiii, xiiii
viii	93-108		xv, xvi
ix	124-111	}	xvii, xviii
x	117-116	}	
xi	137-150		xix
xii	151-166		xx
xiii	167-182	}	
xiv	183-197	}	xxi, (xxii), (xxiii)
xv	198-212+	}	
xvi	213-228		l
xvii	-229-242+		li, lii, liii
xviii	243-262	}	lv, lvi
[Gap in MS]		}	

xix	263-278 }	lvii, (lviii), (lix)
xx	-279-292+ }	
xxi	293-304	lx, (lxi), (lxii), (lxiii)

Only John Ireland and the *Buke of the Chess* are long enough to extend over several gatherings. Items xix, xx and l fill a gathering exactly. The items enclosed in brackets are small 'fillers' of the type commonly used to complete sections. Apart from these only related material appears in the same gathering or group of gatherings: the historical xv and xvi, and xvii and xviii; the animal fables li and lii, and the interlude liii; and the tales lv and lvi.

It is very likely that this correlation was maintained in the parts now lost. Plausible groups are made up of xxiiii-xxvii, poems of Henryson and Dunbar, with xxviii perhaps a filler; xxix-xxxi, related texts, then a series of (?small) ballads, xxxii-xxxviii; xxxix and xl, animal fables; xli the Dunbar-Kennedy *Flyting*; xlii-xlviii Henryson's fables, then two (?small) poems, xlviii and xlix; lxiiii Ralf Colȝear; lxv a romance; lxvi and lxvii poems of Dunbar, with four (?small) poems lxviii-lxxi.

A reasonable inference from this correlation is that the manuscript consisted of a series of more or less independent fascicles.[9] There is physical evidence to support this. First, the folding of sheets the wrong way round and related errors in gatherings v-vi and ix-x (see above (iii)) imply that these gatherings were, at least for a time, not securely sewn into a volume. Second, a scribal subscription occurs at the end of or after the principal item in most of the inferred fascicles (see below IV), again suggesting their independence. Finally, several pages are considerably more soiled than normal, and the great majority of these would have been on the outside of the inferred fascicles: ff.1r, 17r, 76v, 77r, 124r, 137r, 150v, 151r, 167r, 213r, 247r, 304v. Of the others, f.182v is the end of a gathering but not of a fascicle, and ff.123v and 257r are in the middle of gatherings. Whatever the explanation of these, it can hardly be doubted that the fascicles had a separate existence for long enough to allow them to get dirty.

9 This is now a well-recognised phenomenon. See P.R. Robinson, 'A Study of Some Aspects of the Transmission of English Verse Texts in Late Medieval Manuscripts' (Oxford B.Litt., 1972), and 'The "Booklet": a self-contained unit in composite manuscripts', *Codicologica,* iii (1980).

IV. Scribes

The *communis opinio* is that the manuscript was written by one scribe, John Asloan. Certainly the greater part of it was, as is attested by a series of subscriptions:

f.40v (end of i-xii)	explicit p*er* manu*m* Johan*n*is Asloan
f.76v (end of xii(*bis*))	script*us* p*er* manu*m* Joh*ann*is Sloane
f.92v (end of xiiii)	script*us* p*er* M. Jo. Asloan
f.166v (end of xx)	p*er* M. Jo. Asloan
f.209v (end of xxi)	p*er* M. Jo. Asloan
f.228v (end of l)	p*er* M. Joha*n*nis Asloan
f.235v (end of li)	p*er* M. Jo. Asloan
f.290 (end of lvii)	writtin be þe hand of Jhon Asloan
f.300v (end of lx)	p*er* M. Jo. Asloan

The unabbreviated 'per manum' of the first two, with the Scots equivalent at f.290, and the genitive 'Johannis' at f.228v suggest with scarcely any possible doubt that 'per M.' elsewhere stands for 'per manum' also, not the more obvious 'per Magistrum'.

How then should we interpret the note on f.150v (end of xix): 'per M G Myll'? If it is taken in conformity with Asloan's habit as 'per manum G Myll', then this item alone must be attributed to another scribe, G. Myll. If, on the contrary, it is taken as 'per Magistrum G Myll', Myll may be the author or translator of *The Spectacle of Love.* The latter is the prevailing view. However, if we look more closely at the handwriting of item xix and that of the rest of the manuscript, it can be seen that though they are not dissimilar in general, being characteristic secretary bookhands, there are differences. That of xix is more angular, and more letters are formed with two strokes; the ink is a richer brown. Also this item constitutes gathering xi, unique in the manuscript in having 14 leaves. I am sure that Myll is the scribe. However, he must be contemporary with Asloan, and indeed working in conjunction with him, for the paper he uses is the same as Asloan uses in gatherings vii-x and xii.[10]

John Asloan or Sloan, has been plausibly identified by van Buuren[11] with a notary public in Edinburgh, attested from 1518 to 1530; he is likely to be the same person as the one who appears as procurator and witness from 1499 to 1526. She further traces

[10] Van Buuren, ed. of the *Sevyne Sages*, at 9-10, notes the difference in handwriting, but fails to draw the obvious conclusion.

[11] *English Studies*, xlvii (1966), 365-72, and edition of the *Sevyne Sages.*

other copying activity by him in parts of Bodleian Library, MS. Douce 148 (*Troy Book*), whose subscription says it was 'written and mendit at the Instance of ane honourable chaplane Schir Thomas ewyn in Edinburgh', and in eleven folios of NLS, Adv. MS. 19.2.3 (Andrew of Wyntoun's *Chronicle*).

G. Myll, on the other hand, has not been traced; van Buuren suggests that the scribe of xix (unnamed on her view) might be a clerk of Asloan's, and this is quite possible. One Gilbert Myln occurs as a witness in 1520;[12] he or another of the same name appears as a notary public in Lanarkshire in 1545-50.[13]

The only original decoration in the manuscript is rubrication of titles, initials and Latin quotations in items i, vii, xii (*bis*), xxi (beginning), lv and lvi (beginning). Elsewhere some spaces for initials have been left, with guide-letters; in many of these cases the letter has been inserted in black ink at a later date. Rubricated initials (E, I, T), cut from a vellum manuscript, have been pasted to ff.4, 52v, 77, 93, 175, 179v, 188v and 195v, certainly long after the manuscript was written.

V. Date

None of the scribal subscriptions (see above IV) is dated. Other indications of the date of writing, of varying strength, can be adduced.

(i) Asloan's biography (above IV) would allow any date in the first three decades of the sixteenth century, and could not rule out one slightly beyond these limits.

(ii) The addition (compared with the other, older version of the text) of the name of James V on f.95, 'our sou*er*ane lord Iames þe fyft þ*at* now Is', shows that this passage was not written earlier than 9 September, 1513 (or later than 1542). Whether this addition was due to Asloan or taken over from his source is not determinable.

(iii) The terminal date of item xviii is likewise the end of August, 1513. The same proviso applies as in (ii).

(iv) The dates of composition of the other items, in so far as they are known, are given in I above. Neither Dunbar, Henryson

[12] *The Protocol Book of John Fowler, 1514-1528*, ed. M. Wood (SRS, 1944).

[13] *The Protocol Books of Dominus Thomas Johnsoun, 1528-1578*, ed. J. Beveridge (SRS, 1920).

nor Kennedy can be later than 1510. None of the others is much if at all later than 1500.

(v) In so far as the papers used can be compared with dated examples (see above III (ii)), they mostly appear to belong to the approximate period 1515-25. *a* is slightly later (1521-7), *e* rather earlier (1508-14); but I should be reluctant to draw conclusions about relative order of writing from this.

(vi) It has been suggested that Asloan copied some of his pieces from the Chepman and Myllar prints; two of the four in question (the *Porteous of Nobleness* and Lydgate's *Complaynt*) are dated 1508, so that if the suggestion can be proved the Asloan manuscript can be no earlier than that year. It should be recalled that the lost items xxvi, xli and lxv were also printed by Chepman and Myllar, and the same has been proposed for xxiiii and lxiiii.

(a) *Porteous of Nobleness* (Asloan xiii, C&M I). The print is incomplete and only ff.90v-92 of the manuscript appear in it. There are very few substantive variants. I have noted only seven. In three of these Asloan is wrong: p.182 l.2 (*Asloan MS*) 'p*ro*thecall' for 'prodigal', l.7 omission of 'gret', p.183 l.22 omission of 'man'. However, in the remainder C&M are wrong: p.182 l.5 'as' for 'is', l.8 'laif for' for 'laif of', p.183 ll.11-12 'as' for 'ffor sobirness is', l.14 omission of 'no*ch*t'.

(b) Holland, *The Howlat* (Asloan l, C&M fragment). There are very few variations. C&M appear to be wrong l.553 'with' for 'wicht'.

(c) Henryson, *Orpheus and Eurydice* (Asloan lv, C&M VIII). Again the texts are very close. I find only two substantive errors in Asloan: ll.307 'Thai' for 'That' and 554 'fele' for 'tell'; and four in C&M: ll.3 'ancester' for 'ancestry', 328 'und*er*' for 'eft*er*', 400 'on' for 'of', and 527 'ar' for 'is'.

(d) Lydgate, *Complaynt* (Asloan lx, C&M VI). The texts here diverge to a greater extent; in many instances it is not clear that one is better than the other. But of those where I would venture an opinion I find Asloan in error ten times: ll.13 'disport' (from 10) for 'despite', 33 'bemes' (from 35) for 'leves', 93 'portes' for 'poetes', 138 'on' for 'myne', 268 'exeiss' for 'excuse', 335 'goddess' for 'gaddis', 437 'Iche' for 'I', 538 'displey' for 'diseobey', and 609 'lond' for 'bond'; while C&M are wrong 12 times: ll.11 'gray' for 'gay', 45 'londe' (from earlier in the line) for 'wod', 48 'breste' (from 49) for 'thrist', 225 and 231 'caulde' or 'cold' for 'causs', 236 'desterue' (perhaps from 235 'deserf') for 'me sterf', 249 'myserabile if' for 'misbeleif', 281 'ryght' for 'licht', 305 'hight' for 'my*cht*', 359 'to kokes' for 'in colcos', 373 'slade' for 'schad', 398 'long' (from 'strong' earlier) for 'lond', 443 'gete' for 'gret', 509 'if' for 'or', 591 'mys' for 'amyss', and 605 'the' for 'to'. Also the anonymous poem before the colophon (also in the Bannatyne manuscript) is not in Asloan.

In theory there are two possible explanations for these discrepancies: 1) neither Asloan nor C&M is a copy of the other; 2) one is a copy of the other and has corrected the errors of the source by conjecture, while making other errors. It would be hard to prove either of these, though I should think the probability lies with 1), at least in (d). Certainly it cannot be safe to regard 1508 as the earliest possible date of Asloan on this ground.

Given the existence of fascicles, it cannot be assumed that the manuscript was written at one time or in the order it was given later. Thus 1513 is the *terminus post quem* only for the two items xv and xvii (though probably also for xvi and xviii in the same fascicles); an earlier date for other parts cannot be ruled out. That the earlier limit of 1508 for items also printed by Chepman and Myllar is unsafe has just been shown. The watermark evidence is not precise. Asloan's life is not well enough known to allow even a guess at the point when he was most likely to have written the manuscript. And yet despite the uncertainties the commonly accepted date of 1515-25 cannot be far from the truth.

V. History

In the early sixteenth century the Edinburgh notary John Asloan wrote a series of fascicles containing a miscellany of works in prose and verse, religious and secular. Some time later he put them in order, numbered the items and compiled a contents-list (in which liiii is already out of place). Given this later activity it is a little more likely that he made the manuscript for himself, rather than on commission for another (as was the case with Douce MS. 148).

For almost two centuries nothing is known of the manuscript. The names 'William Murray' and 'William Leslie of Balquhain' in sixteenth-century hands appear on ff.40v and 166v: 'per me gulielmum Murray manu mea et non' and 'I William Leslye of bollquhan grantis me to haff rasavit fra þe hand'; pen-trials, but whether by owners or others is totally unknown; the latter will refer to the person of that designation who died in 1571. Other deleted or cropped notes of the sixteenth or seventeenth century occur on ff.76v, 98, 151 and 198.

The next fact is the ownership of Alexander, 2nd earl of Kincardine, and all that is known of that is his transmission of the manuscript, through his daughter Elizabeth, to his grandson Alexander Boswell. Kincardine (1629-80) was a royalist who shared the Dutch exile of Charles II, during which he married a Dutch heiress, and was later rewarded by being appointed a Privy Councillor, a Commissioner of the Treasury and a Lord of Session. Intellectual interests are shown by his being a foundation fellow of the Royal Society, and Gilbert Burnet describes him as 'the wisest and worthiest man that belonged to his country'.[14] But there is no indication as to where or how he might have acquired the Asloan manuscript. Alexander Boswell of Auchinleck, Senator of the College of Justice, did take an interest in the manuscripts in his library. In 1731 he wrote notes on the old laws of Scotland in a manuscript of them (now NLS, Adv. MS. 25.4.14). In 1740 he wrote his name in the volume of English romances which four years later he presented to the Advocates' Library and which ever since has been known as the Auchinleck manuscript (NLS, Adv. MS. 19.2.1). For the Asloan manuscript, as well as signing it in March, 1730 (f.i), he prepared the second contents-list (f.ii) and foliated the volume; also, in the journal of his better-known son James we have a pleasant picture of him in old age reading part of it, which incidentally tells us the provenance: 'I had read with my father an old Scots chronicle in a manuscript collection which belonged to Lord Kincardine, his grandfather. It was curious reading and improved me in the habit of reading old writing.'[15]

The manuscript remained in the Boswell family till 1966, but not without adventures. Sir Alexander Boswell, 1st Bart., grandson of Lord Auchinleck, was also interested in at least some of the contents. It was he who had the manuscript bound by Abram Thomson in or about 1812 (above II). At his own Auchinleck Press he printed the text of items xii (*bis*) and xvi in 1818. He lent this and other manuscripts to the distinguished record scholar Thomas Thomson, who edited item xviii, and from whom after Sir Alexander's death in 1822 they were reclaimed by James A. Maconochie, advocate, one of the trustees of his son. However,

[14] *History of My Own Time* (1724-34), i, 166.

[15] For 28 September 1776, *Boswell in Extremes 1776-1778*, ed. C. McC. Weis & F. A. Pottle (1971), 34.

Maconochie apparently did not return them to Auchinleck, but retained them among his own books. He died in 1845, and his library was sold by Peter S. Fraser, bookseller in Edinburgh. But no manuscripts were disposed of at this time; and in 1867 Fraser sold the Asloan manuscript privately to another bookseller, William Paterson, in whose possession it still was in 1876.[16] Soon after, however, it was, by what means is not clear, restored to the Boswell family. On 29 June 1882 Jessie Jane, Lady Boswell (widow of the 2nd Bart.) gave it to her son-in-law Richard W. Talbot, who recorded this on f.i of the manuscript. His first wife was Emily Harriette Boswell, the 2nd Bart.'s second daughter and co-heir, who died in 1898. Talbot, having succeeded in 1883 as 2nd Baron Talbot de Malahide (in the United Kingdom peerage, also 5th Baron Talbot of Malahide in the Irish peerage), died on 4 March 1921. The signature of his son, James Boswell Talbot, 3rd and 6th Baron, dated March 1921, is also on f.i. On his death without issue in 1948 the title went to a cousin, while the Asloan manuscript was left to his wife. She deposited it on loan in the British Museum for several years and in 1966 sold it to the National Library of Scotland.

---

[16] This is an outline summary of the complex series of events which are fully narrated in David Laing, *PSAS*, xii (1878), 72-87, and in 'Minutes of the evidence adduced to the House of Lords in the claim of Sir Frederic John William Johnstone, Bart., to the Earldom of Annandale, 21st July, 1876'; both are reprinted in T. G. S[tevenson]'s 'Introductory Notice' to the reprint of *The Auchinleck Chronicle*, ed. Thomas Thomson, (Edin., 1877).

THE CATHEDRAL CLERGY OF DUNKELD IN THE EARLY SIXTEENTH CENTURY[1]

Ian B. Cowan
with
Michael J. Yellowlees

Since a recent survey of Scottish material in the Vatican archives, much more is known about the organisation of the medieval church in Scotland in general and in the diocese of Dunkeld in particular.[2] The names of the clergy who served the cathedral in various capacities from the twelfth century until the Reformation in the mid-sixteenth can be established with some certainty and the identities of many of the diocesan clergy can also be ascertained for numerous parishes.[3] Their tenure of office and the bitter struggles which occasionally characterised their search for benefices are frequently documented, as are sometimes their educational qualifications and blood relationships with kings, magnates and commoners. Little, however, is known about their daily lives and how they measured up to their vocation as priests.

This is a fact which is common to all Scottish dioceses, with one exception, that of Dunkeld. In this case, here one of the canons, Alexander Myln,[4] not only wrote an account of the lives of the bishops of Dunkeld, but added to it a pen-picture of his fellow

---

[1] This paper was originally delivered at the AGM of the Society of Friends of Dunkeld Cathedral on 14 April 1988. Permission to reproduce it, in slightly amplified form, has kindly been granted by Mrs Anna Cowan and Mr J.J. Robertson, the literary executor of Professor Cowan. Thanks are also due to Michael Moss, Glasgow University Archivist, and to Professor Allan Macinnes for their help in uncovering it.

[2] A wealth of information is contained in the draft calendars of materials in the Vatican archives held by Glasgow University; see I.B. Cowan, 'The Vatican Archives: a report on pre-Reformation Scottish material', *SHR*, xlviii (1969), 227-42. A synopsis of the Scottish cases in the Manualia of the Sacra Romana Rota, which includes 28 cases from Dunkeld between 1464 and 1560, is currently being prepared for publication by Mr J.J. Robertson.

[3] For the cathedral dignitaries, see Watt, *Fasti*, 93-126. There has been no study of the Dunkeld Cathedral clergy in the first half of the sixteenth century, but lists of dignitaries, canons and chaplains in the Reformation period are contained in M.J. Yellowlees, 'Dunkeld and the Reformation' (Edinburgh University Ph.D., 1990), 339-55.

[4] *DNB*, xiv, 2-3; *Camb. Reg.*, pp.lxxxviii-xcvi; *DSCHT*, 616.

canons and their deputies—the vicars choral—shortly after the death of Bishop George Brown in January 1515.[5] Amongst Brown's achievements Myln listed the refurbishment of the cathedral and the construction of the palace on Loch Clunie, the bridge over the Tay and St George's Hospital. The hospital was restored following the discovery in an old diocesan register of a forgotten hospital prebend from the lands of Ferdischaw. These revenues combined with those of Logiebride to provide a hospital with a master, who was responsible for seven poor folk. Myln enjoyed a particularly close relationship with Brown, attending him on his death-bed and then acting as his executor.[6]

Who were these clergy and how did they fit into the daily life of the cathedral? First and foremost, it should be understood that the bishop had no formal authority within a church which at first glance might appear to be his rightful charge. Instead, he could officiate only as a simple member of a chapter which constituted the ruling of the body of the cathedral in both spiritual and temporal matters. Even this concession was not universal: although the bishop of Dunkeld was accepted as a member of the chapter the archbishop of Glasgow was effectively debarred from such a position. Nevertheless at Dunkeld, as elsewhere, the dean held pre-eminence.[7]

The dean, as head of the chapter which constituted the clergy of the cathedral, was assisted by various other dignitaries—the chanter or precentor who was responsible for the song school and the cathedral services; the chancellor who looked after the cathedral's library as well as its writing house or chancery; and the treasurer who was custodian of the cathedral's jewels and precious objects, which at Dunkeld included the famous Columban relics reputedly removed to Ireland or the Western Isles at the Reformation. To these four principal persons could be added the archdeacon, the 'eyes and ears of the bishop' who was responsible for discipline among the diocesan clergy, and also a varying number of canons including a sub-dean and sub-chanter; these numbered seventeen in all at Dunkeld and as a body were

[5] A. Myln, *Vitae Dunkeldensis Ecclesiae Episcoporum ... ad annum MDXV* (Bann. Club, 1823; later edition, 1831). The period covering George Brown's episcopate is translated in *Dunkeld Rentale* (SHS, 1915).

[6] *Dunkeld Rentale*, 314-15, 318-20.

[7] As well as the dean there were four rural deans established in the late fifteenth and early sixteenth centuries to oversee discipline in the various parts of the diocese: *Dunkeld Rentale*, 304; Watt, *Fasti*, 102-06, 122-4.

responsible for the services of the cathedral, the election, in theory, of new bishops and decisions in chapter affecting the day-to-day running of the church. Of these duties, only the daily services committed the canons to residence, which, with the exception of the dean, did not statutorily exceed three months per year. Even this limitation could be overcome by the use of deputies, known as vicars-choral.[8]

If, for the most of the medieval period these officers and their deputies are shadowy figures not only at Dunkeld, but in all other Scottish dioceses, this veil lifts for a moment in Myln's account of his colleagues. Of the dean, George Hepburn, he writes that he exercised his office and did not leave the church of Dunkeld. One suspects that he is speaking of the statutory six-month residence expected from the president of the chapter, for Myln records that on every day of his residence he appeared devoutly among his brethren at high mass; at Lent he even presented himself for compline. Christian charity was also among Hepburn's virtues for besides daily alms, he provided each week a boll of meal for certain decrepit poor folk in the city. When there was a dearth in the country he ordered porridge to be supplied every day, whether he was present or not, to the poor who came for it, to each in good measure.[9] Hepburn was also responsible for the establishment of a foundation for a number of Dominican students, whose success was later applauded by the chapter.[10]

The precentor, James Fenton, was deemed to be no less virtuous, for he gave to the church a white silk cope and founded two chaplainries in the parish church of Perth. Despite Myln's avowal that he too resided at Dunkeld unless the bishop ordered otherwise, Perth appears to have been the fulcrum for his activities. There he maintained a large household where 'he furnished the necessaries of life to honest men of his kin'—an interesting insight not only to social provision in medieval Scotland, but also a commentary on how many youths were prepared for service in the church. Nevertheless, Fenton was equally at home in Dunkeld where he refurbished a house on the banks of the Tay as his manse while at the same time adorning the canons' cloister.[11]

---

[8] J. Dowden, *The Medieval Church in Scotland* (Glasgow, 1910), 74-5.
[9] *Dunkeld Rentale*, 320-22; Watt, *Fasti*, 105.
[10] W. Moir Bryce, *The Blackfriars of Edinburgh* (Edinburgh, 1911), 28.
[11] *Dunkeld Rentale*, 322-3; Watt, *Fasti*, 109.

The chancellor, George Brown, was a cousin of the bishop. Few Scottish cathedral chapters lacked some of the current bishop's relations; no one would have expected otherwise. He also founded a conventional chaplainry, although on this occasion one with an educational bias as the holder was expected to rule a grammar school which would supply the church with youths instructed in grammar.[12] His presence in the diocese must, however, be considered more doubtful for whereas the precentor had utilised his administrative talents as chamberlain of the bishop of Dunkeld,[13] Brown's merits led for a time to his appointment as chamberlain of the archbishop of St. Andrews.[14]

Fewer skills appear to have been found in the treasurer Walter Small. Though described as 'the best penman of his time' in every style of writing, Small's concern appears to have been more orientated towards converting his manse, which he inherited as 'an old-fashioned, Highland manse' into the best available, after that of the dean.[15] Similar secular traits and nepotism were displayed by the archdeacon, George Ferne, Bishop George Brown's nephew; although he failed to found a chaplaincy, he did present a cope to the church and repair and refurbish his manse.[16]

Of the simple canons, two held offices of some distinction. David Abercrombie was sub-dean, while another kinsman of the bishop, David Balbirnie, acted as sub-chanter. Even Myln can find little to say in the latter's favour, although he is described as 'very entertaining company'.[17] The sub-dean, on the other hand, was obviously a trained lawyer who was appointed commissary general in one of the bishop's courts and who, it is alleged, 'effectually punished the excesses and crimes of the Highland folk'.[18]

Of the other simple canons, who were maintained by prebends or livings, some based on the revenues of parish churches and others on the rents of lands, all in one way or another demonstrate the continuing strengths of the medieval church at a time when some historians allege that Reformation was but a stone's-

---

12 *Dunkeld Rentale*, 323; *RMS*, ii, 3482.

13 The chamberlain was generally a layman but during the sixteenth century clerical appointees became more common. He enjoyed a special position within the bishops's household as his chief adviser. *Dunkeld Rentale*, 322.

14 *Dunkeld Rentale*, 18.

15 ibid., 323-4; Watt, *Fasti*, 114.

16 *Dunkeld Rentale*, 324; Watt, *Fasti*, 121.

17 *Dunkeld Rentale*, 324-5; Watt, *Fasti*, 118.

18 *Dunkeld Rentale*, 324; Watt, *Fasti*, 117.

throw away. What traits characterised these canons? Clearly, many were trained canon lawyers, who directed their talents in this direction rather than to purely spiritual duties. Among these can be found canons who served as official-principal of St. Andrews, commissary of the official principal of St. Andrews, commissary general of Dunkeld and official of Dunkeld; the latter, Walter Brown, was Myln's mentor for three years, during which time the author himself had held the office of clerk and notary in his court.[19] Trained lawyers, one of whom is described as an excellent textualist, were clearly to the forefront amongst the canons, who must have been frequently absent from the cathedral on their legal duties. A number of canons were also noted for their ability to speak Gaelic. The use of the local idiom was encouraged by Bishop Brown who, as well as appointing Gaelic-speaking canons, arranged for Gaelic-speaking friars to preach and hear confession in the Highland parts of the diocese.[20]

Devotion, nevertheless, was not entirely lacking and the foundation of chaplaincies and gifts to the church were commonplace. Among gifts made to the church of Dunkeld were silver gilt chalices, silver cruets and a paten with a representation of the cathedral's patron, St Columba. A cope of blue damask, a candlestick of brass and altar coverings all added to the richness of the cathedral furnishings.[21] Chaplaincies were not only founded at Dunkeld, but further afield at Loch Clunie, Edinburgh, Perth, Tullilum and St. Andrews.[22] In other ways too, many of the canons added to the riches of the church.[23] One at least, the prebendary of Ferdischaw, excelled in music and in 'the playing of organs'. Others showed their devotion by their care for the poor, one of the canons at least being generous with both money and food. Self-comfort, however, was equally to the fore. Most of the canons

---

[19] *Dunkeld Rentale*, 326-7; Watt, *Fasti*, 125.

[20] *Dunkeld Rentale*, 304, 313. Bishop Brown's encouragement of Gaelic is dealt with more fully in J. MacQueen, 'Alexander Myln, Bishop George Brown and the chapter of Dunkeld', in *Humanism and Reform: The Church in Europe, England and Scotland, 1400-1643*, ed. J. Kirk (Oxford, 1991). It is interesting to note that even 300 years after Myln's time the General Assembly was still grappling with the same linguistic and cultural problems, namely that it was not possible to have a 'Highland mouth without a Highland tongue'. *New Statistical Account*, x, 1010; NRA, Atholl Manuscripts 224, bdle 1227.

[21] *Dunkeld Rentale*, 314.

[22] ibid., 212, 214, 216, 239, 270, 311, 328; *HMC Athole* (1891), vii, 710-11.

[23] Myln's account of his fellow canons is given in *Dunkeld Rentale*, 325-9.

are praised for having rebuilt or repaired their manses[24] and, if true, the canons' manses and the town of Dunkeld itself must have taken on a radically new appearance in the early sixteenth century.[25] Many of these manses housed kinsmen of the canons. One prebendary, although his income was not large, maintained a number of friends in his household. He was, it is noted, 'most cheerful company at the board'. Life was not an eternal round of prayer for yet another canon 'loved to take his cheer and honest wit and merriment', while another of his fellow canons kept open house in Highland fashion when in residence. That is not to say that the canons did not take their duties seriously. The prebendary of Forgandenny 'often rose in the middle of the night to perform the office of Lauds, celebrated mass daily when morning began, and after hearing high mass later, devoted the rest of the day to judicial work, study and reading in the law and theology'. At least one other, the prebendary of Alyth, who (it is admitted) by nature possessed a quick temper, had expressed his piety by going on pilgrimage to Rome, perhaps in atonement for the strict discipline which he had exercised at home where, it is recorded, he had rooted out 'abominable sins in Atholl and Drumalbane'.[26] Clearly, many of the canons were men of this world and were not entirely pre-occupied with the next. Nevertheless, the overall impression of the canons of Dunkeld at this point of time is of a community who, if not unmindful of creature comforts, fulfilled their obligations to church and society to the best of their ability.

Whatever their concern to meet these obligations, it is nevertheless clear that it was their deputies who, on very slender stipends, bore what Myln describes as the 'burden and heat of the day'.[27] In consequence, they too required secondary occupations, if at a somewhat more lowly grade than that enjoyed by the canons. Once again legal duties prevailed. Two vicars choral were

---

[24] Within a few decades of the Reformation many of the manses were again in a state of disrepair or had been sold or excambioned. *RMS*, v, 70.

[25] Some impression of the sixteenth-century town and cathedral may be gained from John Slezer's drawings in *Theatrum Scotiae*; see K. Cavers, *A Vision of Scotland. The Nation Observed by John Slezer, 1617 to 1717* (HMSO, 1993), 41. The location of many of the manses can be found on a plan of Dunkeld entitled 'Sites of the old and new mansion houses of Dunkeld belonging to the Atholl family, 1832': SRO, RHP 10560.

[26] *Dunkeld Rentale*,, 326-7, 328-9.

[27] ibid., 329.

advocates in the consistorial court, one acted as a notary, while another was a consistorial clerk. Most apparently had been trained in canon law. Naturally, however, their professional vocation lay in the field of music. Assessments of their ability in this aspect of their careers include descriptions of individual vicars choral as 'a pillar of the choristers and a sedulous observer of canonical hours', 'a chorister steady in the chant—very expert in the ordinary', and of another who was 'steady and correct in all manner of chanting and a pillar of the choir'. Yet another was 'highly trained in the theory of music as well as in the art of singing'. Choral singing at Dunkeld was obviously of an exceptionally high standard and the cathedral was well-known for its antiphonary in honour of the Blessed Virgin Mary with its polyphonic settings for the ordinary of the mass and anthems.[28]

Like their *alter egos*, the vicars choral in other respects were not unmindful of their duties. Patrick Gardiner, one of the chaplains of Abernyte, provided clothing, furniture and food for the poor, but family obligations naturally prevailed. Two vicars tended their mothers, while another, Alexander Richardson, maintained a household in which he brought up promising boys of his kin—another confirmation of how children were prepared for service in the church, some entering religious houses, others the priesthood and some prepared for choral service. Some vicars apparently had their own houses, although some may have lodged with the canon for whom they deputised. Do-it-yourself repairs were not unknown even in the sixteenth century and William Lacock worked very hard out of doors, 'especially at repairs to the houses of the founders of his chaplaincy'. All appear to have been literate, one writing in a very good style, while yet another, as might be expected in the diocese of Dunkeld, had a 'knowledge of the Irish tongue'.[29] If less qualified than the members of the chapter, the vicars choral clearly ran them a close second.

This unique picture of a Scottish cathedral, which had been revived in the twelfth century and renovated early in the fourteenth century, may be viewed as an act of *pietas*. It undoubtedly does not tell the entire truth, but even within these agreed limits it does illustrate that the cathedral of Dunkeld at this period was

---

[28] ibid., 329-31; C.R. Borland, *A Descriptive Catalogue of Western Medieval Manuscripts in Edinburgh University Library* (Edinburgh, 1916), 113; J. Purser, *Scotland's Music* (Edinburgh, 1992), 83-4.

[29] *Dunkeld Rentale*, 330.

still a live and vibrant institution.[30] This vibrancy, which may later have mellowed into complacency, was temporarily rekindled in the decade following the Reformation. The opposition of Bishop Robert Crichton and his largely orthodox Catholic chapter, however, was insufficient to stem the tide of Protestantism. Within little more than a decade after 1560 the new Kirk had established an adequate ministry within much of the diocese and had deposed the bishop and most of his dignitaries.[31] The benefices pertaining to the cathedral were appropriated by the crown or local nobles, including those of the choristers, which became 'vakand by ressoun the singing of the said priestis ceassis'.[32] Yet, viewed from the early decades of the sixteenth century, the cataclysm of the Reformation, even within fifty years of its attainment, would have seemed to Myln and his fellow canons not only unthinkable, but also unattainable.

---

[30] Cowan & Easson, *Religious Houses*, 205-06.

[31] J. Kirk, *Patterns of Reform: Continuity and Change in the Reformation Kirk* (Edinburgh, 1989), 328. M.J. Yellowlees, 'The ecclesiastical establishment of the diocese of Dunkeld at the Reformation, *IR*, xxxvi (1985), 74-85; idem, 'Dunkeld and the Reformation', 278-9.

[32] *RSS*, vi, 955.

THE INVENTION OF TRADITION, HIGHLAND-STYLE

William Gillies

In the sixteenth century the house of Argyll had a foot in two worlds, being on the one hand deeply involved in the court and administrative life of the Scottish realm, and at the same time playing a fully integrated part in the world of Gaelic politics in Ireland and Scotland.[1] The Gaelic dimension of the Campbells in time withered away at the highest levels in terms of their own family aspirations, and likewise became marginalised in the Gaelic consciousness. Yet their policies continued to be a prime determinant of developments over a great part of the Highlands while, at less exalted levels, Campbell lairds and their families continued a life-style comparable to that of other members of the minor gentry of the Highlands. This, however, was not yet the case in the sixteenth or earlier seventeenth centuries, when we know the house of Argyll itself to have actively cultivated Gaelic learning and culture, in keeping with the political image and ambitions of the family.[2] This study is concerned with genealogy, an important aristocratic concern at any time; more particularly, with the way in which claims regarding family origins formed a currency whereby contemporary political preoccupations and ambitions could be expressed. The matter to be discussed forms a relatively clear-cut episode within the not uncomplicated story of Campbell origins.[3]

In the medieval Gaelic world a family's status could be measured in terms of the alliances they could command, their expectations as regards marriage ties, or the numbers and standing of those who were their followers. It might also be expressed in genealogical terms, in accordance with a well-articulated and widely-understood dialectic developed over the centuries by the Gaelic literati. For a variety of reasons the learned genealogies of the Campbells are particularly instructive in this respect.[4] Both the Campbells' involvement in Scottish affairs as a whole and the

---

[1] J. Dawson, 'The fifth earl of Argyll, Gaelic lordship and political power in sixteenth-century Scotland', *SHR*, lxvii (1988), 1-27.

[2] W. Gillies, 'Some aspects of Campbell history', *TGSI*, l (1976-8), 256-95.

[3] W.D.H. Sellar, 'The earliest Campbells—Norman, Briton or Gael?', *Scot. Stud.*, xvii (1977), 109-25.

[4] Gillies, 'Some aspects', 280-85.

tendency for Gaelic genealogical learning and Scottish historiography to become interactive in the sixteenth century make an investigation of this area a pertinent addition to the more familiar themes of the Scottish Renaissance.[5]

In the dialectic of the learned Gaelic poets and historians, eminence was expressed in terms of nearness to the senior line of Milesian invaders who, in the *Leabhar Gabhála Eireann* (the pseudo-historical 'Book of the Conquest of Ireland'), were supposed to have established Gaelic rule in Ireland and held the High Kingship of Ireland in the prehistoric period.[6] It is worth noting that this pseudo-historical edifice was dynamic in the sense that it was continually being worked over and revised in detail by the medieval historians: to reconcile, for example, the inconsistencies which kept springing up between the tenets of the general theory and the genealogical claims of individual families and kindreds. In particular, it could respond to fluctuations in family fame and fortune; for a family pedigree could be 'unplugged' from its existing connection within the schema and plugged in again via a different connection to reflect a material change in the status of the family in question. Thus the latest learned Irish sources showed the Campbells as descended from a Milesian ancestor—from Lugaid, son of Ith, son of Míl of Spain, who was considerably more of an 'establishment' figure than the ancestors whose claims are discussed below. This promotion reflected the Irish learned poets' and historians' acceptance of the Campbells as a family worth taking seriously in the last century before the collapse of the medieval Gaelic polity.[7]

This pragmatic flexibility was achieved in various ways. For instance, it could be attained by creating extra younger sons or brothers at key points within the Milesian framework, as hooks on which to hang additional family lines. Such procedures are not confined, of course, to the medieval exponents of the Milesian myth. They have been part of the stock-in-trade of creative genealogists from biblical and classical times down to the present

[5] W.D.H. Sellar, 'Highland family origins—pedigree making and pedigree faking', in *The Middle Ages in the Highlands*, ed. L. Maclean of Dochgarroch (Inverness, 1981), 103-16.

[6] R.M. Scowcroft, '*Leabhar Gabhála*—part I: the growth of the text', *Eriu*, xxxviii (1987), 81-142; and idem, '*Leabhar Gabhála*—part II: the growth of the tradition', *Eriu*, xxxix (1988), 1-66.

[7] See Geoffrey Keating's *History of Ireland* (vol. i, ed. D. Comyn; vols. ii-iv, ed. P.S. Dinneen, Irish Texts Society, 1902-14), ii, 285, 383. In the former reference *Mac Ailín* is for *Mac Cailín.*

day. But they flourished spectacularly in the Gaelic context on account of the scale of the edifice and the multitude of vested interests in it. An alternative procedure, more strictly applicable to the Gaelic model, was available in the case of families which had sprung up—as it were from nowhere—in relatively recent times. This involved assigning them ancestors from amongst the invaders who had peopled Ireland in the period before the coming of the Milesian Gaels. Thus, for instance, the families known to the Irish genealogists as *Breatnaigh Eireann* ('The Britons of Ireland') were said to derive from the stock of Nemed (later spelling Neimheadh), i.e. from surviving members of an antediluvian colony which had been driven out of Ireland by the Fomorians (who in their turn were driven out by the Tuatha Dé Danann, who in their turn were subjugated by the Milesians). The genealogists had recourse to the fiction that they had fled into exile in Britain, whence they were deemed to have 'returned' to Ireland in historical times. This segment of Irish pseudo-history was of relevance when the Campbells were first adjudged suitable to be connected up with the genealogical 'system'; for some of the Nemedian exiles were deemed to have stayed on in Britain, and to have had issue there.[8]

If the genealogical origins claimed over the centuries for the house of Argyll are gathered together, a first impression can only be one of astonishment at the multiplicity of explanations offered. The number of distinct traditions as to their origins is indeed great, and a considerable degree of variation remains even when a chronological framework has been established for the rise and fall of the principal orthodoxies. This study is concerned solely with the learned Gaelic tradition: as opposed, on the one hand, to the popular Gaelic tradition and, on the other hand, to the non-Gaelic antiquarian tradition which sprang up in the seventeenth century.[9] Even within this more limited sphere of activity, there is evidence for a considerable degree of variation. The particular concern here is with a group of genealogies whose date of composition corresponded to the highest level of prestige attained by

[8] W. Gillies, 'The "British" genealogy of the Campbells', forthcoming in *Celtica*, xxiii (1994).

[9] Sellar, 'Earliest Campbells', 112 ff; cf. also W. Gillies, 'Heroes and ancestors', in *The Heroic Process*, ed. B. Almqvist, S. O Catháin and P. O hEalaí (Dublin, 1987), 57-74. The earlier or alternative traditions occurring within the learned tradition, which are equally excluded from the present discussion, are those designated *MS 1467* and *MacFirbis* by Sellar (117 ff).

the Campbells in the Gaelic world. Sandwiched between an earlier, less elaborated group of learned genealogies and a succeeding group which begins to show the influence of popular and exotic concerns, this group seems to reflect the activities of the MacEwen professional poets and historians to the earls of Argyll, and to have had its vogue during the ascendancy of this learned family, in the sixteenth and seventeenth centuries.[10]

The version of the Campbell genealogy under discussion occurs in several incomplete or imperfect sources, from which it is possible to deduce its complete form with a fairly high degree of confidence. It is proposed to begin by setting it out in the form of an edition based on the extant sources, and then to proceed to a discussion of those features of its contents and construction which are of interest for the mentality and materials of the Gaelic professional poets during the last centuries of the classical early modern period.[11]

The sources, in chronological order of compilation, are as follows:

(1) The copy of the lost NLS MS. 72.1.32 (i.e. Kilbride XXXII: see D. MacKinnon, *A Descriptive Catalogue of Gaelic Manuscripts* (Edinburgh, 1912), 217-21), printed by W.F. Skene in *Collectanea de Rebus Albanicis* (Edinburgh, 1847), 360 (cf. idem, *Celtic Scotland* (2nd edn., Edinburgh, 1888-90), iii, 458). The original was apparently compiled during the earldom of Gilleasbuig, 4th earl of Argyll, with whom the genealogy ends, between 1530 and 1558. The text printed by Skene in *Collectanea* suffers from some obvious misreadings, but the genealogy he printed in *Celtic Scotland* is a composite, and the earlier printing is hence preferred for present purposes.[12] It is designated K, and the lost original *K.

(2) NLS MS. 72.1.36, written in 1690-91, contains several pieces of syllabic verse to seventeenth-century earls of Argyll, including the poem *Triath na nGaoidheal Giolla-easbuig* ('Gilleasbuig is the prince of the Gaels'), addressed to the 8th earl.[13] This poem contains at

---

[10] On the MacEwens, see A. Matheson, 'Bishop Carswell', *TGSI*, xlii (1953-9), 182-205 (200-03).

[11] W. Gillies, 'Gaelic: the classical tradition', in *The History of Scottish Literature, Vol. I (Origins to 1660)*, ed. R.D.S. Jack (Aberdeen, 1988), 245-62.

[12] Sellar, 'Family Origins', 104 ff.

[13] W.J. Watson (ed.), 'Unpublished Gaelic poetry—IV., V.', *SGS*, iii (1931), 139-59 (see 142-51).

stt. 26-32 a summary of the descent of the house of Argyll from Adam which clearly belongs with the Kilbride version. Although it only mentions a handful of names from our section, it provides some valuable name-forms and generation gaps. Since the poem contains a pretty certain allusion to the 8th earl's elevation to the rank of marquis,[14] its composition may be dated between 1641 and 1661; shortly after the former date, one suspects. The genealogical section of the extant poem is designated W hereafter, and the full genealogy that lies behind it *W.

(3) NLS MS. 72.2.2, a collection of pieces of diverse origin, includes a version of the Campbell genealogy written in a late seventeenth- or early eighteenth-century hand. The latest name in the genealogy is that of Gilleasbuig, 9th earl, who was 'Mac Cailein' from 1661 to 1685, and it was presumably written between those years.[15] This source is designated N.

(4) MacLagan MS. 196 (in GUL) contains a Campbell genealogy which, although written by James MacLagan himself, claims to be *o laimh Dho[nnchaidh Ui] Mhuirghesain* ('from the hand of D[uncan] O Muirgheasain')—a valuable reference in that it connects the pedigree with one of the families of the Highland literati, if not that of the MacEwens themselves. The Donnchadh mentioned here may have been the 'Duncan McIldonich, MacLeod's Irish poet' who received 20 merks 'of gratuity allow'd him after MacLeod's decease ... for an Epitaph made upon him' in 1706.[16] At all events, this genealogy terminates, like N, to which it is closely related, with the 9th earl. It is here designated M.

None of these sources depends directly on another, and there are some inconsistencies in their testimony. Nevertheless, they

[14] *Os tú as uaisle don fhuil Bhreatnuigh / tar bhéas iarla d'ardaigh sdair.* 'Since you are the noblest of British blood, whom history has exalted beyond the rank of earl ...' (st. 35*ab*).

[15] The genealogy, which occurs at p.40 of the MS, was printed in part by Watson, 'Unpublished Gaelic poetry', 140.

[16] Quoted from A. Morrison, 'The Contullich papers, 1706-20', *TGSI,* xliv (1964-6), 310-48 (see 321); cf. W. Matheson, *The Blind Harper* (Edinburgh, 1970), p. xlviii, and N.M. Bristol, 'The O'Muirgheasain bardic family', *Notes & Queries of the Society of West Highland and Island Historical Research,* vi (1978), 3-7. That an exemplar in Gaelic script lies behind MacLagan's version is suggested by the reading *Fearghga* (in the section immediately above the 'British' section) which must surely be a misreading of *Fearghus*a, i.e. with the Gaelic *us*-contraction (written 'ȝ')being taken as a *g* by someone who was not conversant with Gaelic scribal practices.

may fairly claim to be grouped together when compared with other phases of genealogical activity by the Campbells or on their behalf. They are to be regarded as giving the 'authorised version' of the Campbells' own poet-historians in the sixteenth and seventeenth centuries, and, by extension, the official doctrine about ultimate Campbell origins which was to be disseminated by the learned poets as a professional caste.[17] Given that the main thrust of Campbell genealogical claims, already established before the sixteenth century, was of descent from King Arthur and inheritance of the 'leadership of the Britons' (by contrast with the MacDonalds' Dalriadic and Milesian claims and the MacLeods' claims to inherit a Norse title to supremacy), the main innovation of the group presently under consideration was the elaboration of the pedigree from King Arthur, who is already present in the earliest genealogy extant,[18] up to the point at which it could be tied into the framework of *Leabhar Gabhála*. The junction point was that already mentioned in the case of the 'Britons of Ireland', the eponymous Briotan son of Fergus Red-side, son of Neimheadh. Having filled in that gap, the Campbell genealogists were able to draw on established doctrine to fill in the rest of the genealogy, from Briotan up to 'Adam son of God'.[19]

Here, then, is the reconstructed genealogy from Arthur up to the eponymous Briotan son of Fearghus Leithdearg. In the left-hand column are given in regular spellings (i.e. normalised to a classical early modern Irish standard) the genealogy as it may be supposed to have been in *K (the lost original of K, as previously explained). In the right-hand column are given significant variants from K, W, M and N.

(m.) Artú(i)r	Artuir (Artair *N*) an bhuird chruinn *MN(W)* m. Iomhair *add. MN*
m. Ambróis	Ambhrois *W*, Ambhroish *M*
m. Constaintín	Considin *K*
m. Aingeil (?)	Amgcel *K*, Aincheil *MN*

[17] The truncated version of the Campbell genealogy found in the Black Book of Clanranald (p. 176; printed in A. Cameron, *Reliquiae Celticae* (Inverness, 1892-4), ii, 301) reflects lack of sympathy (given the Black Book's MacDonald orientation), lack of interest (given the decline of the 'Gaelic dimension' of the Clan Campbell by the end of the seventeenth century), or a combination of these factors.

[18] i.e. 'MS 1467' (NLS Gaelic MS 72.1.1), which refers to 'Arthur son of Uther' (*mac Uibuir* MS) and calls him 'King of the world, without doubt'.

[19] Printed by Watson, 'Unpublished Gaelic poetry', 140.

m. Thoísigh (?)	Toisid *K*
m. Cormaic (?)	Conmuic *K*, Chomhruisg *M*, Comhruirg *N*
m. Constaintín	Considin *K*
m. Artúir na Láimhe	*sic MN*; na l... *K*
m. Láimhfhinn (?)	Larnailin *K*, Laimhlin *MN*
m. Thoísigh (?)	Toisid *K*
m. Artúir Láimhdheirg	Arar *W*
m. Bhéinne Briot	*sic MN*; Benbriot *K*
m. Artúir	
m. Alldóid (?)	Allairdaid *K*, Allaroid *M*, alla roid *N*
m. Artúir [...]	Artuir .h.e. *K*, Artuir Fhuith Eaglui[..] *M*, Artuir fhat eaglaisi *N*
m. Lámhdhóid	Laimh roid *M*
m. Fhionnlogha	Fionlug *K*
m. Artúir Oig	
m. Fhir Mhara	
m. Artúir Mhóir	
m. Bhéinne Briot	Banebriot *K*
m. Bhriotuis	Briotus *K*, Bhriotain *M*
m. Bhriotain a quo Breatnaigh	o bhfuilid (bhuilid *M*) *MN*; Braodn (*sic*) *K*, Breatanaich *M*

It will be noted that there is relatively little variation as to the order and number of the generations above the latest Arthur—much less than occurs in the proto-historical section of the Campbell genealogy, for example.[20] This gives reason to believe that the surviving versions of our section are quite close to the form in which it was created. On the other hand, there are some divergences as to the precise forms indicated, and also some suggestions of common errors. The data available do not permit the reconstruction of a definitive stemma, but it will be sufficient for present purposes to record the impression that the surviving sources derive from a copy of the original composition, and that the later witnesses, M and N, derive from a further copy, now lost, which incorporated some editorial reworking. (This conclusion is reinforced by consideration of the other sections of the genealogy.) While the existence of this background of textual

[20] The addition by M and N of *mhic Iomhair* between the latest Arthur and 'Ambrós' is the only serious divergence of this sort. The implications of this omission will be discussed in a moment.

transmission must be borne in mind, it need not act as a deterrent as regards the present enquiry. In fact, it is possible to explain the principles of construction of this section of the genealogy in quite a detailed way. There are a handful of difficulties, but they can be whittled down to the point at which the scheme shows through beyond doubt.

In order to understand the construction of this section of the genealogy, a start may be made by recognising that its author's fundamental motive was to fill a void.[21] In the chronological scheme of the medieval Irish antiquarians, the invasion of Ireland by Neimheadh and his followers, their subsequent expulsion by the Fomorians and the colonisation of parts of Britain by Briotan were set in remote prehistoric times; whereas on any reckoning one had to cope with the 'fact' that King Arthur had flourished at the end of the Roman period within the Christian era. The author would seem to have proceeded in the first instance from two basic beliefs: the bald assumption that his patrons were 'British', and the strategic relevance of the name 'Arthur'. He then constructed the genealogy by a mixture of multiplication (involving replication or cloning of the basic data) and addition (involving importation of fresh data by association). In the following presentation the discernible categories are analysed in sequence; it is not pretended that the pedigree-maker's thought-processes have been replicated in detail.

(1) When noting the Arthurs who recur every few generations in the section under review it is necessary to recall the name-giving habits of Gaelic families in later times. It would have been perfectly natural for a Campbell pedigree-maker used to the Colins and Archibalds of the Early Modern period to attribute similar conservatism to the era he was creating. (The same thing can be seen happening in the later fictions of Campbell pre-history, where Duibhne is the strategic name that gives rise to a whole series of characters.) Similarly, the assignment of the epithets *mór* and *óg* to the first two Colins of the 'historical' period is an example of a familiar tendency amongst the Highland shen-nachies to assign the epithet *mór* '(the) Great' to the eponymous ancestor and *óg* '(the) Young(er)' to the next bearer of the

[21] Compare the later elaboration, following very similar principles, of the period from 'King Arthur' down to the earliest historical Campbells, as detailed by Sellar, 'Earliest Campbells'.

numinous name. This practice was naturally exploited when it came to differentiating the multiplicity of Arthurs. For the rest, one needed a sprinkling of appropriate-sounding epithets to break the monotony implicit in further replications of the strategic name, and to impart an air of authenticity to the genealogy. One needs to look no further than the proliferation of epithets attaching to the Colins and Archibalds of later times to exemplify the practice of recording (and where necessary creating) epithets in order to distinguish characters and provide the more shadowy figures with an element of personality. This explains the presence of 'Arthur the Younger' and 'Arthur the Great' and suggests the psychology underlying the other Arthurs. They are: 'Arthur of the Hand' (*A. na láimhe*), 'Arthur Red-hand' (*A. láimhdhearg*), one Arthur with an opaque and perhaps textually corrupt epithet (*A. f[...] e[...]*), and one plain Arthur (the son of Alldóid), whose distinguishing feature is perhaps his unique lack of an epithet.[22]

(2) Intermingled with the Arthurs are names evocative of the 'British' connection, which had its own eponyms to contribute. While Briotán (i.e. Briotán Máel, son of Fearghus Leithdearg) was an obvious recruit to the genealogy, he was not the only eponym of the Britons known to the medieval Gaelic literati, or even the

---

[22] The undifferentiated Arthur may not be original to the genealogy. While the appropriateness of the name *Alldóid* ('Mighty-fist') is supported by reasons to be given shortly, the MSS may suggest something else. Bearing in mind the association of Arthur in later Campbell tradition and in Gaelic Arthurian texts with a place called 'the Red Hall' (located at Dumbarton) one might speculate that the MS readings point to something like **Artu(i)r an Alla Ruaidh* ('A. of the Red Hall'). Admittedly, the Red Hall elsewhere involves *dearg* '(blood-)red' rather than *ruadh* '(russet-)red'; but the famous *Craobhruadh* 'Red-branch (Hall)' of the Ulster Cycle of tales could conceivably have exerted an influence. (On these matters, see W. Gillies, 'Arthur in Gaelic tradition. Part II: romances and early lore', *Cambridge Medieval Celtic Studies*, iii (1982), 49, 69.) Alternatively, but with the Dumbarton connection still in mind, it could be suggested that *Alla Cluaidh* 'of Dumbarton' might originally have been intended. (Compare Scottish Gaelic *mac (t)alla* 'echo' (literally 'son of a rock/hall') for the genitive singular form *alla* and for confusion between the old word for 'rock' and the loan-word *(h)alla/talla* based on English 'hall'.) There is also a difficulty about the style of the Arthur who is named as father of *Alldóid.* I cannot make much sense of the readings of M and N, except that they would appear to contain *eaglaise* 'of a church' while *K may have contained an abbreviated or contracted version of the same appellative. Conceivably, the MSS reflect a copyist's misreading of an original *scéithe glaise* 'of the green shield', and somehow echo the 'green shield' of the Brutus Greenshield (*viride scutum*) whose father Ebraucus founded Dumbarton in Geoffrey of Monmouth. (See *Historia Regum Britanniae,* ii, 7; cf. J.S.P. Tatlock, *The Legendary History of Britain* (London, 1950), 164.)

best supported one in medieval Gaelic writings. That honour went to Britus mac Isicoin (i.e. Brutus, son of Ascanius), who appears in such widely differing sources as the Irish version of the Nennian *Historia Brittonum,* in the Irish version of *Sex Aetates Mundi,* in the *Leabhar Gabhála* itself, and in the Scottish-oriented *Duan Albanach.*[23] Our pedigree-maker has simply availed himself of the duplication of eponyms and made one the son of the other. In the same frame of mind he has imported 'Béinne the Briton', a character from early Irish literature.[24] Béinne then receives two slots in the genealogy by a simple duplication.

(3) Arthur's immediate ancestry is usually given at the beginning of Arthurian romances in Gaelic. In these sources it standardly appears as 'Arthur, son of *Iobhar,* son of Ambrose, son of Constantine', where *Iobhar* corresponds in Gaelic tradition to Uther (Pendragon).[25] The genealogical sequence of these sources has clearly been founded on the regnal sequence in Geoffrey of Monmouth's *Historia Regum Britanniae.* There is a slight complication here, in that K and W, our two earlier witnesses, omit Iobhar, and make Arthur the son of Ambrós, while M and N have the significantly differing Iomhar as Arthur's father. Here it must be borne in mind that Iobhar was already present in the Campbell genealogy before our genealogist set to work: he appears in the early fifteenth-century pedigree contained in 'MS 1467', in the alternative sixteenth-century pedigree contained in the Book of Genealogies of the Irish genealogist MacFirbis, and in a genealogical reference in an early sixteenth-century bardic poem in the Book of the Dean of Lismore.[26] The reading of M and N, the later sources, may be explained as an attempt to square the genealogy with the more widely accepted tradition as to Arthur's paternity; a subsidiary aim may have been to provide a connection whereby the Clann Iomhair (MacIvers) of Glassary

[23] See D.N. Dumville, 'The textual history of "Lebor Bretnach": a preliminary study', *Eigse,* xvi (1975-6), 255-73, for the eleventh-century 'Irish Nennius', which seems to be the main intermediary by which subsequent Gaelic tradition became acquainted with Brutus.

[24] See Gillies, 'Arthur', 70-71.

[25] ibid., 50, 71-2.

[26] The testimony of *W may be inferred from statements in W: 'Arthur ... son of Ambrose' (stt. 10*a*, 19*ab*); cf. also the ten generations said to separate Arthur from Arar Láimhdhearg (st. 29). For 'MS 1467' and MacFirbis, see Sellar, 'Earliest Campbells', 117. For the poem in the Dean's Book, see W.J. Watson (ed.), *Scottish Verse from the Book of the Dean of Lismore* (Edinburgh, 1937), p.116, st. 22*d*, where we should read *artur vᶜ ewir* for Watson's '*artur vᶜ eriv (?)*'.

could be attached to the Campbell genealogy.[27] The problem is therefore to explain why Iobhar is absent in K and W. Was he deliberately omitted by the creator of our version of the genealogy, or inadvertently left out by a copyist who was followed by our sources? Since reference to Arthur's Round Table can in general be taken as a sign of indebtedness (direct or indirect) to Geoffrey of Monmouth, and since the poem upon which we depend for *W contains ample evidence for acceptance of the Round Table, it might be guessed that the creator of the pedigree must likewise have had access to the 'standard' Gaelic doctrine of the time. Moreover, he had no reason to shorten the pedigree; quite the reverse, in fact. It is therefore difficult to envisage an accidental omission at this juncture; yet it is difficult to suggest any reason why Iobhar should have been omitted deliberately. But at all events, the identification of *Historia Regum Britanniae* as the ultimate source of Ambrós and Constaintín is reasonably secure; their immediate provenance may have been a literary one.[28]

(4) With the remaining names it is necessary to proceed more cautiously. It is noteworthy that of the epithets attached to the Arthurs in the body of the genealogy the two transparent ones involve mention of a 'hand': *Artúr na láimhe* 'A. of the Hand' and *Artúr láimhdhearg* 'A. Red-hand'. It may be suggested that some traditional or antiquarian link between 'Arthur' and 'hand' was known to our pedigree-maker, and that it spurred him to include some more names involving 'hand'.[29] On this hypothesis, it should be possible to account for other names occurring in the genealogy and containing *lámh* 'hand' or *dóid* 'fist', i.e. *Láimhfhionn* 'White-hand(ed)' and *Alldóid* 'Mighty-fist' (if it is correct to extrapolate them from our sources) and *Lámhdhóid* 'Fist-hand' (if that is what is intended).

(5) The last-mentioned names belong to a class of 'utility' names which recur in various literary and genealogical sources in Gaelic literature, their common denominator being simply that

---

[27] For the MacIvers cf. *Highland Papers*, ii, 82; W.D.H. Sellar, 'Family origins in Cowal and Knapdale', *Scot. Stud.*, xv (1971), 21-37, and idem, 'Earliest Campbells', 115, 119.

[28] Cf. Gillies, 'Arthur', 50. The Constantine who appears further up the genealogy may simply be a doublet of the first; see below, however, for an alternative suggestion regarding Constantine.

[29] Could the *lám Artúir* ('hand of A.') which slew 840 Saxons at Arthur's twelfth battle (see J.H. Todd, *The Irish Version of the Historia Britonum of Nennius* (Dublin, 1848), 110-12) be the germ from which this theme developed?

they convey suitable connotations and associations. While it is thus impossible to be certain where a learned Gaelic historian working in the sixteenth century might have come by his knowledge of them, it may be recorded, for what it is worth, that forms of *Láimhfhionn* and *Lámhdhóid* occur in texts relating to the ancestry of the kings of Scots, where one can also find forms of *Fear Mara* ('Man of the Sea', itself an 'utility' name with the connotation of 'incomer' in the dialectic of the genealogies) and of *Fionnlugh* (perhaps 'White/Bright/Fair Warrior'); while the same sources would provide the possibility of associating the difficult *Amgcel/Aincheil* (MSS) with forms of *Ainbhcheallach*, and the equally perplexing *Conmuic/Chomhruisg/Comhruirg* (MSS) with forms of *Conaing*.[30]

(6) Last of all, *Toisid* (MSS) may simply be for Gaelic *tóiseach* or *toíseach* 'leader'. Names for 'ruler', like names for 'lawgiver' or 'warrior', are to be expected in any tradition of creative genealogy. On the other hand, it might just represent an unnoticed doublet of *Constaintín*.[31]

To sum up, the principles of construction visible in this version of the Campbell genealogy consisted of the elaboration of a couple of basic themes according to principles which are familiar enough from other Celtic, and indeed non-Celtic, examples of the genre. The two basic themes were '(King) Arthur' and 'Briton', and the principal types of elaboration were (1) duplication (sometimes with differentiation by the addition of evocative epithets), and (2) importation of names with appropriate associations from literary and (pseudo-)historical sources. These could be supplemented by 'off-the peg' space-fillers from the resources of the genealogical tradition.

The sources drawn on are to some extent identifiable, though questions, especially questions of immediate provenance, remain. There are a couple of hints that the author of our genealogy may have had access to some items of oral-traditional knowledge; but

---

[30] See, for example, *Chron. Picts-Scots*, 134-5; cf. Anderson, *Early Sources*, i, p. clvii; M.O. Anderson, *Kings and Kingship in Early Scotland* (Edinburgh, 2nd edn., 1980), 237. The fact that there are Constantines in the Scottish king-lists as well as in Geoffrey of Monmouth could perhaps have been the spark that caused this source to come under the scrutiny of the Campbell genealogists. One should stress, however, that the 'utility names' recur widely in Irish literary and antiquarian sources.

[31] Given the similarity of *t* and *c* in the Gaelic script, and the presence of the spelling *Considin* in K, one could imagine *cōsid*¯ (i.e. con*sid*in) being taken as *tósid*, or similar.

it is evident that his first instinct was to seek his inspiration in learned (i.e. written) sources.[32] Some shared textual errors suggest that the surviving sources share a common ancestor derived from the original composition; but their relative homogeneity suggests that the transmission was fairly short and self-contained. The date of composition is hard to calculate with certainty, but most probably fell within the first half of the sixteenth century. It may well be associated with the arrival of the MacEwen bardic family as official poets and historians to the earls of Argyll.[33]

[32] Note the stress which is laid on ancient, learned tradition in the poem containing W, which refers to *slán croinice* 'the guarantee of chronicle' (st. 34*b*), *cuimhne druadh* 'the memory of sages' (st. 19*d*), and *ughdair* 'authorities' (st. 32*a*). Such references do not, of course, preclude the possibility that a fairly near relative of the poem's MacEwen author had created at least part of the genealogy *de novo*! Hints of oral-traditional sources include the 'Red Hall' (*ex emendatione*) and the curious form *Arar* in W (stt. 29*b*, 30*a*), which I can only explain as an oral derivative of a (presumably Cumbric) form of the name Arthur borrowed before the twelfth-century loss of /þ/ from the Gaelic consonant system.

[33] Reasons for this belief are set out in Gillies, 'The "British" genealogy of the Campbells'.

GLASGOW UNIVERSITY LIBRARY'S COPY OF ROBERT RICHARDSON'S *EXEGESIS IN CANONEM DIVI AUGUSTINI*

Stephen Rawles

Anyone interested in Rabelais will inevitably connect a Scot living in Paris in the 1530s with Panurge and his outburst in 'Scots' in chapter nine of *Pantagruel*.[1] Anyone interested in Rabelais inevitably has at least a passing interest in the printer Chrétien Wechel, who printed the first edition of the *Tiers Livre* in 1546 as well as the volume under scrutiny here.[2] Anyone interested in Rabelais who is confronted with a book which used to belong to the real Bibliothèque Saint Victor in Paris will inevitably think of the spoof catalogue of that institution, also in *Pantagruel*,[3] especially since the book under discussion here was written by a visitor to the Abbey of Saint Victor. The subject of the Scots in Paris has been considered by several scholars. Geneviève Guilleminot-Chrétien of the Bibliothèque Nationale is currently working on the output of Chrétien Wechel for the 'grand Renouard'.[4] The Library of Saint Victor would be worth several books in itself.[5] I shall therefore confine myself largely to the considerable

[1] The chapter numbering of *Pantagruel* varies according to the edition cited. Reference is made here to the earliest known edition of the work, printed by Claude Nourry in Lyons (n.d). See Rawles and Screech, *New Rabelais Bibliography* [*NRB*], (Geneva, Droz, 1987), 1. However, the 'Scots' of Panurge did not appear until 1533 (*NRB*, 7), in the first edition printed by François Juste, who was probably Rabelais's preferred printer, at least for the first two books. The only known copy of this 1533 edition was destroyed during the allied bombing of Dresden in 1945, so that the earliest surviving edition to contain it is the Juste edition of 1534 (*NRB*, 8) of which one of the four known copies is also in GUL (C8v; f.24v).

[2] *NRB*, 28

[3] *Pantagruel*, ch. 7.

[4] *Imprimeurs & libraires parisiens du XVIe siècle: ouvrage publié d'après les manuscrits de Philippe Renouard* (Paris, 1964-).

[5] See Alfred Franklin, *Les anciennes bibliothèques de Paris: églises, monastères, collèges, etc*, 3 vols. (Paris, Imprimerie Impériale, 1867-73). i, 135-85; *Le catalogue de la bibliothèque de l'abbaye de Saint-Victor de Paris de Claude de Grandrue, 1514*, ed. Gilbert Ouy *et al.* (Paris, CNRS, 1983). The 1514 catalogue is now in the Bibliothèque Mazarine, MS 4184. A later catalogue of the printed books, made by Etienne Regnard in 1623 is now in BN, MS lat.15169. I have not been able to check whether this edition is listed there.

bibliographical interest of the Glasgow volume, with passing reference to the tangents of wider interest which it generates, even if it was Rabelais who attracted me to it.

The volume is briefly described as follows:

Richardson, Robert: *Exegesis in canonem divi Augustini,* Paris, Chrétien Wechel, 1530.

Collation
18m° in 6's and 4's: aa^{6}bb-cc^{4} A-V$^{6/4/4/4}$ X-Z^{4} a-Aa$^{6/4/4/4}$ Bb^{4} AA^{6} BB-CC^{4} DD-GG$^{6/4/4/4}$ HH^{4} [$4/3/3/3 (-aa1H2+A5) signed] 264 leaves, ff.[*14*] 1-214 [*36*] [K2 signed K2; k signed K; GG2 signed GG3]

Contents
aa1r: title (in a compartment = Renouard 1123;[6] see fig.1); aa1v: woodcut of crucifixion; aa2r: dedication to Alexander Mylne, and prefatory matter, ending cc3r; cc3v-cc4v: blank; A1r: text, ends Bb4r; Bb4v: colophon: dated 'Anno M.D.XXX. Mense Januario'; AA1r: 'Junioribus confratribus celebrerrimorum coenubiorum Canbuskenalis Scouensis (*sic*), & aliorum ordinis sancti Augustini Frater Robertus Richardinus S.P.D.'; BB2v: 'Alphabetnm (*sic*) religiosorum, à nenerabili (*sic*) Thoma Caupis ordinis sancti Augustini'; DD6r: 'Sequuntur orationes de actibus Christi secundum ferias distinctis ...'; HH3v: 'Talis ordo alphabeti in hoc servatus est libro' (table of gatherings; see fig.2); HH4r: colophon (same setting of type as on Bb4r); HH4v: Printer's mark (=Renouard 1111).

Typography
The main text is in italic on the Aldine model, 85 mm for 20 lines; the type page measures, typically, 85mm (93 mm over the head and direction lines) by 45 mm (A2r).

Glasgow University Library
Pressmark TCL 415. Bound in nineteenth-century calf. The pages as cut are 113 by 75 mm overall. Title page has the stamp: BIBL. S. VICT. and in manuscript: Ex alta Bibliotheca S. Victoris Parisiensis; this wording is also found on the verso of the fly leaf (see fig.1). On HH3v in a sixteenth-century hand: Ex libris fratris Robertus Boursier (?) Victorini (see fig.2). More recently the volume belonged to the Library of Trinity College, Glasgow, and passed to the University of Glasgow in 1974. The volume was presented to Trinity

[6] Phillipe Renouard, *Les marques typographiques parisiennes des XVe et XVIe siècles* (Paris, Champion, 1926).

College in 1881 by Dr W.G. Blackie, according to a note on the fly-leaf.

Other copies
BL; BN; CUL; NLS.

The biography of Robert Richardson (who is also listed as Richardinus, Robertus, and Richardin, Robert), canon of Cambuskenneth, near Stirling, is dealt with by the *DNB*,[7] by G.G. Coulton in the introduction to his edition of the *Exegesis*,[8] and, in particular and as so frequently with Scottish figures of this period, by John Durkan.[9] Richardson was, of course, only one of many Scots to study in Paris during the early sixteenth century, of whom Buchanan is probably the best known. For the purposes of this short article, the chief interest lies in the fact that Richardson was sent to Paris by the dedicatee of the *Exegesis*, the abbot of Cambuskenneth, Alexander Mylne,[10] during which time the work was published. The printer Chrétien Wechel was a native of Herentals near Antwerp, who had established himself in Paris in 1526, and whose publishing career lasted until 1553.[11] His relationship with Rabelais was confined to the production of the first edition of the *Tiers Livre*, and, indeed, it seems likely that he was involved in a lawsuit with Rabelais at about the time of the publication.[12] I have found nothing about the Brother Robert whose signature appears on the Glasgow copy, but so far as the Bibliothèque Saint Victor is concerned we are on surer ground. It was quite simply one of the great libraries of Paris in the sixteenth century, and retained its status until the French Revolution, when it was broken up. Rabelais's spoof catalogue is a delightful and typical extravaganza of word-play, satire and implied intellectual comment. Notwithstanding his satire, it is difficult to believe that a scholar of his calibre did not have reason to exploit the resources of the Abbey,

---

[7] vol. xlviii, 242. Richardson is dealt with very briefly at the end of an entry for another figure of the same name.

[8] Richardinus, *Commentary*.

[9] J. Durkan, 'Robertus Richardinus and *STC 21021*', *TEBS*, iii (1957), 83-4; idem, 'Scottish "evangelicals" in the patronage of Thomas Cromwell', *RSCHS*, xxi (1983), 127-56.

[10] On Alexander Mylne, see *DNB*, vol. xl, 2-3; Coulton, ibid. See also, index in McRoberts, *Essays*, and the entry in *DSCHT*.

[11] See E. Armstrong, 'The origins of Chrétien Wechel re-examined', *Bibliothèque d'humanisme et renaissance*, xxiii (1961), 341-6; H. Elie, 'Chrétien Wechel, imprimeur à Paris', *Gutenberg Jahrbuch*, xxix (1954), 181-97.

[12] See *NRB*, 28.

and it is tempting to speculate whether Rabelais and Richardson did not meet in the library—Rabelais is thought to have been in Paris studying medicine at the same time that Richardson was there.

But alongside all the more normal interest of a work such as this, there is the element of bibliographical curiosity. It is very possible that this is the first book to have been printed in the octodecimo format. That is to say that each sheet in the book had 18 leaves or 36 pages. The format was relatively common in later centuries[13] but has not, so far as I know, been recorded in any book earlier than this. It was certainly highly experimental in 1530.

At first sight the sequence of gatherings seems anomalous—the 264 leaves 'ought' to be divisible by 18, to indicate the use of a whole number of sheets, but they are not; in fact the book involves the use of fourteen and two thirds sheets of paper per copy. Furthermore it is easily established that the sheets of 18 leaves were cut into four different parts before folding and binding, making one gathering of six leaves and then three of four leaves each, and that the 'standard' sequence of the four gatherings from each sheet was 6/4/4/4. The gatherings in the book do not, however, reflect this sequence regularly. The preliminaries account for only 14 leaves, before the text proper starts with the first 'standard' sequence on A1r. Reference to the contents, and a knowledge that it was common in the sixteenth century to print the preliminaries last (at least in the first edition of a work), is helpful. It will be seen that cc3v-cc4v are blank, and that the final gathering of the whole work, signed HH, consists of only four leaves, following the standard 6/4/4/4 sequence of gatherings DD-GG. This indicates that aa-cc and HH were probably printed together on one sheet, making the requisite 6/4/4/4 combination to fill a sheet. If this is what happened, then only two odd areas remain. These are: a) $R^6S\text{-}V^4$, followed by $X\text{-}Z^4$, followed

[13] Joseph Moxon, *Mechanick Exercises on the Whole Art of Printing* (1683-4) does not mention the octodecimo. The octodecimo is illustrated in the illustrations to the *Encyclopédie* in 1769, both as the awkward 18m° in half sheets, and in the more usual whole sheet imposition in 12's and 6's: *Recueil de planches sur les sciences, les arts libéraux, et les arts mécaniques...* 7e volume (Paris, Briasson and Le Breton, 1769): 'Imprimerie en caractères', planche VIII, 20-22. By 1808, Stower in *The Printer's Grammar,* refers to 'works of that size' (i.e. 18's in half sheets) 'which are now constantly printing' while many of the other impositions he gives are recognised by him as unusual. By a happy coincidence John Durkan's *Bibliography of George Buchanan* reveals another 18m°, this time in 10s and 8s, in the edition of the Psalms with the *Jephthes* and the *Baptistes,* published in Aberdeen in 1672.

by a^6b-d^4; and b) x^6y-Aa^4, followed by Bb^4, followed by AA^6BB-CC^4, followed by DD^6EE-GG^4.

Of these two apparently strange sequences, b) is easily explained by assuming that Bb (the last gathering of the main *Exegesis* text) was printed on the same sheet as AA, BB, and CC, making a 'standard' 6/4/4/4 pair of eighteen-page formes. The only difficulty would then be the correct ordering of the gatherings at the binding stage, for which guidance was available in the register on HH3v (where the correct sequence of aa, bb, cc and HH is also explained).

Section a) is far more difficult to deal with. At first sight one could assume that a 6-leaf gathering is missing, but the foliation, the register of gatherings on HH3v, and the text all clearly indicate that no such gathering was meant to precede gatherings X-Z. The explanation might be that the printer, faced with an unfamiliar imposition pattern, wished to begin the second alphabetical sequence of signatures with a new sheet, but this implies a willingness to waste a third of a sheet of paper per pair of formes in the process. However, if this explanation is correct, then he had gained confidence by the end of the second full alphabetical sequence, when, if the explanation of b) is also correct, he was prepared to vary the sequence for the sake of beginning the new work on AA1r with a new alphabetical run of signatures. There is no evidence to suggest that the copy had been cast off for simultaneous setting and printing from A1 and a1 (or perhaps X1).

It will be noted that in the Glasgow copy, at least, there is a considerable number of misprints, even in the parts transcribed above.[14] Wechel's compositors and readers were not good, especially, perhaps, with Scottish names. But the person responsible for imposition 'sub scuto Basiliensi' was certainly blessed with ingenuity when he instigated this new format. The most dyed-in-the-wool bibliographical enthusiast would be hard put to suggest that the use of octodecimo format for Richardson's work has any necessary significance to its meaning, except perhaps that its overall size meant that it was a comparatively cheap book. Rabelais, the Bibliothèque Saint Victor and bibliographic curiosity notwithstanding, the *Exegesis* certainly adds to the evidence for the Scottish presence and potential influence in Paris at a crucial point in Renaissance and Reformation history.

[14] I have not examined any other copy to corroborate this evidence, but Coulton is blunt: 'To have corrected [Richardson] and his printer would have been a hopeless task ...' (p. xxx).

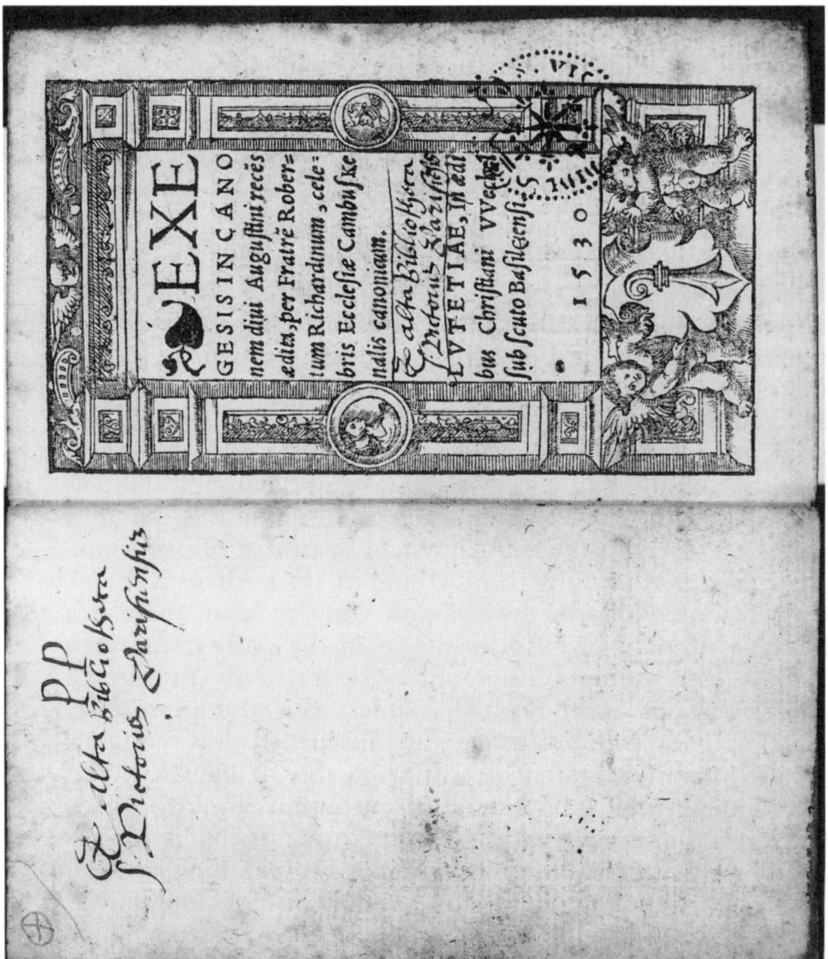

Fig. 1 Richardson, Robert, *Exegesis in canonem divi Augustini*, Paris, Chrétien Wechel, 1520, aa1r and facing flyleaf.

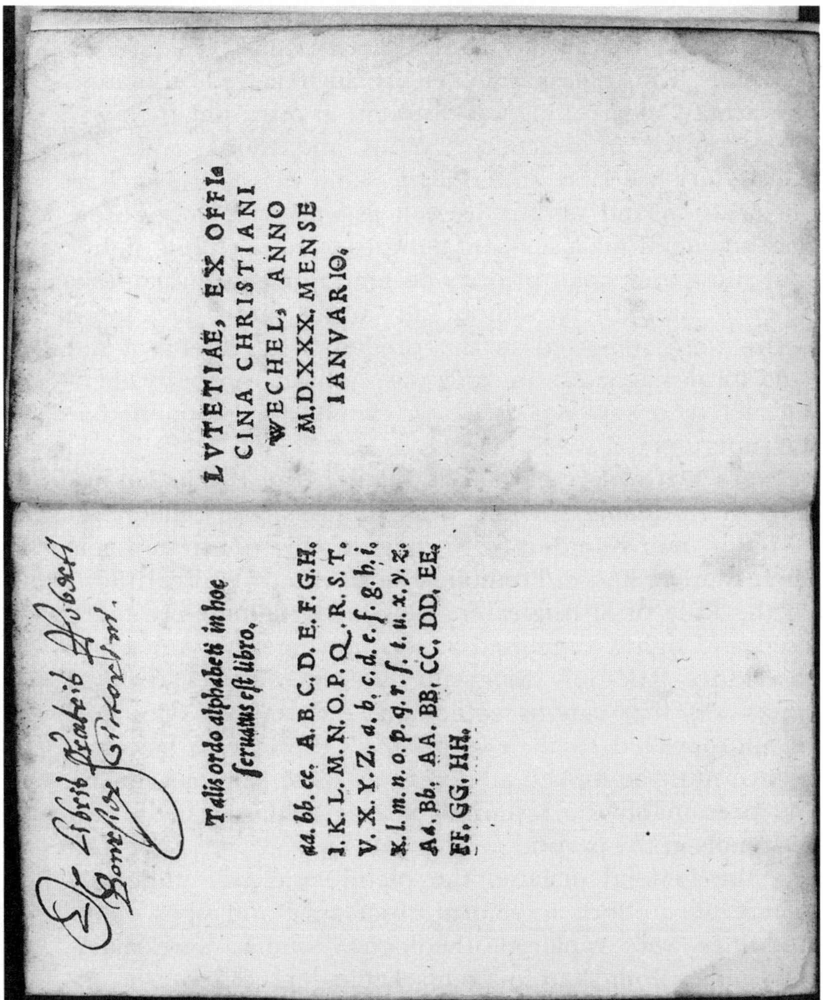
Talis ordo alphabeti in hoc ſeruatus est libro.

aa. bb. cc. A. B. C. D. E. F. G. H. I. K. L. M. N. O. P. Q. R. S. T. V. X. Y. Z. a. b. c. d. e. f. g. h. i. k. l. m. n. o. p. q. r. ſ. t. u. x. y. z. Aa. Bb. AA. BB. CC. DD. EE. FF. GG. HH.

LVTETIAE, EX OFFICINA CHRISTIANI WECHEL, ANNO M.D.XXX. MENSE IANVARIO.

Fig. 2 Richardson, Robert, *Exegesis in canonem divi Augustini*, Paris, Chrétien Wechel, 1520, HH3v-HH4r.

CANONS REGULAR AND THE REFORMATION

Mark Dilworth OSB

In the late Middle Ages, houses of canons regular and monasteries of monks strictly so called had grown to be very like each other. The canons were priests living a monastic life, while monks —by definition, living a monastic life—usually received ordination as priests. Even if their calling was different in principle, their way of life was similar in practice. Canons and monks alike, in sixteenth-century Scotland, suffered the same vicissitudes such as inflation, taxation and warfare as well as what can only be described as a general malaise. Communities were declining rather than flourishing and small priories became non-conventual, that is, a superior lived there without any other monk or canon. Monasteries were subjected to the predatory attentions of the crown and local magnates: not only was monastic property alienated, but men who were not monks or canons were appointed as monastic superiors.

There were two orders of canons regular: the Black Canons, also called Augustinians, and the White Canons, also called Norbertines (after their founder, St Norbert) or Premonstratensians (after their mother house, Prémontré in northern France). Both followed the Rule of St Augustine, though the latter were more centralised and tightly organised as well as somewhat stricter in their observance. The only important difference between canons and monks was that canons could and did serve as vicars in parishes appropriated to their monastery. Even here, however, the evidence must be looked at closely, as some canons with the title (and presumably the revenue) of a parochial vicar did not serve personally in the parish.

Despite the general malaise, the picture was not uniformly black. There were efforts to reform observance and signs of vitality. Buildings were repaired, theological studies were maintained and music flourished to a remarkable degree. Scottish canons regular played a part in Reformation controversies before 1560 and made a substantial, though uneven, contribution to the ranks of Protestant clergy.

The most important and conspicuous sign of vitality was the

founding of St Leonard's College by the canons of St Andrews.[1] This Augustinian house was the wealthiest in Scotland and had the largest monastic community. As it was a cathedral priory, its superior was only a prior, but he enjoyed the use of pontifical insignia and ranked above all Scottish abbots. Prior James Hepburn founded St Leonard's in 1512 as a college of St Andrews university. He had been a secular cleric, not a canon, before his appointment as prior in 1483; he was also motivated by personal ambition and deeply involved in church politics. Nevertheless the foundation was a sign of Augustinian vitality and desire for reform.

A monastic reform movement emanating from the Augustinian monastery of Windesheim in the Netherlands had coalesced to some extent with the efforts of a remarkable man, Jean Standonck, to reform university life for clerical students.[2] His aim was to produce priests dedicated to study and to austere poverty; the place which exemplified his ideals was the College of Montaigu in Paris. The founding of St Leonard's as a 'College of Poor Clerks' owed much to this ideal, and John Annand, a St Andrews canon and possibly the first principal of the new college, had known Standonck well. The principal was to be a canon appointed by the prior, and visitations were to be conducted by the prior and conventual chapter. St Leonard's was in large measure an appendage of the priory, situated within the monastic confines, endowed with priory revenues and aimed at recruiting and training young canons. The students, whether Augustinians or not, were treated as novices, under strict discipline and secluded from outside influences that might hinder their formation.

St Leonard's gradually won acceptance within St Andrews University and parity with the other colleges. Paradoxically, given the origins of its ethos, it played a significant part in preparing the ground for the Scottish Reformation. According to the historian Calderwood, a student imbued with Reformation principles was said to have drunk of St Leonard's well, while John Knox records two such alumni who were forced to flee abroad. The first, Alexander Alane, a St Andrews canon, was born in Edinburgh in 1500,

[1] For St Leonard's see J. Herkless & R.K. Hannay, *The College of St Leonard* (1905); *St A. Acta*, xliii ff; J. Durkan 'The cultural background in sixteenth-century Scotland', in McRoberts (ed.), *Essays on Scottish Reformation*, 293-5.

[2] See also Richardinus, *Commentary*, xiii ff; H. Rashdall, *The Universities of Europe in the Middle Ages* (1905), i, 520-21n; iii, 412-13.

determined at St Leonard's in 1515 and fled to Germany in 1532. His career as a Lutheran theologian under the name of Alesius is too well known to need elaboration here. The other, Master John Fyfe, who determined at St Leonard's in 1522 and was licenciate in 1524, may also have been a canon. He too fled to Germany but eventually, according to Knox, returned to St Andrews.[3]

Not everyone at St Leonard's was Protestant in sympathy. John Annand, a distinguished academic, remained a staunch Catholic, willing to enter into controversy for his beliefs, so much so that Knox dubbed him 'a rotten Papist'. He was principal of St Leonard's in the 1540s.[4] Then in 1559-60, under a later principal, John Duncanson, the college staff went over to the Reformation side.

The Augustinian abbey of Cambuskenneth likewise played a part both in efforts towards Catholic reform and in Protestant reformation. Alexander Mylne, a notable churchman and lawyer provided as abbot in 1519, clearly took his monastic duties seriously. In June 1522 he wrote to the abbot of the celebrated Augustinian house of St Victor in Paris, asking if he might send some of his novices to study there. St Victor had been influenced by the reform movements associated with Windesheim and Jean Standonck. One of Mylne's canons, Robert Richardson, was at St Victor by 1527. Born in 1491 and a near relative of Alesius, he is probably the man of that name who determined at St Leonard's in 1520.[5]

Richardson is best known through the commentary he wrote on the Rule of St Augustine, *Exegesis in Canonem divi Augustini*, published at Paris in 1530. It is a strange compilation. In a dedicatory letter to Abbot Mylne, he says that the latter often wrote to him at Paris asking for information on reformed religious observance and for a short commentary on the Rule, and he also claims that the young canons at Cambuskenneth, Scone and other houses had often put questions to him about Augustinian observance. The erudite Mylne, even if he did make these requests, was surely unimpressed by the book. Quite apart from the careless printing and mangled Latin (for some of which

[3] Knox, *History*, i, 15, 23; Calderwood, *History*, i, 83-4, 96; *St A. Acta*, 316, 340, 346; Herkless & Hannay, *St Leonard*, 56, 99, 123, 203; see also J. Durkan, 'Heresy in Scotland: the second phase, 1546-58', *RSCHS*, xxiv (1992), 320-65.

[4] Knox, *History*, i, 83; Herkless & Hannay, *St Leonard*, 57, 119, 220.

[5] *Ep. Regum Scotorum*, i, 335-7 (the translation in *Camb. Reg.* pp. xc-xci has some inaccuracies); *St A. Acta*, 332.

at least the printer rather than Richardson was surely responsible), the volume is replete with general moralising, unintelligent formalism and extravagant denunciation of corrupt monastic observance, while being very short of factual detail. It is usually impossible to tell how widespread the alleged general (rather than particular) abuses were and whether he is referring to Scotland or France. One abuse mentioned often, however, is canons having private property, which he rightly condemns as incompatible with true monastic life.[6]

We do not know how many canons of Cambuskenneth in fact went to St Victor. Richardson is not mentioned in any Cambuskenneth documents known to us, nor are two other men who were perhaps with him in Paris: Robert Logie and Thomas Cocklaw or Gibson.[7] Logie was a brother or kinsman of Gavin Logie, who is credited by Knox with teaching reformed doctrine at St Leonard's. Robert Logie was certainly a canon, being mentioned in Richardson's *Exegesis* and being said to have 'brought up' the novices at Cambuskenneth.[8] Cocklaw served as a priest at Tullibody, a parish appropriated to Cambuskenneth and only a few miles distant. Richardson and Logie were both at Cambuskenneth in August 1531, when Abbot Mylne lifted a sentence of excommunication (probably monastic excommunication from table and choir) imposed on them for disobedience.[9]

A few years later, however, Richardson was at Rome in the service of Cardinal Ghinucci, who in the late 1530s acted as James V's agent in the Roman curia. In Italy Richardson was, in John Durkan's words, 'clearly canvassing for support for Henry's divorce'[10] and from late 1535 he was corresponding with Thomas Cromwell, Henry VIII's principal agent in spiritual matters. He went to England and in June 1540 became a naturalised Englishman. He was provided with an English safe-conduct to Scotland in September 1541. We know nothing further about this, but in June 1543 he was the English king's envoy to Governor Arran,

---

[6] Richardinus, *Commentary*, Index s.v. Property.

[7] For the careers of all three, see J. Durkan, 'Scottish "evangelicals" in the patronage of Thomas Cromwell', *RSCHS*, xxi (1982), 134-7, 148-9. Other references are additional.

[8] Richardinus, *Commentary*, 127, where his name has been latinised as Longensis; Knox, *History*, i, 15; Calderwood, *History*, i, 83-4, 124 (where John Richardson is no doubt an error for Robert).

[9] Durkan, 'Cultural background', 299n.

[10] Durkan, 'Scottish evangelicals', 135.

who received him kindly, heard him preach and promised him a living. Richardson went on to St Andrews to confer with Cardinal Beaton. This was the time of Arran's brief rapprochement with Henry VIII and Reformation principles. By November, however, Arran had ceased to support good preachers of the Word of God and was persecuting them. Richardson had to flee to England,[11] where he was a minister until his death at a ripe old age. In 1540 Logie and Cocklaw both became Protestant preachers in London, and four years later they were naturalised. Cocklaw had married secretly, was accused of heresy and condemned to imprisonment for life in January 1540 but managed to escape, while Logie smuggled out the treasure hidden by Cocklaw.[12]

Robert Logie was associated with Thomas Forret, canon of Inchcolm and vicar of its appropriated parish at Dollar. Foxe and Calderwood have a lively account of Forret's altercation with the bishop of Dunkeld, in which of course Forret is on the side of the angels in upholding the value of Scripture. He had studied at Cologne, matriculating in 1515, then became a regular canon. He is said to have been converted to Protestantism by reading St Augustine and to have influenced the younger canons at Inchcolm in that direction. He was burned for heresy in Edinburgh in March 1539.[13]

Two other canons are recorded as being in trouble for heresy. Donald Makcarny, Premonstratensian of Holywood near Dumfries, was accused of various heretical views before the inquisitor in Glasgow in 1539. Freely and uncoerced, he abjured them and was absolved. William Forman, Augustinian of Holyrood, was charged with heresy and in November 1543 ordered to enter into ward once again 'within his chalmer within the Palice of Halyrudehouse'. In the event he was warded with Cardinal Beaton. Nothing further is known except that before this, in 1540-41, Forman was vicar of Balmaghie in Kirkcudbright, an appropriated parish of Holyrood, and was deceased vicar in 1557.[14] Nor do we know if either man's views judged heretical were in any way connected with Protestantism. It is perhaps safe to say, however, that

---

11 *LP Henry VIII*, xvi, no. 1190; xviii, pt. 1, nos. 478, 638, 696; pt. 2, no. 392.

12 Calderwood, *History*, i, 123-4; *RSS*, ii, 2858; Haws, *Parish Clergy*, 239.

13 Calderwood, *History*, i, 124-9; Pitcairn, *Trials*, i, 210-15; Durkan, 'Cultural background', 320.

14 J. Durkan, 'Some local heretics', *TDGAS*, 3rd ser., xxxvi (1959), 71. Pitcairn, *Trials*, i, 330*; SRO, CH 5/3/1, f.301v; NP 1/14, f.169v.

here were two canons not content to remain within the limits of what was theologically safe and acceptable.

In the decades before the Reformation, canons in at least some monasteries were competent in theology and a number of them had studied at universities in Scotland and abroad. In at least two houses, St Andrews and Cambuskenneth, monastic reform and theological studies were linked. At Cambuskenneth, significantly, there was also reconstruction of the fabric. A transaction in August 1520 took place in Abbot Mylne's new hall (*nova aula*); a year later the church, graveyards, chapter-house and cloister were dedicated and the high altar consecrated.[15] As for Premonstratensians, there were moves by their general chapter over the three decades between 1505 and 1534 to conduct visitations of the Scottish houses (aimed at maintenance of monastic discipline and observance, if not specifically at reform) but nothing seems to have resulted.[16]

Holyrood's dependent priory at Trail (St Mary's Isle) on the Kirkcudbright coast had been non-conventual for some time. Evidently it ceased to have a canon of Holyrood as prior, for in 1512 James IV informed the Pope that he wanted the priory, which had been removed from the control of the abbot of Holyrood, to be reunited with the parent abbey or at least to be held by the abbot as a commend. In this case, commendation would be a legal device allowing the abbot to hold a second benefice simultaneously. In 1526 Rome provided Holyrood to a new abbot, William Douglas, and granted him Trail *in commendam.*[17] When Douglas died in late 1528, however, the subprior and community of Holyrood presented one of their number, John Lamb, as prior of Trail and were rebuked by the privy council for going against the royal nomination to Rome. A royal nominee duly received the benefice.[18] In another vacancy thirty years later, in March 1558, the Holyrood chapter presented one of their number, William Heslop, to the bishop of Galloway for collation as prior.[19] Again it was to no avail, but clearly this

---

[15] *Camb. Reg.*, 296, 122.

[16] M. Dilworth, 'Franco-Scottish efforts at monastic reform, 1500-1560', *RSCHS* (forthcoming, 1994); N. Backmund, 'The Premonstratensian order in Scotland', *IR*, iv (1953), 30-32.

[17] *James IV Letters*, no. 426; Brady, *Episcopal Succession*, i, 182-3.

[18] SRO, RH 6/1034; CH 8/7; *ADCP*, 288.

[19] SRO, RH 6/1749A.

community of canons had sufficient self-confidence and cohesion to stand up for their rights against both king and pope.

There is general agreement that in the mid-sixteenth century 'a very high standard of musical culture existed in Scotland'. Some of the finest musicians at this very time were Augustinian canons. The most notable was Robert Carver (c.1487-1566), canon of Scone and composer of sacred music. He showed 'a remarkable degree of musical imagination and sensitivity' and was 'one of the greatest contrapuntists of his day'.[20] Two other composers were Andrew Blackhall (Holyrood) and David Peebles (St Andrews). The latter, described as 'ane of the principall musitians in all this land', composed a canticle in four parts in 1530; a fifth part was added c.1547 by one of his disciples, Francis Heagy, at one time a novice at St Andrews.[21] Another St Andrews canon, James Baldovy, was recorded in 1543 as 'skilled in the art of music'.[22] Ten years later, in February 1553, the provost and bailies of Cupar granted licence to Alexander Bellenden to become a canon of St Andrews although he was the provost's 'feit servant...to play on the organis and sing in the quer'.[23] At Inchmahome Priory, the commendator and canons granted a canon's portion for life to Alexander Scott, musician and organist, 'for the decoir of our queir in musik and playing'.[24] By this act they showed that they were willing to have one less canon in the community in order to retain the services of a gifted musician.

There was, however, a sharp difference of opinion as to the fittingness of elaborate music in Augustinian monasteries. Robert Richardson, in his usual intemperate way, condemned the protracted and, to him, time-wasting mass settings in vogue in Scotland and England. He wanted to have one note only for each syllable, as in the masses of a shining light of their order, 'abbatis sancti Columbae'. One presumes that the word 'insulae' has been omitted and that he is referring to an abbot of Inchcolm (St

[20] A. Oldham, 'Scottish polyphonic music', *IR*, xiii (1962), 54, 58. Carver is last recorded on 27 March 1566 (SRO, RH6/2025). See also J. MacQueen, 'Alexander Scott and Scottish court poetry of the middle sixteenth century', in *Procs. Brit. Acad.*, liv (1968), 95-8; J. Durkan, 'Education in the century of the Reformation', in McRoberts, *Essays*, 149-50.

[21] *MBXV*, pp. xv-xvi, 205, 207.

[22] *St A. Acta*, p. clix. See n.30, below.

[23] SRO, B 13/10/1, ff.117v-118. Dr Durkan kindly provided this reference and a transcript.

[24] *Fraser Papers*, 223-4; MacQueen, 'Alexander Scott', 103-04.

Colm's Inch). Most writers presume that this is John Elwand or Elliot (1505-32), though his predecessor Thomas Inglis (1492-1505) has also been suggested. Inglis must be the abbot of Inchcolm given royal licence in 1498 to go abroad 'to the skulis for science and knauledge'.[25] It is tempting to conclude that he went to the Continent to enhance his musical skills.

In the event, Richardson's view prevailed in Scotland. Carver's magnificent compositions were buried in oblivion for four centuries, though they are again being performed and acclaimed in our own day.[26] His fellow canons Peebles and Blackhall, however, were called on to use their expertise in the production of the Scottish Psalter of 1566. In so doing they rendered a notable service to reformed worship in Scotland by using the musical skills they had exercised before 1560 in Augustinian monasteries. Peebles, it is true, 'wes not earnest': he had to be nagged by Thomas Wood, a former monk of Lindores, into performing the task and was commanded by Lord James Stewart, bastard son of James V, half-brother of Queen Mary and commendator of St Andrews, to keep the music plain.[27]

When the Reformation gained the ascendancy, the canons of St Andrews made an outstanding contribution to the new Kirk.[28] Their commendator James Stewart was a committed Protestant. St Leonard's College embraced Protestantism, as did the subprior John Winram. The community in 1555 numbered at least 31, and at least 32 if James Baldowy is to be distinguished from James Pardawy.[29] Nine new canons were recruited shortly before 1560;

---

[25] Richardinus, *Commentary*, 78-81, 142-3; *Inchcolm Chrs*, 240-41. For omissions of 'Insulae', see ibid., 59, 94.

[26] One might mention Mr D. James Ross, who has led performances and also written on Carver: *Musick Fyne: Robert Carver and the Art of Music in Sixteenth Century Scotland* (Edinburgh, 1993).

[27] D. Laing, 'An account of the Scottish Psalter of A.D.1566', *PSAS*, vii (1866-8), 448-55; *MBXV*, pp. xv-xvi. There is some circumstantial evidence that Peebles remained a Catholic at heart, although he married after 1560 (NLS, Adv. 17.1.3, 2nd section, f.7).

[28] M. Dilworth, 'The Augustinian chapter of St Andrews', *IR*, xxv (1974), 25-30. Other references are additional to this. The lists in Haws, *Parish Clergy*, give the relevant information for vicars and Protestant incumbents. See J. Dawson, '"The face of a perfyt reformed kyrk": St Andrews and the early Scottish Reformation', in J. Kirk (ed.), *Humanism and Reform: the Church in Europe, England and Scotland, 1400-1643* (1991), 413-35, for the suddenness of the impact of the Reformation on St Andrews.

[29] Robert Ogilvie, vicar of Leuchars from 1544 and signing with the St Andrews canons in 1570 (SRO, NP 1/26, f.103) is to be added to the number before

most, if not all, were young and the majority studied at St Leonard's. In 1560 the community numbered possibly 40-41, and certainly 33 are recorded after that date.

Winram became Protestant superintendent of Fife, 15 canons became ministers in the new Church (16 if Robert Acheson, minister of Ayr, is the canon of that name),[30] five served as readers or exhorters. All of these five served in parishes appropriated to the priory, four of which were in Fife and thus not far distant: Lathrisk, Forgan, Portmoak and Kennoway. The reader at Lathrisk later moved to Rossie and the fifth canon served at Inchture; these two parishes were not far north of the Tay. Of the 15 ministers, 12 were in parishes appropriated to the priory; and geographically, seven served in Fife and three north of Tay. Two canons, vicars at Dull and Leuchars respectively, enjoyed parochial revenues while making no contribution to the reformed Church,[31] but no canon of St Andrews took a stand in favour of Catholicism. The Augustinian community thus played an important role in the early formative years of the reformed establishment in the east of Scotland, as well as making other significant contributions. St Leonard's became an avowedly Protestant school, while the priory gave generous financial help to the reformed cause. Last but not least, the Augustinian chapter became part of the Protestant diocesan structure.

Information on monastic communities in the mid-sixteenth century is gleaned chiefly from documents, usually feu charters, signed by the community. Not all invariably signed, however, and a missing canon has to be added if he is attested before and after the date in question. Documentation at Cambuskenneth is scarce. In 1445 18 canons signed; in 1546 15 signed, three of them with *Frater* before their name, denoting presumably that they were junior members not yet ordained priest.[32] In 1557-8 there were 17

---

and after 1560. Baldowy was vicar of Fowlis-Easter until 1557; Pardawy was vicar of St Andrews 1553-7. Baldowie and Pardovan are names of different origin (Black, *Surnames*, 46, 646).

[30] The canon 'maid ane [Protestant] sermond' at Kelso in 1553 (*Mary of Lorraine Corresp.*, 368) and signed with the community in 1555. The minister of Ayr 1559-61 is of unknown antecedents and could be the canon.

[31] A list and map of appropriated churches are in P. McNeill and R. Nicholson (eds.), *An Historical Atlas of Scotland c.400-c.1600* (1975), 146-7.

[32] *Camb. Reg.*, 311; *Laing Chrs*, no. 505, where for Ascin read Asone. See Black, *Surnames*, 236, s.v. Eason.

canons, including two signing as *Frater*.[33] Seventeen are found after 1560, three of them not attested before 1560.[34]

Three Cambuskenneth men served in the reformed Kirk from 1567: James Dalmahoy as exhorter (later as reader) at Cambuskenneth, Andrew Row as exhorter at Lecropt, and David Hagye as reader at Kincardine. All three churches were appropriated to Cambuskenneth and near the abbey. John Painter, on the other hand, presumably continued to hold the vicarage of Clackmannan without serving in the new Kirk. Caution is always needed in identifying parish incumbents at this period. If no document gives explicit identification, or narrows the choice by using 'Dene' or some other qualification, one can only judge by probabilities: for instance, if the name is uncommon, or the parish is near the monastery or appropriated to it, and so on. The three readers/exhorters mentioned can safely be identified as Cambuskenneth canons, but there is no positive reason for so identifying Robert Bell, reader at Polwarth in Berwickshire. Robert Mackieson, explicitly termed a professed canon of Cambuskenneth, is known to us from no monastic source: his goods were escheated in May 1568 because he was at Langside on the Queen's side.[35] All in all, Cambuskenneth's contribution to the Reformed establishment was meagre.

Documentation on Holyrood is more plentiful. There were at least 23 canons in 1531;[36] in 1537 besides 21 signing a document there were three who then or later were canon-vicars: William Forman (Balmaghie), John Wilson (Kinneil) and Stephen Moffat (Tranent).[37] Thereafter the community declined; in 1546 only 13 (excluding the three vicars) are recorded.[38] There was little new

---

[33] *Camb. Reg.*, xxxv; *Laing Chrs*, no. 687, with the addition of David Hagye signing in 1546 and found after 1560.

[34] SRO, GD 124/1/976; SRO, GD 86/194, where Robert Bell is visible under UV lamp; *Laing Chrs*, no. 904. To these must be added William Brown and George Johnston, attested as having died after 1560 (SRO, E 4/1, f.44/49) and Robert Mackieson (for whom see below).

[35] *RSS*, vi, 283, 863.

[36] SRO, GD 1/202/6, signed by 21. To these should be added Thomas Ryklynton (Riccalton) and Alexander Wilson, who signed in 1530 (NLS, Ch. 4768) and 1537.

[37] SRO, RH6/1155. The latter three signed in 1531. For Forman, see also n.14, above.

[38] SRO, GD 103/1/39. George Broychtoun and Thomas Ryblynton in 1545 (*Binns Papers*, no. 39) are surely misreadings of Crichton, Ryklynton.

recruitment and the abbey suffered damage at English hands in 1544 and 1547. Only ten besides the vicars are found in 1552.[39] Nevertheless, Holyrood made a recovery. In 1558 12 canons, three of them new, signed the document presenting William Heslop as prior of Trail, and there were three canon-vicars, with George Crichton succeeding William Forman at Balmaghie: a total of 16.[40]

Thirteen of these certainly survived 1560. Nine signed monastic documents, the others are recorded in public records or as vicars.[41] Three of the four signing for the first time in 1558 gave steady service as reformed ministers: Peter Blackwood in Fife, then Aberdeen; Alexander Forrester, mainly in East Lothian; and Andrew Blackhall, the musician, mainly in Inveresk. One gets the impression that the Holyrood canons were polarised concerning the Reformation, with some adding 'Dene' and others 'Minister' to their signature in the same document. In 1565 Queen Mary confirmed and renewed a grant of petty commons to five canons, apparently the whole resident community apart from the prior.[42] Three canons (James Abercrombie, William Heslop and John Ged) were put to the horn in 1571 by the regent and privy council for not compearing to answer the charges against them;[43] one wonders if religious matters were in question. Heslop could be the same man found as reader in 1574-6 at Stow, a fair distance south of Holyrood and not one of its appropriated churches.

As for the vicars, George Crichton held Kirkcudbright as well as Balmaghie until his death in 1571.[44] John Wilson, who renounced popery in February 1560, was celebrating mass and Catholic sacraments in 1564 but continued to hold the vicarage of Kinghorn-Easter.[45] Stephen Moffat was vicar of Tranent, where Alex-

---

[39] SRO, GD 45/13/275 (the transcript of which in *Holyrood Liber*, 158, misreads David Gudson's name as Anderson) with the addition of William Heslop, who signed in 1531 and after 1560. The Alexander Forrester invested as vicar of Kinneil, a Holyrood appropriation, in 1552 is not the canon but a clerk of St Andrews diocese (cf. Haws, 140). See also Cowan and Easson, *Religious Houses*, 90.

[40] SRO, RH6/1749A. Two other ghosts should be eliminated: Andrew Watson, *recte* Wilson, in 1556 and Alexander Harpar in 1558 (*Laing Chrs*, nos. 645, 693). Harpar is a modern addition in the original by someone trying to read Alexander Harkas' signature.

[41] SRO, RH6/1904, 2128; *RSS*, v, 2142.

[42] *RSS*, v, 2142.

[43] SRO, PC1/6, pp. 29-30; *RPC*, ii, 91.

[44] *RSS*, vi, 1148-9.

[45] *STAKSR*, 11-13. 193; *RSS*, v, 3093; vi, 870.

ander Forester was minister, until he was deprived in 1574 for not signing the Confession of Faith.[46] All three enjoyed parish revenues but did not serve in the Kirk. Holyrood gave three ministers to the reformed establishment but also offered some not entirely passive resistance.

Inchcolm, off the Fife coast, suffered far more than Holyrood from enemy action during the English invasions of the 1540s and never recovered. Documentation is very scarce. Eight canons signed in 1538, 14 (the same eight with a further six) in 1541.[47] English forces occupied the island in 1547, the canons went to the mainland and it is not known to what extent monastic life was ever resumed at Inchcolm. Only four canons, all of whom had signed in 1541, are found in later documents. Thomas Espleyne, William Harvey and John Brownhill signed or are mentioned in the late 1550s, then the last-named and Andrew Angus signed in 1578.[48] Angus was vicar of Leslie and served as reader there from 1562, while Brownhill was reader at Dalgety in 1574. Both churches were in Fife and appropriated to Inchcolm. It is possible that John Brown, Inchcolm canon 1538-41, was the reader of that name at Kinghorn (Fife) 1563-74 but, given that the name was so common, such identification can only be conjectural. The state of Inchcolm at this crucial time suggests an important conclusion: that a monastery could not make an important contribution to the post-1560 Protestant establishment unless it had been in a healthy state in the pre-1560 Catholic period.

At Scone 15 canons signed in 1544,[49] and there were 15 in 1548.[50] Sixteen are found in August 1559,[51] of whom all but one certainly survived 1560.[52] Five signed for the first time in the late 1550s. There can be little doubt in identifying two of these newcomers as ministers from 1567: Thomas Morison in Scone and Thomas Cruikshank in Lundeiff (Kinloch), not far to the north. James Pitcairn served as reader in Scone from 1567, and John Blair was reader in 1568 at Kinfauns, near Scone, before

---

46 *RSS*, v, 2432; vi, 2608, 2776.

47 *Inchcolm Chrs*, 68-73.

48 ibid., 212, 96, 216.

49 SRO, RH6/1351; *Scone Liber*, 206-07.

50 SRO, RH6/1442, with John Baldowy and John Blair, who signed in 1544 and 1559.

51 *Bamff Chrs*, 89, with Robert Purves and Thomas Morison, who signed in March 1557 or 1558 (SRO, RH6/1701—day of month missing) and after 1560.

52 SRO, RH6/1851, 2025; *Bamff Chrs*, 104.

moving further away to Benvie. None of the Scone vicars served in the Kirk. Henry Abercrombie, the prior, was vicar of Logierait as well as holding the prebend of Kildonan in Caithness, but almost certainly he resided in Scone. William Abercrombie, the subprior, held Redgorton and William Hepburn held Invergowrie and Logie (Dundee). The James Hepburn who was vicar of Blairgowrie, appropriated to Scone, was not, however, the canon of that name.[53]

The history of Pittenweem, a dependent priory of St Andrews, did not follow the general trend. Having sunk to being a benefice held by the archbishop of St Andrews, it became an Augustinian house once more and in 1541-2 had a community of a prior and nine canons. No new novices were received, however, so that in 1558 only five are recorded, of whom only two are known to have survived 1560.[54] Of the five canons in 1558, Thomas Wright is unlikely to be the reader at Kirkinner (Galloway) in 1574 and James Murray to be any of the four readers or ministers of his name. James Murray, canon of Monymusk, however, can confidently be identified as minister of Monymusk and Kinerny from 1563. The small Augustinian house at Monymusk had suffered from internal troubles and serious damage to the fabric, leaving only James Murray and one other there in 1550.[55]

At Inchaffray there were sixteen canons in April-June 1554.[56] Twelve of them are found after 1560.[57] One man, William Melrose, was from 1567 minister of Findogask and Trinity Gask, then in 1574 of Fowlis-Wester. Three served as readers: Alexander Murray at Kinkell from 1567; William Ruthven at Trinity Gask after being presented to the vicarage in 1572; and George Spens at Madderty in 1574, having held the vicarage of Kinkell, possibly since before 1560. The other pre-Reformation vicars did not serve in the Kirk: William Oliphant held Trinity Gask from 1551 until his death in 1572, while Patrick Murray was vicar-portioner of

[53] The vicar died in 1576, whereas the canon was alive in 1586 (SRO, E 4/2, f.27). This source gives Hepburn's surname only, but William Hepburn, canon-vicar, had died in January 1580 (*RSS*, vii, 2192). The identification in Haws, 26, should be corrected.

[54] M. Dilworth, 'Dependent priories of St Andrews', *IR*, xxvi (1975), 57-61.

[55] ibid., 61-4.

[56] *Inchaffray Chrs*, p. xcix; *Inchaffray Liber*, p. lvii, with William Oliphant signing in 1536 (*Laing Chrs*, no. 407) and found after 1560.

[57] *Inchaffray Chrs*, p. xcv; SRO, RH6/1944. with two vicars: Oliphant and Patrick Murray.

Fowlis-Wester in 1558 and presumably held on to the benefice.[58] He was still receiving his canon's portion in 1579. All these churches were within a few miles of the abbey, and all except Findogask were appropriated to Inchaffray. It seems reasonable to identify Dene Patrick Murray in Newraw with Patrick Murray of Newraw; both occur in April 1563. Murray not only received emoluments from church revenues but used them to found a landed family.[59]

The Border abbeys suffered greatly from English incursions in the sixteenth century. At Jedburgh there were ten canons in 1528, but thereafter never so many. Only four survived 1560; one of them, William Moscrop, an elderly man, was minister in 1563 of a group of parishes round Holyrood's cell at Trail. The community at Dryburgh remained larger than that at Jedburgh during this period. There were 17 canons in addition to absent vicars in 1537-8. Recruitment more or less ceased, but at least 12 are found after 1560. The careers of six are relevant. John Turnbull, vicar of Lessuden (St Boswells) from before 1560, eventually became reader there; George Haliburton, vicar of Gullane from 1560 at least, was in arrears with his third 1566-72 but was reader there in 1574; John Chatto, vicar of Pencaitland from c.1560, was deprived of the benefice in 1577 for not making the Confession of Faith. Robert Milne, reader at Mertoun 1574-6, had been summoned before the privy council in 1569 for exercising his priesthood, together with two other canons, James Jameson and Mungo Wilson.[60] Mertoun was appropriated to Dryburgh and only two miles distant; Lessuden was even nearer. The modicum of assistance given by Dryburgh canons to the reformed establishment was, at best, tardy.

All the communities outlined above were Augustinian, except for Premonstratensian Dryburgh. The Premonstratensians also had a cathedral priory, Whithorn, not as large or as wealthy as St Andrews but a prestigious place of pilgrimage as the burial-place of St Ninian. There were at least 26 canons besides the prior in 1508.[61] Of a number of documents signed by canons in 1530-37,

---

[58] J.R. Todd, 'Pre-Reformation cure of souls in Dunblane diocese', *IR*, xxvi (1975), 32; *Inchaffray Chrs*, p. c.

[59] *Inchaffray Chrs*, pp. xcv, c; *Inchaffray Liber*, 120-31, esp. 126.

[60] M. Dilworth 'The Border abbeys in the sixteenth century', *RSCHS*, xxi (1983), 234-8.

[61] SRO, RH6/730. The summary in *Wigt. Chrs*, 26, omits Patrick Peirson and Adam McClellan, who also signed.

one shows that there were 20 in 1533.[62] Five documents of 1553-9 are signed by 19 canons, with 17 occurring in 1555 and 1556.[63] Ten canons are found for the first time in these years, though Frederick Bruce, appearing as subprior in June 1557 and holding the vicarages of Toskerton and Soulseat (not appropriated to Whithorn) in 1558, was clearly no newcomer. In the document of October 1555 a notary signed for John Rig, professed canon, as he was unable to write. He evidently set about learning, however, as his scrawled signatures in 1556 and 1557 show.[64]

Only 11 of the 19 canons are found after 1560.[65] Bruce is recorded as resigning Toskerton in March 1560, leaving seven unaccounted for, which seems a very high proportion for natural wastage. The survivors in the priory must have been subjected to conflicting religious influences: the bishop, Alexander Gordon, was actively Protestant, while the prior, Malcolm Fleming, was, at least for some time, actively Catholic. John Martin, vicar of Gelston from 1542,[66] was in arrears for the third of this vicarage and Longcastle in 1567-72 and did not serve in the Kirk. John Stewart, recorded at Whithorn from 1555, is very unlikely to be either the Master John Stewart presented in 1541 to the vicarage of Minigaff, not a Whithorn appropriation, or the John Stewart who was vicar of Kirkdale and notary public in 1552.[67] It is a very common name, and the exhorter at Minigaff 1563-72 is surely the long-standing vicar and not the canon.

Six canons did, however, serve as readers. To take them in chronological order, Ralph Pearson was vicar of Kirkmaiden in 1560 and reader there from 1561 until his death in 1569. William Telfer, vicar at Cruggleton, was reader there from 1562 but also, together with Prior Malcolm Fleming, publicly celebrated Ca-

[62] SRO, GD 99, Box 7, 2/2, with Andrew Stevenson found in 1508 and 1537 (ibid. Box 1) and William Vaus found in 1508 and deceased vicar in 1541 (*RSS*, ii, 4313). Other signed documents are in GD 99/4/14,15; Box 1 (unnumbered); Box 7, 2/3; NLS, Adv. 29. 4. 2/1, ff.136-40, 143. Summaries and names are printed in *Wigt. Chrs,* nos. 20-25, 265 (in no. 25 Carnis is a misreading of Talefer).

[63] SRO, RD 1/2, f.170; GD 99/7, with Ralph Pearson, John Martin and William Telfer, found in 1533 and after 1560. See also SRO, GD 99, Box 2: GD 138/1/84; RH6/1773. Summaries and names are in *Wigt. Chrs,* nos. 33 (where for Rf Peirsoun read ff[inla] Peirsoun), 35, 347.

[64] References as in n.63, above. *Wigt. Chrs,* no. 347 misreads Rig's name as Creig.

[65] SRO, GD 138/1/97, 99, 103 etc; G. Donaldson 'The Galloway clergy at the Reformation', *TDGAS,* 3rd ser., xxx (1953), 42-59.

[66] *Wigt. Chrs,* no 81.

[67] SRO, GD 138/1/79.

tholic mass at Cruggleton in 1563, as part of an organised defiance made by over forty clergy drawn from the dioceses of Glasgow and Galloway of the legislation on church services and worship.[68] George Stevenson was reader at Longcastle in 1563, then on the death of Ralph Pearson in 1569 succeeded as reader and vicar of Kirkmaiden. John Johnston, vicar at Whithorn itself, was reader there in 1563. On his death in 1566, Adam Fleming succeeded him as vicar and reader. A fellow canon, John Kay, who made a fraudulent but unsuccessful attempt to be appointed vicar at Whithorn, became reader at Glasserton in 1570. A seventh should perhaps be added: in December 1591, when George Mure was presented to the vicarage of Kirkmaiden, the formula added that he was to be examined on his suitability to be a reader.

The five churches served by these readers were all Whithorn appropriations, and the furthest distant was only half a dozen miles from the monastery. No Whithorn canon became a minister; in fact in 1574, when ministers were charged with the oversight of churches served by readers, four canons (Fleming, Telfer, Kay, Stevenson) were readers in a group of four neighbouring parishes (Whithorn, Cruggleton, Glasserton, Kirkmaiden) under the supervision of ministers who were not canons. This cathedral priory's contribution to the Reformation, unlike that of St Andrews, was not significant.

Tongland, also Premonstratensian, was annexed to the bishopric of Galloway; in other words. the bishop was its commendator. It was thus linked with Whithorn priory and there seems to have been some exchange of officials between the two communities. Tongland had 12 canons in 1537[69] and the same in 1557.[70] Eight of these are found in 1564 and later.[71] Six of the eight served in the Kirk. William Scharpro was reader at Tongland in 1563, then exhorter and finally minister with the oversight of other churches. In 1563 Patrick Grant was reader at Kirkdale and James McCulloch reader at Toskerton. James Mair was reader at Twynholm 1567-71. Thomas McCutrie was from 1567 reader successively at Galtway (Trail), Kirkchrist and Kelton. The last man, Edward Hering, became reader at Tongland between 1574 and

[68] Pitcairn, *Trials*, i, 427-8*.

[69] *Wigt. Chrs*, no. 24a, with James Mair found in 1536 (SRO, RH6/1132) and 1557.

[70] SRO, RH6/1712-13 (*Wigt. Chrs*, no. 346).

[71] *Laing Chrs*, nos. 772, 801. 'William of Tongland' in the latter is a misreading of 'Vicar of Tongland' after William Scharpro's name.

1576. Apart from Tongland itself, none of these churches was appropriated to the abbey, though most were annexed to monasteries of canons. Only Twynholm and McCutrie's three churches were very near Tongland. Mair (Twynholm) no doubt continued to live in the abbey, where he was subprior in 1568.[72]

At Holywood (Premonstratensian) there were ten canons in 1558,[73] seven signing and three vicars: Robert Welsh at Tynron, Andrew Haning at Dunscore, Mungo McGhie at Holywood. These parishes were three of the five appropriated to the abbey. Eight canons, including the three vicars, are recorded after 1560. When Andrew Haning died in 1562 without having served in the new Kirk, he was succeeeded at Dunscore by John Welsh, who was exhorter there 1563-72. Robert Welsh was reader at Tynron from 1561 but died in June 1568.[74] McGhie was reader at Holywood from 1567. All four were designated 'Dene' or 'Dompnus', the style of religious men. Two others can reasonably be identified as serving in the Kirk: William Haning, reader at Lochrutton 1563, and John Little (not recorded before 1560) exhorter at Troqueer 1563 and exhorter/reader at Lochrutton 1567-74. These two parishes were near Holywood though not appropriated to it. John Logan, however, reader at Colvend 1568-9 and its neighbouring parish of Lochkindeloch (New Abbey) 1570-74, is surely the monk of New Abbey and not the canon of Holywood.[75]

Canons belonging to other monasteries held vicarages after 1560 or served in the Kirk, but in no great numbers. Ten canons of Inchmahome (Augustinian) signed a document in 1526. Of these, eight signed in 1548, seven in 1553 and five in 1555, but no others.[76] In addition James Thomson, who signed in 1526, had become vicar of Leny by 1549.[77] Only two of these are recorded after 1560, but a further four canons, signing in January 1563 and later,[78] must have entered the abbey before 1560. The only one

---

[72] SRO, RH6/2126.

[73] SRO, GD 103/1/49. The calendar in *PSAS*, xli (1906-07), 331-2, no. 49, misreads William Haning as Hannay.

[74] SRO, RH6/1869; CC 8/8/1, ff.344-5. John Welsh, Robert's executor, signed himself in Latin as minister of Dunscore but is termed exhorter in church documents.

[75] *Laing Chrs,* nos. 700-02, 1235. He was in trouble in 1590 for celebrating Catholic mass and sacraments (*BUK,* ii, 770; *RPC,* iv, 522).

[76] SRO, RH6/985; GD 86/162; NLS, Adv.29.4.2/7, ff.115-18; *Fraser Papers,* 223-4; Fraser, *Menteith,* 333-5.

[77] Todd, 'Dunblane diocese', 32.

[78] *Dryburgh Liber,* p. xxvi; *Laing Chrs,* no. 881. In Fraser, *Menteith* , 362-3, the

who served in the Kirk was William Stirling, reader at Port of Menteith 1569, exhorter at Aberfoyle 1571-73, reader at Kippen 1574. All three churches were within a few miles of Inchmahome. Master Alexander Drysdale, vicar of Leny in 1562, was apparently not a canon. The only monastic document in which he features distinguishes between him, the vicar, and the community, who consented to an assedation of vicarage property made by him.[79]

At Soulseat (Premonstratensian) conventual life seems to have virtually ceased. Only two canons are found in 1539 and 1544.[80] One of these, Thomas Galletly, survived 1560, as did two others, John White and James Thomson.[81] White, vicar of Kirkmaiden in Rhinns, appropriated to Soulseat, was in arrears with his third 1567-72 but was reader there 1574-6.[82] James Thomson held the vicarage of Soulseat itself and was reader there 1563-74.

Fearn, the only Premonstratensian house not in southern regions, is not well documented. Eight canons signed in 1526, and five, none of them the same, in 1558-9. The only one recorded after 1560 is David Reid, subprior 1550-76.[83] There is no positive reason for identifying John Young, signing in 1558-9, as the exhorter at Invernairn (Nairn). The houses of canons not so far mentioned can be ignored, as they had become non-conventual some time before 1560.[84]

It is surprising that so few canons, apart of course from the St Andrews community, became Protestant ministers. Jedburgh and Monymusk, houses where conventual life had virtually if not entirely ceased, provided one each; at Tongland one man advanced his status, from reader and exhorter to minister; there was one at Inchaffray. Only Holyrood with three and Scone with two had more than one. Readers (and exhorters) were much more numerous, with the majority serving in churches in the vicinity appropriated to their monastery. Probably many continued to live in their monastic quarters; they retained their monastic portion and, as readers, either received a stipend in

ten canons signing are all of Dryburgh, with the exception of the subprior of Inchmahome (see Dilworth, 'Border abbeys', 237).

[79] NLS, Adv. 29.4.2/7, ff.119-22.

[80] *Wigt. Chrs,* 110, 111.

[81] SRO, E 4/1. f.45v

[82] See also *Reg. Min.*, 89.

[83] *Laing Chrs,* nos. 354, 878, 935; NLS, Adv. 29.4.2/11, f.242.

[84] M. Dilworth, 'The commendator system in Scotland', *IR,* xxxvii (1986), 56-7, 72.

addition or kept the entire revenue of their vicarage. Their duties as readers were not onerous. There is need for dispassionate judgement. Undoubtedly they rendered useful service to the Kirk in those crucial early decades, but their objective commitment (that is, as measured by their labours or their hardships) was not great. This perhaps helps to explain how a Whithorn and a Dryburgh canon served as readers but also exercised their Catholic priesthood.

Vicars display a wide range of reactions to the Reformation. None became a minister. Some became readers quickly, others more tardily. The majority did not serve, but they paid their third. Then come those who were seriously in arrears with their third, or were deprived for refusing to sign the Confession of Faith, or were in trouble for exercising their priesthood. One can only speculate on their mental attitudes and their motives, but they were not more eager to serve in the Kirk than their unbeneficed brethren. This of course applies only to vicars appointed before 1560 or fairly soon after, not to Protestant clergymen given a vicarage as their stipend.

Just as the condition of monasteries of canons in 1560 differed widely from house to house, so too did each monastery's contribution of ministers and readers. In this there is no discernible difference between monasteries of canons and of monks properly so called. In fact Arbroath and Lindores, both Benedictine, supplied four ministers each, more than any house of canons except St Andrews. The driving force in producing the Protestant Psalter came from another monk of Lindores, Thomas Wood, its committed and forceful editor. Two conclusions from the evidence serve to put the situation into perspective. The more pastoral ethos of the canons, as compared with monks, did not lead them to accept the Reformation more readily, and the reason for the willingness of St Andrews canons to become ministers should rather be sought in factors peculiar to that house. Secondly, the contribution made by canons regular (St Andrews always excepted) to the Protestant establishment, although not very notable, was far and away greater that any stand they made for Catholicism.

THE INTERACTION BETWEEN LITERATURE AND HISTORY IN QUEEN MARY'S EDINBURGH: THE BANNATYNE MANUSCRIPT AND ITS PROSOPOGRAPHICAL CONTEXT

Theo van Heijnsbergen

Introduction

The significance of prosopography or 'collective biography'—a collection of data concerning a set of people who are grouped together on account of some common denominator—lies particularly in its collective element. It reveals patterns which would be lost in more traditional forms of biography that focus on one historical figure, and yields a dynamic model with a wider and more organic range. In Scottish history, the need has recently been voiced for studies of this kind—network histories, histories of families, minor clergy and lesser gentry as well as urban histories—while further publication of biographies of Mary Queen of Scots or Robert Burns as well as narratives of the '45 'ought to be banned by statute under heavy penalties'.[1] Moreover, prosopographical research neutralises fossilised methodological errors. For example, the historical phenomenon of the Reformation itself has been too frequently used as a given starting point in an attempt to come to grips with the events of the Reformation, a reversal of historical cause and effect that leads to circular argumentations and self-fulfilling prophecies. In contrast, data-based studies can remedy this defect by reversing the process, uncovering historical patterns before rather than after constructing abstract historical concepts.[2]

The Bannatyne Manuscript (1568) is without question the most important literary document of early Scottish literature. Its copyist, George Bannatyne (1545-1607), has for centuries been

[1] M. Lee, 'The daughter of debate', *SHR*, xlviii (1989), 79.

[2] J. Durkan, review of M. Lynch, *Edinburgh and the Reformation* (Edinburgh, 1981), in *IR*, xxxiv (1983), 89. G. Donaldson, *All the Queen's Men: Power and Politics in Mary Stewart's Scotland* (1983) likewise contributes towards a more refined understanding of that period by means of prosopographical research.

hailed as the saviour of Scottish medieval literature; in the words of Sir Walter Scott, 'George Bannatyne had the courageous energy to form and execute the plan of saving the literature of a whole nation'.[3] This judgement, however, needs to be modified or at least qualified, even if only because it might suggest that it was the isolated effort of one individual genius that was responsible for the collection. If Bannatyne personally selected and ordered the poems in his manuscript, this in itself indeed shows that he was at least in some way interested in creative writing; moreover, he copied into the manuscript a handful of poems of his own making. There is nothing in George Bannatyne's life after 1568, however, that even remotely suggests a sustained interest in literature: he became a businessman and does not seem to have spent any more time or money on literary affairs. Even so, it is fortunate for Scottish literature and history that he was the son of a well-to-do burgess of Edinburgh and thus had the leisure and the means to copy over 750 pages of vernacular poetry into what is now known as the Bannatyne Manuscript (henceforth BM).[4]

George's mother also gave birth to twenty-two other children, and the Bannatyne family consequently required a substantial number of godparents. George Bannatyne drew up a list of these godparents in a 'memoriall buik' (henceforth MB), together with the names of the spouses of his brothers and sisters and what seem to have been family patrons.[5] The appendix given below is a checklist of names taken from that document; in the following discussion, this list and the names it contains are referred to simply as 'the MB', while an asterisk is added to a personal name to indicate—whenever appropriate or desirable—that the person in question occurs on this list.

The BM has come down to us through the descendants of the compiler, several generations of merchants and civil servants preserving the manuscript in their private possession for more than two centuries. It is a 'family manuscript' in many other respects: some half-dozen poems in it were composed by the scribe

---

[3] 'Memoir of George Bannatyne', in *Memorials of George Bannatyne MDXLV—MDCVIII* (Bann. Club, 1829), 11.

[4] For details of the manuscript and its diplomatic and facsimile editions, see Bann. MS., *Bann. MS.* and *Bann. MS.* (*fac*).

[5] 'The memoriall buik of certane evidentis and vthiris writtis concernyng George Bannatyne anno 1582', printed in *Memorials of George Bannatyne*, 25-42, and in *Bann. MS.*, i, pp. cxlii-cxlviii.

himself, but two poems that have the name 'Bannatyne' attached to them are distinctly more competent than the others and might perhaps be attributed to a relative.[6] Moreover, a James Bannatyne and a Patrick Bannatyne actually feature in Sempill's 'The defence of crissell sandelandis', one of the poems of contemporary relevance in the BM; considering the description of James Bannatyne in this particular poem ('ffor men of law I wat nocht quhome to luke / auld James Bannatyne wes anis a man of skill'), this is almost certainly a reference to James Bannatyne, George Bannatyne's father, who was indeed a man of law.[7] Furthermore, the MB features the coat of arms of the Bannatynes of Corehouse on its front page—the younger branch of the Bannatynes of Kames to which George Bannatyne's family belonged—while the only illustration in the BM is a coat of arms of the Bannatynes of Kames. Both documents thus underline George Bannatyne's keen awareness of the fact that his own family was part of a larger structure of family relations.

It seems, although precise details are missing, that the Bellendens were also descended from the Bannatynes of Corehouse, which helps to explain the prominent position of the Bellendens in both BM and MB.[8] The Bellendens take pride of place in the MB, while throughout the BM we find strategically placed poems of John Bellenden (c.1490—c.1548), the brother of Mr Thomas Bellenden* and uncle of Sir John Bellenden of Auchnoull*. John Bellenden, described by David Lindsay as the most promising vernacular poet of the 1530s, was also that most fundamental of literary humanists, a translator of classical texts (Livy's 'History of Rome') as well as of Boece's *Scotorum Historiae* for James V, over which Boece himself 'cast a friendly eye'.[9] Such texts and channels of transmission suggest a continuity of thought within an intellectual setting that was urban as well as courtly, with Renaissance as well as medieval elements. Bellenden's greatest predecessor as translator was Gavin Douglas, whose 'Prollog of the fourt buik of Virgell' at an early stage of copying concluded the

[6] 'As Phebus bricht in speir merediane' and 'No woundir is althocht my hairt be thrall', *Bann. MS. (fac)*, ff.230v-231r, 234.

[7] *Bann. MS. (fac)*, ff.124r-125v, ll. 63, 78.

[8] E.A. Sheppard, 'John Bellenden', in *The Chronicles of Scotland, compiled by Hector Boece*, ed. E.C. Batho and H.W. Husbands (STS, 1941), ii, 419-20; *Bann. MS. (fac)*, f.357v; *Bann. MS.*, i, pp. clxxi-clxxiii.

[9] 'The Testament and Complaynt of the Papyngo', in Lindsay, *Works*, i, 57, ll. 49-54; J. Durkan, 'Early humanism and King's College', *AUR*, xlviii (1980), 267.

BM (ff. 291r-294v) before another section of poems was added. The prominent placing of these humanist poets in the manuscript, at both beginning and end, shows that George Bannatyne was aware of where the avant-garde of a vernacular Renaissance was to be located. At the same time, other sections of the manuscript, such as the cluster of poems of advice to princes at the end of book two (ff. 87v-96v) or the fables in book five, have a more traditionally medieval flavour.

In conjunction with the BM, the list of names in the MB reflects the interactions of a mid sixteenth-century family of merchants and legal clerics with other townspeople: local administrators who became national figures, merchant lairds, professional legal men, royal servants and secular clergy. The list also shows the fluctuations of Catholic and Protestant sympathies within this group of people. Considered collectively, these names provide a cross-section of the public figures on whom the Stewart monarchs had come to depend for the increasingly complex administration of the country. Many of them were university-trained men with roots in the educated circles at previous courts, and had been the recipients as well as promoters of the twin concerns of Scottish humanism, education and legal reform. By contrast, the aristocracy, frequently tied up with dynastic interests furth of Edinburgh, formed a separate power in many respects, and were not likely to act as civil servants. To all intents and purposes, and regardless of whether we view the BM as a collection prepared for the press or merely for circulation in manuscript among a select group of friends or relatives, this list of names provides the most detailed checklist available as to who might have constituted the audience for such a manuscript. Moreover, the poems in the manuscript mirror to a remarkable extent the contrasting yet not mutually exclusive cultural, political and religious identities of the various names in the MB; this confirms the assumption that underlies the present paper, namely the complementary relationship between the historical data on the one hand (the names from the MB) and the literary manuscript on the other.

THE BANNATYNE FAMILY

George Bannatyne's grandfather was John Bannatyne, the king's 'lovit daily servitour'. In addition to being a writer to the Signet, he also acted as notary public throughout the reign of James V, occasionally together with his son James, George Bannatyne's father; in the same period he also received regular payments for his labours as a writer in the offices of the Exchequer and the Treasurer. In 1538, John and his son James were appointed 'tabularis of all summondis to be persewit befor the lordis of counsale and sessioun' for life; this was confirmed in 1543.[10]

George's father, James Bannatyne of Formanthills and the Kirktoun of Newtyle (1512-84), was admitted a burgess of Edinburgh in 1538. Apart from being a writer to the Signet and tabular or keeper of the rolls, he was also Deputy Justice Clerk under Sir John Bellenden of Auchnoull* and a member of the town council. In addition to his duties as a servant of the crown, he was also a well-to-do merchant, and his son George was in due time himself admitted to the Edinburgh merchant guild.[11] Several members of the family followed a legal career in administrative bodies such as the Chancery and the Signet; several of George's brothers became writers to the Signet, while a William Bannatyne acted as a notary public alongside George Bannatyne's father.[12] Another position that ran in the Bannatyne family was that of searcher of customable skins. On 16 February 1543 this post was granted to John Bannatyne, George Bannatyne's uncle, and his son William; after the latter's death at Pinkie, the vacancy was filled by James Bannatyne, elder (George's father) and his son James. Furthermore, Laurence, George's eldest brother, received the gift of tabulary in 1554 together with his father; the same happened to Thomas, another brother, in 1557 and again in 1583.[13] Thomas was eventually appointed one of the Lords of the

---

[10] *Bann. MS.*, i, pp. xxi and xxxii-xxxv. John Bannatyne as writer to the Signet and "daily servitour": *RSS*, ii, 1416. As notary public: *RMS*, iii, passim.; a John Bannatyne acted as a notary for Cardinal Beaton: M.H.B. Sanderson, *Cardinal of Scotland: David Beaton, c.1494-1546* (Edinburgh, 1986), 107. As writer to the Exchequer: *ER*, vols. xiv-xvii, passim.; *TA*, vols. vi-viii, passim.; tabular: *RSS*, ii, 2726; iii, 248.

[11] James Bannatyne occurs as Deputy Justice Clerk on 30 November 1562 (*RSS*, v, 1158); he was succeeded at his death by his son Thomas (see below). Society of Writers to the Signet, *Society of Writers to His Majesty's Signet* (Edinburgh, 1936), 71; *Edinburgh Burgesses*, 45. On town council: Lynch, *Edinburgh*, 228.

[12] *RMS*, iii, 3035 (15 Dec. 1544); 3301 (15 Aug. 1546); *Writers to His Majesty's Signet*, 71.

[13] Customable skins (i.e. the skins on which export duty was payable to the Exchequer): *RSS*, iii, 95, reconfirmed on 7 March 1543 (*RSS*, iii, 131); *RSS*, iii, 2444 (20 Sept. 1547). James Bannatyne, elder, and his son, Mr James, are re-appointed to the same position on 11 October 1567 (*RSS*, vi, 28). Tabular: *RSS*, iv, 2757; v, 230; viii, 1304.

College of Justice as Lord Newtyle, and his son James was again a writer to the Signet and appointed Deputy Justice Clerk in 1595.[14] To this pattern of mercantile and legal affairs, George Bannatyne's voluminous manuscript provides the extra dimension of letters, in which his father's and grandfather's links to the world of books played an important role.

The Edinburgh printers

Most recent studies of the BM conclude that the manuscript was originally meant to be printed. Leaving the literary discussions on this subject aside for the moment, the names in the MB provide sufficient reason to consider this a plausible theory.[15] To start with, they show that the Bannatynes were in close touch with printers in Edinburgh. In the early years of the sixteenth century, the first printers in Scotland, Chepman and Millar, included a substantial amount of literature in their output. Although Millar, the actual professional printer, is a shadowy figure, we know more about his partner, who provided the money. Walter Chepman of Ewerland was a merchant, an entrepreneur involved in all sorts of trades, with making money a main priority. Printing was not his only or even main occupation, and it was not one of his financially most successful enterprises. He may have had some interest in literature and printing for its own sake, but he seems to have lost interest in the troubled days after Flodden.[16] Apart from his occupations as a man of business, Chepman acted occasionally as notary and was a clerk in the office of the king's secretary; he is one of the earliest recorded writers to the Signet ('before 1494'), and as such was a colleague of 'gud gentill Stobo', the poet whose death is deplored by Dunbar in his 'Lament of the Makaris'.[17]

---

[14] G. Brunton and D. Haig, *An Historical Account of the Senators of the College of Justice* (Edinburgh, 1832), 218-19; *Bann. MS.*, i, p. lxiv.

[15] The idea that the BM was meant to be printed is an old one, but has most recently been revived by A.A. MacDonald, 'The Bannatyne Manuscript—A Marian Anthology', in *IR*, xxxvii (1986), 36-47; idem, 'The printed book that never was: George Bannatyne's poetic anthology (1568)', in *Boeken in de late Middeleeuwen*, ed. J.M.M. Hermans and K. van der Hoek (Groningen, 1993), 101-10; see also J. Hughes and W.S. Ramson, *Poetry of the Stewart Court* (Canberra, 1982), 22.

[16] R. Dickson and J.P. Edmond, *Annals of Scottish Printing* (Cambridge, 1890; reprint Amsterdam, 1975), 14-22; *ER*, xiv, p. cxiii.

[17] *Writers to His Majesty's Signet*, 27, 107; Dickson and Edmond, *Annals*, 13; Kinsley, 180, l. 86.

Connections with the legal profession ran within the Chepman family in a context and pattern similar to that of the Bannatynes, and so it is not surprising to find John Bannatyne and Walter Chepman appearing together as public notaries as well as acting jointly as witnesses to legal transactions. In 1527 they were paid for dictating and writing the rolls in the Exchequer's office, a task in which Dean James Kincragy* was also frequently involved.[18]

George Bannatyne's father, James Bannatyne, shared Walter Chepman's combination of legal training, landed possessions and a mercantile way of life as well as an interest in 'affairs of letters', and he was regularly in touch with other Edinburgh figures who were connected to printing and books. As initial evidence of a familial literary interest one might point to various Latin and vernacular verses copied into a manuscript of the *Regiam Maiestatem* owned by John Bannatyne in 1520 and later by his son James, George's father.[19] The latter was in 1541 appointed searcher of foreign ships, in order to stop heretical writings from being smuggled into Scotland. In its own right, this appointment may have stimulated his (and his son's) interest in books and manuscripts; what is important in the present context is the fact that the appointment as searcher was a joint one, together with Thomas Davidson, an Edinburgh printer who in the same year was appointed by Mr James Foulis of Colinton to print the acts of three parliaments.

James Foulis, whose son and heir Henry Foulis of Colinton* features in the MB, was a neo-Latin poet who had been appointed together with Mr Adam Otterburn and the renowned vernacular poet David Lindsay to prepare the welcome speech 'with the words in Fransche' to Mary of Guise on her arrival in Edinburgh in 1538; among the twelve persons who were to represent the city at this occasion, 'accowterit and arrangit in gownis of veluott with thair pertinentis', we find John Carkettill*, Mr Thomas Marjoribankis*, Simon Preston* and George Henderson*, while among those who were ordered to 'awaitt vpoun the grathing of thair rowmes in skaffetting personages and ordour' appears 'James Bassenden*, for the Netherbow', which in a nutshell shows that the Bannatyne family was indeed in touch with the upper

---

[18] *RMS*, ii, 2872, 3239 and 3498; *ER*, xv, 387, and for Kincragy, passim.; see also 'Preface', p. lxi. Moreover, John Bannatyne appears as a witness in instruments of sasine to Walter Chepman in *RMS*, ii, 3872 and in *Protocol Book of John Foular, 1503-1513*, ed. M. Wood (SRS, 1941), 723, 760.

[19] NLS, Adv. MS 25.5.9.

layer of Edinburgh society.[20] James Foulis and Thomas Davidson were no strangers, for only a few years earlier Davidson had printed some of Foulis's Latin poems. In 1542 Thomas Davidson, the printer, was granted the premises of the deceased John Cockburn, previously granted to Walter Chepman and his wife. Chepman was no longer alive at this date but his wife is of interest to us: her name was Agnes Cockburn*, and the name appears as a Bannatyne godmother in 1540. She enjoyed special tax privileges owing to her husband's work, and is regularly styled 'our lovit oratrice and wedo' in the royal accounts.[21] Considering the professional connections between Bannatyne and Chepman and the links of the Bannatynes to various royal servants as outlined above and below, the Bannatyne godmother is most likely to have been the printer's wife.

Further connections between the MB and the printing establishment of sixteenth-century Edinburgh can be discovered. The coat of arms of Walter Chepman's first wife, Marion Carkettill, firmly links her with another prominent figure in the MB, John Carkettill of Finglen*.[22] Again, James Bassintyne* is the name of the father of the printer Thomas Bassenden—the name Bassintyne as spelt in the MB being a frequent corruption of the name Bassenden or Bassindene. The printer was indeed the son of one James Bassenden, his mother being Alison Tod, another surname that appears in the MB, and the identification of the Bannatyne godfather as the printer's father becomes even more likely if we consider the document in which James Bassenden, burgess of Edinburgh, 'sett to Andro, Erle of Rothes, ane ludgeing in Shortis Close beside the Nether Bow in Edinburgh', James Bannatyne functioning as cautioner for payment of the rent. The Nether Bow was the area in which the premises of Edinburgh printers were usually located, and Thomas Bassenden was no exception: his house was on the south side of the High Street in the Nether Bow.[23]

---

[20] *RSS*, ii, 4275 (22 Oct. 1541); *Edin. Recs.*, ii, 89-91 (17 July 1538).

[21] Aldis, no. 19; *RSS*, ii, 1584, 3577, 3822 and passim.; her testament was recorded on 24 July 1565 (SRO, CC 8/9/1).

[22] The coat of arms of Marion Carkettill, still visible in Walter Chepman's aisle in St Giles', is clearly linked to that of Carkettill of Finglen; see R.R. Stodart, *Scottish Arms* (Edinburgh, 1881), i, 83, and ii, 148. W. Anderson, *The Scottish Nation, or, the Surnames, Families, Literature, Honours, and Biographical History of the People of Scotland*, 9 vols. (Edinburgh and London, 1859-63), ii, 260.

[23] *DNB*, iii, 374-5. SRO, CS 7/20, ff.196, 303. James Bassenden, burgess of

The Bellenden family

As indicated above, an important connection between the Bannatynes and literature ran through the Bellenden family. Circles of relationships rather than personal convictions account for many of the events and alignments in Scottish life in this period, and to the Bannatynes, or at least to George Bannatyne, the Bellenden connection was of the greatest importance.[24] Not only does the name 'Bellenden' appear in the MB among the godparents, but three distinguished representatives of the Bellenden family head the MB in a class of their own (see appendix), in a striking parallel to the above-mentioned prominent position of the poems by John Bellenden in the BM. This lay-out of the MB suggests the Bellendens were looked upon or even acted as a kind of patron family to the Bannatynes. The position of George's father as Deputy Justice Clerk meant that he worked directly under the Justice Clerk, Sir John Bellenden of Auchnoull*, and the 1570s and 1580s saw an increase in the interactions between the Bannatynes and the Bellendens. The two families had a shared interest in various tracts of land in and near Leith and Holyrood; many charters relating to such lands as granted to various sons of James Bannatyne by Sir Lewis Bellenden*, who succeeded his father as Justice Clerk in 1576, provide illustrations of such interests. Moreover, after James Bannatyne's death in 1584, Sir Lewis Bellenden appointed James's son, Mr James Bannatyne, as Deputy Justice Clerk.[25]

The first references to the Bellenden family in Edinburgh date from the 1460s, when the grandfather of Thomas Bellenden* acquired land in the adjacent burgh of the Canongate. In the sixteenth century, the Bellenden family combined service to the crown with legal careers; their connections to the court were numerous and their offspring distinguished. From c.1484 to 1500, Robert Bellenden was abbot of Holyrood, where we also find Adam Bellenden as prior and Walter Bellenden as one of the ca-

---

Edinburgh, also had a son called James (*Edinburgh Burgesses*, 49-50). That 'James Bassenden of the Netherbow' was related to the printer is also suggested by J. Sanderson, 'Two Stewarts of the sixteenth century. Mr William Stewart, poet, and William Stewart, elder, Depute Clerk of Edinburgh', in *The Stewarts*, xvii (1984), 37 and n. 96.

[24] Donaldson, *All the Queen's Men*, 5.

[25] *RSS*, viii, 1339, 2443. For Bannatyne and Bellenden connections, see also 'Roxburghe Muniments. Appendix: Calendar of Bellenden Papers', National Register of Archives Scotland 1100 (microfiche), passim.

nons. The latter's nephew, the poet John Bellenden, was clerk of expenses in the king's household until he was cast from royal service 'be thame that had the court in gouerning / as bird but plumes heryit of hir nest'; later he became, *inter alia*, archdeacon of Moray (1533-8) and precentor of Glasgow (1537-47).[26] He was the son of Patrick Bellenden, parish clerk of the Canongate and steward to Queen Margaret Tudor from 1509 until his death in 1514, and Marion Douglas, nurse or 'kepar' of the infant James V and as such a colleague of the poet David Lindsay, who was at that time 'maister uscher' to the young king. Apart from the name of the mother, there are several indications that the Bellendens were in touch with the Douglases, which must have added to their literary baggage. Patrick Bellenden and Marion Douglas received a grant of land in Berwickshire from Archibald Douglas, 'Bell the Cat' and 5th earl of Angus, in 1493, and it is not surprising to find the poet John Bellenden connected to Gavin Douglas, son of the 5th earl and another renowned makar: on 5 November 1520 John Bellenden witnessed a contract between Gavin Douglas (as bishop of Dunkeld) and Elizabeth Auchinleck, Gavin's sister-in-law, on the latter's entry to the convent of Sciennes. Bellenden remained a Douglas supporter all his life, and his sister Katherine succeeded David Lindsay's wife, Janet Douglas, as royal seamstress.[27]

The poet's older brother, Mr Thomas Bellenden*, appears as a Bannatyne godfather in 1540. In 1510 he was studying logic in Paris under Robert Galbraith, professor of law and later Senator of the College of Justice. His fellow students there were James Foulis and George Henderson of Fordell*, and, while in Paris, James Foulis dedicated verses to his brother-in-law George Henderson of Fordell* and to Thomas Bellenden*, printed in Robert Galbraith's *Quadrupertitum*, a book which in itself was dedicated to James Henderson of Fordell, the Justice Clerk and father of George.[28] This Robert Galbraith, lawyer, has been

---

[26] *Bann. MS. (fac)*, f.4v, ll. 31, 35-6. For the Bellendens, see J. Ballantyne, 'Mr Thomas Bellenden of Auchnoull (c.1490-1547)', typescript in SRO; P. Anderson, *Robert Stewart Earl of Orkney, Lord of Shetland, 1533-1593* (Edinburgh, 1982), ch. 3; Sheppard, 'John Bellenden', 411-61. I am grateful to Mr Ballantyne for access to this typescript.

[27] *Scots Peerage*, ii, 61-2; Lindsay, *Works*, iv, p. xi; Ballantyne, 'Mr Thomas Bellenden', 3.

[28] A dedicatory letter to James Henryson of Fordell appears on verso of the title page of Galbraith's *Quadrupertitum* (1510). Verses in honour of Thomas Bellenden appear on the title-page and on f.126v; the lines dedicated to George Henderson likewise appear on f.126v, and can also be found in Foulis's own vol-

identified as the 'Galbreith', named in the list of poets presented by David Lindsay in his 'Testament of the Papyngo'. A Lord of Session, he was also advocate to Margaret Tudor in 1528, rector of Spott (which was a Chapel Royal prebend) and treasurer of the Chapel Royal from 1528 to 1532 and as such a successor of John Mair and Andrew Durie.[29] To this circle of learned men we should also add Mr Thomas Marjoribankis*, procurator of the Scottish nation at Orléans in 1517, a position also held in 1512 by James Foulis. David (later Cardinal) Beaton arrived in Orléans in 1519, and it was probably there that the 'continuing friendship' between Marjoribankis and Beaton began; in later years Marjoribankis regularly took care of the Cardinal's business. One of the first advocates of the Court of Session in 1532, Marjoribankis was provost of Edinburgh in 1541 and was appointed Clerk Register in 1549 as successor to the deceased James Foulis.[30]

Mr Thomas Bellenden* was director of Chancery for a brief period in 1513, and he was made an ordinary Lord of Session in 1535 together with Mr Arthur Boece, brother of Hector Boece, the scholar and author of *Scotorum Historiae.* He was appointed director of Chancery and Keeper of the Quarter Seal on 10 September 1538; his appointment as Justice Clerk followed in December 1539. Mr Thomas was also entrusted with important diplomatic missions: in early 1540 he was commissioned, together with Henry Balnaves*, to negotiate with the English on Border affairs. In a report on this to Thomas Cromwell, the dedicated Protestant secretary to Henry VIII, the English commissioners describe Bellenden as gentle and sage, and 'inclined to the English point of view on religious matters'; they also reported that according to Bellenden the Scottish king

ume of Latin verse, which was dedicated to Alexander Stewart, the King's illegitimate son, archbishop of St Andrews and pupil of Erasmus, and containing poems in honour of Patrick Panter and James Henryson of Fordell; see J. Durkan, 'The beginnings of humanism in Scotland', *IR*, iv (1953), 7-8, and J. IJsewijn and D.F.S. Thomson, 'The Latin Poems of Jacobus Follisius or James Foullis [sic] of Edinburgh', in *Humanistica Lovaniensia*, xxiv (1975), 133.

[29] 'Testament of the Papyngo', Lindsay, *Works*, i, 57, l. 47; Durkan, 'Beginnings', 7; Ballantyne, 'Mr Thomas Bellenden', 2; W. Menzies, 'Robert Galbraith, 148-–1543', in *Aberdeen University Library Bulletin*, vii (1929), 204-13; A. Broadie, *The Circle of John Mair: Logic and Logicians in Pre-Reformation Scotland* (Oxford, 1985), esp. 4-5; *DNB*, xx, 372; Watt, *Fasti*, 339.

[30] C. Rogers, *Estimate of the Scottish Nobility during the Minority of James VI* (Grampian Club, 1873), 95-9; Anderson, *Scottish Nation*, vii, 114; *The Faculty of Advocates in Scotland, 1532-1943*, ed. F.J. Grant (SRS, 1944), 144; M.H.B. Sanderson, '"Kin, Freindis and Servandis". The men who worked with Archbishop David Beaton', *IR*, xxv (1974), 45; Sanderson, *Beaton*, 12, 53.

> was gretely geven to the reformation of the mysdemeanours of Busshops, religious personnes and preistes ... so muche that by the Kinges pleasure ... they have hade ane enterluyde played in the Feaste of the Epiphane ... before the King and Quene at Lighqwoe, and the hoole Counsaile spirituall and temperall. The hoole matier wherof concluded upon the declaration of the noughtines in religion.

After this, James is reported to have told the bishops to reform their lives, or else he would ship the proudest of them to England. Bellenden asked the English commissioner 'to send him, by secret means, an abstract of all acts, constitutions and proclamations which had been passed in England concerning the suppression of religion, etc., with the intention that James would study these'.[31]

In this period, a group of men in favour of a limited programme of religious reform, centred around men like Thomas Bellenden*, Henry Balnaves* and Robert Galbraith seems to have enjoyed royal protection. A brief look at Bellenden's colleague, Henry Balnaves of Halhill*, provides additional insight into the kind of connections that the Bannatynes had with this group at the close of the reign of James V.[32] Although born of poor parents in the burgh of Kirkcaldy, Mr Henry Balnaves studied in St Andrews and in Cologne, and later acted as procurator, occasionally working for Cardinal Beaton in the 1530s. In 1538 James V appointed him Lord of Session, and in 1539, the same year in which he became godparent to James Bannatyne's first-born child, he had already aroused the jealousy of the clergy (on account of his career and the royal preferments bestowed on him) as well as their suspicion (on account of his quasi-Protestant views). In 1543, Bellenden and Balnaves were prominent supporters of Governor Arran's short-lived 'godly fit', together with David Lindsay, the poet and Lyon King of Arms, and the laird of Grange. As secretary of state, Balnaves was one of the leading figures in Arran's 1543 government, and his name is especially connected with the passing of the Act of Parliament that permitted the reading of the Bible in the vernacular. Consequently, Cardinal Beaton had come to love this early Protestant 'worst of all', and after Arran's 'reconciliation' with Beaton,

---

[31] Ballantyne, 'Mr Thomas Bellenden', 2-7. The Epiphany interlude may refer to an embryonic version of Lindsay's 'Satyre'; see C. Edington, 'Sir David Lindsay of the Mount: Political and Religious Culture in Renaissance Scotland' (St Andrews Ph.D, 1991), 99.

[32] Edington, 'Lindsay', 277, 329-31.

Balnaves was arrested.[33] Following his release, Balnaves acted as an English agent, and received an English pension. After the assassination of Cardinal Beaton in 1546, Balnaves joined the rebels in St Andrews Castle, and was eventually declared a traitor and forfeited; after the rebels at St Andrews had finally surrendered in July 1547, he was sent, together with John Knox, in a galley to France. By 1555, however, after receiving a pardon from the regent, Mary of Guise, he had returned to Scotland to offer her his legal services. Balnaves was a steadfast but moderate Protestant; he eventually became one of the principal reformers, and together with George Buchanan he was appointed in 1563 to revise the 1560 text of the *First Book of Discipline*. Knox, who later edited Balnaves's *The Confession of Faith* (published posthumously in 1584), calls him a very learned and pious man, and Sadler was similarly positive about him. Knox also speaks favourably of Thomas Bellenden*, calling him a man of counsel, judgement and godliness.[34] Finally, Bellenden and Balnaves also have a literary interest in their own right. The last recorded activity of Thomas Bellenden is his work in 1546 as copyist of Gavin Douglas's translation of Virgil's *Aeneid* into the Lambeth MS, while the name of 'Balnaves' has been appended to a poem in the BM. In the Maitland Folio manuscript this poem is attributed to 'Johnne balnaves', and although this rules out the Bannatyne godfather himself as the author, the appearance of this relatively uncommon surname in the BM (which names only a handful contemporary Scottish poets) in conjunction with Henry Balnaves's prominent position in the MB is unlikely to be coincidental, and suggests that personal links between the two families were the channel of transmission of this text.[35]

It is important that Balnaves and Bellenden appear as godparents to James Bannatyne's two eldest sons in the years 1539 and 1540. University graduates and reform-minded jurists,

---

[33] R. Chambers, *Biographical Dictionary of Eminent Scotsmen* (Edinburgh, 1875), i, 78-9; Sanderson, *Beaton*, 26, 87, 90, 174, 271; Spottiswoode, *History*, i, 144; Anderson, *Scottish Nation*, i, 229-30; Edington, 'Lindsay', 96-8, 114-15, 300, 338.

[34] *DNB*, iii, 91-2; I.D. McFarlane, *Buchanan* (1981), 215; *The Scottish Correspondence of Mary of Lorraine, 1542-1560*, ed. I.A. Cameron (SHS, 1927), 404; C. Rogers, *Three Scottish Reformers* (English Reprint Society, 1874), 18; Knox, *Works*, i, 105, 106; Knox, *History*, i, 48. On Balnaves, see also H. Watt, 'Henry Balnaves and the Scottish Reformation', *RSCHS*, v (1935), 23-39.

[35] Ballantyne, 'Mr Thomas Bellenden', 13; 'O gallandis all I cry and call', *Bann. MS. (fac)*, ff.138r-139v; *Maitl. Folio MS.*, i, 355-9.

anxious to reform society without irrevocably breaking the values which underpinned it, they suggest the social and political sympathies of the Bannatynes, which were clearly with progressive but non-radical men of the middle. The public figures in the MB were picked from the ranks of those who were trying to preserve the intellectual inheritance of the nation, which included that of the Church: apart from men like Thomas Bellenden*, Balnaves* and Marjoribankis*, this circle would include Adam Otterburn; David Lindsay; Robert Galbraith; Robert Richardson, the Augustinian reformer; Hector Boece; Robert Reid, bishop of Orkney; Giovanni Ferrerio, the Piedmontese humanist who was brought to Scotland by Reid and who lived in Scotland from 1528 to 1537 and again from 1540 to 1545, lecturing to the monks of Kinloss on, amongst others, Erasmus, Melanchthon, and Rudolph Agricola; William Stewart, bishop of Aberdeen; and Laurence Telfer*, treasurer of Dunkeld, who appears together with Henry Balnaves* as godparent to James Bannatyne's eldest son.[36] Laurence Telfer was brother-in-law to the better-known Andrew Halyburton, conservator of the Scottish staple in the Low Countries, who has left us his 'Ledger' covering business transactions from 1492 to 1503. Laurence Telfer's own account has also been preserved, which shows that he was a merchant as well as a clergyman. He was the successor of Patrick Panter as secretary to the King, and in 1533 James V tried in vain to secure a chaplaincy for him. Clearly in royal favour, he is styled an experienced and erudite man, a faithful servant of both James IV and V.[37]

The above survey shows that, at the end of James V's reign, the Bannatynes were clearly in touch with the intelligentsia as well as with men of affairs. Such men were increasingly in charge of the machinery of government in a period in which the power of the aristocracy was gradually coming to be challenged. The BM stands as a kind of index to the cultural activities of these groups, much

[36] Durkan, 'Beginnings', 14-17; J. Kirk, 'Clement Little's Edinburgh', in *Edinburgh University Library 1580-1980: A Collection of Historical Essays* (Edinburgh, 1982), ed. J.R. Guild and A. Law, 7-8; Edington, 'Lindsay', 85; J. Durkan, 'Giovanni Ferrerio: religious humanism in sixteenth-century Scotland', in *Studies in Church History. Vol. XVII: Religion and Humanism,* ed. K. Robbins (Oxford, 1981), 181-94.

[37] *Ledger of Andrew Halyburton, 1492-1503,* ed. C. Innes (Edinburgh, 1867), pp. xxvi, lxiii, 17-27; *James V Letters,* 67, 247-8. Telfer owned copies of Pliny Secundus, *Epistolarum libri novem* (Venice, 1510) and Seneca, *Tragedie* (Paris, 1512); see Durkan & Ross, *Libraries* (NLS, interleaved copy, shelf mark SU8).

of its contents belonging to a more aristocratically and clerically dominated medieval heritage but preserved by a new, socially dominant cultural elite, which was largely made up of a secularised urban oligarchy. These men and women, as well as the BM itself, were thus true cultural intermediaries.

Thomas Bellenden's son and heir, John Bellenden of Auchnoull*, was appointed director of Chancery on 17 January 1543, and in 1547 succeeded his father as Justice Clerk. He amassed a great deal of property, and became a central political figure; although he eventually joined the reformers, he was never a committed Protestant, but always remained first and foremost a crown servant. He was employed by Mary of Guise as mediator between her and the Lords of the Congregation, and he, after 1560, occasionally negotiated with the Kirk on behalf of the crown. Knox claims that Bellenden had once been 'not the least ... amongis the flatteraris of the court'. Nevertheless, he has also been referred to as a traitor to the Marian cause, one of the 'creatures of Murray'.[38] John Bellenden of Auchnoull* fled from Edinburgh after the Riccio murder, but on 18 May 1566, barely two months later, he was 'permittit to purge himself of the slauchter of umquhile seinyeour David ... and was fund clene'. John Bellenden's court connections were impressive: his first wife was Margaret Scott, the daughter of the first marriage of Marion Scott*, one of the ladies-in-waiting to Mary Queen of Scots; in 1555 he married, secondly, Barbara Kennedy, a favourite of Mary of Guise, and in later years Mary Queen of Scots was a party to his third marriage contract in 1565 to Janet Seton, promising him 1000 merks of tocher; the Queen and her four Maries also attended his daughter's wedding.[39] This royal interest, as well as Bellenden's political career, show that he was a prominent member of the court, who took care to marry into the royal household and into families with a tradition of loyalty and service to the crown.

---

[38] *RSS*, iii, 39, 2313; *DNB*, iv, 187-8; Knox, *Works*, ii, 414; Keith, *History*, i, 208, 217; ii, 69, 78; G. Chalmers, *The Life of Mary, Queen of Scots* (2nd edn., 1822), iii, 427, 443; G.W.T. Omond, *The Lord Advocates of Scotland* (Edinburgh, 1883-1914), i, 34, quoting Tytler, *Inquiry*, ii, 102.

[39] R. Douglas, *The Baronage of Scotland* (Edinburgh, 1798), 518; *Diurnal*, 100; Anderson, *Scottish Nation*, i, 282-3; *TA*, x, p. xxx; *Scots Peerage*, ii, 65-6; J. Harrison, *The History of the Monastery of the Holyrood and of the Palace of Holyrood House* (Edinburgh and London, 1919), 104. *TA*, vii, 445, gives Margaret Scott as the name of the nurse to one of James V's sons who died in infancy in 1541, and, considering Bellenden's court connections, this may well be his wife.

John's eldest son, Lewis Bellenden*, succeeded his father as Justice Clerk. He donated five French books to the library of James VI in March 1576; he was a Lord of Session, and in 1589, having been an ambassador to negotiate the royal marriage, he accompanied James VI to Denmark for the wedding. Finally, the other Thomas Bellenden* in the MB, identified as 'tutor of Kilconquhar', was a son of the third marriage of John Bellenden of Auchnoull*. He married Marion Gilbert*, the widow of Thomas Bannatyne, Lord Newtyle (George Bannatyne's brother), and also succeeded him as Lord of Session in 1591, which once more confirms the close links between the Bellenden and Bannatyne families outlined above.[40]

The Maitland family

This short survey of the Bellenden family brings out the latter's characteristic combination of national careers in crown service together with a highly-developed interest in literature and learning. The same pattern and ambitions, though on a more humble level, can be traced in the history of the Bannatynes, showing that literary interests, like politics, trade and particular crafts, ran in families. The Maitlands were another family of modest background, who nevertheless produced prominent legal men and statesmen who were also poets. At their head stood William Maitland, a great favourite of James IV, who died with his king at Flodden. His son, Sir Richard Maitland (1496-1586), was a student of law in France and of literature and philosophy at St Andrews. A royal servant under James V, Arran, Mary of Guise, Mary Queen of Scots and James VI, his offices included that of Lord of Session and Keeper of the Privy Seal during the Guise regency as well as under Mary Queen of Scots, and Keeper of the Great Seal under James VI. Maitland was also a substantial vernacular poet, who collected and preserved vernacular poetry in a manuscript now known as the Maitland Folio, second in importance only to the BM; he also wrote a history of the house of Seton (his father married a daughter of George Lord Seton).

---

[40] *Scots Peerage*, ii, 66, 68-70; 'The Library of James VI in the hand of Peter Young, his tutor, 1573-1583', ed. G.F. Warner, in *SHS Miscellany* (SHS, 1893), i, p. liii (note also the name of John Bellenden, p. xlv); Anderson, *Scottish Nation*, i, 283; RMS, vi, p. 319, n.1; Brunton and Haig, *Senators*, 218-19.

Documents of Maitland's time as well as his own poetry reveal a wise, humanitarian character respected by all sides—*pace* one allegation by Knox, who claims that Maitland, in the 1540s, was bribed into letting Beaton escape. His special status is marked by the fact that he was the first to be allowed to nominate his successor on the bench when old age finally overtook him in 1584; it is interesting to learn that he chose Sir Lewis Bellenden of Auchnoull*, which indicates the interaction of these literate families.[41]

Maitland's children displayed both the political as well as the literary interests of their father: his eldest son William was the well-known 'Secretary Lethington', nicknamed 'Mitchell Wylie' (after Machiavelli), who in 1567 married Mary Fleming, one of the four Maries, an illegitimate daughter of James V and a lifelong favourite of the Queen, and he himself became one of the principal supporters of Mary during the Civil War. The second son, John, was Keeper of the Privy Seal in 1567 until forfeited in 1571, and was in Edinburgh Castle along with his elder brother when it fell, while another son, Thomas, wrote an encomium on Alexander Arbuthnot, printed in the *Delitiae Poetarum Scotorum.* Finally, the Maitland Quarto, another important manuscript of Middle Scots poetry, was copied by Sir Richard's daughter, Mary. The Maitlands were connected to other families generally characterised by their loyalty to the crown—such as the Setons, Flemings and Bellendens, and it is in these court-related circles that Middle Scots literature as we have it was produced and preserved. The BM stands at the intersection of these families and wider national concerns; while attempting to do away with moral and social wrongs in pre-Reformation society, men like Thomas Bellenden* were equally concerned with preserving from that same period those political and social structures that they considered valuable. The poems in which Richard Maitland laments the new abuses of the post-Reformation period clearly echo the balanced criticism of both Protestant and Catholic abuses as voiced in 1562 by Alexander Scott in his 'New Year Gift' poem to the Queen, the central political statement in the BM. The overriding concern of these poets was the national 'common weill', a social and civic rather than political or religious priority, which makes them the true successors of David

---

[41] Anderson, *Scottish Nation*, vii, 74-5; Chambers, *Eminent Scotsmen*, ii, 87.

Lindsay; in this respect, it is significant that the one poem by Richard Maitland that is included in the BM is a reworking of part of Lindsay's *Monarche.*[42]

From the mid-1540s to the mid-1560s

The names entered in the MB for the years 1542 to 1548 reflect the realities of a socially and politically unsettled country, beset by English invasion, political factionalism and the beginnings of a Protestant movement. Exact identification of these names is difficult since they are neither distinctive as names in themselves nor do they seem to be related to figures that have left a mark on contemporary history as individuals. However, collectively they do tell a story; they show how the Bannatynes in this period moved predominantly in merchant circles, and were in touch with families like the Telfers, Patersons, Fishers and Rhynds. The Telfers (James Bannatyne's in-laws) and Fishers were prominent merchant families in the first half of the sixteenth century. John Fisher* and George Telfer* had a vessel taken by the Spaniards in the early 1520s, while William Fisher*, James Bannatyne's 'eme', was a money-lender in Edinburgh in this period; together with Nichol Cairncross, the second husband of Marion Scott*, he lent money to Cardinal Beaton as well as to the government. A Thomas Paterson* and a Robert Paterson* (George Bannatyne's brother-in-law) were also merchants, while the Rhynds were a prosperous family of goldsmiths; Thomas Rhynd* was deacon of the goldsmiths for two years and in 1526 went to Flanders to purchase an image of the Lady of Loretto for the goldsmiths' altar in St Giles'. The Irelands on the list, possibly related to Mr David Ireland, advocate, are more difficult to pin down, but they clearly intermarried within the circle of Bannatyne connections: Christian Ireland* married Thomas Rhynd*, while Marion Ireland* married Mr John Abercrombie*. The name of Tod is again that of

---

[42] G.R. Hewitt, *Scotland under Morton, 1572-80* (Edinburgh, 1982), 27; *Maitl. Folio MS.*, i, 34-6, 37-40; *Bann. MS. (fac)*, p. xxi, and ff.12r-14v, 90r-92r. On Thomas Maitland, see W.S. McKechnie, 'Thomas Maitland', *SHR*, iv (1907), 274-93. For further details of the Maitland family, see M. Loughlin, 'The career of William Maitland of Lethington, c.1526-1573' (Edinburgh University Ph.D. thesis, 1991), esp. ch. 1. For William Maitland's reputation, see idem, 'The Dialogue of the Twa Wyfeis', in this present volume.

a merchant family, and David Tod* can be found engaged in both national and international trade.[43]

There is little evidence of Protestant sympathies in the names of this period, with its unsettled economical and political climate. The latter is perhaps best illustrated by the disillusion voiced by Adam Otterburn with regard to political relations between England and Scotland; the opportunity for a new alliance, as promised in the two Treaties of Greenwich of 1543, had temporarily vanished amidst the rigours of the 'rough wooing'. The MB, however, shows signs of renewed vigour from 1548 onwards. The names become less anonymous, and include adherents of both the old and the new faith, although a chronological perspective shows that the names linked to the Protestant establishment of Edinburgh begin to come in gradually, gaining in godly repute as time passed. Alexander Guthrie* is the first name we meet on the list with a solidly Protestant record. He was already a leading figure of the Protestant element in Edinburgh in the 1540s, and his wife, Janet Henryson, was one of Knox's 'dear sisters'. Guthrie was on the Edinburgh town council almost continuously from 1557 to 1580 and was known to his enemies as 'King Guthrie'. As common clerk of the burgh, he was ordered into ward by the 1559 loyalist council under the Catholic Lord Seton, and in 1560 he acted as informant of Randolph, the English ambassador. He was summoned to appear in court for joining Moray's rebellion in 1565, and was banished in March 1566 in connection with the murder of Riccio, but he was granted a remission later that year.[44]

A similar Protestant figure was Mr James McGill of Rankeillor Nether*. Eldest son of Sir James McGill, Lord Provost of Edinburgh, he was appointed Clerk Register by Mary of Guise on 25 June 1554 (succeeding Mr Thomas Marjoribankis*), and appointed ordinary Lord of Session on 20 August of the same year. Late in 1559 McGill joined the reformers, but was nevertheless included in Mary's privy council when she returned from France in 1561. It was in the house of McGill that laymen and ministers met to decide on how to react to Mary's mass-services. Like John Bellenden of Auchnoull*, Alexander Guthrie* and

---

[43] *James V Letters*, 387; Sanderson, *Beaton*, 59, 136; Lynch, *Edinburgh*, 347; *Edinburgh Burgesses*, 393; J. Durkan, *Protocol Book of John Foular, 1528-1534* (SRS, 1985), p. xii; SRO B/22/1/21 (Protocol Book Alexander Guthrie, elder, vol. 2), f.126, 23 May 1562; *TA*, ix, 435; *ADCP*, 308.

[44] *DNB*, xlii, 343; Lynch, *Edinburgh*, 15, 278, 282, 331-32; idem, 'The two Edinburgh town councils of 1559-1560', *SHR*, liv (1975), 124, 130, 138.

John Knox, McGill fled the capital when Mary returned to Edinburgh after the 1565 crisis.[45] He was later 'delatit' for the slaughter of Riccio and lost the post of Clerk Register, but was soon pardoned and returned to the Queen's administration in 1567, through the intercession of Moray, with whom he had been engaged on several embassies to England. It was in this period that the Bishop of Mondovi complained about the fact that both McGill* and Bellenden of Auchnoull* remained in the royal household, and he labelled McGill 'plebeo, inventore d'ogni male' ('a man of no family and contriver of all evil'). James McGill married Janet Adamson, who, like Guthrie's wife, was a personal ally of Knox and remained a radical Protestant after her husband's death; she was the sister of William Adamson, younger, a prominent Protestant of the 1540s who had married Agnes Bellenden, the younger sister of John Bellenden of Auchnoull*.[46]

There are also a few 'minor' Protestants in the MB. James Millar* was a writer to the Signet and Deputy Justice Clerk. He was suspected of being involved in the assassination of Riccio and was listed among the Edinburgh burgesses to whom remission was granted for the murder. In 1571, during the civil war, he was denounced as a rebel by the Queen's lords.[47] Thomas Thomson of Duddingstoun* was appointed royal apothecary for life under the Governor Arran in 1545, and he also served as such during the regency of Mary of Guise. Himself a town councillor (1558-59 and 1560-61), he was a source of problems to Seton's council in 1559, and Randolph complained in November 1561 that he was 'much cumbered' by this 'mischievous man ... a playne anabaptiste'. Later he was 'a prominent and active Protestant figure in the burgh until his death in 1572'.[48] For Robert Henderson* there are two possible candidates: a master flesher from the 1530s until c.1559, and a barber-surgeon who served on the town council in 1557-8, 1573-5 and 1583-4. That the Bannatyne godfather is

---

[45] Lynch, *Edinburgh*, 116, 304-05; J.H. Burton, *The History of Scotland* (new edn., Edinburgh, 1897), iv, 34; Chalmers, *Life of Mary*, iii, 427. The McGills were a family of legists; see Grant, *Faculty of Advocates*, 132.

[46] *Papal Negotiations with Mary Queen of Scots during her Reign in Scotland, 1561-1567*, ed. J.H. Pollen (SHS, 1901), 272, 278; Lynch, *Edinburgh*, 276, 283, 366; *Scots Peerage*, ii, 64.

[47] *Writers to His Majesty's Signet*, 261; *Laing Chrs*, 695, 737; Omond, *Lord Advocates*, i, 31; Lynch, *Edinburgh*, 116, 283, 305.

[48] *RSS*, iii, 1313; Lynch, *Edinburgh*, 74, 284, 357; Lynch, 'Two Edinburgh town councils', 124, 131, 134.

the surgeon is suggested by the latter's occurrence as a witness to a contract made by George Bannatyne's father in 1577. He was an active Protestant, and his is the last name in the list of those who on 24 December 1566 were granted a remission for the murder of Riccio.[49]

Alexander Guthrie*, Thomas Thomson*, James McGill*, Robert Henderson* and James Millar* were all involved with the Protestant cause in Edinburgh in the 1550s and 1560s, while figures like John Bellenden of Auchnoull* and Simon Preston*, though on good terms with the royal establishment, were at least nominal Protestants. Even more revealing is a comparison between the names in the MB and those on the list, drawn up in 1562, of 160 'faithful brethren' who were donors to a new poor hospital in the burgh: the large section of 29 lawyers and professional men on that list especially catches the eye, yielding seven names from the MB (Robert Scott, Neil Laing, James Bannatyne, Alexander Guthrie, John Young, James Millar, and James McGill); from the ranks of the merchants we may add Thomas Henderson, William Paterson and Thomas Thomson, while Thomas Hamilton of Priestfield, John Carkettill, Marion Scott and Robert Henderson, barber, also appear.[50]

In marked contrast to Protestants like Guthrie or McGill are the names of men in the MB who had become entrenched in the system of royal patronage and church prebends. As royal favourites, they were either connected to the royal household or held church livings which were in the patronage of the crown. What accentuates the Bannatyne connections even more is that so many of the latter group of secular churchmen can be connected to an explicitly cultural context; they were prebendaries of institutions like Trinity College, the rich collegiate church just outside Edinburgh which received much attention from successive Stewart monarchs, and the Chapel Royal at Stirling, a main centre for both devotional and profane literature. James Kincragy*, dean of Aberdeen, has already been mentioned in

---

[49] *Bann. MS.*, i, p. lxxxiv; D. Hay Fleming, *Mary Queen of Scots* (1897), 502-03; Lynch, *Edinburgh*, 271, 282.

[50] Lynch, Edinburgh, appendices ii and v, clearly show the overlap between the names from the MB and the Edinburgh Protestants. See also idem, 'The "faithful brethren" of Edinburgh: the acceptable face of protestantism', in *Bulletin of the Institute of Historical Research*, li (1978), 194-9. For Thomas Hamilton of Priestfield, see Brian Hillyard, '"Durkan & Ross" and beyond', in this present volume.

connection with his work in the office of the Exchequer, as a combination of an ecclesiastic and a civil servant. He fulfilled many public and semi-religious functions and must have been a close colleague of John Bannatyne, for he was frequently engaged in writing and dictating the rolls in the 1520s and 1530s. He was also conservator for the College of Justice and provost of the collegiate church of St Mary on the Rock in St Andrews from 1496 until his death in 1539, a post that, in the process which led to the re-foundation of the Chapel Royal by James IV in 1501, came to be connected to the deanery of the Chapel Royal. He was also prebendary of Spott from 1499 to 1507, another Chapel Royal prebend at this re-foundation.[51]

A similar figure was Robert Denniston*, brother germane of Mr John Denniston, a favourite of James V. As 'familiar servitor to the king', this John Denniston was in 1530 presented with the prebend of Balmaclellan in the Chapel Royal of Stirling, the same benefice that was presented to the poet Alexander Scott in 1539. His demission on 18 March 1531 should be read in conjunction with a letter by James V (28 March 1531) asking the Pope to nominate 'the King's well-beloved clerk John Denneston' to the rectory of Dysart, a benefice annexed to the collegiate church of St Mary on the Rock. A few years later we see James trying to help John Denniston, of the bed-chamber, in retaining three incompatible benefices. James also proposed to appoint Denniston as the new archdeacon of Dunblane in November 1542.[52] John Denniston, deceased, was succeeded as rector of Dysart in 1547 by his brother germane, Robert Denniston*. On 23 June 1535 Robert Denniston was presented with the prebend of Ayr Tertio (Dalmellington) in the Chapel Royal, vacated by George Clapperton*; a few months later Robert Denniston resigned the prebend of Ayr Quarto, another Chapel Royal prebend. On the basis of the books they owned, John and Robert Denniston*, rectors of Dysart, together with—among others—James Foulis, can be ranked among the intellectual society of higher clergy and academics. Apart from *The New Actis and Constitutionis of Parliament* and St Augustine's *Enarrationes in psalmos*, Robert also possessed copies

[51] *ER*, vols. xv-xvii, passim.; Patrick, *Statutes*, 295; Watt, *Fasti*, 333, 372; *ADCP*, 492; *RSS*, i, 383 and 1474; C. Rogers, *History of the Chapel Royal of Scotland* (Grampian Club, 1882), pp. xxxiv, cxxxiv, 14, 15, 25, 26.

[52] Haws, *Parish Clergy*, 59; *TA*, vii, p. xxxix; *James V Letters*, 190, 196, 374, 445; Watt, *Fasti*, 90.

of Seneca's *Opera* and of Ptolemy's *Geographicae*; the latter had in 1548 been in the possession of John Steinston, protonotary and precentor of Glasgow (and as such a colleague of several Bellendens, including the poet John Bellenden) and was later owned by his friend Edward Henryson, lawyer and classicist.[53]

There are more names from the MB that can be connected to the Chapel Royal. The uncle of James Bannatyne, Mr Laurence Telfer*, treasurer of Dunkeld and canon of Aberdeen, in 1538 resigned the rectory of Creichtmont, a prebend of St Machar's Cathedral, Aberdeen, in royal patronage, to his relative, Mr Arthur Telfer*. The latter also held the chaplaincy of the royal chapel of the Blessed Mary of Rattray from 18 February 1543 until 31 October 1545, when he resigned it to John Bannatyne, George Bannatyne's uncle; John Bannatyne and Arthur Telfer* were both prebendaries of Trinity College as well.[54] Since Arthur Telfer was also vicar of Aboyne as well as titular vicar of Inchture, we are clearly dealing with a pluralist. He was also a 'concubinarius', who had at least four bastard sons, yet he signed the 'counsel' of the cathedral chapter of Aberdeen which requested its bishop 'to show good and edificative example, in special in removing and discharging himself of the company of the gentlewoman by whom he is greatly slanderit.' This was done at the provincial council in 1549, at which another Bannatyne godparent of a similar type was present, namely George Clapperton*.[55] In 1535 Clapperton had been presented to the subdeanery of the Chapel Royal, a position he held until 1574, and in 1540 he was also appointed provost of Trinity College. This post had become vacant after the decease of James Kincragy*, and had originally been granted to Robert Erskine, brother to the King's secretary, Mr Thomas Erskine, who

---

[53] *RSS*, ii, 499, 852, 926, 1704 (see also 'Index of Offices'); *RSS*, iii, 2436; J. MacQueen (ed.), *Ballattis of Luve 1400-1570* (Edinburgh, 1970), p. xl; Durkan & Ross, *Libraries*, 3-4, 20, 88. James Denniston, son of John and Robert Denniston's brother William, provost of Linlithgow and Keeper of Linlithgow Palace, married Margaret, the daughter of Mr Thomas Bellenden* (*Scots Peerage*, ii, 64). For Henryson, see below, p. 211.

[54] Mr Arthur Telfer is referred to as James Bannatyne's 'gudsir bruder' by George Bannatyne, *Bann. MS.*, i, p. cxliv; *RSS*, ii, 2737-8; *RSS*, iii, 76, 348, 1395; Black, *Surnames*, 765. On Sir John Bannatyne, prebendary of Trinity College, see *Registrum Domus de Soltre*, ed. D. Laing (Bann. Club, 1861), and *RSS*, vi, 857.

[55] Haws, *Parish Clergy*, 7, 52, 110; C.H. Haws, 'The diocese of St Andrews at the Reformation', *RSCHS*, xviii (1972-4), 120; J.H.S. Burleigh, 'The Scottish reforming councils, 1549 to 1559', *RSCHS*, xi (1955), 199-200. *RSS*, iv, 778; Patrick, *Statutes*, 107.

was, like Clapperton, connected to both Trinity College and the Chapel Royal. Clapperton was clearly a pluralist enjoying royal favour: apart from his Chapel Royal and Trinity College livings, he was titular vicar of Wemyss and parson of Kirkinner. Moreover, from 1538 until the death of James V in 1542 he was almoner (an office which also sometimes carried the duties of librarian) to the King, in which capacity a livery was made for him in 1541. Most interesting in the present context is the fact that he can be identified as a vernacular poet: the Maitland Folio includes his 'Wa worth mariage'.[56]

A similar figure to Arthur Telfer*, Robert Denniston* and George Clapperton* was Sir William Makdowell*, who combined service in the royal household with various church benefices. In addition, however, his involvement in cultural events throws an interesting light on the Bannatyne circle. He was Master of Works to the Queen, and was appointed chaplain of the palace of Holyrood in November 1554, which suggests that he was in the favour of Mary of Guise, who immediately set about restoring Holyrood as a royal palace when she became regent on 12 April 1554. On 1 January 1560 Makdowell was presented to the vicarage of Leswalt, and from 1561 to 1572 was vicar of Inch, Leswalt, Holyrood and Dalmeny, as well as chaplain of St Nicholas in St Giles'; this is clearly the profile of a pluralist who was not likely to serve in person in any remote parish. As Master of Works, Makdowell was paid in his capacity as 'makar of the playing-place' for a play staged at the Tron on 10 June 1554. Only a few months later, Makdowell was building the stage and the 'Quenis grace hous on the playfeild ... and the playars hous, the jebbettis and skaffauld about the samyn' for the famous performance of David Lindsay's 'Satyre of the Thrie Estaitis', performed on 12 August 1554 'besyde Edinburgh, in presence of the Quene Regent and ane greit part of the Nobilitie'. Makdowell was clearly involved in a brief 'court & culture' revival under Mary of Guise in the years 1554 and 1555, which also included the staging of plays by William Lauder.[57] This was a cultural revival in which the town of

---

[56] *RSS*, ii, 1703; Haws, 'Diocese of St Andrews', 119; *James V Letters*, 406; Watt, *Fasti*, 340; *TA*, vii, p. xxxii; *Maitl. Folio MS.*, i, 243-4.

[57] Master of Works: *Edin. Recs.*, ii, 269, 271; *TA*, x, passim.; *RSS*, iii, 2604; *RSS*, iv, 2835, 2839; Haws, 'Diocese of St Andrews', 121; B.L.H. Horn, 'List of references to the pre-Reformation altarages in the parish church of Haddington', in *East Lothian Trans.*, x (1966), 42; Lindsay, *Works*, i, 398; iv, 139-43; *Edin Recs.*, ii, 206.

Edinburgh and the royal court mutually complemented one another, cultural preferences blending in with political compromise.

This complex pattern of church appointments and patronage reveals further circles with which the Bannatyne family had connections. Apart from the Chapel Royal and Trinity College, various names on the MB can also be connected indirectly to Holyrood Abbey. In addition to the Bellendens (see above), this would include the second husband of Marion Scott*, Nicoll Cairncross, the Edinburgh merchant seen earlier, whose relative Robert Cairncross was commendator of Holyrood and a 'noted royal adviser', while Nicol Ramsay* was brother germane to Sir John Ramsay, canon of Holyrood.[58]

Landed gentry

The above survey shows that the Protestant flavour of the list of names in the MB was balanced by firm links with elements of the old establishment such as the royal household and the Catholic Church. The representatives of the landed gentry in the MB complete this picture, especially through their long-standing allegiance to the royal cause. Knox listed the Scotts of Balwearie among the few Fife families that collaborated with the French, 'ennemyes to God and traytouris to thair countrey', and William Scott of Balwearie* is indeed recorded as a pro-French laird in the 1540s, and again in 1560. He was the subject of royal gratitude in 1540 for having remained 'continewly in our service with our derrest fallow the quene in Sanctandrois'. He heard mass in December 1560 and fought on Mary's side at the battle of Langside, on account of which he was charged to appear before the privy council. His father, of the same name, had acquired a large estate; he had been 'familiar servitour' and 'consilliarius' to the king, and at the institution of the College of Justice in May 1532 he was nominated the first senator on the temporal side. Thomas Scott of Pitgorno, 'gentleman of the king's hous' and half-brother of

[58] Anderson, *Robert Stewart*, 5; SRO, B 22/1/14 (Protocol Book of Alexander King, vol. 1), ff.53 and 62, 23 April and 6 June 1549. Both Nicol and Robert Cairncross were related to the Cairncross family of Colmislie: W. Stephen, *History of Inverkeithing and Rosyth* (Aberdeen, 1921), 142; Lynch, *Edinburgh*, 291; Dowden, *Bishops*, 226; SRO, CC 7/49, f.168. On the church livings held by the Bannatynes, see n.77 below.

the Bannatyne godfather, was another great favourite of James V, and was appointed Justice Clerk in 1535.[59] The third husband of Marion Scott*, the 'trusty cousin' of William Scott of Balwearie*, was George Henderson of Fordell*, mentioned above as fellow student of Mr Thomas Bellenden* in Paris. He was provost of Edinburgh and regularly passed to Flanders and France with merchandise; he died at the battle of Pinkie in 1547. His successor, his grandson James, was a great favourite of James VI, and the family was rewarded for faithful service to him and previous Stewart monarchs. An instance of this would be the protection provided by the laird of Fordell and Sir John Bellenden of Auchnoull* in 1566 to John Scott, the schoolmaster, ex-chaplain and notary who had been protected from the Protestants by the Queen herself in 1564.[60]

Loyalty to the crown was likewise a feature of Henry Foulis of Colinton*, son of the poet James Foulis, and of Patrick Hepburn of Waughton* and his ancestors. The latter was among the lairds in the 'party of revolution' in 1559 and attended the Reformation Parliament on 1 August 1560. Nevertheless, together with some other Hepburns, he held Dunbar Castle for his kinsman, the 4th Earl of Bothwell, after the latter's defeat at Carberry in 1567. As a consequence of this, he had to surrender his house and was ordered to appear before the regent and council. Shortly after this he was exiled, and in 1572 he was still 'under sentence of forfeiture' for his allegiance to Mary. In 1580, Waughton was on the assize deciding Morton's fate, a jury clearly loyal to the Stewarts and anti-Morton in sentiment; Morton protested especially against the inclusion of Waughton, who had served with Grange in France.[61] The Bannatyne family had long-standing connections with these Hepburns of Waughton, possibly going back to the late fifteenth century, when a Patrick Hepburn was writer to the Signet. Moreover, Patrick Hepburn, bishop of Moray and kinsman of Waughton, was appointed Keeper of the Signet in 1524. That the Bannatynes knew this bishop appears from a document recording the

---

59 'Journal of the siege of Leith', in *Two Missions of Jacques de la Brosse*, ed. G. Dickinson (SHS, 1942), 122; *ADCP*, 383, 389, 489; Anderson, *Scottish Nation*, viii, 406; Donaldson, *All the Queen's Men*, 107; *TA*, xii, 126 and 218; *RMS*, ii, 761, 1472; Brunton and Haig, *Senators*, 19.

60 Stephen, *Inverkeithing and Rosyth*, 142; *ADCP*, 224, 479, 561-2.

61 Douglas, *Baronage*, 87; Donaldson, *All the Queen's Men*, 40, 84, 104, 162; *APS*, ii, 526; *APS*, iii, 6; *TA*, xii, 78, 80, 219; *Court Book of the Regality of Broughton and the Burgh of the Canongate, 1569-1573*, ed. M. Wood (SRS, 1937), 302; Hewitt, *Scotland under Morton*, 22, 199.

sale in 1559 by Patrick Hepburn, bishop of Moray, of the lands of Little Balquhomerie and Formonthills to George Bannatyne's parents; Patrick Hepburn of Waughton* was a witness to the contract.[62]

John Carkettill of Finglen*, who has already crossed our path as a relation of Walter Chepman's first wife, was a close ally of Patrick Hepburn of Waughton*, with whom he occurs regularly in the records, most notably in the years 1567-8, when Carkettill can be found on the side of the Queen's men together with these Hepburns. But his name is in another way tied up with an important figure mentioned above: he was charged with the murder of Robert Galbraith, the above-mentioned lawyer and poet, who was killed on 27 January 1544 'vpon ane festivall day in time of divine service before noon in the kirkyard of the gray friars within the burgh of Edinburgh'; Carkettill was eventually ordered to pay a sum of 2000 merks in compensation.[63]

What characterises the Bannatyne connections as well as the BM as an enterprise in itself is especially a concern for continuity, both in social, cultural and intellectual terms: figures such as Balwearie*, Waughton* and Fordell* indicate that loyalty and service to the monarch were characteristic features of those whose names can be found in the MB. Allegiance to the crown was frequently based on family traditions or on vested interests rather than on political opinion, and moderation ran in such families, especially the more prominent ones. The leading merchants, together with the lawyers, were 'the pillars of the new kirk' in the 1560s, but at the same time their loyalties clearly lay with the crown.[64] The merchants in the MB from the 1540s, like the lairds, yield a surprisingly large number of connections in the later period with the Queen's party. Although much more information needs to be unearthed, this applies especially to the Fishers and the Patersons. For their part, David Tod* and his wife, Elizabeth Young*, have both been identified as Catholics, the latter being present at the baptism of the child of John Charteris, younger, at Holyrood in December 1561. This is another reminder of the close links between merchants and printers, since this John

---

[62] *Writers to His Majesty's Signet*, 32, 190, 377; *RMS*, iv, 1348.

[63] *TA*, xii, 28, 80; *Inchcolm Chrs*, 189; SRO, CS 7/8, ff.386-87 (I owe this reference to the date of Galbraith's death to Mr John Ballantyne); SRO, RD 1/2, ff.148-9; *ADCP*, 537, 638.

[64] Lynch, *Edinburgh*, 180; the sympathy of the older merchant establishment was with the Marian cause (ibid., 146, 203, 207, 219).

Charteris was the brother of the merchant and bookseller Henry Charteris, who financed the printing by John Scot of *The warkis of David Lindsay* in 1568.[65]

An important change overtook these middling ranks of Scottish society in the period between the 1540s and the 1560s. In the 1540s, the landed gentry and the merchant establishment largely still moved in and reflected traditional, semi-feudal patterns of loyalty or a civic concern with social order. Increasingly, however, the fast-growing legal circles of Edinburgh, represented in the MB in great number by writers, advocates and other clerks, looked upon the sovereign as the juridical, political and cultural centre of the realm rather than as a charismatic personality topping the feudal order. Several generations of legal training lay behind the emergence of this new, centralist dimension which was added to the old, habitual loyalties to the crown, and these men were often statesmen and courtiers rather than lawyers.[66] At the same time, the Bannatynes also picked up new discourses of power and culture, and forged links with the new, Protestant establishment. Moving in this way among 'new men', printers, poets, merchants, 'politicians' and lairds made George Bannatyne eminently suitable to capture the transmission as well as the transformation of the products of a disappearing cultural élite as it gradually gave way to a new one. The above survey shows that the Bannatynes had been in touch with those figures who could be said to guard the national cultural heritage, and, following naturally from these connections and concerns, the BM, a few decades later, survives as the major reflection of such a cultural process.

Central concerns and pragmatic measures

The social stability maintained in most of the years from 1550 to 1565 not only yielded an almost bloodless Reformation but also created the opportunity for progress. It has been argued that in these years 'a healthy civic Catholicism' developed into 'a civic

[65] Lynch, *Edinburgh*, 288, 293. For Charteris's preface to the *Warkis*, see Lindsay, *Works*, i, 397-405.

[66] This development, originating in the reign of James IV with its successful educational and administrative reform in conjunction with the advent of printing, had in the reign of James VI led to 'a *noblesse de robe*, made up of men drawn from the lairds, the cadet branches of noble houses, and the Edinburgh legal fraternity, through which he governed': M. Lee, review of J. Wormald, *Lords and Men in Scotland: Bonds of Manrent, 1442-1603* (Edinburgh, 1981), in *Scotia*, x (1986), 31.

Protestantism', implying that the Protestantism of the 1560s, like the Catholicism of the 1550s, was motivated to a considerable extent by national or local priorities rather than any specific religious aim. Minding 'their particular', 'the religion of Edinburgh', proved more important than any religious dogma, and the merchant-dominated 'faithful brethren' of 1562 subscribed first and foremost to a local, communal concern.[67] In attempts to remedy pre-Reformation short-comings while at the same time boosting the position of Edinburgh as the largest centre for overseas trade and administrative capital of the realm, these same people contributed towards the establishment of educational and legal institutions. A new vogue for civic improvement underpinned the growth of the professions.

Thus, the books of Clement Little, an advocate who became a moderate Protestant 'through Erasmian humanism and reformist Catholicism', formed the nucleus of the library of Edinburgh's 'tounis college' founded in 1582, and this same, emerging institution benefited from the attempts by Robert Reid and Mary of Guise to introduce 'higher education' to Edinburgh. Robert Reid, abbot of Kinloss, bishop of Orkney and Lord President of the Court of Session, was a pivotal force in the group that included Kincragy*, Galbraith, Laurence Telfer*, Ferrerio, Foulis and Marjoribankis*; he drew up a new constitution for Orkney Cathedral in 1545 which included provisions for teaching, and he left a considerable sum of money in his will towards the promotion of learning in Edinburgh, appointing James McGill* as one of three men to counsel the executors of his educational plans.[68] Reid's name is also connected with another initiative that may be considered a sign of civic health combined with cultural and intellectual progress on the eve of the Reformation—the royal lectureships. Mary of Guise, who deplored the 'laik of cunning men' in her realm, created these lectureships in 1556 to the 'untellabill proffet of our leigis'; she appointed Alexander Sym and Edward Henryson as the royal lecturers, and as part of their duty they gave public lectures on Greek and law in the Magdalen Chapel in Edinburgh's Cowgate. Henryson is of special interest to us in that he was the second husband of Helen Swinton*. He had been recommended as a Greek scholar to Reid by

[67] Lynch, *Edinburgh*, 30, 216, 222; Calderwood, *History*, v, 177-8.

[68] Kirk, 'Clement Little's Edinburgh', 17; D.B. Horn, 'The origins of the University of Edinburgh', *EUJ*, xxii (1966), 213-25, 297-312.

Ferrerio in 1555, and had been employed in the household of Henry Sinclair, dean of Glasgow and later bishop of Ross; he was acquainted with Henry Scrimgeour and Ulrich Fugger, to whom he taught Greek and to whom he dedicated one of his works.[69]

It is characteristic of the practical partnership struck in the mid-1550s between the crown and the legal establishment that these lectureships were a royal initiative executed by lawyers; this pragmatic focus on learning must have appealed to all parties. In addition, through such practical concerns, men like Henryson, Marjoribankis, Foulis, Otterburn, Galbraith and the Bellendens formed a new Edinburgh-centred network in which learning was cultivated, and through them families like the Bannatynes had access to continental learning and culture. A sample piece of evidence for the cultural process involved is a letter from Mr George Bellenden, the illegitimate son of Mr Thomas Bellenden*, to 'his verie good lord and broder my Lord Justice Clerk of Scotland' (i.e. John Bellenden of Auchnoull*).[70] This letter shows the desire for learning and continental scholarship among the people connected to the Bannatynes as well as the channels through which such contacts were established: Mr George is studying Aristotle under Petrus Ramus in Paris and living in a 'pensioun' in the Rue St Jacques; he has come to Paris with some Scottish merchants, through whom he has sent reports back home; he has obtained cheap accommodation through the services of these and other 'factours' as well as through James Nisbet, servant to the Treasurer; finally, he hopes to be able to make the planned contact with John Lesley, bishop of Ross, who was in France at this time. Through such channels of communication, Mary's subjects continued to develop the intellectual and cultural inheritance of earlier periods.

With the same eye for practical compromise as that which went into educational progress, the Protestant élite of the 1560s was always alive to the notion that compromise with Mary or with Catholics was more beneficial to the well-being of Edinburgh (and thus to themselves) than taking a hard line. The social milieu that had fostered the BM in the 1560s had little to gain

[69] J. Durkan, 'The royal lectureships under Mary of Lorraine', *SHR*, lxii (1983), 73-8. Anderson, *Robert Stewart*, 26, 32-3; Durkan, 'Beginnings', 16; Durkan & Ross, *Libraries*, 4, 13; C.P. Finlayson, *Clement Littill and his Library* (Edinburgh, 1980), 9-11; Grant, *Faculty of Advocates*, 100; Kirk, 'Clement Little's Edinburgh', 10.

[70] HMC, *Report on the Laing Manuscripts*, i, 20-21.

from an outright conflict, and therefore practised moderation in both political and religious matters, concentrating primarily on issues like trade, legal reform, and education, preferably in co-operation with the crown. This pragmatic middle course, however, was not appreciated by more outspoken Protestants. Consequently, men of the middle—like Mr Simon Preston of Craigmillar*—present characteristically ambiguous profiles. Although he was a respectable member of the Protestant establishment at the time of his appointment as provost of Edinburgh in 1565, there are nevertheless several indications that Preston maintained connections with the old establishment. He enjoyed Mary of Guise's favour and lent her money, and he was the second husband of Janet Beaton, Cardinal Beaton's relative who was on good terms with the Queen. Preston acted on several occasions as Mary's trustworthy agent, and, on the outbreak of Moray's rebellion in August 1565, Mary replaced the Protestant Lord Provost of Edinburgh with Preston, and, against the town council's wishes, insisted on his re-nomination in 1566; moreover, she included him in her privy council. Randolph called Preston a 'rank papist', while Knox labelled him 'a right epicureane' for adhering to the Queen after the Riccio murder, but admitted that after the Darnley marriage Preston 'shewed himself most willing to set forward Religion, to punish vice, and to maintain the Commonwealth'. In the same vein, James Melville classified 'legal politicians' like David McGill, brother of James McGill*, as clever but disdainful of the ministry and 'without all sense of God'. Even Alexander Guthrie, firmly on the Protestant side, was suspected of Marian sympathies, and he had to defend himself in subsequent years against repeated accusations that he secretly favoured the Queen.[71]

The Protestantism of these public figures frequently represented a social or political choice rather than religious conviction, which seems to have been a secondary, 'applied' interest. Any condemnation of the collocation of traditional Queen's men and Protestants in the MB as a break in Bannatyne family logic or an instance of calculated opportunism on their behalf would reflect

[71] *DNB*, xlvi, 312-14; Lynch, *Edinburgh*, 118, 221, 331-2; Sanderson, *Beaton*, 119; Sir W. Fraser, *The Scotts of Buccleuch* (Edinburgh, 1878), i, 554, and ch. 10; M. Wood, *Lord Provosts of Edinburgh, 1296-1932* (Edinburgh, 1931), 22-4; Knox, Works, i, 236; ii, 511. Melville: as quoted in D.B. Smith, 'Sir Thomas Craig, feudalist', *SHR*, xii (1915), 279.

a defect in our own retrospective perception, largely due to the superimposition of later events on this period. These names from the MB belong together by the fact that they covered the middle ground between polarised opinions—a position reflected by many of the individual poems that found their way into the BM and by the internal structure of the BM—as well as by their consistent attention to legal reform and to a continuity of administration. Nor was Mary hostile to 'a Protestantism characterised by civic responsibility and social conservatism';[72] her own dealings with Rome during her personal reign illustrated that her position as monarch was dearer to her than her faith. It is at this overlap of priorities that a party of the middle can be located, and it is in this context that the MB, viewed in conjunction with the BM and its literary contents, confirms the theory that 'there must have been a party willing to go to great lengths to compromise; if we are to accept Sir David Lindsay as still orthodox, such a party has to be postulated.'[73] It involved those who had merged Christian or Erasmian humanism containing Lutheran elements with a native tradition of learning that focused particularly on education and legal reform, a mixture that might be termed civic humanism. Thus, the names from the MB and the connections radiating from it in various directions indeed constitute a 'republic of letters', with poets like Scott and Maitland as its spokesmen, representing a humanism that was concerned with the 'common weill' (John Bellenden's translation of *res republica*) and with the concept of a nation, based on the underlying notion that 'men were born for the sake of men'.[74] Bannatyne's 'intelligent conservatism' and the 'mediating emphasis' of his editing form the literary expression of such concerns, aimed at a treasured Renaissance good, the golden mean. In this way, the MB as well as the BM thus suggest a different paradigm for the history of the period. People like the

[72] Lynch, *Edinburgh*, 104.

[73] J. Durkan, 'The cultural background in sixteenth-century Scotland', in McRoberts, *Essays*, 314.

[74] Durkan, 'Cultural background', 294-5 (focusing on Robert Galbraith's use of Cicero's lines 'Homines hominum causa nati sunt, ut interesse alii aliis prodesse possint' in a letter to Henderson of Fordell); idem, 'Beginnings', 7; Edington, 'Lindsay', 178, 241, 246-9. On Robert Galbraith's work as a 'casualty of the Reformation', see A. Broadie, *The Tradition of Scottish Philosophy* (Edinburgh, 1990); idem., 'Philosophy in Renaissance Scotland: loss and gain', in *Humanism in Renaissance Scotland*, ed. J. MacQueen (Edinburgh, 1990), 75-96. On the confluence between literature, legal training and the concept of a nation, see also M. Lynch, *Scotland. A New History* (2nd edn., 1992), 259-61.

Bellendens and Simon Preston* represent the concern for a political consensus on which to build a nation—an impulse that has frequently been drowned out in later historiography by louder but more marginal voices.[75]

But the centre did not hold. One early, major indication of the growing estrangement between Mary and the 'middle' section of the Edinburgh establishment is the remarkable number of Bannatyne connections that was apparently deeply involved in the plot against Riccio (McGill, Bellenden of Auchnoull, Guthrie, Millar, Robert Henderson). For the BM and its contents, it is vital to realise that by the time George Bannatyne finished copying it in December 1568—after Mary's deposition, her imprisonment on Lochleven, her escape and the disastrous defeat at Langside—the common ground between various factions had been almost totally eroded. The rhetoric of Mary's proclamation after her escape from Lochleven in 1568 exemplified this in highly emotional language; she listed among the 'oppin traitouris ... airis to Judas, sones of Sathane ... Maisteris Hendrie Balknawis, James M'Gill ... and the rest of that pestiferous factioun, quhome ... we promovit, and oft pardonit thair offences.' As a result of the above cultural and political 'input', the BM reflected a culturally conservative impetus yet at the same time tried to meet new political demands, and in his editorial self-censorship Bannatyne 'genuflected towards the prevailing ideology, while maintaining his personal integrity'.[76]

In the years immediately following the deposition of the Queen, the two factions within the King's party that had jointly vanquished the Marian cause rapidly drifted apart. The secularisation of learning, which had made men like Mr Thomas Bellenden* and Robert Galbraith instrumental in preparing the way for reform, by the same token now began to separate the Protestant

---

[75] G. Kratzmann, 'Sixteenth-century secular poetry', in *The History of Scottish Literature. Vol. I: Origins to 1660*, ed. R.D.S. Jack (Aberdeen, 1988), 111. Note that George Bannatyne went to St Mary's College in St Andrews (1558-1561), Archbishop Hamilton's instrument for internal reform (*Bann. MS.*, i, p. lxxxvi).

[76] Pollen, *Papal Negotiations*, 273; A.A. MacDonald, 'Censorship and the Reformation', in *File. A Literary Journal*, i (1992), 8-16; for further discussions of Bannatyne's censorship, see idem, 'Poetry, politics and Reformation censorship in sixteenth-century Scotland', in *English Studies*, lxiv (1983), 410-21; idem, 'Catholic devotion into Protestant lyric: the case of the *Contemplacioun of Synnaris*', in *IR*, xxxv (1984), 58-87; idem., 'Religious poetry in Middle Scots', in *The History of Scottish Literature*, Vol. I, ed. Jack, 91-103; idem, 'Marian Anthology'; idem, 'The printed book'. On Mary, her poets and her moving away from the 'golden mean', see R.D.S. Jack, 'Mary and the poetic vision', in *Scotia*, iii (1979), 35-40.

establishment of Edinburgh from the new Kirk. Many of the leading Protestants resisted the radicals' insistence on the autonomous authority of the Kirk and on egalitarian ministerial parity on account of the concomitant loss of power this would involve for those already established in the higher ranks of the hierarchy. For the same reason, they resisted the radicals' claims to ecclesiastical revenues; many of these Protestant merchants and men of affairs had appropriated former Catholic church property and positions which they were reluctant to surrender, while, in educational spheres, they considered former church livings to be highly suitable as bursaries for students; the Bannatynes benefited from such dealings as well.[77] Consequently, many of the more moderate reformers and humanists who supported the Protestant movement in the 1560s in this period 'came to abhor "a perfect reformation"; brought up on Luther they wanted a laicised church and were offered instead a clericalised state'. Just as their ancestors in the 1550s and 1560s had favoured a reformation outwith the Catholic Church but 'within the framework of duly constituted authority in the state', their moderate descendants of the 1580s emphasised the 'acceptance of legally constituted government or authority' and were anxious to avoid disruptions like the ultra-Protestant Ruthven Raid in 1582 or the Stirling Raid staged by the Earl of Gowrie in 1584.[78]

Pragmatic, irenic Protestants, in their political struggle against more radical forces, found themselves increasingly taking over the role of the Queen's men, who had formed the politically and socially conservative power in the 1560s. As a result, the differences between these pragmatists on the one hand and the Melvillian radicals in the Kirk on the other hardened into irreconcilable opposites, and the names from the MB in the post-Marian years resisted kirk authority with increasing vigour. These advocates, writers and leading merchants, who habitually served as elders on the Edinburgh kirk session, found themselves more and

---

[77] J.H. Cockburn, 'Parochial clergy of the medieval diocese of Dunblane', *Journal of the Society of Friends of Dunblane Cathedral,* viii (1960-61), 120-21; idem, *The Medieval Bishops of Dunblane and their Church* (Edinburgh and London, 1959), 277. George's uncle, John Bannatyne, had enjoyed various church livings before the Reformation (Trinity College, Restalrig, St Michael's altar in Crieff), and after his death in 1569 his relatives appropriated these sources, exchanging them within the family; *RSS,* iii, 76, 1515; iv, 3196, 3316; vi, 824, 831, 857, 1223; vii, 258, 1183; viii, 712, 806.

[78] Durkan, 'Cultural background', 317; Donaldson, *All the Queen's Men,* 7-8, 149.

more at loggerheads with the smaller men and younger merchants who had been appointed to the unpopular job of deacon, a development which unwittingly made the session a breeding ground for radicalism. Mr Thomas Craig (on whom see below), who apparently had 'stubbornly Catholic inclinations' was charged with fornication; James Nicoll* was fined by his fellow councillors for fornication with his servant; John Young*, writer, was charged with misbehaviour towards a minister and Henry Nisbet* was accused of 'irreverent and sklanderous speiches'.[79]

Henry Nisbet* was a close friend of the Bannatyne family: he married George Bannatyne's eldest sister Jonet, was a witness to the will drawn up by George Bannatyne's mother (26 June 1570) and was in 1580 made tutor to the 'bairns' of James Bannatyne, younger. During the civil war, his brother William Nisbet* (died 1585), the first husband of George Bannatyne's wife, had been a leading Queen's man. Henry, a successful merchant, was already in the mid-1580s an ardent supporter of James VI's ecclesiastical policies and a firm opponent of the more radical presbyterians.[80] James Nicoll*, Thomas Aikenhead* and Henry Nisbet* were three of the four bailies appointed by the crown to the council of 1583-4, in the royalist backlash which followed the collapse of the Ruthven regime in the summer of 1583. On the same royal leets of 22 and 24 September 1583 is also to be found William Nisbet*, Henry's brother, who was appointed a councillor. Thomas Aikenhead* and James Nicoll* have been selected as examples of merchants who dissociated themselves from more traditional trades and merchandise and instead became more interested in money-lending and in land as an object of speculation.[81]

These Bannatyne connections were clearly in royal favour; in their conservative concerns and their impatience with the demands of the Kirk, people like Henry Nisbet* seem to have shared common ground with figures like Neill Laing*, a pre-

---

[79] Lynch, *Edinburgh*, 42, 47 (n.51), 93; Wood, *Lord Provosts of Edinburgh*, 33; SRO, CH 2/450/1 (Buik of the General Kirk of Edinburgh), f.8r.

[80] *Bann. MS.*, i, pp. lxvi, lxxii; *RSS*, vi, 1899; M. Lynch, 'The origins of Edinburgh's "toun college": a revision article', *IR*, xxxiii (1982), 4, 5, 9; Lynch, *Edinburgh*, 346, 158, where Henry Nisbet's replies to the veteran Protestant Edward Hope can be read as 'the manifesto of the moderate faction'; J. Geddie, 'Sculptured stones of Edinburgh. The Dean group', in *BOEC*, i (1908), 86-92.

[81] Lynch, *Edinburgh*, 257-8; M.H.B. Sanderson, 'The Edinburgh merchants in society, 1570-1603: the evidence of their testaments', in *The Renaissance and Reformation in Scotland. Essays in Honour of Gordon Donaldson*, eds. I.B. Cowan and D. Shaw (Edinburgh, 1983), 188.

Reformation pluralist who had consolidated his position in the establishment, and who also had close personal ties to the Bannatyne family, turning up with Henry Nisbet* as witness to the testament of George Bannatyne's mother. Neill Laing*, scribe to Governor Arran, was made clerk of coquet for life on 12 April 1543 and appointed Keeper of the Signet in 1547 as successor of Mr John Denniston, rector of Dysart. He is identified as 'one of the Pope's Knights, about the Time of the Reformation' in a short 'satyr' on him by one of the sons of Sir Richard Maitland of Lethington.[82] He indeed seems to have been a man who shared little common ground with the post-Reformation Kirk, to judge from an entry in the 'Buik of the General Kirk of Edinburgh' which epitomises the 'crabbit' relations between the Kirk and many of the names on the MB in the 1570s and 1580s. It is reported that Laing

> had all to gidder violatit and transgressit the actis and ordinance of the kirk maid anent mariage inhebeting and forbydding nocht only supperfluous and ryatus bancatting bot als the pompius convoy of the bryd growme and brid ... and fordir it is declarit that the day foirsaid the said Sir Neill said and declarit the wardis following in greit disdane and disspyt that he rather wald be of the devillis kirk nor be of the kirk of this burgh and that he sould neuir be ane member tharof and wald nocht knaw the samin as the kirk and that the elderis and deaconis wer bot fallowis with sic vther maist opprobrius and disspytfull wordis sounding to the lik purpoiss and effect.[83]

Later generations

A selective look at the offspring of the Bannatyne connections confirms the notion that in the MB are to be found many of the originators of early-modern Scottish literature and learning. Katherine Bellenden, sister of Mr Thomas Bellenden* and of the poet John Bellenden, was the grandmother of John Napier, the inventor of logarithms; it is little known that this renowned mathematician also wrote vernacular poetry. Henry Nisbet* was the ancestor of the Nisbets of Dean, of which family Alexander

---

[82] *Bann. MS.*, i, p. lxvi; *RSS*, iii, 205; *TA*, xii, passim.; *Writers to His Majesty's Signet*, pp. xi, 46; *James Watson's Choice Collection of Comic and Serious Scots Poems*, ed. H.H. Wood, 2 vols. (STS, 1977-91), i, 54; ii, 129-30.

[83] SRO, CH 2/450/1 (Buik of the General Kirk of Edinburgh), f.50v; Laing later admitted the 'making of the pompious convoy' but denied 'thair wes ony supperfluouis banketting' (see also f.42r).

Nisbet, author of *A System of Heraldry*, was a direct descendant. Robert Scott*, himself the subject of a laudatory epitaph by Alexander Montgomerie, was the grandfather of John Scott of Scotstarvit. Scotstarvit wrote Latin poetry, and edited the *Delitiae Poetarum Scotorum* (1637), by far the most valuable collection of Scottish verse in Latin. He married Anne, eldest sister of the poet William Drummond of Hawthornden, was knighted in 1611 and made a Lord of Session in 1617.[84] Thomas Hamilton of Priestfield, younger, merchant, son of Thomas Hamilton of Priestfield*, elder, was a Queen's man, and bailie on the Queen's party council in 1571; he was in later years selected by the king to be raised to the bench as Lord Priestfield. His son was Sir Thomas Hamilton, a famous advocate nicknamed 'Tam of the Cowgate'; having been knighted in 1603, he was the first Earl of Haddington and Earl of Melrose. John, younger son of Thomas Hamilton*, elder, was a secular priest and author of theological works; he was professor of philosophy in the College of Navarre and rector of Paris University as well as tutor to the Cardinal de Bourbon.[85]

Katherine Bellenden, younger, the daughter of Mr Thomas Bellenden*, was the mother of the famous jurist and Latin poet, Sir Thomas Craig of Riccarton, who was a godfather to George Bannatyne's eldest grandchild. His first extant piece of Latin poetry is the epithalamium for Mary's marriage to Darnley, written at a time when he had recently been appointed Deputy Justice Clerk (i.e. working like George Bannatyne's father under the Justice Clerk, John Bellenden of Auchnoull*). Here, literature and legal studies meet again within the Bannatyne circle in what seems to be an instance of a Marian court culture. Although he was educated under the supervision of his uncle John Craig, Knox's colleague at St Giles', Thomas Craig's training in French legal humanism made his work a crucial plea for a powerful,

---

[84] D. Irving, *The History of Scottish Poetry* (Edinburgh, 1861), 471-3; *Bann. MS.*, i, p. clxxiv; J.W.L. Adams, 'The Renaissance poets: (2) Latin.' in *Scottish Poetry: A Critical Survey*, ed. J. Kinsley (1955), 89; *The Poems of Alexander Montgomerie*, ed. J. Cranstoun (STS, 1887), 221; Anderson, *Scottish Nation*, viii, 412; Douglas, *Baronage*, 572; T.G. Snoddy, *Sir John Scot, Lord Scotstarvit: his Life and Times* (Edinburgh, 1968), 12-13, 49.

[85] Lynch, *Edinburgh*, 245, 332-3; *The Staggering State of Scottish Statesmen from 1550 to 1650 by Sir John Scot of Scotstarvet*, ed. C. Rogers (Grampian Club, 1872), 79; *Scots Peerage*, i, 677; K.M. Brown, 'The nobility of Jacobean Scotland 1567-1625', in *Scotland Revisited*, ed. J. Wormald (1992), 72; Fraser, *Haddington*, i, 10-24, 34-6. On Sir Thomas Hamilton, see also Brian Hillyard, '"Durkan & Ross" and beyond', in the present volume.

centralised monarchy based on a professionally-run administration, thus separating legal jurisdiction from territorial or other powers. This illustrates how royal power was linked to the rise of the legists, and Craig's *Jus Feudale* stands at the end of a tradition that had emerged at the beginning of the century among the 'patrons of civic virtue' centred around Robert Galbraith, including, among others, Thomas Bellenden*, George Henderson of Fordell* and Thomas Marjoribankis*.[86]

The son of William Stewart* and George Bannatyne's sister, Catherine, was Sir Lewis Stewart of Kirkhill, whose godfather was Sir Lewis Bellenden*. Stewart of Kirkhill, a loyal servant of the royal Stewarts, was a renowned advocate who acquired many historical manuscripts, including the 'Liber de Cupro', Bower's revised text of Fordun's *Scotichronicon.* Finally, in 1606 George Bannatyne and George Heriot, elder, were godfathers to their joint grandchild, George Foulis. Heriot's son, George Heriot younger, was the royal banker and jeweller who had an apartment assigned to him in Holyrood Palace. He is now better remembered as 'Jinglin' Geordie', the man who bequeathed his fortune to the foundation of Edinburgh's well-known Heriot's Hospital.[87] It is an apt conclusion of the survey of the MB with its many godparents that it was through the descendants of this George Foulis, George Bannatyne's own godchild, that the BM finally came into the possession of the Advocates Library.

The poets

It is striking to see how many of the names from the MB can be connected to the world of literature. In addition, the 'inside information' concerning persons from the world of the Edinburgh legal and administrative élite in poems such as the one by Sempill mentioned above—which, apart from James and Patrick Banna-

---

[86] *Bann. MS.*, i, p. cxlviii. Craig's *Henrici Illustrissimi Ducis Albaniae Comitis Rossiae etc. et Mariae Serenissimae Scotorum Reginae Epithalamium* was published by Lekpreuik in 1565 (Aldis, no. 47). On Craig, see J.W. Cairns, T.D. Fergus and H.L. MacQueen, 'Legal humanism and the history of Scots law: John Skene and Thomas Craig', in *Humanism in Renaissance Scotland,* ed. Macqueen, 48-74; Smith, 'Sir Thomas Craig', 271-302; *DNB,* xii, 448-50; Durkan, 'Cultural background', 315. As Justice Depute: *RSS,* v, 1892 (18 Jan. 1565).

[87] Anderson, *Scottish Nation,* i, 283; Sanderson, 'Two Stewarts', 38; idem, 'Robert Stewart of Atholl, son of the Wolf of Badenoch', *The Stewarts,* xvii (1986), 145-6; *Bann. MS.*, i, p. cxlix.

tyne, also mentions Alexander Guthrie* and David McGill, brother of James McGill*—suggests a specific audience for this poetry as well as a particular discourse that had developed in a milieu that apparently relished such invectives and satires, and of which George Bannatyne must have formed a part. These interactions between text and context closely resemble those between William Dunbar and his more exclusively courtly audience half a century earlier, a relation between poet and audience that may well have been deliberately imitated by the urban Bannatyne circle.

The notion of such a coterie is confirmed by the links between the names from the MB and the contemporary poets who dominate the BM; as shown above, there were close personal links between these Stewarts, the Bellendens and the Bannatynes. Moreover, these Stewarts had pronounced links to the world of literature. William Stewart, elder, had an interest in books: he possessed 'warklumis belanging to the binding of bukis', and he actually received money for binding the town's books in 1560. Among his clients as notary we find many Edinburgh printers and related figures, while his son Robert Stewart, macer, incurred a debt of £400 to a London bookseller. The number and variety of books that William Stewart, elder, owned is similarly indicative of such literary interests: legal works, French and Latin grammars, a Greek Testament, but also—among others—'Metamorphoses in Inglische of Ovid', 'De Sonnetis' and 'Auld storeis in Frensch', and it is interesting to see that among those who borrowed books from him we find Mr William Roberton, the Catholic master of the 'hie scole' who, with the support of a cross-section of the burgh's professional men, successfully resisted attempts to dismiss him after 1560. But the most intriguing connection between these Stewarts and Middle Scots literature lies in their descent from the poet William Stewart; William Stewart, elder, was almost certainly the natural son of the poet of the same name by Janet Hepburn, the aunt of Patrick Hepburn of Waughton*, which tightens the Stewart links with the BM even more. In his poetry, William Stewart gratefully acknowledged the gift of a horse to him (perhaps an instance of literary patronage) by Patrick Hepburn, 3rd Earl of Bothwell, which proves there was indeed a connection between the poet and this branch of the Hepburns.[88]

The close connections between the Bannatynes, Bellendens,

[88] Sanderson, 'Two Stewarts', 34-8; A.A. MacDonald, 'William Stewart and the

Hepburn of Waughton and the Stewarts explain the inclusion in the BM of the poetry of William Stewart, whose presence in the BM as a contemporary lyricist ranks second only to that of Alexander Scott, and the theory of Stewart's verse being enjoyed by such a particular set of prominent men and women in Edinburgh is in fact confirmed by the existence of similar links between the Bannatyne circle and this other makar. Scott's poetry, like Stewart's, is almost exclusively found in the BM; his lyrics clearly dominate the 'ballatis of lufe', which seems to have been the first section of the BM that Bannatyne put together; finally, as stated above, Scott's New Year poem to Queen Mary forms the major political statement of the anthology.[89] Considering this remarkably prominent presence of Scott in the BM, it is interesting to find 'Alexander Scott, servant to his majesty' as one of three witnesses on 18 November 1573 in a document in which George Bannatyne is entered as heir to an annualrent of 50 merks of the lands of Lufnes, belonging to Patrick Hepburn of Waughton, James Bannatyne's 'superior'. A later deed records that in Stirling on 9 March 1576 Alexander Forrester of Garden registered an obligation to infeft Alexander Scott, younger, in an annualrent pertaining to Alexander Scott, elder, 'servitur to the kingis majestie', present 'lyfrentar' of that annualrent, and failing the said Alexander, younger, to his brother, John. The latter piece of information reinforces the hypothesis that this Alexander Scott, elder, is the Chapel Royal poet of that name, for in 1549 the poet legitimated his two sons, Alexander and John. Considering the proximity in date and the similarity in description between the 'Alexander Scott, servant to his majesty', who was a witness to the document from 1573 involving George Bannatyne, and the Alexander Scott, 'servitur to the kingis majestie' in the 1576 obligation, it is most likely that both documents refer to one and the same person, the poet and Chapel Royal prebendary; in other words, Scott was a personal acquaintance of the Bannatynes.[90]

court poetry of the reign of James V' (forthcoming). Stewart listed his books at the beginning of his 'Notarial notebook', now NLS, MS 19312 (I owe this reference to Mrs Joyce Sanderson).

[89] On the theory that the 'ballatis of lufe' form the original nucleus of the BM, see MacDonald, 'Marian Anthology'.

[90] *Bann. MS.*, i, p. lxxxiv; *RMS*, iv, 395; SRO, RD 1/16, f.77/1. Alexander Scott, elder, father to Alexander Scott and John Scott, is also described as both 'lyfrentar' and musician in NLS, Ch. B. 1876, dated 18 June 1582. The most recent survey of Scott's biography can be found in MacQueen, *Ballattis of Luve*,

In addition, Scott's personal history links him to several other names connected to the MB. He was presented to the Chapel Royal prebend held by John Denniston, and the legitimation of his two sons coincides with a spate of similar actions which may be related to the provincial church council of 1549. Other members of the old establishment, including Arthur Telfer* and Robert Denniston*, legitimated their offspring in the same period. Interestingly, Scott's legitimation was followed by that of one Dom. Henry Fethy; Fethy is also the name of the poet whose verses in the BM make him the third contemporary vernacular lyricist from this period, after Scott and Stewart.[91] This man, Dom. John Fethy, organist and chanter of the Chapel Royal, was paid for tuning the organs of St Giles' in 1554-5, and here, too, his path crosses that of Scott, for on 31 January 1556, Alexander Scott received a pension from Edinburgh town council to sing in the choir and play the organ 'for the yeir to cum alanerlie'. Other entries show that much attention was paid to the repair of the Edinburgh song school from April 1554 onwards, and the appearance of Scott and Fethy in this context (like that of William Makdowell*) was part of the revival of cultural activities in the capital; Scott was again paid for singing in the choir on 10 January 1558. His appearance side-by-side with Fethy in the BM thus mirrors their physical proximity in St Giles' itself. Their personal lives also intertwined with that of Bannatyne godparents; for example, Mr John Abercrombie*—a 'ubiquitous' and 'leading lawyer', acting as procurator in the separate Commissary Court of the Chapel Royal at Stirling—on 25 May 1557 acted as procurator for John Fethy, chanter of the Chapel Royal, with Alexander Scott as witness, together with several Chapel Royal prebendaries.[92]

All in all, the names from the MB yield direct, solid links to prominent poets whose presence dominates the BM. Apart from making the links between the BM and the MB even tighter, this also provides an answer to the question of where Bannatyne

---

pp. xxxvi-xlvi; additional biographical details will be provided in the present writer's thesis on the poetry of Scott (forthcoming).

[91] *RMS*, iv, 342, 395, 478; *RSS*, iii, 2969.

[92] MacQueen, *Ballattis of Luve*, p. xxxii; Watt, *Fasti*, 337; *Edin. Recs.*, ii, 192, 236, 358; *Edinburgh Records. The Burgh Accounts*, ed. Robert Adam (Edinburgh, 1899), i, 234; J. Cameron Lees, *St Giles', Edinburgh* (Edinburgh and London, 1889), 81-2, 353-4; S. Ollivant, *The Court of the Official in Pre-Reformation Scotland* (Stair Soc., 1982), 59-62. The 1557 document: SRO, CS 7/15, ff.24r-26r (I owe this reference to Mr. John Ballantyne).

found his 'copeis awld mankit and mvtillait' out of which he copied the BM: he found them among the same people whose names later went into his 'memoriall buik' and who formed a humanist 'republic of letters' that considered literature to be a vital component of a national heritage.[93]

Appendix

List of names in George Bannatyne's 'Memoriall Buik' (MB)

Some of the names have been modernised; the information in square brackets is additional to the printed extracts of the MB in 'Memorials of George Bannatyne', 25-42, and in *Bann. MS.*, i, pp. cxlii-cxlviii.

Sir Lewis Bellenden, Justice Clerk
Sir John Bellenden of Auchnoull, knight
Mr Thomas Bellenden, tutor of Kinneuchar [Kilconquhar]

Godfathers of James Bannatyne, George Bannatyne's father:
Mr James Kincragy, dean of Aberdeen (1512)
John Lichtoun (1512)

Godparents of George Bannatyne's brothers and sisters:
Mr Laurence Taillefeir [Telfer], treasurer of Dunkeld (1539)
Mr Henry Balnaves of Halhill (1539)
[Isobel] Windeyettis, spouse of John Fisher (1539)
Mr Thomas Bellenden (1540)
Mr Simon Preston (1540)
Agnes Cockburn (1540)
Thomas Hamilton of Priestfield (1541)
Jonet Purves, spouse of Mr Thomas Marjoribankis (1541)
Elizabeth Young, spouse of David Tod (1541)
George Taillefeir [Telfer], elder (1542)
Agnes Liddardaill (1542)
Dame Paterson (1542)
John Paterson, son of Thomas Paterson (1544)
Jonet Fisher (1544)
Jonet Ireland (1544)
George Taillefeir [Telfer] (1545)
William Fisher (1545)
Mavis Fisher (1545)
James Corsby [Crosbie] (1546)
James Bassintyne [Bassindene] (1546)
Agnes Bannatyne (1546)
John Young, writer (1547)
Christian Ireland, relict of umquhile Thomas Rynd (1547)
Margaret [no surname reported] (1547)

---

[93] *Bann. MS.*, i, p. xxiv.

Sir George Clapperton, provost of Trinity College (1548)
Marion Scott, relict of George Henderson of Fordell (1548)
Isobel Rynd, spouse of Sir Neill Laing (1548)
Sir Robert Danielstoun [Denniston], parson of Dysart (1551)
Agnes Blackstock (1551)
Marion Ireland (1551)
John Carkettill of Finglen [Fingland] (1553)
Catherine Windeyettis (1553)
Jonet Rynd, spouse of John Young, writer (1553)
Sir John Bellenden of Auchnoull, Justice Clerk (1555)
Mr Arthur Taillefeir [Telfer], parson of Crythmond [Creichtmont] (1555)
[Helen] Swinton, spouse of Mr Robert Heriot (1555)
Patrick Hepburn of Waughton (1556)
Alexander Guthrie, burgess of Edinburgh (1556)
[Margaret] Barton, spouse of Thomas Thomson, apothecary (1556)
Sir William Makdowell (1557)
Katherine Henderson, spouse of Thomas Henderson (1557)
Margaret Taillefeir [Telfer] (1557)
Mr Henry Foulis of Colinton (1559)
Catherine Ireland (1559)
Christian Abercrombie, daughter to Mr John Abercrombie (1559)
Robert Scott, writer (1560)
John McNeill, writer (1560)
Catherine Murray, spouse of Nicoll Ramsay (1560)
Henry Nisbet (1562)
James Millar, writer (1562)
Elizabeth Danielstoun [Denniston], spouse of Sir Neill Laing, Keeper of the Signet (1562)
Mr William Scott of Balwearie (1563)
Mr James McGill, Clerk Register (1563)
Margaret Lundie, Lady Waughton (1563)
Robert Paterson (1564)
Isobel Bannatyne (1564)
Jonet Bannatyne (1564)
Robert Henderson (1565)
Margaret Taillefeir [Telfer] (1565)

George Bannatyne also recorded the spouses of his brothers and sisters:
[Marion Gilbert]
Robert Paterson
James Nicoll
Thomas Aikenhead, bailie
James Bannatyne, younger
William Stewart, writer
Henry Nisbet
Isobel Mauchan, relict of William Nisbet, bailie
Margaret Hay, daughter to Alexander Hay, Clerk Register
Marion Blyth
Sarah Johnston
Helen Rutherford

'THE DIALOGUE OF THE TWA WYFEIS': MAITLAND, MACHIAVELLI AND THE PROPAGANDA OF THE SCOTTISH CIVIL WAR

Mark Loughlin

> On xxx day of Aprile at þe houre þat þe sone had passit þe guis cruve as I lay resting in a chalmer þair come in twa wyfeis and sat down to þe drink. I can not tell þair names for þair wes not ane hoill in þe dur þat I myt see þame throw it and I durst not oppin for scaring of þame but hald my ear and harkit þair talke as þai spake at large thinking na man hard thame.... I baptisit þame as Maister Johnne Mair usit to baptise hors and maris in hys logyk. The ane A, the uþir B and here without longer prologue I begyn my taill.[1]

The Scottish civil war of 1567-73 has in recent years, thanks largely to much needed and long overdue analytical study, been rescued from its status as a footnote in Scottish history. It is beginning to be recognised as one of the major turning points in Scotland's religious and political history. One of the many benefits of this recent research into the civil war is the recognition of the part played by propaganda. Indeed the immense output of party propaganda is one of the most outstanding and distinct features of this bitter internecine dispute, which divided the nation at least nominally into two clearly defined parties, professing allegiance to Mary Stewart and to her infant son James, although—as in many civil wars—allegiances often crossed and confounded party lines. A decade earlier, propaganda had also played a conspicuous role in the Reformation crisis and it has been claimed that a 'novel appeal to public opinion' was made by both sides during that dispute.[2] The propaganda of the civil war, however, saw a development of that novel appeal, which, if it differed little in its conservative emphasis on the commonweal and defence of the realm, contrasted sharply in its bitterness, intensity and volume.

---

[1] See PRO, SP 52.17.77 for the original of this nine-page dialogue; cf the nine-line entry in *CSP Scot.*, iii, 139.

[2] G. Donaldson, *Scotland: James V to James VII* (Edinburgh 1965), 102.

The extract from the prologue to 'The Dialogue of the Twa Wyfeis' given above provides an intriguing opening to one of the most curiously neglected pieces of civil war propaganda. 'The Dialogue' exemplifies many of the themes of the propaganda offerings of both sides during the conflict, as well as shedding new light on the legendary association of Maitland of Lethington with Niccolò Machiavelli and the whole question of Machiavellian influence in Scotland.

Unquestionably, the greatest significance of 'The Dialogue' lies in the fact that it offers arguably the earliest and most detailed exposition of the popular Scottish interpretation of the political principles of Machiavelli. The notorious Italian seems to have become an *idée fixe* amongst civil war propagandists and 'The Dialogue', for its part, depicts William Maitland of Lethington, the Scottish Secretary of State, as the Machiavellian 'scole master', the brains behind the 'glaikit cumpane' of the Queen's men, indoctrinating them with the wisdom of 'Michaivell Wylie' which, according to 'The Dialogue', Maitland had imbibed from the teaching of John Mair at the University of St Andrews.

The wyfeis' conversation makes it abundantly clear that the popular Scottish reputation of Machiavelli was no different from the popular image which the Italian earned elsewhere. The opprobrium heaped upon Machiavelli's work is not the least of the many ironies of the early modern age. Machiavelli had merely put into print what politicians across Europe had been practising long enough, yet the general view was that it was clearly a very bad thing to embrace in theory the unsavoury realities of the practice of political power. Consequently, self-righteous indignation and a certain amount of hysteria surrounded any imputation of Machiavellian influence and, by the time of the civil war, Machiavelli was a by-word for atheism, tyranny, treachery and deceit. 'The Dialogue' is the perfect embodiment of that, delineating in great detail the alleged political principles of Machiavelli in its castigation of the entire Queen's party as his disciples.

'The Dialogue' provides further evidence to support the view that there were two conflicting traditions of Machiavellian interpretation in Scotland.[3] One was relatively informed, through actual acquaintance of Machiavellian texts, and the other was a

[3] Fowler, *Works*, iii, pp. cvii-xcix. R.D.S. Jack, *The Italian Influence on Scottish Literature* (Edinburgh, 1972), 86, argues that Fowler's translation of *Il Principe* was an attempt to gain a fairer assessment of Machiavelli's political position.

cruder, more popular interpretation promulgated by the propagandists. Copies of *The Prince* and the *Discourses* were almost certainly circulating in Scotland long before 1594, which is the date of the inventory made of the library of Bishop Adam Bothwell, who possessed French translations of three Machiavellian texts.[4] As early as 1553 the first French translation of *The Prince* was dedicated to James, 2nd earl of Arran and duke of Châtelherault, then the Governor and second person in the realm, by the learned companion of Ronsard, Gaspar d'Auvergne.[5] Indeed it has been convincingly argued that it can hardly be doubted that *The Prince*, either in translation or in its original form, was widely known in cultured and court circles in Scotland throughout the second half of the sixteenth century.[6] Thomas Maitland's (Lethington's younger brother) masterly *jeu d'esprit* of 1570, in which he poked fun at the King's party's obsessive tarring of the Queen's party as Machiavellian disciples, provides further evidence to support this view. The remark he put in the mouth of Blair, the clerk, that 'Matchiavel is an evile booke and I would he had beene burnt seven yeeres since', suggests that Machiavelli was circulating in printed form in Scotland well before the 1590s, when William Fowler made use of d'Auvergne's text for his translation into Scots.[7]

Maitland himself suffered the same dichotomous interpretation given to Machiavelli. He was commonly branded, not a little crudely, as the Italian's Scottish counterpart. Even his family's name lent itself to the caricature. The name Maitland originates from the French *maltalent* which translates roughly as evil genius.[8] This was the role foisted on Maitland by contemporaries and later generations alike. This popular image, however, requires refining. While there is much in Maitland's career which supports the propagandists' exaggerated view of him as treachery incarnate,

[4] Fowler, *Works*, iii, p. xcvii, and *Warrender Papers*, ii, (SHS, 1931), 396. See also Brian Hillyard, '"Durkan & Ross" and beyond', no. 34, in this present volume, for another example of a library of approximately the same period with a copy in it of a work of Machiavelli (here his *Discourses*, in a 1588 edition).

[5] I am grateful to John Durkan for advice in this matter. Fowler, *Works*, iii, p. xciv.

[6] ibid., iii, 46.

[7] Bannatyne, *Memorials*, 5-13. For the Machiavelli tradition, Fowler, *Works*, ii, 69-164. Jack, *Italian Influence*, 86, also confirms the view of M. Praz, *Machiavelli and the Elizabethans* (1928), 6, that Fowler was not the first to introduce Scots to *Il Principe* or the works of Machiavelli as a whole.

[8] G.W.S. Barrow, *The Anglo-Norman Era in Scottish History* (Oxford, 1980), 80.

there is also a good deal of evidence which suggests that Maitland was conversant with the actual principles of Machiavelli as laid out, for example, in D'Auvergne's text.

The best evidence for this comes from Maitland himself. In July 1570, he articulated his basic political premises in a letter to the earl of Sussex.[9] As well as revealing the influences of Zeno, Aristotle, Plato, Cicero, the Jurists and St Paul, Maitland's rationale bears a striking resemblance to Machiavelli's insistence, found in chapter 25 of *The Prince* and also in *The Discourses*, on the need to adapt policy to particular circumstances and environments. Maitland was certainly no stranger to Italian cultural influences and in this respect a parallel can be drawn between him and one of his predecessors in the office of Secretary, Sir Thomas Erskine, who had been a student at Pavia.[10] The Scottish secretariat was a notable centre of humanist influence throughout the late fifteenth and sixteenth centuries. Maitland himself was known for his ability to quote Italian proverbs and was acquainted with the Italian humanist Pietro Bizzari, who had dedicated one of his works to Maitland.[11] It was in all probability Machiavelli to whom Maitland was referring when he told Sussex:

> I remember I have redde in a good author one that in his time was no prentice in the politique science beinge from his youth brought up in that trade, it was never praised in those that were excellent in the government of the commonwelthe to remaine always perpetuallie in one opinion but as in sailinge it is a chief point of the master's arte in ruling his shippe to applie his course as the stormie blastes of winde and wether shall dryve him so in the politique actions of all states tyme must beare a great swinge to teache men how farre they may follow the trade they have begonne or where they shall change to direct their course an other waie.[12]

Maitland's entire career is illustrative of his firm grasp of this precept. As contemporaries were wont to observe, Maitland always had more than one string to his bow. This pragmatic, almost statesmanlike philosophy bears little resemblance to the unsophisticated popular Scottish interpretation of Machiavelli, which was

---

[9] Maitland's tussle with Sussex was a prolonged one throughout the summer of 1570, but see especially SP 52.18.61, SP 52.19.5. (I and II), and SP 52.19.9. (I and II).

[10] *ADCP*, p. xxxviii.

[11] J.Durkan, 'The library of Mary Queen of Scots', in M. Lynch (ed), *Mary Stewart: Queen in Three Kingdoms* (Oxford, 1988), 76-7.

[12] SP 52.19.5. I.

certainly not based on the close scrutiny of any particular Machiavellian text. Nor does it bear any resemblance to the popular image or reputation of Maitland.

It seems remarkable that a document so rich in literary, historical and political interest as 'The Dialogue of the Twa Wyfeis' should have been so neglected. Part of the reason for this neglect is a *caveat* to the historian to consult the primary rather than the secondary source. For the dialogue is actually catalogued in the printed volume of the *Calendar of the State Papers of Scotland* for 1569-71.[13] Yet no one appears to have investigated any further the editor's brief nine-line entry, which tells us merely that this dialogue attacks the conduct of several of the leading combatants of the civil war. Consequently, the twa wyfeis have lain undisturbed in the State Paper collection of the Public Record Office in Chancery Lane. Actual consultation of the original source reveals that this nine-line entry hardly begins to do justice to a nine-page manuscript, written very closely but anonymously in Scots prose in classic dialogue form, from a heavily pro-King's party perspective. While the *Calendar* entry relates that the dialogue criticises Châtelherault, Huntly, Athol, Lesley, Boyd, Culross, Borthwick and Yester, the editor, not recognising the Machiavellian allusions to the 'Secretare', failed to spot that Maitland, who then stood at the head of the Queen's party, was the principal target of the piece. 'The Dialogue' does indeed attack the leading lights of the Queen's party, whilst warmly toasting the immortal memory of the recently assassinated Moray, who was apparently turning in his grave at the lamentable state of the realm; but it is Maitland, the Machiavellian 'scole master', who is its chief target.

What was the occasion of 'The Dialogue'? In this respect, a great deal of information can be gleaned from the endorsement of the manuscript made by Sir William Cecil and dated 30 April 1570. This immediately enables 'The Dialogue' to be placed reasonably accurately in the proper context of the civil war. By April 1570 the civil war had reached a critical stage, and the prospects of a victory for the Queen's party were at their highest. The chief reason for this was undoubtedly the assassination in January 1570 of the Regent and leader of the King's party, Mary's half-brother James Stewart, earl of Moray. Since his brilliant mili-

---

[13] *CSP Scot*, iii, 139.

tary triumph over Mary at Langside in 1568, Moray had managed to hold the King's party together despite facing increasing opposition, but his assassination left it in disarray. Moray, so often depicted as the biblical captain of Israel, had—to continue the biblical metaphor—left his flock untended as sheep without a shepherd. The King's party was not only leaderless but directionless. It faced a constitutional crisis over what Maitland termed the question of the 'regiment of the realm'[14] and its right to appoint another regent to replace Moray. Even more alarming, the prospect of only uncertain support from England was a source of little comfort. The result was that the initiative had swung very much to the Queen's party, which, with Maitland at its head, was conducting a vigorous recruitment campaign which enabled them to claim, at the time of 'The Dialogue', the support of 32 earls and lords in Parliament. It could also boast of a lieutenancy of Argyll, Châtelherault and Huntly over the realm, a triumvirate representing a formidable range of territorial support for the Queen's party across northern and central Scotland.

Although the supremacy enjoyed by the Queen's party proved to be remarkably shortlived, due largely to the substantial English invasion mounted in the summer of 1570 under the earl of Sussex—an expedition not often accorded the significance which it merits[15]—the Queen's party in April 1570 nevertheless posed a very real threat to the survival of an increasingly nervous and fragile King's party. 'The Dialogue' should be viewed in the context of the panic of the King's party at a time of intense debate over the regiment of the realm, when at rival conventions their opponents consistently boasted stronger support and the prospect of a settlement on pro-Marian lines seemed more likely than at any point since 1568. It belongs to the same nervous climate of thought that produced Buchanan's 'Admonitioun to the Trew Lordis', as well as such effusions as 'The Poysonit Schot', 'The Cruikit Leidis the Blinde', 'The Bird in the Cage', 'The Hailsome Admonitoun' and 'The Admonitoun to the Lordis'.[16] In April 1570, it appeared that Moray's assassin had dealt a fatal blow not only to Moray but to the King's party as well.

If the occasion of 'The Dialogue' was the King's party's fear that they were about to lose control over the regiment of the realm,

---

[14] ibid., iii, 169.

[15] *Diurnal*, 177-8.

[16] *Satirical Poems*, i, 132-8, 128-31, 160-64, 165-9, 139-43, respectively.

the next question to be asked is why was Maitland its principal target? It is not difficult to answer. The King's party propagandists recognised the position Maitland enjoyed in the Queen's party: if he was not its titular head he was certainly the brains behind the operation. Maitland, eldest son of Sir Richard Maitland of Lethington, east Lothian laird, privy councillor, judge, historian, poet and collector of poetry, had attended St Leonard's College in 1540 and was at the University of Paris in 1542. He had been Scotland's principal Secretary of State since 1558,[17] and by 1570 had amassed an unparalleled wealth of diplomatic and political experience. Gifted intellectually, he was familiar with Italian, Latin, Greek and French literature. According to George Buchanan, in the 'Chameleon', Maitland allegedly possessed the power to 'easilie flatter and imitat everie manis countenance, speche and fassoun and subtill to draw out the secreittis of everie manis mind'.[18] Although Buchanan poured scorn on the view that Maitland's pen was worth 'ten thowsand men',[19] the amount of time and energy he spent trying to belittle Maitland suggests otherwise.

Richard Bannatyne, personal secretary to John Knox and a bitter critic of both Maitland and the Marians, put it succinctly when he said of Maitland's importance to the Queen's Party: 'the secretare is the saule and without whom and whose counsell they can do no moir than the whelis can do without the extrie'.[20] On another occasion Bannatyne pithily acknowledged the danger Maitland posed to the King's party in his ability to 'lay a plaster over the wound of variance'[21] which lay at the heart of the Queen's party. The mixed motives lying behind the coalition of Queen's men was a recurrent feature in the propaganda of their opponents. There were many Marians whose allegiance owed little to a desire to see Mary restored to her full powers in Scotland. Bannatyne, however, knew only too well that Maitland could mould the Queen's party into a dangerously cohesive force. His complaint probably stemmed in part from envy: the King's men

---

[17] M. Loughlin, 'The Career of Maitland of Lethington c.1526-73' (Edinburgh University Ph.D. thesis, 1991). The opening chapter details Maitland's academic and cultural background.

[18] Buchanan, *Vernacular Writings*, 37-53.

[19] ibid., 53.

[20] Bannatyne, *Memorials*, 15.

[21] ibid., 38.

lacked someone of Maitland's ability to hold together their own party, in which sincere support for the infant James was at least as questionable as the Marians' support for his mother.

Maitland of Lethington, known in contemporary international circles as 'The Scotch Cecil',[22] was the principal target of 'The Dialogue of the Twa Wyfeis' for the same reason as he was the principal target of so much King's party propaganda. It was because he was perceived as the most dangerous threat to them that the best wits of the King's party spent so much time and energy denouncing him. King's party propaganda that made no passing, scathing mention of Maitland was conspicuous by its absence at this time. 'The Crukit Leads The Blinde', 'The Bird in the Cage', in common with Buchanan's notorious 'Chameleon', were all aimed specifically at Maitland as the 'very soul of the Queen's party'. Similarly, a string of Sempill's ballads, all printed by the industrious Robert Leprevik, such as 'Maddies Lamentatioun' and 'Proclamation' and 'The Poysonit Schot', and the tract, 'Admonition to the Trew Lordis', confirm Maitland's guiding influence over the Queen's party and his hold over Athol, Hume, Grange, Seton, Châtelherault and Huntly, and offer a begrudging tribute to his powers of political guile. Yet there was more than a hint of envy amidst the resentment:

> They say he can both quhissil and cloik
> and his mouth full of meill.[23]

That Maitland of Lethington was depicted as the champion of the Queen's party is an apposite illustration of the complex irony of the civil war and of the sheer volatility of party allegiance during it. Although he stood in 1570 as the virtual head of the Queen's party, he had not always done so. In 1567 he had been one of those directly responsible for manufacturing Mary's fall from power and the attempts to strangle the nascent Queen's party at birth.[24] Maitland actually admitted in 1570 that Mary's deposition and the coronation of her son James could not have been done without him or his secretarial expertise: 'Ye and farther without me they had nather the knowledge, wisdome nor the moyen to perform the same'. He went so far as to issue a complete con-

[22] *CSP Spain*, i, 492.
[23] 'The Cruikit Leidis the Blinde' in *Satirical Poems*, i, 128-31.
[24] Loughlin, 'Maitland', 256.

fession of his guilt in so doing: 'for my owin part I confes I did very evil and ungodly in the upsetting of the kingis authority for he can never be justlie king sa long as his mother lives'.[25]

Consistency of allegiance was not a feature of Maitland's conduct during the civil war but he was far from alone in this. While the propagandists tried to denounce Maitland as the supreme waverer, the 'scurvy scholar of Machiavelli's lair' whose reputation went before him:

> The Quene his doingis sair did rew
> and richt sa did hir Mother:
> The counsall kennis if he was trew
> To him that was hir brother[26]

it was not wise of them to summon the ghost of Mary of Guise. Maitland's betrayal of her may well have been the most spectacular coup of his career; he had arranged her downfall while acting as her envoy at the treaty of Cateau-Cambrésis. Yet if loyalty to Mary of Guise was to be a criterion of membership of the King's party, there were few who could honestly have qualified. The above extract from Sempill's 'Bird in the Cage' also highlights the dogmatic public façade of the King's party, which maintained that it was actually acting in Mary Stewart's best interests. Even the charge that Maitland had betrayed the Regent Moray would have been difficult to sustain. The dynamic partnership which the two men had shared since 1559 had clearly collapsed during the opening year of the civil war, and most impartial observers would recognise that the 'Good Regent' was at least as responsible as the Machiavellian secretary for their split.

Given Maitland's acknowledged political influence, it is not too difficult to see why the King's party delighted in making Maitland's new found allegiance and political life as uncomfortable as possible. No one succeeded better in this respect than George Buchanan, who was at the very heart of both the anti-Marian and anti-Maitland propaganda machine. The tracts, *Detectio* and *Actio,* were both valuable weapons in a relentless campaign to reduce domestic and foreign support for Mary through the constant sullying of her reputation. Some indication of the importance of Buchanan's campaign can be gleaned from the pen of Cecil, now Lord Burghley, writing in 1572: 'It were not here amiss to have

[25] Bannatyne, *Memorials*, 126-7; Calderwood, *History*, iii, 79-87.
[26] *Satirical Poems*, i, 129.

divers of Buchanan's little Latin books to present if needs were to the King of France and likewise to some noblemen of his council'.[27] This also draws attention to the fact that there were at least two distinct languages of propaganda—Latin, chiefly directed at the international arena, and the vernacular, aimed at a domestic audience. Similarly, while accepting the view that the increase in the use of propaganda in the Reformation period marked a growth of sorts in appeal to public opinion, Burghley's comment suggests that the prime audience of civil war propaganda was still the small, influential élite who controlled the means of power. In this respect, Burghley's comment is a timely reminder of the wider European dimension in which Scottish affairs were all but invariably cast throughout the sixteenth century. The outcome of Scotland's civil war lay not in the hands of its own people but in those of external forces—in this case France and England.

That Buchanan was also at the nucleus of the anti-Maitland machine is abundantly clear from one of the most famous pieces of civil war propaganda, his vitriolic but brilliant 'Chameleon'. While it is true that Maitland managed to seize the 'Chameleon' at the Edinburgh press of Robert Leprevik, and it was not until after the civil war that it was finally printed, it is generally accepted that the 'Chameleon' enjoyed a wide circulation in manuscript form, possibly in the same way that 'The Dialogue' appears to have done.[28] The 'Chameleon' viciously lampooned Maitland's capacity to change his hue whenever a selfish need arose, claiming he was capable of camouflaging himself like a chameleon in any colour bar red and white, the symbols of courage and purity. There is little need to go into that well-known work in detail here but perhaps an extra twist in Buchanan's bitterness towards Maitland, which was strictly a post-1567 phenomenon and stood in sharp contrast to his earlier warm regard for the Secretary, can be detected. It is possible that Buchanan, through his mother Agnes Heriot, was loosely related to Maitland through the marriage of Maitland's sister to James Heriot of Trabroun, himself a loyal Queen's man.[29]

Was Buchanan the author of 'The Dialogue'? This cannot be ruled out but speculation as to the authorship is inconclusive. It

---

27 *CSP Scot*, iv, 367.

28 Buchanan, *Vernacular Writings*, 40.

29 I.D. MacFarlane, *George Buchanan* (London, 1981), 19-22; *Scots Peerage*, v, 298.

bears the stamp of Buchanan and was certainly produced at the same time as his 'Admonitioun to the Trew Lordis', a pamphlet designed to ensure Elizabeth sent much-needed military aid to offset the Queen's party's superiority, but 'The Dialogue' could just as easily be the work of Bannatyne. Similarly, many of 'The Dialogue's' terms of reference are not unfamiliar to the anonymous author of the *Historie and Life of King James the Sext.* References to the Queen's party as the 'lords of the meill mercat' can be found in the pages of that work, as can a description of Maitland as 'sufficientlie studiet in the preceptis of Nicolas Machiavel'.[30] The analogy of Maitland as the 'scole master' and his house as the 'scole' is one that Buchanan used, whilst the derogatory references to John Mair are also reminiscent of Buchanan's later contempt for his former master.[31] Similarly, the references to Maitland's 'heid of wit' are familiar to readers of Bannatyne as one of his favoured epithets for his arch-enemy.[32] This uncertain provenance of 'The Dialogue', however, does nothing to diminish its value as a striking illustration of many of the major themes of the propaganda of the civil war.

Before proceeding to a specific examination of 'The Dialogue', it should be noted that Maitland was not the only member of his illustrious family who figured in the propaganda warfare waged by the two parties. In it, the entire Maitland family figured prominently as victims, perpetrators and protesters. Maitland's father. Sir Richard, whose reputation as a poet and as one of the greatest collectors of English and Scots poetry has recently begun once again to receive some attention, denounced what he regarded as a highly unsavoury development. He attacked in his poem 'Of the Malyce of Poyetis' those:

> Poyetis and makaris þat ar now
> off grit despite and malice ar so fow

who sought the defamation 'of mony gude honest men insetting forth þair bukeis and þair rymes'. Sir Richard warned of the retribution awaiting such authors from their victims, who could well confront them saying:

> think on ye maid of me ane ballat

---

30 *HKJVI*, 51.
31 MacFarlane, *Buchanan*, 402-03.
32 Bannatyne, *Memorials*, 32 and passim.

> now for your reward I shall break your pallat.

But it was the wider, harmful effect such attacks had on the community as a whole that really concerned him:

> Dispytfull poyettis sould not tholit be
> in commoun weillis or godlie cumpane.[33]

As on many other occasions, his three sons—William, John (the future Secretary and Chancellor) and Thomas—chose not to follow their father's advice.

While William was the butt of much of the King's party propaganda, it was his younger brother, Thomas, who provided one of the most brilliant satirical attacks on behalf of the Queen's party. His masterly pasquinade, referred to earlier, ridiculed the leading protagonists of the King's party including the late Regent Moray, his faithful secretary John Wood, John Knox, James McGill, Lindsay of the Byres, Wishart of Pittarow and James Haliburton tutor of Pitcur and their nefarious aspirations.[34] It hit several raw nerves and was bitterly and angrily denounced by Knox in the pulpit. It was perhaps in revenge that Buchanan used the character of Thomas Maitland in his renowned anti-Marian treatise *De Jure Regni*, which, although not printed until 1579, seems to have enjoyed a wide circulation much earlier than this in manuscript form.[35] Interestingly, this major work was also modelled on the dialogue form.

The third Maitland brother, John, the future Secretary and Chancellor of the realm, also seems to have inherited his father's literary bent and took an active part in propaganda warfare. 'Ane schort inveccyde maid againis the delyverance of the erle of Northumberland' is one of three poems attributed to him at this time.[36] It is to be doubted that the earl of Morton, the principal target of the poem and a man not known for his clemency, would have shown John the mercy that he did in 1573 had he known him to be the author. The poem depicted Morton as the Scottish Judas who, along with his kinsman Lochleven and other stalwarts of the King's party including Colville of Cleish, Pitcairn, Lindsay,

[33] *Poems of Sir Richard Maitland* (Maitland Club, 1830), 79-80; cf A.A. MacDonald, 'The poetry of Sir Richard Maitland of Lethington', *East Lothian Trans.*, xii (1972), 7-19.

[34] Bannatyne, *Memorials*, 5-13.

[35] MacFarlane, *Buchanan*, 392-415, esp. 393.

[36] *Satirical Poems*, i, 248-53.

Mar, McGill and Orkney, were responsible for the treacherous deed. It was Morton, however, displaying the traditional Douglas avarice, who was chiefly responsible:

> Fals miscreant Mortoun, febill and unkind,
> Thy wretchit hairt could never schame eschew
> Thou never was upricht, trustie, nor trew
> To friend, to fo, nor to na other man,
> on sic vyild treasoun vengeance man ensew
> on the and all thy fals degenerat clan.

The *coup de grâce* of this diatribe against Morton was the assertion that 'Had Christ himself been in the Percy's room, I wight ye would have playit Judas' part, gif Caiaphas had offert you the sum'.[37] Such bitter, exaggerated and personal invective was typical of the propaganda of the period. The heavy strains of self-righteous indignation, together with appeals concerning the defence of the realm, the commonweal and religion, can be found in abundance throughout the works of both parties.[38]

Attention however must be re-focused specifically on 'The Dialogue'. The tantalising prologue explains that the work is modelled on the example of John Mair's logic classes, with the speakers termed respectively 'A' and 'B'. The 'taill' begins with the twa wyfies safely ensconced in an Edinburgh tavern, drink in hand, ready to put the world to rights. The dialogue itself begins innocently enough, with the wyfeis expressing the seemingly habitual view that things had never been worse, goods never more expensive and the weather positively apocalyptic, 'as if Domesday be neir', before launching into severe censure of the 'lords on the meill mercat', the Queen's party. It was they 'who herd everie day and convene as bairnis to þe scole up in þe secretaris house to learne wisdome, for þai say he hes ane heid of wit'. Maitland, it transpires, is imbuing the 'glaikit cumpane' with the principles of Machiavelli, which he had learned from John Mair at St Andrews.

The wyfeis' description of the activity in Edinburgh's High Street is a perfectly accurate account of the events in the spring of 1570, when the town houses of Morton and Maitland provided the rendezvous for the King's and Queen's parties respectively. By

---

[37] ibid., i, 252.

[38] ibid., i, nos. 16-39. Although this is chiefly King's party propaganda, the Queen's party were no less busy. See for example, the industrious output of Thomas Bassenden, Queen's party printer in Edinburgh, in M. Lynch, *Edinburgh and the Reformation* (Edinburgh, 1981), 316.

contrast, the wyfeis' allegation that John Mair taught Machiavelli's thought seems far-fetched, although it is perfectly possible that Maitland, as a student at St Leonard's in 1540, may have encountered the East Lothian scholar who taught at St Salvator's from 1536 to 1553.[39] The attack on Mair, however, is the strongest evidence to suggest that Buchanan may have been the author of 'The Dialogue'.[40]

It was the wyfeis' contention that Maitland was responsible for the corruption of the Scots lords by teaching them the erroneous precepts of Machiavelli. An extract illustrating this is given below.

> A: Quhat new lerning teiches that buke of þairis ?
> B: Now mony new thingis as schowis þe grit folie of our forbearis and first quhow ane king should be brocht up.... The first precept is that he be of na religion for þai say that religion is to men as ane bogill to bairnis and kepis þaime fra mony plesouris and makes þame towart in fearing of punicion in ane vþir warld for thingis done in this warld. Nixt that ane man suld cast him alwayes to win geir and care not on quhat faschoning. For ane pourr man is bot ane schadow of ane man and silver is ane manis saull, lyfe and paradyse—þe qlk þai move be þe buke of pocalppis þat sayis that paradys is all beildet of gold and precious stanes. The third principall poynt is þat þe best net in þe warld to tak fuills is ane fair promise, ane subscription and ane fals aith.

As an accurate appraisal of the political principles of Machiavelli this leaves a great deal to be desired, but that is hardly the point. It seized on the popular perception of Machiavelli to slur the entire cause of the Queen's party as a Machiavellian ruse. The Queen's men were motivated by completely selfish desires. The cause of Marian restitution was nothing but 'ane cloik to uther crymes.... The quenis auctority is pretendit be al and menit be nane.' This last gibe hits at the heart of the fundamental debate earlier acknowledged as to the true rationale behind the Queen's party. The wyfeis were sure that Mary's restoration was not really intended and they pointed to the basic implausibility of such an aim: 'For how can þai put hir in auctority þat can not put hir in

[39] I am grateful to John Durkan for advice on this point; but see the entry on Mair in *DNB*.

[40] 'Admonitioun to the Trew Lordis' in Buchanan, *Vernacular Writings*, 24, offers corroborative evidence for this view. There is also a most striking similarity between Buchanan's criticism of the Queen's party for having 'no god bot geir' and the wyfeis' condemnation of the same party's Machiavellian belief that 'ane man suld cast him alwayes to win geir'.

hir own chalmer', before proceeding to launch an acerbic attack on the Machiavellian motives of specific Queen's men.

The Hamiltons were prime targets and Châtelherault's motives in particular were challenged with the constitutionally correct statement, 'for he that be ane King most first be Duke'. The view was put forward by one of the women that the Duke 'and his bairnis ar bot ane nest of fuilles' but her drinking partner was quick rightly to point out 'howbeit he seme to yow he hes mony poyntis of Machiavellis wisdome ... he cares not for religioun, for na ayth nor princis ... he estemis silver uver al thingis'. The wyfeis' uncomplimentary characterisation of Châtelherault was not without some justification, as any student of this period can vouch. The Machiavellian comparison was particularly apposite, given the fact, noted earlier, that the first French translation of *The Prince* had been dedicated to him. Similarly, the sincerity of Châtelherault's attachment to Mary is questionable in the light of his instructions to David Chalmers to ensure foreign support for his own appointment as Regent in the event of Mary not being restored.[41]

Other Queen's men did not escape the wyfeis' opprobrium. Argyll and his close associate Boyd were lampooned as 'ye gook and hir titling'. Argyll was 'ane scoler of Machiavellis' whilst Boyd had 'past twa universities' in Machiavellian deceit. The military power of Argyll was alluded to, with his redshanks being equated to 'ane of the plagues of Egypt'. Cassillis, Argyll's cousin, was dismissed as an inconstant waverer, which seems a more than fair assessment but curiously he was also alleged to be guided by the obscure Andrew Gray, 'his heid of wit'. Hume was described as Maitland's slave whilst the Machiavellian abilities of Maitland's younger brother (either Thomas or John) were criticised. Herries, it was alleged, was so conversant with the principles of Machiavelli that if Maitland died he would be his perfect replacement as 'scolemaster'. Borthwick and Yester were described as 'lustie young men' who regrettably 'ar gydit by þair sheip'. Somerville was 'abill to infect ane army' and the consequence of his consorting with the Hamiltons was greatly feared. Oliphant, along with Eglinton and Marischal, were allegedly being bought with

[41] I am grateful to Dr Julian Goodare for information on Chalmers' activities, which can be traced through *CSP Scot.*, iii, esp. pp. 246-7, for his instructions from Châtelherault for France and Spain.

French money. Crawford was acknowledged as a member of the Queen's party, although—again quite accurately—it was said that 'few of the Lindsays followis him'.[42] Athol's allegiance was neatly and accurately described as 'nither heit nor cauld, he fisches on the brayis and out of dangear... firme to na partye and reddye to bayth'.

The wyfeis also offered certain qualifications on the powers of 'the King of the north', Huntly. Although his ability to 'bring him alane mair than al þe contrary pairte may be' was admitted, the wyfeis believed that his influence, like that of his father before him, would be limited by the traditional 'northland habit.... which is ginourly trew þat þai cum lait, bringis few, and bydis schort tyme'. Yet Huntly, with his rival administration in the north, posed a far more potent threat than the wyfeis predicted, as Lennox, who would shortly succeed as Regent, was only too well aware.[43]

'The Dialogue' closed with the expression of the wyfeis' firm belief that justice would prevail, with the King's men triumphing over their evil enemies. The chief reason for their confidence was the straightforward *raison d'être* of the King's men, in contrast to the Queen's party which was riddled with particularism despite the pretence of devotion to Mary. 'Þe maintaining of þe Kingis auctority and to do justice ane thing favorit by þe haill body of Scotland be þame that are nolder giltie of þe King nor regent's slauctor' was in stark contrast to their motley, Machiavellian opponents, 'sum murthiraris of þe King, sum muthiraris of þe regent and sum of bayth', who harboured 'þe quene of Inglandis rebellis the said being enemies to God and to þe king of Scotland'. With the comforting thought of the impending defeat of the Queen's men, the wyfeis returned to their drink.

Whilst the specious nature of many of the wyfeis' partisan allegations must be acknowleged, not least their insistence on the altruistic single-mindedness of the King's party, 'The Dialogue' nevertheless illustrates several of the major characteristics of civil war propaganda. Its factual inaccuracies are particularly symptomatic of the extremely subjective literary output of both parties. More positively, its consistent attempt to identify the Queen's party as contemptuous of religion, as enemies to both God and

[42] F.D. Bardgett, *Scotland Reformed: the Reformation in Angus and the Mearns* (Edinburgh, 1989), 127-35, confirms this point.

[43] SP 52.17.77 and A.L. Murray, 'Huntly's rebellion and the administration of justice in north-east Scotland, 1570-73', *Northern Scotland*, iv (1981), 1-6.

Scotland, is in keeping with the great efforts of both sides to portray themselves as the true upholders of the religion and the defenders of the commonweal. This is despite the fact that the most cursory of glances through the ranks of both parties—at any time during the civil war—shows conclusively how unsatisfactory the notion of the conflict as a war of religion is.

Religious affiliation exercised very little influence as a determining factor of party allegiance during the civil war. This fundamental fact was accepted even by several leading English and Scottish divines. Edmund Grindal, archbishop of York and future archbishop of Canterbury, seems to have grasped it better than most: 'For each party even when the dispute was at the highest, professed as they still do, the doctrine of the gospel'.[44] John Spottiswoode, superintendent of Lothian, lamented the fact that the Queen's party enjoyed the support of 'such as were esteemed the principal within the flock'.[45] Argyll was certainly one of those. Few had a more distinguished Protestant pedigree than him, yet for the vast majority of the civil war he was opposed to the authority of the King. Conversely, the consistent support of the Catholic, Lord Sempill, for the King's party along with the allegiance up to 1570 of Athol, shows that the King's party, despite pretences to the contrary, was never the exclusive preserve of the elect.[46]

There were those, of course, who preferred to take a simpler, confessional view of the proceedings. Bishop John Jewel of Salisbury believed the King's party to 'cherish the pure religion and the gospel and depend on us, the other are enemies to godliness and friends to popery and are inclined towards the French'.[47] The notion of a holy war gathered strength as the cause of Mary became more desperate, and reached new heights after the St Bartholomew's Massacre of August 1572. In August 1571, Bishop Parkhurst informed the Zurich-based reformer, Henry Bullinger, that 'the true religion is flourishing in Scotland. But the nobles are sometimes quarelling with each other not on account of religion to which all parties are favourable but for the custody of the King'. By 1573, however, Parkhurst preferred to

---

[44] H. Robinson (ed.), *The Zurich Letters* (Parker Society, 1852), 210.

[45] Calderwood, *History,* ii, 438.

[46] G. Donaldson, *All the Queen's Men: Power and Politics in Mary Stewart's Scotland* (1983), 98-9.

[47] *Zurich Letters,* 228.

describe to Bullinger the triumph of 'the godly Scots' over 'the papists'.[48] He was not alone in seeing the fall of Edinburgh Castle in terms of an international Protestant triumph. In a letter to Leicester of May 1573, the earl of Huntingdon saw the victory in Edinburgh as compensation for the loss of the Huguenot stronghold of La Rochelle.[49]

The King's party clearly felt there were advantages to be gained, in terms of both domestic and English support, in identifying the restoration of Mary with the restitution of Catholicism. It spent a good deal of time portraying itself as the Protestant party, forcing the Queen's party to devote an equal amount of its literature to the refutation of 'malicious calumnies' that it intended 'the subversioune and alteratioune of the stait of trew religioune and danger to the professoris thairof'. On the contrary, it was the Queen's men who were the protectors of the 'commoun weill and libertie of thair native cuntrie', who not only 'hes professit and does profess the same trew religioune' but 'war of the first and chiefest instrumentis of the promotioune, continowance and establishing thairof'.[50]

Some brief comments remain to be offered on the literary techniques employed in 'The Dialogue'. The dialogue form was a familiar enough weapon in both literary reminiscences and political disputations in sixteenth-century Scotland. Its exponents ranged from the wandering scholar Florence Wilson (Volusenus), dreaming in exile of his homeland in Moray, to the uncompromising John Knox, in a lengthy account of his debate with Maitland about the Queen's mass in the General Assembly in 1564.[51] Perhaps the classic example is Buchanan's *De Jure Regni*, which recruited Thomas Maitland in a debate with the author. Amongst the most notable in Scots prose form and arguably the closest exemplar for the 'Twa Wyfeis' is William Lamb's *Ane Resoning*.[52] Unlike many other dialogues, however, the best lines

[48] ibid., 256-7; *Letter Book of John Parkhurst, Bishop of Norwich, 1571-5* (Norfolk Record Society, 1975), 62.

[49] *CSP Scot.*, iv, 557.

[50] Bannatyne, *Memorials*, 27-31; *Diurnal*, 188.

[51] Florence Wilson, *De animi tranquilitate* (Lyons, 1543). For Knox's debate with Lethington, see Knox, *History*, ii, 108-15, 116-30. See also R.J. Lyall, 'Vernacular prose before the Reformation', in *The History of Scottish Literature*, i (Aberdeen, 1988), 163-82; R.D.S. Jack, 'The prose of John Knox: a re-assessment', *Prose Studies*, iv (1981), 239-51.

in the 'Twa Wyfeis' are not kept to one of the parties. The wyfeis alternate in offering each other pearls of wisdom. Yet perhaps of greater significance for the literary historian is the fact that the author of 'The Dialogue' chose to express his argument through the female persona. This again was not an uncommon literary device. Perhaps the best-known example from this period is 'The Lamentatioun of Lady Scotland', printed in 1572, in which the wife of 'John the Commounweil' laments the condition of her realm,[53] but William Dunbar had also chosen to speak with women's tongues in 'The Twa Cummeris'.

Whilst the twa wyfeis certainly do much lamenting and complaining, perhaps their nearest literary and social cousin is Sempill's 'Maddie of the Kailmarket', who also figured prominently in civil war propaganda.[54] During the course of their dialogue, the wyfeis stress that they are acquainted with Maddie, whose 'Lamentatioun' and 'Proclamation' were printed by Leprevik in 1570. The wyfeis actually mention Maddie during the course of their dialogue to illustrate one of their points. The incidental allusion to Maddie also suggests that the anonymous author was not as ignorant of the works of Machiavelli as his main exposition of Machiavelli's principles suggests. In criticising the devious conduct of the influential James Balfour, who in 1567, like Maitland, had been at the forefront of the campaign to depose Mary but had since (again like Maitland) changed sides and (unlike Maitland) was to change sides once more to the King's party, one of the wyfies put forward the view that while it was correct for Maddie to sell different wares in the market place according to the season, such latitude was not to be afforded to the politicians. This comment, found in the last pages of 'The Dialogue' and far removed from the wyfeis' main, exaggerated exposition of Machiavellian principles, shows a clear familiarity with the political expediency that both Maitland and Machiavelli advocated.

One last amusing point on the use of the female persona in this dialogue is that the anonymous author (undoubtedly male) chose in his conclusion to allow the wyfeis to voice their recognition of the place of women in society. Incisive political commentators they may be, but the pragmatic wyfeis are also aware that events

---

[52] William Lamb, *Ane Resonyng of ane Scottis and Inglis Merchand betuix Rowand and Lionis*, ed. R.J. Lyall (Aberdeen, 1985).

[53] *Satirical Poems*, i, 226-39.

[54] ibid., i, 144-55.

are beyond their control. In common with so many of their sex throughout history their greatest concern is the avoidance of widowhood:

> A: Quhat will be the end of all this?
> B: Lat ws sely [*or* ?foly] wyfeis drink away sorow, and men mell with þe rest as þai think best. God belovet of all that folowis. Gif my man wer slane þis nycht I haif ane uthir in his steid.
> C: Cummer, þat is þe forsyt and wisdome that wyfeis suld steik be.

While on one level the author may well have been firmly reminding his audience where the woman's place was—and certainly the twa wyfeis can be viewed as comic stereotypes, characterised as they are as gossiping complainers worried about being left on the shelf—there is also a much deeper motive behind their admission of themselves as 'sely wyfeis'. The author, through the wyfeis, has laid down a clear challenge to his audience. Simple gossips the wyfeis may have been, but they were none the less able to recognise the Machiavellian deceit that lay behind the Queen's party when 'the queenis auctority is pretendit be al bot menit by nane'. The author was demanding that his male audience take up the baton that his 'sely wyfeis' had so clearly laid down, both in their denunciation of the Queen's party and in their admission that it was up to the men to 'mell with þe rest as þai think best'.

In conclusion, the wyfeis deserve to be rescued from the neglect of the past 400 years and reunited with their female literary cousins. 'The Dialogue', too, while it does not belong to the voluminous printed output of Robert Leprevik or Thomas Bassenden, deserves to be acknowledged as a classic and informative piece of civil war propaganda.[55] It sheds significant light on the question of how early the Scots were familiar with both the actual and popularised ideas of Machiavelli and it can provide the basis for a much needed refinement of the view of Maitland of Lethington as Scotland's Machiavelli.

---

[55] M. Lynch, *Scotland: A New History* (1991), 220; idem, *Edinburgh*, 316.

THE REGENT MORTON'S VISITATION: THE REFORMATION OF ABERDEEN, 1574

Allan White OP

What is often counted one of the most romantic of historical events, the escape of Mary Queen of Scots from her island prison in Lochleven in Fife in May 1568, precipitated five years of civil war in Scotland. During that time political life was governed by disputes between the supporters of Mary's young son, James VI, collectively known as the King's party, and the coalition of Mary's allies known as the Queen's party.[1] Confusion was often worse confounded during these years by frequent changes in the composition of both factions. The tide turned in favour of the King's party, however, with the succession of the Earl of Morton as Regent on 24 November 1572. By the beginning of 1573 there was little real prospect of Queen Mary's return from her English imprisonment and her party amongst the aristocracy was ready to negotiate terms with the new regent. In February 1573, the Marian leaders gave an undertaking to accept the authority of the young King James VI (1567-1625). The Pacification of Perth, as it was called, was an agreement forged by the Scottish magnates to establish a coherent constitutional settlement which would promote stability whilst leaving as much as possible of the traditional patterns of power intact.

Mary's chief supporters were James Hamilton, 2nd earl of Arran, duke of Châtelherault, and George Gordon, 5th earl of Huntly. The Hamiltons drew their power from a large network of kinship and vassalage stretching from Linlithgow to Renfrewshire but concentrated mostly in the west. The second earl had been an important player on the Scottish political stage since the death of James V in 1542. His descent from James II, which gave him a claim to be heir presumptive to the throne after the infant Queen Mary, led to his nomination as Governor of the kingdom in 1543. His policy of religious and political alliance with Henry VIII's England provoked widespread hostility. His subsequent change of

[1] For the civil war, see G. Donaldson, *All the Queen's Men: Power and Politics in Mary Stewart's Scotland* (1983), 83-126; I.B. Cowan, 'The Marian civil war', in *Scotland and War, AD79-1918*, ed. N. Macdougall (Edinburgh, 1991), 95-112.

tack and support for association with France gained him the French duchy of Châtelherault. For the next thirty years or so he pursued a wayward policy which earned him a reputation for inconstancy.

The Gordons were a powerful family which had begun life in the Borders and in the fifteenth century had transferred its centre of operations to the north-east of Scotland. In a relatively short time the Gordons managed to establish themselves as the leading magnates in the area, a position they were to hold until the seventeenth century. Their political leanings were characterised by a strong conservatism which, after the Reformation, was often overtly sympathetic to Catholicism. The Gordon connection in this period included within it William Gordon, Catholic bishop of Aberdeen and chancellor of its University, who remained resident in the bishop's burgh of Old Aberdeen until his death in 1577. The influence of the Hamiltons and the Gordons was a perennial threat to any government with which they chose to disagree. The conclusion of an agreement with these two magnatial interests together with their supporters gave Morton the space in which he could begin to render his power effective throughout Scotland. Since he could not completely dislodge the Gordons or the Hamiltons from power Morton devoted his attention to limiting, as much as possible, their influence in their own territories.

One of the targets of the Regent's displeasure was the royal burgh of (New) Aberdeen, which had at times found itself as the reluctant centre of operations for Huntly's campaign against the King's party.[2] For over 30 years the burgh had tried to tread a fine line between dependence on the Gordons and their supporters amongst the local lairds, which would have earned them the hostility of the central government, and outright opposition to the same group which would have alienated the burgh from its hinterland. During the civil war of 1567-73 the Gordons had used the economic resources of Aberdeen as a useful means of support for the Queen's party. Its port, one of the busiest in Scotland, together with its regular contact with the maritime centres of France and northern Europe, was a valuable component in foreign diplomatic adventures. The burgesses of Aberdeen were not above benefiting from this trade, but were for ever casting

[2] A.L. Murray, 'Huntly's rebellion and the administration of justice in north-east Scotland, 1570-73', *Northern Scotland*, iv (1981), 1-6.

glances over their shoulders anxious at the potential price for all of this. It was clear that, once the fortunes of the Marian party began to decline after 1571, there would be a day of reckoning. Morton, like some of his predecessors, believed that Gordon power in the north-east would need to be challenged if not entirely eradicated if the King's rule was to enjoy any sort of security. An incidental advantage would be that the doctrines of the Reformation might be more successfully planted in what was a traditionally conservative area. A further consideration determining Morton's interest in punishing the Queen's party and those associated with it was his pressing need for money to pay off the considerable debt incurred during the conduct of the war.

Regent Morton's visitation

Morton was unable to devote his full attention to Aberdeen until the late summer of 1574. In an attempt to minimise magnatial interference in the proceedings, Huntly was kept in relative isolation in the west of Scotland.[3] The earl's fearsome kinsman and lieutenant, Adam Gordon, was safely out of the way in France where Morton was content to leave him, believing that he would do less harm there than at home.[4] The absence of Huntly and his more belligerent kinsmen gave Morton a somewhat freer hand than he would have otherwise enjoyed. The Regent clearly intended his visit to Aberdeen to be exemplary. In many ways his visitation bore a resemblance to previous punitive expeditions to the north-east undertaken by Queen Mary in 1562 and the Protestant Regent Moray in 1569. In 1562 Mary had provoked the fifth earl's father, known as the 'pope of the north-east', into revolt. She had hoped that by humbling her most powerful Catholic subject Queen Elizabeth and her Protestant subjects might be more amenable to the idea of naming Mary as heir to the throne of England. In 1569, after Mary had fled to England, her half-brother, the Earl of Moray, came to Aberdeen as Regent of the kingdom to reassert royal power and to attempt to implement some of the changes wrought by the Reformation. The urban elite which controlled the town council had proved to be as conservative in their religious sympathies as the earls of Huntly and

[3] *RPC*, ii, 420, 423.
[4] *CSP Scot.*, iv, no. 788.

had attempted with a discreet determination to oppose as much Protestantisation of the burgh as possible.

Like Mary in 1562, Morton brought along the English ambassador so that full reports of his activity in the north-east could be conveyed to Queen Elizabeth in London.[5] The earls of Rothes, Buchan and Errol, together with a fairly full complement of advisers, were also present, to stress the comprehensiveness of support for the Regent and to ensure that the Queen's remaining supporters would be suitably overawed. In case there was doubt left in anybody's mind, the Regent also issued a proclamation ordering levies within the sherriffdoms of Fife, Kinross, Perth, Forfar and Kincardine, all of them reliable areas from a religious and political point of view, to meet him at Brechin and to accompany him to Aberdeen. In the hope of fairly rich pickings in the north, a large clerical staff was transported to assist him in the execution of the judicial business.[6] In the event, the sums of money collected by the Treasurer were not as great as he had hoped: how much this was due to an attempt at reconciliation and how much to a desperate shortage of cash in the region is not quite clear.[7]

The burgesses of Aberdeen faced the prospect of a visit from the Regent with some degree of alarm. It was the third time in a little over a decade that they had received a visitation from the central government and each of the two previous expeditions had induced severe disturbance within the local polity. In previous conflicts in which the authority of central government had been challenged, the burgesses of Aberdeen had habitually attempted to preserve their links with whatever government was in power. In the opening shots of the Reformation crisis in 1559-60, the burgesses had adopted the cautious approach of not wishing to undertake anything against the authority of the regent, Mary of Guise. In 1562, in the events leading to the defeat and death of the 4th earl of Huntly at the hands of the Queen's troops at the battle of Corrichie, the burgh had remained punctiliously loyal to the Queen and had rejected any attempt to involve it in rebellion against the crown. There was an earlier precedent for this course of action in the crisis of 1543, when the Earl of Arran, as Governor

---

5 *CSP Scot.*, v, no. 15.

6 *TA*, xiii, p.xv.

7 A. White, 'Religion, Politics and Society in Aberdeen, 1543-1593' (Edinburgh Univ. Ph.D., 1985), 272-5.

of the kingdom, had attempted to seal an alliance between Scotland and England. On this occasion the 4th earl of Huntly, unquestionably the most powerful magnate in the region, had ranked himself with the Queen Dowager, Mary of Guise, and the pro-French party opposing the Anglophile policy of the Governor. When Huntly had attempted to include the provost and burgesses of Aberdeen amongst his allies he had found, to his dismay, that they took the Governor's side, seemingly challenging his authority in the region in the process.

The same patterns obtained during the political crises of the late 1560s and early 1570s. Huntly, with the support of his network of kin and dependants, was one of the chief bastions of the Queen's party during the civil war whereas the royal burgh of Aberdeen was, in so far as prudence allowed, a supporter of the King's party. Politics, both national and local, counted for more than religion in this strategy, which ignored the apparent convergence of conservative religious opinion between Huntly, his Gordon affinity and the burgess aristocracy of Aberdeen. Needless to say, such a consistent pattern of policy spread over more than a generation should place a question mark against those who claim that the royal burgh of Aberdeen was governed by Huntly's placemen, slavishly obedient to him in both civil and religious matters. The members of the Aberdeen patriciate appear to have had definite opinions of their own as to where their interests and those of the realm lay. Such a vision included a strong concern for control over their own destiny; their actions were not always to be determined by the interests of the Gordon alliance system in the north-east. It was possible for Aberdeen, which was by far the largest burgh in the north-east and had since the fourteenth century been acknowledged as one of the 'four great towns of Scotland',[8] to aspire to a certain independence of policy although it may not always have been possible for it to secure independence of action. One of its main considerations in maintaining links with central government was to avoid a lapse into the status of a pocket burgh under the control of the earls of Huntly or other rival magnates in the region.

Ironically, in 1574 Morton was visiting a burgh which had, technically at least, remained loyal to the king during the civil war,

[8] See M. Lynch, M. Spearman and G. Stell (eds.), *The Scottish Medieval Town* (Edinburgh, 1988), 4, 240, 268-9, 272-5.

although it would be true to say that the burgesses had been prudent in the exercise of valour and had not always exerted themselves noticeably in James's cause. Far from suffering at the hands of the earl of Huntly, they had derived a measure of immunity and prosperity from his occupation of the burgh in 1569, when it had been turned into the centre of the rival Marian administration in the north. Their plea that they had been coerced into contributing to the Queen's cause rang somewhat hollow in the Regent's ears. Huntly's surrender at the Pacification of Perth in effect left them friendless, since they had not done much to support either party. Morton realised that the burgh was dependent for its autonomy on a renewed alliance with central government. He capitalised on Aberdeen's vulnerability by wringing as much money as possible out of its inhabitants. A glance at the list of the compositions exacted by the justice ayre which accompanied his visit to Aberdeen in 1574, taken together with his general policy in the north-east, suggests that he was implementing a novel policy of conciliating his enemies whilst plundering his friends.

One of Morton's chief political levers against the burgh and a principal reason for suspecting it of disaffection was its failure to implement what might be called 'the spirit' of the reformed religion. In many ways the machinery and discipline of Protestantism had been established in the town, but its exercise had been so tightly controlled as to be rendered almost completely ineffective. A Protestant minister, Adam Heriot, had been recruited at the time of the Reformation parliament of August 1560 and a kirk session had duly been set up, somewhat belatedly, on the eve of Queen Mary's visit in 1562. Morton's visitation in 1574 and the religious measures which stemmed from it pinpointed what was lacking in the reformed settlement of Aberdeen, which fell far short of a 'perfyt reformed kirk', such as had been established in the hot-house atmosphere of St Andrews in 1559.[9] When Morton arrived in Aberdeen, he found a community dominated by Catholic survivalists and conservative sympathies. The burgesses had managed to maintain this way of life by an astute use of the political skills they had acquired during the

[9] See J. Dawson, '"The face of a perfyt reformed kyrk": St Andrews and the early Scottish Reformation', in J. Kirk (ed.), *Humanism and Reform: the Church in Europe, England and Scotland, 1400-1643* (Oxford, 1991), 413-35.

previous half century of dealings with central government: masterly inactivity combined with judicious temporising. It was clear that for the Reformation to take root and thrive in Aberdeen a whole infrastructure of power, patronage and kinship would have to be dismantled. The incidental effect of such drastic action would have been to render the burgh ungovernable, temporarily at least. It would also have jeopardised the collection by Morton of the financial exactions which he so desperately needed. The Regent's actions fell short of such radical courses, but only just. By imposing a heavy composition on the burgh, Morton shook the confidence of the burgesses in the closed corporation which had hitherto preserved the town from hardship. In a further series of actions directed at the religious polity of the burgh, he warned that a measure of conformity was necessary if the authority of the burgh establishment was to continue to be upheld by the crown.

In Scotland, as in England, Catholicism survived best in those regions which were remote from the central government's control and surveillance, and where public authority was concentrated in relatively private hands. Such areas as the north-east in general, and Aberdeen in particular, marked as they were by the conventions of traditional seigneurial authority, offered ideal territory for the survival of Catholic beliefs and practices. The social framework of the region was overwhelmingly conservative and the rhythms of popular culture were still marked by the observances which had given shape and meaning to the cycles of daily life. The religious revolution of 1560 had not yet been matched by an equivalent social revolution; in many areas popular culture remained relatively unchanged save that it lacked the public forms of Catholicism. A significant body of opinion in Aberdeen retained Catholic habits but was at a loss how to articulate them or the basic instincts which they represented under the new dispensation. As a result, there were a number of surviving customs and much civic ceremony to give great offence to the regent when he arrived in the town in 1574.

At the head of Morton's instructions designed to eradicate Catholic customs was the demand that the council inhibit the celebration of festival days in the town.[10] In the kind of Catholicism that depended on a complex of social practices, the

---

[10] *RPC*, ii, 390.

observances of traditional holidays could be as significant as other, more obvious devotional practices. It was a common experience for burghs to find the suppression of Catholic practices difficult in those institutions where social and religious identities overlapped. The craft guilds are prime examples of religious societies which were deprived of their traditional means of publicly expressing their solidarity by the Reformation. In many towns, they preserved some vestiges of their Catholic ethos by refusing to work on the customary religious holidays of the burgh. In February 1574, the deacons of the cordiners, the websters, tailors and baxters were ordered by the kirk session to see that their members did not observe any holy day or festival 'quhilk wes usit of auld tyme befor'. The only holy day to be marked was the Sabbath.[11] This prohibition may not have had much effect since in January 1576 there was a sizeable demonstration of conservative sentiment when all of the burgh's craftsmen refrained from working on Christmas Day.[12] Aberdeen was not the only burgh to face such difficulties with its craftsmen, for even in the bracing Protestant air of St Andrews similar problems were encountered.[13] The close confines of the craft guild lent opportunities for conservative practices to survive.[14]

Attachment to the rhythms of the pre-Reformation Christian year also made its appearance in another burgh institution, the grammar school. In 1569, the council had granted a Latin petition from the pupils of the grammar school that they should be allowed to enjoy the usual Christmas holidays.[15] In April 1574, as part of the Protestantising policy of the kirk session, it was ordained that this practice should be suppressed. Clearly some inhabitants of the burgh continued to cling to the custom since the session ordered that if parents refused to send their children to school on these days they should be reported to the authorities.[16] The position of the grammar school master in this conflict is not recorded, yet he was an interesting figure in his own right.

The master of Aberdeen's grammar school was Master John Henderson, a Catholic and a graduate of King's College, Aber-

---

[11] *Aberdeen Ecc. Recs.*, 16.
[12] *Aberdeen Council Register*, ii, 25.
[13] *STAKSR*, i, 387-90, 404.
[14] M. Lynch, *Edinburgh and the Reformation* (Edinburgh, 1981), 56-9.
[15] *Aberdeen Council Register*, i, 366.
[16] *Aberdeen Ecc. Recs.*, 16.

deen. In 1549 King's College, Aberdeen was visited by its rector, Alexander Galloway. Galloway stipulated in his visitation charge that Henderson was to be entrusted with the task of reporting on all of those scholars who were absenting themselves from the liturgy in the college chapel.[17] Since the acts of the visitation record a reluctance of the theology students to go on to receive holy orders, and we know from other sources that a number of these same students went on to serve as ministers in the reformed Church, Henderson's religious leanings may be presumed to have been orthodox.[18] This impression is confirmed by his departure for France in the company of James Cheyne of Arnage in 1573, when measures against Catholic sympathisers in burgh institutions were being intensified.[19] A schoolmaster at a burgh school was a powerful figure with great scope for influencing his pupils.[20] A Catholic schoolmaster in a conservative burgh had an ideal opportunity of delaying the impact of the Reformation on his pupils and perpetuating some traces of Catholic belief and customs. Henderson's quitting Aberdeen for France demonstrated how necessary it was for the new Kirk to establish itself within the close-knit burgh institutions which could act as breeding grounds for crypto-Catholicism. Edinburgh was to confront this problem directly, if unsuccessfully, in its attempts to dismiss William Roberton, its Catholic schoolmaster.[21] Henderson's withdrawal was to save Aberdeen similar trouble.

The ordering of the parish kirk of St Nicholas in Aberdeen also gave the regent a clue to the state of religious opinion in the burgh. Although it had been stripped of its vestments, plate and even its chandeliers, many of the more solid fixtures remained in position. The organ was still intact in 1574; despite an earlier instruction from the council that it should be dismantled, the burgh treasurer had not seen to its removal. During his visit to the town, Morton ordered that the organ be broken up and disposed of as quickly as possible. Mindful of the investment of capital and conscious that it might fetch a good price if sold, the council asked John Black to see to its careful dismantling. The choice was

---

[17] *Aberdeen Fasti*, 264

[18] White, 'Religion, Politics and Society in Aberdeeen', 108-10.

[19] J. Durkan, 'Early humanism and King's College', *AUR*, clxiii (1980), 259-79, at 272.

[20] M.E. James, *Family, Lineage and Civil Society: A Study of Society, Politics and Mentality in the Durham Region, 1500-1640* (Oxford, 1974), 101-02.

[21] Lynch, *Edinburgh*, 100-01.

poignant since Black had formerly been the master of the song school and must often have played it in the days before 1560.[22] Black had originally refused to conform to the Reformation settlement or to attend the reformed liturgy in the parish kirk of St Nicholas, and in this he was different to most of its other chaplains. Instead, he took up foreign trade for some years. It was only ten years after the Reformation that he agreed to accept the changes. His apparent change of mind may have been influenced by his acquisition of a wife, a decisive step for a former priest.[23]

As well as the organ, the choir stalls and the carved timber choir screen were also remarkable survivals of pre-1560 liturgical arrangements. The stalls were removed in accordance with the regent's orders; they were not destroyed but simply moved to another part of the church. The choir screen remained intact along with the rood loft until the 1590s, when the church was divided into two so as to accommodate separate parish congregations.[24] Although most of the side altars had been removed, the reredos of at least one of them was still standing in 1584.[25] Even though the building may have been less richly furnished than it had been in 1560, it still bore the essential outlines of a Roman Catholic church.

Despite being confronted with a direct order from the regent to re-order their parish church and eradicate some of the remaining traces of Catholic practice in the burgh, the council still temporised in the hope of being able to avoid total compliance.[26] At some point after Morton's departure, word must have reached him that his orders had not been obeyed. His response was a stern letter asking the burgesses for an explanation. In their reply they hastened to reassure him by stating that only the casing of the organ remained to be broken up and the choir stalls, along with the screens at the backs of all the altars, had been removed, save one which had been retained to keep draughts off the backs of the necks of the congregation whilst at prayer.[27] In his efforts to enforce his policies in Aberdeen, Morton was faced with the famil-

---

22 Aberdeen City Archives, MS Council Register, xxiv, ff.159, 273.
23 White, 'Religion, Politics and Society in Aberdeen', 174-6.
24 Ms. Council Register, xxxvi, f.556
25 *Aberdeen St Nicholas Cartularium*, ii, 386.
26 *Aberdeen Ecc. Recs.*, 19-20.
27 SRO, GD 149/265, pt. 3, f.33. I am grateful to John Durkan for directing me to this source.

iar problem of central government in the sixteenth century; he needed reliable local agents. Aberdeen's government was a closed society and there was, as yet, no possibility of breaking into it or replacing the current administration with one more to his liking. The urban patriciate, even though it had a Protestant minority within it, seems to have believed that it was better for them all to hang together otherwise they would all have hanged separately.

There were a number of reasons moving Aberdeen's burgesses to delay the removal of some of the trappings of Catholicism. First and foremost was the fact that many remained to be convinced that Protestantism had come to stay. Just as in England, where many parishes together with their clergy seem to have hoped for a Catholic restoration and retained their altars and images, so did Aberdeen.[28] The survival of images was a matter of particular displeasure to the regent during his visit to the burgh in 1574.[29] In response to his complaints, the burgesses were forced to dispose of those that survived, although some may have been hidden away in the hope of better days. When replying to Morton's enquiry about the results of their implementation of his orders, the burgesses wrote to him that they had confiscated a respectable number of statues and crucifixes and burnt them.[30]

On the whole, there does not seem to have been a great wave of iconoclasm in Aberdeen. The considerations moving the burgesses in the direction of preservation of such articles were not purely devotional but also, to some extent, economic. The adornments of the parish church represented centuries of burgh investment and it was not fitting that such endowments should be lightly disposed of. Their concern for the beauty of holiness was not indiscriminate and it may have been that the economic motive and the sense of pride of place outweighed any strict devotion to religious relics or ornaments as such. In June 1560, Andrew Buk, son-in-law of the provost of Aberdeen, had broken into the Cistercian abbey of Kinloss, some 75 miles to the north, and carried off the bells 'hersis, pillaris, standing chandlaris, lettronis and other brazen work'.[31] Yet he was one of the substantial group

---

[28] C. Haigh, 'The continuity of Catholicism in the English Reformation', *Past and Present,* xciii (1981), 39-40.

[29] *Aberdeen Ecc. Recs.*, 19-20.

[30] SRO, GD 149/265, pt. 3, f.33

[31] *Wodrow Misc.*, 341-55, 396: there were, in addition, 89 readers, most of whom were conforming ex-Catholic clergy.

of burgesses who objected to the arrival of the Reformation in Aberdeen in 1560 and opposed the spoiling of Aberdeen's friaries.[32] For Buk, as for others, it was possible to be iconoclast abroad and iconodule at home. The Menzies family, a kin group with strong conservative and Catholic opinions which monopolised many of burgh offices, including the key post of provost, also maintained a similarly self-interested approach. In benefiting from the sale of the treasures of the burgh's parish church, the Menzies showed how it was possible to combine deep conservatism and opposition to change with a cool and pragmatic approach to ecclesiastical property, seeing it as an asset to be realised in advance of competitors, especially if the latter happened to be members of the central government.[33]

Catholicism in the north-east after 1560

The survival of Catholic sympathies in the north-east was undoubtedly promoted by the conservative instincts of the earl of Huntly. Although not a Catholic himself, the fifth earl realised the importance of the forms of Catholicism to key members of his gentry clientage. Catholicism gave expression to the ideals of communal solidarity, local consciousness and pride of place. For the lairds of north-east Scotland as for many of the barons and squires of northern England, Catholicism seemed the 'natural religion'.[34] Protestantism, as it then stood, seriously short of ministers—in 1574 there were 24 ministers in the 105 parishes of the diocese of Aberdeen[35]—and exceedingly underdeveloped institutionally could not express the political and social realities of Aberdeen or the north-east. The conservative lairds and the equally conservative burgesses of Aberdeen distrusted Protestantism as an alien and divisive force. Its stress on a particular kind of participation, together with its tendency towards the egalitarian involvement of the congregation in the exercise of discipline, threatened the long-accepted notions of order and hierarchy in local society. After the Reformation the idea of the

32 SRO, Acts and Decreets, xxviii, f.50.
33 *Aberdeen Council Register*, i, 319.
34 White, 'Religion, Politics and Society in Aberdeen', 203 ff.
35 M.E. James, 'The concept of order and the Northern Rising 1569', *Past and Present*, lx (1973), 82.

'community' of the realm came to be understood in a different way. The increased emphasis on individual and personal morality, as signs of a life of that true virtue which alone qualified an individual to bear rule in society, ran contrary to contemporary understanding of how urban and rural government should function.[36] Catholicism in the north-east was not simply a religious sentiment but a social settlement. In order to dislodge this pattern of society to replace it with another an alternative machinery of government was necessary if social change was to be engineered and the conservative framework of life dismantled.

The Earl of Huntly's influence may have appeared as a threat to the liberties of Aberdeen, but it was a positive benefit to those who wished to continue their Catholic way of life. Two patterns of Catholicism developed in the north-east: the seigneurial and the civic. In many ways one conditioned the growth and preservation of the other. At the heart of the piety and practice of both was the celebration of the mass, which was widely available in and around both burghs of Aberdeen for several decades after 1560. The efforts of Protestant ministers and successive outraged General Assemblies to plant the reformed faith in the area were gravely hampered by the survival of mass centres in and around the burgh of Aberdeen. In 1572 the General Assembly complained angrily about the celebration of mass in Old Aberdeen.[37] In 1587 the situation had still not improved since the Assembly issued another lament that year about the regular celebration of mass in the chancellor's house in Old Aberdeen.[38] The chancellor in 1572 and 1587 was the same man, Master Alexander Seton, a brother of William Seton of Meldrum and connected, through his mother, with the Gordons of Haddo.

A number of significant strands of local social and political life met in Alexander Seton: the ecclesiastical and the noble. Seton was a notable worker for the Marian cause during the civil war and when Morton appeared in Aberdeen in 1574 Seton was one of those he was keenest to interview. Seton wisely chose not to appear and as a result was put to the horn.[39] Lord Seton, another prominent Marian who had been provost of Edinburgh at the time of the Reformation crisis of 1559-60 and whose main sphere

[36] White, 'Religion, Politics and Society in Aberdeen', 191 ff.
[37] *BUK*, i, 254.
[38] *BUK*, ii, 716.
[39] *RPC*, ii, 398.

of interest lay in East Lothian, appears to have maintained an establishment in Old Aberdeen during these years. It was there that he offered shelter to old Lady Northumberland after the unsuccessful rising against Elizabeth in the north of England. Whilst enjoying his hospitality he was able to enjoy the additional benefit of hearing daily mass.[40] There were also a number of conservative lairds' houses in the vicinity where a Catholic priest could count on a welcome and where he could find small Catholic congregations.[41] Occasionally the owners of these houses were prosecuted for non-conformity. In 1575 Lady Jean Gordon, lady of Fyvie, was put on trial for hearing mass,[42] and a summons was also issued against Lady Aboyne for allowing mass to be said in her house at Craig of Boyne, and at her lodgings in Turriff and Aberdeen.[43] Even devotional articles associated with traditional Catholic piety appear to have been readily available in Aberdeen and the surrounding countryside. Some years after the civil war a Jesuit priest was able to report that rosaries were on sale at a fair in Turriff.[44] In this way Aberdeen and its hinterland offered ample opportunities for those who wished to attend mass to do so in comparative security. Despite occasional prosecutions, Catholic practices were able to continue as long as Huntly and his affinity provided the political and social framework under which their fellow-conservatives could shelter.

A further factor encouraging the survival of Catholic customs was the abiding presence and continued influence of Catholic clergy. Before the Reformation the clerical population had been relatively high; it has been estimated that the ratio of clergy per head of the population of Old Aberdeen, which had both a cathedral chapter and a university, may have stood at one in four at the time of the Reformation.[45] There was certainly no expulsion of clergy from either Old or New Aberdeen after 1560. Provided that the clergy were prepared to give the minimum of conformity they were allowed to live peacefully and enjoy their pensions. In 1575 there were at least five former chaplains of St Nicholas' kirk living in the royal burgh.[46] There were also former

---

40 *CSP Scot.*, iii, no. 302.
41 *BUK*, ii, 717.
42 SRO, JC 26/1/24.
43 SRO, JC 26/1/26, 28, 29.
44 *Catholic Narratives*, 162.
45 White, 'Religion, Politics and Society in Aberdeen', 141.
46 MS Council Register, xxviii, f.542.

members of the burgh's three religious houses. On occasion the council was even willing to maintain them if they fell on hard times. A Carmelite, Richard Gordon, was ordered to be supported by the chief men of the burgh in 1566, whilst one of the former chaplains of the parish church was also given the comparatively secure job of the newly- established lighthouse.[47] By appointing the former chaplain to this office the council was continuing the practice of employing ecclesiastics in the burgh's service.

One of the most notable of the former clergy to remain in Aberdeen was the ex-prior of the Carmelite house, John Failford. After the Reformation Failford found refuge in the provost's house where he was later described as a servant.[48] However, he must have lived in circumstances of comparative ease since he was able to receive books from abroad and to lend sizeable sums of money to other former Catholic clergy.[49] He is registered as drawing his friar's pension during these years, which suggests a measure of conformity.[50] However, the consistent association of various branches of the Menzies family with Catholicism suggests that he may have served as a domestic chaplain, possibly even using the altar vessels of the parish church which Patrick Menzies had purchased after the Reformation.[51] By making use of such services the conservative burgesses were claiming for themselves the same facilities as the conservative aristocracy and initiating the process of Catholic withdrawal to the confines of the urban household.

Another social grouping within the burgh community which fostered and sustained a conservative outlook was the household, centred as it was round the family and kinship group. One of the measures taken by Morton against continuing conservatism was specifically directed against Catholic households in the town, more particularly against the households of prominent Catholic burgesses. The web of family alliances and business associations centring on the council chamber, and latterly on the kirk session, encouraged a close sense of cooperation amongst the burgh's urban aristocracy, a sense which included toleration for trad-

[47] *Aberdeen Council Register*, i, 362.
[48] *Spalding Misc.*, ii, 43.
[49] *CSP Scot.*, iv, no. 168; Ms. Council Register, xxvii, f.172.
[50] *Thirds of Benefices*, 97, 154, 220.
[51] *Aberdeen Ecc. Recs.*, 14, 22.

itional beliefs and practices. Catholicism was so deeply ingrained in the upper ranks of burgh society that a full-scale attack on it, apart from being highly impractical, would have undermined the customary forms of government. The regent recognised this necessary fact of political life by publicly ordering the bailies to ensure that religious conformity and discipline should reign in their own homes as well as in the town as a whole.[52] The regent issued a powerful rebuke, but he realised that he was not strong enough to remove them from office.

Of the four bailies called to account by Morton in 1574 two had close links with Catholicism thorough their wives, whilst one made no secret of his opposition to the Reformation. Master Patrick Rutherford was connected to the ruling Menzies family through his wife, Marjorie, the daughter of Provost Thomas Menzies.[53] Master George Middleton's wife belonged to the Catholic family of Irvine of Drum. She consistently refused to accept the new religion despite being brought before the session on a number of occasions before finally submitting in June 1574, a date significantly close to the regent's visit to the burgh.[54] The third bailie, Gilbert Menzies of Coull, had originally opposed the advent of the Reformation and had maintained his position ever since. During the early months of 1574 his recalcitrance had earned him a spell of imprisonment in Edinburgh, from which he was only released on the understanding that he would come to communion and give confession to his faith when he returned home.[55] Despite being brought before the regent and his council twice in Edinburgh, he maintained his defiance on his return to Aberdeen and was once more rebuked by Morton on his visit to the burgh.[56] Gilbert was the provost's son, and once again there were limits to the amount of discipline that could be exercised against the essential pillars of government within the burgh. It was thus apparent that there was no prospect of strengthening or even creating a Protestant establishment, until such 'house churches' operating an alterative system of Catholic sacramental practice were rooted out.

Obviously the narrow base from which Protestantism operated

52 ibid., 19.
53 Aberdeen City Archives, MS Burgh Register of Sasines, xii, 21 July 1561.
54 SRO, RH3/20, f.34.
55 *RPC*, ii, 343.
56 *Aberdeen Ecc. Recs.*, 19.

within the burgh was rendered considerably narrower by the degree of Catholic representation on the town council, a degree of representation which was inevitably reflected in the composition of the kirk session. Three of the bailies summoned before Morton in 1574 for allowing Catholic practices in their households were also members of the kirk session of 1573.[57] The danger faced by the town's minister and the small number of committed Protestants within the burgh was that the political and religious institutions of the burgh would simply become extensions of the burgess households and that the equally powerful conservative influences operating from within those households would be used to delay, if not entirely inhibit, the growth of Protestantism in Aberdeen. The chief aim of the Protestant party, once Morton's power was assured, was to break the influence of the Catholic household and its stranglehold on the life of the Kirk. Encouraged by the single-mindedness of John Craig, who had arrived as the town's minister from Edinburgh by way of Montrose in 1573, and intimidated by the presence of Morton and the privy council, the oligarchs of Aberdeen set about reluctantly dismantling the obstacles placed in the way of further reformation. Even the Menzies family, robbed of external allies and threatened at home with ruin and excommunication, was forced to give some public subscription to the new kirk.

In many ways Morton's visit to Aberdeen in the late summer of 1574 could be counted as a success for the Protestant cause. Much of the work in the direction of the purification and clarification of the Protestant machinery of the town had been achieved through the combination of external pressure and the efforts of the internal Protestant group within the burgh. By the end of 1574 drastic changes had been wrought within the burgh of Aberdeen. The previous fourteen years had seen three visitations by the central government; the first bringing about the fall of the earl of Huntly in 1562; the second in 1569 the purge of the remaining Catholic reaching staff at King's College, and the third in 1574 the partial eclipse of the Menzies family and their enforced public adherence to the new Kirk. Gradually the area for conservative manoeuvre was whittled away and the foundations of a Protestant polity within the burgh strengthened. At the close of the year Aberdeen had established the framework of a

---

57 SRO, RH3/20, f.19.

stable reformed system of discipline. Under the guidance of John Craig and with the support of central government and local sympathisers it was to prove hard for the conservative faction in the town to regain its former position of absolute dominance. Morton had proved in 1574 that even the kirk session could act as a restraint, a goad or a focus of opposition to the town council. The session was an alternative representative body allowing a way into public life for the professionally and economically secure, but not enormously wealthy, merchants. The question of religion was not settled in Aberdeen in 1574, but its boundaries became more clearly delineated. Over the next twenty years this process was to be taken further, and chiefly by men who had to struggle to find a voice in the council chamber.

1574 also marked a significant point in the development of the Catholic community in the north-east. It was another stage in the withdrawal of Catholicism to the relatively private world of recusancy. Until 1574 Catholicism, albeit in the form of survivalism rather than missionary endeavour, had maintained a high profile in Aberdeen and represented a viable alternative to the established Kirk. After 1574 it was compelled to adopt a less public stance and as the number of priests trained before 1560 declined, to be only intermittently replaced by priests trained in foreign seminaries, the sacramental life on which Catholicism depended for its identity and strength was seriously threatened and starved of vigour. The character of Catholicism in the years after 1574 was to be marked by a sense of decline and insecurity, its strength in the burghs of Aberdeen was to decline accordingly.

SOME HELPES FOR YOUNG SCHOLLERS A NEW SOURCE OF EARLY SCOTTISH PSALMODY

Kenneth Elliott

A Scottish didactic publication of 1602, *Some helpes for young Schollers in Christianity* by John Davidson, printed in Edinburgh by Robert Waldegrave, gives an unexpected and perhaps unique insight into the world of Scottish church music of the period. A copy of this small and extremely rare octavo volume is preserved in GUL.[1] The following is a brief description of its contents:[2]

[parchment binding]
[fly-leaf v: MS inscriptions] Gifted by the Right [scored out] much honourable [scored out] honoured Sir Robert Sibbald to Mr Jameson Lecturer of history in the University of Glasgow [last eight words lightly scored out] Octr 18 1712
A1r [title-page] Some helpes...
A1v To the Reader
A2r The Epistle Dedicatory / To his loving flock of Salt-prestoun...
A2v [refers to]...this daye seauen yeare, to wit; 16. day of Nouember 1595, the firste time I spake among you... [at end of Epistle] 16 Nouember, 1602...
A5r [biblical quotations]
A6r Some helpes for young Schollers...
F1v Lord in great grief [Psalm 130] [with music]
F4r Psalme CXVII / O all ye Nations [with music]
F6v [blank]
[fly-leaf: blank]
[parchment binding]

The last two items are particularly interesting from the musical point of view, when placed in their historical context. The first printed Scottish psalter appeared in 1564, containing metrical texts by English and Scottish versifiers, with matching psalm-tunes drawn from an international repertoire. Thereafter, until the

---

[1] GUL, Special Collections, Bi7- 1.21. It measures 140 × 85 mm. According to *STC*, this is the only surviving copy.

[2] There is an incomplete transcription printed in W. Jameson, *Mr. John Davidson's Catechism* (1708). An incomplete transcription is also printed in C. Rogers, *Three Scottish Reformers* (Grampian Club, 1876), 132ff. No location of the original print is given. J.P. Edmond, 'Bibliographical gleanings, 1890-93', *PEBS*, i (1890-95), no. 17, p.12, also wrongly states that it is 'printed entire' in that volume. Again no location is given. Aldis refers to this article, but yet again no location of the source is given.

early seventeenth century, there followed many similar publications, mostly in Scotland (but two in Middelburg, Zeeland), and all presenting simply the psalm-tunes with their texts. Meanwhile Thomas Wood, a former monk of the Tironensian house at Lindores who became a reader in the reformed Church, began to compile his harmonised manuscript psalter[3] at St Andrews between the years 1562-6, for which he commissioned material notably from the composer David Peebles of St Andrews, but also from John Angus of Dunfermline, Andrew Kemp of St Andrews and Andrew Blackhall, who at this time was residing in Musselburgh.[4] This is how Wood describes his commissions:

> ... I wes ever requeisting and solisting till thay wer all set, and the canticles (lyk as veni creator, the sang of Ambros, the sang of mary etc) I oft did wreat to maister andro blakehall; to Ihone Ang*us* and sum andro kemp set, sa I notit tenors [i.e. the psalm-tunes] and send sum to mussilbrough, and sum to du*n*farmling, and sa wer done...[5]

It seems probable that Wood's harmonised psalter was intended for publication, along the lines of those that were appearing in France and England at the time. But harmonised settings of the psalm-tunes had to wait several decades in Scotland before reaching print. Alongside the series of Scottish printed psalters, several contemporary manuscript sources include psalm-settings, notably Duncan Burnett's Music-Book[6] of c.1615, which contains some 40

---

[3] Sometimes described as 'The St Andrews Psalter', and surviving in two (the second incomplete) widely dispersed sets of part-books. See 'Music of Scotland, 1500-1700', *MB* XV, ed. K. Elliott, song-texts ed. H.M. Shire (3rd edn., 1976) (*MB* XV) for locations of most of these. The two sets are henceforth referred to as TWC_1, TWC_2, TWQ, TWA_1, TWT, TWB_1, TWB_2. [C,Q,A,T,B = *cantus, quintus, altus, tenor, bassus.*] See n.27 for TWA_2, and my article on Wood in *New Grove*.

[4] See my articles in *New Grove* on David Peebles (fl.1530-76), John Angus (fl.1543-95), Andrew Kemp (fl.1560-70) and Andrew Blackhall (c.1535-1609).

[5] Extract from TWT, 166-7, printed complete in H.G. Farmer, *A History of Music in Scotland* (1947), 162-3, in modern spelling. Complete passage in original spelling in K. Elliott, 'Music of Scotland, 1500-1700' (Cambridge University dissertation, 1961), along with detailed accounts of the sources mentioned in the present article. The musical forms associated with psalmody in Scotland were (i) chordally harmonised settings of Proper Tunes (i.e. psalm-tunes associated with a particular metrical psalm-text or canticle), (ii) similarly set Common Tunes (psalm-tunes to which any psalm in common metre could be sung), (iii) Psalms in Reports (vocal imitative settings of proper tunes), (iv) Lessons on the Psalms (instrumental consort settings of proper psalm-tunes), and (v) Anthems (imitative vocal settings of metrical psalm-texts). For further discussion of these, see K. Elliott and F. Rimmer, *A History of Scottish Music* (1973), 25-32.

[6] NLS, MS 9447, ff.140v-161r.

settings by Andrew Kemp, and other sets that are anonymous and unique.[7] It was not until 1625 that harmonised versions of the psalm-tunes began to appear in printed psalters in Scotland, first in the group of Common Tunes in a psalter published in Aberdeen. Others followed in Aberdeen (1633) and Edinburgh (1634), culminating in the great Psalter of 1635 (Edinburgh), for which Edward Millar of the Chapel Royal of Scotland edited the music. It is strange that *Some helpes* was never mentioned (even in a footnote) in such exhaustive bibliographical work as that of Maurice Frost,[8] which describes in great detail printed sources and identifies origins of individual texts and tunes.

These lines of enquiry enabled tune and text of Psalm 117 in *Some helpes* to be traced to Scottish and English psalters respectively. But the tune, text and setting of Psalm 130 seemed to be quite new. With a view to establishing the identity or even authorship of this material, it seemed worthwhile to investigate the career of the remarkable sixteenth-century church leader John Davidson, the author of the book under discussion here. John Davidson (c.1549-1604) was born in Dunfermline and educated at St Andrews University, where he became regent of St Leonard's College in 1567. He subsequently became well-known as a fiery and controversial preacher and produced several printed religious and poetical works. Soon after 1573 he fell foul of Regent Morton for criticising the latter's unfair means of securing benefices, and chose to reside abroad until 1577. In 1579 he was installed as minister of the parish of Liberton near Edinburgh.[9] Meanwhile Morton was arrested on 31 December 1580 on accusation of complicity in the murder of Lord Darnley. Davidson visited him in prison in April 1581 and a reconciliation seems to have resulted. But Morton was eventually executed in June 1581. Davidson fled to England 'to escape the troubles of the period', but during the period of the radical Ruthven administration in 1582-3 he officiated in various local churches in or near Edinburgh, including the second charge of Holyrood.[10] By 1595 he had become minister of Prestonpans, where he erected a new

---

[7] E.g. the addenda after 1615 to TWC_1 (194-200), TWT (186-92), the Rowallan Cantus Part-Book, c.1627-37 (ff.47v-53r), EUL MS La.III.488, and the William Stirling Cantus Part-Book, 1639 (ff.35r-42v), NLS MS 5.2.14.

[8] M. Frost, *English & Scottish Psalm & Hymn Tunes, c.1543-1677* (1953).

[9] Scott, *Fasti*, i, 170.

[10] ibid., i, 27.

church, manse and school 'for teiching Latine grek and hebrew towngis and Language and for Instructing of youth in virtue and learning'.[11] The next news of him comes in 1602, with the publication of *Some helpes*, which was closely linked with this last foundation. He died in 1604.[12]

Davidson's career shows similarities to that of the late sixteenth-century Scottish composer Andrew Blackhall (c.1535-1609). Originally a canon of Holyrood Abbey, Blackhall after the Reformation became minister of Liberton in 1564.[13] About this time he contributed three psalm-settings and one canticle (possibly two, for there are conflicting ascriptions) to Thomas Wood's anthology.[14] In 1569 he composed the anthem 'Of mercy and of judgement both' (Psalm 101), 'giffin in propyne [i.e. as a tribute] to the kyng',[15] perhaps representing a bid for promotion at court.[16] In 1574 Blackhall was appointed to Inveresk parish church,[17] and a year later composed another anthem 'Blessed art thou' (Psalm 128):[18] in Wood's words, 'Psalme icxxviii set & send be blakehall to my L*ord* mar at his first mariadge with my L*ord* of ang*us* sister'.[19] In 1578 Morton commissioned Blackhall to set as an anthem the metrical version of Psalm 43, 'Judge and revenge my cause, O Lord'.[20] To use Wood's words again: '...at the earnest sute of L*ord* morto*n* quho p*re*sentit the sa*m*in [to] kyng Jamis the saxt at stirling in the moneth of february as I understand, yeir of god imv^c^lxxviii'. This text had already appeared in significant and emotive political circumstances as the motto on the banner of the Confederate Lords (with Morton among them) at Carberry Hill in 1567.[21] Evidently Morton used musical as well as political means in a vain attempt to clear his name of suspicion of Darnley's mur-

---

[11] ibid., i, 387; viii, 99.

[12] *DNB*, xiv, 125-7.

[13] Scott, *Fasti*, i, 170; see Dilworth, 'Canons regular', in this present volume.

[14] Psalms 68, 76, 121, 'The humble sute of ane sinnar', 'Ane prayer' (also, but possibly in error, attributed to Angus in TWC_2).

[15] TWC_1, TWC_2, TWQ, TWA_1, TWA_2, TWT, TWB_1, TWB_2.

[16] H.M. Shire, *Song, Dance and Poetry of the Court of Scotland under King James VI* (Cambridge, 1969), 69-71.

[17] Scott, *Fasti*, i, 324. Inveresk includes Musselburgh in its parish.

[18] *MB* XV, 10.

[19] This information curiously does not seem to match names and dates in *Scots Peerage*.

[20] *MB* XV, 11.

[21] See further K. Elliott, 'Scottish music of the early reformed Church', *TSES*, xv, pt.2 (1961), 21; and Shire, *Song, Dance and Poetry*, 70.

der, and to find favour with the young King in 1578. In 1579 an important Act of Parliament was passed 'For instructioun of the youth in musik'[22] in which responsibility for teaching music was officially passed to the burghs of Scotland. A theoretical and possibly didactic 'Art of Music' of about the same date may be linked with this reorganisation. It contains, among many identifiably Scottish musical examples, several possibly Scottish psalm-settings and what seems likely to be a setting by Blackhall of Psalm 18 in reports. It has all the characteristics of the composer's style.[23]

In the early 1580s, Blackhall seems to have been a member of the 'Castalian Band' of poets and musicians at King James's court, led by the poet Alexander Montgomerie, who had recently converted to Catholicism.[24] There he set to music Montgomerie's *The banks of Helicon*, which became the musical as well as the literary prototype for later poems-with-music in the same stanza form,[25] notably Montgomerie's *The Cherrie and the Slae*, which appeared partially in print in 1597.[26] And in the recently recovered second copy of Wood's *Altus* part-book[27] there is an inscription that provides evidence for the earliest known use of Blackhall's setting of the Helicon tune to be sung to Sir Richard Maitland's *Ane ballat of the creatioun of the warld*: Maitland's 'ballat' had been described in the Bannatyne Manuscript (1568) as 'maid to the tone of the ba*nk*is of helecon'.[28] Blackhall lived in Inveresk / Musselburgh at least until 1594, and most likely remained there until his death in 1609.

Several striking parallels emerge between the careers of the two men. Apart from their close contemporaneity, they both had links with the court. Their spheres of activity were also very close, even overlapping. The parish of Liberton, recently vacated by Blackhall, was taken over by Davidson in 1579. The printer of *The*

---

[22] *APS*, iii,174.

[23] 'The Art of Music': see *MB* XV for location and Elliott, 'Music of Scotland', 265-73, for description of contents and provenance; complete edition and commentary in J.D. Maynard, 'An Anonymous Scottish Treatise on Music from the Sixteenth Century', (Indiana University dissertation, 1961). Music by Blackhall published in *MB* XV and *Fourteen Psalm-Settings of the Reformed Church in Scotland*, ed. K. Elliott (1960).

[24] Shire, *Song, Dance and Poetry*, 80-99.

[25] ibid., 163ff; *MB* XV, 49.

[26] Shire, *Song, Dance and Poetry*, 117ff.

[27] K.Elliott, 'Another one of Thomas Wood's missing parts', *IR*, xxxix (1988), 151-5.

[28] *Bann. MS*, ii, 26.

Cherrie and the Slae, for which Blackhall made a musical setting, was Robert Waldegrave, who also published *Some helpes.* But perhaps the most vivid links are those with the Earl of Morton. And yet John Davidson seems—initially at least—to have been the stricter, more uncompromising reformer, while Andrew Blackhall saw fit not only to support Morton, but also set a tune associated with the Catholic poet Alexander Montgomerie's *The Cherrie and the Slae* in the early 1580s. Perhaps the most significant later coincidence is the proximity of their parishes: Saltpreston (later Prestonpans) is next door to Musselburgh and Inveresk. What more natural than that John Davidson should invite his distinguished neighbour to contribute some musical material to his new publication with a strongly local interest?

The text of Psalm 117 first appeared in the English Psalter of 1562, where it is attributed to the English versifier Thomas Norton and directed to be sung to the proper tune for Psalm 95.[29] Another tune was introduced for it in later English psalters. The version composed by the Scot John Craig replaced it in the first Scottish Psalter of 1564 and was used in all subsequent Scottish psalters.[30] And so the present text would seem to be a unique appearance of Norton's verses in a Scottish publication. According to Frost, the tune first appeared in its present melodic form in Scottish 1615, being a much altered and shortened version of the tune for Psalm 23, first published in English 1579 and then in all later English psalters.[31] In Scottish 1615 it is included in a group of Common Tunes and entitled 'London', as it was in all later seventeenth-century printed Scottish psalters. All of these have a flat key-signature. The present version would therefore antedate the first 'official' appearance of the tune by thirteen years, and contains characteristically Scottish rhythmic subtleties smoothed out in later psalters.[32]

As for the setting for four voices of Psalm 130, it has not so far proved possible to trace the text, tune or setting to any other source, English or Scottish, printed or manuscript. Closer inspection of the verses and the music reveals similarities to contemporary practice, and also certain possible pointers to authorship. For example, Davidson wrote and published both prose and

---

29 Frost, *Psalm & Hymn Tunes*, 13-14.
30 ibid., 178.
31 ibid., 86-7.
32 Elliott and Rimmer, *History*, 32.

poetical works.[33] In the latter field, his pieces range from *A Memorial of the Life of two Worthye Christians composed in retirement in Argyll* (c.1575), published eventually by Waldegrave in 1595, which rarely rises above the level of doggerel, to *Ane Schort Discurs of the Estaitis quha hes caus to deploir the Deith of this Excellent Servand of God* (1573), which shows a reflection, however pale, of Castalian[34] phrase and alliteration:

Thy lemand Lamp that schew sic licht,
Was gude Johne Knox, an man upricht,
Quhais deith thow daylie m[a]y deploir.
His presence maid thy bewtie bricht,
And all thy doings did decoir...

The present psalm-verses do not appear in contemporary published psalters; but they do seem to be a cut above the rest of the current routine metrical psalm-versifications and may possibly be attributed to Davidson himself. There are again a few familiar alliterations, such as 'For free forgivenesse', 'haill hope', 'stay in all my strait', 'wayteth on his will', that also recall the Castalian style. The tune seems also to be unique, as does the setting, neither appearing in any contemporary printed or manuscript collection of psalmody. Certainly a number of psalm-tunes of later sixteenth-century Scotland cannot be traced to other sources and are therefore possibly the work of Scottish composers. The same is true of many anonymous psalm-settings.[35] Authorship of a psalm-tune may be difficult to establish, but a psalm-setting is perhaps slightly more feasible. There are details in this one that are reminiscent of the musical characteristics of Blackhall's anthems of the 1560s and 1570s, including the skilled part-writing and modulation that mark it out immediately as the work of a professional musician, and at least two details of technique: the decorated cadence/resolution figure 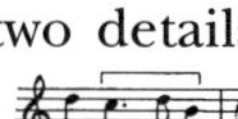 that seems to occur nowhere else in the work of later sixteenth-century Scottish composers, but appears often in Blackhall's anthems and is so reminiscent of contemporary English anthem style; quaver passing notes, that are conspicuous by their absence from the settings by, say, Peebles and Kemp; and a characteristic treatment of

[33] Rogers, *Three Scottish Reformers* contains Davidson's 'poetical remains' and *Some helpes*, though the latter omits the music and gives only verses 1-4 of 'Lord in great grief', and no music for 'O all ye Nations'.

[34] For discussion of 'Castalian' style see Shire, *Song, Dance and Poetry*, 80ff.

[35] Elliott and Rimmer, *History*, 30.

dissonance and of harmonic sequence involving first-inversion chords. All are small details, but together they mount up. These features occur in the surviving identified psalm-settings by Blackhall.[36]

Waldegrave's *Some helpes* provides interesting evidence about contemporary Scottish music printing. This English printer and publisher settled in Edinburgh in 1590 with royal patronage. He had produced many theological works in England, had spent a brief time in France in 1589, and among many subsequent publications in Scotland included King James's *Daemonologie* (1597) and *Basilikon Doron* (1603).[37] There are, unusually, two styles of music type-setting in *Some helpes*: the one for Psalm 117 is large and beautiful, reminiscent of, for example, Byrd's *Cantiones sacrae* of 1589 and other contemporary English and European prints, but unlike any previous or later Scottish music publications. Where did that beautiful type come from, and what became of it? The other, for the part-setting, is, on the other hand, similar to the small and rather crabbed type of the 1615 Scottish psalter and many other Scottish and English psalters of the period. There are also many errors of type-setting: missing and misplaced accidentals, missing rests, a missing note and clef, symbols on the wrong stave, wrong line, and so on. Waldegrave obviously had a lot to learn about printing part-music. But the role of publishing psalters with harmonised versions passed to other printers in Scotland, notably Andro Hart of Edinburgh and Edward Raban of Aberdeen.

The names in the manuscript inscription on the fly-leaf provide fascinating information about the subsequent history of this book. Sir Robert Sibbald (1641-1722), presbyterian, physician and antiquary, somewhat unsure as to how to describe himself (if it was he who wrote the inscription), was author of an important natural history of Scotland, founder of the Edinburgh Botanic Gardens, the first professor of medicine at Edinburgh University and President of the Edinburgh Royal College of Physicians. He briefly became a convert to Catholicism but later 'repented of [his] rashness and resolved to... return to the church [he] was born

---

[36] So far Blackhall has to his credit five (possibly six) psalm-settings/canticles, one (possibly two) psalm(s) in reports, three anthems and one part-song. Other psalm-settings may await identification in the anonymous MS sets and even in the 1635 Psalter, which names composers (including Blackhall) only in the Preface.

[37] *DNB,* lix, 20-22.

in'.[38] Mr [William] Jameson (fl.1689-1720) is loosely described as Lecturer or Professor in History at Glasgow University. A presbyterian, he was much occupied with the episcopal controversies of the time.[39] He describes in his Introduction to *Mr John Davidson's Catechism* (1708) how he sought out a copy of *Some helpes* ('so worn out of Print, that it is well nigh as rare as an old Manuscript') from Sir Robert Sibbald in 1706. The latter allowed Jameson the use of it, 'and from that this Impression is taken Word for Word...only some musical Notes for Psalms could not conveniently be here set down...'. In his Introduction, he examines the evidence for Davidson's alleged episcopal interests.

Jameson's reluctance to have had any music printed is somewhat puzzling. The technique was certainly available in Scotland, as the work of John Forbes, printer in Aberdeen and recent publisher of his renowned *Songs & Fancies* (1662-82) and the small set of *Common Tunes* (1666-1706) shows. Regarding the acquisition of *Some helpes* by GUL, the manuscript 'Records of Donations to the Library' between 1692 and 1712[40] mention Jameson's edition of it under 'Mr. William Iamison Professor of History in the Colledge of Glasgow ... Mr. John Davidsons Catechism &c. Edinb: 1708...'. It is now untraceable. Jameson must have donated the original copy of *Some helpes* at some point after that: it is now listed in the earliest printed catalogue, *Catalogus impressorum librorum in Bibliotheca Universitatis Glasguensis* (1791). It is clear that this volume might never have survived but for Jameson's curiosity, Sibbald's generosity, and in turn Jameson's gift.

What, then, can be deduced from this apparently 'simple' musical source, and its apparently complex content? First of all, that John Davidson probably wrote at least one rather fine psalm translation. Do others exist elsewhere? Versions by Alexander Montgomerie[41] and Sir William Mure of Rowallan[42] are the nearest equivalents. Further, Blackhall may well add another psalm-setting if not a new psalm-tune to his score. It may also be suggested that Blackhall probably edited—even partially composed—the twelve Scottish Common Tunes that were brought together for the first time in the Scottish Psalter of 1615, published, signif-

[38] *DNB*, lii, 179-81.
[39] *DNB*, xxix, 235-6.
[40] GUL, MS Gen.1110.
[41] *The Poems of Alexander Montgomerie*, ed. J. Cranstoun (STS, 1887), vol. i.
[42] *The Works of William Mure of Rowallan*, ed. W. Tough (STS, 1898), vol. ii.

icantly, in Edinburgh. Four of them had already appeared severally in earlier psalters between 1564 and 1592, eight were new, and all were given characteristic titles such as 'French' or 'Martyrs'.[43] They appeared, often with additions, in later Scottish and English seventeenth-century psalters, and were to remain at the very heart of Scottish psalmody of the reformed Church until the present day. Their author may well have been Andrew Blackhall. And finally, *Some helpes* of 1602 assumes a special significance not only in becoming the first Scottish source of a printed psalm-setting, but also the earliest example so far recorded of part-music ever printed in Scotland.

[43] Frost, *Psalm & Hymn Tunes*, 36, 255ff.

Figs. 3 (left) and 4 (right) *Some helpes for young Schollers in Christianity* (Edinburgh: Robert Waldegrave, 1602), Left: F5r; Right: F6r.

APPENDIX

Psalme Cxvij.
['London Tune']

[edited by ANDREW BLACKHALL?]

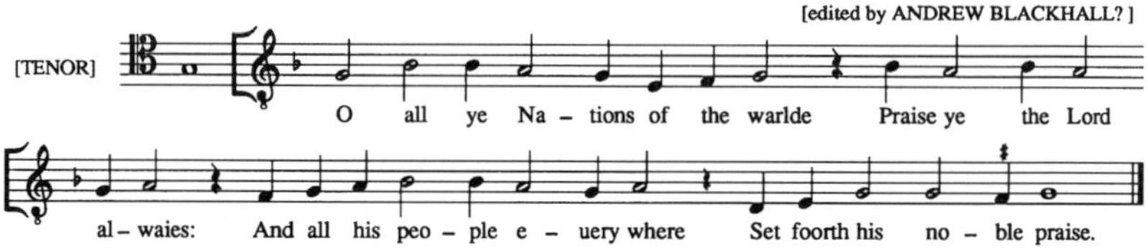

[Psalm 130]

[set by ANDREW BLACKHALL?]

Lord in great grief I call to thee,
and say, Lord heare my cry:
vnto the voice of my request,
thine eares with speede apply.

Our sins Lord, if thou mark straitly
Lord, then wha can indure:
For free forgiuenesse is with thee,
thy worship to procure.

Wherefore I wait vpon the Lorde,
my verry saule doth wait:
Yea my haill hope is in his word,
as stay in all my strait.

My saule does to the Lord aspire,
mair earnestly then they:
That watching all the night desire,
to see the breake of day.

Let Israel Gods people, thus,
wait still the Lord vpon:
For with the Lord much mercie is,
and great redemption.

Wha will redeeme true Israel,
that wayteth on his will:
Fro*m* al their sins both great &
smal,
and saue them from all ill.

'MELVILLIAN' REFORM IN THE SCOTTISH UNIVERSITIES

James Kirk

'I think', wrote Martin Luther in 1520, 'that pope and emperor could have no better task than the reformation of the universities, just as there is nothing more devilishly mischievous than an unreformed university'.[1] Luther's appeal epitomised the search for a new educational programme—a programme of humanist teaching for the citizen as well as cleric—designed to replace the traditional values of scholasticism. This attack on teaching practice coincided with the assault on religious practice. Accepted beliefs in philosophy and theology were rigorously re-examined: divine truth no longer seemed amenable to scholastic reasoning.

The sixteenth century, as a whole, witnessed this renewed expression of the twin ideals of educational progress and ecclesiastical reform. These two themes of renaissance and renewal helped shape the humanist tradition, and they were seen to represent much that was fundamental to the Christian life. These ideals, of course, were shared by Catholics and Protestants alike, though deep and irreconcilable divisions emerged over the different ways through which these ideals should ultimately be attained. In Scotland, good Catholics like Archibald Hay and Archbishop Hamilton in St Andrews, Archbishop James Beaton in Glasgow, Bishop Reid of Orkney and Ninian Winyet, Linlithgow schoolmaster, all advocated a reform of morals and practice, and a revival of learning as part of their reappraisal of Christian values within the existing house of God; and sound Protestants like John Knox, John Douglas in St Andrews, John Row in Perth and George Buchanan, a humanist of European reputation, demanded a far more radical solution in the expectation that this alone would provide the necessary firm foundation for the task of reconstructing God's house on earth.[2]

---

[1] *Luther's Primary Works*, ed. H. Wace and C.A. Buchheim (London, 1896), 230.

[2] J. Durkan, 'The beginnings of humanism in Scotland', *IR*, iv (1953), 5-24; J. Durkan, 'The cultural background in sixteenth-century Scotland', *IR*, x (1959), 382-439; J. Durkan, 'Education in the century of the Reformation', *IR*, x (1959), 67-90; J. Durkan, 'Early humanism and King's College', *AUR*, xlviii (1980), 259-79;

With the Reformation, a re-formed church, professedly purged of the accretions of centuries, replaced the old ecclesiastical structure, and the reformers claimed that they had restored at last 'the grave and godly face of the primitive church'.[3] The appeal was for a return to first principles, a return, that is, to the teaching, organisation and example of the Early Church itself. By applying the new philological tools of biblical criticism, sound learning and educational enlightenment were seen to bring fresh insights and a new understanding of the church of the New Testament which, in turn, was viewed by many including Calvin as the model for the church in all ages. The humanism of the Scottish Reformation was substantially a Calvinist humanism: the reformers in their *First Book of Discipline* of 1560 planned to reorganise the whole field of education; and before the century ended two new university colleges had come into being at Edinburgh and New Aberdeen, and two more were projected for Orkney and Fraserburgh.[4]

It is a fact of almost universal currency that John Knox, apart from helping to set up the Kirk, wanted to establish a school in every parish; and indeed much of that vision became a reality in the course of the seventeenth century. But as Knox's successor, Andrew Melville has fared less well in popular imagination. He still remains an essentially enigmatic character. When he is remembered at all, it is usually in the form of some such epithet as 'the father of Scottish presbyterianism' or possibly even as 'episcoporum exactor', the thrower-out of bishops; or as the man who addressed King James VI as 'God's sillie vassal'.[5] To some, Melville was none other than a troublemaker, a distasteful little man, argumentative and overbearing, who returned home from Geneva intent on upsetting good order in the Kirk by attacking the newly created Protestant bishops and so initiating a period of controversy in the church. This was Archbishop Spottiswoode's assessment, and Spottiswoode, who once considered Melville as 'more

J.K. Cameron, 'The Renaissance tradition in the reformed Church of Scotland', *Renaissance and Renewal in Christian History*, ed. D. Baker (Oxford, 1977), 251-69; J. Kirk, 'The religion of early Scottish Protestants', in *Humanism and Reform*, ed. J. Kirk (Oxford, 1991), 361-411.

[3] Knox, *Works*, i, 306; ii, 264.

[4] Cameron, 'Renaissance tradition', 253; *FBD*, 129-55; D.B. Horn, *A Short History of the University of Edinburgh* (Edinburgh, 1967); G.D. Henderson, *The Founding of Marischal College, Aberdeen* (Aberdeen, 1947); *APS*, iii, 214 (Orkney); *Frasers of Philorth*, i, 154; ii, 263-9; *RMS*, v, 2117; vi, 1167; *BUK*, iii, 958 (Fraserburgh).

[5] Melville, *Diary*, 52, 370.

like a madman than a divine', had been a student at Glasgow under Melville's principalship before Melville left for St Andrews.[6] Indeed, Melville's ecclesiastical policies have sometimes been subjected to such criticism that an examination of his educational reforms has gone almost by default. All this serves only to obscure an assessment of his wider contribution.

The twin themes of educational and ecclesiastical renewal, so conspicuous in Knox, were certainly central to, and no less dominant in, Melville's outlook. Although he is largely remembered for his contribution to presbyterianism, there is good reason for believing that in his own day his educational reforms were far more innovating than any changes he may have urged in the Church. Nor is there really any paradox here. The Reformation Kirk claimed to be in the tradition of the 'best reformed churches' on the continent: it had experienced a thorough reformation in both theology and polity. Melville himself had been absent from Scotland for much of the 1560s, but after his homecoming in 1574 he sought not to oppose Reformation principles but rather, by applying them, to correct some defects in the Church's operation. His influence in the Church, though by no means negligible, can be exaggerated. Nor was his influence necessarily disruptive in itself. What he tried to ensure was that the Church, when confronted with the powers of the world, did not lose sight of its earlier idealism; and he offered attractive solutions to outstanding problems.[7]

In education, however, Melville's innovations ought to be accorded a rather greater significance, for, unlike the Church, the reformation of the Scottish universities, intended in 1560, had come to very little in the years immediately after 1560. In some cases, they seemed but half-reformed, and in other instances they appeared altogether unreformed in both an educational and ecclesiastical sense. Knox, who showed such solicitude for the schools, was understandably suspicious of the universities as the intended nurseries of the ministry. His warning in 1572 not to submit the Church to the judgment of the universities was timely advice in view of their tardy reformation.[8] Even in 1578, parlia-

---

[6] Spottiswoode, *History*, ii, 200; iii, 183; J. Kirk, *Archbishop Spottiswoode and the See of Glasgow* (Glasgow, 1988).

[7] J. Kirk, *Patterns of Reform* (Edinburgh, 1989), 352ff.

[8] Knox, *Works*, vi, 619; J. Kirk, 'John Knox and Andrew Melville: a question of identity', *Scotia*, vi (1982), 14-25.

ment still saw a need 'to reform sic thingis as soundis to superstitioun, ydolatrie and papistrie' in the universities.[9] In any event, it was Andrew Melville the academic, and not John Knox the parish minister, who took the universities in hand by introducing far-reaching changes in both curriculum and structure, and by integrating the universities more successfully in the wider work of the reformed Church.

Melville's own background was at once humanist and reformist. Born in 1545, the youngest son of an Angus laird whose family showed reforming sympathies, Melville was schooled in Latin and (somewhat exceptionally) in Greek grammar at Montrose by a French schoolmaster, and equipped for more advanced studies in Arts, on the eve of the Reformation, at St Mary's College, St Andrews, where he won distinction, so it was said, as 'the best philosopher, poet and Grecian of anie young maister in the land'.[10] His humanism was already in the making. Thereafter, Paris provided further instruction in the humanities, especially in the oriental languages, at the Royal Trilingual College; then on to Poitiers to pursue law and undertake some teaching there, before ending up professing Latin in the Geneva of Theodore Beza, whose divinity lectures he attended. In Geneva, he came into contact with Walter Travers and Thomas Cartwright, the future English presbyterian leaders. Yet unlike the two Englishmen, he showed no enthusiasm to return home. After all, his kinsman Henry Scrimgeour was professor of law at Geneva, and it was only when the Regent Mar failed to persuade the elderly Scrimgeour to take up a teaching post at home that Melville was urged to return so that his native land might benefit from the services of a distinguished scholar. His purpose on returning, therefore, was not to remodel the Church but to revitalise university teaching which had fallen on hard times, and was sorely in need of fresh life. Melville helped to provide a new direction and fresh approach.[11]

Invitations from Glasgow and St Andrews led him to choose the former university in order that, as his nephew expressed it, he

---

9 *APS*, iii, 98.

10 Melville, *Diary*, 38-9; J. Durkan & J. Kirk, *The University of Glasgow, 1451-1577* (Glasgow, 1977), 262ff.

11 Melville, *Diary*, 39-45; Durkan & Kirk, *University of Glasgow*, 266-72; see also J. Durkan, 'Henry Scrimgeour, Renaissance bookman', *TEBS*, v (1978), 1-31.

might 'sie the beginning of a collage ther'.[12] Certainly, on arriving, he found neither an outgoing principal nor teaching staff other than the lonely figure of Peter Blackburn who taught according to the St Andrews pattern. Before the Reformation, with the notable exception of John Major, Glasgow had few teachers of distinction, and after 1560 the university had contracted almost to the point of withering away, though teaching never quite ceased. Neither a royal donation in 1563 nor the town's intended new foundation for the university in 1573 succeeded in reversing this downward trend. Only drastic reconstitution under Melville and a realistic benefaction by King James VI in a charter of new erection in 1577 saved Glasgow from extinction. So spectacular, indeed, was the revival under Melville's principalship that St Andrews and Aberdeen soon decided to adopt features of Melville's successful experiment at Glasgow where teaching methods and subject matter alike were revolutionised.[13]

These were the fruits of Melville's earlier continental training. Paris, with its international reputation in education, Poitiers, famed for its law school, and Geneva, the home of international Calvinism—each had provided Melville with a distinctive intellectual stimulus, and together they did much to shape the direction and content of his thought. As a humanist centre in Paris (initially possessing no buildings of its own), the Royal Trilingual College, founded by Francis I in 1530, provided specialist teaching by royal lecturers in Greek, Hebrew, mathematics and eventually Latin (a model imitated by Mary of Guise when she sponsored royal lectureships in Edinburgh in the 1550s). At the Trilingual College, Melville absorbed the anti-scholastic philosophy of Peter Ramus, the educational reformer and convert to Protestantism, whose teaching (at Ave Maria and then as principal of the College des Prèsles and as royal lecturer) had upset the pedagogic world with its revolutionary approach to logic and by its application to education as a whole. He also attended the philosophy lectures of Turnebe, an anti-Ramist, the mathematics classes of Charpentier, Ramus's bitter critic, and those of Duhamel and Forcadel, as well as hearing Mercier, Cinquarbres and Salignacus on Hebrew, Baudouin on law and Duret on medicine. Yet it was Ramus, above all, and not his opponents, who fired Melville with enthusiasm.

---

[12] Melville, *Diary*, 47; Durkan & Kirk, *University of Glasgow*, 272.
[13] Durkan & Kirk, *University of Glasgow*, 272-340.

Poitiers, his next choice, also had Ramist (and Scottish) connections, strengthened through the influence of the Guise family, particularly Charles of Lorraine, once conservator of ecclesiastical privileges at Poitiers, and Ramus's great protector and patron, until the latter's profession of Protestantism by 1561. Even at Geneva, Melville had opportunity to hear Ramus lecture on Cicero's *Orations*, but when Beza, a convinced Aristotelian, prevented Ramus from teaching at Geneva, Melville significantly followed Ramus to Lausanne during the summer of 1570. On his returning to Scotland it was wholly predictable that Melville should apply his own version of Ramist teaching, as his nephew explained, 'in sum Universitie and profess thair as the King's Lectors in Parise'. Glasgow, therefore, provided the opportunity for Melville to introduce his far-sighted experiments in teaching methods.[14]

The transformation began with a studious revision of the curriculum and the appointment of a new teaching staff. This enabled specialist teaching to be introduced, as the *First Book of Discipline* had once recommended,[15] and so replace regenting, the outmoded system whereby a regent teacher took his class through the whole Arts curriculum. Glasgow became the first Scottish university to abolish regenting. Alongside these changes came the adoption of new Ramist texts in logic, rhetoric, geometry and arithmetic. Instruction in Greek, Hebrew and the unfamiliar Syriac and Chaldaic languages (deemed necessary for scholarly biblical exegesis) was quickly established by Melville, and so too were classes in history, geography (cosmography) and astronomy; metaphysics, by contrast, was discarded as unprofitable.[16]

The introduction of compulsory Greek for first-year students in Arts was startlingly novel. Not even the *First Book of Discipline*, which had prescribed Greek for divinity students, had contemplated that. Yet it was in accord with the humanist programme of educational reform on the continent. Only with the Renaissance had the classical Greek authors become readily available in western Europe in the original Greek texts. And in Scotland, Melville introduced to the Arts course at Glasgow the Greek literature of Homer, Hesiod, Isocrates, Pindar and numerous other writers who during the Middle Ages had been largely lost to the west in

---

14 ibid., 267, 269, 276-80; see also J. Durkan, 'The royal lectureships under Mary of Lorraine', *SHR*, lxii (1983), 73-8.

15 *FBD*, 138ff.

16 Durkan & Kirk, *University of Glasgow*, 275ff.

either Latin or Greek. The importance of these literary preoccupations was clearly stressed by Melville as principal. The whole emphasis was on the *studia humanitatis*, the liberal arts: classical grammar, rhetoric, poetry, history and moral philosophy. Pure philosophy was considered too abstract and speculative, too theoretical and technical, and of little practical relevance to life. Scholastic philosophy was rejected for its failure to communicate persuasively. The quest was for useful knowledge, to recover the wisdom of the ancient world and by its application in education to equip man to lead a virtuous life on earth. Rhetoric and the pursuit of eloquence were now promoted by Melville at the expense of logic, which humanists like Valla, Agricola, Ramus and Nizolius had attempted to reform and reorganise. Medicine and law ceased to be taught at Glasgow, but theology, in an age of Reformation and Counter-Reformation, remained of central importance. On the whole, a narrowly professional training was apparently abandoned in favour of a broader, more general, humanist approach.[17]

The revised curriculum epitomised the new humanist and Ramist values designed to replace the old scholasticism. Aristotle's philosophy, significantly, was now to be studied from the original Greek (not Latin) texts. Physics was to be taught from Plato as well as Aristotle. The humanist belief in returning to the original sources, freed from the shackles of scholastic commentaries, is yet again apparent. The particular appeal of Ramism, which Melville brought to Glasgow, lay partly in its call for clarity, its claim to provide a simplified method for communicating ideas, its protest against scholastic philosophy by jettisoning the cluttered commentaries of the schoolmen, and not least in its aim of reforming the whole field of education, so giving it a much more practical relevance to everyday life. The new Ramist logic based on a method of arranging and classifying ideas in almost symmetrical fashion into dichotomies seemed to offer a short-cut designed to help the preacher, lawyer, physician and mathematician solve their difficulties in communicating, instructing and persuading. This was of particular importance in an age of questioning and controversy, where teachers and learners alike were expected to master the intricacies of ornate Renaisance Latin as the accepted mode of

[17] P.O. Kristeller, *Renaissance Concepts of Man* (New York, 1972), 121; Durkan & Kirk, *University of Glasgow*, 312ff.

expressing ideas often difficult enough to grasp in the vernacular.[18]

The Scot Roland MacIlmaine—the first in England to publish Ramus's *Dialecticae* and the first to offer an English translation (1574)—eagerly explained:

> how easye it is above all others to be apprehended, how thou shalt applye it to all artes and sciences and shortlie, that no arte or science may eyther be taught or learned perfectlie without the knowledge of the same.[19]

Ramist method seemed to serve a very practical purpose; hence its popularity.

In Scotland, Melville was the first academic to introduce Ramist literature as part of the official curriculum; and writers who have attributed earlier Ramist influences to Arts teaching at St Andrews[20] on the slender ground that MacIlmaine was a St Andrews graduate were unaware that MacIlmaine proceeded to Paris, where he appears on the rector's lists in June 1571,[21] at a point, that is, when Ramus had returned to Paris and was reinstated as principal of the College des Prèsles and as royal lecturer, before his death in the St Bartholomew massacres of August 1572.

In St Andrews, at that stage, there is no record of Ramist teaching. The existence in the library of a heavily annotated copy of the *Georgics*,[22] owned by a student, conceivably a Scot, who attended Ramus's lectures in 1555, presumably in Paris, certainly testifies to Ramus's popularity but it does not sustain a belief in early Ramist teaching in St Andrews, for the book itself, bound in the mid-nineteenth century with a copy of Horace, *De arte poetica ad Pisones* (Paris, 1550), entered the library belatedly at a date between 1867 and 1892. At the Reformation, the foremost philosopher in St Andrews was the decidedly Aristotelian John Rutherford, who, after teaching at Bordeaux, Coimbra and Paris, had

---

[18] Durkan & Kirk, *University of Glasgow*, 276-8, 313, 369.

[19] *The Logike of the Moste Excellent Philosopher P. Ramus Martyr, translated by Roland MacIlmaine* (1574), ed. C.M. Dunn (Northridge, Cal., 1969), 3.

[20] W.S. Howell, *Logic and Rhetoric in England* (Princeton, 1956), 183, 188;

[21] W.A. McNeill, 'Scottish entries in the *Acta rectoria Universitatis Parisiensis* 1519 to c.1633', *SHR*, xliii (1964), 78.

[22] Paris, apud Thomam Richardum, 1554 (colophon dated 1550), bound with Horace, *De arte poetica ad Pisones*, Paris, ex typographia Matthaei Dauidis, 1550. I am grateful to Mr R.N. Smart, Keeper of Muniments, University of St Andrews, for drawing my attention to this item in 1977, and to Mrs Christine Gascoigne, Keeper of Special Collections.

returned to teach humanity at St Mary's, at Archbishop Hamilton's invitation, before becoming principal of St Salvator's College after the Reformation. As Rutherford was also professor of philosophy in the public schools, Melville as a student would have had an opportunity to hear his lectures, which seem to have followed the teaching of Nicholas de Grouchi, Rutherford's own teacher, whom Rutherford is said to have accompanied to Portugal, along with George Buchanan. Rutherford's own treatise in logic *De Arte disserendi*, published in Paris in 1557, and in Edinburgh in 1577, firmly adhered to Aristotelian principles, and was critical both of the sophistry of current commentators and the frivolous questions of recent dialecticians, possibly an allusion to the New Academicians and to the circle of Peter Ramus.[23] Melville's own regent at St Andrews is said to have been Alexander Ramsay, apparently a mistake for William Ramsay, who became Rutherford's colleague at St Salvator's, and who may have taught at St Mary's (as Rutherford had done) during the dislocation of the Reformation when Melville attended St Mary's in 1560. Nor is there evidence of any Ramist influence in Ramsay's career; rather the reverse. His background was Melanchthonian. In 1544, he had matriculated at Wittenberg, apparently as tutor to James Balfour, later of Pittendreich. Thereafter, he joined Rutherford on the continent and taught in Portugal and at Bordeaux, before returning to St Andrews, where his knowledge of Greek, as his books reveal, was likely to interest Melville.[24]

More significantly, perhaps, John Douglas, the provost of St Mary's, who encouraged Melville in his studies, had once taught in the College des Prèsles where he appears on record in 1530, though shortly afterwards he moved to Montaigu. Yet as Douglas remained a philosophy teacher at Paris till returning to St Mary's in 1547, he must have been aware of Ramus, who left Ave Maria, though still banned from teaching philosophy, to become principal of the College des Prèsles in 1545. But again no Ramist connection with St Andrews can be established. Indeed, the existence of prescribed Ramist texts at St Andrews, on present evidence, dates only from the 1580s after Melville's decisive intervention there.[25]

---

[23] J. Durkan, 'John Rutherford and Montaigne: an early influence', *Bibliothèque d'humanisme et renaissance*, xli (1979), 115-22.

[24] Durkan & Ross, *Libraries*, 137; Dempster, *Historia*, ii, 561.

[25] *Evidence, oral and documentary, taken by the Commissioners appointed by King George IV, for visiting the Universities of Scotland*, 4 vols. (London, 1837), iii, 194.

Plainly the Scottish centre from which these new influences first spread was Glasgow. There the introduction of Ramist principles had met with little resistance as Melville had carefully chosen and trained his team of teachers. Yet, significantly enough, criticism was voiced by the one existing member of staff, Peter Blackburn, a St Andrews man and an Aristotelian of the Paduan school, whom Melville sought to win over, though something of a compromise may have been devised with Blackburn's appointment as professor of physics, an area where Aristotelian texts remained fundamental. In logic and rhetoric, however, Ramist works were introduced, and metaphysics ceased to be taught. The humanities took precedence over the philosophies: the emphasis was on Greek grammar (Latin was presupposed), rhetoric, to which logic was now allied, moral philosophy, history and geography, mathematics and astronomy, two subjects largely independent of the Aristotelian tradition, on physics or natural philosophy, still rooted in Aristotle, and finally theology, where Melville predictably resisted Aristotelian philosophical influences. All this was essentially Melville's personal achievement, and it contrasted sharply with the town's intended foundation of 1573 which had earlier prescribed an Arts course devoted to the philosophies: logic, moral and natural philosophy and metaphysics.[26]

More determined opposition to Melville's innovations was forthcoming in St Andrews with its multi-collegiate structure, where Melville as head of a theological college, St Mary's, lacked the commanding position he once held at Glasgow. Yet his advice, with that of others, for remodelling St Andrews university on lines akin to Glasgow's pattern of specialist teaching was incorporated in the new foundation of 1579. The revised syllabus for Arts teaching in St Leonard's and St Salvator's more closely resembled the Glasgow model than, say, the proposals resulting from Regent Morton's visitation of St Andrews in 1574 or even those of the *Book of Discipline* in 1560 (which proposed, for St Andrews, teaching logic, mathematics, physics and medicine in one college, moral philosophy and civil law in another, and divinity and the tongues in a third). In 1579, the new St Andrews curriculum aimed at equipping students with 'perfite knawledge of humanite and trew philosophie'. Compulsory Greek for first-year students was

[26] Durkan & Kirk, *University of Glasgow*, 253-4, 279-81; J. Durkan, 'The early history of Glasgow University Library: 1475-1710', *The Bibliotheck*, viii (1977), 102-26, at 108.

followed by rhetoric to be taught by the 'schortest, easiest and maist accurate' method; only 'the maist proffitable and needful pairtis of the logiks of Aristotle', with his *Ethics* and *Politics*, were to be studied, again from the Greek text, together with Cicero's *Offices*; and finally physics was to be taught from the original Greek. Metaphysics, of course, was excluded, but curiously there was no word of history, geography or even mathematics, though a mathematician undoubtedly existed.[27]

Once installed in St Mary's, Melville launched a scathing attack on Aristotle in his public lectures in theology and in disputations, which provoked the scholastic philosophers of St Leonard's to respond until after several years of 'mikle feghting and fascherie', Melville convinced them of the need to study Aristotle more critically from the Greek text, freed from the clutter of scholastic commentaries. This was, of course, the method already prescribed in the charter of new foundation for St Andrews, which had also directed the principal of St Leonard's to lecture four times a week on the philosophy of Plato. Here was a move designed perhaps to counteract any excessive Aristotelianism or, at least, to achieve a synthesis between the two philosophers. Yet little, it seems, was achieved here, for almost at once the principal was released from professing Plato.[28]

Rhetoric continued to be defined in traditional, non-Ramist, terms as 'invention, disposition and elocution' (whereas Ramists assigned the first two topics to logic alone). Even so, by 1588, a visitation disclosed that Ramist texts in rhetoric and arithmetic had come into use at St Salvator's (if not at St Leonard's), though St Mary's alone had successfully introduced specialist teaching. At the same time, the dominance of the Aristotelian tradition showed signs of weakening; and as late as 1616, long after Melville's downfall, the philosophy lecturers in St Andrews had to be reminded 'to insist more in Aristotele his text and the questiounis rysing properlie thairupon, than in uther questiounis quhilk oftymes ar bothe impertinent and unprofitable'. All this might suggest that during

---

[27] *Evidence*, iii, 183ff; SRO, PA10/1, Papers relating to the Visitation of St Andrews University (unfoliated); *FBD*, 137ff; Durkan & Kirk, *University of Glasgow*, 288, 290-91; R.G. Cant, 'The New Foundation of 1579 in historical perspective' (St John's House Papers, ii, 1979); J.K. Cameron, 'The refoundation of the University in 1579', *The Alumnus Chronicle of the University of St Andrews*, lxxi (1980), 3-10; J.K. Cameron, 'Andrew Melville in St Andrews', *St Mary's College Bulletin*, xxii (1980), 14-25.

[28] Melville, *Diary*, 83ff, 122-4; *Evidence*, iii, 184, 191.

the Melvillian interlude, teachers had become somewhat neglectful of Aristotle's primacy.[29]

Aberdeen also showed interest in Melville's educational reforms. There Melville found a ready ally in his presbyterian colleague, Alexander Arbuthnot, the principal of King's College, who agreed with Melville in 1575 on a common line of action. Accordingly, the new foundations at Glasgow and St Andrews were followed by a projected new foundation for King's in 1583 which conformed to the Glasgow plan. But Arbuthnot's death in 1583 postponed a reorganisation for more than a decade. And when change came in 1597, King's already had a rival in Marischal College, founded in 1593, which also adopted Melville's scheme for Glasgow. Here the fifth Earl Marischal was following the example set by his grandfather, the fourth earl, who had witnessed the Glasgow charter of new foundation in 1577.[30]

The lingering conservatism of King's, which frustrated wholesale reform till 1597, is attributable to several factors: to the death in 1583 of Principal Arbuthnot, the main promoter of change; to the onset in 1583 of the conservative, and anti-presbyterian, government headed by the earl of Arran which, ruling in name of James VI, postponed sanctioning in 1584 the intended new foundation; and to a preference among conservatives for adhering to Bishop Elphinstone's original foundation of 1497, thereby retaining the offices of canonist, civilist and mediciner, which the new foundation intended to abolish. Another factor inhibiting change was the dominance in north-eastern Scotland of the earls of Huntly and Erroll. At the Reformation they had frustrated Protestant efforts at reforming the university until the Protestant Regent Moray managed to overpower Huntly's interest by 1569, so enabling Catholic incumbents to be deposed and Protestant staff under Arbuthnot's principalship to be installed.[31]

What happened at King's on Arbuthnot's death, in the absence of record evidence, may only be surmised, but the possibility cannot be excluded that the influence of the northern earls again prevailed. In June 1587, Arbuthnot's successor as principal, Walter

---

[29] *Evidence*, iii, 184, 193-4, 200.

[30] Melville, *Diary*, 53, 139; Durkan & Kirk, *University of Glasgow*, 288-9; D. Stevenson, *King's College, Aberdeen, 1560-1641* (Aberdeen, 1990), 29ff.

[31] G. Donaldson, 'Aberdeen University and the Reformation', *Northern Scotland*, i (1974), 129-42; J. Durkan, 'George Hay's Oration at the purging of King's College, Aberdeen, in 1569: commentary', *Northern Scotland*, vi (1984-85), 97-112.

Stewart, appeared on record with 'certain prebendaries, canons and masters of the said college', granting the earl of Erroll a feu of the kirklands of Slains, property annexed to King's College as endowment by James IV; and the continued existence of Nicholas Hay as civilist may also indicate Erroll's influence; but while the disposition of college property and exercise of patronage might readily fall into noble hands, it is less than clear that the prevailing political climate wholly stifled curricular reform and innovation at King's. At the same time, it may be regarded as scarcely fortuitous that parliament's approval of the new foundation for King's in 1597 should immediately follow the downfall of Huntly and Erroll in 1595. Nor, for that matter, is it surprising that the strongly Protestant Earl Marischal, who supported the reforms of 1583 and who saw Huntly and Erroll as his rivals, should seek to enhance his own prestige by founding his own college in 1593, not indeed in Old Aberdeen in Gordon territory but in the adjacent burgh of New Aberdeen, which was fast developing at the expense of the old burgh where the cathedral and King's College lay.[32]

In practice, whatever their autonomous status, the two colleges in Aberdeen shared the same university chancellor: David Cunningham, once dean of the Faculty of Arts at Glasgow during Melville's principalship, became university chancellor *ex officio* in 1577 as bishop of Aberdeen. Again, Peter Blackburn, who left the Glasgow College in 1582 to become minister (and later bishop) of Aberdeen, was active in planning the proposed Aberdeen foundation of 1583, and he subsequently served as dean of the Faculty of Arts (though apparently at different times) for King's and Marischal Colleges. The Glasgow influence was indubitably strong; in dedicating his *De Aeterna Dei Praedestinatione Aphorismi Theologici* to Andrew Melville in 1591, the Aberdeen graduate, Robert Howie, recalled how Blackburn had brought to Aberdeen the spirit of Melville's teaching at Glasgow.[33]

Whether Ramism at that point had gained a decisive foothold at Aberdeen is hard to establish in the absence of university records; but there are indications that it had. The 'old laws' of King's College, 'promulgated of new in 1641', prescribed Ramus in logic and

[32] *RMS*, v, 1449.

[33] G.D. Henderson, *The Founding of Marischal College, Aberdeen* (Aberdeen, 1947), 16, 18, 29-30, 56-61.

Talon in rhetoric; and two graduates from King's in 1584—John Johnston and Robert Howie—are known to have pursued Ramist studies abroad.[34] Besides, Peter Blackburn, whose conversion from Aristotelianism is credited to Melville, significantly left his copies of Aristotle at Glasgow, and at Aberdeen he acquired a Ramist edition of Cicero's *De Oratore* by Omer Talon, and also a copy of Nizolius, another anti-Aristotelian writer.[35] All this suggests that the humanist assault on Aristotle had firmly entered Aberdeen. It was also a sign of the reforming tendencies at work that Walter Stewart, who as principal was required to teach theology, should acquire Ramus's *Commentaries on the Christian Religion* and that his copy should be inherited by his successor, David Rait.[36]

Melvillian influences undeniably were present, too, in the Edinburgh College, founded in 1582.[37] Its first principal, Robert Rollock, had studied Hebrew under James Melville (Andrew's nephew) at St Andrews and had taught philosophy at St Salvator's College. Rollock also acquired a knowledge of biblical philology which Andrew Melville had promoted in St Andrews. 'Learne the wordis', Rollock once remarked, 'for all the doctrine rysis of the wordis'. His Ramist tendencies are apparent both in his logical analyses of scripture and in his criticism of Aristotelian scholasticism. In the earliest surviving statutes of 1628, which preserved elements of earlier teaching, the works of Ramus and his disciple, Omer Talon, appear as prescribed texts for logic and rhetoric. Moreover, Rollock's assistant, Duncan Nairn, who taught classics, was a graduate of 1580 under Andrew Melville's regime at Glasgow, and was accounted 'a man of great learning'. Not surprisingly, perhaps, much of the curriculum followed Melville's pattern, notably its emphasis on Greek and its exclusion of metaphysics, though the study of human anatomy at Edinburgh was plainly new, and with so small a staff the introduction of specialist

---

34 *Aberdeen Fasti*, 231; *Letters of John Johnston and Robert Howie*, ed. J.K. Cameron (Edinburgh, 1963), pp. xvi, xxv, xxix, xlvi, 35ff.

35 *Glasgow Univ. Munimenta*, iii, 409-10; AUL, *De Oratore* (Paris, 1553), signature dated 1581, shelf-mark: Ð87515/O Tal; Nizolius, *sive Thesaurus Ciceronianus* (Lyons, 1581), inscription dated 1585, shelf-mark: Ðf873103/ Niz. I am grateful to the Keeper of Special Collections for this information.

36 Stevenson, *King's College*, 43-5.

37 For the best account, D.B. Horn, 'The origins of the University of Edinburgh', *EUJ*, xxii (1966), 213-25, 297-312.

teaching could not then be contemplated.[38]

The selection in 1583 of Rollock as first master of the newly-founded College of Arts in Edinburgh had clearly an immediate and sustained impact in shaping the pattern and content of instruction offered by the college within the general framework approved by the town council. Rollock's nomination for the post had been strenuously canvassed by James Lawson, Knox's chosen successor as minister in Edinburgh and the presbyterian ally of Andrew Melville in the Church.[39] Lawson himself was well placed to offer considered advice, for his earlier career had been centred on the universities. As a student, he had entered St Andrews University with Andrew Melville in 1559, and on graduating had proceeded, as tutor to the sons of the Countess of Crawford, to the University of Paris.[40] Thereafter, he had spent some months with his pupils at Cambridge before returning home to become regent in February 1569 in St Mary's College, St Andrews, only to be promoted sub-principal of King's College, Aberdeen in July 1569.[41] In securing the services of Rollock for Edinburgh, Lawson plainly took the initiative by sending Rollock 'a most courteous letter, entreating him to undertake the duty'; and when Rollock accepted, Lawson approached the town council 'where his influence was very great, and informed them that there was no person better qualified for the charge of the university than Rollock'. Evidently impressed, the council sent two commissioners to meet Rollock in St Andrews where he was teaching as regent in St Salvator's College, 'entreating him not to fail the Council in so sacred a cause' and persuading him to come to Edinburgh for an interview with the council where 'matters were arranged between them without the least difficulty'.[42]

A contract drawn up in September 1583 required Rollock to take up his appointment on 14 October, according to the town

---

[38] Melville, *Diary*, 86; Rollock, *Works*, i, pp. lxxxix-xcv, 318, 388; *University of Edinburgh Charters, Statutes and Acts of the Town Council and the Senatus 1583-1858*, ed. A. Morgan (Edinburgh, 1937), 60-63; Durkan & Kirk, *University of Glasgow*, 291-2, 359.

[39] Rollock, *Works*, p. lxii; Melville, *Diary*, 33, 52, 55, 144.

[40] *St Andrews Univ. Recs.*, 267; Lord Lindsay, *Lives of the Lindsays*, 3 vols. (London, 1849), i, 329-33; NLS, Crawford Muniments, MSS 3/2/4-5, 3/2/12; a booklist (n.d.), 14/2/6, contains several works by Ramus and Talon. The MS material, now in NLS, was examined in the John Rylands University Library, Manchester.

[41] *RSS*, vi, 518, 663.

[42] Rollock, *Works*, i, p. lxiii.

council's 'ruills and injunctiouns quhilk sall be given unto him'. If, after a year, he was dissatisfied with his stipend, Rollock could appeal to James Lawson, John Preston, one of Edinburgh's commissaries (whose wife was the widow of Clement Little whose library later became the nucleus of the university library),[43] and John Sharp, the advocate, whose advice the council would accept. Despite the changing political complexion of the ruling élite within the burgh and the country, as the government of the radical Ruthven lords who were sympathetic to the presbyterians gave way in the summer of 1583 to the earl of Arran's conservative 'anti-presbyterian dictatorship', Rollock indisputably remained the approved candidate for what was, in effect, principal of the college.[44]

Lawson's man got the job (despite Lawson's departure with the presbyterian leaders to England where he died in London in October 1584). Nor did the change of town council on 1 October 1583, from one directly influenced by the Ruthven lords in the elections of October 1582, to one of a more conservative character under Arran's domination, have any immediate effect on Rollock's position as master of the college; Alexander Clerk continued as provost (an office he had held since 1578) and William Little, Clement's brother and an indefatigable campaigner for establishing a college, was among the new bailies elected. Indeed, on 16 October 1583, Little along with another bailie was required to convene those appointed by the council 'to set downe and devyse the ordour of teaching with the discypline to be keipit in the College now erectit'.[45] The town council might seek to stipulate the subjects for instruction but it was scarcely equipped to dictate to Rollock how the prescribed subjects should be taught; and it would be rash to assume, as one writer has done,[46] that Rollock's teaching automatically conformed to a conservative and traditional mould, in accord with the changing political climate, and at

[43] J. Kirk, 'Clement Little's Edinburgh', *Edinburgh University Library, 1580-1980: a Collection of Historical Essays,* eds. J.R. Guild and A. Law (Edinburgh, 1982), 1-42.

[44] Rollock, *Works,* i, p. lxiv; see also Edinburgh City & District Archives, MS Edinburgh Town Council Minutes, vol. vii, 15 Nov. 1583, 7 Feb. 1584.

[45] Calderwood, *History,* iv, 65, 201-08; *Edin. Recs.,* iv, 249-56, 292-3, 300; Kirk, 'Clement Little's Edinburgh', 22-6.

[46] M. Lynch, 'The origins of Edinburgh's "Toun College": a revision article', *IR,* xxxiii (1982), 3-14.

variance with the innovations detectable, with varying emphases, at Glasgow, St Andrews and Aberdeen.

In a public lecture on 1 October, the day of the council's elections, Rollock delivered his inaugural address 'in the presence of a crowded audience'; thereafter students, as they enrolled, were subjected to an entrance examination; and those who failed to exhibit proficiency in classics were assigned for further instruction not to the burgh's grammar schoolmaster but to Rollock's assistant, Duncan Nairn, whom the incoming council had appointed 'secund masiter' in November 1583. The son of Duncan Nairn at Bannockburn mill, the new member of staff, like Rollock himself, was a Stirlingshire man; yet he was recruited not from Rollock's own students in St Salvator's College, St Andrews but from Melville's innovating régime at Glasgow, where he had obtained what was, in effect, a bursary for seven years and had graduated in first place in 1580. As a persistent critic of Arran's government, Andrew Melville with fellow presbyterians had fled to England in 1584, but Edinburgh's new town council was clearly prepared to accept a promising candidate, reputed 'a man of great learning and elegance of manners', from Melville's Glasgow, with its reputation for progressive and radical innovations in teaching methods and content. In short, Nairn, who had been reared at Glasgow on Ramist rhetoric and logic, was considered the appropriate choice for assisting Rollock at Edinburgh.[47]

For Rollock, Nairn's appointment from Glasgow was apposite. Despite a recent claim discounting Ramist teaching at Edinburgh under Rollock's principalship,[48] there is clear evidence that Rollock himself was an enthusiastic supporter of Ramist theories. It has been argued, somewhat narrowly, that the only indication of Rollock's attitude towards Ramism rests on a short and ambiguous passage in one of Rollock's sermons, in which Rollock denounced Aristotelian scholasticism and accused its followers of turning 'the gospel of Jesus to Aristotle, all thair writings are bot spreitles. Thair is not sa mekle as ane smel of the spreit of Jesus in them all'. By itself, Rollock's criticism is inconclusive proof of his attachment to Ramist principles and is liable to be misinterpreted unless placed within the broader framework of Rollock's teaching.[49] One

[47] Rollock, *Works*, i, pp. lxiv-lxvi; *Edin. Recs.*, iv, 305; Durkan & Kirk, *University of Glasgow*, 359, 376.

[48] Lynch, 'Toun College', 9-13.

[49] ibid., 9; Rollock, *Works*, i, 388.

clue, however, which ought not to be dismissed so readily, is Rollock's own preference for logical analyses of scripture, a familiar, though not exclusively, Ramist pursuit.

The concept of 'logical analysis' seems to have developed first among Ramists and was put to good effect by Johannes Piscator in his planned analysis of every book of the Old and New Testaments. To presbyterians, in particular, part of the appeal of Ramus lay in the claim that Ramist dialectic was a more effective method than the logic of the schoolmen for interpreting scripture, and that Ramist rhetoric seemed more relevant when it came to preaching the pure Word of God. Rollock's own application of the techniques of logical analysis to scripture is clearly revealed in his writings. Among his many theological works, several were specifically devoted to interpreting the true meaning of scripture by logical analysis. These include his *Analysis Dialectica ... in Pauli Apostoli Epistolam ad Romanos*, printed in Edinburgh by Robert Waldegrave in 1594, his *In Epistolam S. Pauli ad Romanos ..., Commentarius Analytica methodo conscriptus*, published in Geneva in 1596, his *In Epistolam Pauli Apostoli ad Philemonen Analysis Logica*, issued in Edinburgh by Waldegrave in 1598 (another edition of which, with additional notes and corrections, was produced by the famous Ramist divine at Herborn, Johannes Piscator himself, in 1601), Rollock's *Analysis Logica in Epistolam Pauli Apostoli ad Galatas*, which appeared posthumously in 1602, and his *Analysis Logica in Epistolam ad Hebraeos*, printed in Edinburgh in 1605. Rollock's own students at Edinburgh, from the outset, were encouraged to apply this method for a more exact understanding of the meaning of the Bible; and Charles Ferme, who graduated from Edinburgh in 1587 to become minister at Fraserburgh and principal of the ill-fated college there, followed his master's example by producing his own *Analysis Logica in Epistolam Apostoli Pauli ad Romanos*, 'in qua omnia verba, sententiae et phrases difficiliores ex sacris scripturis exacte, solide et dilucide explicantur', a work printed posthumously in Edinburgh in 1651.[50]

At the very least, the possibility that Rollock was a Ramist cannot be so readily excluded as some have done. Nor is it sufficient simply to rely on the guidance of Thomas McCrie (1772-1835),

---

[50] W. Ong, *Ramus, Method, and the Decay of Dialogue* (Cambridge, Mass., 1958), 8, 298-9; P. Miller, *The New England Mind* (New York, 1939), 328-9; Rollock, *Works*, i, pp. lxxxix-xcv; C. Ferme, *A Logical Analysis of the Epistle of Paul to the Romans*, ed. W.L. Alexander (Edinburgh, 1850).

who judged that Rollock's 'understanding was not led astray by admiration of the Ramean logic', though McCrie himself was less dismissive than some of the Ramist influence on Rollock.[51] Besides, attempts at extrapolating Rollock's approach to teaching at Edinburgh on the basis of his background at St Andrews, so far, have proved unrewarding. It is true that, as an undergraduate, he had studied, and later taught, at St Salvator's College, where the Aristotelian, John Rutherford, was principal; but it is also true that, as a postgraduate student and teacher, Rollock had devoted himself to studying theology in St Andrews at a time when Andrew Melville, as the new Ramist principal of St Mary's College in the university, gave public lectures in divinity, and Rollock also came into close contact with James Melville (the principal's nephew), who taught him Hebrew. In any event, Rollock's own regent at St Salvator's was not the anti-Ramist provost but John Carr, himself a product of the regime and 'a man of the greatest learning', who helped Rollock, or so it was said, to advance 'so rapidly in the study of philosophy that he was equalled by few and surpassed by none of his fellow students'.[52] While it is possible that Carr might have taken an independent or less committed line than his teacher, it was scarcely permissible for him, had he so wished, to depart significantly from Rutherford who was not only an authority on logic but also provost of the college, at least until Rutherford's retirement in 1577, which occurred just before Rollock's graduation.[53] By the 1580s, however, some Ramist literature had penetrated St Salvator's and gained a foothold as prescribed texts in certain subjects, though not apparently in logic itself.[54]

Yet even before Melville's arrival in St Andrews in 1580, there is evidence of disagreement within the University on how logic should be taught. At St Leonard's College, James Melville's regent, William Collace, in the early 1570s had opted to use his own compendium of traditional fare;[55] and by 1576 efforts were underway to introduce and enforce a more unified approach when it was 'ordanit that the principall maisteris of ilk college sall continewe

[51] T. McCrie, *Life of Andrew Melville* (Edinburgh, 1819), 387.

[52] Rollock, *Works*, i, p. lxi; Melville, *Diary*, 86.

[53] Watt, *Fasti*, 384; *St Andrews Univ. Recs.*, 175, 179, 285 (where his graduation is dated 1578); St Andrews University Archives, MS SS 110 E2 (where Rollock is depicted in 1577 as 'Maister' and as 'student' of St Salvator's College).

[54] *Evidence*, iii, 194.

[55] Melville, *Diary*, 25.

and ether be commoun consent sall agrie upone ane compendium of logik and phisik quhilk thai sall subscryve ... and in caice thai agre nocht everie ane sall delyver ane compendium as thai think to be usit in tym cuming and thai ar certifeit gif thai fail in the premissis ane compendium salbe prescryvit unto them quhilk thai salbe compellit to be techit in tyme cuming ondir the pane off deprivatioun'.[56] All in all, Rollock's career in St Andrews offers few clear pointers to his plans for Edinburgh.

A more informative guide to teaching patterns established at Edinburgh is forthcoming in the *Disciplina academiae Edinburgenae ... prout observata sunt multis retro annis*, compiled by 1628 and preserving, as the title suggests, elements from the college's early years, which significantly reveals the inclusion, as part of the curriculum, of Ramist logic and the rhetoric of Omer Talon, Ramus's disciple.[57] The problem remains, however, whether the Ramist content in the curriculum of 1628 was present as early as the 1580s. Convincing proof of Rollock's devotion to Ramism from the start of his career at Edinburgh is disclosed by one of Rollock's students, John Adamson, later himself to become principal of Edinburgh University. Adamson, who graduated under Rollock's principalship in 1597 and was then appointed to the staff, had been taught by another Edinburgh graduate, Charles Ferme, who, as a student, had entered the college about 1583 or 1584, for he graduated four years later with 47 other students in the college's first graduation ceremony in 1587. In his life of Ferme, Adamson, who had first-hand knowledge of the early curriculum, disclosed that 'under Rollock's guidance' Ferme studied 'Greek grammar and the Greek authors, the *Dialecticae* of Ramus (to which Rollock attached the greatest value, as an instrument so admirably adapted to the study of logic, that no one, in his opinion, who was ignorant of it could either excel in synthetical, or know anything of analytical, reasoning); the rhetoric of Talon, the *Logica, Physica* and *Ethica* of Aristotle, the teaching of John of Holywood's *De Sphaera*, the Catechism of Ursinus, the commonplaces of theology, the analysis of certain Epistles of sacred scripture and the rudiments of the Hebrew tongue'.[58] In addition, besides the study of arithmetic and geography, Rollock's Arts course also provided

[56] SRO, PA10/1, Papers relating to the Visitation of St Andrews University, 1574-76 (unfoliated).
[57] *Charters, Statutes and Acts*, 60-61, 63.
[58] Ferme, *Logical Analysis*, pp. xii, 25-6.

instruction in human anatomy—hence, no doubt, his acquisition of Galen[59]—and Saturday afternoons were devoted to Beza's *Questiones*, which prompted Rollock to publish 'a short analysis to assist the memory of the students'.[60]

In essentials, Rollock's programme for the 1580s bears some striking similarities to the revised and expanded curriculum of the 1620s, not least in the emphasis on Greek, Ramist logic, Talon's rhetoric, Hebrew grammar and logical analyses, as well as the study of human anatomy. In all, Adamson's account of Rollock's teaching practice lends no support for the unfounded claim that Rollock eschewed Ramist values and sided with the anti-Ramist camp. Rollock, in short, was a Ramist and is credited with teaching Ramist method in the college from his arrival. In doing so, he was plainly rejecting and reacting against Rutherford's philosophical emphases at St Andrews and adopting a programme more akin to Melville's Ramist innovations at Glasgow and elsewhere. The Edinburgh curriculum of the 1580s was emphatically not a reiteration of the old, unreformed curriculum of St Salvator's College in St Andrews, as is sometimes claimed. By contrast, Rollock's prescription of Greek for first-year students and his introduction of Ramist method and Hebrew grammar closely followed Melville's example and experiments in Glasgow. There was little, indeed, which can appropriately be described as conservative or narrowly scholastic in the humanist-inspired curriculum which Rollock introduced at Edinburgh.

Besides, the conservative influence of Arran's government (sometimes misinterpreted as a determining factor in relations with the college) was wholly transitory: appointed chancellor of the kingdom in May 1584, Arran found himself dismissed from office in December 1585; neither he, nor the town council elected during his regime, had any significant role to play in revising teaching methods or in changing personnel. Besides, it is often overlooked that the college itself remained closed on account of plague for more than half the duration of Arran's short period in power as chancellor of the country: in May 1585 Rollock and Nairn informed the town council that 'the haill students, throw the

[59] Galen, *Aliquot opuscula* (Lyons, 1550), in NLS. I am grateful to Dr Robert Donaldson and Mr Julian Russell for supplying this information in 1983.

[60] Rollock, *Works*, i, pp. lxv-lxvi. The curriculum depicted here by Henry Charteris is complemented by Adamson's more precise account of the authors used for instruction.

feir and bruit of the pestilence, hes left the scholes and thairby thai haif nathing to do'. The council then granted the two masters leave 'to depairt and visy thair freindis for a seasoun', and only in February 1586 (after Arran's downfall in December 1585, and the return of the presbyterian exiles from England) did classes in the college resume in an atmosphere decidedly more sympathetic to the presbyterians.[61]

With varying success Andrew Melville's reforms had affected each of the Scottish universities. In Glasgow, in King's and Marischal Colleges, Aberdeen, and in Edinburgh, the emphasis was on Arts teaching with additional instruction in theology undertaken by the principal himself. In Glasgow, St Andrews and Aberdeen, the charters of new foundation had recognised the need to reform studies and introduce specialist teaching. And in all the Scottish universities, an attachment to Ramism, which Melville promoted, played a part in reorganising methods of study.

There is, however, another aspect of Melville's humanism which needs emphasis: this was Melville, the theology professor and biblical scholar, who held the ecclesiastical office of doctor, which according to Calvin was one of the four essential ministries granted by God to the church. This fourfold ministry was upheld in the *Second Book of Discipline*, to which Melville contributed, in 1578. Melville therefore sat on the courts of the Church, and his duty as doctor was to interpret scripture aright by applying the tools of philology to exegesis. He was 'to oppine up the mynd of the Spirit of God within the Scripturis', as the *Second Book of Discipline* explained in 1578.[62] The biblical texts had to be studied in their original tongues: the Old Testament in Hebrew, Syriac and Chaldaic; the New Testament in Greek and Syriac. Here Melville's expertise revitalised theological training first at Glasgow and then at St Andrews.

It is sometimes said that Melville's reforms met with scant success at St Andrews; but such a judgment seems too hasty. St Mary's College, as a divinity school, is a lasting reminder of his work.[63] It is, of course, quite true that the *First Book of Discipline* in 1560 had

---

[61] *Handbook of British Chronology*, eds. E.B. Fryde, D.E. Greenway, S. Porter and I. Roy (London, 1986), 183; *Edin. Recs.*, iv, 421, 448-9.

[62] *The Second Book of Discipline*, ed. J. Kirk (Edinburgh, 1980), 187.

[63] Cameron, 'Andrew Melville in St Andrews', 14-25.

intended creating a divinity college there,[64] and in 1569 John Hamilton, the surviving Catholic archbishop of St Andrews, had suggested setting aside St Salvator's College for that purpose.[65] Yet it was Andrew Melville and Thomas Smeaton, his successor at Glasgow, who succeeded in their efforts to have an 'anti-Seminarie' established in St Andrews. As Melville himself expressed it, he was appointed 'for reforming of the universitie and erecting of a colledge of divinitie for the profession of learned tongues and theologie against the seminaries of Rems and Rome'.[66] The format he devised for St Mary's was an expansion of his theology course at Glasgow based on an intensive study of the tongues and biblical exegesis.

In the tradition of Luther and Calvin, Melville resisted the influence of scholastic philosophy on theology; and he helped secure in 1583 the General Assembly's condemnation of those aspects in Aristotle's 'doctrine directlie impugning the grounds of religioun'.[67] By contrast, Ramus's anti-metaphysical approach offered clarity and order in analyses of scripture, and was effectively used by Melville's presbyterian colleagues, Robert Rollock and Charles Ferme. In Melville's own eyes,

> theology is the wisdome of divine things inspired according to divine truth by God, and committed to His servants by the Word pronounced in Christ and consigned in the Old and New Testaments by the prophets, apostles and evangelists as far as it was expedient to be revealed to His glory and the good of the elect. This sacred scripture is perfect, clear in itself, its own interpreter, the supreme judge of all controversies; it is of divine authority, comprehended in the canonical and God-inspired books of the Old and New Testaments, written down in Hebrew and Greek letters, editions of which alone are authentic, from which to resort to Latin or vernacular editions in controversies is practically foolish and impious'.[68]

As with Rollock, philology was seen to be the key to divine truth. There was no tendency to elevate reason to a position equal with revelation.

Indeed, themes decidedly critical of Aristotle were often selected for disputations, over which Melville presided, in St Mary's Col-

---

[64] *FBD*, 138.

[65] St Andrews University Archives, MS UY 812.

[66] Melville, *Diary*, 76; McCrie, *Melville*, 487.

[67] *BUK*, ii, 640-41.

[68] A. Melville, *Scholastica diatriba de rebus divinis...* (Edinburgh, 1599), aphorismide III.

lege. Divinity students were asked to debate 'whether the dialetic method of question and response described by Aristotle ... can fruitfully be transferred to theological disputations', 'whether contradictions can be solved without the teaching of Aristotle's *Elenchi*', 'whether a truth in philosophy can contradict a truth in theology', 'whether logical ideas can be equated with theological ideas, and whether rhetoric and logic should be drawn from scripture itself'.[69]

In all of this, Melville seems to have diverged from the Italian Aristotelianism of Beza's Geneva where the influence of Peter Martyr, Girolamo Zanchi, Lambert Daneau and others helped shape the new reformed scholasticism, with its emphasis on metaphysics. The Genevan Academy, under Beza's direction, had over fifty Aristotelian works, but few indeed by Ramus or Talon.[70] Beza's own devotion to Aristotelian philosophy had led him to refuse Ramus a teaching post in the Academy, and so Melville had followed Ramus for a spell to Lausanne.[71] Even Henry Scrimgeour, Melville's relative in the Genevan Academy, had studied at Padua;[72] but Melville was schooled in a very different philosophical tradition. In church government, however, if not in philosophy, Melville sided with Beza in defending the Calvinist polity when it came under attack by Ramus, who veered towards congregationalism; and his strenuous defence of ecclesiastical independence places Melville firmly in the tradition of Oecolampadius, Bucer, Calvin and Beza.[73]

For more than three decades, Melville remained the dominant figure in Scottish theological education, and for a spell the universities were headed by men sympathetic to the Melvillian cause. But the success was short-lived. In the Church, Melville lost the battle with King James's bishops (three of whom were also university chancellors), and he himself was imprisoned in London and then exiled to France.[74] In the universities, conservatives came into their own again. Specialist teaching was abandoned in the early seventeenth century, and regenting returned. In other ways, too, Melville's pioneering reforms suffered an eclipse. An interest in scholasticism and in metaphysics, which Melville had eschewed,

---

69 ibid., Progymnasmata.
70 A. Ganoczy, *La bibliothèque de l'Académie de Calvin* (Geneva, 1969), passim.
71 Durkan & Kirk, *University of Glasgow*, 271.
72 Durkan, 'Henry Scrimgeour', 5.
73 Kirk, *Patterns of Reform*, 232ff.
74 McCrie, *Melville*, 282ff, 320ff.

came to the fore again. A restored Aristotelianism emerged triumphant in all the principal reformed academies throughout Europe, except in parts of France where the appeal of Calvin's humanism still remained strong, and it was in France, at Sedan, that Melville chose to teach in exile.

As a result of continuing debates among Protestants themselves and in further encounters with Catholic opponents, the appeal to scripture was seen to be insufficient to resolve disputes. The difficulty lay in discovering the true meaning of scripture. By adopting the philosophy of the real Aristotle and Plato, which the humanists and Paduans in Italy had revived, truth, certainty and precise definition might be properly attained. Consequently, in reformed theology, reason became as important as faith and revealed truth. This was an approach very different from that which Melville had encouraged.

The re-emergence of metaphysics at Glasgow was fostered in 1615 with the appointment as principal of Robert Boyd, who had already displayed an interest in scholasticism at Montauban. Glasgow students, like John Livingston in 1620, were once more subjected to 'logick and metaphysick and the subtilties of the schoolmen'. Increasingly, the College library was stocked with scholastic commentators: Zabarella and Rubio in logic; Clemens Timpler and Pedro de Fonseca in metaphysics. Ramism was plainly overshadowed by this new scholasticism, but it did not entirely vanish. Ramism continued to be taught, for example, at Aberdeen in the 1640s. Besides, many of the new systematics like Keckermann, Burgersdijck and Alsted, who came into vogue, preserved and improved elements of Ramus's logical method in their efforts to reform the shortcomings of the old scholasticism. In 1621, the Edinburgh printer, Andrew Hart, still found a ready market when he published the Ramist *Rhetoric* of Omer Talon.[75]

Even here, the Melville tradition, it seems, did not altogether evaporate; and in the continued emphasis on studying Greek and Hebrew, it certainly remained strong. Only in the eighteenth century, however, with the abolition of regenting and an acceptance of specialist teaching, were Melville's teaching methods for the universities finally vindicated.

---

[75] Durkan & Kirk, *University of Glasgow*, 277, 372; Durkan, 'Glasgow University Library', 108-09; J. Durkan, 'King Aristotle and old Butterdish: the making of a graduate in seventeenth-century Glasgow', *College Courant*, lxiii (1979), 18-24; Howell, *Logic and Rhetoric*, 272-3, 282-3, 309; W. Ong, *Ramus and Talon Inventory* (Cambridge, Mass., 1958), 130.

PREACHING TO THE CONVERTED? PERSPECTIVES ON THE SCOTTISH REFORMATION

Michael Lynch

For David Calderwood, the most influential of the presbyterian historians of the first half of the seventeenth century, the year 1596 was *annus mirabilis*, when the Scottish Church achieved 'her perfectioun and the greatest puritie that ever she atteaned unto, both in doctrine and discipline'. The years that followed were those of the fall, and a 'doolefull decay' of the Kirk which lasted until its reawakening in a 'second Reformation' in 1638.[1] For Sir James Balfour of Denmilne, royalist historian but sharp critic of Charles I, who was also writing from hindsight (in the 1650s), the most remarkable feature of 1596 was not the dishing of the Kirk's radical ministers, which merits only brief mention, but the steep rise in the price of grain.[2] The price rise, which came to Scotland later than it reached England, was used by Catholic propagandists from the 1570s onwards as a sign of the affliction which had gripped the country since the Reformation of 1560. The year 1597, however, which saw the second recantation of the earl of Huntly and news almost 'every day' of the defection of Catholic minor nobles or lairds in the north and north-east, marked, for some Catholic commentators, the 'triumph' of the Protestant ministers.[3] For them, the period of Catholic resurgence, which had since 1579 seen a marked increase in the missionary activity of seminary priests and Jesuits, some evidence of the re-emergence of popular Catholic practices and devotions and the appearance of a militant Counter-Reformation Catholicism amongst some of the nobility, was over; it was a view which closely corresponded to the dismay which later greeted the flight of the Catholic earls from Ulster in 1601.[4] The 'facts' of history have seldom been at greater variance, but a highly selective, radical presbyterian canon of history established itself in the course of

---

[1] Calderwood, *History*, v, 387-8. See D. Mullan, *Episcopacy in Scotland: the History of an Idea, 1560-1638* (Edinburgh, 1986), 78.

[2] Balfour, *Works*, i, 398, 400.

[3] *Catholic Narratives*, 160, 232-3; *Spalding Misc.* iv, pp. lix-xlii.

[4] K. Brown, 'In search of the godly magistrate in Reformation Scotland', *J. Ecc. Hist.*, xl (1989), 574-5; *Catholic Narratives*, 137-225; J. Durkan, 'William Murdoch and the early Jesuit mission to Scotland', *IR*, xxxv (1984), 3-11.

the seventeenth century as a new orthodoxy. It has greatly influenced the agenda used by historians ever since to analyse the longer-term process, spread over three or four generations after 1560, of the implementation of the Reformation in Scotland.

It has been Calderwood's vision of history, buttressed by the works of other radical presbyterian polemicists such as John Row and Thomas Scot, usually creations of the period between 1625 and 1635 or later, which has held a remarkable sway over Scottish ecclesiastical historians ever since.[5] Yet these were not the generally accepted views of the mid-1590s held at the time, even amongst Melvillian commentators. In March 1596, the General Assembly had declared that in many parts of the land 'the people ly altogether ignorant of their salvatioun'. For many radicals, such as Alexander Hume, minister of Logie near Stirling, the Kirk had by the early 1590s shown distressing evidence of having already fallen into decay from the early 'measour of perfectioun' it had enjoyed soon after the Reformation of 1560, which had then been acclaimed by both John Knox, in the well-known passage in the preface to Book IV of his *History of the Reformation,* and by the General Assembly itself, in its barbed ratification of the Second Helvetic Confession of 1566. In similar vein, Robert Pont, one of the veterans of 1560, pointed, in a sermon to the Assembly in 1594, to the sharp contrast between the 'bold confession' at 'the beginning of the Reformation' and the present timidity of both Church and state in combatting 'idolatry in sundry parts of the land'.[6]

But one myth replaced another, as the time served. The early 1590s had seen, according to the General Assembly itself, some 400 benefices left unfilled, with certain areas more poorly provided than in the 1560s, a fall in clerical incomes and the steady dilapidation of benefices, mounting fears of an increase in recusancy and Catholic practices and increasingly 'cruel oppression' of tenants through rent rises and evictions, made worse by severe climactic conditions. This was the period which became,

---

[5] Row, *History*; the bulk of the manuscript was completed by 1634. Scot, *Apologetical Narration*; the work was written sometime after 1625. Little study, however, has been made of Calderwood or the other presbyterian historians of this period, except, for somewhat different reasons, by D. Allan, *Virtue, Learning and the Scottish Enlightenment* (Edinburgh, 1993).

[6] *BUK*, iii, 876; i, 90; Calderwood, *History*, v, 416; ii, 331-2; Alexander Hume, 'Ane Afolde Admonitioun to the Ministerie of Scotland' (1609), *Wodrow Misc.*, 569-90, at 588; Knox, *History*, ii, 3; Wodrow, *Biog. Colls.*, I, i, 190-91.

for a later generation, a golden age. It has remained so ever since.

Some of these fears were doubtless exaggerated. The natural currency of a church which preaches *semper reformanda* is exaggeration, periodic paranoia and a literature of despair and lamentation, whether it was the Melvillian offensive of the 1580s and 1590s, puritan preachers in Elizabethan England or pastors in Lutheran territorial churches in Germany in the same period.[7] Yet there can also be little doubt that the 1590s were in many ways a watershed, for Scottish society and government as well as for the Church. The institutions of a feudal kingdom were put under immense strain by a variety of pressures, including population increase, price inflation, the bankruptcy of the crown, escalating feud, two sets of noble rebellions (each of which resorted to playing the card of religious militancy), and the frantic efforts of various groups in society to discover their status or keep it amidst a complex of bewildering change.[8] This is the context in which the confrontation between Kirk and crown needs to be understood; it may also help explain why the crown's assault on the radical Melvillian faction within the Kirk met with such striking success. The crisis of the 1590s afflicted almost all sections of Scottish society, including both ministers and the institution of the Kirk itself.

In the orthodox, presbyterian canon of history, the sharp debate between James VI and Andrew Melville at Falkland Palace in 1597 over the 'two kingdoms' epitomised the clash between two irreconcilable views of church and state. Yet the debate over 'two kingdoms', about which the reformed Church had since 1559 shown itself to be in at least two minds, was not a simple, stark struggle between Kirk and crown, for even amongst the Melvillians there were sharp differences, not least over the vexed question of the Kirk's representation in parliament. This was an issue on which even Andrew and James Melville, uncle and

[7] P. Collinson, *The Religion of Protestants: the Church in English Society, 1559-1625* (Oxford, 1982), 190-91, 196, 199-205, 221-6; G. Strauss, *Luther's House of Learning: Indoctrination of the Young in the German Reformation* (Baltimore, 1978), 268-99; also idem, 'Success and failure in the German Reformation', *Past and Present*, lxvii (1975), 30-63.

[8] There is no single study of the crisis of the 1590s. The most useful recent works which examine aspects of it are J. Goodare, 'Parliament and Society in Scotland, 1560-1603' (Edinburgh Univ. Ph.D., 1989); R.R. Zulager, 'A Study of the Middle-Rank Administrators in the Government of King James VI of Scotland, 1580-1603' (Aberdeen Univ. Ph.D., 1991); and K.M. Brown, *Bloodfeud in Scotland, 1573-1625* (Edinburgh, 1986).

nephew, sharply disagreed. Some ministers, like the lairds, demanded a place in parliament, the institution which James VI himself called the 'head court of the king and his vassals', to make sure of their place in society. For them, the interaction between the two kingdoms was more important than their separation. It was in 1590, when the King addressed the General Assembly, that the prospect had taken on a new reality.[9] In fact, never was the Kirk so united as when it was acting in concert with the crown—or so it would have seemed to contemporaries until 1610 or perhaps as late as 1618.

Against this background, the period between c.1600 and 1620 saw the Church taking serious stock of itself. The myth of the perfection of the first Reformation was subjected to critical scrutiny. For some veterans, like Robert Pont, it was to a great extent a story of missed opportunities and broken promises, usually made by the nobility.[10] For John Spottiswoode, who had been taught by Andrew Melville at Glasgow University in the late 1570s and had shared in the wave of radical expectation of the 1580s before accepting the archbishopric of Glasgow in 1603, the Reformation had been marked by an excess of zeal, which had resulted in the plunder and destruction of many churches, libraries and ecclesiastical treasures.[11] There was growing criticism in this period as well of the amount of effort made by many ministers in the basic work of catechising; the Linlithgow Assembly of 1608, in a soul-searching analysis of the causes of a further resurgence of papistry 'in all the quarters of the kingdom', partly blamed the negligence of the parish clergy in the work of catechising, especially of children, and partly the admission of too many raw recruits, straight from university, into the ministry. To these criticisms could be added the death-bed tract of Alexander Hume, a minister with a good Melvillian pedigree, who in 1609 sharply attacked some radical ministers for negligent or perfunctory discharge of their parochial duties.[12] It may be wondered whether he had in mind 'busie men', such as James Melville, who

[9] See Calderwood, *History*, v, 106; *BUK*, iii, 762-78. For representation of the Kirk in parliament, see *CSP Scot.*, x, no. 691 (1592). For the lairds and parliament, see Goodare, 'Parliament and Society', 37, 62.

[10] See Robert Pont, *Against Sacrilege; Three Sermons* (Edinburgh, 1599: Aldis 314).

[11] Spottiswoode, *History*, i, 372.

[12] ibid., iii, 193-4; *BUK*, iii, 1051-6; the Assembly had voiced the same criticisms in 1601 (ibid., iii, 964); *Wodrow Misc.*, 586-8.

spent so much time in pursuing the affairs of the Kirk in Edinburgh and elsewhere that he was obliged to employ the young local schoolmaster to act as locum for the 'daylie attendance and comfort' of his Anstruther congregation for some six months of the year.[13] Preaching to the converted had become a habit for the bulk of the Melvillian clergy, settled in fairly comfortable circumstances in the better-paid benefices of Lothian and Fife and in the universities.

Much ink has been spent, from the time of Calderwood onwards, in deploring the motives of the new Jacobean episcopate. Too little has been devoted to the efforts made by James's new bishops to redress what was widely regarded as a very real crisis of parish provision, which had its roots in successive failures since the early 1580s to secure a full and permanent augmentation of ministerial stipends. Most of these bishops had first entered the parish ministry in the difficult years of the 1580s and many of them had a past record of militant ecclesiastical politics.[14] Most were not natural civil servants, fond of 'courting', but they had by the later 1590s become convinced that reform under the king provided a better prospect for the Kirk than the endless process of petitioning the civil power. Indeed, they were probably right, for by 1630 the cumbersome process of the augmentation commissions had begun to take a real grip of the complex problem of ministerial provision.[15] By then, too, the privy council, which devoted fully a quarter of its business in 1629-30 to the harrying of Catholic recusants, had shown itself to be a dogged instrument in the battle against papistry in the darker corners of the land.[16] The reading of history backwards, from the crisis of 1637-8, has dealt unkindly with the very real achievements of the Jacobean episcopate. It seems likely that it largely won the propaganda battle in print of the 1620s against the radical wing within the Kirk, partly because it could rely on the power of censorship. Certainly it was the episcopal party which landed the first effective blows: William Cowper, bishop of Galloway, made the first serious

---

13 Melville, *Diary*, 7.

14 W.R. Foster, *The Church before the Covenants: the Church of Scotland, 1596-1638* (Edinburgh, 1975), 57; Mullan, *Episcopacy*, 114.

15 W.H. Makey, *The Church of the Covenant, 1637-1651: Revolution and Social Change in Scotland* (Edinburgh, 1979), 108-14; idem, 'Presbyterian and Canterburian', in R.A. Mason (ed.), *Scotland and England, 1286-1815* (Edinburgh, 1987), 160-64; Foster, *Church*, 159-67.

16 ibid., 191; *RPC* (2nd series), iii, pp. xi-xviii, 186-8.

attempt at a history of the Church since the Reformation to justify a particular polity.[17] It had made real strides forward in the battle against Catholicism, especially in the north-east and south-west.[18] In the north-east, too, major advances had been made in the provision of university education under the new broom wielded at King's College by Patrick Forbes, bishop of Aberdeen from 1618 to 1635 and, like Spottiswoode, another former student of Andrew Melville; by his death the College's finances had been restored, its staff enlarged and teaching overhauled, as part of what Forbes saw as a desperate struggle against the Catholic menace.[19]

This was the concerted episcopal programme which was undermined by the liturgical innovations of 1636 and 1637, an inability to dominate the printing press as thoroughly as in the 1620s and a failure of nerve in the crisis which followed the Prayer Book riot of 1637. It was, as a result, the radicals who were able to claim for themselves the role of leaders in the battle against papistry, ironically citing within the National Covenant the King's or 'Negative' Confession of 1581 and its blanket condemnation of 'all contrarie religion and doctrine, but cheifly all kynd of papistrie in generall', as well as reclaiming presbyterian polity as the basis of the 'true Church of God'. It was a calculated rewriting of history. Its success should not be allowed to obscure the patterns of a continuing reformation, which had, ironically, probably begun in the 1620s to take a real grip of some of the seemingly intractable problems of ministerial provision and religious discipline.

Plantation of the ministry

How persuasive is the evidence of a steady consolidation in the inculcation of the tenets of Protestantism amongst parish congregations in the period between 1560 and 1620? The

[17] eg. William Cowper, *The Bishop of Galloway, his dikaiologie* (London, 1614); see Mullan, *Episcopacy*, 136-7.

[18] ibid., 162-4; A. Macinnes, 'Catholic recusancy and the penal laws, 1603-1707', *RSCHS*, xxiii (1987), 27-30, 35, 37-44. B. Maclennan, 'Presbyterianism challenged: a Study of Catholicism and Episcopacy in the North-East of Scotland, 1560-1650' (Aberdeen Univ. Ph.D., 1977) lists known Catholic recusants in the area.

[19] D. Stevenson, *King's College, Aberdeen, 1560-1641: From Protestant Reformation to Covenanting Revolution* (Aberdeen, 1990), 61-93.

progress of the Reformation, in the sense of the hard business of catechising and evangelising, has tended to be measured by the growth of a parish ministry. By the end of 1561, within twelve months of the compilation of the final draft of *The Book of Discipline*, about 240 members of the ministry had been planted in parishes.[20] This 'remarkable accomplishment',[21] even if it was distinctly more evident in some areas rather than others—Angus and the Mearns alone accounted for a quarter of it[22]—has been convincingly demonstrated.[23] The initial impetus made by the Kirk in the plantation of a parish ministry in parts of the Highlands by the 1570s, while less striking, was nevertheless a 'creditable achievement'.[24] There has, however, been little effort made to trace the process of the consolidation of a parish ministry over the next two generations. By the 1620s, it is sometimes said, every parish in Lowland Scotland was provided with a minister, who, more often than not by then, was a graduate.[25] In the Highlands, the qualifications of most ministers were by the 1620s on a par with their brethren serving Lowland parishes.[26] The journey between these two points, however, was uneven and difficult. By the 1580s and certainly by the 1590s, a number of factors had complicated its path.[27]

Comparatively little attention, too, has been given to the essential instruments of catechising, and still less to patterns of piety amongst the literate classes. There have been some differences which have arisen amongst historians as to the numbers of reformed ministers who could speak Gaelic. Yet preaching was less important in the long haul towards catechising than the vital instruments on which the clergy in Lowland Scotland increasingly relied: the availability in cheap editions of the psalms, the Creed and the catechism in the vernacular. The difficulty here is largely to do with scattered evidence. Yet no general thesis of the com-

---

[20] J. Kirk, *Patterns of Reform: Continuity and Change in the Reformation Kirk* (Edinburgh, 1989), 130.

[21] ibid., 130.

[22] F.D. Bardgett, *Scotland Reformed: the Reformation in Angus and the Mearns* (Edinburgh, 1989), 88-9.

[23] In the diocese of Dunkeld, 90 per cent of parishes were filled by 1574: M.J. Yellowlees, 'Dunkeld and the Reformation' (Edinburgh Univ. Ph.D., 1990), 25-57.

[24] Kirk, *Patterns of Reform*, 462.

[25] Foster, *Church*, 132.

[26] Kirk, *Patterns of Reform*, 487.

[27] Further analysis of this subject must await the publication of the 'Books of Assumption' by Dr J. Kirk.

parative successes and failures of the Reformation in the three quarters of a century after 1560, such as has distinguished the study of most other Protestant Reformations in northern Europe, has been attempted. This is a modest attempt to pose some of the likely questions. Distinctly fewer answers, however, can as yet be established.

The confident statistics relating the planting of ministers conceal a more sober reality, which was well recognised by contemporaries. The remarkable initial impetus of the early 1560s, bolstered by the recruitment both of substantial numbers of clergy from the old pre-Reformation Church and a significant cohort of men trained in the law,[28] was not sustained. The placement of a minister or reader in a parish was the beginning of the long process of catechising and evangelising, not its end. Few contemporaries by the 1580s shared the confidence of some modern historians that the plain teaching of the Gospel, by minister or reader, would be enough. As elsewhere in Europe, there was an initial period which saw a flurry of activity, with the establishment of a reformed ministry in about a quarter of the country's parishes within 15 months of the Reformation parliament of August 1560.[29] This gave way to a more gradual process of consolidation, which by 1574 saw almost 90 per cent of parishes outside the Highlands filled, although in three cases out of four the incumbent was a reader.[30] The next stage, as elsewhere, was a crisis of provision, which began to set in from the late 1570s onwards, when conforming clergy began to die off.

That crisis seems to have taken two forms. One, to which we shall return later, was essentially about the quality of teaching and preaching and its limited success in reaching the ignorant or ungodly bulk of the population. The other lay in provision itself. In a number of areas, such as Dunkeld, Dunblane, Angus and the Mearns and on Shetland, more parishes were vacant in the 1590s than in the 1560s or 1570s.[31] In other cases, such as Ross and in

[28] Kirk, *Patterns of Reform*, 148-51; Haws, *Parish Clergy*, pp. v-xv.

[29] Kirk, *Patterns of Reform*, 130; Bardgett, *Scotland Reformed*, 88. Cf. E. Cameron, *The European Reformation* (Oxford, 1991), 396-7.

[30] 'Register of Ministers and Readers in the Kirk of Scotland from the Book of the Assignation of Stipends, 1574', *Wodrow Misc.*, 319-96.

[31] *BUK*, iii, 803-04. For statistics of parishes in these areas in the period 1560-74, see I.B. Cowan, *The Scottish Reformation* (1982), 159-81; Yellowlees, 'Dunkeld and the Reformation', 30-36 (summarised at 305-06); Bardgett, *Scotland Reformed*, 87-92, esp. 90; C. Haws, 'Parish clergy in the dioceses of Dunblane and Dunkeld at the Reformation', *Proceedings of the Conference of Scottish Studies*, ii (1974), 16-17.

the Merse, where there were still fourteen unfilled parishes in 1593, improvement had been only marginal.[32] The surprising element in this comparison is that it embraces both areas where there had been an initial surge of provision (such as in Dunkeld, Angus and the Mearns and Shetland), and regions where early progress had been much more modest. The most striking deficiencies which are evidenced, however, lay on the western border; Nithsdale had 17 parishes unfilled in 1608 compared to six in 1574 and in Annandale the vacancies amounted to 28, compared to 15 in 1574.[33]

The underlying reasons for this pattern are not far to seek. The early 1560s had seen two considerable windfalls for the new Church. The large numbers of conforming Catholic clergy had maintained a continuity of service in many parishes, made up for the shortfall of 'learned men' and, because most remained as readers, had not overstrained the Kirk's limited financial resources. In Nithsdale in 1574, 18 of the 23 clergy had been readers.[34] The initial recruitment of notaries and other professional men, which was paralleled elsewhere in Europe,[35] was another once-for-all phenomenon which was not to be repeated. The early pattern of recruitment to the Protestant ministry had a double, but paradoxical effect: it provided a more substantial initial presence in the parishes than might otherwise have been achieved; but it also merely postponed for a decade or so a basic problem of manpower. Because many recruits must have been men in middle age or older that difficulty would overtake the Church before it had enough young, trained graduates to fill all its parishes. The result was a serious shortfall, which lay at the root of the Kirk's anxieties in the 1590s. By then, its worsening economic problems meant that there was a new brain drain, of unemployed young graduates forced abroad to seek employment.[36] The Church perceived all around it the limitations of the Protestant mission, but it had neither the means nor the manpower to meet its own exacting standards—unless the state would provide.

---

32 *BUK*, iii, 803-04; cf. Kirk, *Patterns of Reform*, 465-7.

33 *BUK*, iii, 1061-2; Calderwood, *History*, vi, 765; *Wodrow Misc.*, 396.

34 ibid., 389-90, 396.

35 See eg. R. Po-Chia Hsia, *Social Discipline in the Reformation: Central Europe, 1550-1750* (1989), 31, for Electoral Saxony; also Cameron, *European Reformation*, 391.

36 *BUK*, iii, 879; Melville, *Diary*, 333.

The concentration on the role of the more prominent of the ministers has obscured the potentially important roles of four other groups in the second and third generations after 1560. They include the lawyers, who had risen to a new prominence in both central and local affairs in the last quarter of the century;[37] the ordinary parish ministers, especially those working away in the dark corners of the land, and the readers, the unsung foot soldiers of the Kirk, often despised or distrusted by the ministerial elite in the General Assembly; and the members of the Jacobean episcopate, vilified both by their contemporary opponents and by the presbyterian propagandists of the next generation and after.

What role was played by readers, the foot soldiers of the kirk in its first generation? They accounted for 70 per cent of the ministry in 1574 (excluding Argyll): 699 out of a total of 988. The fact that readers remained in such numbers contradicted the blueprint sent down in 1560 in the *First Book of Discipline*, which had envisaged the post of reader as a recruiting device for the ministry itself; by 1567, the recommendation that a reader should be dismissed if he did not show promise of becoming better qualified for full ministry was forgotten, and more rather than fewer readers were recruited in the following years.[38] How plausible is the claim that the whole of the early reformed clergy—readers and exhorters as well as preaching ministers—were 'all but invariably ... depicted as "ministers"', able to convey the simple truth of the Gospel?[39] If that is so, it makes Scotland a distinct exception to much experience of a reading ministry elsewhere. In Ireland, for example, the established Church in the 1560s was also mostly made up of reading ministers who 'simply read the service book to the congregation and ... many were incapable even of that'.[40] That was certainly the view taken by the

[37] See Zulager, 'Middle-rank Administrators', 62-5, 69-70, 72-6; also G. Donaldson, 'The legal profession in Scottish society in the 16th and 17th centuries', *Juridical Review*, new ser., xxi (1976), 1-19.

[38] *Wodrow Misc.*, 396; M. Lynch, 'Calvinism in Scotland, 1559-1638', in M. Prestwich (ed.), *International Calvinism, 1541-1715* (Oxford, 1985), 248-9; R.M. Healey, 'The preaching ministry in Scotland's *First Book of Discipline*', *Church History*, lviii (1989), 344; M. Dilworth, 'Monks and ministers after 1560', *RSCHS*, xviii (1974), 216-20.

[39] Kirk, *Patterns of Reform*, 117. Cf. Thomas Scot, who made a sharp distinction in his *Apologetical Narration* between the temporary device of readers and a 'reading ministry'.

[40] H.C. Walshe, 'Enforcing the Elizabethan settlement: the vicissitudes of Hugh Brady, bishop of Meath, 1563-84', *IHS*, xxvi (1989), 362; see also A. Ford, *The Protestant Reformation in Ireland, 1590-1641* (Frankfurt-am-Main, 1987), ch.1.

General Assembly itself in the 1590s. When it characterised over 400 parishes as 'destitute of the Word' in 1596,[41] the Assembly meant that they were either vacant *or* served only by readers. It is difficult to see how one generation of readers could act as effective evangelists whereas the next was incapable.

Yet there may well have been two vital differences between these successive generations. In the 1560s and 1570s, the new ministry depended heavily for its effectiveness on the quality of the pre-Reformation clergy; drawn as they were from monks, canons regular and friars as well as from the secular parish ministry, who ranged from beneficed priests to underpaid curates, quality was a variable commodity. The Catholic clergy who conformed may have shed their faith (though a few clearly did not), but they could hardly change their natural gifts as pastors—for good or bad. It is likely that the new Protestant readers were most effective either where there was a continuity of service in the parish or where, in the case of regular clergy, their religious house had been in a healthy state before 1560. In the case of parishes served by Augustinian canons, both conditions sometimes applied.[42] In a real sense, the strengths and weaknesses of the old Church were visited upon the new in the first generation after 1560.

Readers had always been the low-paid workers of the Kirk, but no group within it suffered more from a fall in income in the inflation-ridden years of the last quarter of the sixteenth century, by when, it has been estimated, a minister's salary set at £100 in 1560 would have had to have risen fourfold to maintain its purchasing power. In 1585, the 11 readers in Ross were paid between £20 and a miserable £4. Even in the 1620s, many readers were still being paid £20 per annum. These were sums which compared badly with stipends in the poorest parts of the Church of Ireland; there, it was recommended by the Irish council in 1604, the minimum stipend for a preaching minister was set at £30 sterling (£360 Scots) and at 20 marks IR (£107 Scots) for a reader.[43] Ministers in the Scottish Church, by contrast, were

---

[41] *BUK*, iii, 876; Calderwood, *History*, v, 416; cf. J. Kirk, 'The Development of the Melvillian Movement in Late Sixteenth Century Scotland' (Edinburgh Univ. Ph.D., 1972), 385n; G. Donaldson, *The Scottish Reformation* (Cambridge, 1960), 94.

[42] See Dilworth, 'Canons regular and the Reformation', in this present volume, at n.48.

[43] Makey, *Church of Covenant*, 107; Kirk, *Patterns of Reform*, 466; Foster, *Church*, 194; S.G. Ellis, 'Economic problems of the Church: why the Reformation failed in Ireland', *J. Ecc. Hist.*, xli (1990), 239-65, at 254.

faring distinctly better. Their average stipend in the early 1620s, it has been calculated, was £360; this was perhaps uncomfortably close to the minimum of £333 laid down by the commissioners of 1617 and 1621 and it is likely that the average for ministers north of the Tay was rather lower, but a real improvement had been made since the 1590s. By the mid-1630s, the average augmented stipend stood at almost £550.[44] The poverty of livings in large upland parishes, characterised by sparse and scattered settlement of population, which marked the church in much of Ireland and Wales, was a fact of geography which impeded both clerical incomes and the spread of the gospel.[45] It was the work of the augmentation commissioners, however slow or piecemeal, which allowed the Scottish Church to escape the cycle of rural poverty and its consequences which so afflicted its sister churches in Ireland and Wales.

It is as well to remember that the original level of income enjoyed by the ministry in the generation after the settlement of the thirds of benefices in 1562 was skewed by the fact that only one in four were ministers. With strictly limited resources, the reasonable stipends enjoyed by the few depended on the pittances paid to the many. Thus the Kirk had by the 1590s been caught in a trap, even if it was not one of its own making. The appointment of more and more ministers might in theory bring about a faster spreading of the Word, but it would also risk the impoverishment of a substantial section of the parish clergy. And that, it is likely, would be counter-productive. In the parish of Lenzie near Glasgow, where the annual stipend in 1596 was just £48, and the vicarage worth a further twenty merks, the local presbytery detected only a 'miserabill congregatioun' and 'all kind of impietie for laik of exercise of the Word of God'.[46] In the absence of decisive local lay patronage, the road to improvement came only from the crown's promise to augment low stipends.

Not the least of the effects of this decisive ratio of ministers to readers in the 1560s was that it postponed for a generation a profound financial crisis for the Church. In 1581, the General

[44] Makey, *Church of Covenant*, 109-12.

[45] Ellis, 'Economic problems', 254; G. Williams, *The Welsh Church from the Conquest to the Reformation* (Cardiff, 1962), 283-4, 287.

[46] 'Extracts from the Register of the Presbytery of Glasgow, 1592-1601', *Maitland Misc.*, I, i, 79, 92-3. In the case of Lenzie, the promise was quickly fulfilled. In 1601, the Register of Assignation and Modification of Stipends recorded an increase in stipend from 253 to 600 merks; see Foster, *Church*, 156, 160.

Assembly proposed to square this uncertain circle of provision by reducing the number of parishes from over 1,000 to 600. It was against the same background of cost-cutting that the Melvillian 'New Foundation' for King's College, Aberdeen proposed cuts in the teaching staff of 57 per cent. The Melvillian reforms, both in the parishes and the universities, were indelibly marked by the spectre of severe economic retrenchment.[47] In the parishes, the Kirk drew back from the implementation of such a radical programme of rationalisation. It hirpled on, largely funded by the grant made by Queen Mary in 1566 of the smaller (and unappropriated) benefices, which provided a lifeline but not a means to fund a new-style, fully professional ministry. The steady increase after the 1580s in the proportion of ministers to readers—539 ministers and 129 readers were assigned stipends in 1596—combined with other factors to threaten to bring down the average income of rural ministers. By the 1590s, there were complaints in the Assembly that the economic problems of the Church had produced a new brain drain: young, qualified scholars were being forced abroad to find employment. It was hardly surprising that the promises made by the crown from 1590 onwards for the augmentation of stipends were so seductive.[48]

There is a tendency, by the end of the century, to describe the ministers as a discrete class, subject to similar pressures and enjoying the same *esprit de corps*.[49] The fact that this may have been more true of the generation of the 1630s than that of the 1580s and 1590s lies at the root of the problem. By the 1590s, the economic problems of the Church were multiplying. An active market in land and the prospect of the creation by the crown after the act of 1587 of temporal lordships out of the old episcopal and abbatial estates—the so-called 'lords of erection'—threatened to introduce a substantial, new element of lay patronage over many benefices.[50] For various reasons, there was greater disparity amongst the incomes of ministers in the 1590s than in the 1560s. Additionally, some ministers were subject to taxation and thus

---

[47] *BUK*, ii, 480-87; J. Kirk (ed.), *The Second Book of Discipline* (Edinburgh, 1980), 104-05; Stevenson, *King's College*, 47.

[48] It is likely that the number of readers was higher than 129 in 1596 for 900 parishes, excluding Argyll and the Isles should have been encompassed: Foster, *Church*, 153, 193. See also *BUK*, iii, 879.

[49] R. Mitchison, 'The social impact of the clergy of the reformed Kirk in Scotland', *Scotia*, vi (1982), 1-13.

[50] Kirk, *Patterns of Reform*, 424-5.

exposed to the surge in royal taxation in the 1590s.[51] Faced by such a range of pressures, some had resorted to setting their benefices in tack or feu, which provided short-term relief but made an overall remedy more difficult to find; the economic problems of the Church in the 1590s were not wholly dissimilar to those experienced in the 1530s, which had also seen rising taxes demanded by the crown.[52] The 1590s saw a clergy riven both by external pressures and by the byzantine complexity of the structure of the benefices system, which left a division within the ministry between fully and only partly beneficed clergy not unlike the gap between beneficed priests and curates or vicars which had hampered the pre-Reformation Church. By the 1630s, however, a measure of parity had been achieved, largely through the efforts of the crown's augmentation commissioners. It had been the Melvillians who claimed that minsters were poor, but it was the crown and its commissioners which had by the 1630s typically made the rural minister one of the most prosperous members of the local community.[53]

The story of the plantation of a parish ministry, when taken beyond the Reformation generation, becomes more complicated rather than less. That maxim applies to financial provision and patronage as well as to the basic appointment of a ministry in the parishes. The depth of the problems faced by the second and third generations serves to underline the thought that the truly radical solutions were found, not amongst the Melvillian establishment, but by James VI's government and episcopate. It is a conclusion which contradicts presbyterian orthodoxy but which should not surprise recent students of Jacobean Scotland.

The Melvillian party

The dynamic—or the spectre—of a Melvillian party in the Kirk has absorbed many historians' attentions. The history of the post-Reformation Church in its vital second and third generations, between the 1580s and the 1620s, has, as a result, often become focussed on a struggle between contending parties within the Kirk, at the expense of more measured consideration of the

51 J. Goodare, 'Parliamentary taxation in Scotland, 1560-1603', *SHR*, lxviii (1989), 35; idem, 'Parliament and Society', 243-4.

52 *BUK*, iii, 848-9.

53 Makey, *Church of Covenants*, 106-22; Foster, *Church*, 164-7.

progress of the basic process of catechising and evangelising Scottish society. Analysis of that struggle itself has not moved much beyond an acceptance of the terms laid down by controversialists, who mostly rewrote history after 1638. Questions such as 'How large was the Melvillian party?' or 'why did it lose influence so readily after 1597?' have been addressed only by the committed, of either camp. It has been claimed that the Melvillians numbered some 155 in the 1590s, yet 68 per cent of them were concentrated in Fife, Lothian and the Merse.[54] The membership of the Assembly in the 1580s corresponded closely to Melvillian areas.[55] A scrutiny of voting in the General Assembly and petitions addressed to parliament between 1578 and 1610 reveals that it was rare for the radical Melvillian ministers to muster more than about 55 votes though, more commonly, their support stood somewhere in the forties; on particularly controversial issues, their strength could fall to single figures.[56] Only history, as recreated in the generation of David Calderwood, would credit them in such circumstances with moral victory.

The General Assembly, in short, seems—like parliament in the same period—to have voted differently on different issues.[57] When the crown, however, went too far—as when six radical ministers were tried for treason by the privy council and imprisoned in 1605 for convening an illicit meeting of the General Assembly—a petition of protest signed by some 300 to 400 ministers resulted.[58] The protesters included some of James's newly created bishops. But a sympathy vote was far removed from the hard facts of ecclesiastical politics: these Melvillian radicals had seen just 30 of their colleagues turn out to support them at their trial earlier in the year.

Was the balance of power within the Assembly decisively shifted by the device, so diligently exploited after 1597 by James VI and Sir Patrick Murray, the 'apostle of the north',[59] of moving its meeting place to areas where the northland ministers might attend in significant numbers? Initially, the influx of ministers from the north was comparatively modest: of the 91 ministers who

---

54 Kirk, 'Melvillian Movement', 384-5, 389-90, 558-667.
55 ibid., 393.
56 See eg. Calderwood, *History*, vi, 16, 376, 491.
57 Goodare, 'Parliament and Society', ch. 1.
58 Scot, *Apologetical Narration*, 148-57.
59 Melville, *Diary*, 403.

attended the Assembly held at Holyroodhouse in 1602, just 34 per cent came from north of the Tay, whereas 43 per cent were from Fife, Lothian and the other areas to the south and east of the Tay, and a further 23 per cent came from Glasgow or the south-west.[60] Yet even then, as Melville revealingly claims of a vital vote in the Perth Assembly of February 1597, there was no in-built majority, for the Melvillian cause lost only 'by a few votes ma'.[61] The decisive factor, then as before, was a split within Melvillian ranks.[62] It was not until 1610, in the meeting held at Glasgow, that the ministers from north of the Tay attended in as large numbers as those from the south.[63] It was the faultlines within Melvillianism rather than the swamping of its meetings with compliant poodles of the court which made the General Assembly so vulnerable to royal manipulation.

One of the most striking features of the Melvillian party was its tactical incompetence amidst the *perestroika* forced upon it in the period of royal intervention between 1597 and 1610. The party had relied since the later 1570s on the device of the moderator's privy conference to arrange the agenda and the practice of taking silence in meetings of the Assembly to mean assent. Repeatedly, after 1597, its business managers were out-manoeuvred, and nowhere more regularly than in the business of the election of a moderator; at the Montrose Assembly in 1600 and the Linlithgow Assembly in 1608, it was infighting amongst Melvillian rivals which allowed in the sole court nominee.[64]

The *annus mirabilis* of 1596 began with the celebrated case of David Black, who was defended by the Assembly against a charge made by the privy council of seditious preaching. Here is another example of how the *cause celèbre* distorts reality, for the remarkable feature of Black's case was that he found much support amongst the members of the Assembly; repeatedly in the years between 1584 and 1596, hotheaded ministers had either been rebuked or left to their own devices. In 1586, for example, James Gibson, minister of Pencaitland, had been dismissed from office 'by maniest vottes' in the Assembly for a sermon which rivalled

---

[60] *BUK*, iii, 974-9; Kirk, 'Melvillian Movement', 393n.
[61] Melville, *Diary*, 403, 411.
[62] *BUK*, iii, 974-9; Kirk, 'Melvillian Movement', 393n.
[63] *BUK*, iii, 1085-91.
[64] Melville, *Diary*, 469, 754.

Black's for its seditious content.[65] The surprise in 1596 was that the Assembly did not think better of its actions.

Yet how representative was the General Assembly, either of Scottish society as a whole or of the reformed ministry? There are only a few sederunts in this period. When these become more widely available, in the 1640s, it becomes clear that even then, in the hothouse atmosphere of the Wars of the Covenant, only one minister in three ever attended the Assembly, and far fewer still attended more than once.[66] It is likely that in the period between 1560 and 1610, the proportion was slimmer still. According to Calderwood, some 84 ministers were present at meetings of the Assembly between 1578 and 1581: 27, amounting almost to a third of them, were from Lothian; a further 21 came from the universities, almost all of them from St Andrews or Glasgow; 15 came from other parts of Fife and ten from Ayrshire. James Melville, doyen of the Melvillian establishment, estimated that between 1574 (the year of Andrew Melville's return to Scotland) and 1603, a total of some 100 ministers and 1,000 lay commissioners attended some 50 meetings of the Assembly.[67] The relative figures are instructive. In little more than a generation, perhaps one in 12 of the ministry attended the General Assembly; the fact that considerably more laymen did so suggests that they attended a good deal less regularly. The Assembly fell considerably short of being a general meeting of either church or nation. The success of James VI lay more in persuading the ministers themselves than in the tactic of intruding a new phalanx of lay supporters of the court into the Assembly. At Linlithgow in December 1606, over 130 ministers attended alongside 35 lay members. At the same venue two years later, Melvillian fears were heightened by the attendance of just 40 lay supporters of the court, despite a 'very frequent' presence of ministers.[68] Why were the ministers so susceptible to royal persuasion? Presbyterian propagandists have laid a series of false trails, innuendo and black propaganda. Bribery, that familiar stock-in-trade of Scottish history, is blamed by Melville, and Calderwood, Row and Scot repeat and embroider the same

[65] ibid., 253.

[66] D. Stevenson, 'The General Assembly and the Commission of the Kirk, 1638-51', *RSCHS*, xix (1974), 59-79.

[67] Wodrow, *Biog. Colls.*, I, i, 179-80; Calderwood, *History*, iv, 527-9; Melville, *Diary*, 605.

[68] *BUK*, iii, 1022; Melville, *Diary*, 729, 754.

accusations; 50 merks, according to Row, was enough in 1610 to persuade the minister of Aberdour to succumb to the court.[69] Yet a more persuasive answer lies in the volatile circumstances of the period. In 1590, the young King (then 24 years old and just married), promised to maintain the unique doctrinal purity of the 'sincerest church in the world', to drive papistry out of his kingdom and to consider an increase in minsterial stipends. The threefold plank of Jacobean strategy was laid out. The Assembly erupted into 15 minutes of rapturous applause.[70]

The turning-point for the Melvillian cause is hard to date with precision. The surprising fact about the protest vote in the Perth Assembly against the Five Articles is that it was so modest in numbers—just 45 ministers voted against.[71] The road to eventual revolution, in 1638, has often had the effect of a spotlight, blinding historians to anything other than the question of the origins of the revolt 20 years before it happened. Reading history forwards, as it happened for most contemporaries, the more immediate question to settle is why, both in the Perth Assembly of 1618 and in the parliament of 1621, the crown was able to assemble fairly comfortable majorities?[72] The dissenters at Perth numbered no more than the standard Melvillian protest vote. The court in 1621 saw off a concerted protest, by then exacerbated by fears of new and unprecedented levels of taxation. When was it that the radical ministers managed, in the celebrated phrase of Balfour of Denmilne, to 'capture the conscience of the nation'?[73] It is sometimes claimed that the petition of grievances collected by the dissident minister, Thomas Hogg, at the time of Charles I's visit to Scotland in 1633, marked a turning-point. Yet the petition's *cri de coeur*, which would by 1638 become familiar radical property, of the overthrow of the constitution of the Kirk since 1596 and its demand for a return to its 'golden age' of 1592-6, still seems to have counted for less than the secular grievances embodied within the 'Humble Supplication' addressed to the

---

[69] ibid., 802; Calderwood, *History*, vi, 626; Row, *History*, 287-9; Scot, *Apologetical Narration*, 224.

[70] Calderwood, *History*, v, 105-06.

[71] ibid, vii, 332; I.B. Cowan, 'The Five Articles of Perth', in D. Shaw (ed.), *Reformation and Revolution* (Edinburgh, 1967), 160-77.

[72] J. Goodare, 'The Scottish parliament of 1621', *Historical Journal*, xxxvii (1994, forthcoming). I am grateful to Dr Goodare for access to this paper.

[73] Balfour, *Works*, iii, 426-7.

King by parliament.[74] The answer seems, again, to lie in the circumstances of 1637-8, later to be cast in the role of a 'second Reformation'.

A POPULAR REFORMATION?

In Scotland, it is necessary to separate the question of the patterns of a continuing Reformation—its successes, difficulties and failures in the three generations or so after 1560—from an internal struggle for control of the post-Reformation Church between two factions which did not, for the most part, disagree over doctrine and vied only over polity and the degree of contempt in which they held papistry. The capture of the 'conscience of the nation' by the radicals in 1637-8 had the effect of handing the authorised version of the Kirk's internal wranglings to David Calderwood and his heirs, but it also involved a rewriting of the process of the Reformation itself. The basic pattern that historians of late sixteenth-century reformations elsewhere might expect—of a middle-aged crisis of frustrated expectations—was transformed into the creation of a golden age cruelly snatched from the Kirk in 1596 by an Erastian state and its fellow travellers in the ministry. The task which confronts the modern historian is to try to reassemble, from contemporary evidence, the problems and stresses which bestrew the ongoing, hard work of evangelising a scattered population in a country which was distinctly localist, both in its power structures and its sense of place. Or, if the presbyterian polemicists are to be believed, two alternative set of questions pose themselves. Did Scotland in the first thirty years of its Reformation experience a more successful planting of Protestantism than elsewhere in Europe, and if so why? And what effect did the loss of power by the Melvillians in the period between 1596 and 1637 have on the progress of that Reformation?

The problem in Scotland is not that of dating the 'failure' of the Reformation, as has, for example, been notably done for Ireland,[75] but of seeking more detailed and better nuanced answers

---

[74] A.I. Macinnes, *Charles I and the Making of the Covenanting Movement, 1625-41* (Edinburgh, 1991), 129-30, 132-3.

[75] See K. Bottigheimer, 'The failure of the Reformation in Ireland: une question bien posée', *J. Ecc. Hist.*, xxxvi (1985), 196-207; A. Ford, 'The Protestant Reformation in Ireland', in C. Brady and R. Gillespie (eds.), *Natives and Newcomers: Essays on the Making of Irish Colonial Society, 1534-1641* (Dublin, 1986), 50-74; Ellis 'Economic problems'.

as to the reasons for its success, and of trying to date the phases of that emerging phenomenon. It is, however, as well to remember that the Scottish Church was distinctly aware of the tribulations of its sister church in Ireland for Scots after 1610 made up a significant number of its clerical recruits.[76] To paraphrase (and suitably amend) Karl Bottigheimer's conclusion about Ireland: the Reformation need not and might not have succeeded, and to assume otherwise is to attribute to Scotland a pervasive 'character' which it may, indeed, have acquired, but which was itself a changeable and changing product of other circumstances.[77]

How early, for example, did the new Kirk take on the character of a national church? One of the strengths of the pre-Reformation Church—amidst its many flaws—had been the fact that the Church had been the guardian of the archives of the nation; Scotland's historians had, almost without exception, been clerics.[78] The Reformation of 1559-60 began, not as a national uprising, but as a revolt of the provinces.[79] As early as October 1559, the Protestant rebels had claimed to act as the 'Church of Scotland'. Yet the first meeting, in December 1560, of what would later come to be called the 'General Assembly' was of representatives of the 'particular kirks of Scotland'.[80] The new reformed clergy, like the nobles or lairds, represented what contemporaries regarded as their own 'countries'.

One of the possible ways to address Dr Bottigheimer's question is to try to establish when the new Church was able to substitute a new religious patriotism to replace that promoted by the medieval Church. There was a notable wave of patriotic publishing in the period after 1570, initially stimulated by the Protestant printer, Robert Lekpreuik, but it took the form of the reprinting of the classic works of late medieval Scotland, most notably Blind Harry's epic poem, *The Wallace* and Barbour's *The Brus*. Some ministers, such as John Johnston and Andrew Melville himself, made minor contributions to this vogue for the writing and reading of histories of Scotland.[81] Yet their works were as secular in their outlook as George Buchanan's *History*. The first attempt to integrate the

[76] Ford, *Protestant Reformation in Ireland*, 137.
[77] See Bottigheimer, 'Failure of Reformation in Ireland', 207.
[78] D. McRoberts, 'The Scottish Church and nationalism in the 15th century', *IR*, xix (1968), 3-14.
[79] M. Lynch, *Scotland: a New History* (2nd edn., 1992), 197.
[80] Knox, *History*, i, 255; *BUK*, i, 3.
[81] Lynch, *Scotland*, 260; see Aldis, nos. 82, 98.

story of the new Church into the general history of Scotland came from the pen of William Cowper in the 1610s. Hard on his heels was David Calderwood, who first devised the later important metaphor of a 'suffering mother Church' about 1620.[82] The battle of the books of the 1620s, however, has been little studied, or has been skewed by a determined, but highly selective hunt for the origins of covenanting thought.[83] Yet out of the propaganda struggle, as in Ireland, came a new notion of a national church, which claimed to trace its descent back to the nation's first Christian missions. Both Spottiswoode and Calderwood claimed the 'culdees' and Columba as their own. The culdees, twelfth-century resisters of Rome, would become one of the less likely symbols of the Covenanting revolution.[84]

Because Scotland was still such a patchwork of distinct localities, generalisations about the spread of Protestantism in Scottish society after 1560 are inherently risky. Recent research has tended to suggest different local reformations, each progressing at its own speed, partly because of the distinctive problems which each had to face. Few, if any, localities experienced the overnight reformation undergone by St Andrews in June 1559.[85] Yet the example of this small university town, which was untypical even of burghs of a similar size, is frequently cited, not least because it possesses the only complete kirk session record for the period between 1560 and 1600.[86] The more Scotland's 'urban reformation' is studied, the more varied it has become.

---

[82] For Cowper, see Mullan, *Episcopacy*, 136-50. For Calderwood, see eg. *The Speech of the Mother Kirk of Scotland to her Children* (1620).

[83] See eg. S.A. Burrell, 'The covenant idea as a revolutionary symbol: Scotland 1596-1637', *Church History*, xxviii (1958), 338-50, and idem, 'The apocalyptic vision of the early Covenanters', *SHR*, xliii (1964), 1-24.

[84] M. Lynch, 'National identity in Ireland and Scotland, 1500-1640', in C. Bjørn, A. Grant, and K. Stringer (eds.), *Nations, Nationalism and Patriotism in the European Past* (Copenhagen, 1994), 109-36, at 114-16, 123-4. The battle between Spottiswoode and Calderwood, each claiming for his party the Celtic origins of the Kirk, was paralleled in Ireland. Counter-Reformation Irish Catholicism, orchestrated by a new Jesuit mission, was in the 1630s also rediscovering its Celtic origins, with St Patrick cast in the role of a Jesuit some 14 centuries before his time. Archbishop Ussher was alternatively claiming the Protestant Church of Ireland as the true heir of Patrick: see Ford, *Protestant Reformation in Ireland*, 221-2; S.G. Ellis, *Crown, Community and the Conflict of Cultures, 1470-1603*, (1985), 218.

[85] J. Dawson, '"The face of ane perfyt reformed kyrk": St Andrews and the early Scottish Reformation', in J. Kirk (ed.), *Humanism and Reform: the Church in Europe, England and Scotland, 1400-1643* (Oxford, 1991), 413-35.

[86] *STAKSR*; but see Dawson, 'St Andrews', 434-5, who emphasises both its untypicality and the slightness of the impact made by it on the surrounding countryside of north-east Fife.

In Perth, John Knox benefited from a distinctive history of anti-clericalism in the town and two decades of unusually sharp tension between merchants and craftsmen.[87] If Perth's reformation profited from the presence of a local Protestant noble in Lord Ruthven, who ran the burgh through a group of cadet lairds on the council, Dundee, in contrast, benefited through having none, since the conservative earl of Crawford preferred to cultivate his interests in the north rather than in Dundee itself. In the case of Aberdeen, the burgh appointed a reformed minister soon after the Reformation parliament of 1560 to assuage a Protestant minority within the town, but delayed establishing a kirk session until the eve of a royal progress in 1562, and fundamental reform was delayed until after a further visit, this time by the 'godly Regent' Morton in 1574.[88] In Edinburgh, where there was, unusually, a purge of Catholics from civic office in 1560, the new Protestant caucus brought to power by the Reformation crisis paradoxically lost power steadily to more moderate opinion in the years which followed. Edinburgh's threefold pattern of the slow growth of militant Protestantism, the crystallisation of moderate Protestant opinion and the re-emergence of Catholicism, especially amongst the craft guilds, was broken only by the Protestant regency of the earl of Moray after 1567 and, more decisively, by the civil war of 1568-73, which in its later stages had the capital as its fulcrum.[89] By the 1580s, however, Edinburgh's progress from a centre of distinct Catholic piety to a stronghold of 'precise' Protestantism— rather like that of Norwich, a town similar in size—was near-complete.[90]

If a general urban pattern existed, it resembled some aspects of the late city reformation in Germany, where religious reform also tended to come from the magistrates above rather than the

---

87 M. Verschuur, 'Merchants and craftsmen in sixteenth-century Perth', in M. Lynch (ed.), *The Early Modern Town in Scotland* (1987), 36-54.

88 See A. White, 'The impact of the Reformation on a burgh community: the case of Aberdeen', in Lynch (ed.), *Early Modern Town*, 81-101; idem, 'The Regent Morton's mission: the Reformation of Aberdeen, 1574', in this present volume.

89 M. Lynch, *Edinburgh and the Reformation* (Edinburgh, 1981), 215-22; idem, 'The Reformation in Edinburgh: the growth and growing pains of urban Protestantism', in J. Obelkevich, L. Roper and R. Samuel (eds.), *Disciplines of Faith* (1987), 283-94.

90 The different paths taken by the urban reformations in Perth and Edinburgh, which had sharply contrasting social structures, with the late starter more easily achieving a more 'precise' Protestantism, seems to parallel the patterns in Hull and Leeds: see C. Cross, *Urban Magistrates and Ministers: Religion in Hull and Leeds from the Reformation to the Civil War* (University of York, 1985).

people below, and to be linked to outside forces.[91] The lateness of the growth of significant popular Protestantism in most of Scotland's towns, which also had its counterpart in cities such as Colmar and Hagenau, surely stemmed from a simple fact which has gone largely unremarked in Scottish Reformation historiography—the flight of so many intellectuals and clergymen in the 1530s and early 1540s.[92] Most did not return. This lost generation of evangelical reformers did sterling work throughout much of northern Europe and Scandinavia, but in their homeland charismatic preachers were left in distinctly short supply, both before and after the Reformation of 1560. It was only in the second half of the 1570s that the shortfall began to be made good.

In rural areas, the progress of Protestantism was undoubtedly slower, though patterns of Reformation were no less diverse. In 1568, Lord Herries sharply contrasted the nature of reform in towns and countryside, where 'learned men are lacking'.[93] The locality where the general progress of Protestantism was most notable was Fife, but it was at its most impressive in the chain of coastal parishes, often based around a small seaport. Such was Anstruther Wester where James Melville became minister in 1586. In the larger, more remote inland and upland parishes of Fife, however, progress was distinctly slower and more mixed: the General Assembly complained in 1587, by which time all Fife's parishes had been filled for over twenty years, of infrequent attendance and the persistence of superstitious practices in many parts of the shire.[94] It is likely that Fife's reformation had had an unusual initial boost through the conversion to the Protestant ministry of 20 of the Augustinian canons of St Andrews, who were accustomed to regular service in the parish churches appropriated to the Abbey. Yet conformity, it is also likely, had its price. Ambiguous seems to be the best word to describe the process of Protestantisation in the abbot's burgh of Dunfermline, where both the burgh and its Benedictine abbey remained dominated by the same tight-knit corps of families before and after 1560. The

---

[91] K. von Greyerz, *The Late City Reformation in Germany: the Case of Colmar, 1522-1628* (Wiesbaden, 1980), 196-201.

[92] I am grateful to Dr John Durkan for generously giving me access to an unpublished paper on Scottish Protestant exiles. Part of it appeared as J. Durkan, 'Heresy in Scotland: the second phase, 1546-1558', *RSCHS*, xxiv (1992), 320-65.

[93] *CSP Scot.*, ii, no. 743.

[94] Dawson, 'St Andrews', 432-4; Kirk, *Patterns of Reform*, 153; *BUK*, ii, 719.

same family of Durie produced both the pre-Reformation abbot and the post-Reformation monk who would after 1567 become a radical Protestant minister of Edinburgh. Three other Benedictine monks became readers in the reformed Church, but also, it was reported, continued to say the office of their order into the 1580s.[95]

In the diocese of Dunkeld, the speed with which a reformed ministry was established was rather sharper than in the neighbouring diocese of Dunblane; by 1567 three-quarters of Dunkeld's 68 parishes had a Protestant ministry and by 1574 the figure had risen to no less than 90 per cent.[96] The origins of its new Protestant ministry are instructive: over 60 per cent were ex-Catholic clerics, most of them parish clergy who made up the bulk of the post-1560 reading ministry; but as in Fife, there was a substantial phalanx of Augustinian canons, who had been accustomed before 1560 to serving parish churches appropriated to their house; and the diocese, which after 1560 fell under the jurisdiction of the superintendent of Fife, based in St Andrews, experienced an unusually large influx of ministers or fresh young graduates from outside, to counter the influence of the Catholic bishop, Robert Crichton, who remained based in Dunkeld itself.[97] Here was a local reformation which depended on the determined importation of radical elements from outside but also drew on the instinct of local clergy to conform.

A somewhat different pattern was drawn in the superintendent's area immediately to the north and east. In Angus and the Mearns, both the spread of Protestant ideas amongst the gentry before 1559 and the satisfactory establishment of a reformed ministry after 1560 were more notable in Angus than in the Mearns, to its immediate north. Even so, the overall pace of change in its 91 parishes was a good deal sharper than in Dunkeld: by 1561 the new ministry there numbered 60—a remarkable figure which accounted for about a quarter of the complement of the whole Church at that time—and by 1563 it stood at 88. Here too, an early settlement of a Protestant ministry was achieved partly through the appointment of young graduates

[95] See Dilworth, 'Canons regular', in this present volume; also idem, 'Monks and ministers', 216-20.

[96] Yellowlees, 'Reformation in Dunkeld', 25-57, 278-80; cf J.R. Todd, 'The Reformation in the Diocese of Dunblane' (Edinburgh Univ. Ph.D., 1973).

[97] Yellowlees, 'Reformation in Dunkeld', 33-43, 49-50, 53-4.

to the ministry, in such numbers as to be greeted with criticism in the General Assembly, but the vast bulk of the incumbents, in contrast to Dunkeld, were local men.[98] In both these cases, recent research has confirmed a local reformation which established a notably early parish ministry. There was, however, in each case a price to be paid a generation later for early achievement. In Angus and the Mearns, 20 parishes were vacant in 1593. In Dunkeld, 19 parishes were unprovided in 1593 and matters had not improved by 1614.[99] The crisis of provision which the 1590s brought meant a long period of hard work and retrenchment to recover lost ground.

The distinctive patterns of recruitment to the ministry in the 1560s had probably increased the common dilemma faced by clergy of the second and third generations in many reformations in other parts of northern Europe. In many areas of Scotland, the new Church had quickly established a presence in the parishes and secured a basic conformity to the precepts of Protestantism. But conformity was only a first step, albeit an essential one to take. The Reformation had come about largely through a network of personal contacts, between Protestant lairds and preachers, within the circle of kin or friendship or the ambit of common trade or profession. In Angus, its success largely stemmed from the degree to which it conformed to a deeply conservative 'lairdly culture'.[100] In taking on what Knox called a 'public face' after 1560, the Church was confronted by a rather different problem—of how to extend to the many what had characteristically been the intense conviction of the few.[101] In Angus, which saw not only a tight-knit circle of Protestant lairds before 1559 but even perhaps also the establishment of a 'privy kirk', conviction was none the less confined to about 30 lairds; the shire as a whole had some 300.[102] Regular attendance after 1560 was, for most ordinary parishioners, probably largely confined to the rites of passage and an

[98] Bardgett, *Scotland Reformed*, 88-9, 95.

[99] *BUK*, iii, 803-04; Kirk, *Patterns of Reform*, 468.

[100] Bardgett, *Scotland Reformed*, 157.

[101] Cf R. Whiting, *The Blind Devotion of the People* (Cambridge, 1989), 171; C. Haigh, (ed.), *The English Reformation Revised* (Cambridge, 1987), 213-14; See also Cameron, *European Reformation*, 415-16, but his treatment of Scotland, at 385-8, is distinctly conservative and at variance with his treatment of other reformations.

[102] Lairds and magnates in Angus and the Mearns are listed in F.D. Bardgett, 'Faith, Families and Factions: the Scottish Reformation in Angus and the Mearns' (Edinburgh Univ. Ph.D., 1987), 725-63.

annual communion; in the small parish of Monifeith, to the east of Dundee, where a reformed ministry had been established since at least 1561, it has been estimated that perhaps 10 per cent of the congregation partook of the weekly diet of worship and preaching in the 1570s. Attendance improved, though only marginally, in the 1580s.[103] Irregular or occasional attendance was not a feature of post-Reformation parish life which was confined to the Highlands. It probably obtained in many, if not most, Lowland rural parishes for some generations after 1560—just as before.[104]

The nature of conformity, which has so exercised historians of the reformations in both Ireland and England, has scarcely been examined in the context of the Reformation settlement in Scotland. Surprise has sometimes been expressed about the willingness of Catholic nobles and lairds to promote or at least not to block the settlement of a Protestant ministry, but this was paralleled in England, even in parts of the north.[105] Conformity, even if it was achieved in Scotland 'with what looks like remarkable speed and ease',[106] brought a different set of problems in its wake for the next generation of Protestant ministers. As they would characteristically have viewed it, conformity implied obedience rather than conviction, and if conviction did not follow, conformity might rapidly dissipate.[107] The surveys made by the General Assembly in the period between 1590 and 1616—ranging from ringing condemnations of the ignorance of the common sort and the lack of spiritual zeal of the landed classes to alarming diagnoses of the recurrence of popular, superstitious practices or the actual spread of Catholicism amongst the nobility—were reflections of a crisis of morale within the ministry itself. They need to be considered both as part of an agonising self-analysis and as reports from the front of the battle against godlessness or papistry. Such an approach may also help explain the violent swings of mood from one Assembly to another.[108] In reality, the danger may well have been exaggerated, for the Jesuits

[103] ibid., 616-17, 621, 689; idem, *Scotland Reformed*, 158-9.

[104] Cf. J. Kirk, 'The Jacobean Church, 1567-1625', in L. MacLean (ed.), *The Seventeenth Century in the Highlands* (Inverness, 1986), 41.

[105] Whiting, *Blind Devotion*, 266.

[106] Kirk, *Patterns of Reform*, 153.

[107] See N. Canny, 'Why the Reformation failed in Ireland: Une question mal posée', *J. Ecc. Hist.*, xxx (1979), 449-50; Bottigheimer, 'Failure of Reformation', 206; Whiting, *Blind Devotion*, 288; Haigh, *English Reformation Revised*, 178-9, 182-3.

[108] See *Catholic Narratives*, 361-74 (1592); *Estimates of the Scottish Nobility during the Minority of James the Sixth*, ed. C. Rogers (Grampian Club, 1873); *CSP Scot.*, ix,

in the Scottish mission chose to target the nobility for reconversion rather than attempt a broader offensive in areas where Protestantism had as yet made only a marginal impact.[109]

Despair, frustration or introspection became the hallmarks of the clergy of the second and third generations after 1560. A rising tide of complaints flooded the records of meetings of the General Assembly and presbyteries, which, taken together, form a devastating commentary on the presumption of the early success of the Reformation at achieving much more than conformity, even in the brightest corners of the land.[110] The first public explosion of anger and frustration seems to have surfaced in the General Assembly of 1587, where there were long and loud complaints, not only about the Catholic threat in the north but about the faults and economic problems of the Church in notably Protestant areas such as the presbyteries of Fife, Dalkeith and Ayr.[111] It is worth noting that the petition of protest from the Assembly to the King was delivered by five prominent ministers—two of them would accept a bishopric by 1600.[112] Another petitioner was Robert Pont, a veteran of the 1560s and one of the few of the leading ministers in the Assembly to have experienced the trials of the godly in the north; for Pont, who had refused the offer of a bishopric in 1587, this was the age of sacrilege.

Pont, too, was the moderator of the Assembly which met in March 1596 to hear a wide-ranging lament about the 'Common Corruptions of all Estates within this Land'; it highlighted 'an universall coldness, want of zeall, ignorance, contempt of the word, ministrie and sacraments'; even where knowledge existed, there was 'no sense or feeling, evidenced by the want of familie exercises, prayer and the word'.[113] If there was an 'evangelical revival' in 1596, it had an air of desperation about it. The evidence, however, is confined to that heartland of Melvillianism, the presbytery of St Andrews, which arranged a revivalist-style gathering of lairds and burgesses from its parishes to subscribe the

---

no. 365; x, no. 35. Cf Whiting, *Blind Devotion*, 267; Cameron, *European Reformation*, 411-12.

[109] Durkan, 'William Murdoch', 5; *Catholic Narratives*, 147, 173, 175-7. Cf Haigh, *English Reformation Revised*, 178-9.

[110] See eg. the records for the General Assemblies of 1587, 1593, 1608 and 1616 (*BUK*, ii, 715-24; iii, 803-04, 1051-6, 1117-29).

[111] ibid, ii, 704-06, 716-24.

[112] ibid, ii, 704.

[113] Wodrow, *Biog. Colls.*, I, i, 190-91; Robert Pont, *Against Sacrilege*; Row, *History*, 172-3.

covenant. Edinburgh declined to follow its example. From the perspective of the radicals of 1638, this was the birth of the protest movement which would culminate in the National Covenant. To contemporaries, it was the public confession of an ecclesiastical establishment which seemed to be losing its grip, both over the Church and the state of religion in the parishes.[114]

It was the Assembly of March 1596 which agreed, against the background of an invasion scare to aid the Catholic earls, to the remarkable stratagem of parish ministers and kirk sessions becoming muster masters of the Jacobean state.[115] The offer of joint action by godly prince and godly people against the spectre of Counter-Reformation papistry was a welcome outlet for a church militant, which was otherwise confronted by seemingly intractable problems of economics, ignorance or indifference. The only systematic offensive made by the Church in the first half of the 1590s in the more difficult battle against mere conformity came in the larger burghs, where there were proposals to split into 'competent congregatiouns' the historic single burgh parish, which, because of population increase, had grown far too large for effective policing.[116] One result was the beginnings of a more systematic provision for discipline; in Glasgow the session first began to make regular examination of parishioners and children, and in 1603, in view of the 'ignorance of the inhabitants', it established it on a weekly basis.[117]

What were the vital instruments of evangelisation? Exposure to godly preaching, the vital drip-feed of Bible, psalter and catechism, and the experience of a new community of reformed worship were the ideal constituent parts of evangelism, but in few places outside St Andrews or some of the larger burghs was there a concerted or early offensive.[118] Preaching remained in short supply in a church which until the 1580s had only one minister to every four parishes,[119] and charismatic preachers, as in England,

---

[114] E.J. Cowan, 'The making of the National Covenant', in J. Morrill, *The Scottish National Covenant in its British Context, 1638-51* (Edinburgh, 1990), 71, 85n; Calderwood, *History*, v, 433-7.

[115] *BUK*, iii, 860.

[116] Calderwood, *History*, v, 172-3.

[117] Wodrow, *Biog. Colls.*, II, ii, 30.

[118] Dawson, 'St Andrews', 414, 434-5.

[119] Robert Pont was especially scathing about the 'great paucity of ministers ... for some years after the Reformation': Wodrow, *Biog. Colls.*, I, i, 164; II, ii, 2; see also F.D. Bardgett, '"Four parische kirkis to ane preicheir"', *RSCHS*, xxii (1986), 195-209.

usually remained in urban pulpits.[120] The difference when a popular preacher did become available could be dramatic. When Robert Bruce (1555-1631), whose sermons from his pulpit in Edinburgh were by 1600 bestsellers in print, was exiled to Inverness in 1622, he attracted listeners from as far away as Ross and Sutherland.[121]

For the hard-pressed readers, who comprised the bulk of rural parish clergy until the 1580s, there were, ironically, fewer instruments of evangelisation available for some time after 1560 than before—unless the decorated walls and stained glass windows of the pre-Reformation era, the instruction manuals for a still largely illiterate peasantry, survived, as they did, for example at the church of Fowlis Easter in Angus.[122] In their place, were the new psalters and catechisms—at least for the literate, who by the end of the sixteenth century probably comprised 25 per cent or less of adult males in a typical rural parish.[123] There is considerable doubt, however, that printed books quickly made up the leeway. An act of parliament of 1579 decreed that every gentleman householder who enjoyed annual rents of £200 or more and every burgess or yeoman who had £500 in lands or goods should own a Bible (the Arbuthnot edition of 1579) and a Psalm book.[124] This was hardly a wide constituency. The average wage of an urban master craftsman was about £40; the testaments only of middling merchants or professional men would have reached the threshold of £500. The average net estate of larger tenant farmers and small feuars (the beneficiaries of the secularisation of monastic lands)

---

120 Whiting, *Blind Devotion*, 247-51, 251.

121 *The Life of Mr Robert Blair* (Wodrow Soc., 1848), 39n; *Sermons by the Rev Robert Bruce* (Wodrow Soc., 1843), 132.

122 T.S. Robertson, 'The church of Fowlis Easter', *Trans. Ab. Eccles. Soc.*, i (1888), 39-42.

123 R. Houston, 'The literacy myth', *Past and Present*, xcvi (1983), 87, 88.

124 *APS*, iii, 139, 211. Even parish churches had difficulty in acquiring copies of the Arbuthnot Bible: D. Shaw, *The General Assemblies of the Church of Scotland, 1560-1600* (Edinburgh, 1964), 228. It cost a prohibitive £4 13s 4d (Calderwood, *History*, viii, 204), rather more than the average collection at annual communion at Monifeith: Bardgett, *Scotland Reformed*, 158. A pre-publication 'offer', at a price of £5, was forced on parish churches in order to subsidise printing costs; the fact that 6s 8d per copy was set aside to cover the cost of collection from parishes may further indicate the hazards of the venture. For details of its publication, see R. Dickson and J.P. Edmond, *Annals of Scottish Printing* (Cambridge, 1890), 283-7, 314-16; P.B. Watry, 'Sixteenth Century Printing Types and Ornaments of Scotland with an Introductory Survey of the Scottish Book Trade' (Oxford D.Phil., 1992), 43-6.

was some £300. Only lairdly society and the upper reaches of the middling sort in the towns—perhaps one urban household in 20—would have been affected by the provisions of this act. It was hardly surprising that editions of the Bible had to be heavily subsidised or that the printing of a Scottish edition was a highly speculative venture, even with a subsidy.[125] Psalters may have begun to proliferate, but there is little sign that this act managed to promote the sale of Bibles. As in England, there is little evidence of extensive Bible reading before the seventeenth century. It was not until the 1640s that Bibles—more usually New Testaments—began to feature in Edinburgh booksellers' inventories in any numbers.[126]

The psalter and the catechism rather than the Bible were the most common, blunt instruments of evangelisation until the mid-seventeenth century. Although the Edinburgh bookseller, Henry Charteris, had fewer than 100, mostly expensive Bibles in stock in 1599, he had 5,400 copies of Calvin's catechism in its simple question and answer form, priced at 2d and intended for use in the 'English' schools which taught children up to the age of seven or eight, as well as 3,300 psalm books of various sorts. By 1645, James Bryson, another Edinburgh bookseller, had no fewer than 5,000 copies of the New Testament in stock and, perhaps more significantly, a further 2,000 copies of a cheaper, abridged children's version.[127] Yet the difficulties which afflicted all reformers, Protestant and Catholic, in what was the age of the catechism,[128] were unnecessarily added to by the Church itself. There was no common, prescriptive catechism after 1560, although Calvin's remained the most commonly used. There was recurrently voiced the complaint that the Kirk need a new 'easy, short compendious catechism' for instructing the 'common sort' which could be made obligatory to own.[129] The history of the period from 1580

[125] M. Sanderson, 'The Edinburgh merchants in society, 1570-1603: the evidence of their testaments', in I.B. Cowan and D. Shaw (eds.), *The Renaissance and Reformation in Scotland* (Edinburgh, 1983), 183-4; idem, *Mary Stewart's People: Life in Mary Stewart's Scotland* (Edinburgh, 1987), 116; Lynch, *Edinburgh*, 52-3, 65n; Watry, 'Sixteenth Century Printing Types', 43.

[126] Whiting, *Blind Devotion*, 190, 183; Lynch, *Scotland*, 258. See 'Collection of the wills of printers and booksellers in Edinburgh between the years 1577 and 1687', *Bann. Misc.*, ii, 259; but cf 243 (Andrew Hart, d.1622), where the inventory does not distinguish New Testaments from other 'buikis for skuilles' in English.

[127] *Bann. Misc.*, ii, 224-5, 259.

[128] J. Bossy, *Christianity in the West, 1400-1700* (Oxford, 1985), 119-20; Collinson, *Religion of Protestants*, 232-3.

onwards is littered with publishing failures, notably John Craig's *Shorte Summe of the Whole Catechisme*, first printed in 1581, which was designed for use by families and in schools, and James Melville's privately financed version, which cost him 500 merks to print and lost him 400.[130] The *Aberdeen Catechism* of 1618, produced after royal initiative and recommended for compulsory use by all families, fared no better.[131]

The publishing history of various editions of different psalters is no less complex than that of the catechism, but success here is likely to have come earlier, for many psalms were based on already well-known tunes. The origins of many of the Wedderburn ballads lie in the 1540s; their popularity before the 1570s is for some historians something of an article of faith but it remains a largely unproven one.[132] By 1613, Robert Blair took his first communion with his Psalm book in his hand. James Melville, in contrast, even though he was brought up in Protestant Angus in the 1560s, was not exposed to the *Gude and Godly Ballads* of the Wedderburn brothers of Dundee until about 1570, when he was twelve and attending grammar school in Montrose.[133] The earliest evidence of popular enthusiasm for singing of the psalms dates from the late 1570s or early 1580s and it comes again from towns.[134] For the conforming rather than the enthusiasts, the psalms probably provided the necessary spoonful of sugar to make the catechetical practice of 'lining'—the rehearsing by a precentor of a metrical psalm, line by line, followed by the congregation—go down. It was a refinement of the practice, which first seems to have developed in larger burghs such as Aberdeen, of readers or school pupils reciting the Ten Commandments, Creed or questions and answers from the catechism for the benefit of 'commoun ignorant people and servands', who repeated in chorus. This was the art of catechising at its most rudimentary, for the reprobate amongst the 'ruder sort', and it seems, as in England, to have been a development of the first decades of the

---

129 *BUK*, iii, 1127.

130 Aldis, 176; *STAKSR*, ii, 848; Melville, *Diary*, 443; Foster, *Church*, 130-31; H. Bonar, *Catechisms of the Scottish Reformation* (1866), 273-85.

131 *BUK*, iii, 1127; Foster, *Church*, 131.

132 A.F. Mitchell, *The Gude and Godlie Ballatis* (SRS, 1897) prints an edition of 1567. A recently discovered copy of an earlier edition of 1565 is being prepared for publication in the STS series by Professor A.A. MacDonald.

133 *Life of Blair*, 7; Melville, *Diary*, 22-3; G. Donaldson, *Faith of the Scots* (1990), 85.

134 Cowan, *Scottish Reformation*, 157-8.

seventeenth century, by which time disillusionment with the persuasive powers of preaching amongst the common sort had firmly set in.[135]

The new rite of communion, in which ordinary bread and wine was served to the congregation sitting at a table by elders and minister alike, was the most striking of all the liturgical changes effected in 1560. Its celebration was a visible and physical demonstration of the congregation of believers.[136] There can be little doubt of the profound spiritual effect which it could have. Both James Melville and Robert Blair, in their autobiographies, give a graphic description of the impact which their first communion, taken at the age of twelve, made on them. These, however, are again accounts of the converted, the 'covenanted and sealed servant', rather than the conforming.[137] Yet, even for those who merely conformed, communion was undoubtedly the climax of the liturgical year.[138]

In most rural areas, communion in practice remained a once-a-year event after 1560, just as it had been before. In 1616, the General Assembly was forced to repeat its recommendation of 1560 that communion should be celebrated four times a year in burghs and twice a year elsewhere.[139] It is well known, from the records of the Synod of Argyll, that communion was very infrequently celebrated, if it all, in many parts of Argyll and the Isles in the 1630s and 1640s.[140] There is a good deal of evidence, however, to suggest that, even outside the Highlands, practice fell well short of the norm set by the Assembly, both in town and countryside. In Perth, communion was celebrated twice a year only from 1595, when a second minister was appointed.[141] In Glasgow, communion seems generally to have been held only once a year until 1631, and twice yearly from then until 1638.[142] In Ayr, there were complaints made to the Assembly in 1587 that petty feuds induced some parishioners to refuse the Christian

135 W.D. Maxwell, *A History of the Worship in the Church of Scotland* (Oxford, 1955), 110-11; *Aberdeen Ecc. Recs.*, 38 (for 1604).

136 See Dawson, 'St Andrews', 422-3.

137 Melville, *Diary*, 23; *Life of Blair*, 6-7.

138 See Bardgett, *Scotland Reformed*, 158-9; communion offerings were commonly ten times greater than the average weekly collection.

139 *BUK*, iii, 1128; Calderwood, *History*, viii, 106.

140 D.C. MacTavish (ed.), *Minutes of the Synod of Argyll, 1639-1651* (SHS, 1943), see eg. 36, 451.

141 *Spot. Misc.*, ii, 272-3, 311.

142 Wodrow, *Biog. Colls.*, II, ii, 27-30.

fellowship of communion.[143] Infrequency of communion was a standard feature of the frequent complaints in the General Assembly about the inability of the Church to evangelise the godless, far-flung corners of the land; in 1608, for example, it was claimed that in many parts of Ross and Caithness as well as in parts of the Borders, such as Annandale and Eskdale, communion had never been celebrated since 1560.[144] In circumstances such as these, the stratagem of making communion a test of conformity for suspected Catholics, as was attempted by the privy council in 1629, made considerable sense.[145] Yet, even where communion was established, the Assembly remained repeatedly troubled by the 'irreverent behaviour of the vulgar sort' at its celebration. In that sense, little, it seems, had changed since similar injunctions of Catholic provincial councils in the 1550s.[146]

Two last evangelical instruments need to be considered—schools and the family itself. The scattered evidence available tends to yield up conflicting impressions. The reformers in 1560 had understandably been wary of becoming too dependent on the household as a medium of instruction. Yet, in places where Protestantism had been nourished before 1559 in the houses of nobles or lairds, the habit proved hard to break. The Ayrshire laird, Robert Campbell of Kinzeancleuch, a convinced Protestant since the 1540s, supervised a daily examination of his own family and a weekly one of his servants in the 1560s.[147] The enthusiasm of the nobility for godly exercise, however, perceptibly waned in the next generation.[148] It is difficult to discover much about the teaching of the basic precepts of Protestantism within the households of the common sort other than by noting the persistent suspicion of the Kirk that it was seriously deficient.[149]

The natural failings of the household obliged the Kirk to put more weight on its own supervision of the provision of basic schooling, in the various kinds of vernacular and 'adventure' schools. But here, too, there lay gaps in the programme of cat-

---

143 *BUK*, ii, 722.

144 ibid., iii, 1061; Calderwood, *History*, vi, 774.

145 *RPC* (2nd series), iii, pp. xi-xviii, 186-8; Foster, *Church*, 191n.

146 *BUK*, iii, 1141; see 'Register of the Kirk Session of Stirling', *Maitland Misc.*, i, 129-30, for one such case in 1597 of 'rash and sudden cuming to the tabill, spilling of wyne', and 'thrusting and shouting' after communion. Cf. Patrick, *Statutes*, 175-6; Bossy, *Christianity*, 68-71, 128.

147 Calderwood, *History*, iii, 312.

148 Brown, 'Christian magistrate', 579.

149 See eg. *BUK*, iii, 873.

echising of the young. Although the Kirk often acknowledged that the minds of children had to be captured by the age of six, by which time they should be able to recite the Creed, Lord's Prayer and Ten Commandments by heart,[150] the means usually lay in the schoolroom rather than within the community of worship. Often, as in Glasgow, children under the age of eight were discouraged from attending services because of the disruption they caused.[151] And the bulk of children who attended some kind of school would leave by the age of eight or nine to begin work, with some seven or eight years to pass before they received their first communion. For the favoured élite of boys who attended grammar school, there was a closer supervision of their spiritual development. Those such as James Melville, son of an Angus laird and minister, who was sent away from home to not one but two grammar schools in succession, took first communion, by contrast, as they neared the end of their schooling at the age of twelve.[152] The two-tier education system, to an extent, virtually enshrined the contrast between the truly converted and the merely conformist.

Until recently, a pessimistic view was taken of the state of Scottish schooling outside the towns, partly based on the seemingly damning returns made by parishes in 1627, complaining of the lack of schools or their poor state.[153] A new survey, using more extensive record, has suggested that there may have been about 700 schools in early seventeenth-century Scotland, even if they were spread unevenly across the country's 1,000 or so parishes.[154] A significant number, however, were not parish schools, but may have been based in the houses of lairds. The issue for the Kirk was thus partly about the foundation of new schools but also about exercising proper control over existing schools; the Assembly was particularly anxious in 1616, the year of the act of the privy council ordering the establishment of a school in every parish, to extend control over sewing and other girls' schools.[155] Little is

---

150 ibid., iii, 1052, 1127; Spottiswoode, *History*, iii, 193-4.

151 Wodrow, *Biog. Colls.*, II, ii, 17.

152 Melville, *Diary*, 15-23.

153 *Reports on the State of Certain Parishes in Scotland, 1627* (Maitland Club, 1835).

154 J. Durkan, 'Education: the laying of fresh foundations', in J. MacQueen (ed.), *Humanism in Renaissance Scotland* (Edinburgh, 1990), 123-30; a collated list of schools in 16th and 17th century Scotland, made by Dr Durkan, is forthcoming in the SRS series.

155 *BUK*, iii, 1120; Foster, *Church*, 194-7; Lynch, *Scotland*, 259.

known of the schoolmasters of this period, although some also acted as readers. They, however, were probably the most vital instruments of all in laying the foundations of a popular Protestantism. Their achievements, however, are necessarily to be measured in decades rather than years.

THE CONSOLIDATION OF THE REFORMATION

Any analysis of the consolidation of the Scottish Reformation during the complex reign of James VI (1567-1625) needs, above all else, to grasp the nettle that society was changing, but complexity was its hallmark rather than simple speed. How quickly or early did the new reformed Church, as has recently been claimed, establish via the chain of church courts a new set of links between centre and localities, which was not replicated in secular jurisdictions?[156] Alternatively, how early is it possible to sustain the claim that the parish, with its kirk session, replaced the barony, with its baron court, as the natural centre of local life?[157] The second claim seems easier to sustain than the first, although the higher survival rate of kirk session records over those of baron courts may still make the inference hazardous. In many cases, the ethos of the session was, in any case, derived from that of the baron court, which was the natural, local institution to serve as a model.[158]

The links between kirk sessions and General Assembly were occasional rather than regular, even after the establishment of prebyteries. It was to remedy this weakness that informal commissions of the General Assembly, forerunners of a more formal body which would emerge in the complex years of the Wars of the Covenant of the 1640s, developed in the later 1580s; a small team of influential Melvillian ministers regularly met in Edinburgh to lobby the court, privy council and meetings of parliament or

---

[156] J. Wormald, *Court, Kirk and Community: Scotland, 1488-1625* (1981), 132-9, 165. The less frequent meeting of the General Assembly between 1597 and 1618, and in places other than the capital, entirely changed the nature of the contact between the Assembly and the lesser courts of the Church.

[157] ibid., 138, 139.

[158] Bardgett, *Scotland Reformed*, 96, 102, shows that this was the case in the parish of Monifeith. There, too, the term 'session' was not used before 1581, with 'Assembly' being preferred.

convention.[159] The commissioners to the General Assembly were more than a pressure group; they also for a time in the early 1590s became the agents of the state. They were given blank signet commissions by the privy council to enforce a range of laws, including poor relief, witchcraft and even the deprivation of unsuitable ministers.[160] These arrangements depended, not on a separation of the 'two kingdoms', but on their ability to confer amicably. James Melville, in writing his *Diary*, which was a sustained essay on the perils of Erastianism, found it difficult to justify his own two years of 'courting', which came to an end only in December 1596.[161]

This *modus vivendi* scarcely seems to have survived the fracas of 1596 in a viable form. The famous confrontation between James VI and Andrew Melville at Falkland Palace in September 1596, when the militant reformer tugged the King's sleeve to remind him that he was 'but God's sillie vassall', was an outburst which took place during one of the regular, intimate meetings between representatives of the two kingdoms. It was out of the breakdown of this *modus vivendi* that there emerged a doctrinal theory of a separation of the powers, which was an exaggeration of practical reality.[162] What Melville—or the crisis of 1596—had done was to remove himself from the inner circle of court and privy council. Removing themselves from the court was for the 'forward' ministers a last, futile gesture of protest; in that respect, they were no different from nobles.

The Melvillians were replaced, in royal counsel, by other ministers, who were very different from the much-criticised 'tulchan bishops' appointed in the 1570s. Most were gifted and much respected within the Church and many had a record of militancy. These new civil servants of the Jacobean state were part of a broader royal campaign of more regular intervention in the localities.[163] New thinking about the nature of civil power would seem to suggest that the extent of the links which by the 1590s emanated from privy council or parliament to the localities have been much underestimated: commissions from both bodies

---

[159] D. Stevenson, 'General Assembly and the Commission of the Kirk', 63-4; Makey, 'Church of the Covenants', 88-93.

[160] Goodare, 'Parliament and Society', 125-6; *RPC*, iv, 753-4.

[161] Melville, *Diary*, 328-9.

[162] ibid., 370-71; Lynch, *Scotland*, 228.

[163] Goodare, 'Parliament and Society', ch. 3.

granted power to enact legislation at local level ranging from university reform to a witch hunt. The much-vaunted 'Golden Act' of 1592, which restored the liberties of the Church, did so, in effect, under licence from parliament. The granting of commissions from the secular arm to the religious blurred the boundaries between the two kingdoms. The initiative was passing from ecclesiastical to secular jurisdiction. At stake was control of the parish, as the local agency of legislation and regulation. The consolidation of the Reformation, in short, had to take place, for good or bad, in the context of a closer working relationship between Church and state.

By the 1590s, a complex social tapestry had been woven which added fresh complications to the relationship between the Church and its natural patrons, the greater and lesser magistrates, of various kinds. Some generalisations can safely be made. The royal court, which had briefly flowered as a model of Calvinist piety in the second half of the 1580s, was by 1596 giving the Assembly cause for complaint, and criticism of it from the pulpit was the pretext for the fracas of December 1596.[164] Its removal to London, nevertheless, left a vacuum. Godly lesser magistrates were, the Melvillians themselves acknowledged, in distinctly short supply after the execution of that 'pearl of godliness', the earl of Gowrie, in 1584 and the death of the earl of Angus in 1588.[165] Both the Assembly and English Protestant diplomats were so alarmed at the prospect of a revival of Catholicism amongst the nobility as to commission a series of surveys of their religious leanings.[166] The initiative in the localities, however, had by now passed to lesser landed families.

The history of the emergence of a popular, rural-based Protestantism, in areas such as Fife and the so-called 'radical southwest',[167] during the course of the first four decades of the seventeenth century has as yet hardly been explained.[168] One example must suffice, but it may be instructive. In Stewarton, in northern Ayrshire, a parish which had had a reader since at least 1567 and a

---

164 Calderwood, *History*, v, 408-09.

165 Melville, *Diary*, 315; Brown, 'Christian magistrate', 557-8; Lynch, 'Calvinism', 246-7.

166 See Rogers, *Estimates of Nobility*.

167 G. Donaldson, 'Scotland's conservative north', *TRHS*, 5th ser., xvi (1966), 65-79.

168 But see R.A. Bensen, 'South-west Fife and the Scottish Revolution: the Presbytery of Dunfermline, 1633-1652' (Edinburgh Univ. M. Litt., 1978).

(non-resident) minister since 1574, a religious revival seems to have been generated in the early 1620s by a visiting preacher; it spread, via the weekly market centre of Irvine which was some nine miles away, to other parishes in Cunningham. It was the repeat, some fifty years later, of a process of the dissemination of ideas through a network of natural communications which is usually held to have brought about the initial spread of Protestantism. Here, however, that process may have begun only after the licensing of Stewarton as a market centre in 1623; it was the seventeenth century, it needs to be remembered by ecclesiastical historians, which saw the emergence of a new rural infrastructure of market centres in the form of burghs of barony or regality, which must have provided a more efficient communications network not available to the first two or three generations of Protestant reformers.[169] The fact that a Stewarton 'revival' was necessary in the 1620s is a reflection of the 'glass ceiling' which the first Reformation had come up against by 1590.

The dynamics of the process of parish regeneration which took place in the early seventeenth century are likely to have been complicated, and to have involved bishops as well as 'precise' ministers. William Cowper, bishop of Galloway between 1612 and his death in 1619, who bore the brunt of much presbyterian venom in print, claimed, with some justice, that it had been he and his fellow bishops who first planted kirks in parts of Galloway, Annandale and the Borders.[170] That was a striking achievement, at least measured by the much more modest efforts of the Jacobean church in the remote, upland regions of Ireland in the same period,[171] but a late conversion, combined with feelings of social tension peculiar to the remote south-west,[172] may well have released popular forces outside the control of the ecclesiastical establishment. A new generation of radical ministers, such as Samuel Rutherford, who moved to the parish of Anwoth in Kirkcudbrightshire in 1627, inherited a society brought to the brink of a new populist Protestantism.

If the later history of Scotland's rural reformation is little

---

169 *Life of Blair*, 19; see Kirk, *Patterns of Reform*, 152. Stewarton had had a reader since at least 1567. Shotts was another fairly remote, upland parish which experienced a 'revival', also through Monday market preaching, in 1630: G.S. Pryde, *The Burghs of Scotland: A Critical List* (Glasgow, 1965), 313; J.K. Hewison, *The Covenanters*, 2 vols. (Glasgow, 1913), i, 205.

170 Mullan, *Episcopacy*, 125, 136.

171 Ellis, 'Economic problems', 248, 255-6.

172 Makey, *Church of the Covenants*, 166-78.

known, there is already by the 1580s ample evidence, in some of the larger towns, of a popular, grass-roots Protestantism, which was increasingly gaining a radical edge. In this process, experience of office in the kirk session seems to have been significant. In the Edinburgh general session, by the 1610s, humble master craftsmen or small merchants (who usually served as deacons) were willing to risk debating Scripture and the perils of Erastianism with their social betters.[173] Yet real conviction, as distinct from conformity, was probably still confined to the minds or households of the few rather than the many. James Melville complained bitterly that the novel phenomenon of the fast, first ordered by the Edinburgh presbytery in 1590 when the King was away in Denmark, was observed only in the 'houses of the godly' in the capital after his return.[174]

In some burghs, there were also signs, as in England, of a new anti-clericalism, which found different ways of manifesting itself: in Perth, for example, accusations of libel against minister, reader or session clerk were common from the 1590s on; so was leaving in the middle of the Sunday service before the blessing and other violations of the Sabbath.[175] In part, these reflected a popular resentment of the more fortunate urban ministers, who were accused of 'living like lairds'; but there were also traces of a new conflict between minister and kirk session on the one hand and the town council and burgh establishment on the other, anxious to lay claim to some of its old, accustomed rights of ecclesiastical patronage. Major market centres such as Perth had much to lose from strict Sabbatarianism, which would have precluded the transport of goods or animals to a Monday market. The fact that burgh councils had shed the influence of nobles, who were in 1609 banned by parliament from holding burgh office, made the tension over jurisdiction within towns all the sharper.[176]

Yet it was also in the late 1580s and the 1590s that a new consolidation of the urban reformation can first be traced. It took the form of an increasing determination on the part of kirk sessions and presbytery to grasp the nettle of religious discipline. It took place—and this was part of the explanation for its increasing urgency—against a background of sharply rising popu-

---

173 ibid., 155-6; Lynch, 'Calvinism', 240-41.
174 Melville, *Diary*, 277.
175 *The Chronicle of Perth, 1210-1668* (Maitland Club, 1831), 9, 63, 72, 80, 90.
176 Lynch, *Early Modern Town*, 64-5.

lations in the larger burghs. The expectations of some historians—both Protestant and Catholic—of the efficiency of kirk session discipline in the years immediately following the Reformation seem inflated.[177] It was relatively easy to police the incorporated guilds, for there the guild's own council as well as the officers of burgh and session could pursue miscreants. Yet that covered, at best, only a half of adult males in large towns; journeymen, day labourers, unincorporated craftsmen, such as the Edinburgh candlemaker eventually caught in 1575 who admitted never having attended communion since 1560,[178] could more easily evade the system of communion tickets which had evolved since the Reformation. Masterless women, who may have made up some 18 per cent of all households, were an even greater concern to kirk sessions than masterless men; the visitations established in Glasgow after 1600 were instructed to pay particular attention to 'solitary women'.[179] Ecclesiastical historians may well also have substantially underestimated the mobility of the urban and rural labour force; at harvest time, Perth had to accommodate an extra 2,000 men and women labourers in the 1580s.[180]

It is thought that there was a general increase in Scotland's population of some 50 per cent in the 'long century' between 1500 and 1650. In some of the larger towns, however, both the scale and the speed of population increase sharply exceeded that. The prospect of ministers having to cope with congregations of 3,000 souls or more, turning churches into sheepfolds for the ignorant, first became a matter for serious concern in the 1580s.[181] The Edinburgh presbytery in 1592 made a census of the adult communicants in the capital and found exactly 8,000, sufficient, it felt, for eight separate model parishes rather than the ad hoc, fourfold division of the historic single parish of St Giles, with which the burgh had muddled through since 1560. By 1598, the presbytery settled for four, separate parishes, each with its

---

[177] See Kirk, *Patterns of Reform*, 282-3; A. Ross, 'Reformation and repression', in McRoberts, *Essays*, 388-96.

[178] SRO, CH2/450/1, MS Buik of the General Kirk of Edinburgh, 1574-5, f.67r.

[179] Wodrow, *Biog. Colls.*, II, ii, 8. See also 'Register of Kirk Session of Stirling', 129 (1597), 134 (1600), 459 (1621), for suspicion of single female householders.

[180] MS Perth Kirk Session Register, NLS, Adv. MS 31.1.1, 23 Nov. and 14 Dec. 1584.

[181] Lynch, *Scotland*, 171, 173; Melville, *Diary*, 188.

own minister.[182] Edinburgh's population increased by some 60 per cent between then and the 1630s, but in the south-east parish, where building of the new Tron Church began in 1636, the number of households more than doubled over the same period.[183] The appointment of a second minister to Perth in 1595 provoked ambitious plans in the session for a weekly visitation of households; not surprisingly, in a town with some 4,000 souls, the reality fell far short of that.[184] In Glasgow, the scale of population increase was as great—surpassing anything experienced again in urban Scotland until the end of the eighteenth century; 4,000 communion tickets were issued in 1595 and no fewer than 6,200 by 1653.[185]

The evidence for Glasgow seems to point to a formidable apparatus of kirk session discipline being developed over the course of the first four decades of the seventeenth century, during a period of rapid population increase. In the 1580s, no less than 11 of the members of the kirk session were graduates, suggesting much the same cosy club as marked the session in St Andrews. This was not the kind of body likely to be capable of evangelising society. Yet in the 1590s, collections doubled and they increased fourfold again by the 1630s; it was an impressive achievement, even in a period of price inflation. By the 1640s, examinations were being held twice a week, with a more active role being given to session elders and deacons. In 1600 each family was supposed to be visited four times a year; by the 1650s it was once a month, with each of the burgh's parishes sub-divided into 18 units with between 19 and 24 families in each.[186] What seems to have happened, in the kirk session as in burgh government as a whole, was a far more systematic involvement of the middling orders in urban society in the regulation of urban life; the burgh, as in Aberdeen, might devise the office of constable; the kirk session used both deacons and elders in the essential but tedious business of examination and visitation.[187]

---

182 The population figures for the eight projected Edinburgh parishes are given in M. Lynch, 'Whatever happened to the medieval burgh?', *Scottish Economic and Social History*, iv (1984), 7.

183 W.H. Makey, 'Edinburgh in mid-seventeenth century', in Lynch (ed.), *Early Modern Town*, 192-218.

184 *Spottiswoode Misc.*, ii, 272-4.

185 Wodrow, *Biog. Colls.*, II, ii, 25, 30, 46-50, 56-7.

186 ibid., II, ii, 30.

187 G. Desbrisay, 'Authority and discipline in Aberdeen, 1650-1700' (St Andrews University Ph.D., 1989).

Seventeenth-century urban society was distinctly different from that of the sixteenth.[188] It was far better suited to the task of overseer of the parish state.

The early seventeenth century was an age of controversy, marked by fierce exchanges between contending clerical parties about the polity of the Church, as well as a period of deep anxiety for the godly about the state of the mostly passive audience in ordinary congregations. It is hardly surprising that this 'declining age'[189] was also one which saw a multiplication of spiritual autobiographies, a new vogue for handbooks of practical divinity and the growing sale of published sermons, especially on subjects such as grace, salvation and redemption. As elsewhere, in England and continental Europe, the deficiencies of exterior discipline in bringing about a new Jerusalem encouraged a retreat into the spiritual inner self.[190] This instinct was not confined to one clerical party or another and it was shared by laymen as well as ministers. Robert Blair, later an active Covenanter, encouraged his students at Glasgow University in the early 1620s to 'study piety' rather than philosophy.[191] Yet a number of the Jacobean bishops were also earnest practitioners of practical divinity and the works of divines such as William Cowper, Patrick Forbes and John Abernethy, bishop of Caithness 1616-38, were prominent, especially in the period between 1615 and 1630.[192] The popularity of such works amomgst the laity is an important part of the evidence for the growth of a new 'middling sort' in society, often professional men, which formed a new reading public in this period.[193] Some 60 religious works were published in Scotland in the 1620s and that figure almost doubled in the next decade.[194] A good deal more were imported, both from England and the Continent. This was the period which first saw an increase in Bible reading, as measured by the numbers of New Testaments in the stock

[188] Lynch, *Early Modern Town*, 28-9.

[189] 'A True Narratioune of the Declyneing Aige of the Kirk of Scotland': see Melville, *Diary*, 503ff.

[190] Bossy, *Christianity*, 133. With others, such as Robert Pont and John Napier of Merchiston, it induced an active pursuit of the prospect of the millenium: see A.H. Williamson, *Scottish National Consciousness in the Age of James VI* (Edinburgh, 1979), 23-31.

[191] *Life of Blair*, 32, 35.

[192] Mullan, *Episcopacy*, 164-5.

[193] Lynch, *Scotland*, 257-62; idem, 'Renaissance and Reformation', in R. Mitchison, *Why Scottish History Matters* (Saltire Soc., 1991), 30, 33.

[194] M. Steele, 'The "politick Christian": the theological background to the National Covenant', in Morrill (ed.), *Scottish National Covenant*, 31-67, at 50-51.

of Edinburgh booksellers. The evidence suggests that these individual journeys of the soul took place despite and not because of the ecclesiastical controversies of the age.

All of this may add up to a religious revival, but it was one of the intelligentsia rather than of the 'common sort'. There were some local revivals from about 1620 onwards, but they were usually confined to a specific locality, which was often upland or remote. In such cases, like that of Stewarton, Protestantism was 'born again' and gained a much sharper evangelical edge. In other cases, notably in the far south-west, Protestantism gained its feet only in the early decades of the seventeenth century; late conversion produced a reformation marked by a strong streak of social discontent and popular fervour. If there was a 'people's reformation' in Scotland, it seems more realistic to locate it in the 1620s and after rather than in the decades either side of 1560. A populist tone had begun to infect some craftsmen and small merchants as early as the 1580s, especially in Edinburgh, but it was a relatively isolated phenomenon before 1610. More significant, it has been argued, were distinct signs, even if they were as yet confined to a handful of larger burghs, that the arm of the parish state was acquiring more muscle from about 1610 onwards; the long process of evangelisation and session discipline was at last beginning to tell, through the more concerted use of elders and deacons. The basic system of schooling, however, was still struggling to cope with mass evangelisation, even if there were signs in some Lowland areas of improvement after about 1610.

Taking these developments together, answers to the question of how long the reformation—when defined as a process of catechising and conversion—took begin to pinpoint the third and fourth decades of the seventeenth century. By then, three of the most important moulds of Scottish Protestantism—a pursuit of the millenium and the mysteries of divinity amongst an intelligentsia; a militant tendency which had both a rural and an urban face; and a formidable apparatus of discipline organised by the 'middling sort' in society—were beginning to set. The remarkable events of 1637, coincidentally in that very thirty-eighth year of the century which John Napier of Merchiston had calculated as the date of the millennium, brought these developments together, in a combustible mix. The 'second Reformation' was sparked off by the imminent expectation of the second coming of Christ. It was a popular revival on a larger scale than ever seen before. As such, 1637 was not—despite the enormous efforts of presbyterian historians such as Calderwood to make it so—1596 born again.

'M. ALEX: BOYDE.'
THE AUTHORSHIP OF 'FRA BANC TO BANC'

Robert Donaldson

The Scots vernacular sonnet that commences 'Fra banc to banc' is generally regarded as having reached a high standard of achievement in its form. From the year 1900, it has been reprinted on numerous occasions, always with the traditional attribution to Mark Alexander Boyd. Although this attribution is perfectly reasonable and, indeed, probable, it is possible to raise some questions about it, and, in view of the poem's importance, there seems some justification for devoting a few pages to setting out and considering the evidence on which the attribution can be based and the reasons for the questions. Thereafter we might expect to be in a position to accept the attribution, if we do accept it, taking due account of the relevant circumstances and with whatever reservations we may think justified.

Prior to the editions of the twentieth century, the text of 'Fra banc to banc' survived, so far as is known, in three versions, which are reproduced here as illustrations. The printed version, the only known copy of which is in NLS (pressmark RB.s.82), may be dated 'circa 1600', probably earlier rather than later. The other versions, both in manuscript, are also in NLS (pressmarks MS.25417, f.144r, and Wodrow MS. 4to, CIV, f.1r). MS. 25417 is among the Newhailes Papers, acquired by the Library in 1978, and the text, dated 20 January 1787, is clearly a direct transcript of the print, exact save for a few minor variants in spelling and punctuation. The latter manuscript may have been part of, or associated with a letter (on the back are the remains of a seal), and was probably written in the latter half of the eighteenth century. In some points of detail the text of this manuscript differs (to its disadvantage) from that of the print, but only in the first line is there any significant divergence of meaning. 'Fra banc to banc fra vod to vod I rin' in the print has become 'Frae banc to banc [or, possibly, 'bane to bane'], frae void to void I rin' in the manuscript. The word 'vod' in the print should certainly be read as 'wood', although to misinterpret it as 'void' is perhaps understandable, and it is possible that the change in the sense of line 1 in the manuscript stems from such a misinterpretation. If true, this supposition would imply that the 'Wodrow'[1] manuscript text had been copied from an original that retained the print's spelling 'vod'—possibly from the print itself, or, if it were written after 20 January 1787 (which is possible rather than probable), from the Newhailes transcript. As a textual authority, at any rate, the print is unique.

It is also unique inasmuch as only one copy of it is known to have survived. For some time before it was acquired by NLS,[2] this copy was in the possession of the Boyds of Penkill (Mark Alexander's own family).[3] Twentieth-century readers were introduced to it by Sir Arthur Quiller-Couch, who printed the poem in *The Oxford Book of English Verse* (1900), and by W.P. Ker, who copied it and passed the text to Bowyer Nichols for inclusion in *A Little Book of English Sonnets* (1903). Although Quiller-Couch was probably right in describing his original as 'unpublished', it is certainly printed, not manuscript (as is stated in at least three books).[4] Reprinted and briefly discussed by Wittig,[5] Spiers,[6] and R.D.S. Jack,[7] mentioned by James B. Caird[8] and no doubt by others, the sonnet has been studied from the literary point of view by Professor Ian Ross in his article, 'Sonneteering in sixteenth-century Scotland',[9] Professor Jack in his thesis, 'The Scottish Sonnet and Renaissance Poetry',[10] and Dr Ruth McQuillan in her anthology,

[1] So-called for convenience. The hand in which it is written is eighteenth-century, but, as will be specified below in greater detail, at some unestablished time it has been inserted at the beginning of a volume of seventeenth-century manuscripts in the collection of Robert Wodrow (1679-1734).

[2] It was purchased with the aid of a grant from the Friends of the National Libraries, to whose *Report* for 1965 the author of the present paper contributed a note in which was included, in very brief form, some of the material now presented. Acknowledgment is made to the Friends of the National Libraries for permission to 'recycle' it.

[3] See D.C. Anderson's genealogical tables, no. III, in *Annals of the House and Family of Boyd by F.R. Cameron* (Edinburgh, duplicated typescript, 1963), 145-6. Also S. Clarke, *The Boyds of Penkill and Trochrig* (Edinburgh, 1909), 37.

[4] *The Oxford Book of Scottish Verse, chosen by J. MacQueen and T. Scott* (Oxford, 1966), p. xvii; T. Scott, *Late Medieval Scots Poetry* (1967), 176; *The New Oxford Book of English Verse*, ed. H. Gardner (Oxford, 1972), 947.

[5] K. Wittig, *The Scottish Tradition in Literature* (Edinburgh, 1958), 128-9.

[6] J. Spiers, *The Scots Literary Tradition* (2nd rev. edn., 1962), 88-9.

[7] R.D.S. Jack, *A Choice of Scottish Verse, 1560-1660* (1978), 158, 179.

[8] J.B. Caird, 'Some reflections on Scottish literature', *Scottish Periodical*, i, 1 (Edinburgh, 1947), 17-18.

[9] *Texas Studies in Literature and Language*, vi, 2 (Austin, 1964), 266-8.

[10] R.D.S. Jack, 'The Scottish Sonnet and Renaissance Poetry' (Edinburgh Univ. Ph.D., 1968), 22-4.

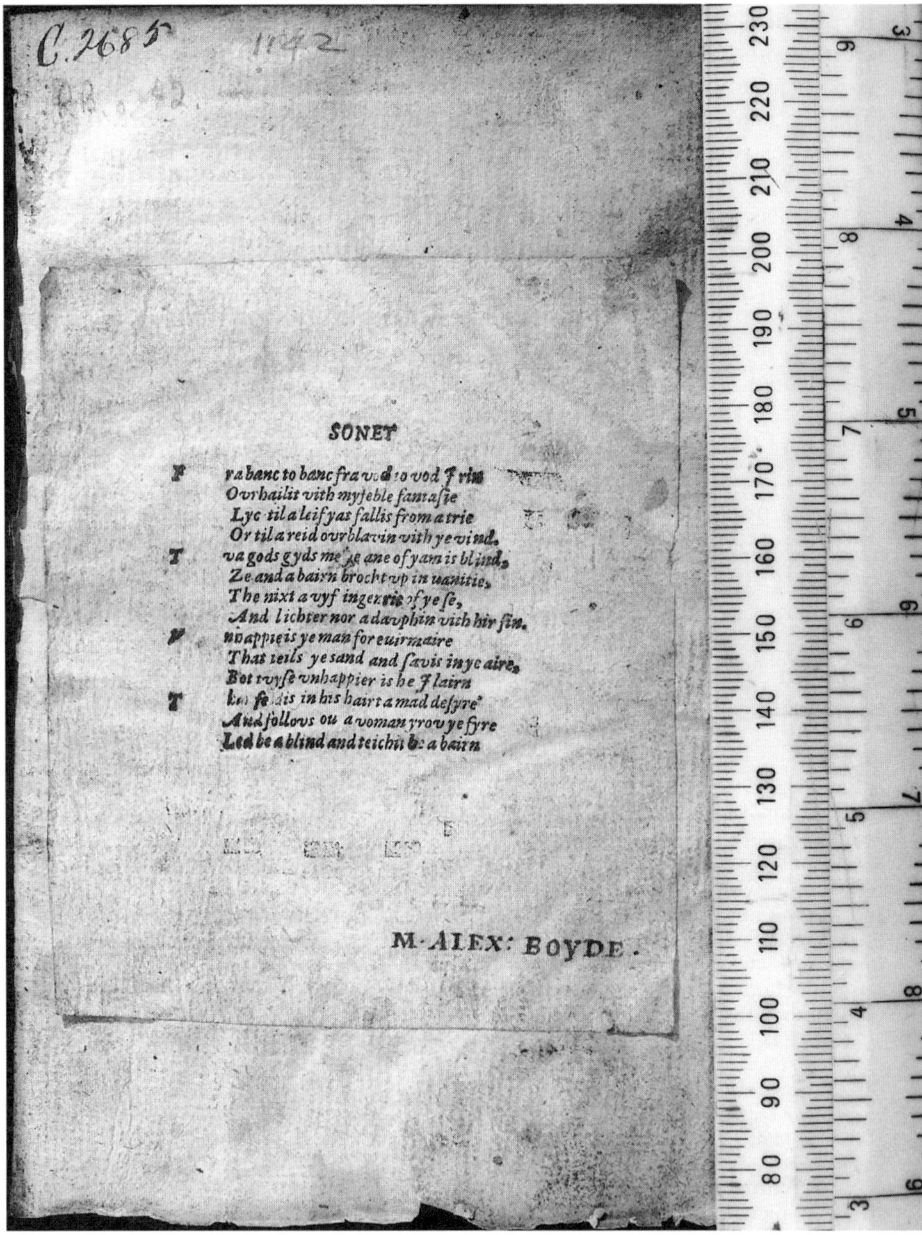

SONET

F ra banc to banc fra vod to vod I rin
Ovrhailit vith my feble fantasie
Lyc til a leif yat fallis from a trie
Or til a reid ovrblavin vith ye vind.
T va gods gyds me ȝe ane of yam is blind,
Ze and a bairn brocht up in uanitie,
The nixt a vyf ingenrie of ye se,
And lichter nor a davphin vith hir fin.
V nhappie is ye man for euirmaire
That teils ye sand and savis in ye aire,
Bot tuyse unhappier is he I lairn
K en se dis in his hairt a mad desyre
And follovs on a voman throv ye fyre
Led be a blind and teichit be a bairn

M·ALEX: BOYDE.

Fig. 5. 'Fra banc to banc' [La Rochelle? c. 1600]. Printed on slip of paper pasted to endpaper of a copy of David Chalmers of Ormond, *Histoire abbregee de tous les roys*, etc., Paris, 1579. (NLS, RB.s.82.) Actual size.

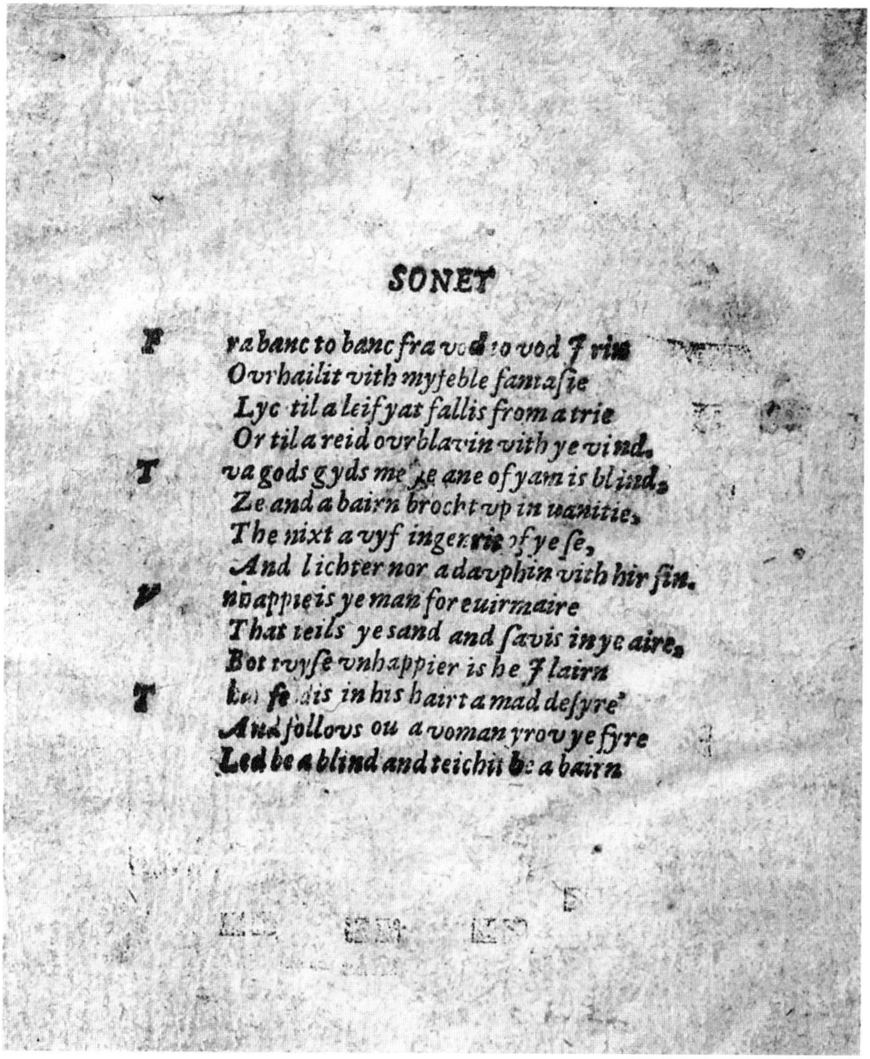

SONET

Fra banc to banc fra vod to vod I rin
Ourhailit vith my feble fantasie
Lyc til a leif yat fallis from a trie
Or til a reid ourblavin vith ye vind.
Tva gods gyds me ye ane of yam is blind,
Ze and a bairn brocht up in vanitie,
The nixt a vyf ingenrit of ye se,
And lichter nor a dauphin vith hir fin.
Vnhappie is ye man for euirmaire
That teils ye sand and savis in ye aire,
Bot tuyse vnhappier is he I lairn
That feidis in his hairt a mad desyre
And follovs on a voman throu ye fyre
Led be a blind and teichit be a bairn

Fig. 6. Enlargement of part of Fig. 5.

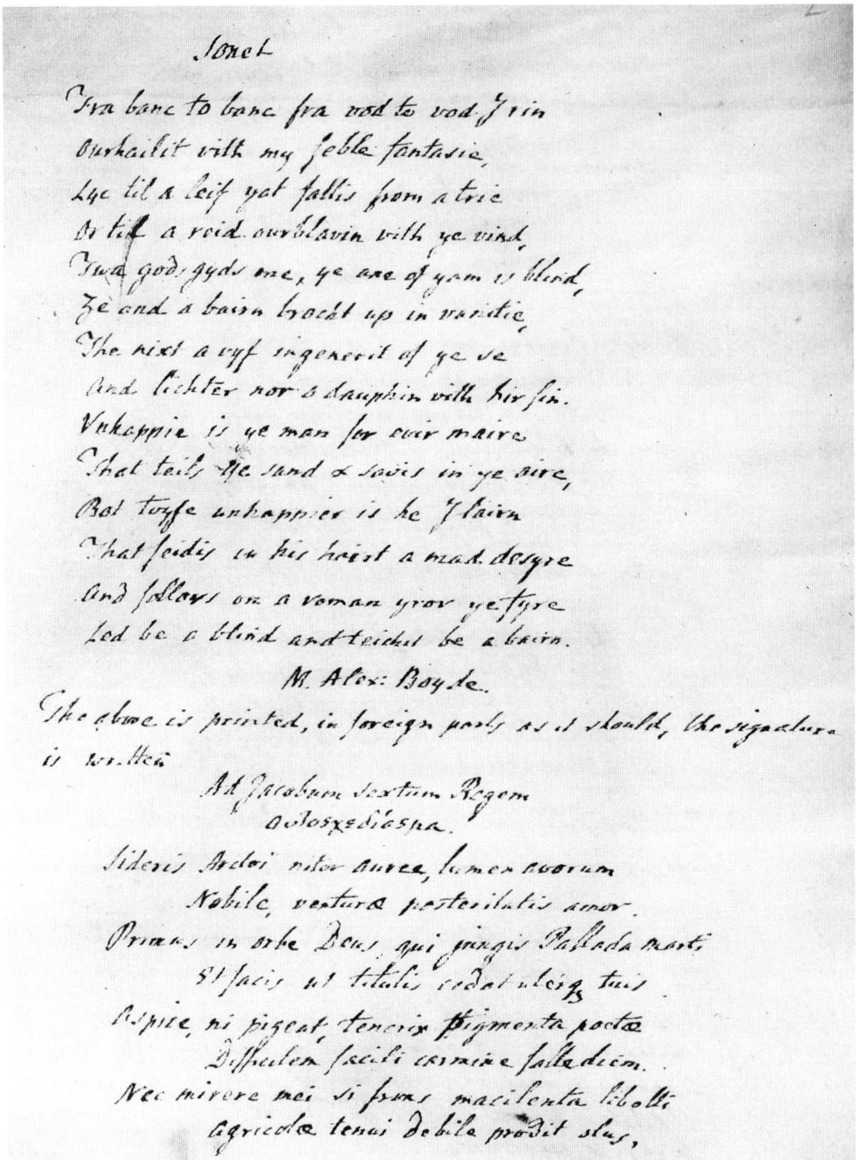
Sonet

Fra banc to banc fra vod to vod I rin
Ourhailit vith my feble fantasie,
Lyc til a leif yat fallis from a trie
Or til a reid ourblavin vith ye vind,
Twa god gyds me, ye ane of yam is blind,
Ye and a bairn brocht up in vanitie,
The nixt a vyf ingenerit of ye se
And lichter nor a dauphin vith hir fin.
Vnhappie is ye man for evir maire
That teils the sand & savis in ye aire,
Bot tuyse unhappier is he I lairn
That feidis in his hairt a mad desyre
And follows on a voman throw ye fyre
Led be a blind and teichit be a bairn.

M. Alex: Boyde.

The above is printed, in foreign parts as it should, the signature is written

Ad Jacobum Sextum Regem
αὐτοσχεδίασμα.

Sideris Arctoi nitor aurea, lumen avorum
Nobile, venturae posteritatis amor.
Primus in orbe Deus, qui jungis Pallada marti,
Et facis ut titulis cedat uterque tuis.
Aspice, ne pigeat, teneri pigmenta poetae
Difficilem facili carmine falle diem.
Nec mirere mei si frons macilenta libelli
Agricolae tenui debile prodit olus,

Fig. 7. 'Fra banc to banc'. Manuscript of poem and associated notes, dated 20 January 1787, among Newhailes Papers. (NLS, MS. 25417, f. 144 r.) Reduced to 70 per cent of original size.

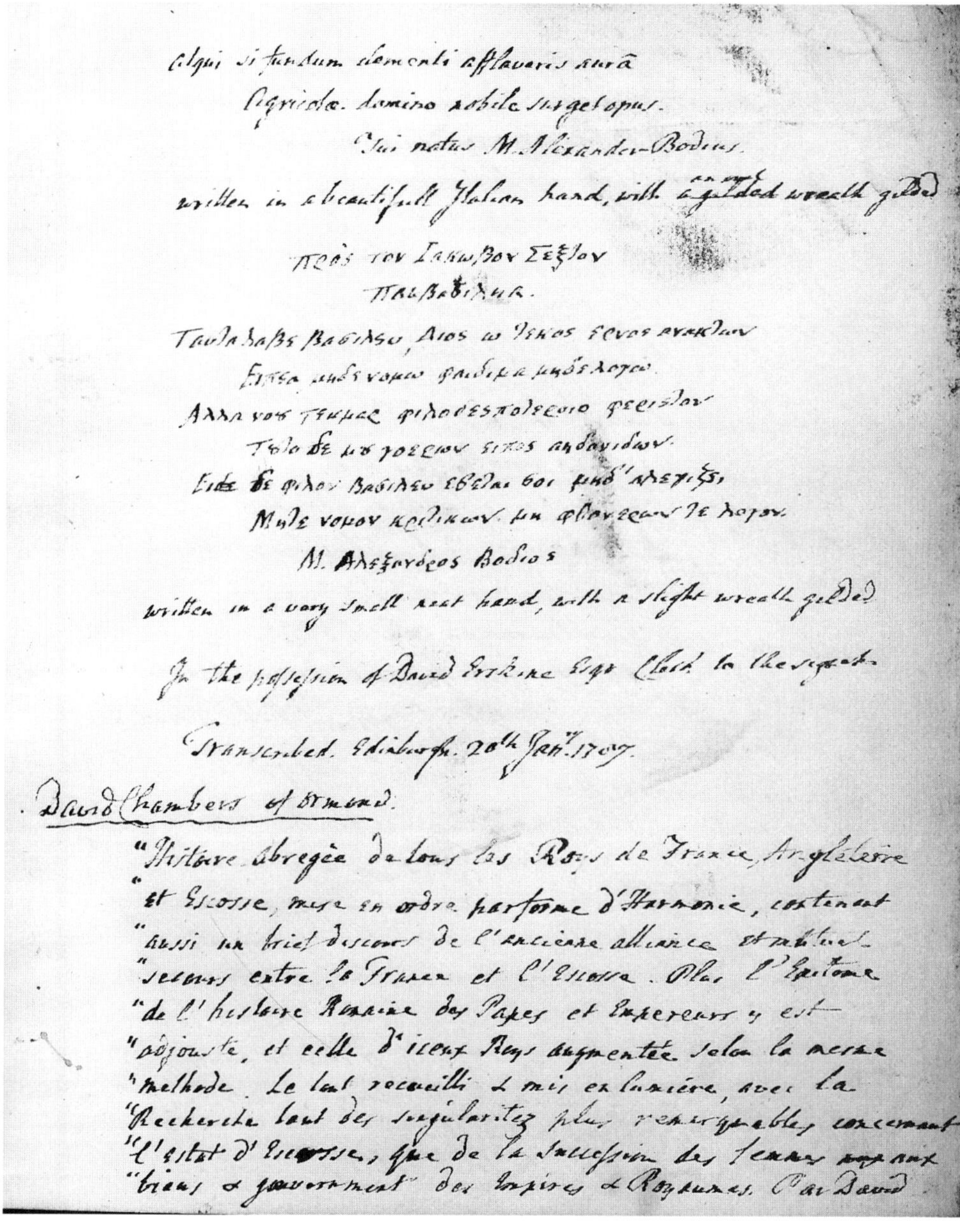
Atqui si fundum clementi afflaveris aura
Agricolæ domino nobile surget opus.
Cui notus M. Alexander Bodius.

written in a beautifull Italian hand, with an ornamented wreath gilded

[illegible]

M. Αλεξανδρος Βοδιος

written in a very small neat hand, with a slight wreath gilded

In the possession of David Erskine Esqr Clerk to the signet.

Transcribed. Edinburgh. 20th Jany 1707.

David Chambers of Ormond.

"Histoire abregée de tous les Roys de France, Angleterre
"et Escosse, mise en ordre par forme d'Harmonie, contenant
"aussi un brief discours de l'ancienne alliance et mutuel
"secours entre la France et l'Escosse. Plus l'Epitome
"de l'histoire Romaine des Papes et Empereurs y est
"adjousté, et celle d'iceux Roys augmentée selon la mesme
"methode. Le tout recueilli & mis en lumiére, avec la
"Recherche tant des singularitez plus remarquables concernant
"l'estat d'Escosse, que de la succession des femmes aux
"biens & gouvernement des Empires & Royaumes. Par David

Fig. 8. NLS, MS. 25417, f. 144 v. Reduced to 70 per cent of original size.

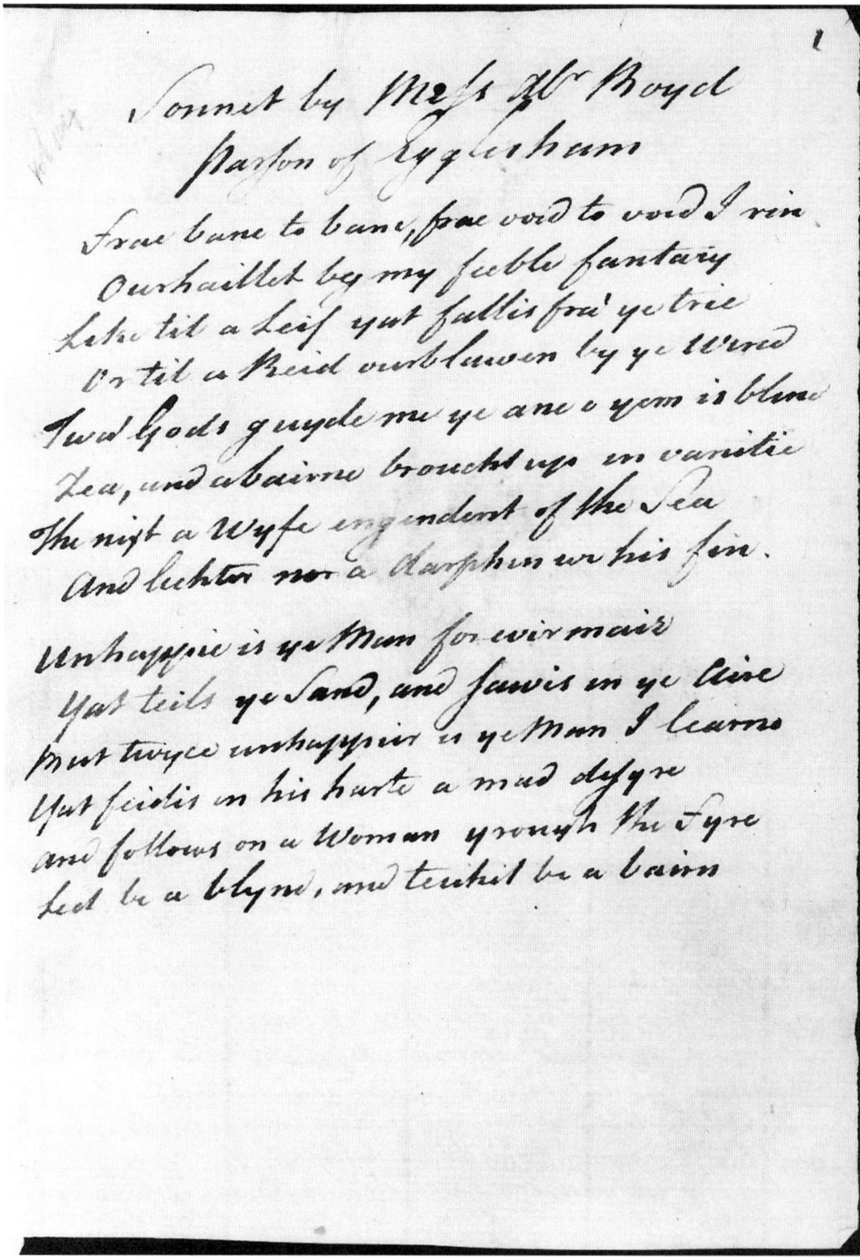

Sonnet by Mr Alr Boyd
Parson of Eglesham

Frae banc to banc, frae void to void I rin
Ourhailled by my feeble fantasy
Like til a Leif yat fallis frae ye tree
Or til a Reid ourblawen by ye Wind
Twa Gods guyde me ye ane o yem is blind
Yea, and a bairne brought up in vanitie
The nixt a Wyfe engendert of the Sea
And lichter nor a Dolphin wi his fin.

Unhappie is ye Man for evir mair
Yat teils ye Sand, and sawis in ye Aire
But twyce unhappier is ye Man I learne
Yat feidis in his harte a mad desyre
And follows on a Woman throuch the Fyre
Led be a blynd, and teichit be a bairn

Fig. 9. 'Fra banc to banc'. Eighteenth-century manuscript. (NLS, Wodrow MS.4to, CIV, f. 1r.) Actual size.

The Galliard Book of Shorter Scottish Poems from the 14th to the 20th Century.[11]

The original print itself and its provenance have been described by Sir James Fergusson in a letter entitled 'The text of Boyd's "Sonet"', in *TLS* of 12 May 1950. The print is on a small piece of paper measuring 102x83 mm., the verso of which is blank. Both composition and presswork are poor, and the impression from the quadrats used as bearers at the foot, which would have been covered for finished work, suggests that the print may be a form of proof.[12]

The paper on which it is printed is pasted inside an octavo volume containing three works by David Chalmers of Ormond (1530?-92), who was created a Lord of Session by Mary, Queen of Scots in 1565 and occasionally attended meetings of the privy council; he later suffered forfeiture and exile for adherence to her cause. The works, in which he is styled 'Chambre', are *Histoire abbregee de tous les roys de France, Angleterre et Escosse, La recerche des singularitez plus remarquables concernant l'estat d'Escosse,* and *Discours de la legitime succession des femmes aux possessions de leurs parens,* all published at Paris in 1579. They are preceded by three blank leaves, the two first conjugate, and the last, which might have been expected to have been conjugate with the upper pastedown, seemingly a singleton, as, consequently, is the upper pastedown itself. To the recto of the first of the three blank leaves is pasted the print of 'Fra banc to banc', and to the rectos of the other two are pasted calligraphic transcripts, partly gilded, of the Latin and Greek dedications to King James VI from Boyd's *Epistolae heroides et hymni,* the printed version of which was published in 1592. The paper on which these transcripts are written is different from the piece on which 'Fra banc to banc' is printed. The verso of the first is blank, the verso of the second may contain some marks in ink, but, without floating it off the mount, it is not possible to decipher what, if anything, the marks signify.

The last printed leaf of the book is followed by 39 leaves in five octavo quires (wanting the final leaf) of what seems to be the same paper as the initial three leaves. The lower pastedown may be the eighth leaf of the fifth quire, but it is impossible to be sure

---

11 *The Galliard Book of Shorter Scottish Poems from the 14th to the 20th Century,* ed. R. McQuillan (Edinburgh, 1991), 24, 25, 68, 69.

12 This suggestion was put to me, independently of each other, by Mr Harry Carter and Mr J.H. Loudon.

because of the condition of the volume. The first 18 of these 39 leaves are occupied by a text in manuscript, entitled 'Excerptions out of a little thin book in octavo entituled; A Memorial of Monarchs, from Bute to King Charles'. The original text from which these 'excerptions' were made has not been identified, either as to author or as to the (possibly printed) edition, a copy of which must have occupied the 'little thin book in octavo'. There may be some connection with the entries (in French) for English monarchs in the *Histoire abbregee*, but the manuscript entries are far from an exact translation of the French, nor is the *Histoire abbregee* a 'little thin book' (it contains about 250 leaves); the term 'excerptions', however, might just be an acceptable description of the relationship of the manuscript entries to the printed *Histoire abbregee*, if the words 'translated' and 'abstracted' were added to it. The terms of the title of the 'excerptions' preclude a time of composition earlier than the accession of King Charles I in 1625. On the recto of the first leaf of the manuscript after the titleleaf there has been transcribed the dedication, 'To the Right Honourable Lionel Viscount Cranefield, Earle of Middlesex, &c.' Lionel Cranfield (1575-1645) became Earl of Middlesex in September 1622. In 1624 he was impeached, condemned, and, although pardoned in 1625, was not restored to his seat in the House of Lords until 1640.[13] It is difficult to be sure to what extent and over what period his misfortunes might have inhibited the dedication of a work to him, and all that is certain is that the book must have been written not before 1625 and not after 1645. Therefore the manuscript 'Excerptions' cannot (like the original) have been written before 1625, but (unlike the original) might have been written after 1645. The first appearance recorded in the *OED* of the word 'excerption' in the sense intended in the manuscript is dated not later than 1618,[14] and Sir James Fergusson described the manuscript as 'written in an English hand of the early 17th century'.[15] The title of the manuscript is in the same hand as the text, which does not seem to have been completed in accordance with the title's intentions, ending, as it does, with the heading for King James VI and I, and having no text to cover the reign of that monarch, nor that of his suc-

[13] *DNB*, s.v. Cranfield, Lionel, earl of Middlesex.

[14] My attention was kindly drawn to the *OED* reference by Dr Jean Robertson (Mrs J.S. Bromley).

[15] *TLS*, 12 May 1950, 293.

cessor, Charles I. The 21 leaves following the 'Excerptions' are blank, although to the lower pastedown is pasted a strip of paper described by Sir James Fergusson as 'bearing a mutilated line of manuscript in a Scots hand of the 16th century, which reads, "... [rem?]ainit there with a great part of his army."' On the reverse of the strip, in the same or a similar hand, is written, 'aforesaid [h?]e [made?] them to be kept [am...?]'. There is no indication of when the strip was pasted down. Nor is much to be learned from the watermarks in the sheets that precede and follow the printed text-block. The watermarks do not match anything in Briquet, Churchill or Heawood,[16] and near misses (for what they are worth) point to a French source between the late sixteenth and mid seventeenth century. Since cropping for binding has cut slightly into the text of the 'Excerptions' manuscript, it was probably written before being bound into the volume,[17] and it appears, therefore, that the likeliest conclusion that can be reached, on the basis of generally inconclusive evidence, is that the assembling of the text-block and the extra leaves with their manuscript contents and paste-ons took place during the second quarter of the seventeenth century.

The dimensions of the binding leather itself do not suggest that it was prepared for any volume other than the one that it now encloses, including the additional leaves. The binding is of vellum, strengthened by two paper leaves of an unidentified work, possibly theological, printed in black letter, probably in the sixteenth century. The upper pastedown is stained black. On it are inscribed (partly gilded) some characters, and a wreath, which resembles those that surround the calligraphic transcriptions of the dedications in the *Epistolae heroides.* Only some of the characters are legible. A group, consisting of a line of capital letters with confusing flourishes, written from bottom to top of the page near the inner margin, might be deciphered as 'CLAUD DANTO', a suggestive possible reading, bearing in mind that one of Mark Alexander Boyd's associates was the writer, Claude Dantonet, author of 'une Paraphrase poétique des Lamentations de

---

[16] C.M.Briquet, *Les filigranes,* ed. A. Stevenson, 4 vols. (Amsterdam, 1968); W.A. Churchill, *Watermarks in Paper in Holland, England, France, etc., in the XVII and XVIII Centuries* (Amsterdam, 1935); E. Heawood, *Watermarks mainly of the 17th and 18th Centuries* (Hilversum, 1950).

[17] This line of reasoning was first explored by Dr T.I. Rae, to whose notes I am indebted.

Jérémie, La Rochelle, 1602'.[18] If the reading and identification were correct, they might suggest a possible association with Boyd of the pastedown paper, like the items pasted to the upper flyleaves, although without necessarily establishing that this material was associated with this copy of the Chalmers book before the present binding was assembled and applied in or after 1625. Boyd, it should be noted, makes a reference to the *Histoire abbregee* in his 'Discours civiles sur le royaulme d'Escosse'[19], but this, while showing that he knew the work, does not prove that he owned a copy, still less this copy. The binding's spine,which has been repaired, is titled in black ink (mostly on and probably at the time of the repair—in all likelihood during the nineteenth century): 'Les Roys/ de / FRANCE / ANGLETERRE / et / ESCOSSE / [rule] / DAVID CHAMBRE / [rule] / *PARIS 1579*', and on both upper and lower covers there is an armorial shield in gold (not a block but assembled from impressions of small tools and fillets), identified in 1950 by Sir James Fergusson as the arms of the Seton family. 'Unfortunately', continues Sir James, there is 'no record or tradition of how the book came to Penkill. It bears on the first flyleaf recto and verso figures in pencil and ink showing that in the nineteenth century it passed through the hands of more than one bookseller; and it seems probable that it was bought by Spencer Boyd of Penkill, who restored and refurnished the house nearly 100 years ago.'

As Sir James Fergusson observed, the armorial shield identifies the book as having once been in the possession of a member or members of the family of Seton, but it does not reveal which member or members. One possibility might be Alexander Seton (1621?-91), son of the 3rd earl of Winton, who, prior to his ennoblement as Viscount Kingston in 1651, might have used the

[18] E. and E. Haag, *La France protestante*, tome IV (Geneva: Slatkine Reprints, 1966), 204. Other relevant references are Sir David Dalrymple, Lord Hailes, *Sketch of the Life of Mark Alexander Boyd* ([Edinburgh, 1786 or 1787]), 22, which contains the phrase, 'his [Boyd's] friend Danconet'; Boyd's own *Epistolae quindecim* (Bordeaux: Simon Millanges, 1590), 90 and 107, where he writes, 'Ad Publium Claudium Dantonetum amicum'; and his *Epistolae heroides et hymni* (Antuerpiae [or rather La Rochelle: Jérôme Haultin] 1592), which, on p. 167, contains his short letter to 'P.C. Danthoneto'. The *DNB* entry for Mark Alexander Boyd seems to have created a curious hybrid, 'Pietro Florio Dantoneto', by merging the identities of the Italian, Pietro Florio, and the Frenchman, Claude Dantonet.

[19] Boyd's 'Discours civiles' seems to exist only in manuscript; it is one of the texts in the volume that is titled on its spine, 'M.A. Bodii opuscula', collected by Sir Robert Sibbald (NLS, Adv. MS. 15.1.7, f.182r).

form of arms stamped on the covers. In the course of his 'grand tour' (1636-40), he passed, probably in 1639 or 1640, through La Rochelle, where, some forty years earlier (as we shall see), the sonnet may have been printed. If he had come upon the volume and/or any of the insertions, he might have brought them to Scotland with him, and had them bound as they are now. This, however, is pure speculation, as is also the possibility that the volume, in its present state, might have later passed to Sir Alexander Seton, Lord Pitmedden (1639?-1719), the judge who, according to Wodrow, possessed a vast and curious library.[20] Lot 323 on page 87 of *A Catalogue of Valuable Books which belong'd to Sir Alexander Seaton of Pitmedden, Baronet, lately deceased* (Edinburgh, 1719) is 'Chambre (Dav.) Seig. d'Ormond, Ecossais, Histoire abregée de tous les Roys de France, Angleterre & Ecosse'. Thus Pitmedden possessed a copy of the Chalmers book, which was bought by Mr Lumsdale for 15 shillings, according to a manuscript note in the NLS interleaved copy of the catalogue,[21] but not necessarily this copy. Lord Pitmedden was one of a number of legal luminaries produced by the Seton family,[22] but he ought not to have been the one to have had the arms put on the covers, and consequently, to have been, most probably, the first Seton owner, since the arms are certainly not his.

In contrast to the lack of certainty regarding the ownership of the volume during the two first centuries of its existence, there is a piece of evidence that seems to locate it exactly in the year 1787. This evidence is contained in two conjugate leaves of laid paper, each measuring 228×187 mm., within the collection of Newhailes papers acquired by NLS in 1978.[23] On these leaves there is a text of the sonnet, evidently copied directly from the print, although there are a few variants in spelling and punctuation. It is followed

---

[20] *DNB*, s.v. Seton, Sir Alexander, Lord Pitmedden; George Seton, *Memoir of Alexander Seton, Earl of Dunfermline* (Edinburgh, 1882), 16; cf. T.I. Rae, 'The origins of the Advocates' Library', in *For the Encouragement of Learning*, ed. P. Cadell and A. Matheson (Edinburgh, 1989), 13, referring to G. Brunton and D. Haig, *An Historical Account of the Senators of the College of Justice* (Edinburgh, 1836), 407, which quotes 'an unreferenced Wodrow source'.

[21] NLS, MS. 3802, p.87, lot 323.

[22] See Seton, *Memoir of Alexander Seton*, esp. the genealogical tables.

[23] NLS, MS. 25417, ff.144-5. At the beginning of the file that contains the leaves is a list of contents that begins: 'Lord Hailes, Sketches of Papers in periodical publications'; the contents of the leaves, however, are not mentioned by R.H. Carnie in his article, 'Lord Hailes's contributions to contemporary magazines', in *Studies in Bibliography* (Charlottesville, Virginia), ix (1957), 233-44.

by transcripts of the two calligraphic transcripts of dedications that are pasted to the flyleaves of the Chalmers volume described above, and these, in turn, are followed by a transcript of the title of Chalmers' work and a brief note on the work and its author, all seemingly in the hand of Sir David Dalrymple, Lord Hailes (1726-92). Immediately after the sonnet is written, ' In the possession of David Erskine Esqr Clerk to the Signet. Transcribed 20th Janry. 1787.' Apparently, therefore, on this day, the Chalmers volume, with its 'Boydean' accretions, was in Edinburgh in the possession of David Erskine, and available to Lord Hailes for the copying of extracts.

Apart from common membership of the Scottish legal establishment, there does not seem to be a connection between the families of Erskine and Seton, nor is there one between the families of Erskine and Boyd.The route by which the volume passed from Seton to Erskine to Boyd is unclear. David Erskine, Clerk to the Signet, was a son of Professor John Erskine of Carnock and Cardross (1695-1768), who held the Chair of Scots Law at Edinburgh University and was the author of two frequently reissued treatises on the law of Scotland. David himself had three sons, the third of whom (also David) had a family. There does not, however, seem to be evidence of a connection between any of them and Spencer Boyd, laird of Penkill (Sir James Fergusson's reasonable choice as the member of the family most likely to have the kind of interest that would have prompted the acquisition of the book for its own sake or as a family heirloom), nor, for that matter, any other member of the Boyd family.

So much for the conditions under which the printed text of the sonnet has descended to us, and, as a corollary, the Hailes manuscript copy of 1787. There is even less certainty about the provenance of the eighteenth-century 'Wodrow' manuscript text. It is written in black ink by an unidentified writer on one side of a piece of laid paper measuring 166×116 mm., the verso of which is blank apart from the remains of a seal. The paper is inserted at the beginning of a quarto-size manuscript volume containing works by Master Andrew Boyd (c.1567-1636), minister of Eaglesham, bishop of Argyll, and, in fact, a distant relative of Mark Alexander Boyd himself.[24] The manuscripts in this volume, written in the seventeenth century, were preserved by the anti-

[24] Cameron, *Annals of Boyd*, 142, 145.

quary, Robert Wodrow, and the volume, together with many others from Wodrow's collection, came to the Advocates' Library towards the end of the eighteenth century (some are known to have been received in 1792). The paper containing the sonnet may have been associated with the Wodrow volume before or after its accession to the Advocates' Library. Its present binding, and the attachment to guards of all the leaves (including the one with the sonnet), dates from 1935, ten years after it had passed, with the rest of the stock of the Advocates' Library, except the legal collections, to NLS.[25]

Direct evidence regarding the authorship of the sonnet consists of the subscription to the printed text and the heading of the 'Wodrow' manuscript. The subscription, 'M. ALEX: BOYDE.', is not itself set in type, but is written in block capitals in a hand that might or might not be that of the poem's presumed author. It bears no obvious relationship to any other hand among the manuscript additions to the book into which the print has been pasted. The heading of the 'Wodrow' manuscript text reads, 'Sonnet by Mess Alr Boyd, parson of Egglisham'. There is, as we have seen, at least a possibility that the writer of this text had the print before him, and, if so, he has taken the 'M.' of the subscription to mean 'Messire' or 'Master', not 'Mark'.

If we assume that the truth about the authorship can be related to the subscription and/or the heading—assume, that is, that they are not both quite wrong and that the author was not somebody entirely unidentifiable from them—there would appear to be four possible interpretations of the evidence:

(i) that the subscription refers to one Master Alexander Boyd who was not Mark Alexander;

(ii) that the author was Master Andrew Boyd, minister of Eaglesham;

(iii) that the sonnet was written by Mark Alexander Boyd, but that the subscription stands for 'Master Alexander Boyd';

(iv) that the sonnet was written by Mark Alexander Boyd, and that the subscription stands for 'Mark Alexander Boyd'.

To argue for no. (i) requires the identification of somebody called Alexander Boyd who can be shown to have been more

[25] NLS, Wodrow MS. 4to, CIV. Wodrow's 'Life' of Andrew Boyd, to be distinguished from this collection of papers, is now in GUL, and is the source of the extracts printed in J.B. Craven, *Records of the Dioceses of Argyll and the Isles, 1560-1860* (Kirkwall, 1907), 50-80.

likely to have written the sonnet than Mark Alexander. There are at least two Alexander Boyds recorded in Scottish academic circles in the late sixteenth and early seventeenth centuries. One is the Alexander Boyd who appears as a bachelor and intrant in St Andrews University Bursar's Book of November 1560 to November 1562;[26] the other is the Magister Alexander Bodius who was a regent at the University of Glasgow in the early seventeenth century and who left 1,000 merks for the renovation of the University buildings in 1613.[27] Enquiries at both universities have elicited no reason to believe that either of these two men composed the poem. Somewhat later laureations listed in *Glasgow Univ. Munimenta*, include the name 'Alexander Boyd' in 1619 and 1622, but its owners do not seem to be otherwise recorded in print.

The second possibility is the only one based entirely upon the heading of the eighteenth-century 'Wodrow' manuscript. There can be little doubt that the 'Mess Alr Boyd parson of Egglisham' of this heading is a confusion of a hypothetical 'M.... Alexander Boyd' with Master Andrew Boyd, minister of Eaglesham. (The only other Boyd recorded as having been in charge of Eaglesham is Thomas, Andrew's son.)[28] Such confusion naturally renders the heading suspect as evidence for the authorship of the sonnet, and the only other argument that can be advanced in favour of Andrew Boyd is the fact that he is known to have written a sonnet called 'Vanitie'[29] and some other verses in Latin and English;[30] their style, however, is not reminiscent of 'Fra banc to banc'. But even if Andrew did not write 'Fra banc to banc' and Mark Alexander did, Andrew, as a relative, may conceivably have had in his possession after his kinsman's death in Scotland in 1601 the piece of paper containing the print, perhaps pasted into the Chalmers volume, perhaps not. He might even have made a copy of the text, a copy which, no less plausibly than the print itself, may be postulated as the basis of the eighteenth-century

[26] *Acta Facultatis Artium Universitatis Sanctiandree, 1413-1588*, ed. A.I. Dunlop (Edinburgh, 1964), 415.

[27] J. Coutts, *A History of the University of Glasgow* (Glasgow, 1909), 113, 251.

[28] Scott, *Fasti*, iii, 386.

[29] NLS, Wodrow MS. 4to, CIV, no. 4; printed, but titled, 'A dialogue from Lucian', in Craven, *Records of the Dioceses of Argyll and the Isles*, 72.

[30] NLS, Wodrow MS. 4to, CIV, no 3; *Ad augustissimum monarchum Carolum carmen panegyricum* (Edinburgi: R. Junius, 1633 (*STC*, 3443)); Craven, *Records of the Dioceses of Argyll and the Isles*, 76-7.

'Wodrow' manuscript. Such a hypothesis could explain the association of the work with Andrew Boyd, an association which might help to account for the manuscript's confused heading. Unfortunately, this hypothesis runs counter to the earlier proposition that the poem did not come to Scotland in the possession of Alexander Seton, later Viscount Kingston, until about 1640, four years after Andrew Boyd's death. As has been stressed, however, both scenarios are no more than speculative. Either may be true, both may be false.

The third possibility is compatible both with the 'M. ALEX: BOYDE.' of the subscription and the 'Mess Alr Boyd' of the heading, if the latter is taken apart from the designation, 'parson of Egglisham'. If it is accepted, both must be interpreted as 'Master Alexander Boyd', and that individual must be identified as Mark Alexander, who was apparently prouder of his assumed name, 'Alexander' (after Alexander the Great),[31] than of his given name, 'Mark', and who was sometimes referred to simply as 'Alexander'.[32] Support for this possibility can be found in the volume of Sir Robert Sibbald's notes and drafts on Scottish writers entitled on the spine, 'Sibbaldi Bibliotheca Scotica', which is now in NLS. Under the heading, 'Alexander Bodius', Sibbald includes the text of a brief biography that seems to be that of Mark Alexander, although the subject is referred to as 'natione Scotus in Baronia Ranfroensi natus', whereas *Scotia illustrata* declares 'Natus est in Gallovidia'. The brief biography relates that, after studying at Glasgow University, 'Magisterii titulum de more accepit'.[33] Even if, therefore, there is no evidence that Mark Alexander graduated at any of the seats of learning that he attended on the Continent,[34] this statement adds some weight to the notion that, correctly or not, he may have been styled 'Master' from time to time.

Perhaps that notion need not be regarded as incompatible with the fourth possibility, which holds that the subscription 'M.

---

[31] Hailes, *Sketch of the Life of Mark Alexander Boyd*, 21-2.

[32] NLS, Adv. MS. 15.1.7, f.220. See also the inscription on the engraved portrait by Thomas de Leu, which appears among the plates at the end of some copies of Sir Robert Sibbald, *Scotia illustrata* (Edinburgi, 1684).

[33] NLS, Adv. MS. 33.5.17, f.78v.

[34] Paris, Orleans, Bourges and Toulouse, according to *DNB*. I am indebted to the librarians of the Universities of Paris (Sorbonne) and Toulouse, and the Director of the Archives du Cher, Bourges, for kindly searching their records on my behalf.

ALEX: BOYDE.' should be read as 'Mark Alexander Boyd', a reading which is supported by the use of the abbreviation 'M' in signatures among the Mark Alexander Boyd papers assembled by Sibbald,[35] and in the title and dedications of the *Epistolae heroides et hymni.* It may well be that in some (perhaps most) renderings of the name 'M' represents 'Mark', but in others it represents 'Master' or 'Magister'.

Apart from the doubts raised by the nature of the subscription to the print and the heading of the 'Wodrow' manuscript, the main reason for questioning the traditional attribution of the authorship of the sonnet is the apparent lack of any other vernacular verse in manuscript or print by Mark Alexander Boyd. His known writings are in Latin, Greek and French, and the poem in English addressed to Patrick Sharp, which is cited as an original by Florence Robertson Cameron,[36] is in fact a translation from the Latin of some lines from 'Thymbra' in the *Hymni.*[37] It seems unlikely that a poem of the quality of 'Fra banc to banc' could represent a unique effort by the author in its particular language and form. Yet there is nothing similar among Boyd's known surviving writings, which consist of (i) the two published volumes, *Epistolae quindecim* (Bordeaux: Simon Millanges, 1590),[38] and *Epistolae heroides et hymni* (Antwerp, 1592);[39] (ii) the substantial collection of Mark Alexander Boyd papers made by Sir Robert Sibbald in the seventeenth century, which was acquired by the Advocates' Library and is now in NLS;[40] and (iii) a small volume of late sixteenth-century manuscript leaves (which includes material that was printed in *Epistolae quindecim*), sold by Sotheby on 19 July 1960, lot 404, under the title 'Epistolae, Elegiae,

---

35 NLS, Adv. MS. 15.1.7, ff.225-6. A subscription to one of the documents actually reads, 'Tui amantiss. M. Alex: Boyde.', in cursive script, however, not block capitals (f.226r). Even so, it offers some support for the claim to authenticity of the subscription to the early print.

36 Cameron, *Annals of Boyd,* 27.

37 *M. Alexandri Bodii epistolae heroides et hymni,* 120.

38 The only known surviving copy is now in the Bibliothèque de la Ville, Bordeaux. The work bears the dedication, 'Clarissimo viro Roberto Bodio a Badneto', who was probably Robert Boyd, laird of Badenheath (also spelt, *inter alia,* 'Badenhet', near present-day Cumbernauld), a younger son of the fifth Lord Boyd (H. Cleland, *Blairlin District and the Clelands* (Kirkintilloch, 1934), 18-26: 'The Boyds of Badenheath and Blairlin').

39 There are copies in NLS, BL and BN.

40 NLS, Adv. MS. 15.1.7.

Epigrammata, etc.', and later acquired by NLS.[41]. Among these writings, however, and in the volume of Sir Robert Sibbald's notes and drafts entitled 'Sibbaldi Bibliotheca Scotica', referred to above,[42] there are pieces of relevant information.

As a collector of Mark Alexander Boyd material, Sibbald was fortunate in being related to the Boyd family through his mother, Margaret, who was the daughter of the advocate, Robert Boyd of Kipps, and, less directly, through his uncle, Dr George Sibbald, who married the widow of Robert Boyd of Trochrig, Principal of Glasgow University.[43] In 1671, it was Sibbald, according to a note pencilled beside the manuscript text, who was the recipient of a letter signed, 'Votre tres-humble serviteur et cousin.—J. Boyd de Trochvregge'. This 'J. Boyd', who is identified by another pencilled note (qualified, however, by a question mark) as 'John Boyd of Trochrig', possibly the son of Principal Robert Boyd,[44] wrote, 'I had communicatioune with my cousin the Laird of Pinkull anent ... our long-agoe-deceassed cousin, Mr, A, B, who (being but a youth himselfe [the Laird, that is] [at] the tyme of his [Mark Alexander's] deceasse) told me all he knewe of him ... I could possiblie shawe vnto you somvhatt of my fathers manuscript ... that might conduce vnto the accomplishment of your desinge and desyre'.[45]

It is possibly from this source that Sibbald obtained the short biography of Mark Alexander Boyd that he set down in manuscript among his notes under 'Vitae illustrium Scotorum', and in print (somewhat augmented) in *Scotia illustrata.*[46] The text contains notes on works said to have been written by Boyd, and includes the statement, 'Ad vernaculae poeseos principatum tan-

---

[41] NLS, MS. 20759. Lot 404 in Sotheby's catalogue of the sale on 19 July 1960 is listed under 'other properties', so no indication of its previous ownership appears.

[42] NLS, Adv. MS. 33.5.17.

[43] J.A. Inglis, *The Monros of Auchinbowie* (Edinburgh, 1911), 204-05 of the chapter, 'The Boyds of Kipps'; *DNB*, s.v. Boyd, Robert, of Trochrig'; Sir Robert Sibbald, *Vindiciae Scotiae illustratae* (Edinburgi, 1710), last leaf: 'Libri authoris impressi'.

[44] See Cameron, *Annals of Boyd*, 145-6.

[45] NLS, Adv. MS. 15.1.7, f.236r.

[46] NLS, Adv. MS. 33.5.17, ff.245v-248v; Sibbald, *Scotia illustrata, pars 2a specialis*, tom. ii, 2-4. The exact origin of Sibbald's text is not clear. Lord Hailes (*Sketch*, 19) calls it 'a little tract by James Boyd, son of the archbishop of Glasgow, containing Memoirs of his cousin Mark Alexander'. No such James Boyd is recorded in Anderson's genealogical tables in Cameron, *Annals of Boyd*, in which only Robert Boyd, later Principal of Glasgow University, appears as a son of the

dem aspiravit et sine controversia est adeptus'.[47] In his *Sketch of the Life of Mark Alexander Boyd,* Lord Hailes derives from these notes an inventory of Boyd's works, in which, on the strength of this statement, he includes a category which he defines as 'Poems in the Scottish language'. He adds, rather acidly, 'They are immoderately extolled by the author of the Memoirs [i.e. the biography published by Sibbald]; but as he estimates the verses of Boyd that are extant [the Latin and Greek ones] much above their real value, we cannot rely on his judgement with respect to verses that are now lost [the presumptive vernacular ones]'.[48]

Hailes seems to have been less than overwhelmed by Mark Alexander's literary achievements, although he was prepared to give credit where credit was due. On page 11 of the *Sketch* he writes, 'The fame of Boyd's works is, in a great measure, traditional; and, if I mistake not, has chiefly rested on his own testimony, to which his panegyrists gave implicit belief'; yet on page 14 he concedes that 'we must own the Hymni to be, upon the whole, a work of merit', and on page 25, after translating part of a letter of Boyd's on theological subjects, the original of which is in NLS,[49] he concludes, 'Were there nothing of the works of Boyd extant but this letter, we might still pronounce him to have been a man of genius.' In assessing the views that Hailes expresses in the *Sketch,* it has to be remembered that, in this work, he makes no mention of 'Fra banc to banc', and it seems most likely that, when he was writing it, he had not yet come upon the sonnet. The transcript in the Hailes manuscript[50] of the sonnet and other

archbishop, whose own name was James, nor in 'Collections upon the Life of Mr James Boyd of Trochredge, Tulchan Archbishop of Glasgow' (Wodrow, *Biog. Colls.*, 203-30), where one other son (Thomas) is mentioned. Sir Robert Sibbald, in the heading of his manuscript text, states that it was written by James Boyd, rhetorician, the brother of his [Sibbald's] grandfather. The grandfather can only be the advocate, Robert Boyd of Kipps, whose daughter, Margaret, was Sibbald's mother, but the chapter, 'The Boyds of Kipps', in Inglis, *Monros of Auchinbowie*, 194-210, records only John and Stephen as the brothers of Robert. Furthermore, even if Anderson's and Inglis' information as to genealogy were incomplete, there is no certainty that James Boyd of Kipps (if he existed) could be identified with Hailes' James Boyd of Trochrig (if he existed), son of the archbishop of Glasgow. In the text of this life of Mark Alexander, as printed in *Scotia illustrata*, Sibbald does not refer to James Boyd, rhetorician, as author, and merely states that it was contained in a manuscript that he [Sibbald] had obtained thanks to his family connections with the Boyds.

47 NLS, Adv. MS. 33.5.17, f.247r; Sibbald, *Scotia illustrata, pars 2a specialis,* tom. ii, 3.

48 Hailes, *Sketch of Life of Mark Alexander Boyd,* 20.

49 NLS, Adv. MS. 15.1.7, f.233.

50 NLS, MS. 25417, ff.144-5.

material inserted in the NLS copy of Chalmers' *Histoire abbregee* is dated 20 January 1787, and, although Hailes' *Sketch* bears no date of printing, and most of the modern major library catalogues assign it to 1787, the Advocates' Library catalogue of 1873, which was closer to Hailes in date and memory, gives 1786. Whichever of these dates is correct, it would seem that Hailes was more likely to have been working on the *Sketch* in 1786 than in 1787. Indeed, it would not be surprising if his work on the *Sketch* triggered the surfacing of the volume and the consequent copying from it of the relevant texts. Be that as it may, there seems to be no record of Hailes' opinion of the sonnet, nor of his views on its authorship.

In Boyd's adulatory address to King James VI, with which he prefaces his *Epistolae heroides et hymni*, there is a passage that might lead one to suspect that he composed some verses in the vernacular. In the *Sketch* Hailes represents the passage as follows:

> After having praised the King for his affability and greatness of soul, and mentioned the renown of his natural talents and singular learning, he [Boyd] descants, with much exultation, though under a shew of modesty, on the transcendent merit of his own Latin verses; and then adds, "Petrarca and Tasso have borne away the palm for poetry in their native language, as Ronsard has done in his: I should certainly have attempted to rival them in that species of writing, *had not your Majesty, by your ingenious and excellent compositions, precluded me from all hopes of reputation.*"[51]

Interpreted literally, this indicates that Boyd would have liked to have written in the vernacular and rivalled the achievements of the poets mentioned, but did not do so because the king's writings had already, as it were, stolen his thunder. One might well, however, imagine that Boyd had, in fact, tried his hand at vernacular verse. If that is the case, he either did not publish his efforts (possibly, but not very credibly, out of modesty in the face of royal prowess), or did have them printed, but failed thereby, so far as can yet be established, to secure their survival, except for the sonnet. Another possibility is that he tried to have them printed, but (again with the exception of 'Fra banc to banc') failed.[52]

---

[51] Hailes, *Sketch of Life of Mark Alexander Boyd,* 9-10; *M. Alexandri Bodii epistolae heroides et hymni* (1592), leaves Aiir-Aiiiir.

[52] This is perhaps an appropriate point at which to mention a pamphlet, entitled *Sonet by Mark Alexander Boyd* (Leiden, 1991), which contains a translation of

A pointer to the authorship of the sonnet may be obtained by considering the typography of the print together with what is known of the movements of Mark Alexander Boyd. He was the son of Robert Boyd of Penkill; also a nephew of James Boyd of Trochrig, minister of the Barony Church and titular archbishop of Glasgow; and also, more distantly, related to Robert, 5th Lord Boyd.[53] After some turbulent years at the University of Glasgow and the court of King James VI, he made his career mainly in France as a scholar, poet and soldier of fortune. His itinerary, so far as is known, between approximately 1580 and 1595, was Paris, Orleans, Bourges, Lyons (followed by an interlude in Italy), Lyons, Toulouse, Bordeaux, La Rochelle, Fonteney.[54] In the early 1590s he was at Bordeaux and La Rochelle. The latter town was the centre of activity of the printing and type-casting family of Haultin, the former the home of the printer, Simon Millanges, who is known to have purchased type from Haultin.[55] In 1592 was published Boyd's *Epistolae heroides et hymni*, with the imprint 'Antuerpiae', but using some types and ornaments that were almost certainly cut by Haultin; and featuring a titlepage device that is the same as the one on the books listed by Desgraves[56] as

---

the sonnet into Dutch by Adriaan van der Weel, accompanied by a printing of the Scots text and a brief note on Mark Alexander Boyd, contributed anonymously by Dr Peter Davidson. Dr Davidson's note concludes with the conjecture that the sonnet is 'all that survives of what appears to have been a projected volume of Boyd's Scots works, to have been printed in France at the end of the sixteenth century', but 'abandoned in obscure and violent circumstances'. Dr Davidson gives no source for his conjecture, and I have been unable to find one. Until such a source comes to light, the conjecture, and whatever plausible surmises might follow from it, must remain speculative, as also, for want of supporting evidence, must Sir James Fergusson's suggestion of 1950, that 'The leaf may have been ... extracted from a miscellany of poems by various authors', a proposal consistent with the authorial subscription being appended, as it is, to an individual poem.

[53] See Cameron, *Annals of Boyd*, 145-6.

[54] Hailes, *Sketch of Life of Mark Alexander Boyd*, 2-8.

[55] E. Labadie, *Notices biographiques sur les imprimeurs et libraires bordelais* (Bordeaux, 1900), 77.

[56] L. Desgraves, *Les Haultin, 1571-1623* (Geneva, 1960), p.xxxvi. Reproductions of the ornament on the titlepage of *Epistolae heroides et hymni* appear in Desgraves, nos. 78, 106, 121 (*bis*), and 122 (*bis*); a reproduction of the ornament at the head of leaf Aiir appears in, for example, no. 125, and of the ornamental initial on the same leaf in no. 258 (p.142); of the type ornaments at the head of page 1 in no. 132 (p.78); of the ornament on p.79 also in no. 132 (p.79); and reproductions of the ornament at the head of p.149 in nos. 106, 115, and 136 (*bis*). The roman type on pp.33 and 87 of the *Epistolae* appears in Desgraves, no. 83 (the text roman) and no. 132 (the smaller text roman on p.79); the larger roman on leaf Aiiir and p.152 appears as the text roman in Desgraves, no. 88, and the large capitals of line 2 of the titlepage appear in Desgraves, no. 96 (p.50, col.1).

clandestine publications of Jérôme Haultin bearing the false imprint, 'A Anvers, par Herman Mersmann, 1591.' Two years earlier, in 1590, Millanges printed at Bordeaux, employing at least some material cut by Haultin,[57] Boyd's *Epistolae quindecim quibus totidem Ouidij respondent.* There is, finally, reason to suppose that the type with which the sonnet was printed was cut by Pierre Haultin,[58] and, although it is true that Haultin sold founts of his type to printers in England and Scotland, the failure to set the letters 'k' and 'w' in the sonnet (substituting for them 'c' and 'v') suggests a French composing case, and the misprinting of 'ou' for 'on' in line 13 (even allowing for the common error of turned letters)[59] could suggest a misreading of copy by a French compositor.[60]

To sum up *pro* and *contra*: doubt may be cast on the contention that Mark Alexander Boyd was the author of the sonnet by (i) the nature of the subscription to the earliest version of the text, which is not printed along with the text, but added in manuscript on no specified authority, (ii) the existence of a later manuscript version with a heading which is self-contradictory but which seems to identify Master Andrew Boyd, minister of Eaglesham, as author, and (iii) the absence of any other surviving writing by Mark Alexander Boyd in Scots vernacular. Against these sources of doubt can be set some relatively weighty counter-arguments. (i) The sonnet may well have been printed at La Rochelle, in an area of France with which Boyd had other associations. (ii) Although the subscription is not printed, its form corresponds with the style of subscriptions that appear in some of the Boyd papers in NLS. (iii) There is evident confusion in the manuscript's heading between the names of Alexander and Andrew, which renders it

---

[57] I have seen the book only in microfilm, but, even so, at least three of its ornaments can be seen to match reproductions in Desgraves, nos. 5 and 132.

[58] The type of the sonnet is the small italic illustrated by Desgraves at no. 40. In correspondence Mr Matthew Carter kindly informed me that he had found it in other Haultin imprints (not illustrated by Desgraves). He added that it does not seem to have been widely distributed, and, although it may have been used by other printers, these would probably only have been such as had direct dealings with the Haultins (e.g. Millanges). As for the origin of the type, Mr Carter considered that 'this face can tentatively be assigned to Pierre Haultin on the grounds that it occurs in his printing and cannot be proved to have been cut by anyone else'.

[59] See R.B. McKerrow, *An Introduction to Bibliography* (2nd imp. with corrections, Oxford, 1928), 257-8.

[60] *TLS*, 12 May 1950.

suspect as an authority. (iv) While no extant example of any other writing in the Scots vernacular by Boyd has been found, Boyd would not have been the only artist to have to his credit only one known surviving work in a particular form. (v) A tradition that Boyd had written more in the vernacular seems to have survived in the Boyd family from the early seventeenth century, to be accepted by Sibbald and even by the more sceptical Lord Hailes, although no example has ever come to light. It cannot be said that, on the whole, the available evidence radically undermines Mark Alexander Boyd's traditional status as the author of 'Fra banc to banc'. Unless and until any further evidence can be brought to light, or the present evidence can be convincingly reinterpreted, this seems to be the attribution that ought to be accepted.[61]

[61] My thanks are due to members of the staff of NLS for help with problems posed by bookbinding techniques, heraldry, obscure Latinity and handwriting difficult to decipher and identify.

'DURKAN & ROSS' AND BEYOND

Brian Hillyard

For any member of staff of the National Library of Scotland involved in the acquisition and cataloguing of early printed books, *Early Scottish Libraries* by John Durkan and Anthony Ross[1]—often referred to as 'Durkan & Ross'—soon becomes an indispensable work of reference. Listing, by order of owner (in three sequences: bishops, other individual owners, institutions) all printed books known to its authors as having been in Scottish ownership before the Reformation, this is one of the first aids one reaches for when struggling with an early, possibly Scottish, signature written in a pre-Reformation printed book. With the help of 'Durkan & Ross' and, indeed, frequently of John Durkan himself, many inscriptions have been identified in existing or newly acquired NLS stock or sometimes in books being considered for purchase. In this way 'Durkan & Ross' has been continually refined and expanded with reference to the holdings of NLS, a process that has happened also in other libraries.[2]

'Durkan & Ross' is certainly an ever-growing working-tool, and at a guess its growth is not slowing down, but rather accelerating. Reference tools of this kind can acquire a life of their own, but it would be wrong to assume that it is merely this inward-looking use of 'Durkan & Ross' for its own enlargement which is providing the impetus in the search for more data. David Pearson, in his useful

---

[1] J. Durkan and A. Ross, *Early Scottish Libraries* (Glasgow, 1961); expanded from *IR*, ix (1958), 5-167.

[2] The material has been published in a number of articles: J. Durkan and R.V. Pringle, 'St Andrews additions to Durkan & Ross: some unrecorded Scottish pre-Reformation ownership inscriptions in St Andrews University Library', *The Bibliotheck*, ix (1978-9), 13-20; J. Durkan, 'Further additions to Durkan and Ross: some newly-discovered Scottish pre-Reformation provenances', *The Bibliotheck*, x (1980-81), 87-98; J. Durkan and J. Russell, 'Additions to J. Durkan and A. Ross, *Early Scottish Libraries*, at the National Library of Scotland', *The Bibliotheck*, xi (1982-3), 29-37; J. Durkan, 'Addenda to 'Further additions to Durkan and Ross'', *The Bibliotheck*, xi (1982-3), 57-8; J. Durkan and J. Russell, 'Further additions (including manuscripts) to J. Durkan and A. Ross, *Early Scottish Libraries*, at the National Library of Scotland', *The Bibliotheck*, xii (1984-5), 85-90. T.A.F. Cherry, 'The library of Henry Sinclair, bishop of Ross, 1560-1565', *The Bibliotheck*, iv (1963), 13-24, includes some corrections and additions (pp. 19-23).

pamphlet on provenance indexes,[3] which, by the way, describes 'Durkan & Ross' as 'an invaluable work for which there is no English equivalent', not only documents the comparative lack of available provenance indexes but also illustrates growing interest in this area of bibliographical studies. He is certainly correct about this. Catalogues of early printed books or manuscripts now routinely have provenance notes and indexes; if not, reviewers want to know why not. Moreover, there is increasing interest in including both notes on and the indexing of provenance in machine-readable library catalogues, which should eventually bring to our attention a larger number of items from a larger number of sources, enabling listings such as 'Durkan & Ross' to be expanded. This enhanced status of provenance information is most appropriate at a time when the Leverhulme Trust has made a handsome grant for research towards *A History of the Book in Britain*, which Cambridge University Press has agreed to publish, in six volumes.[4] This is not to say that the projected *History* has stimulated provenance studies; it may be, rather, that students of provenance have provided ready support for the idea of the *History*. If more British bibliographers are now interested in studying provenance than was previously the case, it could be partly because in the light of the achievements of retrospective British bibliography—most notably the machine-readable *Eighteenth-Century Short Title Catalogue* (*ESTC*)—they see less scope for enumerative bibliography.

In a prefatory note to *Early Scottish Libraries* the editors wrote that the work was 'intended to serve as a pilot list which will be extended from time to time, as research continues, by the publication of new material in *The Innes Review*', and also commented: 'It is hoped eventually to list manuscripts as well as printed books, and to extend the chronological limits of the survey backwards into the earlier middle ages'. In 1978 *The Bibliotheck* published its first supplementary listing, and the editor invited further contributions, noting that 'ownership inscriptions recorded in these articles will be incorporated in due course in a future

---

[3] D. Pearson, *Provenance Indexes for Early Printed Books and Manuscripts: A Guide to Present Resources* (Huntingdon: The author, 1987).

[4] Part of the Leverhulme Trust grant is being used to support a research programme (Research Fellow: Margaret L. Ford) to record British ownership of books and manuscripts 1400-1557. For a brief report see *Publishing History*, xxix (1991), 69-70.

second edition of Durkan & Ross'.[5] Nor has the original idea of including manuscripts been forgotten, for in 1985 *The Bibliotheck* published some additions that included manuscripts and an editorial note welcomed supplements including or devoted to manuscripts from all sources.[6]

With a reference book of this kind new editions are needed from time to time, and we have seen that a second edition was mentioned at least as long ago as 1978. But no new edition should be regarded as definitive; each one is a superior working-tool serving as a basis for the next edition. The text should be held on disk, and updated disks or interim print-outs could be made available at the main centres of research. Thanks to modern printing technology, it might become a more financially viable option than it has been hitherto to bring out limited published editions by setting them from disk.

Once new editions are being seriously considered, changes other than additions can be considered. There will be no shortage of suggestions: here I confine myself to two points. The first stems from the needs of those researchers who want to pass beyond the superficial listing of the books owned by an individual and assess the intellectual influences exerted on that person through his library, or need perhaps in a particular case to trace in an author's library the sources for his own writings. This requires some examination of the texts he possessed. If we could assume that 'Durkan & Ross' informed us of the presence of annotations by the owner, and no annotations were noted, we would not need to see the actual copy owned; other copies would suffice. But while finding the inscribed books in the locations recorded should be easy enough ('Durkan & Ross' usually gives shelfmarks), the shortage of bibliographical details sometimes makes it more difficult to find other copies. Which of the undated Basle editions—there are at least three—of Robert Caracciolus, *Sermones quadragesimales de poenitentia* did William Elphinstone and Hector Boece own (pp. 34, 77)? Fortunately, this book is in Aberdeen University Library, and Mitchell's catalogue of the incunabula held there gives us the answer: *Gesamtkatalog der Wiegendrucke* 6077

[5] J. Durkan and R.V. Pringle, 'St Andrews additions', 13.

[6] J. Durkan and J. Russell, 'Further additions (including manuscripts)', 85. John Durkan serves on the Editorial Committee of the Corpus of British Medieval Library Catalogues (The British Library in association with The British Academy), and is working on the Scottish volume to appear in this series.

= [Basel: Berthold Ruppel, about 1480].[7] Or how easily would somebody outside New College, Edinburgh, find a copy of '*Expositio hymnorum.* Rouen. *Circa* 1500' (p. 66)?[8] And could another Aberdeen University Library book, 'Gabriel Biel, *De fastis Christi sermones* n.p. c. 1519' (p. 83), be safely identified as Basle, 1519 = *Index Aureliensis* *119.123, if Drummond had not described it adequately?[9]

Examples like this show that a case can be made out for including sufficient bibliographical details to assist in the firm identification of other copies. Printers and formats should always be given, and preferably collations unless already available. In fact, since the first publication of 'Durkan & Ross', bibliographical control of early printed books has improved. There are various union and other catalogues for sixteenth-century foreign books, including the *Index Aureliensis*,[10] the *Répertoire bibliographique*,[11] Voet's Plantin Press bibliography,[12] and Adams for Cambridge libraries,[13] while for British books we can refer to the recently completed second edition of *STC*.[14] For the fifteenth century there is a growing number of reference books, backed up by the British Library's *Incunable Short-Title Catalogue* (*ISTC*), which is fast becoming a world-wide union catalogue.[15] References to such

[7] W.S. Mitchell, *Catalogue of the Incunabula in Aberdeen University Library* (Aberdeen, 1968), 62 (now Inc.167).

[8] New College Library, Edinburgh, tVK 74 EXP (title leaf and some other leaves damaged). *Expositio hymn[orum.] Per totum anni circulum.* Impressum Rothomagi [i.e. Rouen] p(er) Richardum Goupil impensis Jacobi le Forestier eiusde(m) urbis bibliopole, [c.1510]. 8vo. ff.lxxxvi,[2]. A-L^8. Publication details taken from colophon on L8r. Title page contains Jacques le Forestier's device: L.C. Silvestre, *Marques typographiques*, 2 vols. (Paris, 1868), no. 552. From the *Répertoire bibliographique*, which does not record this book, it would appear that Goupil's career began at around the time Le Forestier's ended. The only other book I know of in the publication of which both Goupil and Le Forestier were involved is an edition of Dionysius Cato dated 2 July 1510 (*Répertoire*, 130 Goupil 1).

[9] It is in fact the only recorded edition. The identification can be made from *A Short-Title Catalogue of Books Printed on the Continent of Europe, 1501-1600, in Aberdeen University Library*, compiled by H.J.H. Drummond (Aberdeen, 1979), item 617.

[10] *Index Aureliensis: Catalogus librorum sedecimo saeculo impressorum* (Aureliae Aquensis, 1962-, in progress).

[11] *Répertoire bibliographique des livres imprimés en France au seizième siècle*, 30 vols. (Baden-Baden, 1968-80). H.L. Baudrier, *Bibliographie lyonnaise*, 12 vols. (Lyons, 1895-1921) remains indispensable.

[12] L. Voet, *The Plantin Press (1555-1589)*, 6 vols. (Amsterdam, 1980-83).

[13] H.M. Adams, *Catalogue of Books Printed on the Continent of Europe, 1501-1600 in Cambridge Libraries*, 2 vols. (Cambridge, 1967).

[14] *STC*, 2nd edn., 3 vols. (1976-91).

[15] For recent descriptions of the *ISTC* see, for example, L. Hellinga and J.

descriptions can take the place of bibliographical descriptions in the way that they have already done for incunables,[16] with the additional advantage that at the same time they often provide details of other locations. Where published descriptions are not available, adequate details should of course be given.

My second point arises from considering 'Durkan & Ross' in the context of the history of Scottish libraries. The success of 'Durkan & Ross' is underlined by the relative paucity of published information for the immediately following period.[17] It should come as no surprise to find that 'Durkan & Ross' is of great value for this following period also, for, as Anthony Ross pointed out (introduction, p. 8), the survival of the books listed in 'Durkan & Ross' is in great measure owed to the booklovers of subsequent centuries—men like Charles Lumsden (both father and son) of Edinburgh and Robert Baillie of Glasgow—who took these books into their own libraries whence eventually most of them have come into institutional ownership. Therefore the later provenance information given in the descriptions is extremely valuable for the history of book collecting in Scotland, and should always be included, as in fact usually seems to have been the practice. It follows that a comprehensive index to all the provenances mentioned in 'Durkan & Ross' would greatly increase its usefulness in this respect, and would be most welcome.

In the post-Reformation period, library catalogues, whether in manuscript or, in due course, printed (the 1627 catalogue of the poet William Drummond's library as presented to Edinburgh University Library is the earliest such Scottish printed catalogue),[18] became more frequent in Scotland. Nevertheless, the reconstruction of libraries from inscribed books remains important. One such library may appropriately be mentioned here as it

---

Goldfinch, 'Ten years of the *Incunable Short-Title Catalogue* (*ISTC*)', *Bulletin du bibliophile*, 1990, no.1, 125-32; M.C. Davies, 'The *Incunable Short Title Catalogue* (*ISTC*)', *Bulletin of the Society for Renaissance Studies*, vii (1990), 1-7.

16 D.E. Rhodes, *A Catalogue of Incunabula in all the Libraries of Oxford University outside the Bodleian* (Oxford, 1982), provides an excellent example. He records provenance and other copy-specific information tied to succinct bibliographical identifications using references to published descriptions.

17 Some of the points made here have already been noted in B. Hillyard, 'Working towards a history of Scottish book collecting', in *Six Centuries of the Provincial Book Trade in Britain*, ed. P. Isaac (Winchester, 1990), 181-6.

18 *Auctarium bibliothecae Edinburgenae, sive catalogus librorum quos Guilielmus Drummondus ab Hawthornden Bibliothecae D. D. Q. anno. 1627* (Edinburgh, 1627).

takes us back nearly into the 'Durkan & Ross' period. In 1987, NLS acquired from the Haddington family library at Tyninghame House 345 volumes which were believed to have been in the library of Thomas Hamilton, the first earl of Haddington (1563-1637).[19] These volumes could be identified as his because he signed them with whatever was his appropriate title at the time, whether as M. [i.e. *Magister*] T. Hamilton (until 1603), Sir T. Hamilton (from 1603), Lord Binning (from 1613), Earl of Melrose (from 1619) or Earl of Haddington (from 1626).

As the library of the first earl of Haddington, these books represent an early seventeenth-century Scottish library, and because of the first earl's changes of title and his use of them in inscribing his books it is possible to separate out various strata of his collecting and so reconstruct as the earliest, pre-1603, stratum an almost entirely late sixteenth-century library. But it is possible that some of the books belonged to a Scottish library of a generation earlier or at least were the first earl's earliest acquisitions of the pre-1603 stratum. For the collection includes 31—listed below in the Appendix (31 volumes, 45 items, in all)—signed 'MTHamiltoun' (fig. 10) or 'MTH' in an italic hand which unlike the different, more rounded 'MTHamilton' (fig. 12) bears little resemblance to 'STHamilton' (fig. 11).

If we look at the origins of these books with the italic signature, we find that they consist of 26 works published in Paris, eight in Lyons, four in Geneva, two each in Antwerp and London, and one each in Orleans, Montbéliard, and Frankfurt. This pattern is quite different from that which emerges from the first earl's collection proper:[20] while rich in French imprints, it is not overwhelmingly so, and there are over 80 books from London and quantities also from Germany and Italy. Also worth noticing in the present group

---

[19] For the life of the first earl see Fraser, *Haddington*, i, 34-188. The books now form a special collection (shelf-mark 'Tyn.') in NLS, and it is their numbers within this collection that are used here for reference. On the circumstances of acquisition, with some brief details, see B. Hillyard, 'Books for the National Library from Tyninghame House', *Scottish Book Collector*, vi (June/July 1988), 26-7. Attention had been drawn to the importance of the collection by H. Trevor-Roper, *Tyninghame Library* (privately printed, 1977), but its earlier fame is shown by Patrick Fraser Tytler, *An Account of the Life and Writings of Sir Thomas Craig of Riccarton* (Edinburgh, 1823), 263, referring to 'the various notes and observations collected by him [*sc. the first earl*] in the course of his studies, and the marginal adversaria yet seen upon his books'.

[20] A handful of books are known which left Tyninghame House before the recent dispersal, but their small number suggests that we do possess the greater part of his library.

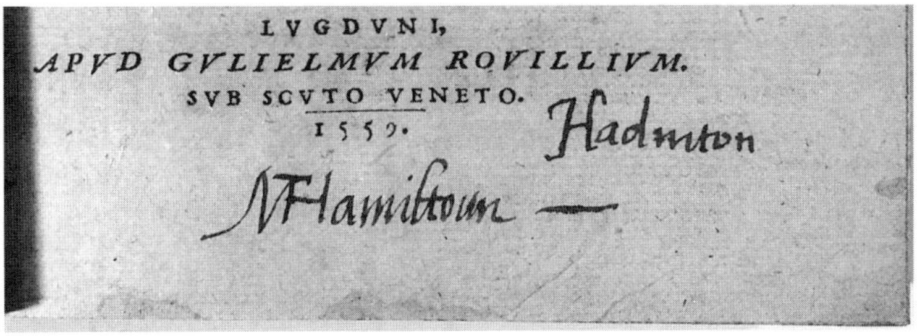

LVGDVNI,
APVD GVLIELMVM ROVILLIVM.
SVB SCVTO VENETO.
1559.
Hadinton
MTHamiltoun —

Fig. 10 DIO CASSIUS. *Romanae historiae libri ... XXV. nimirum à XXXVI. ad LXI* (tr. G. Xylander). Lugduni: apud Gulielmum Rouillium, 1559. (NLS, Tyn.39). With the signatures of 'MTHamiltoun' and the Earl of Haddington.

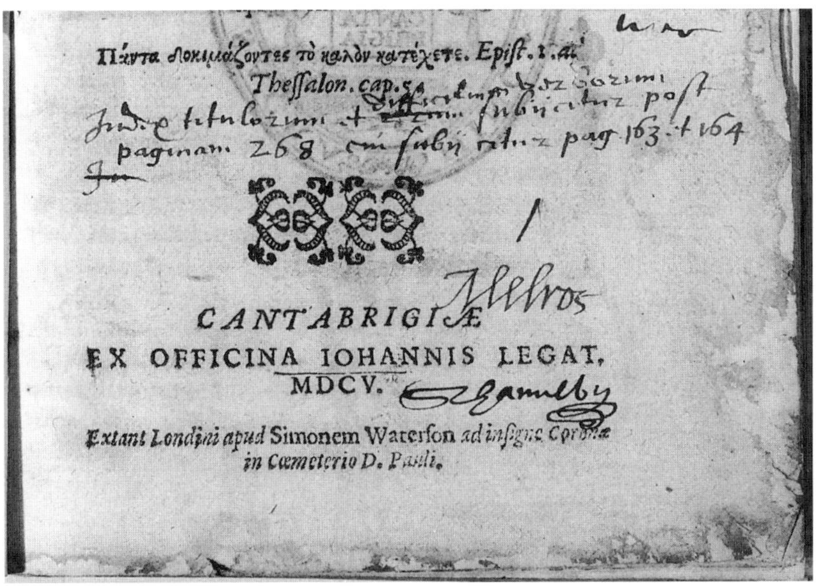

Πάντα δοκιμάζοντες τὸ καλὸν κατέχετε. Epist. 1. ad Thessalon. cap. 5.
Melros
CANTABRIGIÆ
EX OFFICINA IOHANNIS LEGAT.
MDCV.
Extant Londini apud Simonem Waterson ad insigne Coronæ in Cœmeterio D. Pauli.

Fig. 11 Cowell, John. *Institutiones iuris anglicani ad methodum et seriem institutionum imperialium compositae & digestae.* Cantabrigiae: ex officina Iohannis Legat, 1605. (NLS, Tyn.24). With the signatures of Sir T. Hamilton and the Earl of Melrose.

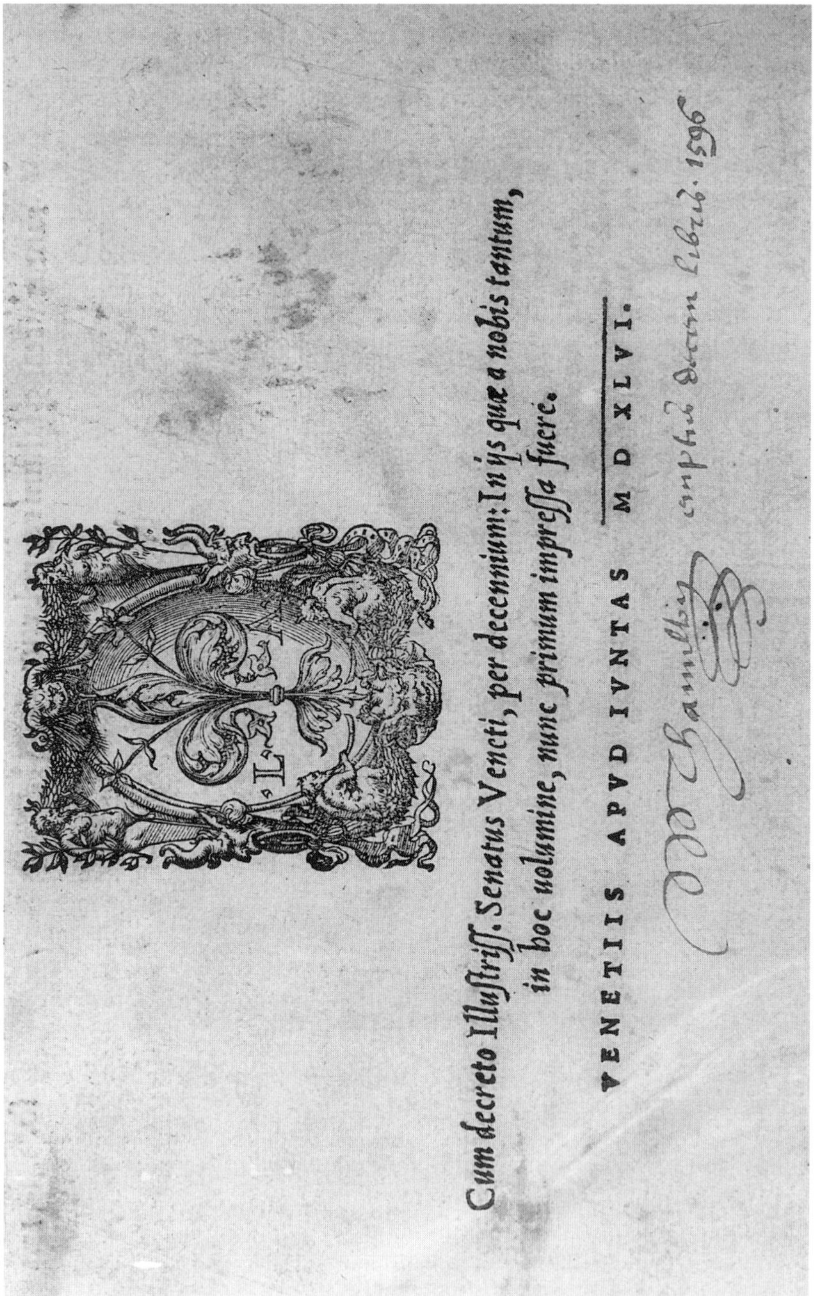

Cum decreto Illustriss. Senatus Veneti, per decennium: In ijs quæ a nobis tantum, in hoc uolumine, nunc primum impressa fuere.

VENETIIS APVD IVNTAS M D XLVI.

Fig. 12 ROLANDINUS, de Passageriis. *Summa totius artis notariae.* Venetiis: apud Iuntas, 1546. (NLS, Tyn.283). With the signature of M(agister) T. Hamilton.

is the high number of texts of Greek—albeit in translation—and Latin authors (302 is a French-Latin dictionary). Moreover, 141(1-3), 215, 219(1-5), and 226(1-8) could be categorized as students' textbooks; indeed 215 and 219(1-4), as also 226(1) and 226(4), are printed by Thomas Richard, printer to the University of Paris. 215, 219(1-5), and 226(8)—as also 10, 22, 32—have manuscript notes, some of them probably taken down at lectures.[21] These textbooks or annotated texts are all French imprints (one published in Orleans, three in Lyons, the remainder in Paris), and none is later than 1570. An attractive explanation for these characteristics of this group of books is that 'MTHamiltoun' acquired them as a student in France, where in the sixteenth century Scots often went to pursue their studies, as indeed we shall see was the case with both the first earl and his father.

To return to the signatures, the latest publication date of any of these books is 1588 (34), and this shows that the italic signature was in use as late as that year. We could say that it was the first earl's signature and that subsequently he changed it to the more rounded form of which the earliest attested use is 1596 (283, fig. 12).[22] Otherwise the most that can be said—which amounts to very little—about the date when the first earl adopted the rounded form is that it was sufficiently before he was knighted in 1603 to account for the books inscribed with that form. There is no reason, therefore, why he should not have persisted with the italic form until 1588 or even some years later. It is worth bearing in mind the italic character of the later 'Melros' signature and of the inscription 'emptus decem libris. 1596' (283, mentioned above) as suggesting that the first earl could well have used an

[21] No. 22, an interleaved copy of eulogies of Roman citizens collected out of Cicero by Jean Papire Masson, carries on a blank leaf facing the dedication an inscription relating to a Frenchman's studies at the College of Navarre in the University of Paris: 'Vincentius Fererius(?) Noviodunensis in florentissima Navarraea palaestra scolasticus sub eruditissimo praeceptore d(omi)no de Morarmier(?) Parisiense'. No. 32, a copiously annotated edition of Vegetius, carries on the verso of the title page details about the origin of some of these notes: 'Annotationes Nicolai Le Sueur in hunc libru(m)' (for Nicolas Lesueur, c. 1540-94, see *Biographie universelle*, xxiv, 340).

[22] No. 283 is inscribed a second time, in the same rounded form, beneath the colophon, 'MTHamilton emptus decem libris. Edr apr. 1596'. Non-italic 'MTHamiltoun' is also found in 228, which is inscribed 'ffor Maistre Thomas Hamilton of Drumcairn Lord of ye session in Edinbourgue from Paris ye last of marche 1594': but it would be incorrect to assume that Hamilton inscribed it in 1594, as is shown by 197 which has a similar presentation inscription with the same date but has no earlier inscription than 'Melros', i.e. not before 1619!

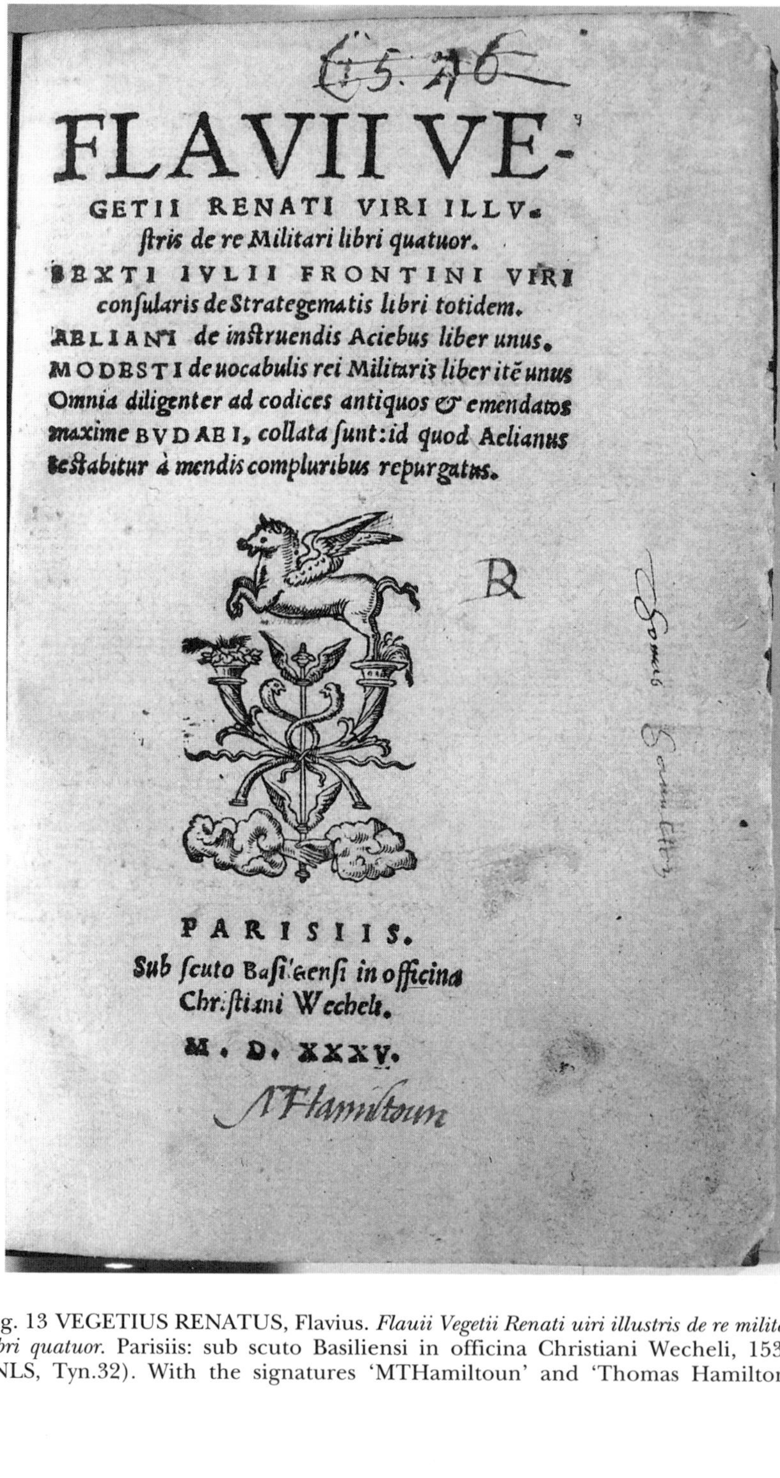

FLAVII VE-
GETII RENATI VIRI ILLV-
ſtris de re Militari libri quatuor.
SEXTI IVLII FRONTINI VIRI
conſularis de Strategematis libri totidem.
AELIANI de inſtruendis Aciebus liber unus.
MODESTI de uocabulis rei Militaris liber itē unus
Omnia diligenter ad codices antiquos & emendatos
maxime BVDAEI, collata ſunt: id quod Aelianus
teſtabitur à mendis compluribus repurgatus.

PARISIIS.
Sub ſcuto Baſilienſi in officina
Chriſtiani Wecheli.
M. D. XXXV.

MTHamiltoun

Fig. 13 VEGETIUS RENATUS, Flavius. *Flauii Vegetii Renati uiri illustris de re militari libri quatuor.* Parisiis: sub scuto Basiliensi in officina Christiani Wecheli, 1535. (NLS, Tyn.32). With the signatures 'MTHamiltoun' and 'Thomas Hamilton'.

italic signature. The fact that there is only one probable instance of a book containing both these forms of signature (310),[23] might be seen as possible support for the hypothesis that there is only one man's signature here on the argument that if the italic signature were not the first earl's, he would have wanted to add his own signature, and there would be more books with both signatures: but if the books had belonged to somebody else and become available to the first earl only in or after 1603, that is after he had ceased to use either form of the M. T. Hamilton signature, that would explain the facts equally well.

Ownership of these books would suit the first earl, though admittedly not, as we shall see below, exclusively so. He was a student in Paris from 1581 to 1587, where he is assumed to have studied classics and philosophy.[24] While there he associated with one of his uncles, John Hamilton, a graduate of St Andrews who taught philosophy at the College of Navarre in the University of Paris from about 1574 and became Rector of the University in 1584.[25] The identification therefore provides a reasonable working hypothesis. Unfortunately, no proof in the form of a pre-1588 italic signature attested as the first earl's can yet be produced.[26] This is not totally unexpected, as young men who have not attained to positions of responsibility have less occasion to sign documents.

Some rather ambiguous evidence is presented by 32, a collection of texts on military strategy printed in Paris in 1535, which is inscribed in the usual way with italic 'MTHamiltoun' beneath the imprint but also has, written sideways half-way up the righthand side of the title page, the inscription 'Thomas Hamilton' (fig. 13). This is not the usual position of one of the first earl's inscriptions (even when there are several of them), and it does not look like the first earl's mature hand (note also the omission of any title). If this is the first earl practising his signature as a boy, the italic signature could be his own later

---

[23] The italic signature is slightly different from the usual one but is probably in the same hand.

[24] Fraser, *Haddington*, i, pp. 35-6.

[25] ibid., i, 15-17; *DNB*, viii, 1079-80. See also Fraser, *Haddington*, i, 63-4, for a 1597 letter of uncertain authorship which refers to 'Mr. Thomas Hamilton, brought up in Parise with that apostat, Mr. Johne Hamiltoun'.

[26] Dr Ian Grant, National Register of Archives (Scotland), who is relisting the Haddington Muniments, kindly informs me that so far he is unaware of any relevant documents.

signature.[27] But would a boy have acquired this volume? It might be easier if the italic signature is that of a previous owner, to whose books the first earl had access.

If—for whatever reasons—the italic 'MTHamiltoun' signature is not the first earl's, whose might it be? As these books came fairly early into the first earl's library, the signature must be that of a member of the family. Thomas Hamilton, the first earl's grandfather, is ruled out because he was killed at the battle of Pinkiecleuch in 1547.[28] The most obvious possibility is Thomas Hamilton, the first earl's father.[29] Probably born in about 1540, he married (for the first time) in 1558, and was made a burgess of Edinburgh in 1561. In April 1568 he was in Paris,[30] 'probably pursuing the study of law'.[31] Back in Scotland by September 1569, when he was sitting on the burgh council of Edinburgh, he was later to be overtaken in his career by his son, the future first earl, who became Lord Drumcairn in 1592, whereas the father was created a Lord of Session (Lord Priestfield) only in 1607. He died about 1613.[32] After his death his books—if they had been kept separately hitherto—might have found their way into his son's library. Perhaps the obvious point needs to be made that the first earl's father would have had books and that as there was a family library some of his books would be expected to survive as part of it. While this remains a possibility, there is no proof that the italic signature is Lord Priestfield's; and in so far as the signature in a letter which he wrote on 13 April 1571 should probably be read as 'Thomas Hammilton' (*sic*), this might count as evidence against the identification.[33]

---

[27] On p.282, at the end of Frontinus's *Strategemata*, in the same hand that has annotated the *Strategemata* throughout (which is different from the hand that has anotated the earlier part of the volume, Vegetius), there is an inscription 'Octob. 1587'. It is impossible not to recall that this is a year—the last year—when the first earl was in Paris, but nothing can be deduced from this.

[28] Fraser, *Haddington*, i, 14-17; George Hamilton, *A History of the House of Hamilton* (Edinburgh, 1933), 413.

[29] Fraser, *Haddington*, i, 17-24; Hamilton, *House of Hamilton*, 414-15; M. Lynch, *Edinburgh and the Reformation* (Edinburgh, 1981), 208, 210, 332-3.

[30] See the letter dated 1 April 1568 sent to him in Paris, printed in Fraser, *Haddington*, ii, 115-16.

[31] Fraser, *Haddington*, 18, who, however, cites no specific evidence for this.

[32] Fraser, *Haddington*, 24, says 'probably dead before 1612'. but see the evidence cited by Hamilton, *House of Hamilton*, 415, for dating his death to after 27 July 1613.

[33] The letter is printed in Fraser, Haddington, ii, 201-02. The original is PRO, SP 52/20, item 25, which I have seen in photocopy.

Perhaps one day new evidence will enable the owner to be firmly identified. In the meantime we are fortunate to possess here a group of books clearly connected with higher education in Paris in the second half of the sixteenth century, and quite possibly used in Paris by a member of the Hamilton family. These books, with their annotations, deserve further detailed examination by students of intellectual history. From the Scottish angle, one book is of particular interest, William Davidson's *Institutiones luculentae in totum Aristotelis organum logicum* (219(4)), an introduction to Aristotle's *Organon* which has recently been praised for its luminous clarity.[34] The success of this work, which was previously recorded in a rare 1560 edition[35] and in an even rarer 1567 epitome,[36] is now underlined by this hitherto unrecorded 1561 edition. In William Davidson's preface, dated 24 September 1560, he says that he has been teaching philosophy in Paris for seven years, that is since 1553. Unlike his brother John Davidson, who returned from France in 1556 to become Principal of Glasgow University and embraced the Reformation in 1559, William remained a Catholic (his book is dedicated to Archbishop Beaton) and stayed behind in Paris, being appointed Regent at Ste Barbe College in 1558.[37] He continued to teach philosophy there until ordered to stop in September 1568.[38] Whoever annotated this copy of William Davidson's book could have done so from its author's lectures.[39]

Appendix of Volumes inscribed with Italic 'MTH' or 'MTHamiltoun' in the NLS Tyninghame Collection

Books are identified via bibliographical references, where available, to Adams, *Index Aureliensis, Répertoire bibliographique,* Voet, Baudrier, and *STC* (2nd edn.); for full details of these works see nn.10-14, above.

[34] A Broadie, *The Tradition of Scottish Philosophy: A New Perspective on the Enlightenment* (Edinburgh, 1990), 85.

[35] M.A. Shaaber, *Check-list of Works of British Authors Printed Abroad, in Languages other than English, to 1641* (New York, 1975), D5, recording only two copies, both in Oxford: Bodleian Library and Pembroke College.

[36] Shaaber D6, recording Bodleian Library copy only. Shaaber incorrectly gives the date as 1563.

[37] J. Durkan & J. Kirk, *The University of Glasgow 1451-1577* (Glasgow 1977), 216-17, 232-3, 266.

[38] J. Crevier, *Histoire de l'université de Paris,* 7 vols. (Paris, 1761), vi, 235.

[39] I am grateful to my colleagues Elspeth Yeo and Julian Russell for their advice throughout, although the final responsibility is my own.

Where no references are available, collation and foliation/pagination are recorded following Adams's method. All the inscriptions recorded occur on the title pages of the books. Early shelf-marks from the Tyninghame Library have not been noted. Accents have been transcribed as/where found.

[**1**] VIDA, Marco Girolamo. *Marci Hieronymi Vidae Cremonensis, Albae episcopi opera.* Lugduni: apud Ant. Gryphium, 1578. 8vo (Adams V698).
Inscribed 'MTHamiltoun'.

[**10**] PASQUIER, Etienne. *Des recherches de la France.* 2 vols. A Orleans: par Pierre Trepperel, 1567. 8vo. I. ff.115. a-q^8 p^4 (p4 blank); II. ff.122. ā^8 ē^8 i^4 A-P^8 Q^6 (i4, Q6 blank).
Inscribed 'MTHamiltoun'. MS table of contents in each volume.

[**22**] MASSON, Jean Papire. *Io. Papirii Massoni elogia ciuium Romanorum, ex Cicerone collecta.* Parisiis: ex typographia Dionysij à Prato, 1570. 8vo. ff.(24). A-F^4.
Inscribed 'MTHamiltoun'. Many MS notes.

[**23**] SAINTE-MARTHE, *Scévole de. Scaeuolae Sammarthani consiliarii regis, et aerarii apud Pictones antigraphei, poëtica paraphrasis in sacra Ca(n)tica ... [etc.].* Lutetiae: ex officina Federici Morelli, 1575. 8vo. ff.68. A-R^4.
Inscribed 'MTH'.

[**28**] ESTIENNE, Henri. *L'Introduction au traite de la conformite des merueilles anciennes auec les modernes. Ou, traite preparatif à l'Apologie pour Herodote.* [Geneva: H. Estienne], Mars 1579. 8vo (Adams S1774).
Inscribed 'MTHamiltoun' and 'Hadinton'.

[**32**] VEGETIUS RENATUS, Flavius. *Flauii Vegetii Renati uiri illustris de re militari libri quatuor. Sext Iulii Frontini ... de strategematis libri totidem ... [etc.].* Parisiis: sub scuto Basiliensi in officina Christiani Wecheli, 1535. 8vo (Adams V332).
Inscribed 'MTHamiltoun', 'Thomas Hamilton', and (monogram) 'RD'(?); see fig. 13. Many MS notes.

[**34**] MACCHIAVELLI, Niccolo. *Nicolai Macchiauelli Floren. disputationum de republica, quas discursus nuncupauit, libri III.* Mompelgarti [Montbéliard]: per Iacobum Folietum, 1588. 8vo. 654pp. ¶^{8} a-z A-S^8(-S8) (*Répertoire bibliographique* 91 Foillet 4).
Inscribed 'MTHamiltoun'.

[**39**] DIO CASSIUS. Dionis Cassii Nicaei, *Romanae historiae libri ... XXV. nimirum à XXXVI. ad LXI* (tr. G. Xylander). Lugduni: apud Gulielmum Rouillium, 1559. 8vo (Adams D510).
Inscribed 'MTHamiltoun' and 'Hadinton'; see fig. 10.

[**41**] BODIN, Jean. *Les six liures de la republique.* Reueuë, corrigee &

augmentee de nouueau. A Paris: chez Iacques du Puys, 1580. 8vo (*Index Aureliensis* *120.815; Adams B2237).
Inscribed 'MTHamiltoun' and 'Melros'.

[**49**] BENZONI, Girolamo. *Nouae noui orbis historiae, id est, rerum ab Hispanis in India Occidentali hactenus gestarum, & acerbo illorum in eas gentes dominatu, libri tres* (tr. U. Calveto). [Geneva]: apud Eustathium Vignon, 1578. 8vo (*Index Aureliensis* *116.987; Adams B685).
Inscribed 'MTHamiltoun'.

[**59**] MASSON, Jean Papire. *Papirii Massoni annalium libri quatuor: quibus res gestae Francorum explicantur.* Editio secunda. Lutetiae: apud Nicolaum Chesneau, 1578. 8vo (Adams M869).
Inscribed 'MTHamiltoun'.

[**60**] TOLOMEI, Claudio. *Les epistres argentees ou recueil des principalles lettres des sept liures de Messer Claude Tolomeï ... choysiés & traduittes d'Italien.* A Paris: par Nicolas Bonsons, 1572 (achevé d'imprimer: 26 Sept. 1572). 8vo. ff.200. Aa^8 a-z $A-B^8$ $\bar{e}^4$.
Inscribed 'MTHamiltoun'.

[**65-66**] GUICCIARDINI, Francesco. *Histoire des guerres d'Italie* (tr. H. Chomedey). 2 vols. [Geneva]: par Pierre de Saint-André, 1577. 8vo. I. 985pp. π^2 a-z A-Z $Aa-Qq^8$ R^6; II. 904pp. a-z A-Z $Aa-Ll^8$ Mm^2.
Inscribed 'MTHamiltoun'.

[**82**] DES ROCHES, Magdeleine. *Les oeuures de mes-dames des Roches de Poetiers mere et fille.* Seconde edition. A Paris: pour Abel l'Angelier, 1179 [in error for 1579]. 4to. 192pp. (irregular pagination; some foliation between pages 51 and 57). a^4 G3-4 $A-F^4$ G^6 $H-Z^4$ Aa^4.
Inscribed 'MTH' and 'Melros'.

[**99**] LA PRIMAUDAYE, Pierre de. *Academie francoise, en laquelle il est traicté de l'institution des moeurs, & de ce qui concerne le bien & heureusement viure en tous estats & conditions.* Troisiesme edition. A Paris: chez Guillaume Chaudiere, 1582. 8vo. ff.387. $\bar{a}^8$ $\bar{e}^4$ a-z A-Z $Aa-Gg^8$ Hh^4 (Hh4 blank).
Inscribed 'MTHamiltoun'.

[**103**] GUAGNINUS, Alexander. *Rerum Polonicarum tomi tres.* Francofurti: excudebat Ioann. Wechelus, impensis Sigis. Feyerabendij, 1584. 8vo (Adams G1345).
Inscribed 'MTHamiltoun' and 'Melros'.

[**116**] AYRAULT, Pierre. *Petri Aerodii iudicis quaestionum andiumque ducis libell. mag. i.c. decretorum lib. VI.* Parisiis: apud Martinum Iuuenem, 1573. 8vo (*Index Aureliensis* *111.012; Adams A252).
Inscribed 'MTHamiltoun'.

[**126**] PATRIZI, Francesco (1413-1494). *Francisci Patricii senensis de institutione reipub. libri nouem.* Parisiis: apud Ioannem Hulpeau, 1578. 16mo. ff.380. $\bar{a}^8$ $\bar{e}^8$ a-z A-Z Aa-Ff^8 (Ff8 blank).
Inscribed 'MTHamiltoun'.

[**127**] SACRATUS, Paulus. *Epistolarum Paulli Sacrati Canonici Ferrar. libri sex.* Lugduni: apud Matheum Foucherium, 1581. 16mo (Adams S47).
Inscribed 'MTHamiltoun'.

[**128**] TAEGIO, Bartolomeo. *Les doctes et subtiles responces* (tr. A. du Verdier). A Lyon: par Barthelemy Honorat, 1577. 16mo (Adams T51).
Inscribed 'MTH'.

[**129(1)**] SENTENTIAE. *Sententiae Ciceronis, Demosthenis, ac Terentii.* Antverpiae: ex officina Christoph. Plantini, 1572. 16mo (Voet 987).
Inscribed 'MTHamiltoun'.
(bound with)
[**129(2)**] MAIOR, Georgius. *Sententiae veterum poetarum per locos communes digestae, Georgio Maiore collectore.* Antverpiae: ex officina Christophori Plantini, 1564. 16mo (Voet 1619).
No inscriptions.

[**140**] VALERIUS MAXIMUS. *Valerii Maximi, dictorum factorumque memorabilium exempla.* Lugduni: apud Gryphium, 1532. 8vo (Baudrier viii, 67).
Inscribed 'MTH'.

[**141(1)**] FORESTUS, Hector. *Hectoris Foresti Vasionensis iurium doctoris in Ethica Aristotelis ... domesticae praelectiones.* Lugduni: apud Seb. Gryphium, 1550. 8vo (Baudrier viii, 242).
Inscribed 'MTHamiltoun'.
(bound with)
[**141(2)**] FORESTUS, Hector. *Hectoris Foresti Vasionensis ... in quintum Ethicorum Aristotelis domesticae praelectiones.* Lugduni: apud Seb. Gryphium, 1550. 8vo (Baudrier viii, 242).
No inscriptions.
(bound with)
[**141(3)**] FORESTUS, Hector. *Hectoris Foresti Vasionensis iurisconsulti, in Oeconomica Aristotelis ... domesticae praelectiones.* Lugduni: apud Seb. Gryphium, 1550. 8vo (Baudrier viii, 242).
No inscriptions.

[**148(1)**] STAFFORD, William. *A compendious or briefe examination of certayne ordinary complaints ... by W. S. Gentleman.* Imprinted at London: by Thomas Marshe, 1581. 4to (*STC* 23133a).
Inscribed 'MTHamiltoun' and 'Melros'.
(bound with)
[**148(10)**] LOYSELEUR, Petrus de. *The apologie or defence, of the most noble Prince William, by the grace of God, Prince of Orange.* At Delft, 1581 [i.e. London, 1584]. 4to (*STC* 15209).

Inscribed 'MTHamiltoun'. Items (2)-(9) in this volume have imprint dates 1616-1630, and none has any inscriptions.

[**191**] QUINTILIAN. *M. Fabii Quintiliani oratoriarum institutionum libri. 12. vna cum nouendecim siue eiusdem; siue alterius declamationibus.* Parisiis, 1527. 4to (Adams Q27).
Inscribed 'MTHamiltoun'.

[**215**] ARISTOTLE. *Aristotelis ad Nicomachum filium, de moribus, quae Ethica nominantur, libri decem* (tr. N. Gruchius). Parisiis: ex typographia Thomae Richardi, 1561. 4to. ff.138. $*^2$ A-Z Aa-Ll^4 M^2.
Inscribed 'MTHamiltoun'. Many MS notes.

[**219(1)**] PLATO. *Platonis dialogus de philosophia, uel, Amatores* (tr. M. Ficino). Parisiis: ex typographia Thomae Richardi, 1560. 4to. ff.6. A^6.
Inscribed 'MTHamiltoun'. Many MS notes.
(bound with)
[**219(2)**] ARISTOTLE. *Aristotelis & Xenophontis Oeconomica* [includes: *In Aristotelis Oeconomicum scholia*] (tr. J.L. Strebaeus). Parisiis: ex typographia Thomae Richardi, 1560. 4to. ff.8,(4). A-B^4 a^4.
No ownership inscription. Many MS notes.
(bound with)
[**219(3)**] ARISTOTLE. *Aristotelis de republica, qui Politicorum dicuntur, libri VIII* [includes: *Observationes*] (tr. J. Perionius). Aeditio secunda. Parisiis: apud viduam Mauricij à Porta, 1552 (colophon on D4 reads: Parisiis excudebat Thomas Richardus 1552). 4to. ff.107,(24). $\bar{a}^4$ $\bar{e}^4$ i^4 a-z A-D^4; a-f^4.
No ownership inscription. MS notes near beginning only.
(bound with)
[**219(4)**] DAVIDSON, William. *Gulielmi Dauidson Aberdonani institutiones luculentae iuxtà ac breues, in totu(m) Aristotelis organum logicum.* Parisiis: ex typographia Thomae Richardi, 1561. 4to. ff.44. A-L^4.
No ownership inscription. Many MS notes.
(bound with)
[**219(5)**] FRIGILLANUS, Matthaeus. *Matthaei Frigillani Bellouaci in eam disserendi subtilitatem quae ab Aristot. tradita est, facilis & compendiosa introductio.* Parisiis: ex officina Gabrielis Buon, 1560. 4to. ff.17,(1),21-38. A-D^4 E^2 F-I^4 K^2 (E2 blank).
No ownership inscriptions or notes.

[**226(1)**] LITERATUS, Joannes. *Dialecticae familiaris introductio, ad philosophiae studiosos.* Parisiis: ex typographia Thomae Richardi, 1565. 4to. 14,(2)pp. A-B^4.
Inscribed 'MTHamiltoun'.
(bound with)
[**226(2)**] TABULA. *Tabula uniuersam philosophi(a)e partitionem continens.* [*colophon*] Parisiis: ex typographia Dionysij à Prato, 1569. 4to. ff.4. A^4.
(bound with)
[**226(3)**] AURELIUS VICTOR, Sextus. *C. Plinii Secundi Nouocomensis de viris illustribus liber, qui vulgò Cornelio Nepoti ascribitur.* Parisiis: ex officio

Gabrielis Buon, 1560. 4to. ff.23. A-F^4 (F4 blank) The *De viris illustribus* is usually attributed to Sextus Aurelius Victor.
(bound with)
[**226(4)**] CICERO, Marcus Tullius. *M.T. Ciceronis de optimo genere oratorum.* Parisiis: apud Thomam Richardum, 1551. 4to. 8pp. a^4.
(bound with)
[**226(5)**] MURETUS, Marcus Antonius. *M. Antonii Mureti in Ciceronis Philippicas a se innumeris prope locis emendatas scholia.* Parisiis: ex officina Gabriëlis Buon, 1562. 4to. ff.11. a-c^4 (c4 blank).
(bound with)
[**226(6)**] CICERO, Marcus Tullius. *M. Tul. Ciceronis pro rege Deiotaro oratio. Argumentis Francisci Syluij & Barptol. Latomi illustrata.* [Paris]: e typographia Matthaei Dauidis, [between 1546 and 1556?]. 4to. 20pp. a^4 b^6.
(bound with)
[**226(7)**] CICERO, Marcus Tullius. *Topica Marci Tullii Ciceronis ad C. Trebatium, cum Anitij Manlij Seuerini Boëtij, & Ioannis Visorij Coenomani commentarijs.* Parisiis: ex officina Ioannis Palierij, 1542. 4to (*Index Aureliensis* *138.236).
(bound with)
[**226(8)**] CARPENTARIUS, Joannes. *Compendium in communem artem disserendi, per Iacobum Carpentarium collectum, ab ipso authore postremò recognitum.* Parisiis: ex typographia Dionysij à Prato, 1567. 4to. ff.16. A-D^4.

[**302**] ESTIENNE, Robert. *Dictionarium Latinogallicum multo locupletius.* Lutetiae: ex officina Roberti Stephani, 1546. fol. (Adams S1805).
Inscribed 'MTHamiltoun'.

[**310**] BREDERODIUS, Petrus Cornelius. *Thesaurus dictionum et sententiarum iuris ciuilis.* [Geneva]: excudebat Eustathius Vignon, 1585. fol. (*Index Aureliensis* *124.164; Adams B2741).
Inscribed 'MTHamiltoun', 'MTHamilton', and 'Melros'.

GLANVILL RESARCINATE: SIR JOHN SKENE AND *REGIAM MAJESTATEM*

Hector L. MacQueen

The focus of this essay is Sir John Skene's work in the late sixteenth and early seventeenth centuries upon the close link between two medieval legal texts, the Scottish *Regiam Majestatem* and the late twelfth-century English *Glanvill*. Today it is accepted that *Regiam* is fundamentally a copy of *Glanvill*, probably compiled in the fourteenth century.[1] This was not the view of Skene. When he became the first to publish a text and Scots translation of *Regiam*, in 1609, he argued that the work had been put together in the reign of David I, king of Scots from 1124 to 1153, drawing on the attribution to 'king David' in its prologue. *Glanvill*, on the other hand, had been written in the reign of Henry II, king of England from 1154 to 1189, and was accordingly simply a version of *Regiam* adapted to English needs.[2] But even in Skene's own time this was a controverted thesis. The best-known expression of the opposite view of some contemporaries is in the *Jus Feudale* of Master Thomas Craig, advocate of the Scottish bar, where *Regiam* is denounced as 'a blot on the jurisprudence of our country... the work of some obscure plagiarist'.[3]

In Scotland, this was the beginning of a debate which was to endure for some 250 years; my title is drawn from the contribution to it of Lord Stair, first published in 1681, who commented that 'Craig doth very well observe... that these books called *Regiam Majestatem* are no part of our law, but were compiled for the customs of England in 13 books by the Earl of Chester, and by some unknown and inconsiderate hand stolen thence, and resarcinate into those four books which pass amongst us'.[4] 'Resarcinate' is an obscure word derived from the Latin verb

---

[1] The following works are essential: A.A.M. Duncan, '*Regiam Majestatem*: a reconsideration', *Juridical Review*, vi (1961); P.G. Stein, 'The source of the Romano-canonical part of *Regiam Majestatem*', *SHR*, xlviii (1969); A. Harding, '*Regiam Majestatem* amongst medieval law books', *Juridical Review*, xxix (1984).

[2] For this view of Skene's see his annotation of the prologue in his Latin edition of *Regiam* (Edinburgh, 1609), f.7v, and note also his address 'To the Reader' prefacing the Scots edition (also Edinburgh, 1609).

[3] Thomas Craig of Riccarton, *Jus Feudale* (Edinburgh, 1655), I, viii, 11.

[4] James Dalrymple, Viscount Stair, *Institutions of the Law of Scotland*, 6th edn.

sarcio, sarsi, meaning 'to patch, to mend, to botch'. Stair thus conjures up an image of *Regiam* as *Glanvill* patched up and amended, rather badly, to give the appearance of a Scottish work, but not in fact to be relied upon as a source. The ultimate triumph of this view of *Regiam* was to be one of the most important factors in drawing a veil over the medieval law of Scotland from both formal legal and historical points of view; this was, after all, the most important text of that law, yet its contents clearly had to be approached with the greatest circumspection and doubt.[5]

The debate about *Regiam* arising from its association with *Glanvill* thus had all manner of important repercussions for the study and understanding of medieval Scots law. Its immediate significance for Skene and Craig emerges when the context of their discussions is considered. Not only was it part of their efforts, inspired by the techniques of legal humanism, to recover the pure, uncorrupted sources of Scots law,[6] but there was also the backdrop of discussions of a possible union of Scots and English law following the Union of the Crowns in 1603.[7] Did the link between *Glanvill* and *Regiam* suggest that the two laws were not as distinct as many believed?[8] If so, was legal union really the impossibility which so many lawyers in both countries represented it to be? Might such a union not be simply a restoration of the former order of things? Specifically for Scots lawyers, the possibility that *Regiam* followed *Glanvill* may also have hinted that

ed. D.M. Walker (Edinburgh, 1981), I, i, 16. Stair's erroneous reference to the 13 books of *Glanvill* (*recte* 14) appears to have been picked up from *Jus Feudale* (see I, viii, 11).

[5] For an account of the later debates about *Regiam*, see D.M. Walker, *The Scottish Jurists* (Edinburgh, 1985), 16-17; also C. Kidd, *Subverting Scotland's Past* (Cambridge, 1993), 148-150.

[6] For which see J.W. Cairns, T.D. Fergus & H.L. MacQueen, 'Legal humanism and the history of Scots law: John Skene and Thomas Craig', in *Humanism in Renaissance Scotland*, ed. J. MacQueen (Edinburgh, 1990).

[7] On this see B.P. Levack, *The Formation of the British State: England, Scotland, and the Union 1603-1707* (Oxford, 1987); B.R. Galloway, *The Union of England and Scotland 1603-1608* (Edinburgh, 1986); *The Jacobean Union 1604*, eds. B.R. Galloway & B.P. Levack (SHS, 1985). My debt to these three works in what follows is very great. Two earlier articles by Levack on the legal union project of James VI and I remain valuable: 'The proposed union of English law and Scots law in the seventeenth century', *Juridical Review*, xx (1975); and 'English law, Scots law and the Union 1603-1707', in *Law Making and Law Makers in British History*, ed. A. Harding (Royal Historical Society, 1980).

[8] For such a suggestion in an anonymous English source see BL, Sloane MS 1786, ff.100r-104v. This refers to Skene's edition of *Regiam*, so must be post-1609 in date; in correspondence with me, Professor Levack suggests a possible date of 1610 (letter dated 30/9/90).

the contingency which so many of them feared—that legal union would mean a take-over of Scots by English law—was somehow historically justified, while such an outcome might have made the union idea more attractive to English lawyers.

An interesting question is, therefore, by whom was the link between the two texts identified? It seems probable that in Scotland, while it must have been known at least to the compiler of *Regiam* in the fourteenth century, there was no knowledge of *Glanvill* for most of the later Middle Ages and up to the first publication of the text in 1554. Some reason for this supposition will become apparent at a later stage in this article.[9] But for the present it will suffice to note that for a Scots lawyer to become aware of *Glanvill* in the century and a half before 1554 he would have required access to manuscripts which, even amongst English lawyers, were probably not much in use. Although it continued to be 'revered as the earliest book on English law',[10] *Glanvill* had ceased to be important for practising lawyers in England by the fourteenth century, and knowledge of its content (as distinct from its existence) probably faded as a result.[11] Moreover, there was certainly no practical reason before the Union of 1603 why English lawyers should have looked at, or even been aware of, *Regiam*. The greater accessibility of *Glanvill* from 1554, however, made it easier for Scots lawyers to learn that there was some connection between the two texts.

It is therefore plausible to suppose that Skene and Craig were the first to recognise the relationship of *Regiam* to *Glanvill*.[12] But another possibility emerges from consideration of the second edition of *Glanvill*, which appeared in London in 1604. *Glanvill's* modern editor, G.D.G. Hall, describes it as 'substantially a reprint of the first'.[13] Its title is however intriguing: *Tractatus de legibus et consuetudinibus regni Angliae ... Qui nunc imprimitur post 50 annos a*

---

[9] *Regiam* is not the only Scottish text to rely heavily on *Glanvill*. There is also the *Liber de Judicibus*, for which see W. J. Windram, 'What is the *Liber de Judicibus*?', *Journal of Legal History*, v (1984). The date of composition of this work remains obscure, but might throw light on knowledge of *Glanvill* in medieval Scotland.

[10] *The Reports of Sir John Spelman*, ed. J.H. Baker (Selden Society, 1977), ii, 33.

[11] *The Treatise on the Laws and Customs of the Realm of England commonly called Glanvill*, ed G.D.G. Hall (London, 1965), [henceforth *Glanvill*], introduction, p. lxii; T.F.T. Plucknett, *Early English Legal Literature* (Cambridge, 1958), 38-9, 81-2.

[12] Lord Cooper gave the credit to Craig in his introduction to his editions of *Regiam Majestatem and Quoniam Attachiamenta* (Stair Society, 1947), 6.

[13] *Glanvill*, p. lxii.

*priore et prima impressione, quia in pluribus concordat cum antiquo libro legum Scotiae vocato Regiam Majestatem precipue in locis hoc signo-notatis**.[14] The text bears this description out; each chapter is marked, as the title suggests, according to whether or not it also appears in *Regiam Majestatem*.

The interest of the title is confirmed by the preface, a brief introduction from the printer, Thomas Wight, which needs to be quoted in full:

> This booke was first printed above fiftie yeares now since, by the procurement of Sir William Stamford Knight, a very learned judge of the Common place, and hath of many yeares not beene to be had in any shoppe, nor asked for, & little regarded by them which had it, till of late a Professor of the Lawes of this Realme, reading a booke, called Regiam Maiestatem, of the auncient Lawes of the Realme of Scotland, found this and that to agree much, & in many places word for word: And this to be vouched, and mentioned often in that, And therefore perswaded me to print those bookes, to the end that others might know how the same ancient laws of both the realmes did then, and yet doe agree in most points which have not bin altered by statutes in either of these realmes. For the finding whereof, he hath made several Tables but understanding that there is lately brought hither, a larger and perfecter booke of the said Regiam Maiestatem, & other Scottish lawes forbeareth to deliver unto me his booke of Regiam Maiestatem. And therefore I am to entreat you to accept this my labor in good part untill I may get the booke last brought to print: Which if I doe, it shall be so done, as it shall not cause the buyer hereof to buy this againe.

The first point to note is that the information about the 'agreement' between *Glanvill* and *Regiam* is presented very much as a discovery of something hitherto unknown. We have therefore to consider the possibility that it was this publication which drew the relationship of the two texts to the attention of Skene and Craig. Clearly it occurred while each was in the midst of his project. Skene, who had begun his work on *Regiam* in 1575,[15] had made no reference to *Glanvill* in his *De Verborum Significatione* first published in 1597, although other English works were cited.[16] Craig, according to Dr Cairns, started work on *Jus Feudale* sometime in the 1590s, was writing it from 1598 at latest, and was still

[14] The title was first drawn to my attention by Dr J.W. Cairns.

[15] We know this from a note in Skene's hand in the Bute MS, now NLS, Acc 21246, f. 26v: 'Incepit opus, 14 Junii 1575, Jo Skene'.

[16] For example, Sir Thomas Smith (*DVS* s.v. Banrentes, Coroner, Essonium, Placitum, Scaccarium, Varda), John Rastell (*DVS* s.v. Breve, Champert), Thomas Littleton (*DVS* s.v. Hawbert, Sokmannria).

revising the text in 1606.[17] It has been suggested that there are inconsistencies in Craig's treatment of *Regiam*, in that, while on the one hand he denounces it as a source, in his text he draws upon it.[18] Might this be explained by his only becoming aware of its suspect nature after the publication of the 1604 *Glanvill*, and not having completed a full revision of his text before his death in 1608? Further in support of this, his tract of 1605, *De Unione Regnorum Britanniae*,[19] which contains a full treatment of legal union, does not refer to the problems of *Regiam* and *Glanvill*.

A second question which arises from the preface is the identity of the 'professor of the lawes of this realme'. It is clear that 'professor' should not be understood in its restricted modern sense of a university teacher, but rather as meaning simply one who professed, in this case, law. This might involve a teaching function, but more generally is to be seen as an equivalent of our 'practitioner', or 'professional' in the sense of membership of a profession. It is also clear from the context that the 'professor' here was a professor of the laws of England, since 'this realme' is not the 'Realme of Scotland'. The field of candidates is therefore not a small one, although it seems possible to exclude non-lawyers such as John Thornborough, who enthusiastically supported closer union with arguments about the close relationship between the two systems of law.[20] But it can be narrowed down somewhat if we look for English lawyers who at the relevant time might have had both knowledge of *Glanvill* and reason to inquire into Scots law. The latter was of course most likely to arise from the possibility of legal union.

An obvious group with which to begin is the English commissioners appointed for the discussion of union in 1604. Four common lawyers—Sir Francis Bacon, Sir Thomas Hesketh,

---

[17] See J.W. Cairns, 'The *breve testatum* and Craig's *Jus Feudale*', *Tijdschrift voor Rechtsgeschiedenis*, lvi (1988), 311 at 317; also his 'Craig, Cujas, and the definition of *feudum*', in *New Perspectives in the Roman Law of Property: Essays for Barry Nicholas*, ed. P. Birks (Oxford, 1989), 77, and (with Fergus and MacQueen), 'Legal humanism', 56.

[18] See most recently W.D.H. Sellar, 'English law as a source of Stair's *Institutions*', in *Stair Tercentenary Studies*, ed. D.M. Walker (Stair Society, 1981), 140, at 144-5; cf Cairns *et al*, 'Legal humanism', 63-4.

[19] Ed. C.S. Terry (SHS, 1909).

[20] See his two tracts: *The Ioiefull and Blessed Reuniting the two mighty and famous kingdomes, England and Scotland into their ancient name of great Brittaine* (London, 1604), 9; *A Discourse Plainely Proving the evident utilitie and urgent necessitie of the desired happie Union of the two famous Kingdomes of England and Scotland* (London, 1604), 18-19, 31.

Sir Henry Hobart and Sir Lawrence Tanfield—and two civilians—Sir John Bennett and Sir Daniel Dunne—were amongst the commissioners.[21] Perhaps the likeliest candidate amongst these is Bacon (1561-1625), who could claim not only to be an eminent practitioner of the laws of England but also to be one who had professed in the sense of teaching law as a Reader at Gray's Inn as recently as 1600 and wrote a great deal on the topic of legal union.[22] In 1607 he stated in one of his treatises on the legal union that he had 'read, and read with delight, the Scottish statutes, and some other collection of their laws; with delight, I say, partly to see their brevity and propriety of speech, and partly to see them come so near our laws'.[23] But this acquaintance with Scottish legal material must, on his own account, have come after 1604, for in his writing around that time Bacon makes some play of his ignorance of Scots law.[24] If that is accepted at face value, and there seems no reason not to do so, then Bacon must be ruled out as the editor of the 1604 *Glanvill*.

The list of possibilities should not be confined to the English commissioners. For example, a circumstantial, but still not very strong, case may be made out for Sir John Doddridge (1555-1628), who, although not one of the 1604 commissioners, was a member of the conference of the two Houses of Parliament which was appointed in April that year to consider the union,[25] and wrote a tract on the subject which shows that he had at least looked into Scottish legislation.[26] He became Solicitor General in October 1604. An original member of the Elizabethan Society of Antiquaries,[27] Doddridge had a deep historical interest in law and

[21] For a list of commissioners see *Journal of the House of Commons*, i, 208. See also the journal of the commission's proceedings (BL, Add. MS 26635). For Hesketh, Hobart and Tanfield, see W.R. Prest, *The Rise of the Barristers: a Social History of the English Bar, 1590-1640* (Oxford, 1986), 369, 370, 394; for Bennett and Dunne, see B.P. Levack, *The Civil Lawyers in England 1603-1641: a Political Study* (Oxford, 1973), 209, 226.

[22] For Bacon's role in the legal union project see the writings of Professor Levack already cited. The 1600 reading, on the Statute of Uses, is printed in *The Works of Francis Bacon*, ed. J. Spedding, R.L. Ellis & D.D. Heath, 7 vols. (1857-74), vii, 395-445. On Bacon generally, see D. Coquillette, *Francis Bacon* (Edinburgh, 1992).

[23] *Works of Francis Bacon*, vii, 372.

[24] See *The Letters and the Life of Francis Bacon*, ed. J. Spedding (1868), iii, 218-34.

[25] *House of Commons Journal*, i, 172.

[26] J. Doddridge, 'A Breif Consideracion of the Unyon', in *Jacobean Union*, 147.

[27] See R.J. Schoeck, 'The Elizabethan Society of Antiquaries and men of law', *Notes and Queries*, cxcix (1954), 419.

was an admirer of *Glanvill* as one of the 'divers excellent Treatises of the Lawes of this Realme, in the Latine tongue'.[28] His membership of the Middle Temple may perhaps be linked to Skene's honorific admission there (presumably following the conclusion of the proceedings of the commission for union in December 1604)[29] at the reading of George Wrightington in February 1605.[30]

The pre-eminent 'professor' of English law in 1604, by virtue of his series of *Reports* begun in 1600, was undoubtedly the Attorney General, Sir Edward Coke (1552-1634). In April 1604 he and the judges had advised the king that the name Great Britain could not be adopted until there was a union of the laws.[31] The *Fourth Part* of his *Institutes of the Laws of England* also contains a chapter on Scotland, which notes how *Regiam Majestatem* 'doth in substance agree with our *Glanvil*, and most commonly *de verbo in verbum*, and many times our *Glanvil* is cited therein by speciall name'.[32] This passage was not published until 1644 and was probably written in the late 1620s or after, so it cannot be taken as evidence of what Coke knew in 1604; nonetheless it echoes some of the phrases used in the preface to the 1604 *Glanvill*, while the chapter as a whole also uses its argument that originally the laws of England and Scotland were the same, with differences arising as a result of the acts of the two parliaments. This may simply be because Coke had read the preface, rather than because his inspiration lay behind it. It is known that he owned copies of both the 1554 and 1604 editions of *Glanvill*.[33] Indeed he was very enthusiastic about

---

[28] J. Doddridge, *The English Lawyer* (London, 1631), 41.

[29] For an account of the 1604 commission see Galloway, *Union*, 58-76. Note especially its 'amicable social and working relationship' (63).

[30] On Doddridge generally, see *DNB*; Prest, *Barristers*, 357; R.J. Terrill, 'Humanism and rhetoric in legal education: the contribution of Sir John Doddridge (1555-1628)', *Journal of Legal History*, ii (1981); *Jacobean Union*, pp. lxi-iii. On Skene's admission to the Middle Temple, see C.E.A. Bedwell, 'Scottish Middle Templars 1604-1869', SHR, xvii (1920), 100, while for Wrightington see Prest, *Barristers*, 406. On honorific admissions to the Inns, see W.R. Prest, *The Inns of Court under Elizabeth I and the Early Stuarts 1590-1640* (London, 1972), 9-10, 224-7.

[31] E. Coke, *Fourth Part of the Institutes of the Laws of England* (London, 1644), cap lxxv. Professor J.H. Baker has drawn my attention to a MS now in Yale University Library (Law School Deposit) (MS G. R24. 1, ff.149-150), which is a note on the union of the laws, with an autograph annotation by Coke concerning a judicial resolution that the name Great Britain could not be used in legal proceedings. See further Levack, *Formation*, 38-9.

[32] *Fourth Part of the Institutes of the Law of England*, cap lxxv.

[33] *A Catalogue of the Library of Sir Edward Coke*, ed W.O. Hassall (Yale, 1950), no. 379.

the work: he describes it as 'right profitable' in the preface to one of his *Reports*[34] and in another, referring to Glanvill himself, mentions his 'thankfulness to that worthy Judge, whom I cite many times'.[35] Coke also collected Scottish material, although I have not noted any reference to it in his *Reports* apart from a reference to *De Verborum* in his report of *Calvin's Case*, published in 1608, used to conclude that Scots and English law were the same on the point in question.[36] He owned a copy of Skene's *Laws and Acts*, which had *De Verborum* appended. It would be of interest to know when he acquired the book, as *De Verborum* was bound to alert him to the parallels between *Regiam* and early English law. Later on Sir Alexander Hay, secretary to King James, presented Coke with a copy of Skene's Latin edition of *Regiam*. Coke also had a copy of the 1613 London reprint of that work, but obviously these came too late to fix him with the knowledge needed to produce the 1604 *Glanvill*.[37] Enough has been said otherwise, however, to show that he or his inspiration cannot be ruled out of consideration in this regard.

Thus far we have considered the names of English common lawyers. Another group of lawyers practising in England should be borne in mind, however. This is the civilians, the doctors of Roman law who practised in the ecclesiastical and the Admiralty courts.[38] The civilians took a particular interest in the project for a union of the laws (as already noted, two of their number were amongst the English commissioners in 1604), because Scots law was seen as a system strongly influenced by Roman law.[39] Union therefore had the potential to advance the civilians' argument that their law was indeed part of the law of England rather than the malign foreign law generally perceived by the common lawyers.[40] Indeed, some of the civilians, including Bennett and Dunne, the commissioners for union in 1604, were members of the Inns of Court.[41] It is conceivable, therefore, that the reference

[34] I have used the six-volume London, 1826, edition of Coke's *Reports* which brings together all 13 volumes of the Reports (traditionally cited as *Co Rep* preceded by the volume number). For the quotation, see 3 *Co Rep*, preface, p. vii.

[35] 8 *Co Rep*, preface, p. xix.

[36] 7 *Co Rep*, 5a.

[37] For the Scottish works in Coke's library see *Catalogue of the Library of Sir Edward Coke*, no. 433.

[38] The fullest account is in Levack, *Civil Lawyers*.

[39] Levack, *Formation*, 81-4.

[40] Levack, *Civil Lawyers*, 122-57.

[41] Levack, *Civil Lawyers*, 129.

in the preface to the 1604 *Glanvill* to the 'professor of the laws of this realme' need not exclude the possibility that he was a civilian rather than a common lawyer. The possibility is reinforced by the fact that the publisher of the 1604 *Glanvill*, Thomas Wight, who wrote the preface, had very recently been publishing the works of William Fulbecke (1560-?1603), a member of Gray's Inn who, much under the influence of Alberico Gentili (1551-1608), regius professor of civil law at Oxford and an honorary member of Gray's Inn since 1600,[42] had argued powerfully for the reconciliation of the common and the civil laws.[43] Wight held the exclusive right to publish the books of the common law,[44] and it is interesting to find him associated with such ideas.

If the possibility that the professor might have been a civilian is accepted, then there is a case to be made for John Cowell (1554-1611) having been responsible for the 1604 *Glanvill*.[45] In 1604 Cowell held the chair of civil law at Cambridge and was vice chancellor of the university as well as master of Trinity Hall, although he was never amongst the civilians admitted to one of the Inns of Court. It is known that he was working on *Glanvill* at the relevant time and that he had some knowledge of the work of John Skene. The evidence for this is in in his two major public-

[42] For Gentili, see Levack, *Civil Lawyers*, 232; Coquillette, 'Legal ideology and incorporation I: the English civilian writers 1523-1607', *Boston University Law Review*, lxi (1981), 54-63. Gentili also published a tract on the union in a collection entitled *Regales Disputationes Tres* (London, 1605), on which see *Jacobean Union*, 248; but it is innocent of any reference to either *Glanvill* or *Regiam Majestatem*.

[43] Fulbecke's works published by Wight are *A Parallele or Conference of the Civill Law, the Canon Law, and the Common Law of this Realme of England* (in two parts, 1601 and 1602), and *The Pandectes of the Law of Nations: Contayning severall discourses of the questions, points and matters of law, wherein the Nations of the world doe consent and accord* (1602). Fulbecke was also the author of *Direction or Preparative to the Study of Law* (1600). He would be an excellent candidate for the *Glanvill* professor but for the probability that he died c.1603. On him, see Levack, *Civil Lawyers*, 136-7; Prest, *Inns of Court*, 146-8; Coquillette, 'Legal ideology and incorporation', 63-70; R.J. Terrill, 'The application of the comparative method by English civilians: the case of William Fulbecke and Thomas Ridley', *Journal of Legal History*, ii (1981); C.P. Rodgers, 'Legal humanism and English law—the contribution of the English civilians', *Irish Jurist*, xix (1984), 125-7; and the introduction by P. Birks to the 1987 reprint of the *Direction or Preparative*.

[44] See *A Dictionary of Printers and Booksellers in England, Scotland and Ireland, and of Foreign Printers of English Books 1557-1640*, ed R.B. McKerrow (1910), s.v. Wight, Thomas.

[45] For Cowell see *DNB*; S.B. Chrimes, 'The constitutional ideas of Dr John Cowell', *EHR*, xliv (1949); J. Simon, 'Dr Cowell', *Cambridge Law Journal*, xxvi (1968); Levack, *Civil Lawyers*, 137-40, 221; Coquillette, 'Legal ideology', 71-87; and Rodgers, 'Legal humanism', 127-8.

ations, the *Institutiones Juris Anglicani* (1605), and *The Interpreter* (1607). The former sought to rationalise English law within the structure of Justinian's *Institutions*,[46] and it is replete with references to *Glanvill* and other well-known works. The same is true of *The Interpreter*, which, as is clear from its sub-title, *Booke containing the Signification of Words*, was a work in the same genre as Skene's *De Verborum*. It also contains over 70 references to Skene's *De Verborum*,[47] from which he must have been aware of the existence of *Regiam*. Twice he drew on *De Verborum* to suggest 'great affinitie' between Scots and English law.[48] That his knowledge of the materials of Scots law was not merely gleaned from Skene's work may be deduced from the dedicatory epistle of the *Institutiones*, where he mentions the 'undigested mass' of the law of Scotland;[49] certainly a description sufficiently apt to suggest first-hand knowledge of the manuscript tradition, such as was apparently possessed by the professor of Wight's preface. On the other hand, Wight was not the publisher of his two major works, which appeared under the imprint of John Leggat of Cambridge. Further, the collection of books which Cowell bequeathed to King's College, Cambridge, did not include any Scottish works.[50]

It is quite conceivable, however, that the professor of the 1604 *Glanvill* was someone much more obscure than the well-known figures just discussed, such as the person described in the anonymous pro-union tract *Rapta tatio*, also published in London in 1604:[51]

---

[46] For discussion see A. Watson, 'Justinian's Institutes and some English counterparts', in *Studies in Justinian's Institutes in memory of J.A.C. Thomas*, eds. P.G. Stein & A.D.E. Lewis (1983), 182-4; also J.W. Cairns, 'Blackstone, an English institutist: legal literature and the rise of the nation state', *Oxford Journal of Legal Studies*, iv (1984), 331-3, 336-8.

[47] See entries at Adiournment, Advowsen, Assise, Attache, Atturney, Average, Baneret, Bankrupe, Baro, Barrator, Bastard, Batable Ground, Bilawes, Bloodwit, Borow, Bote, Breve, Bullion, Carue of land, Charter, Chawnce medley, Courtesie of England, Demaine, Dereyne, Disclamer, Disseisin, Dower, Einecia, Eyre, Encheson, Eschequer, Feede, Fletwit, Free hould, Garbe, Gardein, Hamsoken, Hariot alias Heriot, Homage, Hue and Crie, Infangthef, King, Librata Terre, Liege, Mahim, Maner, Mariage, Mesuage, Mortmaine, Mulier, Murder, Ordel, Pannage, Perche, Piepowders court, Pourpresture, Rape, Robberie, Sac, Sakebere, Sergeant, Sergeantie, Shyreeve, Soc, Soccage, Sterling, Team, Tenure, Thanus, Vassall, Weife, Wedding, Weights and Withernam.

[48] *Interpreter*, s.vv. Eyre and Gardein.

[49] *Institutiones Juris Anglicani* (Cambridge, 1605), epistle dedicatory.

[50] Information from Mr R.R. Milne, Trinity College, Cambridge.

[51] *Rapta tatio: the Mirrour of his Maiesties present Government, tending to the Union of his whole Iland of Brittonie* (London, 1604), G lv.

> Of this argument, for agreement of both lawes, (except I be deceived) a friend of mine... hath very lately, verie shortly written: comparing the Grandes, the Titles, the rules and right use of both, (as his occasion led him) so learnedly, so fully, and so experiencedly together; as the two common Wealthes may soone be taught, that there is nothing disagreeing in essence betweene them, nothing of the ones substance wanting to the other (the terms and practises only having given the shewe of difference hitherto.)

Another, only marginally less obscure, English figure who could have been involved is George Saltern, whose *Of the Antient Lawes of Great Britain* was published in London in 1605, and who was the first after 1604 to draw attention in print to the parallel between *Regiam* and *Glanvill*, again in the context of an argument for greater unity of the two laws.[52] But this is no stronger evidence of responsibility for the 1604 *Glanvill* than any in the preceding discussion. It does confirm, however, the considerable interest in various quarters in England immediately after 1603 in the Scottish written law and its relationship with the law of England, in general stemming from those who favoured legal union, whether in the form of a combination of the two laws or of the extension of English law to Scotland. The republication of *Glanvill* must be set in that context, even if we cannot yet be firm about the initiator of the project.

The second line of inquiry suggested by the preface to the 1604 *Glanvill* is the question of which manuscript of *Regiam* was used by the professor. Two points about this manuscript are mentioned. First, the agreement between *Regiam* and *Glanvill* is 'vouched and mentioned often' in it; second, there is another 'larger and perfecter' text of *Regiam* lately brought to London. 'Vouching and mentioning' probably indicates annotations of the *Regiam* text to show the parallels with *Glanvill*, but may also refer to a passage found in some, but not all, *Regiam* manuscripts where the name of Ranulf de Glanvill is actually mentioned as holding one opinion on a controverted question in the law of succession, with an opposite view being held by Richard de Luci.[53] The passage comes straight from the text of *Glanvill*, and is a clear indicator

---

52 See especially chapter 11 of the unpaginated work. For further discussion, see Galloway, *Union*, 40.

53 For the passage see *APS*, i, 614-15. Examination of the Bute MS (NLS, Acc. 21246), at f.40v, and BL, Add. MS 18,111, at f.33r, (neither available to the editors of the *APS* edition) confirms the probability that this was part of the Ur-text of *Regiam*. See further H.G. Richardson, 'Roman Law in the *Regiam Majestatem*', *Juridical Review*, lxvii (1955), 167-9.

that *Regiam* was copied from it; its garbling in some later manuscript traditions is evidence of Scottish ignorance of *Glanvill* by the later middle ages.[54] Skene's omission of the passage from his edition was at the root of Hailes' famous denunciation of him in 1767 as 'a careless, if not an unfaithful publisher'.[55]

The 'larger and perfecter' text lately brought to London most likely came in September 1604 with the Scottish commissioners for union, who included both Skene and Craig in their number.[56] It may plausibly be suggested that the text was Skene's own. The professor's copy was of lesser quality, perhaps because it had not been critically edited in the way that Skene's had. There are now in England several manuscripts containing a text of *Regiam Majestatem.* Four are in the British Library,[57] two in the Cambridge University Library,[58] and one in the library of Lambeth Palace.[59] All but one were in England during the eighteenth century,[60] and most were there in the late seventeenth century; but so far it has not proved possible to establish firmly that any of them was available in England in and before 1604.

Some of the possible links are tantalising: one of the British Library manuscripts is in a collection partly formed from the papers of Sir Christopher (1535?-1612) and Sir Henry Yelverton (1566-1629), a father and son who were both prominent common lawyers at the time of the 1603 Union, with the latter being, like Sir John Doddridge, a member of the conference of the two Houses of Parliament appointed to consider the union in April 1604.[61] Again, John Cowell's career owed much to the patronage

[54] On the references in *Glanvill* itself, see R.W. Southern, 'A note on the text of "Glanville"', *EHR,* lxv (1950); Hall's introduction to *Glanvill,* pp. xliii-xlvii; R.V. Turner, 'Who was the author of *Glanvill*? Reflections on the education of Henry II's common lawyers', *Law and History Review,* viii (1990), 119; and J.C. Holt, 'The *casus regis*: the law and politics of succession in the Plantaganet dominions', in *Law in Medieval Life and Thought,* eds. E.B. King and S.J. Ridyard (The Press of the University of the South, 1990), 24-6.

[55] Hailes, *Annals,* iii, 276, 280-83.

[56] The Scottish commissioners are listed in *APS,* iv, 264.

[57] BL, Add. MS 18,111; Harleian 765; Harleian 4700 (described *APS,* i, 189-91); and Addit (Yelverton) 48032.

[58] Ee.4.21 (described *APS,* i, 192-3) and Kk.1.5 (also EUL microfilm, MicM 16/2), described *APS,* i, 199-200.

[59] Lambeth Palace Library MS 167 (described *APS,* i, 202-03).

[60] The one which was not is BL, Add. 18,111, which in the mid-18th century was owned by John Gordon of Buthlaw, the Scottish advocate and antiquary.

[61] See *DNB* for the Yelvertons; for Sir Henry's membership of the 1604 conference, *House of Commons Journal,* i, 172. As well as the *Regiam* MS noted above, the Yelverton collection contains two other Scots law MSS, Add. 48033 and 48050 (the

of Richard Bancroft (1544-1610), the Archbishop of Canterbury whose library of manuscripts is the foundation of the Lambeth collection.[62] On the other hand, neither of the Cambridge manuscripts would have been available to Cowell there, since both appear to have been acquired by the University Library only in the eighteenth century.[63] Armed with the comments in the *Glanvill* preface, however—in particular the reference to the 'vouching and mentioning' of the parallels between Regiam and *Glanvill*—it is possible to narrow our focus down to two of the manuscripts now in England. While most of those already mentioned do include the passage mentioning Glanvill's opinion on the controversial point of succession, none appears to have any other reference to him or the treatise attributed to him. But two manuscripts of *Regiam* now in the Harleian collection in the British Library (nos. 4700 and 765), do contain extensive annotations referring to *Glanvill*, and it is to these that we now turn.

It should be noted first that the Harleian collection was formed from 1705 on.[64] The provenance of the first of our manuscripts (Harley no. 4700) immediately before this cannot yet be determined. But in 1590 it was owned by Thomas Henryson (d. 1638), advocate and later, as Lord Chesters, Lord of Session, who had acquired it from his father, the great civilian and humanist Edward Henryson.[65] Thomas, or someone with a hand very like

---

former probably originally forming a single MS with Add. 48032). The precise provenance of these MSS has yet to be worked out, but they were part of the collection by the end of the 17th century: see E. Bernard, *Catalogi Librorum Manuscriptorum Angliae et Hiberniae* (Oxford, 1697), tom ii, pars i, Bibliothecae Yelvertoniae, nos. 5275, 5276 and 5293; W. Nicolson, *The Scottish Historical Library* (London, 1702), 264-5.

[62] *DNB*, s.v. Cowell, John; M.R. James, 'The history of Lambeth Palace Library', *Transactions of the Cambridge Bibliographical Society*, iii (1959); A. Cox-Johnson, 'Lambeth Palace Library 1610-1664', ibid., ii (1955). The Lambeth MS does not appear in the 1612 catalogue of Bancroft's collection (Lambeth Palace Library Records, F 1 and 2); it is first catalogued after 1700 (ibid, F.39 [f.51, no. CLXVII] and F.40 [f.15, no. CLXVII]).

[63] Ee.4.21 was owned in 1697 by John Moore (1646-1714), bishop of Norwich 1691-1707 and Ely 1707-1714: see Bernard, *Catalogi Librorum Manuscriptorum*, tom ii, pars i, no. 9481, and Nicolson, *Scottish Historical Library*, 265. Moore's collection (which also included the Book of Deer) was given to the University Library by George III in 1715. Kk.1.5 is not listed in Bernard's catalogue of the holdings of the Cambridge library.

[64] See *The Harleian Catalogue*, i, 1-29; C.E. Wright, *Fontes Harleiani* (London, 1972), pp. xv-xxxv.

[65] See BL, Harl. 4700, ff. 4r, 17r, 55r, 68r and 309v. On Edward see J. Durkan,

his, annotated the text of *Regiam* with several references to *Glanvill.* Book III in particular is full of notes stating that passages have been '*exscripta*' from *Glanvill.*[66] In addition, an annotation at the beginning argues that *Regiam* was copied from *Glanvill* in the time, not of David I, but of David II.[67] All this is exceedingly interesting, but it must have been written after the publication of Skene's edition in 1609. The note arguing that *Regiam* was copied from *Glanvill* specifically refutes Skene's contrary view, while other marginalia point out that the manuscript's chapter numbering is different from that '*in libro Skenei*'.[68] This could refer to the manuscript press copy which Skene had had first prepared in 1601-02, but, as will be developed further below, at that time Skene had seen no reason to enter discussion of the relationship between *Regiam* and *Glanvill.* In conclusion, therefore, the notes about *Glanvill* in this manuscript were probably made after 1604, and so it is unlikely that this was the text used by the professor in preparing his edition. It may be observed, however, that it contains the passage about the conflicting opinions of Ranulf de Glanvill and Richard de Luci.[69]

Harley no. 765 is the most likely of the manuscripts now extant to have been that used in preparing the 1604 *Glanvill.*[70] Not only does it contain the passage referring to Glanvill's opinion on succession but it has also been annotated with references to *Glanvill* and indications of which passages are not derived from that source. In addition there is a '*tabula indicando concordantias*' between *Glanvill* and *Regiam,* which produces results virtually (but not quite) identical to those obtained by noting which chapters of the 1604 *Glanvill* are marked as parallel to *Regiam.*[71] Was this one of the 'several Tables' showing the concordance of the two works prepared by the professor of the 1604 preface? If so, then a number of other interesting points about the manuscript become even more significant. First, it contains none of the other texts of

---

'Henry Scrimgeour, Renaissance bookman', *TEBS,* v (1978), 2-4; Cairns, Fergus & MacQueen, 'Legal humanism', 49, 51. On Thomas see *DNB* and G. Brunton and D. Haig, *An Historical Account of the Senators of the College of Justice* (Edinburgh, 1836), 265-6.

66 Book III runs between ff.55r-68r.

67 See f.23r.

68 See ff.57r-v.

69 See f.42v. Henryson annotates the passage with a reference to Hotman.

70 This MS was first brought to my attention by Mr W.J. Windram.

71 Harleian MS no. 765, ff.66v-67r.

Scots law; is this why it was not large and less perfect than other manuscripts? Second, as John Buchanan pointed out in 1937, the manuscript is written on paper bearing the same watermark as the first press copy of Skene's edition (drafted, as already noted, in 1601-02). Buchanan surmised that the manuscript might have been 'prepared under Skene's direction'.[72] But by contrast with the elegant secretary hand of the two press copies prepared for Skene, Harley no. 765 is mainly written in a rather messy cursive script, quite unlike the hands generally found in the later Scottish legal manuscripts.[73] Finally, the provenance of the manuscript can be pushed back before 1705. It was acquired for Harley from the estate of Edward Stillingfleet, bishop of Worcester 1689-99, and it is known to have been in Stillingfleet's library in 1685.[74]

The most significant of these points is the possible link of Harley no. 765 with Skene, and it is to Skene and his first knowledge of the *Regiam/Glanvill* relationship that we now return. When did Skene find out about *Glanvill*? There is no reference in *De Verborum* to suggest that he knew of its existence in 1597. The first press copy of his edition of *Regiam*, to which reference has already been made, makes it clear, however, that by 1601-02 he was aware of *Glanvill* and of a relationship between it and his own text.[75] The text of this press copy was written by Charles Lumsden, minister at Duddingston, between early 1601 and 11 February 1602. The method of work seems to have been that Lumsden wrote up the text, then Skene drafted annotations which were finally copied up by Lumsden in his clear italic hand. Thus Lumsden finished Book 1 on 30 April 1601, Book 2 on 5th May 1601 and Book 3 on 8 June 1601;[76] but the fair copies of the annotations for Books 1 and 2 were only completed on 28 January and 4 February 1602 respectively.[77] The interest of this is that at least twice in these annotations Skene refers directly to *Glanvill*. Both are in the notes

---

[72] J. Buchanan, 'The MSS of *Regiam Majestatem*: an experiment', *Juridical Review*, xlix (1937), 219.

[73] As Buchanan notes (loc cit), ff.8-10 are in a different hand (rather like that of Skene) and on different paper.

[74] See Wright, *Fontes Harleiani*, 316, 386; *The Diary of Humfrey Wanley, 1715-1726*, ed C.E. and R.C. Wright (1966), p. xix; Harleian MS, no. 7644 (Stillingfleet's 1685 catalogue), entry no. 103 (*Liber vocatus Regiam Majestatem*). For Stillingfleet, see *DNB* and D.C. Douglas, *English Scholars 1660-1730*, 2nd edn. (1951), 198-200.

[75] NLS, Adv MS 7.1.10 (described *APS*, i, 208-09).

[76] See ff.17v, 48r and 80r.

[77] See ff.26v and 64r.

to Book 1; the first a correction of corrupt readings by reference to *Glanvill*,[78] the second a note to answer a question left unanswered by *Regiam*.[79] Cosmo Innes also suggests that in this manuscript Skene used *Glanvill* without acknowledgement for the purpose of correcting readings in his texts.[80]

The conclusion which may be drawn from this, particularly if Cosmo Innes' observation is correct, is that Skene had become aware of *Glanvill* as a text with a close relationship to *Regiam* by 1601. But he had not yet seen any consequential difficulties for the traditional view of *Regiam*. At this stage *Glanvill* for him was merely a useful corrective for *Regiam*, a view supported by the belief that *Regiam* should be attributed to David I, with *Glanvill* being the later work. What is interesting, however, is that Skene did not press on to publication, and, indeed, did not complete his annotations. It looks as though Skene broke off that task early in 1602. The second fair copy, which was the basis for the edition of 1609, was not completed until 1608.[81] It seems a fair conclusion that Skene was compelled to think again and to abandon the publication of his text of 1601-02; certainly a much fuller range of references to *Glanvill*, and the argument about the priority of *Regiam*, had found their way into his later published annotations.

Where did Skene obtain his knowledge of *Glanvill*? Although it is not inconceivable that he had access to a manuscript copy, it seems most likely to have been through the 1554 edition. Indeed, the copy which he may have used survives in Edinburgh University Library.[82] The book is extensively underlined and annotated in various hands, including that of Skene or one possessed of very similar writing.[83] Disappointingly, the notes in this hand are mainly mere corrections of the text's Latin, but there is one where the *Glanvill* text is struck out and replaced with the words ultimately printed in Skene's *Regiam*.[84] The many underlinings seem often to

---

[78] See f.23r.

[79] See f.24v.

[80] *APS*, i, 208. The same technique appears to have been used in Harleian no. 765, another factor linking it with Skene: see Buchanan, 'The MSS of *Regiam Majestatem*', 219.

[81] NLS, Adv MS 25.5.8. See *APS*, i, 209, for a brief description. It was the earliest MS accession to the Advocates' Library, being presented by Thomas Skene, advocate and a descendant of Sir John, in 1683: see I.C. Cunningham, 'The Manuscript Collections to 1925', in *For the Encouragement of Learning: Scotland's National Library 1689-1989*, ed. P. Cadell and A. Matheson (Edinburgh, 1989), 119.

[82] EUL, Special Collections, *E.33.61.

[83] See ff.2v (possibly), 14r, 25r, 45r, 50v, 97v, 102r, 104r and 106v.

[84] F.97v.

draw attention to *Glanvill* passages which appear in or are modified in *Regiam.* One of the other annotators has marked in the margins of some chapters of Book 7 the rubrics of the chapter divisions under which the passages so identified appear in *Regiam.*[85] The text is also one where the Glanvill/Luci passage is not included; if Skene used it when working on *Regiam,* then his exclusion of the passage from his edition, and failure (or refusal) to recognise its significance, is a little more understandable than Hailes, perhaps rather uncharitably, was ready to allow.

It is clear that this 1554 *Glanvill* has been marked by various people with *Regiam* in mind. Its provenance before it arrived in Edinburgh University Library is obscure; the name 'Joannes Skene' appears on the title page but in a hand much later than that of Sir John's time, while a Master Alexander, whose surname is now all but illegible, was an earlier owner with writing of a sixteenth-century style.[86] This forename at least suggests the book's long-standing links with Scotland. A plausible hypothesis may be that around 1601 several Scots were becoming aware of *Glanvill,* possibly thanks to this very copy of the 1554 edition.[87] As Skene himself advanced to the annotation of Book III of *Regiam,* he must have recognised that his text had passed from being first, somewhat similar to, second, very similar to, and finally, the same as *Glanvill.* Perhaps at this stage the 'doubts of sindrie learned men' about the authenticity of *Regiam,* to which he refers in the preface of his Scots edition, were being brought home to him, and forcing him to re-think his approach to his task. If so, most probably Craig, and perhaps also Thomas Henryson, were among the learned men in question. Mention may also be made of Robert Pont, a senator of the College of Justice, who in 1604 was arguing in a tract commending fuller union that 'the lawes of

---

85 See ff.45r-48r, 57r.

86 I was initially tempted by an identification of the signature as that of John Skene's brother, Master Alexander (for whom see *Memorials of the Family of Skene of Skene,* 93-5, and *DVS,* s.v. Bothna); but comparison with other known examples of his signature (see *Opera Vergili* (Basle, 1547), now in EUL, Wx 18.57, perhaps Folengo's *Psalterum* (Basle, 1547), also EUL, xC.17.17, and possibly *Opera Tertulliani* (Paris, 1545), now in AUL + 276 Ter) rules this out. I am grateful to John Durkan for these latter references. Another possibility is Master Alexander Shairp (d. 1604), son of John Shairp, first known dean of the advocates and a commissioner for legal union in 1604.

87 Note however that Sir Thomas Hamilton of Priestfield, a senator, lord advocate, and one of the Scottish commissioners for union in 1604, owned copies of both the 1554 and 1604 *Glanvills* (see NLS, Tyn.97(1) and 119(1)). I owe this information to John Durkan.

England and Scotland are almost the same in substance', although without reference to either *Glanvill* or *Regiam*.[88]

But this is not all. If the Harley manuscript no. 765 can be linked, as we have suggested, with the professor of the 1604 *Glanvill*, then, given the manuscript's apparent association with Skene, there must also have been a connection between the professor and Skene. Such a connection is by no means implausible. Skene's *De Verborum* had made him well-known outside Scotland, not just, as we have seen, to Edward Coke and John Cowell, but also to scholars such as Henry Spelman.[89] A possible reconstruction is that the professor of the 1604 *Glanvill* became aware of Skene, *Regiam*, and the parallels of Scots and English law through reading *De Verborum*, established contact, and gained access to Skene's rough copy of his text, from which he compiled his tables and, inspired by the background of the perfection of a union of the laws, pursued the republication of *Glanvill*. Of necessity, this is entirely speculative; but it may gain some support from the apparent fêting of Skene in the Middle Temple early in 1605, and the fact that his Latin edition of *Regiam* was reprinted in 1613 in London by John Bill, Thomas Wight's successor in the monopoly of printing the books of the common law.[90] Bill thus fulfilled a promise which Wight had made in the preface to the 1604 *Glanvill*. Bill was closely associated with the king's printer Bonham Norton,[91] who had entered an obligation with Skene which was still outstanding when the latter died in 1617.[92] Perhaps the origin of these commercial links between Skene and the world of London printers lay in a scholarly exchange on the matter of *Glanvill* and *Regiam Majestatem* conducted in the shadow of the pending union of the crowns. Which of the participants in this exchange should be credited with the discovery probably cannot now be determined, but it seems likely that the professor of the laws of England who was responsible for the 1604 *Glanvill* had played his part before the publication of his work.[93]

---

[88] *Jacobean Union*, 24; see pp. xliv-xlix for discussion. Perhaps Hamilton of Priestfield should also be mentioned (see previous note).

[89] See J.G.A. Pocock, *The Ancient Constitution and the Feudal Law* (Cambridge, 1957, reissued 1987), 95n.

[90] On Bill, see *A Dictionary of Printers*, s.v. Bill, John.

[91] ibid., s.v. Norton, Bonham.

[92] It is referred to in Skene's testament: Register of Testaments, SRO, CC 8/8/49, ff. 309v-310v.

[93] I am indebted in various ways to Professor J.H. Baker, Dr P.A. Brand, Dr

J.W. Cairns, Professor A.A.M. Duncan, Dr J. Durkan, Professor B.P. Levack, Mr W.D.H. Sellar and Mr W.J. Windram, as well as to the Faculty of Advocates for permission to use its Library, and to members of staff in Edinburgh University Library Special Collections Department, the National Library of Scotland, the British Library Manuscripts Department, Lambeth Palace Library, Aberdeen University Library Special Collections Department, and the Libraries of Cornell and Yale Law Schools for invaluable help in the preparation of this article. I wish also to thank Mr R.R. Milne of Trinity College Library, Cambridge, for his assistance. The usual caveats are even more than normally applicable.

SOME RARE SCOTTISH BOOKS IN THE OLD ROYAL LIBRARY

T.A. Birrell

The majority of early Scottish books in the British Library were acquired in the nineteenth century, when the British Museum under Panizzi was pursuing a vigorous and far-sighted acquisitions policy. Most of these books were acquired from libraries of Scottish collectors who had formed their libraries in Scotland.[1] But some of the Museum's rare Scottish books were acquired at an earlier period, and by far the largest group came from the library of King James VI and I (and to a lesser extent from that of Charles I). We think of 'State Papers' as manuscripts: James VI was the first monarch on the English throne who set himself to collect printed dossiers. It is to James's touching faith in the power of the printed word, rather than to his vanity, that we owe the preservation of many of the printed materials of his reign, and of course much of that has Scottish connections.

It would be impossible within the scope of this article to describe all the books of Scottish interest in the Old Royal Library, and attention will therefore be restricted to books that can truly be called 'rare'. For present purposes, rarity can be simply defined as the survival of a book in three (or at most four) copies. The new *STC* enables us to establish this with confidence for all books which come within its terms of reference. For other books, i.e. those by Scottish authors printed abroad in languages other than English, one cannot be so certain of the category of rarity: this problem will be discussed later.

The Old Royal Library was acquired in 1757 by the newly founded British Museum: it included printed books from the reigns of Henry VII to George II (and of course manuscripts dating back to a much earlier period).[2] It has been given the epithet 'Old' in order to distinguish it from the King's Library—the library of George III, acquired by the British Museum in 1823. Henceforth it shall be referred to simply as the Royal Library.

---

[1] There were, for instance, five auction sales at London between 1856 and 1881 of David Laing's library.

[2] For a history of the Old Royal Library see A. Esdaile, *The British Museum Library* (1946) and T.A. Birrell, *English Monarchs and their Books* (1987).

The Royal Library had already suffered some depredations during the Civil War, but it has suffered much more at the hands of librarians. In its early days the British Museum had to raise income by the sale of duplicates. At the outset, duplicates within the Royal Library itself were disposed of, as were duplicates of books already held in the Sloane Library (acquired in 1753). Successive bequests[3] tended to be preserved as entities, and after the acquisition of each new library the Royal (and Sloane) collections were trawled again and again for duplicates: this can be seen in the eight auction sales of BM Duplicates held between 1769 and 1832.[4] Paradoxically, the rare books in the Royal Library have had a better chance of survival precisely because of their rarity, although, as will be seen, there are one or two examples of scandalous disposals of association copies.

To begin with works printed in Scotland, it may be appropriate to start with the example of Alexander Yule, or Julius,[5] master of the grammar school at Stirling from 1578 to 1612, who is recorded by Durkan & Ross[6] as the owner of two books from early Scottish libraries. Yule's output of congratulatory and commemorative Latin verse was considerable. Of the 18 items recorded in *STC*, 16 are in the BL and all belonged to James VI; three of these are unique, and one of them is not in Aldis and has only recently been added to the BL General Catalogue: *Illustrissimae Dominae ... Annabellae Murraviae vitae et mortis Speculum*, 4° Edinb., R. Charteris 1603 (*STC*, 14846.5; BL 1213.k.17(7)).

John Leech (MA Aberdeen) made his debut as a Latin poet with the visit of James VI to Scotland on 1617, and four of his seven publications are connected with this event. *Lachrimae ... in Jacobi I ... recessu de Scotiae*, 4° Edinb., T. Finlason (*STC*, 15371) has survived in only two copies, at opposite ends of the British Isles: one in the Kirkwall Library (now at AUL), and the other in the Royal Library (BL 1070.m.5(4)), a presentation copy to James VI. Leech's *Nemo. Calendis Maii Anno Dom. 1617* (*STC*, 15373), also printed by Finlason, survives in three copies: one, a presentation

[3] Cracherode (1799); Burney (1805); Bentley (1807); King's Library (1823); Colt Hoare (1825).

[4] See *List of Catalogues of English Book Sales, 1676-1900 now in the British Museum* (1915).

[5] The best account of Yule is in A.F. Hutchinson, *History of the High School of Stirling* (Stirling, 1904), although Hutchinson seems quite unaware of Yule's publications in Latin verse.

[6] Durkan & Ross, *Scottish Libraries*, 60, 176.

copy to William Drummond of Hawthornden (EUL De.5.63/1), another, at Sidney Sussex College, probably a presentation copy to James Montagu, bishop of Winchester and translator of the works of James VI,[7] and the third, a presentation copy to James VI, bound in red velvet, with manuscript verses to the King and to the author by David Leech (BL C.136.ee.34). Little is known about Leech.[8] He describes himself as a Selkirk man ('Celurcanus') and in 1620 he was in France, where he met George Chambers ('Fintraeus'), professor of laws and Dean of the Faculty at the Jesuit College of Pont-à-Mousson. Chambers and Leech exchanged Latin verses[9]—humanity evidently transcended the barriers of religion. Leech's collected *Poemata* were published in London in 1620 in two different issues and contained a printed dedication to Charles, prince of Wales. Both issues are common enough: a copy of the first issue, with a manuscript presentation to Charles, left the Royal Library at an early date, was acquired by Wanley for the Harleian Library and is now in AUL. The fact that the Royal Library has retained a copy of the second, and completer, issue suggests that the disposal of the copy of the first issue was deliberate.[10] Another book connected with Leech is John Scot, 'adolescens', *Hodoeporicon*, 4° Edinb. A.Hart 1619, yet another poem on James's departure from Scotland. It was published by the proud father, Sir John Scot of Scotstarvet, together with some poems of his own, and including an exchange of poems with Leech (*STC*, 21856); four copies have survived.[11]

A rare poem connected with Charles I's visit to Scotland is David Wedderburn's *Vivat Rex*, 4° Aberd., Ed. Raban 1633 (*STC* 25194: AUL, GUL, and Charles's copy, BL 1070.m.40(5)). Wedderburn was Rector of the Aberdeen Grammar School from 1603 to 1640: his loyal effusion was probably connected with his

---

[7] I am grateful to Norman Rogers, of the Muniment Room Sidney Sussex College, for this information.

[8] Even to J.F. Kellas Johnstone, who confuses him with Jeremy Leech in *Bibliographia Aberdonensis* (Aberdeen, 1929), 129.

[9] Georgius Camerarius, *Sylva Leochaeo suo sive Lycidae Desiderium; Ioannis Leochaei Scoti Scotiam repetentis, ad Galliam Vale; Georgio Camerario suo, Ioannes Leochaeus Salvere & Valere*, 4° Paris, Iean Laquehay 1620. The only copy is in the Drummond Collection (EUL, De.5.63/5), more probably a presentation from Leech than from Chambers. I am grateful to A.F. Allison for information on Chambers.

[10] I suspect that the disposal occurred during the librarianship of Richard Bentley.

[11] Trinity College, Cambridge: EUL (Drummond Collection); NLS; and James VI's copy, BL 1070.1.28.

efforts to get official sanction for the publication of his Latin grammar book in the same year.[12]

There are yet two more rarities connected with the visit of James to Scotland in 1617. Firstly, Samuel Kellus, *Carmen gratulatorium*, 4° Edinb., A. Hart 1617 (*STC* 14916; BL 1070.l.17): the only other location, besides James VI's copy, is in NLS, on deposit from Blairs—which is odd, as the poem is specifically anti-papist. Secondly, David Lindsay, bishop of Brechin, *De Potestate Principis Aphorismi*, 4° Edinb., T. Finlason, 1617 (*STC*, 21555.28; BL 522.d.1(2): only other copy, in Huntington). This is in fact a theological disputation, with R. Howie as *praeses*, put on for James's benefit at St. Andrews; the text was reprinted in the well-known commemorative anthology of the whole visit, *The Muses Welcome*, ed. John Adamson, fol. Edinb., T. Finlason 1618 (*STC*, 140; BL C.21.d.9, in presentation binding with the royal arms: many other copies in UK and USA).

The next category is of rare books by Scottish authors published in London. The most distinguished author is, of course, James VI himself. There are two unique items, first issues of French translations: *Declaration du serenissime roy ... touchant le faict de C. Vorstius*, 4° London (Eliot's Court Press) chez J. Norton 1612 (*STC*, 9229; BL 859.i.16(3)) with manuscript corrections in the hand of James himself; and *Declaration du ... Roy Jacques I pour le droit des rois*, 4° London, J. Bill 1615 (*STC*, 14367; BL 522.d.1(1))—the leaves are as crisp as the day they left the printer. Although therefore, in strict bibliographical terminology, these two items can be called 'first issues', knowledge of their circumstances reveals that they are in fact simply sets of proofs.

The Scots at the English court provided a steady stream of latinity. The weirdest of all was George Eglisham (fl. 1612-42), whom James VI appointed as his physician in 1618. Eglisham was in Holland in 1612-13, apparently sent by James as a kind of *rapporteur* on the Vorstius case. Besides picking up his medical degree at Leiden, Eglisham was also employed as tutor at the Hague to the young Constantine Huygens and his brother.[13] He

---

[12] See *Bibliographia Aberdonensis*, 263.

[13] Huygens's autobiography is edited by J.A. Worp, *Bijdragen en Mededelingen van het Historisch Genootschap*, xvii (Utrecht, 1897), 1-122. Eglisham had attended the Scots College at Louvain in 1601, and in 1607 he was lecturing at Rouen and quarrelling with the Jesuits there: see *Records of the Scots Colleges*, ed. P.J. Anderson

taught them logic, astronomy, geography and natural philosophy. Huygens had a very low opinion of Eglisham's teaching abilities, and remarked on his use of antiquated scholastic text books, such as Toletanus and Titelmannus—authors to be found in Durkan & Ross, *Libraries.* Huygens describes Eglisham as ' a strange and arrogant man ', a judgement well borne out by *Duellum Poeticum,* 4° London, E. Allde 1618 (*STC,* 7547; BL 1213.k.19(3&4)), which claims that George Buchanan, in his paraphrase of Psalm 104, was guilty of 'impiety towards God, perfidy towards his Prince, and tyranny to the Muses.' The physical make-up of the book is a complete mess: Katherine F. Pantzer, editor of the new *STC,*, comments restrainedly: 'it is not clear what was intended with this book'. The only other extant copy is in EUL (De.6.47). Although it is not included in EUL's catalogue of the Drummond Library, there is a very strong possibility that it was in fact a presentation copy to Drummond: Eglisham has made identical manuscript alterations in both copies.[14] In 1625, after accusing Buckingham of poisoning the King, Eglisham had to flee to Brussels: libelling the living was more dangerous than libelling the dead.

Many works were written quite blatantly in the hope of a pension or of preferment. Alexander Craig of Banffshire (1567-1627) was granted a pension of £400 scots for his *Poetical Essays,* 4° London, W. White 1604 (*STC,* 5958; BL C.39.d.51(1); only other copies Folger and Hatfield House). A.H. Bullen describes the poems as 'very rare and very worthless'[15]—presumably Robert Cecil kept a copy at Hatfield House as a record of what the pension was for. A similar case was that of Thomas Dempster (1579-1625) who published two Latin poems during his brief stay in London. The first (*STC,* 6580.4) combined a panegyric of James with a votive offering to Robert Carr, earl of Somerset, the waning royal favourite: Dempster was a little out of touch with *realpolitik,* and James does not seem to have bothered to keep a copy. James, however, did possess a copy of Dempster's second effort, a collection of New Year verses: *Strena ... ad Illustriss. virum Jacobum Hayum, Baronum de Saley,* 4° London, J. Bill 1616 (*STC,* 6580.7; BL 1070.m.51, only other copy Vatican Library, Barberini GGG. VI.81(14)). It was dedicated to James VI, so Dempster was aiming

(New Spalding CLub, 1906), 8, and Jacques de Montholon, *Plaidoyé ... pour les pères Jesuites,* 8° Paris 1612, 180.

[14] I am grateful to Miss Jean Archibald of EUL for her help.

[15] *DNB.*

at two patrons with one book—and he tried again, successfully, with Cardinal Maffeo Barberini, Cardinal Protector of Scotland, later Pope Urban VIII, who was himself a Latin poet of no mean ability.[16]

Another Latin versifier who had come to London seeking preferment was David Drummond, whose friend at court was Sir Thomas Lake, Latin secretary to James VI and later secretary of state.[17] Drummond's *Xenia Regia*, 4° London, G. Eld 1607 (*STC*, 6162; BL 1213 1.11(1), only other copy Westminster Abbey) and *Xenia ad Jacobum*, 4° ? London, ? 1610 (*STC*, 6163; BL 1213. 1.11(1*), only other copy Huntington) include verses to James; Queen Anne; Prince Henry and Prince Charles; Sir Thomas Egerton; Henry Howard, earl of Northampton; Robert Cecil; James Elphinstone, 1st Lord Balmerino; and finally, 'ad Dominum Thomam Lakeum amicum integerrimum'.

Controversial theology in Latin verse is unusual, but John Gordon (1544-1619) was an unusual man.[18] His grandmother, Jane Drummond, was a natural daughter of James IV, so he could claim kinship with James VI. Though remaining a staunch Protestant throughout his life, he was a loyal supporter of Mary, Queen of Scots, and was a member of her court until the Ridolfi plot. He then served as a gentleman of the privy chamber to three French kings, Charles IX, Henry III and Henry IV; and he was twice married, both times to Huguenot aristocrats. On James's accession to the English throne he published poems in praise both of the Union and of Mary, Queen of Scots, and was rewarded with the deanery of Salisbury Cathedral and took part in the Hampton Court conference. James's library has several of his broadsheet polemics (including a reply in verse to Bellarmine), and one of them is unique: *Papa-cacus* (*STC*, 12063, 4° London, F. Kyngston 1610: BL 860.k.16(2); there is a variant at Balliol). Perhaps the title sounded a little too strong for most people to keep it in their libraries.

An unusual figure of a different plumage was James Maxwell (1581-1640), who graduated MA Edinburgh (1600), a sort of

[16] George Con, *De Duplici Statu* (Rome 1628), mentions that Cardinal Maffeo Barberini was Dempster's patron.

[17] See Drummond's letter to Lake, dated Westminster 12 August 1605, *CSP Dom. Addenda 1580-1625*, 464.

[18] There is a good article on Gordon in *DNB*; see also D.M. Quynn, 'The career of John Gordon', *The Historian* (Albuquerque, 1943).

Scottish Tartuffe: Laud called him 'mountebank Maxwell'. James VI has preserved his elegy on the death of Prince Henry (1610), his epithalamium on the marriage of Frederick and Elizabeth (1613), and *The Golden Art, or the right way of Enriching. Comprised in ten Rules, proved and confirmed by many places of Holy Scripture*, 4° London, W. Leake 1611 (*STC*, 17700: BL 852.g.2; only other copy imperfect, at Folger). The work has been annotated in manuscript and includes the remark, 'This golden art is not worth a fart'; it would be nice to believe that the hand is that of James VI, but unfortunately it is not.

Among the ephemeral tracts in the library of Charles I are several by David Echlin, physician to Anne of Denmark and Henrietta Maria, and a versifier in French as well as in Latin. He dedicated to Henrietta Maria the poem *L'adieu au monde de David Echlin, Medecin de la royne, aage environ de soixante ans, prest a estre taillé de la pierre, au hazard de sa vie*, 4° London, G. Purslowe 1627 (*STC*, 7475; BL C.115.n.13(2), unique); his motto was 'cita mors aut victoria laeta'. The operation was successful, so he followed it up with *Echlin par la grace de Dieu resuscité*, 4° London, G. Purslowe 1628 (*STC*, 7477; BL C.115.n.13(6), other copies at Folger and Yale). Samuel Pepys took a more sober attitude when he was cut for the stone—but when doctors become patients they often tend to over-dramatise. Echlin's funeral elegy on his wife, Philiberta Loubata, was published in 1629 and dedicated to Charles I (*STC*, 7478; BL C.115.n.13(3), only other copy Trinity College, Cambridge), and in the same year he published *Somnium Davidis Echlini ad Carolum Magnae Britanniae Regem*, 4° London, A. Matthews 1629, which was a New Year's gift to the King, and is unique (*STC*, 7480; BL C.115.n.13(7)).

The work of Arthur Johnston (1587-1641), the most famous of all the Scottish Latin poets, is strangely under-represented in the Royal Library. His *Epigrammata*, 8° Aberd. 1632, *Parerga*, 8° Aberd. 1632, and *Musae Aulice*, 8° Lond. 1635, were acquired in 1660 as part of the library of John Morris, master of the London Bridge watermills, and were disposed of in the BM Duplicate Sale of 1788. Two items, however, do still remain in the Royal Library, and they are both unique: *Consilium collegii medici Parisiensis de mania G. Eglishemii*, 8° Paris (*vere* London, W. Stansby?) 1619 (*STC*, 14708.8; BL 1213.k.19(4)), a satire on George Eglisham's *Duellum Poeticum*; and *In obitum Jacobi pacifici ... elegia*, 4° London, M. Flesher imp. N. Butter 1625 (*STC*, 14711; BL 1070.1.12(3)). It is surely remarkable that a funeral elegy on James VI by the leading Scottish latinist should have survived in only a single copy.

Charles I's ownership of a collection of St. Andrews University theses, *Theses aliquot philosophicae ... Praeside J. Barronio*, 4° Edinb., J. Wreittoun 1627 (*STC*, 21555.34; BL 527.c.38, only other copy imperfect, EUL)[19] is not easy to account for. It was dedicated to Sir Thomas Kellie, described as 'Master of the Bedchamber'; perhaps Kellie passed it on to the King.

Charles I's visit to Scotland in 1633 for his coronation at Holyroodhouse, is commemorated by Andrew Boyd, later bishop of Argyll, in *Carmen Panegyricum*, 4° Edinb., R. Young 1633 (*STC*, 3443; BL C.28.g.8(8): other copies GUL and Harvard). A more practical publication connected with the visit of 1633 was that of Charles's chaplain, William Guild (1586-1657), a staunch supporter of the liberties of the Kirk: *The humble Address of both Church and poore to Great Britaines Monarch. For a just redress of the Unity of Churches and the Ruin of Hospitals*, 4° Aberd., E. Raban 1633 (*STC*, 12480; BL 700.e.1(2); only other copy NLS). This was in fact a reissue of the relevant portion of a work published eleven years before: *Issachar's Asse, braying under a double burden; or the Uniting of Churches*, 4° Aberd., E. Raban 1622. Guild was later appointed Principal of King's College, Aberdeen and was the owner of no less than 22 books from early Scottish libraries, listed by Durkan & Ross.

When it comes to the discussion of works by Scottish authors printed abroad, the factor of rarity is more difficult to establish. M.A. Shaaber's *Checklist of Works by British Authors printed abroad, in Languages other than English, to 1640* (New York, 1975), is a most valuable guide, but it is a union catalogue of printed catalogues.[20] But even with that restriction, it is possible to indicate some continental Scottish rarities in the Royal Library.

On a first consideration, Johan Bogusz, baron de Ziemlič, *Διάσκεψις Metaphysica de Unitate*, 4° Sedan 1605 (BL C.29.k.16) may not seem to have much to do with Scotland except for the fact that it has a dedication to James VI and the autograph of Prince Henry on the front pastedown. It is a presentation copy,

---

[19] W. Beattie, 'Handlist of works from the press of John Wreitton', *TEBS*, ii (1941), no. 15.

[20] For instance, Shaaber gives only two locations (BL and Bodley) for George Con, *Premetiae*, 8° Bologna 1621. But A.F. Allison and D.M. Rogers in *ARCR* I also record copies at Göttingen, BN, and Mazarine. There is an extensive and thorough review of Shaaber by A.F. Allison in *MLR*, lxxiii (1978), 588-91.

bound in red velvet, with the royal arms on the covers, and printed on yellow satin; as a university thesis, it was certainly a piece of vanity publishing. The Scottish connection is the fact that the *praeses* of the disputation was none other than Arthur Johnston, at that time professor of logic and metaphysics at Sedan, who had obviously inspired the well-heeled aristocrat to send James a copy.

Andrew Aidie's *Pastoria in decem distributa Eclogas*, 8° Danzig. Martinus Rhodius 1610 (Shaaber A76; BL 1213.k.18(1); other copies at ULC and NLS) is dedicated to the consuls and senators of Aberdeen, and is of considerable poetic merit. Aidie was professor at the Danzig *gymnasium* and later became principal of Marischal College, Aberdeen. He petitioned James VI for preferment in respect of his services at Danzig 'against the Jesuits of Braunsburg, auctors of that most infamous pasquil Bartolus Pacenius', *'Εξέτασις epistolae* (4° Mainz, 1610) by Robert Abercrombie SJ, on the oath of allegiance.[21]

The nuptials of Frederick and Elizabeth at Heidelberg account for two rare items: John Forbes of Corse, *Genethliaca*, 4° Heidelberg, J. Lancellotus, 1614 (Shaaber F168 lists only James's copy, BL 837.k.8(14)) and John Gellie, *Epithalamium*, 4° Heidelberg 1613 (Shaaber G157; BL 837.k.82; other copies at BN and Illinois Univ.).

As far as prose is concerned, James VI's copy of Thomas Cumming, *Theses Theologicae de Sessione Christi ad dexteram Patris ... sub tutela D. Antonii Thysii*, 4° Harderwijk, Thomas Hendricksz 1611, was disposed of as a duplicate in 1769 (Shaaber C478 lists only BL 479.a.19(2), which is the Sloane copy). Cumming was the son of an officer in a Scots cavalry regiment who lost his life in the service of the States General. Cumming's *Album Amicorum* has survived;[22] it gives a vivid picture of his movements. After graduating at Harderwijk, Cumming returned to Aberdeen, then made his way to England and arrived in London in February 1613. James VI was on one of his progresses and Cumming caught up with the king at Thetford and obtained a warm letter of recommendation to the States General in which he was described as a young man who has 'devoted himself to the study and principles of theology'.

[21] *ARCR* I, no. 4 and literature there cited; also *Analecta Scotica*, 2nd series, ed. J. Maidment (Edinburgh, 1837), 337.

[22] Max Rosenheim, *The Album Amicorum* (Oxford, 1910), 298-9; and more fully, J.F. Kellas Johnstone, *The Alba Amicorum of George Strachan, George Craig, Thomas Cumming* (Aberdeen, 1924), 32-47.

Cumming then returned to the Netherlands but did not stay long. In 1614 he passed through Heidelberg (where he obtained a letter of recommendation from Frederick, the Elector Palatine), Frankfurt (where he met Thomas Seget, of whom more anon), and from thence to Herborn-Nassau and Marburg, and back to Heidelberg in 1615; thence to Altdorf, Vienna, Basel and Zurich; by 1619 he had returned to Franeker in the Netherlands. In all his wanderings, the Harderwijk theses would have provided a useful visiting card: James VI took the trouble to preserve them as a reminder of his letter of recommendation. Unfortunately, they had no associations for the British Museum librarian who disposed of them.

John Sharp (c.1572-c.1648) was one of the presbyterian ministers banished for life by James VI in 1606: he became professor of theology at the protestant college of Die, in Dauphiné, from 1608 to 1630. But Sharp did not wish to be forgotten. His first publication *Tractatus de justificatione hominis coram Deo*, 8° Geneva, P. Marcellus 1609 (Shaaber S209; BL 847.h.13(1)) is apparently unique: James must have kept it as part of the man's dossier. Sharp continued to send copies of his publications to the Royal Library (and to Archbishop Ussher in Dublin). Eventually Charles I relented, and Sharp returned to Edinburgh to become professor of divinity in 1630.

A less successful attempt to gain royal favour was that of Thomas Seget.[23] He is first recorded as a convert from Calvinism to Catholicism, attending the Scots College at Louvain in 1596, but he did not stay there long. Armed with a letter of recommendation from Justus Lipsius, he set out for Padua and became librarian to Giovanni Pinelli, and met Galileo in 1599. After the death of Pinelli he seems to have led a wandering life in Europe: a spell in gaol at Venice, then Heidelberg, Hanau, Hamburg, Prague (where he met Kepler), Cracow, Lublin, Rakov, Altdorf, Regensburg, Frankfurt (where he met Thomas Cumming in 1615). He died in Holland in 1628. In 1622, he published his apologia in the form of a little pamphlet, *Thomas Segethus a gravi columnia vindicatus*, 4° Magdeburg, M. Voigt, 1622 (Shaaber S187), with a printed dedication to James VI. He was hoping for a

[23] *Records of the Scots Colleges*, 7; A. Favaro, *Amici e Corrispondenti di Galileo Galilei* (Venice, 1911; repr. 1983), 642-50; Birrell, *English Monarchs*, 48-50. For Seget's visit to Lublin and Rakov in July 1612, see G.G. Zeltnerus, *Historia Crypto-Socinianismi* (Leipzig, 1729) [the diary of Valentine Schmalz], 1196.

job at court, through the good offices of his old friend Thomas Reid (Rhaedus), Latin secretary to the king. There are two copies of the pamphlet in existence: one in the Royal Library (BL C.190.a.30), with a manuscript letter to Charles, prince of Wales, and the other at St. John's College Cambridge (MS S.10),[24] with a manuscript letter to James VI, dated Hamburg, March 1622. The latter copy must have been disposed of as a duplicate from the Royal Library by the end of the seventeenth century.[25]

Finally, though the books are by no means rare in any strict sense, the Scottish associations of the following items are of some interest: Francis Hamilton OSB, *De Sanctorum invocatione demonstratio duplex*, 4° Würzburg, G. Fleischmann 1596 and *Disputatio theologica de legitimo sanctorum culto per sacras imagines*, 4° Würzburg, G. Fleischmann 1597 (Shaaber H73 & 74; *ARCR*, I, 634 & 635; BL 476.a.12(1&2)). The first item is a programme announcing the defence of the thesis, and the second is the disputation itself. The Royal Library copies are inscribed 'G. Strachanus 1604'. George Strachan of the Mearns was one of the most intellectually distinguished of the wandering Scots scholars of the seventeenth century: he was a Latin poet, a distinguished mathematician (a friend of Marinus Ghetaldus of Ragusa), and a pioneer arabist.[26] Strachan's *Album Amicorum* enables us to establish his acquisition of the theses. He left the Scots College, Rome for the last time in January 1604, he was in Venice on 7 March, and by the end of March he had crossed the Austrian Tyrol and arrived at the Scottish Benedictine monastery at Regensburg. The abbot, John James White, and the prior, Adam Makcall, signed his *Album*, and Francis Hamilton, later to be prior, gave him the theses as a souvenir. Strachan then made his way to Paris, where he was employed as a tutor to John Casaubon, eldest son of Isaac Casaubon. Much to his father's grief, John became a Roman Catholic and entered the Capuchins; many of John's books were kept by his father. When Isaac Casòaubon died in London in

---

[24] M. Cowie, *Descriptive Catalogue of the Manuscripts and Scarce Books in the Library of St. John's College Cambridge* (Cambridge, 1842-3), 136. The book is in a white vellum ornamental binding, probably of German origin. I am grateful to Dr Richard Beadle, Librarian of St John's College, for his assistance.

[25] See n.10, above.

[26] *George Strachan, Memorials of a Wandering Scottish Scholar of the Seventeenth century*, ed. G. Dellavida (Third Spalding Club, 1956); Kellas Johnstone, *Alba Amicorum*, 12-13; M. Ghetaldus, preface to *Apollonius Redivivus*, 4° (Venice, 1613); Alexander Anderson, 'Αιτιολογία, 4° (Paris, 1615), 26.

1614, his library was acquired by James VI, and that is the probable channel by which Strachan's copy of Hamilton's theses entered the Royal Library.

It should be possible to draw some tentative conclusions from this very miscellaneous list. Firstly, most of these rarities are ephemeral, being 'occasional' verses or university theses. It may be argued that these are of little intrinsic importance, yet they testify to a vigorous literary sub-culture. If they had not survived, we should have lost part of an historical pattern.

Secondly, printed ephemera are, of their very nature, extremely vulnerable as physical objects: they do not survive unless they are consciously preserved at the time of their production. By the eighteenth century, early Scottish printing was being sought after in England as 'collector's items', but the later collectors were dependent on the books dispersed from early seventeenth-century libraries: individual items of ephemera just did not float about loose for half a century. Of the early seventeenth-century collectors whose libraries have survived more or less intact, James VI was one of the very few who consciously collected ephemera.

Thirdly, it is clear enough that this is a category of books whose primary purpose is to be presented, and whose secondary purpose is to be read: in other words, an extensive form of what may be called 'vanity publishing'. Thanks to the researches of Miss Pantzer, we now know that there were only 87 authors, translators and editors whose names actually appear in the imprints of books up to 1640.[27] But these were all cases where the author's name would serve for commercial advertisement: schoolmasters, writing masters, language teachers, shorthand teachers, musicians, and other forms of patentee. They all wanted to sell their books on the market. In sixteenth- and seventeenth-century imprints, the phrase 'printed for the author' does not imply what it usually does today. The seventeenth-century vanity publisher who was printing his verses or his theses solely for presentation did not put his name on the imprint, nor did he give any sign that his book was in a very limited edition. In the days when labour was cheap and paper was dear, there was not the horrendous discrepancy between unit costs and size of print run that there is nowadays. John Bill, for instance, would not have considered it beneath his dignity as King's Printer to run off 50 or so copies of a *New Year's*

[27] *STC*, iii (1991), 194.

Gift for Thomas Dempster. As well as the factor of physical vulnerability therefore, another reason for the rarity of these ephemera is the simple fact that they were probably printed in very limited editions.

Finally, a most striking feature in this study is the tightly-knit web of patronage and friendship among the Scottish latinists. Their hard-won latinity was their principal asset in a hostile world. And at the centre of that web was James VI and I.

WRITINGS OF JOHN DURKAN, 1931-1994

Peter W. Asplin

Introduction

The following bibliography aims to record all John Durkan's published work, other than items appearing in newspapers. It is, of course, an interim report. No attempt has been made here to record forthcoming publications, and no doubt some earlier writings have been overlooked. The arrangement is by year of publication (or the cover year in the case of some periodicals) and alphabetically by title within each year. Book reviews are recorded at the end of each year's entries and have been given in a standard format rather than replicating the various formats of different journals. Notes have generally been restricted to details of content or authorship, when these are not clear from the title, and the occasional cross-reference to a related publication. Several of his early contributions to *The Innes Review* were published under the pseudonyms of 'Ian Johnson' and 'Robin McLaren' - to disguise the fact that a disproportionate number of articles in that journal were coming from the same pen! These are noted in quotation marks to distinguish them from the real names of other authors.

1931

'Resurrection' (an eight-line poem), *New Statesman and Athenaeum*, new series, i, 508.

1936

'The ABC of escapism', *Blackfriars*, xvii, 116-75.
'New horizons', *Blackfriars*, xvii, 332-42.

1938

Review: '*T.E. Hulme*, by Michael Roberts', *Blackfriars*, xix, 705-06.
Review: '*Le soif (pièce en trois actes)*', *Blackfriars*, xix, 946-8.

1939

'The lesson of standardisation', *Blackfriars*, xx, 125-30.
Review: '*The Left Heresy in Literature and Life,* by Harry Kemp, Laura Riding and others', *Blackfriars*, xx, 824.

1941

Review: '*Sons of the Mistral,* by Roy Campbell', *Blackfriars*, xxii, 213.

1942

'A Greek on art', *Blackfriars*, xxiii, 387-9.
Review: '*Soviet Labour and Industry,* by L.E. Hubbard', *Blackfriars*, xxiii, 325-6.
Review: '*Les guerres modernes et la pensée catholique*', *Blackfriars*, xxiii (*Book Supplement*), 2-3.

1943

'Kierkegaard and Aristotle: a parallel', *Dublin Review*, ccxiii, 136-48.
Review: '*The Fear of Freedom,* by Erich Fromm', *Blackfriars*, xxiv, 192-4.
Review: '*God and Evil,* by C.E.M. Joad', *Blackfriars*, xxiv (*Book Supplement*), pp. viii-ix.
Review: '*God and Philosophy,* by Etienne Gilson', *Dublin Review*, ccxiii, 169-72.
Review: '*God's Will in Our Time. The Report presented to the General Assembly of the Church of Scotland*', *Blackfriars*, xxiv (*Book Supplement*), pp. xv-xvi.
Review: '*Lucky Poet: A Self-Study in Literature and Poetical Ideas,* by Hugh McDiarmid', *Scrutiny*, xii, 72-3.
Review: '*The Many and the Few,* by Paul Bloomfield', *Blackfriars*, xxiv, 157-8.

1944

Review: '*Heritage and Destiny,* by John A. Mackay', *Blackfriars*, xxv, 154-5.
Review: '*Poems 1937-42,* by David Gascoigne. With Drawings by Graham Sutherland', *Blackfriars*, xxv, 312-17.

1946

'Background to the present impasse in poetry', *Dublin Review*, ccxviii, 40-47.
Review: '*Confusion of Faces. The Struggle between Religion and Secularism in Europe. A Commentary on German History,* by Erich Meissner', *Blackfriars*, xxvii, 484-7.

1947

Review: '*La théorie des premiers principes selon Maine de Biran,* by A.M. Monette OP', *Blackfriars*, xxviii, 280-81.

1948

Review: '*Du temps et de l'éternité,* by Louis Lavelle', *Blackfriars*, xxix, 93-5.
Review: '*The Influence of the Enlightenment on the Catholic Theory of Religious Education in France, 1750-1830,* by E.C. Elwell', *Blackfriars*, xxix, 95-6.
Review: '*Les sandales d'Empedocle,* by Claude-Edmonde Magny', *Blackfriars*, xxix, 102-04.

1949

'David Lauxius', *TEBS*, iii (1948-55), 78-80.

'Robertus Richardinus and *STC* 21021', *TEBS*, iii (1948-55), 83-4.

1950

'David Lauxius: a further note', *TEBS*, iii (1948-55), 156-7.
'John Major: after 400 years', *IR*, i, 131-57.
Appendix: 'The school of John Major: bibliography' (140-57).
'Rev. Alexander Gordon', *IR*, i, 68-70.
'Robert Wauchope, archbishop of Armagh', *IR*, i, 48-66.
'The University of Glasgow and the Catholic Church, Part 1', *St Peter's College Magazine* (Cardross), xix, 44-52.
See also following entry.
The University of Glasgow and the Catholic Church. Edinburgh: Scottish Catholic Historical Committee. 16p.
By John Durkan, David McRoberts and James McGloin.
Reprinted from *St Peter's College Magazine*, xix (1950).
[Part 1], 'To 1560', by J. Durkan (1-9).
Review: '*John Knox's History of the Reformation*, edited by William Croft Dickinson', *IR*, i, 158-61.

1951

'Scots College, Paris', *IR*, ii, 112-13.
'The Scottish Minims', *IR*, ii, 77-81.
'William Turnbull, bishop of Glasgow', *IR*, ii, 5-61.
William Turnbull, Bishop of Glasgow. Glasgow: Published for the Scottish Catholic Historical Committee by John S. Burns. [2], 70p; 9 plates.
Reprinted, with bibliography and index, from *IR*, ii (1951).

1952

'Florence Wilson's death: a correction', *IR*, iii, 65-6.
Review: '*The Life and Times of James Kennedy, Bishop of St Andrews*, by Annie I. Dunlop', *IR*, iii, 67-9.

1953

'The beginnings of humanism in Scotland', *IR*, iv, 5-24.
Appendix i: 'Library of Abp. Scheves'. (17-19).
Appendix ii: 'Kinloss Abbey library'. (19-24).
'George Wishart: his early life', *SHR*, xxxii, 98-9.
'Robert Cockburn, bishop of Ross, and French humanism', *IR*, iv, 121-2.
'St Ailred and Paisley', *IR*, iv, 61.
By 'Ian Johnson'.
'Scheves and Kinloss libraries: additions and a correction', *IR*, iv, 119-21.
Amendments to appendices to his 'The beginnings of humanism in Scotland' (1953).
Review: '*The Earlier Tudors, 1485-1558*, by J.D. Mackie', *IR*, v, 63-4.
By 'Robin McLaren'.

1954

'The Catholic survival in the west of Scotland', *St Peter's College Magazine* (Cardross), xxi, 87-91.
'Father Thomas Innes : lost papers', *IR*, v, 78.
By 'Robin McLaren'.
'St. Thomas More and his Scots friar', *IR*, v, 78. [Friar Donald]
By 'Ian Johnson'.
'Scots Carmelites and the French reform', *IR*, v, 141-3.
By 'Ian Johnson'.

1955

'The ordination of John Knox : a symposium', *IR*, vi, 99-106.
By Margot R. Adamson, J.H. Burns, W.J. Anderson and 'Robin McLaren'.
Comments by 'Robin McLaren' (104-06) on a document published in Appendix ii to Peter J. Shearman, 'Father Alexander McQuhirrie, S.J.', *IR*, vi (1955), p.42.
'Relic of Blessed John Ogilvie', *IR*, vi, 148-9.
'The University of Glasgow', *SHR*, xxxiv, 144-7.
Review of J.D. Mackie, *The University of Glasgow, 1451 to 1951.*

1956

'Hospital scholars in the middle ages', *IR*, vii, 125-7.
'Paisley Abbey: attempt to make it Cistercian', *IR*, vii, 60-62.
'Scots in Salerno', *IR*, vii, 123.
By 'Ian Johnson'.

1958

'The Aberdeen Benedictines : a ghost laid', *IR*, ix, 220-21.
By 'Ian Johnson'.
'The Dominicans at the Reformation', *IR*, ix, 216-17.
'Early Scottish libraries', *IR*, ix, 3-167.
By John Durkan and Anthony Ross.

1959

'Care of the poor: pre-Reformation hospitals', *IR*, x, 268-80.
For reprint see 1962 below.
'The cultural background in sixteenth-century Scotland', *IR*, x, 382-439.
For reprint see 1962 below.
'Education in the century of the Reformation', *IR*, x, 67-90.
Appendices: 'Paisley Grammar School' (87-9); 'Linlithgow Song School' (89); 'Schoolmaster at Ayr' (89); 'Scottish pre-Reformation schools' (90).
For reprint see 1962 below.
'The Scottish Universities in the Middle Ages, 1413-1560' (Edinburgh University Ph.D. thesis).
'Some local heretics', *TDGAS*, 3rd ser., xxxvi (1957-8), 67-77.

John MacDowell, Donald Makcarny, William Johnstone, John MacBrair.

1960

'Henry Scrimgeour, Fugger librarian: a biographical note', *The Bibliotheck*, iii, 68-70.
Transcript (69-70) of a brief life by Antoine de la Faye, from Paris, Bibliothèque nationale, Dupuy MS., no 348.

1961

'An Arbroath book inventory of 1473', *The Bibliotheck*, iii, 144-6.
Transcript (146) of 'Richard Guthrie; Books left at Arbroath Abbey in 1473', AUL, MS. 105, f. 139v.
Early Scottish Libraries. Glasgow: John S. Burns. 196p; 48 plates.
By John Durkan and Anthony Ross.
Pp. 5-167 reprinted from *IR*, ix (1958).
Review, including addenda, by William S. Mitchell, *The Library*, 5th ser., xviii (1963), 66-8. See also 1963, 1978, 1981, 1982, 1985, below.
'The library of St Salvator's College, St Andrews', *The Bibliotheck*, iii, 97-100.
Transcripts (99-100) of extracts from St Andrews University Archives, St Salvator's Book, 'B', f. 221r, f. 130r; Acta Rectorum, i, 97; and 'The Catalogue of the Library of St Salvator's College', NLS, Balcarres Papers, vii, f. 101r.

1962

'Alexander Dickson and *STC* 6823', *The Bibliotheck*, iii, 183-90.
'Care of the poor: pre-Reformation hospitals', *Essays on the Scottish Reformation, 1513-1625*, edited by David McRoberts (Glasgow: Burns), 116-28.
Originally published in *IR*, x (1959).
'The cultural background in sixteenth-century Scotland', *Essays on the Scottish Reformation, 1513-1625*, edited by David McRoberts (Glasgow: Burns), 274-331.
Originally published in *IR*, x (1959).
'Education in the century of the Reformation', *Essays on the Scottish Reformation, 1513-1625*, edited by David McRoberts (Glasgow: Burns), 145-68.
Originally published in *IR*, x (1959).
'Foundation of the collegiate church of Seton', *IR*, xiii, 71-6.
'A note on Scottish medieval hospitals', *IR*, xiii, 217-18.
'St Andrews University medieval theological statutes: revised dating suggested', *IR*, xiii, 104-08.
'The sanctuary and college of Tain', *IR*, xiii, 147-56.
'Scots at Franciscan General Chapter in Lisbon', *IR*, xiii, 218-19.

1963

'Additional entries [to *Early Scottish Libraries*]', *The Bibliotheck*, iv, 22-3.
Printed as addenda in T.A.F. Cherry, 'The library of Henry Sinclair, bishop of Ross, 1560-1565', *The Bibliotheck*, iv, 13-24.
'Andrew Leech, Scottish Latinist', *The Bibliotheck*, iv, 24-34.
'Cardinal Farnese and a possible Scots Livy original', *IR*, xiv, 74.
'George Buchanan: some French connections', *The Bibliotheck*, iv, 66-72.
Appendix (69-72) contains transcripts of correspondence.
'Laurence of Lindores: scientific writings', *IR*, xiv, 79.
'Paisley Abbey and Glasgow archives: some new directions', *IR*, xiv, 46-53.

1964

'Buchanan's judaising practices', *IR*, xv, 186-7.
'George Lockhart', *IR*, xv, 191-2.
'A sixteenth-century monastic letter', *IR*, xv, 188-9.
Letter by Dene John Ayr found in St Salvator's College, St Andrews.

1965

'David Lowis or Lauxius of Edinburgh', *The Bibliotheck*, iv, 200-01.
Transcript of letter from Robert Breton of Arras to Lowis (1533?) from *Roberti Britanni Attrebatensis orationes quatuor* (Toulouse, 1536), Epistolarum Liber I, f. 35v.
See also 1949-1950 above.
'St Salvator's College: Castle inventory', *IR*, xvi, 128-30.
Goods placed in St Andrews Castle, 1544.
Review: '*Medieval Libraries of Great Britain*, by N.R. Ker, 2nd ed.', *SHR*, xliv, 150-51.

1966

'Scots national feeling at Constance and Siena', *IR*, xvii, 63-5.
Review: '*Acta Facultatis Artium Universitatis Sanctiandree, 1413-1588*, edited by Annie I. Dunlop', *EHR*, lxxxi, 110-13.

1967

'Scotland, Church of', *New Catholic Encyclopedia* (New York: McGraw Hill), xii, 1235-7.
'History books for schools, xx', *History*, lii, 39-48.
Review: '*John Hus' Concept of the Church*, by Matthew Spinka', *New Blackfriars*, xlviii, 329.

1969

'Three manuscripts with Fife associations: and David Colville of Fife', *IR*, xx, 47-58.
Biblioteca de Palacio, Madrid, MS. II. 2097; Escorial, Latin MS. a.I.10; Municipal Library, Boulogne, MS. no 92.

'David Colville: an appendix', *IR*, xx, 138-49.
Includes transcripts of correspondence. Biblioteca Ambrosiana, Milan, MSS B138 Sup, M86 sussidio(1), O42 Inf (3), Q114 Sup.
See also preceding entry.

1970

'Brown's confession', *IR*, xxi, 169-70.
'The career of John Brown, Minim', *IR*, xxi, 164-9.
'John Francis Maitland, Minim', *IR*, xxi, 163-4.
'John Ogilvie's Glasgow associates', *IR*, xxi, 153-6.
'A Minims obituary', *IR*, xxi, 161-3.
R. Thuillier, *Diarium patrum* (Paris, 1709).
'Notes on Glasgow Cathedral', *IR*, xxi, 46-76.
'Two Jesuits: Patrick Anderson and John Ogilvie', *IR*, xxi, 157-61.

1971

'Grisy burses at Scots College, Paris', *IR*, xxii, 50-52.
'Missing cartularies: the Thomas Innes evidence', *IR*, xxii, 110-11.
'Notes on Scots in Italy. i. George Strachan', *IR*, xxii, 12-18.
George Strachan, Thomas Dempster.

1972

'Archbishop Robert Blackadder's will', *IR*, xxiii, 138-48.
Includes transcript (145-8) by Rosamund J. Mitchell, originally published in *Bolletino dell' Istituto di Storia della Società e dello Stato Veneziano*, i (1959), 175-8.
'The Bickertons: a Dominican connection', *IR*, xxiii, 79-81.
Review: '*John Knox*, by Jasper Ridley', *Catholic Historical Review*, lvii, 526-8.
Review: '*Underground Catholicism in Scotland, 1622-1878*, by Peter F. Anson', *SHR*, li, 204-06.

1973

'Archbishop Blackadder's will: corrigendum and addendum', *IR*, xxiv, 148-9.
See also 1972 above.
Review: '*Records of All Souls College Library, 1437-1600*, by N.R. Ker; *The History of All Souls College Library*, by Sir Edmund Craster, edited by E.F. Jacob; *The Library of Trinity College* [Cambridge], by Philip Gaskell and Robert Robson', *The Library*, 5th series, xxviii, 259-61.

1974

'St Andrews in the John Law chronicle', *IR*, xxv, 49-62.
Transcripts of relevant sections (52-62).
For reprint see 1976 below.

1975

'Archbishop Blackadder's will', *IR*, xxvi, 121.

Further addendum to 1972 above.
'The great fire at Glasgow Cathedral', *IR*, xxvi, 89-92.
Includes transcript of SRO, RH 2/6/2, ff. 102-05, Reg. Aven. 320, f. 599v.

1976

'Paisley Abbey in the sixteenth century', *IR*, xxvii, 110-26.
'St Andrews in the John Law chronicle', *The Medieval Church of St Andrews*, edited by David McRoberts (Glasgow: John S. Burns), 137-50.
Transcripts of relevant extracts (140-50).
Originally published in *IR*, xxv (1974).
'Some Scots in Rome', *IR*, xxvii, 42-8.

1977

'The early history of Glasgow University Library: 1475-1710', *The Bibliotheck*, viii, 102-26.
Paper read at a conference on 'Aspects of rare books', Glasgow University Library, June 1976.
'John Grierson's book-list'. *IR*, xxviii, 39-49.
By John Durkan and Julian Russell.
'Medieval Hamilton: ecclesiastical', *IR*, xxviii, 51-3.
The University of Glasgow, 1451-1577. Glasgow: University of Glasgow Press. xiv, 498p; 5 plates; map.
By John Durkan and James Kirk.
I, 'The old foundation' (1-222), by J. Durkan.
Review by Robert T. Hutcheson, 'Reminder of an inheritance', *The College Courant* (Glasgow), xxix, no. 59 (1977), 9-11.

1978

'Henry Scrimgeour, Renaissance bookman', *TEBS*, v, pt. 1 (1971-4), 1-31.
Transcripts in appendices (25-31):
A. Bayerische Staatsbibliothek, Munich, MS. Clm 10365, f. 22.
B. Bibliothèque nationale, Paris, Collection 500 Colbert MS. 394, f. 24.
C. Bodleian Library, Oxford, MS. Smith 77, 301-03.
D (a). Bodleian Library, Oxford, MS. Cherry 5.
D (b). Bodleian Library, Oxford, MS. Smith 77, p. 29r.
'St Andrews additions to Durkan & Ross: some unrecorded Scottish pre-Reformation ownership inscriptions in St Andrews University Library', *The Bibliotheck*, ix, 13-20.
By John Durkan and R.V. Pringle.
International Commission for the History of Universities: Work in Progress and Publication (for 1977), no. 1. Contributor of 'The British Isles' section. University of Aston in Birmingham.
Review: '*The Church in Italy in the Fifteenth Century*, by Denys Hay', *Scottish Journal of Theology*, xxxiii, 492-3.

1979

'Adam Mure: a biography', *Humanistica Lovaniensia*, xviii, 232-3.

'Adam Mure's "Laudes Gulielmi Elphinstoni"', *Humanistica Lovaniensia*, xxviii, 199-231.
  Edited by John Durkan and W.S. Watt.

'Chaplains in Scotland in the late middle ages', *RSCHS*, xx, 91-103.

'John Rutherford and Montaigne: an early influence?', *Bibliothèque d'humanisme et renaissance*, xli, 115-22.

'King Aristotle and old 'Butterdish': the making of a graduate in seventeenth-century Glasgow', *The College Courant* (Glasgow), no. 63, 18-24.

International Commission for the History of Universities: Work in Progress and Publication (for 1978), no. 2. Contributor of 'The British Isles' section.

Review: '*A Biographical Dictionary of Scottish Graduates to A.D. 1410*, by D.E.R. Watt', *J. of Ecclesiastical History*, xxx, 491.

1980

'Early humanism and King's College', *AUR*, xlviii, 259-79.

'Galloway, Whithorn, Candida Casa ... ', *Dictionnaire d'histoire et de géographie ecclésiastiques* (Paris), xix, columns 889-894.
  In French.

'George Buchanan: new light on the poems', *The Bibliotheck*, x, 1-9.
  Appendix: Three letters of Charles Utenhove.

'Giovanni Ferrerio, Gesner and French affairs', *Bibliothèque d'humanisme et renaissance*, xlii, 349-60.

'The identity of George Thomson, Catholic controversialist', *IR*, xxxi, 45-6.

'Some notes on William Chalmers, philosopher, Jesuit and Oratorian', *IR*, xxxi, 47-8.

International Commission for the History of Universities: Work in Progress and Publication (for 1979), no. 3. Contributor of 'The British Isles' section.

1981

'Further additions to Durkan and Ross: some newly-discovered Scottish pre-Reformation provenances', *The Bibliotheck*, x, 87-98.

'Giovanni Ferrerio, humanist: his influence in sixteenth-century Scotland', *Religion and humanism: Papers read at the Eighteenth Summer Meeting and Nineteenth Winter Meeting of the Ecclesiastical History Society*, edited by Keith Robbins (Oxford: Blackwell. *Studies in Church History*, xvii), 181-94.

International Commission for the History of Universities: Work in Progress and Publication (for 1980), no. 4. Contributor of 'The British Isles' section.

Review: '*The Apocalyptic Tradition in Reformation Britain, 1530-1645*, by Katherine R. Firth; *Scottish National Consciousness in the Age of James VI: Apocalypse, the Union and the Shaping of Scotland's Public Culture*, by Arthur H. Williamson', *Journal of Modern History*, liii, 336-8.

1982

'Addenda to "Further additions to Durkan and Ross"', *The Bibliotheck*, xi, 57-8.
'Bishop Robert Cockburn and the founder of the Minims', *IR*, xxxiii, 71.
George Buchanan (1506-1582), Renaissance Scholar and Friend of Glasgow University: a Quatercentenary Exhibition, Glasgow University Library, 17 May-7 August 1982: Catalogue. (Glasgow: Glasgow University Library). [2], 13p.
By John Durkan, Stephen Rawles and Nigel Thorpe.
Introduction by J. Durkan (1-3).
'Scottish "evangelicals" in the patronage of Thomas Cromwell', *RSCHS*, xxi, 127-56.
'A tincture of humanism', *The College Courant* (Glasgow), lxviii, 26-7.
'*The Trompet of Honour* (Edinburgh?, 1537)', *The Bibliotheck*, xi, 1-2.
International Commission for the History of Universities: Work in Progress and Publication (for 1981), no. 5. Contributor of 'The British Isles' section.

1983

'Contract between Clerk and Lekpreuik for printing the Book of Common Order, 1564', *The Bibliotheck*, xi, 129-35.
Transcript (133-4) from SRO, Edinburgh Burgh Records, Register of Deeds, 1561-70, B22/8/1, ff. 117v-118.
'The date of Alexander Montgomerie's death', *IR*, xxxiv, 91-2.
'The early Scottish notary', *The Renaissance and Reformation in Scotland: Essays in Honour of Gordon Donaldson*, edited by Ian B. Cowan and Duncan Shaw (Edinburgh: Scottish Academic Press), 22-40.
'Medieval Scottish pressmarks', *TEBS*, v, pt 3 (1980-83), 23-4.
'The royal lectureships under Mary of Lorraine', *SHR*, lxii, 73-8.
Includes (77-8) text of SRO, CS7/46, Register of Acts and Decreets, f. 126v.
Review: '*Edinburgh and the Reformation*, by Michael Lynch', *IR*, xxxiv, 88-90.
Review: '*Edinburgh and the Reformation*, by Michael Lynch', *Scottish Journal of Theology*, xxxvi, 269-71.

1984

'The Observant Franciscan province in Scotland', *IR*, xxxv, 51-7.
'The Old College: assets lost and found', *The College Courant* (Glasgow), lxxii, 9-12.
By John Durkan and Lawrence Keppie.
'William Murdoch and the early Jesuit mission in Scotland', *IR*, xxxv, 3-11.

1985

'Further additions (including manuscripts) to J. Durkan and A. Ross, *Early Scottish Libraries*, at the National Library of Scotland', *The Bibliotheck*, xii, 85-90.
By John Durkan and Julian Russell.
'George Hay's Oration at the purging of King's College, Aberdeen, in 1569: commentary', *Northern Scotland*, vi, 97-112.

'Glenluce, Glenlus, Vallis Lucis, ancienne abbaye cistercienne sise dans le Wigtownshire (dioc. Galloway, Écosse)', *Dictionnaire d'histoire et de géographie ecclésiastiques* (Paris), xxi, columns 191-193.
In French.
'Principal John Mair, up-to-the-moment logician: Alexander Broadie, *The Circle of John Mair: Logic and Logicians in Pre-Reformation Scotland,* Oxford, Clarendon Press, 1985', *The College Courant* (Glasgow), lxxv, 51-3.
Protocol Book of John Foular, 1528-1534. (Edinburgh: SRS. SRS, New series, x). [2], xxviii, 223p.
Text edited by John Durkan from abstracts compiled by Helen Armet.
Introduction (pp. vii-xxv).

1986

'The bishops' barony of Glasgow in pre-Reformation times', *RSCHS,* xxii, 277-301.
Map: 'Bishop's barony of Glasgow' (p. 301).
'Glasgow ... ', *Dictionnaire d'histoire et de géographie ecclésiastiques* (Paris), xxi, columns 152-163.
In French.
'Graham (Patrick), évêque de Brechin puis archévêque de St Andrews ...', *Dictionnaire d'histoire et de géographie ecclésiastiques* (Paris), xxi, columns 1044-1047.
In French.
'The French connection in the sixteenth and early seventeenth centuries', *Scotland and Europe, 1200-1850,* ed. T.C. Smout (Edinburgh, John Donald), 19-44.
'James, third earl of Arran: the hidden years', *SHR,* lxv, 154-66.
'Native influences on George Buchanan', *Acta Conventus Neo-Latini Sanctandreani: Proceedings of the Fifth International Congress of Neo-Latin Studies, St Andrews, 24 August to 1 September 1982,* edited by I.D. McFarlane (Binghamton, New York. *Medieval & Renaissance Texts and Studies,* xxxviii), 31-42.
The Precinct of Glasgow Cathedral [Glasgow: Friends of Glasgow Cathedral. *Lecture Series, Glasgow Cathedral,* i]. [2], 12, [1]p.
'Sidelights on the early Jesuit mission in Scotland', *Scottish Tradition* (Guelph), xiii (1984-85), 34-48.
Review: '*Developments in the Roman Catholic Church in Scotland, 1789-1829,* by Christine Johnson', *SHR,* lxv, 213-14.
Review: '*The Jewel,* by Sir Thomas Urquhart, edited by R.D.S. Jack and R.J. Lyall', *SHR,* lxv, 210-11.

1987

'The library of Mary, queen of Scots', *IR,* xxxviii, 71-104.

1988

'The library of Mary, queen of Scots', *Mary Stewart: Queen in Three Kingdoms,* edited by Michael Lynch (Oxford: Basil Blackwell), 71-104.

Originally published in *IR*, xxxviii (1987), see above.

1989

'Edinburgh in 1611: Catholic sympathisers', *IR*, xl, 158-61.

1990

'Education : the laying of fresh foundations', *Humanism in Renaissance Scotland*, edited by John MacQueen (Edinburgh: Edinburgh University Press), 123-60.

1991

'Ian Borthwick Cowan, 1932-1990: a memoir', *The Calendar of Fearn: Text and Additions, 1471-1667*, edited by R.J. Adam (Edinburgh: SHS. SHS, 5th series, iv), 1-8.
Review: '*Cardinal of Scotland: David Beaton, c.1496-1546*, by Margaret H.B. Sanderson', *IR*, xlii, 76-8.

1992 [1994]

'Heresy in Scotland: the second phase', *RSCHS* , xxiv, 320-65.

1993

'Father Anthony Ross OP: a memoir', *IR*, xliv, 113-18.
'Barclay, William (c.1546-1608), legal and political writer', *DSCHT*, 62-3.
'Blackwood, Adam (1539-1613), legal writer', *DSCHT*, 80.
'Burne, Nicol (*fl.* c.1580-90), Catholic polemical writer', *DSCHT*, 111.
'Colville, John (c.1542-1605), RC convert and agitator', *DSCHT*, 197.
'Conn, George (c.1598-1640), papal agent at the court of Charles I', *DSCHT*, 208.
'Dempster, Thomas (1579-1625), RC scholar and academic', *DSCHT*, 239.
'Hamilton, John (c.1540-1610), anti-Protestant writer', *DSCHT*, 390.
'Hay, John (1546-1608), Jesuit controversialist', *DSCHT*, 396.
'Hay, William (*fl.* 1500-40), canonist', *DSCHT*, 396-7.
'Hospitals, Medieval', *DSCHT*, 414.
'Leslie, George ('Father Archangel') (c.1588-c.1637), RC missioner', *DSCHT*, 480.
'Renaissance', *DSCHT*, 706-09.
'Richardson (Richardinus), Robert (1491-1572), early Protestant', *DSCHT*, 719.
'Turnbull, William (c.1400-54), bishop of Glasgow 1447-54, and founder of its University in 1451', *DSCHT*, 832.
'Tyrie, James (1543-97), Jesuit', *DSCHT*, 833.
'Universities ...', *DSCHT*, 842-3.

1994

'Scottish reformers: the less than golden legend', *IR*, xlv, 1-28.

BRILL'S STUDIES IN INTELLECTUAL HISTORY

1. POPKIN, R.H. *Isaac la Peyrère (1596-1676).* His Life, Work and Influence. 1987. ISBN 90 04 08157 7
2. THOMSON, A. *Barbary and Enlightenment.* European Attitudes towards the Maghreb in the 18th Century. 1987. ISBN 90 04 08273 5
3. DUHEM, P. *Prémices Philosophiques.* With an Introduction in English by S.L. Jaki. 1987. ISBN 90 04 08117 8
4. OUDEMANS, TH.C.W. & A.P.M.H. LARDINOIS. *Tragic Ambiguity.* Anthropology, Philosophy and Sophocles' *Antigone.* 1987. ISBN 90 04 08417 7
5. FRIEDMAN, J.B. (ed.). *John de Foxton's Liber Cosmographiae (1408).* An Edition and Codicological Study. 1988. ISBN 90 04 08528 9
6. AKKERMAN, F. & A. J. VANDERJAGT (eds.). *Rodolphus Agricola Phrisius, 1444-1485.* Proceedings of the International Conference at the University of Groningen, 28-30 October 1985. 1988. ISBN 90 04 08599 8
7. CRAIG, W.L. *The Problem of Divine Foreknowledge and Future Contingents from Aristotle to Suarez.* 1988. ISBN 90 04 08516 5
8. STROLL, M. *The Jewish Pope.* Ideology and Politics in the Papal Schism of 1130. 1987. ISBN 90 04 08590 4
9. STANESCO, M. *Jeux d'errance du chevalier médiéval.* Aspects ludiques de la fonction guerrière dans la littérature du Moyen Age flamboyant. 1988. ISBN 90 04 08684 6
10. KATZ, D. *Sabbath and Sectarianism in Seventeenth-Century England.* 1988. ISBN 90 04 08754 0
11. LERMOND, L. *The Form of Man.* Human Essence in Spinoza's *Ethic.* 1988. ISBN 90 04 08829 6
12. JONG, M. DE. *In Samuel's Image.* Early Medieval Child Oblation. (in preparation)
13. PYENSON, L. *Empire of Reason.* Exact Sciences in Indonesia, 1840-1940. 1989. ISBN 90 04 08984 5
14. CURLEY, E. & P.-F. MOREAU (eds.). *Spinoza. Issues and Directions.* The Proceedings of the Chicago Spinoza Conference. 1990. ISBN 90 04 09334 6
15. KAPLAN, Y., H. MÉCHOULAN & R.H. POPKIN (eds.). *Menasseh Ben Israel and His World.* 1989. ISBN 90 04 09114 9
16. BOS, A.P. *Cosmic and Meta-Cosmic Theology in Aristotle's Lost Dialogues.* 1989. ISBN 90 04 09155 6
17. KATZ, D.S. & J.I. ISRAEL (eds.). *Sceptics, Millenarians and Jews.* 1990. ISBN 90 04 09160 2
18. DALES, R.C. *Medieval Discussions of the Eternity of the World.* 1990. ISBN 90 04 09215 3
19. CRAIG, W.L. *Divine Foreknowledge and Human Freedom.* The Coherence of Theism: Omniscience. 1991. ISBN 90 04 09250 1
20. OTTEN, W. *The Anthropology of Johannes Scottus Eriugena.* 1991. ISBN 90 04 09302 8
21. ÅKERMAN, S. *Queen Christina of Sweden and Her Circle.* The Transformation of a Seventeenth-Century Philosophical Libertine. 1991. ISBN 90 04 09310 9
22. POPKIN, R.H. *The Third Force in Seventeenth-Century Thought.* 1992. ISBN 90 04 09324 9
23. DALES, R.C & O. ARGERAMI (eds.). *Medieval Latin Texts on the Eternity of the World.* 1990. ISBN 90 04 09376 1
24. STROLL, M. *Symbols as Power.* The Papacy Following the Investiture Contest. 1991. ISBN 90 04 09374 5
25. FARAGO, C.J. *Leonardo da Vinci's 'Paragone'.* A Critical Interpretation with a New Edition of the Text in the *Codex Urbinas.* 1992. ISBN 90 04 09415 6
26. JONES, R. *Learning Arabic in Renaissance Europe.* Forthcoming. ISBN 90 04 09451 2
27. DRIJVERS, J.W. *Helena Augusta.* The Mother of Constantine the Great and the Legend of Her Finding of the True Cross. 1992. ISBN 90 04 09435 0

28. BOUCHER, W.I. *Spinoza in English.* A Bibliography from the Seventeenth-Century to the Present. 1991. ISBN 90 04 09499 7
29. McINTOSH, C. *The Rose Cross and the Age of Reason.* Eighteenth-Century Rosicrucianism in Central Europe and its Relationship to the Enlightenment. 1992. ISBN 90 04 09502 0
30. CRAVEN, K. *Jonathan Swift and the Millennium of Madness.* The Information Age in Swift's *A Tale of a Tub.* 1992. ISBN 90 04 09524 1
31. BERKVENS-STEVELINCK, C., H. BOTS, P.G. HOFTIJZER & O.S. LANKHORST (eds.). *Le Magasin de l'Univers. The Dutch Republic as the Centre of the European Book Trade.* Papers Presented at the International Colloquium, held at Wassenaar, 5-7 July 1990. 1992. ISBN 90 04 09493 8
32. GRIFFIN, JR., M.I.J. *Latitudinarianism in the Seventeenth-Century Church of England.* Annoted by R.H. Popkin. Edited by L. Freedman. 1992. ISBN 90 04 09653 1
33. WES, M.A. *Classics in Russia 1700-1855.* Between two Bronze Horsemen. 1992. ISBN 90 04 09664 7
34. BULHOF, I.N. *The Language of Science.* A Study in the Relationship between Literature and Science in the Perspective of a Hermeneutical Ontology. With a Case Study in Darwin's *The Origin of Species.* 1992. ISBN 90 04 09644 2
35. LAURSEN, J.C. *The Politics of Skepticism in the Ancients, Montaigne, Hume and Kant.* 1992. ISBN 90 04 09459 8
36. COHEN, E. *The Crossroads of Justice.* Law and Culture in Late Medieval France. 1993. ISBN 90 04 09569 1
37. POPKIN, R.H. & A.J. VANDERJAGT (eds.). *Scepticism and Irreligion in the Seventeenth and Eighteenth Centuries.* 1993. ISBN 90 04 09596 9
38. MAZZOCCO, A. *Linguistic Theories in Dante and the Humanists.* Studies of Language and Intellectual History in Late Medieval and Early Renaissance Italy. 1993. ISBN 90 04 09702 3
39. KROOK, D. *John Sergeant and His Circle.* A Study of Three Seventeenth-Century English Aristotelians. Edited with an Introduction by B.C. Southgate. 1993. ISBN 90 04 09756 2
40. AKKERMAN, F., G.C. HUISMAN & A.J. VANDERJAGT (eds.). *Wessel Gansfort (1419-1489) and Northern Humanism.* 1993. ISBN 90 04 09857 7
41. COLISH, M.L. *Peter Lombard.* 2 volumes. 1994. ISBN 90 04 09859 3 (Vol. 1), ISBN 90 04 09860 7 (Vol. 2), ISBN 90 04 09861 5 (Set)
42. VAN STRIEN, C.D. *British Travellers in Holland During the Stuart Period.* Edward Browne and John Locke as Tourists in the United Provinces. 1993. ISBN 90 04 09482 2
43. MACK, P. *Renaissance Argument.* Valla and Agricola in the Traditions of Rhetoric and Dialectic. 1993. ISBN 90 04 09879 8
44. DA COSTA, U. *Examination of Pharisaic Traditions.* Supplemented by SEMUEL DA SILVA'S *Treatise on the Immortality of the Soul.* Tratado da immortalidade da alma. Translation, Notes and Introduction by H.P. Salomon & I.S.D. Sassoon. 1993. ISBN 90 04 09923 9
45. MANNS, J.W. *Reid and His French Disciples.* Aesthetics and Metaphysics. 1994. ISBN 90 04 09942 5
46. SPRUNGER, K.L. *Trumpets from the Tower.* English Puritan Printing in the Netherlands, 1600-1640. 1994. ISBN 90 04 09935 2
47. RUSSELL, G.A. (ed.). *The 'Arabick' Interest of the Natural Philosophers in Seventeenth-Century England.* 1994. ISBN 90 04 09888 7
48. SPRUIT, L. Species intelligibilis: *From Perception to Knowledge.* Volume I: Classical Roots and Medieval Discussions. 1994. ISBN 90 04 09883 6
49. SPRUIT, L. Species intelligibilis: *From Perception to Knowledge.* Volume II. (in preparation)
50. HYATTE, R. *The Arts of Friendship.* The Idealization of Friendship in Medieval and Early Renaissance Literature. 1994. ISBN 90 04 10018 0
51. CARRÉ, J. (ed.). *The Crisis of Courtesy.* Studies in the Conduct-Book in Britain, 1600-1900. 1994. ISBN 90 04 10005 9
52. BURMAN, T. *Spain's Arab-Christians and Islam, 1050-1200.* 1994. ISBN 90 04 09910 7
53. HORLICK, A.S. *Patricians, Professors, and Public Schools.* The Origins of Modern Educational Thought in America. 1994. ISBN 90 04 10054 7

54. MacDONALD, A.A., M. LYNCH & I.B. COWAN (eds.). *The Renaissance in Scotland.* Studies in Literature, Religion, History and Culture Offered to John Durkan. 1994. ISBN 90 04 10097 0
55. VON MARTELS, Z. (ed.). *Travel Fact and Travel Fiction.* Studies on Fiction, Literary Tradition, Scholarly Discovery and Observation in Travel Writing. 1994. ISBN 90 04 10112 8
56. PRANGER, M.B. *Bernard of Clairvaux and the Shape of Monastic Thought.* Broken Dreams. 1994. ISBN 90 04 10055 5